Gabrielle Roy

A Life

Gabrielle Roy, Fides, 1975. Out of print.

Le Prince et la Ténèbre, short fiction published with etchings by Lucie Lambert, Éditions Lucie Lambert, 1980.

L'Incroyable Odyssée, narrative, Éditions du Sentier, 1981. Out of print.

La Littérature contre elle-même, Éditions du Boréal, 1985.

Le Québec depuis 1930 (co-authorship with Paul-André Linteau, René Durocher, and Jean-Claude Robert), Éditions du Boréal, 1986 [English translation by Robert Chodos and Ellen Garmaise: *Quebec Since 1930*, Toronto: James Lorimer & Co., 1991].

La Génération lyrique, essai sur la vie et l'oeuvre des premiers-nés du baby-boom, Éditions du Boréal, 1992 [English translation by Donald Winkler: *The Lyric Generation, The Life and Times of the Baby Boomers*, Toronto: Stoddart, 1994].

Gabrielle Roy

Roy

A Life

FRANÇOIS RICARD

TRANSLATED BY PATRICIA CLAXTON

M&S

To Marcelle

Originally published as *Gabrielle Roy: Une Vie* by Éditions du Boréal

Copyright © 1996 Éditions du Boréal
English translation © 1999 Patricia Claxton

Canadian Cataloguing in Publication Data

Ricard, François
Gabrielle Roy: a life

Translation of: Gabrielle Roy, une vie.
Includes bibliographical references and index.
ISBN 0-7710-7451-4

1. Roy, Gabrielle, 1909-1983 – Biography.   2. Authors, Canadian (French) –
20th century – Biography.*   I. Claxton, Patricia, 1929- .   II. Title.

PS8535.095Z88213 1999   C843'.54   C99-931232-1
PQ3919.R74Z88213 1999

We acknowledge the financial support of the Government of Canada through
the Book Publishing Industry Development Program for our publishing
activities. We further acknowledge the support of the Canada Council
for the Arts for our publishing program.

Text design by Sari Ginsberg

Typeset in Minion by M&S, Toronto
Printed and bound in Canada

McClelland & Stewart Inc.
The Canadian Publishers
481 University Avenue
Toronto, Ontario
M5G 2E9

1 2 3 4 5   03 02 01 00 99

Who somebody is or was we can know only by knowing the story of which he is himself the hero – his biography, in other words; everything else we know of him, including the work he may have produced and left behind, tells us only *what* he is or was. Thus, although we know much less of Socrates, who did not write a single line and left no work behind, than of Plato or Aristotle, we know much better and more intimately who he was, because we know his story, than we know who Aristotle was, about whose opinions we are so much better informed.

– Hannah Arendt, *The Human Condition*

Overfamiliar metaphor: the novelist destroys the house of his life and uses its stones to build the house of his novel. A novelist's biographers thus undo what the novelist has done, and redo what he undid. All their labour cannot illuminate either the value or the meaning of a novel, can scarcely identify a few of the bricks. The moment Kafka attracts more attention than Joseph K., Kafka's posthumous death begins.

– Milan Kundera, *The Art of the Novel* (trans. Linda Asher)

...a woman [...] looked up and followed me with a long, perplexed and supplicating gaze which never left my memory and never ceased to demand – for years and years – the thing we are all asking for, from the very depths of our silence: Tell about my life.

– Gabrielle Roy, *Garden in the Wind* (trans. Alan Brown)

Contents

Translator's Note

I had the privilege a few years ago of translating Gabrielle Roy's autobiography, *Enchantment and Sorrow* (*La Détresse et l'Enchantement*). As I wrote then in my translator's note, I had to remind myself that "I really did not know her, that she really was not there in the flesh sometimes, telling me her story so that I could pass it on." In that book, she only had time to tell about the first half of her life.

Once again I have had the privilege of listening to her story, this time retold and completed by François Ricard, so I could pass it on. The voice I have been hearing is different, yet the story has been coming through just as clearly – differently, but every bit as clearly – revealing, with insight and perspicacity as well as compassion and affection, the many facets of Gabrielle Roy's work and character.

Many people think, in these days of high technology, that translation should be a simple matter of pushing a button to get what you want. For catalogues and service manuals, and in a more limited way for certain other commercial applications, this can be true, but for literary translation it is not true at all. There is too much cultural variance, author idiosyncracy, contextual nuance, metaphor, allusion, emotional and aesthetic content, and so on, for any programming to be capable of anticipating all the possible combinations.

In 1791, Alexander Fraser Tytler wrote, "I would therefore describe a good translation to be, That, in which the merit of the original work is so completely transfused into another language, as to be as distinctly apprehended, and as strongly felt, by a native of the country to which that language belongs, as it is by those who speak the language of the original work." (*Essay on the Principles of Translation*, 1791, Everyman Edition, p. 8) This is still central in the interpretive school of thought to which I adhere. It follows, in this thinking, that a translation should not be saddled with the rules, customs and conventions of the original language. Not all theorists agree, but that is another subject.

Each translation poses special problems according to the nature of the project. In this, the biography of a writer with many titles translated into English, the first and simplest problem was how and when to introduce the titles of the English translations without making a clutter of titles in the two languages. There was no question of simply dropping the French titles. Gabrielle Roy did not write *The Tin Flute*, for instance, she wrote *Bonheur d'occasion*. It would be absurd to talk about her writing *The Tin Flute*. I have used French or English titles alone where one or the other seemed appropriate, although the easy pattern I had hoped to see emerge never really did. I have sometimes bracketed the English titles where it might be helpful, but not systematically, because it would surely become tiresome. Otherwise, I have tried to inform without too much repetition.

The second problem was that the French book is written in the *présent historique*, which is graceful and has the added merit of blending seamlessly with the many fragments of contemporary quotation. In English the present tense is not acceptable for extended use. For a flashback of limited length, for children's books, for poetry, for highly creative fiction, yes, but not for hundreds of pages of biography. So the *présent historique* had to become past tense and the quotations, whose tense was now different to that of the text, had to be coaxed into blending differently, and as nearly seamlessly as possible.

The third problem presented a more perilous challenge. François Ricard wanted to write a book that would fully satisfy the scholarly reader – giving all the correct bibliographical references and other acknowledgements and examining his subject under various lights – and at the same time appeal to the general reader. This was no small feat, but he achieved it resoundingly, since, as this translation goes to press, the fifth printing of the French book and a new-format paperback edition are in preparation.

However, the general reader in French is more comfortable with a formal, academic style than the general reader in English. This meant that if my translation was to appeal to a corresponding general readership in English, it would need some adaptation to relieve it of the university-lecture-hall tone it was going to have without it.

I want to stress that this adapation has been done with François's full approval and does not imply a "dumbing down" of his writing, just a shift in style from rather formal to more general, which many English-speaking academics favour in the first place. The easiest part called for eliminating unnecessary conjunctive adverbs – "thus," "indeed," "to be sure," "in short," "which is to say," and so on. Besides those I removed myself, my editors found others that were expendable. More comprehensive and complicated but more important was choice of vocabulary. Consider how different the effect is, for instance, between "acquired such urgency" and "became so urgent." Both mean the same thing and neither is obscure, yet to the English ear the second is simpler and more direct, more natural, therefore more relaxed and less formal.

In the English text, Gabrielle is referred to much more often by her first name than in the French. Frequently repeated use of the full name is a French custom. English readers do not need – or like – such constant reminders. The last name only would be too businesslike.

Differences in the way French and English speakers conceive reality lead to some very different manners of expression. Also to differences in the order of expression of ideas. When a French speaker *se promène* or goes for a *promenade*, the recreational aspect of the activity is what is important. The mode of locomotion does not matter, or if it does, it is stated: *en voiture, en vélo, à pied*. In English, however, the mode of locomotion is absolutely essential. To translate one of these expressions, you *must* know whether the recreational outing is a drive, a ride, or a walk. If you do not know, once in a while you can make do with the word "outing," but not too often.

As for differences in the order of expression of ideas, French tends, broadly speaking, to put what is important at the end of a statement, sentence, or paragraph, often as a summation or conclusion of what went before, while English tends to put the important thing first and then elaborate or comment on it. As an example of this comparative importance, in the French and English titles of Gabrielle's autobiography, *La Détresse et l'Enchantement* and *Enchantment and Sorrow*, the order of the two elements is reversed. I shall not anticipate François's discussion of Gabrielle's choice of title, merely observe that, in the dichotomy the title conveys, Gabrielle wants her readers, on balance, to focus more on the enchantment than the sorrow. For English readers, unless "enchantment" is the *first* of the two elements they encounter in the title, their focus will not be what she wants, in fact will be the opposite of what she wants.

Another factor in word order is rhythm. The title *Enchantment and Sorrow* is an example here, too. "Sorrow and Enchantment" is not good rhythm. If importance had required this order, I would have had to find another word or pair of words to make the rhythm right. The rhythm must also be right, of course, in full and extended sentences.

When François handed me a thick bundle of unbound pages of his published biography in French to work from, he had already marked them with corrections in anticipation of the next printing, and he followed them with further corrections from time to time. Some were owing to editorial changes arising from information come to light since the last printing, a few from clarifications that the translation process unearthed, and others from his decisions to delete some redundancies. These changes are entirely in the tradition of Gabrielle Roy herself, who made corrections before every printing and every new edition of her books. I have added occasional small, unobtrusive aids to English readers in order to help situate people, places, and events in common currency on the French scene; for example, five words to identify the missionary Father Zacharie Lacasse. All translations of quotations not otherwise acknowledged are mine.

I would like to express my sincere thanks to François Ricard for his unfailing patience and availability during my work on this translation, his interest in the nuances possible and his help in obtaining them, his assistance in many ways, especially in providing me with quotations from the English translations of Gabrielle's books, saving me months of research – and most of all for an enriching experience that has been one of those that mark a lifetime.

I would also like to thank a number of others for their invaluable information and assistance: Rosmarin Heidenreich of Winnipeg, Maureen Williams of Vancouver, Dr. Desmond Morton of the McGill

Institute for the Study of Canada, Jacqueline Beaudoin Ross of the McCord Museum of Canadian History, and Sister Ann McManus, Sister Maude Elliott, Robert Melançon, Jacques Godbout, Jori Smith, and J. A. McLeod, all of Montreal. Thank you also to my editors at McClelland & Stewart, Alex Schultz and Heather Sangster.

Patricia Claxton

CHAPTER I

*D*aughter of Immigrants

"Un Canadien errant" • The Landry Saga
Tribulations of a Family Man
St-Boniface at Long Last

O n the afternoon of Tuesday, 23 March 1909, the bells of
St-Boniface Cathedral did not ring to announce to the
world the baptism of Marie Rose Emma Gabrielle Roy.[1]
Abbé Duplessis, one of the assistant priests of the
parish, had been so slow with his prayers and ablutions that the ceremony did not end until after the hour of the angelus, too late for the
carillon to ring. For the baby's mother, left at home alone, this silence
was an evil omen.

And yet she had no reason to worry, for the child, born the previous
day, had come into a family that if not well-to-do was at least a fixture in
the community and enjoyed a standard of living envied by many.

"Un Canadien errant"

The baby's father was no longer young to be sure, approaching the age
of sixty, but at this moment in life he had reason to be pleased with
himself and the social standing that, after many a false start, he and his
family had been enjoying for some dozen years now, since the spring
day in 1897 when he had brought his wife and children to settle in
St-Boniface, Manitoba. That day had marked a kind of victory. After
thirty years of wandering, aborted plans, and constant struggle to find a
place and occupation in which to accomplish what he felt he was capable
of, fate was at last being kind and he could consider himself a success.

Until then Léon Roy had in many ways led a typical orphan's life,
though he was not strictly speaking an orphan, just a child who had
rebelled or been rejected and had left his parents to strike out alone,
never to return to the region of his birth,[2] the south shore of the

St. Lawrence River opposite Quebec City in what was then called Canada East. Léon was born there on 1 July 1850 in St-Isidore-de-Dorchester.[3] He was the eighth child of Charles Roy (1803–1900), a farmer, and his second wife, Marcellina Morin (1812–1888). Whether the young man had fled this harsh, impoverished milieu by choice or had been thrown out of his parents' house, history does not say. All that is known is that Léon felt "no tenderness" for his father[4] and at thirteen years of age left the farm and was taken in by the parish priest at Beaumont, who housed, fed, and schooled him in exchange for light work. Then, after several months as a boarder at a classical college in Quebec City, Léon entered the service of a city merchant under whose roof he was an exploited and ill-treated apprentice, but where at least he learned something about the practice of commerce.[5] Finally, having reached adulthood, he chose to leave, like so many other young French Canadians of the day who felt their homeland had nothing to offer.

And like so many others Léon set out for New England. He was a guide and forestry agent in the lumber camps for several years, then went to Lowell, Massachusetts, where his brother Majorique was living. There were plenty of Quebec émigrés working in the spinning and weaving mills of Lowell, as in many other industrial towns of New England. Spying a good business prospect, Léon and a friend opened a small restaurant that also purveyed alcoholic beverages. It was reasonably successful for a time. In the role of genial publican, Léon gladly joined in his customers' libations, which ate into his profits and boded fair to give him bad habits. And so, feeling himself sliding into alcoholism[6] after a number of years and his partner having died, but mostly because growing unemployment was taking a toll on the business, he decided to leave his establishment behind and once again try his luck elsewhere.

At this time, Franco-American communities were receiving a great deal of solicitous attention from legions of priests coming from Quebec to see to the preservation of their language, traditions, and religion. One of their methods was to set up parishes based on the Quebec model, and this was done in almost all the cities and towns with a sufficient émigré population. An even better method was to preach "repatriation" – to persuade the expatriates to return home. This was the surest way for them to escape the two-fold threat of assimilation posed by the secular and materialistic American culture and the fact of living in cities rather than the country, the French Canadian's natural habitat. To this end, working men were offered land in Canada on condition that they agree to become colonists. In the closing decades of the nineteenth century, a small number of families thus left the "little Canadas" of Lowell, Fall River, Worcester, and Central Falls to return to their own country under the wing of colonization companies powered by young priests imbued with the "providential mission" of the French-Canadian people.

Instead of moving back to Quebec, a number of these repatriates chose to go to the Canadian West, where there was potential for much richer farmland and where the Dominion Lands Act of 1872 was offering land ownership very inexpensively on certain minimal conditions involving residence and acreage to be cultivated. The province of Manitoba, created in 1870 and considerably enlarged in 1881, was then officially bilingual and its educational system was confessional, like Quebec's. This led the religious authorities to try to bring about the quickest and most intensive possible increase in the French Catholic population, which, thanks to the work of Monseigneur Provencher, the dedication of the Oblate Fathers and Grey Nuns, and the loyalty of the Métis, had been there since the early nineteenth century. The dream was to re-create another Quebec to the west of English Protestant Ontario, thus equalizing the demographic and political balance in the new Canada born in 1867, or at least tipping the scales in favour of "our race."

This was what gave Léon Roy the idea of selling his restaurant and leaving for Manitoba, taking Majorique with him as well as another of his brothers, Édouard. As a bachelor in the prime of life, free of home-sickness or ties of any kind, his eyes fixed entirely on the future, Léon was just the kind of man the new area needed.

Beginning in the late 1870s, a strong contingent of French Canadians had been building up in the region known as Pembina Mountain, roughly a hundred miles southwest of Winnipeg, where Monseigneur Alexandre-Antonin Taché, the second bishop of St-Boniface, had per-suaded the authorities to reserve two whole counties for them.[7] It was here, in the brand-new parish of St-Alphonse,[8] on 25 March 1883, that Léon "took homestead" when he chose to become the owner of an unoc-cupied lot corresponding in the official register to "the North east quarter of section Four of the 5th Township in the 12th Range West of Principal Meridian in the Province of Manitoba."[9] He then spent almost a year preparing this "quarter section"[10] and building a rudimentary dwelling before moving there on 15 February 1884.

Was this the end of his wandering? Was the orphan by choice at last going to put down roots and begin to live a normal life? This at least was

what Léon believed at the time, and it was in this belief that he decided
to act. He had soon given the finishing touches to his house and barn,
bought animals, put most of his land to the plough, and learned to make
himself known and respected in the community – being able to read and
write and knowing English made it easier for him to win this respect.
Thus in 1885 he circulated a petition regarding the location of the local
post office. The following year his neighbours in St-Alphonse, most of
them French Canadians come like him from the United States, elected
him to the council of the municipality of Lorne (which encompassed
St-Alphonse),[11] while the government entrusted him with the post of
justice of the peace.[12]

But most important of all was to find the wife with whom to achieve
the goal of any life worthy of the name: founding a family. Without this,
material or social success would be meaningless. Léon discovered her
not far from home, in a house in the neighbouring parish of St-Léon.
Her name was Mélina Landry.

The Landry Saga

In Gabrielle Roy's family imagery, there was always a very marked contrast between her father's side and her mother's. Gabrielle always felt
distinctly estranged from the Roys, probably because her father had cut
practically all ties with them himself. To her, this family that she had not
really known[13] seemed to inhabit a shadowy, loveless, joyless world
marked by grim religiosity, a world symbolized by the frightening face
of the Savonarola grandfather, the burner of books,[14] the enemy of
learning, and the dismal countenance of his wife, Marcellina, whose
character one might say heralded those dour, seemingly stony-hearted
women in certain of Anne Hébert's and Marie-Claire Blais's stories.
"We'd never known those two except through [their] awful portraits and
the occasional disclosure let drop by my father. I felt such an antipathy
towards them that I refused to recognize anything about myself in
them," we are told in her autobiography, *Enchantment and Sorrow*.[15]

"I imagined I was descended only from the Landrys," Gabrielle con-
tinues, "a breed in striking contrast, light-hearted, fun-loving, romantic,
even a little fey, as well as gentle, loving, and passionate." The world of
the Landrys enthralled her and appealed to her imagination as totally as
the world of the Roys seemed to her static and inhospitable. To her, the

Landrys' world must be one of light, liberty, unalloyed happiness, one she would never tire of recalling, drawing inspiration first from her mother's stories and later dipping into her own memories. Throughout her life she would continue to add new colours, new voices, new meanings to this world, magnifying and embellishing it to the point of creating a real myth: the myth underlying her very identity and the conception she would have of her own destiny.

The story of the Landrys as told in a chapter of *Enchantment and Sorrow*[16] may have begun in the distant past, first in Acadia and then in Connecticut following the deportation of 1755, but it was in Quebec that it really took shape and became the story of Gabrielle Roy. As shown in the sprawling unfinished novel that she devoted to it later,[17] Gabrielle situated the real beginning of "our family epic,"[18] meaning the site of her own origins, in the hills of St-Alphonse-de-Rodriguez, northwest of Joliette. Here, in her mind, was where the forces governing her own life began to stir, some thirty years before her birth.

It all began in 1881. In this period, the parishes north of Montreal were also being visited by recruiter priests sent by Monseigneur Taché to Quebec to find colonists for Manitoba. One of the most renowned was the Oblate Father Albert Lacombe, who was then *curé*, or parish priest, of Ste-Marie parish in Winnipeg and missionary to the Amerindian nations of the West. At Sunday mass, these envoys of the bishop of St-Boniface spoke glowingly to the Québécois farmers of the fertile Manitoba farms, hoping to persuade them to take part in the great project of French-Canadian and Catholic colonization of Canada's western prairies. To the bishops and the political elite of the period, this was the best remedy for the terrible scourge of emigration to the United States, which was decimating the country districts of Quebec and threatening the survival of the nation. In the words of a propagandist of the period:

> The United States is a foreign land, it is exile; it is "the graveyard of our race," as the valiant Curé Labelle has said. Manitoba [...] is home; it is a land on which our race, instead of atrophying, withering, will grow, vigorous, strong, healthy, valiant, imbued with the religious, social, patriotic and traditional thinking that have created the French-Canadian nationality...[19]

Élie Landry, born forty-six years earlier in the neighbouring Quebec parish of St-Jacques-de-l'Achigan, had been a logger and log-driver before settling on a farm in St-Alphonse-de-Rodriguez. He was among those parishioners who succumbed to the patriotic dream perhaps, but mostly to the prospect of an easier life, less unrewarding work, and a homeland spacious and fertile enough so that their children also might settle down and prosper instead of being squeezed onto cramped, rocky little farms where the only possible prospect was poverty or dispersal. In Manitoba the ground was "even," there were neither trees to fell nor stumps to burn, the frost came late, water was easy to find, and there was no shortage of space. Still, these illiterate peasants needed a good measure of courage – and ambition – to set off into the unknown this way, leaving their houses, neighbours, and relatives behind and starting life over again fifteen hundred miles away, as good as the other side of the world. When people talk about the inertia and conservatism in Quebec's rural society of this period, they too often forget the drive and initiative shown by these emigrants, which cannot be explained by necessity alone.

Élie's wife, Émilie Jeansonne, born also in St-Jacques, had come in her teens to St-Alphonse-de-Rodriguez, where she had married Élie on 9 July 1861. She was now fifty. Understandably, she took some persuading and then was not wildly enthused by the prospect of having to begin again from nothing in a foreign land. All this without considering the couple's seven children. The two oldest boys, Calixte, eighteen, and Moïse, seventeen, were soon taking care of themselves, but there were also Joseph, who was only twelve, Zénon, who was barely ten, and the littlest, Excide, everyone's darling, who was going on six. Then there were the two girls, Rosalie and Émélie. Rosalie had just turned seven, and Émélie, who was called Mélina, was barely fourteen[20] and leaving would mean giving up her studies at the local country school where she was showing an admirable aptitude for learning. But Élie's motives for leaving were stronger than those holding Émilie back.

The journey, as almost invariably, would be undertaken in springtime. When they arrived, the emigrants could thus benefit from the summer season to "settle themselves, begin cultivation immediately, and in the first summer obtain sustenance for the family, sometimes even a surplus," according to a prospectus of the day.[21] Having disposed of all their belongings except the easily transported essentials, Élie and his family, together with several other families from the parish, went first to Montreal and there boarded the train for the West. Stage by stage – the construction of the transcontinental railway was not yet finished – they made their way to Winnipeg, where they were met personally by Monseigneur Taché and Father Lacombe.

If they had had more money, the new arrivals could have bought farms beside the Red River or the Assiniboine. As it was, they were obliged to go farther afield, to the colonization zones where homesteads were still available. They were directed to St-Norbert, south of Winnipeg, where they awaited the make-up of a convoy headed for Pembina Mountain. Then began the final stage of the journey, the most picturesque, the one Gabrielle Roy never tired of recounting. Sitting on their belongings, which were piled into canvas-covered, horse-drawn wagons as in a western movie, the immigrants set out for the West in a slow, winding column along the trail leading them to their destination. The landscape both enchanted and troubled them: the immense sky, the prairie, a distant line of hills to be crossed and beyond it other marvels to discover, other expanses, another horizon line. They slept under the stars or sometimes in some lonely farmhouse where the established colonists would treat them to supper and a little comfort.

At least this was how, in a number of her writings, Gabrielle Roy took pleasure in reconstituting the arrival of her Landry grandparents in Manitoba. The central character, the one through whom the whole episode would be imagined and given poetic colour, was the girl Mélina, Gabrielle's own mother, then in her mid-teens. For the girl, her novelist daughter would tell her readers, this was a true journey of discovery; Mélina was discovering not only a new land and a new way of life but her own being, her yearning for freedom, her capacity for dreaming, and even her feminine condition, since she had reached the age of puberty.

> [My mother] never recovered from her emotions during that trip, and would tell about it all her life. To the point where my own childhood also fell under its spell, as my mother launched again into the old story, holding me on her knees in the big kitchen rocking chair; and I would imagine the pitching wagon and the accompanying rise and fall of the horizon as in a ship at sea.[22]

After three weeks – on 14 June 1881 – the travellers finally reached their destination. At the top of a gentle slope near a small wood, Élie took possession of the site where his family was going to begin life over: the southwest quarter of Section Sixteen in the 9th Range of the 5th

Township.[23] The place was about two miles northwest of the newly founded village of St-Léon, which was the seat of the parish that encompassed the whole region at the time, and where a good many French Canadians had already settled. Their names were Rondeau, Moreau, Major, Lafrenière, Girouard, Toutant, Labossière. The parish priest was an Alsatian, Abbé Théobald Bitsche. Élie and his family spent three years clearing and "breaking" the land,[24] bringing forty acres under cultivation, and replacing the round-log cabin that had been their first dwelling with a fine "house, which was exactly like the one at St-Alphonse-de-Rodriguez."[25] Before long the elder sons, Calixte and Moïse, went into business for themselves, acquiring farms of their own[26] and working on the construction of the new railway line, taking advantage of the rapid development in this region where, west and north of St-Léon, new parishes kept springing up.

In one of these parishes, St-Alphonse, lived Léon Roy, an educated and energetic man. Although rather older than the Landry sons, Léon was soon a frequent visitor at Élie's, where the *curé* of St-Alphonse had drawn his attention to another member of the family, Mélina, who was a fine piece, as the saying went. "She was a dark-haired, healthy, robust girl of medium height."[27] Shortly before, at the age of sixteen, she had entered and spent several months at the convent of the Grey Nuns in St-Boniface, but soon became homesick and dropped her studies and returned home. She had been quietly helping her mother since and preparing for the life awaiting her.[28]

The phase of "conversations on the verandah"[29] and love letters copied from the *Secrétaire des amoureux* lasted barely a year. Then on 23 November 1886, when the harvesting was done and despite Élie's misgivings, the marriage took place in the church of St-Léon.[30] He was thirty-six and she was nineteen.

For Gabrielle, the fact that her parents had been immigrants – people who had left their region of birth to begin their lives over in unknown country – took on increasingly crucial significance with time. She came to see her descent from this "family that was horizon-bound"[31] as one of the keys to her nature and destiny. Convinced that in her own life she was continuing the lives of her parents and grandparents, striving to understand her own nostalgia, her own longings, and searching for the significance of her own acts and an explanation of her writer's vocation and political choices, she never ceased to look to this "wandering [. . .] in our blood,"[32] to this fascination for "the elusive horizon, constantly calling, constantly retreating"[33] felt by the men and women from whom she had sprung, to this need for change and discovery that, she was convinced, was ingrained in her from birth.

Tribulations of a Family Man

After the wedding, Léon Roy led his bride to his farm at St-Alphonse. The young woman was not fond of the house – a cabin of round logs – or of her husband's bachelor habits. Léon was a very busy man besides. His double duties as municipal councillor and justice of the peace often kept him away from home. Mélina would take the least opportunity to visit her parents, and before and after the birth of her children spent sometimes extended periods with them.

The first child, a boy, came into the world nine months after the wedding, on 28 August 1887.[34] He was named Joseph. Next came Anna, who was born at St-Léon at the Landrys' on 25 September 1888.[35]

Léon's life, and therefore Mélina's, now took a new direction. Although having little taste for agriculture – and little talent, perhaps – the new father applied for the "homestead patent," which would make him the owner of his farm. The document was dated 2 October 1887, and the official deeds were issued shortly after, early in 1888.

But at this point the development of the region offered Léon an opportunity to be less dependent on the land and return to the commerce that was closer to his heart. The arrival of the new line of the Northern Pacific and Manitoba Railway was turning St-Alphonse-Sud, the part of the parish in which his quarter section was located, into a village that would soon be given the name Mariapolis.

With an eye on a present and above all future clientele, Léon opened a general store in December 1889, in partnership with his brother-in-law Calixte Landry, who had also given up agriculture. Soon he was having petitions signed calling for the creation of a post office at Mariapolis. The petitions bore fruit and in December 1891 Léon became the first postmaster of the village.[36] Besides the status conferred by this title and the commercial advantage for a storekeeper of having the post office in his establishment, the appointment assured Léon a certain income, since he was also paid for transporting the mail from the railway station to his store. He was to keep this responsibility until his departure from Mariapolis in the autumn of 1893.[37]

But things did not go very well in Mariapolis, and Léon had serious financial difficulties.[38] A consortium enabled Moïse Landry, Mélina's other brother, whom the chronicles portray as a man of many parts – clockmaker, photographer, auctioneer, oculist, and tooth extractor – to seize Calixte and Léon's store, which obliged Léon to go elsewhere to seek his fortune. The little family left for Somerset, a village not far away that had recently been reaping the benefits of proximity to the new railway line. Léon first opened a grocery store in the "Garneau Block," then had a large general store built with living quarters for his family upstairs. It seems he also built a hotel across the road from the railway station.[39] Since Somerset was then part of the parish of St-Léon and was less than two miles from Élie Landry's farm, Mélina now had the pleasure of living near her parents, whom she continued to visit regularly.

Four more children were born during these years, a second boy, who died at three months of age,[40] then three girls: Agnès, who came into the world on 17 November 1891;[41] Adèle, who was born on 30 January 1893 in her Landry grandparents' house at St-Léon;[42] and Clémence, who saw the light of day first at Somerset on 16 October 1895.[43] It was also in this period that Léon embarked on another career that blended perfectly with his shopkeeper activities: politics.

Politics in those days meant partisan agitation. Did Léon become actively partisan out of personal conviction? Family atavism? Did he become so after coming to Manitoba or while he was still in New England? Was his father politically partisan before him? We do not know, but one thing is beyond doubt: Léon Roy was a convinced and very active Liberal.

For a Manitoban French Canadian, belonging to the Liberal party was not without ambiguity. From the moment the Liberal cabinet of Thomas Greenway came to power in 1888, it had embarked on a revision of provincial government practices with regard to French Canadians, culminating in March 1890 with the promulgation by the Manitoba legislature of the "spoliatory laws" abolishing the use of French in the administrative and judicial apparatus and forbidding public support of Catholic schools, all contrary to stipulations in the Manitoba Act of 1870.[44] These developments had major political and legal repercussions throughout the 1890s. In Quebec, they roused indignation and sowed doubt over the future of the Confederation itself. But for those who would later be called the Franco-Manitobans, the impact was far more severe. No less than the entire dream of a bilingual Manitoba embodying an extension of the old French Catholic civilization of the St. Lawrence Valley had been dashed at a single stroke, transforming the vanquishers of yesteryear into a community under siege and those who had believed they had a homeland into foreigners.

A Liberal on the provincial scene, Léon was also in federal politics. As such he was doing battle with the "hangmen" of the Conservative party who had allowed Louis Riel to be executed in 1885, and was a supporter of the new Leader of the Opposition, Wilfrid Laurier, a French Canadian who in the federal election of 1891 had for the first time enabled the Liberals to win a majority of Quebec's seats in Parliament. Laurier, for whom Léon entertained unbounded admiration since the October day in 1894 when he had had a chance to shake his hand, would surely redress the wrong done by Greenway to Franco-Manitobans.

Soon enough, however, the ambiguity dissipated and with the approach of the next election Laurier showed less and less inclination to fly to the aid of the Catholics of Manitoba, anxious not to alienate a Protestant electorate already uneasy at the prospect of seeing a French Canadian accede to the prime-ministership of the country. This was partly why the Liberal opposition in Ottawa attacked the draft "reparation bill" and "remedial act" with which the Conservative cabinet was making a show of invoking the federal disavowal allowed by the Constitution to strike down the Manitoban legislation. The calculation must have been a good one, for Laurier's party was brought to power on 23 June 1896, ending thirty years of virtually uninterrupted Conservative domination. But for the Liberal organizer Léon Roy, things were much less rosy. To the elite of the French-Canadian community and especially the Catholic bishops and clergy, Laurier's election dashed the hopes raised by the Conservatives' disavowal plans, and in their eyes the general store–keeper of Somerset was the scum of the earth. On 2 February 1896, Abbé Noël Perquis, *curé* of St-Alphonse, wrote to Monseigneur Langevin, who had asked him to explain the Conservative candidate's defeat in the last provincial election:

> The one who caused O'Malley to lose the election was without question Léon Roy of Somerset. [. . .] Léon Roy has shown his true face as he needs must in this circumstance and everyone here regards him as a traitor and rank apostate. He deserves it. People wanted to burn him in effigy in Somerset. Decosse, perhaps too charitably, prevented this execution.[45]

The traitor, it was said, had even received $500 from the Liberals to persuade his compatriots to vote in their favour. And when the federal election came, Léon's anti-Conservative ardour remained intact.[46]

Once he had chosen thus to set his fellow Catholics and their pastors against him, Léon had no future as a merchant in Somerset or any other village of the region. From the moment he dared "show his true face" and deviate from solidarity, the community was bound to cast him out.

Did Léon know beforehand what would happen to him? It was not long in any case before he had regained his footing and turned his misfortunes to advantage. As we know, in those days one of the first and most urgent pieces of business for a party newly come to power was to dismiss the civil servants appointed by the predecessor government and replace them with its own friends and organizers. And so, barely a week after the election, Léon took up his finest pen and wrote a long letter to Prime Minister Wilfrid Laurier:

> For reasons of the active part that I took for the liberal party in the riding of Lisgar I have been given much grief [. . .]
>
> Since *messieurs les curés* were greatly opposed to the success of the liberal party we were sent some bigwig gentlemen [. . .] & Monseigneur Larcheveque Langevin who came on his pastoral visit and these gentlemen were all scandalized to see that we had so much confidence in M Wilfrid Laurier and put fear in a lot of our people and told me simply that I would be beggared.
>
> Today my business is being ruined for the reason that I must confess to being the cause of our party winning the election for the local & federal [. . .].

Having thus displayed his "virtues" and stressed his troubles, Léon proceeded to suggest a possible solution:

> Since you are going to be in power and you will perhaps find it necessary to resign some of these Crown land officer and Homestead Inspector gentlemen [,] if it is not too much to ask I would be very grateful to have one of these positions.[47]

Six months later, there had still been no letter from Ottawa, and Léon's position in Somerset was becoming increasingly untenable. The recent compromise over Catholic schools arrived at by Greenway and

Laurier, while appearing to make the 1890 legislation less despotic, in fact confirmed it, making the Liberals even more suspect in the eyes of the clergy and French-Canadian notables. Léon accordingly renewed his appeal to Laurier, but this time also addressed Clifford Sifton, who had just been appointed Minister of the Interior and was therefore responsible for immigration. Mustering his best English, he wrote:

> I was the only French person that did take an active part for our cause in Lisgar and all agree that without my assistance we would have lost the county.
>
> I wish I was in a position to say give this appointment to other of our friends and not to embarrass you with this appeal but the part I have taken for the liberal cause has thrown upon myself the serious displeasure of lots of people in this district and I find my business practically ruined.[48]

The two elected Liberal members for the region who had reaped the benefits of Léon's campaigning and commitment, Macdonell and Richardson, also approached Sifton, who was Laurier's right-hand man in the West and therefore in control of local patronage. From this point on, things began to move. There was some horse-trading between the Liberal back rooms in Ottawa and Winnipeg,[49] in the course of which an appointment as homestead inspector, timber inspector, or forest ranger was considered, and finally Léon pulled down one of two jobs that Sifton had earmarked for "Frenchmen," that of French interpreter at Immigration Hall in Winnipeg. His appointment was dated 1 April 1897 and became effective on the fourteenth of that month.[50]

St-Boniface at Long Last

And so Léon and Mélina were obliged to move for the second time since their marriage. Léon left Somerset rather as a fugitive might, more or less rejected by his fellow citizens, while Mélina moved away from her own family with regret. But at the same time they were freed of the uncertainties of agriculture and retail trade; Léon now had a well-paid, prestigious, and interesting job he could count on for as long as his party remained in power.

The railway station and Immigration offices were in Winnipeg, but the couple chose to live in St-Boniface on the right bank of the Red

River. The town then had fewer than two thousand inhabitants, but even so, with its air of both ghetto and minor metropolis, it was one of Manitoba's important urban centres.[51] It was a ghetto to the extent that, next to the overwhelming Winnipeg, it was a kind of marginal ethnic quarter where francophones were dominant if not the majority, and in any case far more significant proportionately than their number in the population of Manitoba as a whole.[52] But it was a metropolis too in that it played a central role in French and Catholic life throughout the Canadian West, a role that strengthened around the turn of the century as the city grew and modernized. St-Boniface had been the see of an archbishopric since 1871 and was served by several religious communities that operated a hospital and a number of schools. It also had newspapers, retail stores, agencies, some small industry, and services of every kind, besides being the home of the French-speaking elite. It was the image of a peaceful, well-ordered, and pleasant society.

Arriving from the colonial frontier, Léon and Mélina felt both reassured and excited by their new milieu. In addition to the pleasure of finding themselves among people who spoke their language and shared their religious convictions, here they had a more active social life, more comfort, and perhaps better conditions for their children's education and eventual livelihood. When they arrived in the spring of 1897, they rented a red-painted house at the corner of La Vérendrye and Du Collège streets (the latter now Langevin Street) in the north end of town, a neighbourhood known as "la Pointe," inhabited by poor working-class families and Métis.[53] Here on the following September 15, Bernadette was born, the Roys' sixth child.[54] She was soon to be followed by two boys: Rodolphe, who came into the world on 15 July 1899,[55] and Germain, who was born in St-Léon on 9 May 1902.[56]

The father of this growing family, however, had frequently to be away from St-Boniface on account of his work. Bearing first the title of "French Interpreter" and then "Inspector of Colonies," he had very broad responsibilities, acting as a kind of government emissary to the colonists placed in his charge.[57] He met them when they got off the train, guided them through administrative offices, gave them information, comforted them, found them temporary lodgings, and often accompanied them as far as their destination townships, which he would have personally located and inspected in advance. After helping them to choose a piece of farmland, he would continue to advise them through the various stages of settling in. Although his clientele were mostly

French-speaking immigrants, he also looked after colonists of other origins. These included Doukhobors who had come from Russia in the final years of the century and were aided in particular by the writer Leo Tolstoy, and also Galicians, a term used generically at the time for "Ruthenians, Galicians properly speaking, Buckowinians, Poles, Russians, and Slaves."[58] And so around 1898, Léon was actively involved in the settlement of Ukrainian families.[59] A few years later, when demonstrating Doukhobors were giving grief to the authorities, he was among those who helped to calm them.[60]

Included in the duties assigned to him were visiting and inspecting already existing colonies and reporting on them to his superiors at the Immigration Bureau in Winnipeg. His territory covered all the French-speaking townships. At first these remained concentrated mostly in Manitoba, but soon new ones were being created in the "Territories" of Saskatchewan and Alberta (which became provinces in 1905). These too he was expected to visit regularly. On occasion he was even sent into the neighbouring states of North Dakota, Minnesota, and Michigan to recruit colonists among French Canadians living there or to take charge of certain groups of colonists coming from there.[61]

These were years marked by a prodigious influx of immigrants to the Canadian West, originating mostly from Eastern Canada, the United States, and Europe.[62] Taking advantage of the favourable economic conditions at the time, the Liberal government was making settlement of the prairies one of its priorities, led by Laurier and Sifton and in conjunction with the railway companies, which owned vast amounts of land. To this gigantic enterprise, which continued uninterrupted until the outbreak of the First World War, it can be said that Léon Roy made an effective if modest contribution. This is confirmed by the following letter addressed to the immigration commissioner in Winnipeg by the representative of a Dutch group who had come to explore an area in Saskatchewan with a view to possible immigration:

> Prompted by a sense of appreciation, I find it my pleasant duty to express our thanks [. . .] for the splendid service rendered us by Mr. Leon Roy of your office.
>
> We greatly appreciate his knowledge of the country, his fair and impartial advice at all times, his competency as a guide, his display of energy on behalf of the Government and we congratulate your office with the fact that it has men in its service like officer Roy.[63]

While Léon's occupation demanded constant travel and long hours of study and work, it also brought rewards of many kinds to him and his family. The pay was good: from $75 a month in 1897, it rose to $1,200 a year in 1903. This increase reflected the quality of Léon's services and the fact that "the guy has been a good Liberal all his life and fought in our ranks for years. He has been persecuted by our clergy on account of that."[64] Léon also had a railway pass for himself and his family for use on railway lines of the West.

And material benefits were not all. It was also gratifying to have an occupation that made him feel fulfilled. Léon, whose success as a farmer and then retail merchant was doubtful to say the least, who seemed to have little taste for stability and routine and enjoyed action, movement, and personal contact with others, was at last in a position to show what he could do. A combination of social worker, geographer, agronomist, and administrator – and undoubtedly political organizer still – "Officer Roy" led a busy life of multifarious and constantly changing activities. Each train pulling into the station at Winnipeg brought him new acquaintances, new challenges, new journeys. The immigrants looked on him as an important man invested with power and authority, and did not hesitate to place their fate and that of their children in his hands. "Who," asks the narrator in *Street of Riches*, "can ever know what peace of mind, what certitude Papa felt among his [settlers]?"[65] To this feeling of empowerment was added the satisfaction of working for the good of others, of helping to build a better country and a better world. In short, when he was "on the job" – meaning in his office in Winnipeg or even more in the field with his immigrants, where there was no shortage of difficulty, fatigue, and disappointment – Léon Roy must be pictured as a happy man.

For the family too, the father's occupation brought numerous social as well as economic benefits. The government employee, friend of the government in power with access to the archbishop and the local elite, enjoyed an enviable standing in the community that reflected on Mélina and the children as well. There are several indications of this. One is the portrait photograph of 1901 or 1902 showing the little family in all its finery, radiating elegance and middle-class distinction. Another is this item published in the newspaper *Le Manitoba* in October 1902:

> Last Saturday a charming celebration took place at the home of M. Léon Roy on the occasion of the 14th birthday of Mlle Anna Roy. A magnificent

supper was served to the guests. Among those attending were [there followed fifteen or so names of the cream of Liberal society].[66]

Mélina worked hard, taking care of the children, two of whom were still very young, and running the house; meals and housework took up most of her time and her sewing often kept her up late into the night. Still, her life was not without pleasures. Despite Léon's misgivings (he did not consider it desirable for girls to be educated), she put her eldest daughters, Anna and Agnès, then Adèle, Clémence, and soon Bernadette, to board with the nuns, which lightened her domestic burden. She also found it possible to go out fairly regularly, either for shopping or to visit with friends in the neighbourhood. In 1904, following the example of ladies of upper-crust St-Boniface, she even treated herself to a visit to Quebec, her first since leaving St-Alphonse-de-Rodriguez twenty-three years earlier. While there she did the pilgrimage to Ste-Anne-de-Beaupré, saw her childhood friend Priscilla Gaudet, now Sister Octavie of the Sisters of Ste-Anne, and visited her husband's sisters in Lotbinière County and some of her own family connections living in Montreal.[67] It was during this happy period that Léon, as a civil servant, was invited with his wife to attend a ball at the residence of the lieutenant-governor of Manitoba. Although this episode took place before Gabrielle's birth, it was to become one of the highlights of her family history, to the point of casting its magic over the entire Part One of *Enchantment and Sorrow*.[68]

But the surest indication of the family's easy circumstances was Léon's decision in the spring of 1904 to leave the "red house" on La Vérendrye Street, which he had occupied as a tenant for seven years, and build a house of his own. Once again sensing a good deal in the offing, he acquired a large lot at the corner of Deschambault and Desmeurons streets,[69] in a sparsely inhabited part of St-Boniface whose development he himself was to organize. With his contacts and skill in public affairs, he quickly arranged with the city for Deschambault Street to be graded and landscaped, and the work was completed soon after with the laying of wooden sidewalks and the installation of sewers.[70] (Not long after this, when the municipal official in charge of public works was running for mayor, Léon Roy's name appeared in a list of citizens supporting his candidature . . .).[71] After carefully preparing the plans and choosing the building materials, and without the services of a contractor, Léon oversaw the construction of a large, attractive house that met his family's needs and Mélina's wishes. It was Mélina's brother, Zénon Landry, who did the work. The move to 15 Deschambault Street took place on 22 August 1905.[72]

"The father's house," as Adèle was to call it, was superb.[73] On the ground floor, besides the main kitchen and a summer kitchen that also served as a larder, there was an "office" for Léon and a large, carpeted living room in which the upright piano held a place of honour. Upstairs there were five bedrooms and a stairway leading to the attic. There were plaster walls and all the modern conveniences: running water, electricity, and a bathroom. The exterior, painted yellow, was a handsome sight with its three dormers, verandah running the length of two sides, and eight columns with capitals. Léon very quickly surrounded the house with trees and flowers to make it prettier and more hospitable.

> In the open space in front of the house he planted six elm trees [. . .].
> There were rose bushes and an apple tree growing in full sunlight west of
> the verandah, and farther back, oaks and maples. [. . .] He had crimson
> dahlias, white chrysanthemums, deep pink, aromatic carnations, and
> pansies in mixed colours flowering in his flower bed and, along the length
> of the verandah, many-coloured sweet peas and gladioli. But his favourite
> flowers were the roses. [. . .][74]

Could one imagine a pleasanter dwelling and surer sign of prosperity? The house, which had cost over $3,000, was mortgage-free. Léon had just turned fifty-five. Considering the ground he had covered since coming to Manitoba, if not since leaving St-Isidore, he could rightly feel proud of his success. And Mélina too when she looked back over the years. Her relationship with her husband may often have been strained, and the love between them may have been more dutiful than truly joyful, but this good wife and mother could tell herself now that their present well-being had been given her in compensation.

But their well-being was not unclouded. Barely six months after the family moved into the house on Deschambault Street, Agnès, the second-eldest girl, her father's favourite, the one who never left his side when he was at home and whom he lovingly called "Agnèze,"[75] was carried off by meningitis at fourteen years of age.[76] Léon was inconsolable. He bought a plot in the cemetery adjoining the cathedral, in which the girl was the first to be buried. The memory of this death would remain graven in the hearts of the child's parents and sisters as the death of an innocence and sweetness forever lost. But life goes on. Two weeks after Agnès's funeral, Mélina gave birth to another little girl. She was baptised in the cathedral on 4 March 1906, with Joseph and Anna as godfather and godmother, and given the name Marie-Agnès.[77]

The year 1906 was important for Léon and his family in another way, for this was when they acquired their cherished land in Saskatchewan. In the course of his inspection tours, Officer Roy had located a particularly promising area southwest of Regina near the Cypress Hills, where he planned to found a French-Canadian colony. He reserved a number of good pieces of land for himself and his family.[78] Whether his purpose was speculative or he was thinking of bringing his family here to settle some day, we do not know. There is no doubt, however, that Léon paid special attention to this colony. He called it Villeroy (a name that was changed later to Dollard), and he talked to Mélina and the children about it as if it were a kind of paradise. In the family, these remote pieces of land were long regarded as an asset of great worth, representing both the opportunity of a better life and protection from the blows of misfortune.

The children, moreover, did not hesitate long before going there to visit or set up house. Joseph, the eldest son, left St-Boniface to live in Villeroy as soon as it was founded. Early in her marriage, Anna went to live in Dollard for a time. Adèle, Clémence, Rodolphe, and Germain all spent periods there, and much later Gabrielle too paid a crucial visit. In short, for Mélina's children Dollard represented the call of the West, the dream of freedom and prosperity. But it was also to be one of the instruments of their dispersal.

For the moment, however, everything seemed to be going well in "the father's house." Léon was a prominent citizen; illustrating this, Pierre Lardon, known as "the poet of St-Boniface," appealed to "*Bien cher monsieur Roy*" to intervene in his favour with the Lands Office. "I know you have long arms," he wrote, "and that you are also very kind."[79] From a material point of view, what the family had was probably not wealth but it was far from poverty; the Roys wanted for nothing and were better off than most of their neighbours and acquaintances. Thus in 1906, Léon was able to donate $25 – a considerable sum at the time – toward the building of the new St-Boniface Cathedral,[80] and the following year $25 toward "a commemorative gift on the occasion of the Jubilee of His Grace Monseigneur A. Langevin, Archbishop."[81] As for the children, they were numerous, handsome, and healthy. Both the present and future therefore seemed assured.

So, in the summer of 1908, although she had discovered at the age of forty-one that she was pregnant for the eleventh time, Mélina had every reason to be pleased with her family's lot as well as her own. A family of immigrants to be sure, but successful immigrants.

Why then, on the day of Gabrielle's baptism, did she take the silence of the cathedral bells as an evil omen? Was it the child's future that worried her? Or did she have a premonition that something was coming to an end, and soon?

CHAPTER 2

A Singular Childhood

Like an Only Child
Sheltered from Family Tempests
The Gynaeceum
"My Street, My Universe"

person's childhood is not a story that can be told. The best we can do is recount the child's environment – conditions, circumstances, the behaviour of those around – and, at that, we have no way of knowing if this childhood was truly marked by this environment, and, if so, how. As for the rest, which is probably the most important part, we must rely on what time has wrought in the secret confines of each individual's awareness and memory, judging by the images, experiences, fragmentary pronouncements, and faces imprinted in that memory and brought out later by chance or some obscure imperative, once the person has been defined and childhood is long past. All of which is bound to make it difficult to untangle truth from imagination when considering these recollections; that is, to untangle what truly happened from what the person's present memory conceives of the past.

Gabrielle Roy began her own quest for "things past"[1] fairly late, at least in her writings. The first of her texts based on her own past began to appear only in the mid-1950s, when she had reached middle age. These were certain stories in *Street of Riches* (1957) and *The Road Past Altamont* (1966), as well as a number of autobiographical texts such as "Souvenirs du Manitoba" (1954), "Manitoba" (1962), and "My Manitoba Heritage" (1970), and finally some unpublished texts that Gabrielle wrote concurrently with *Enchantment and Sorrow* or earlier.[2]

Gabrielle's picture of her own childhood in these late texts shows two traits that deserve mention. First is the incomplete, fragmentary nature of the picture. Reading these texts from a biographical perspective, one realizes how little there is in them about her childhood properly speaking, the period before the age of ten or twelve. Even in a work as ambitious as *Enchantment and Sorrow*, the "action" really begins only around

25

1920 or 1922, when the heroine is entering adolescence. Her memory operates through brief, unconnected images that reconstitute not so much a linear story as a collage of "moments," glimpses, scraps of life whose chronology is never very precise, as if she were unable to give a sequential account. Thus the narrator's childhood appears to be less a succession of defined events than a climate, an ambience, a psychological and emotional landscape situated outside a time framework, or in a purely subjective time framework having little to do with historical time.

The second, even more remarkable trait, which could well be related to the first, is the degree to which the novelist idealizes her memories of these early years, or at least those she confides to her readers. Once her apparent memory block has begun to dissipate, this part of her life (which was free of notable events, therefore of major trauma) in its succession of fragments seems to her to have been a time of pure grace, a period of unalloyed happiness and enchantment, all of it bathed in light, innocence, and joy. "My sincerest images from my truest pages," she says in 1970, "all come from those days, I imagine."[3] From the days, that is, before the harsh words and the wounds, before the wrongs committed and the guilt. From the days when the deepest, most authentic, and most beautiful part of Gabrielle's being was taking form and finding expression.

Like an Only Child

While Gabrielle Roy surrounds her own childhood with an aura of wonder that to a biographer could be the fruit of re-creation in hindsight, a good deal of it does correspond to the reality – to the extent that this kind of reality can be reconstituted. Considering the context, the doting part played by her mother and other family members, and the little girl's feeling of her own singularity and worth, it can be said that Gabrielle enjoyed a privileged childhood.

As we have seen, she was born into a family that was well regarded and relatively well off. But most important, the family was large and Gabrielle was its last-born. The difference in age between her and her siblings set her apart as someone who was not quite like ordinary people, and who very quickly discovered that she was different, in a class by herself if not chosen for pre-eminence.

When Gabrielle came into the world, the child immediately ahead of her in age, Marie-Agnès, had only just turned three. The following year, however, a dreadful thing happened.

[Marie-Agnès] died, tragically, at the age of four, having set a little fire at the back of the house, which caught onto her starched dress, and in no time the child was all in a blaze. My father was away then amongst his immigrants. The news my mother sent him, telegram and all, never reached him. When he returned home several weeks later, he had no knowledge that the child was dead and buried.[4]

The burial took place in the cathedral cemetery, as with the first Agnès, in the middle of June 1910. Clémence would recall later that there were wild roses on the grave, placed there by a neighbourhood child.

Gabrielle was too young at the time to understand what was happening. "Later," she says, "the tale of the second Agnès's death was told and retold to me many and many a time and I cried endlessly for the company of the little sister I had not known."[5] This episode assuredly left its mark on her early years, if only by accentuating the difference in age between her and the other children. The next youngest was now Germain, who was seven years older than she. Then came Rodolphe, her godfather, who was ten years older. The closest in age among the girls was Bernadette, who was eleven and a half when Gabrielle was born, while Clémence was fourteen and Adèle sixteen. Anna was already married and no longer living in the house.

"The last child in a family is alone," Gabrielle confided to her first biographer, Joan Hind-Smith, "and is in a sense an only child. I had no one to play with because my brothers and sisters were so much older. I was often very lonely."[6] The impressions she retained of her childhood were strongly coloured by this solitude. The stories about Christine's early life in Street of Riches and The Road Past Altamont, for instance, invariably depict the heroine as a solitary child, or as the only one of her age in a world of adults. The same is true of the autobiographical text titled "Ma petite rue qui m'a menée autour du monde," in which there seems to be no child other than Gabrielle living on Deschambault Street or anywhere close. The little girl did have friends near her age in the neighbourhood, but there were none in the family itself, which was almost unheard of for the period and milieu she grew up in.

Yet nothing suggests that this solitude weighed on the child, or that she suffered from it in any way whatever. On the contrary, her rather paradoxical position as virtually an only child in a large family was more likely an advantage. "She became *notre petite* for all of us, father, mother, sisters and brothers," Adèle reports. "And all of us loved, pampered, and coddled her."[7] A recollection confirmed in a letter from Clémence to Gabrielle:

> You were our darling little sister, you know, being the last-born of the family. We really loved you. Maman spoiled you a bit; the poor little love, she's so frail and sickly, so let her be.[8]

The death of Marie-Agnès, sad though it was at the time, served only to reinforce the "only child" aura about little Gabrielle. Becoming in a sense the surrogate for the dead child, who was herself taking the place of "the first Agnès," who had died so shortly before Marie-Agnès was born, Gabrielle appeared to be an even greater treasure, even more deserving of care and affection in the eyes of the family.

The air of fragility surrounding her from the beginning and throughout her childhood, if not later in life, probably owes much to this. "The little girl had the daintiest face, a pretty nose, deep blue eyes and red-brown hair," Adèle recalls. "Although she was not ill, she looked as frail as a tender rosebud," she adds, which induced her mother, one day in 1910, to make haste to have her photographed because "she might die like Marie-Agnès."[9] But the most telling illustration of the very special protection the child enjoyed is still the nickname her family gave her:

> Shortly after I came into the world, my father, because I was of frail health or because he himself – then old and sick – had too great a pity for life, dubbed me "Petite Misère" – "Little Miss Misery."[10]

The above passage is about the fictional character Christine, but it does correspond closely to an episode in Gabrielle's own childhood, as confirmed by the recollections of Adèle, Clémence, and Germain, as well as by other of Gabrielle's writings. It is not certain, however, that the episode occurred "shortly after" Gabrielle's birth. We shall return to this.

The nickname was not entirely owing to the child's weakness of physique. Yes, she was small and frail; yes, she was often short of breath and seemed to suffer frequent indispositions, but her general state of health was far from poor. The sicknesses she contracted when very young were neither worse nor more frequent than those of most other children in a period when systematic asepsis and vaccines were still unknown, and she survived them without major after-effects. She was even more fortunate in this respect than several of her siblings, including the first Agnès, of course, but also Clémence, Rodolphe, and Germain, who had suffered much more serious illnesses – meningitis, typhoid fever, and mastoiditis. The photograph of her with Bernadette taken in 1910 shows her as a bright-eyed baby of eighteen months with slightly curly hair and a face still full and round, not at all the picture of a little person on the point of death.

Yet *Misère* seemed to her family (and later to herself) to be a delicate, rather frail child who was constantly under threat of calamities of all kinds. This "weakness," however, was less a reflection of poor health than an expression and justification of the devotion lavished on the little girl by the family in which she occupied such a very special place, separated from the others and at the same time the focus of all their attention and all their care.

Forty years later, her brother Germain would remember her thus:

> To the brothers and sisters who were more or less ugly ducklings, she seemed of a different world, of a different essence: a fairy or something like that, with her ethereal air, her transparent complexion, her enormous blue-green eyes – with double rows of long dark eyelashes which made a shadowy frame for those deep pools of such a strange hue – and her hair which was curly and of a rich reddish gold. She was the "beauty" and the only "beauty of the Family."[11]

Sheltered from Family Tempests

During Gabrielle's childhood, being the last-born meant having an experience of family life that was very different to that of her older brothers and sisters. Much as the home afforded her siblings the benefits of security and relatively easy circumstances, it was not a household in which tenderness and *joie de vivre* reigned.

There were certainly good times; there were plenty of celebrations, particularly the traditional Christmases recalled later by Anna and Adèle:[12] the masses of food prepared by Mélina, Rodolphe's jokes, the popular music that Anna played on the piano, the old French songs sung by Léon in his "fine, moving" baritone voice.[13] But the most memorable of these festivities took place in the days before Gabrielle was born and were not really seen again after 1910, for the family had begun to disperse. Besides, these moments of grace did not prevent the usual climate in the house from being strained, acrimonious, without great affection among the family members. Clémence, in one of her letters to Gabrielle, speaks even of "a shortage of love" in "the father's house":

> A shortage of love. [...] We couldn't confide in each other. Père Léon who so hated the debts that Maman Mélina got into without telling him. [...] So in the kitchen, that was the scene, you were the littlest, you couldn't remember it all. What I think is that was the reason we were all so edgy. We were all too afraid of our Père Léon.[14]

Léon, who loved his work and felt at ease and happy among "his" colonists, would often return home tired and out of sorts and would give way to rages that terrorized his children, especially his sons, to whom he showed a severity and intransigence that seems to have marked them profoundly, leaving them apprehensive, inclined to flee rather than fight, and more or less embittered toward him.

As for Mélina, who was virtually alone to look after her large family and the running of the house, she too was given to impatience and fits of temper. She felt she was constantly watched by her husband and prevented from leading the life she aspired to. All because Léon was afraid of being short of money, because he had an inordinate need of order and tranquillity in his life, because the religiosity he had acquired as a child had made him distrustful of all "foolery," however harmless. The passing years accentuated not only the difference in the ages of husband and wife but also the differences in their temperaments and expectations from life. "Spats, arguments, flare-ups"[15] were common currency, and the flames were fanned by the father's fatigue and impatience, the mother's secretiveness and discontent, and the often finicky authority that both exercised over the children – the older children at least – in the manner then customary in French-Canadian middle-class families. Things were not always harmonious among the children either; jealousy, cheating, and frustration often set one against another and sometimes left lasting resentments.

In her writings later, Gabrielle would have a strong tendency to water down this discordant atmosphere, even purely and simply to blot it out.

"It's true," she wrote in reply to Clémence, "that our poor father [...] and mother often used to fight. And it's partly true that this past has made us irritable. But look around at other families and you'll see that it's the same thing just about everywhere. There aren't many perfectly united families."[16] Adèle, for her part, proved to be much less reticent and wrote without hesitation about the family frictions and squabbles. Granted, Adèle was much older and the oldest still at home, and had therefore personally witnessed the disharmony between her parents and the tensions tearing the family apart, while Gabrielle had been so young she had mostly been spared the experience. As Clémence told her, "You were the littlest, you couldn't remember all that." Being the last-born and virtually an only child, she was shielded both from parental rages and sibling rivalries. All in the family conspired to pamper the little girl and show her their affection, perhaps in compensation for the "shortage of love" from which they themselves suffered.

By the time Gabrielle was six or seven years old, the family climate had changed greatly. Not only had most of her brothers and sisters left home, taking their dissatisfactions and quarrels with them, but the relationship between her parents was more relaxed, the antagonism of earlier years gradually replaced not by happiness, but by a kind of resignation and truce. Less demanding with the youngest than they had been with the others, less determined – or less able – to maintain strict control over her education, they left her more latitude to escape their authority, develop on her own, and cultivate her own world independently of theirs.

The Gynaeceum

Much later, Adèle, Anna, and even Rodolphe would accuse Gabrielle of having been a spoiled brat, always getting her own way and imposing whatever she wanted on her mother and the rest of the family. Although such accusations are mostly expressions of spite and jealousy, they do not seem unreasonable or entirely unfounded.

The child was spoiled by her sisters more than anyone for as long as they lived at home. Adèle, who was Gabrielle's godmother, was first in line to smother the little girl with cuddling and gifts, but she was closely followed by "the middle girls,"[17] meaning Bernadette and especially Clémence, who, once she had left school, became Gabrielle's "second mother"[18] to a point, playing with her, taking her on picnics in the neighbouring fields, and keeping an eye on her in Mélina's absence.

Besides the three girls there was Mélina's sister Rosalie, who was as smitten with Gabrielle as her nieces were. In 1909, Rosalie was a thirty-five-year-old woman with a history of tortured amorous entanglement. When very young and still living with her parents in St-Léon, she had fallen passionately in love with a Scot by the name of Edward McEachran, the stationmaster at Somerset. The fellow being something of a wastrel and fond of drink, Élie, the girl's father, intervened and forbade his daughter to see any more of her beloved. However, Rosalie, heeding only her heart and determined to convert her Scot, abandoned the paternal hearth and married Edward, only to return to the fold ten years later, proving that Élie had not been mistaken. Edward had turned into an alcoholic and begun to beat poor Rosalie, who then had no choice but to leave him. He departed alone for the United States. But passion was not dead and some time later the young woman went to rejoin her husband, hoping for a reconciliation. Things went from bad to worse, however, so that finally she left Edward for good and returned to Manitoba with her two daughters, Imelda and Blanche.

Rosalie settled in St-Boniface and managed on her own, doing house-cleaning and sewing in order to raise her two children while trying to put the scandal of her failed marriage behind her. She spent a lot of time at her elder sister's, especially when Léon was away. It was she who cared for Mélina before and after Gabrielle's birth, and who carried the baby at her baptism. Since then she had continued to be a frequent visitor to the Roy household, where the girls adored their big-hearted *tantouche*.[19]

Gabrielle's early years were spent in a house full of women and girls, where male presence was increasingly rare and unassertive. Her eldest brother had gone to live in the seclusion of Dollard, while her two others were boarders at classical college. As for her father, he was often absent, first physically on account of his work and then psychologically after 1915 when he was forced into retirement. The child could not understand Léon's situation; he simply seemed to her old, crippled with sorrow, and inaccessible. She had so little contact with him that the slightest show of affection, when perchance he gave way to it, surprised rather than delighted her.

Of all the women around Gabrielle, certainly the most important in her eyes was her mother, she who so filled the little girl's universe that her existence seemed indivisible from her own. This symbiosis, already very strong in Gabrielle's first years, became stronger still when most of the children had left and Léon was in retirement, when – with the father and Clémence both in their respective ways withdrawing increasingly into themselves – mother and daughter seemed to be living alone together in the house, each the only one for the other to talk to and the only companion.

Mélina was forty-five. With her brood now off her hands she had more time than ever to attend to Gabrielle, the only child left to her, and less desire and willpower than ever to resist her demands. Still, remaining close to the customs and sensibilities of country folk, as women often were in those days, she was not in the habit of putting her feelings on display and does not seem to have been a particularly affectionate mother. But she was always there, a bit overpresent even, and made a great deal of room in her life for the little girl. As Elsa does with Jimmy in *Windflower*, she smothered the child with constant attentions, giving her treats and even before she was old enough to go to school spending much time teaching her prayers and reading and writing. Mélina was virtually never away from her daughter, either to visit the neighbours or to go shopping or to weekday-morning mass at the cathedral. Mother and daughter went together to spend several weeks at Pembina Mountain every summer, and Mélina took Gabrielle with her on the infrequent journeys she indulged in, to the sanctuary at Sainte-Anne-des-Chênes, for instance, or Dollard, where she went in the fall of 1914.

From the sole fact that they were always together and most often alone together, a much closer bond developed between Gabrielle and her mother than existed between Mélina and any of her other children. A bond, moreover, that benefited not only "Maman's lil girl," as Clémence put it,[20] but also Mélina, to whom it was consolation for the grief caused her by her older children and the growing solitude in her life. Little wonder in the circumstances that Gabrielle's mother had a tendency to spoil her, giving in to her whims and sparing her chastisement. Gabrielle "spoiled" Mélina too in a sense, far more than did her older siblings, gladdening her mother with her presence and youth.

Gabrielle would retain many pictures from this synergistic closeness. Among those that stand out are shopping forays to the department stores of Winnipeg, walks in the parks, morning masses, and a number of excursions to places around St-Boniface, to St. Andrews, Bird's Hill, or even as far as Gimli on Lake Winnipeg – trips during which the little girl caught her first glimpses of the immigrant faces that would so fascinate her later.

Above all, Mélina's daughter was marked for later life by the countless stories with which her mother kept nourishing the child's imagination and which soon formed an immense oral stockpile that Gabrielle the writer would draw on extensively to enrich her own storytelling.

Mélina would almost always build her stories from memories of her youth in Quebec and her early years in Manitoba. She was clever at imitating gestures and tones of voice. She would unfold her tales from one evening to the next like Scheherazade, connecting them like the chapters of a saga.[21] Christine, the narrator in *Street of Riches*, later said of her mother, "It was [. . .] her fault if I preferred fiction to daily life. She had taught me the power of images, the wonder of a thing revealed by just the right word, and all the love that one simple and beautiful sentence may contain."[22] In the story titled "De quoi t'ennuies-tu, Éveline?" Gabrielle attributes to her heroine this gift of lively narration and talent for enthralling her listeners with moving resurrections of the past.

Mélina's were not the only stories heard in the big kitchen. Léon also had a huge repertory of memories that he would relate with great skill and enthusiasm. But his style was different to Mélina's. While Mélina, at the risk of verging on unlikelihood, would readily embellish her narrations and vary the colours each time as suggested by her propensity for fantasizing and the inspiration of the moment, Léon was a realist, a stickler for exactitude and scrupulous adherence to facts. His stories were shorter, more minutely detailed than his wife's, and often sadder or more disillusioned, their facts appearing unadorned, seen in a light that was sometimes harsh. Of the two stylistic models, Gabrielle's preference was, of course, for her mother's, a style more unfettered, more subjective and poetic, in short more "fictional" than Léon's prosiness. It was Adèle who would follow in her father's footsteps and have above all a documentary conception of literature, and only contempt for what she saw as the inventions and exaggerations with which Gabrielle padded her books.[23]

"My Street, My Universe"[24]

Apart from her mother's constant presence and the immense stockpile of stories she had heard from her, the things of childhood that imprinted themselves most forcefully in Gabrielle Roy's memory, more than people or events, were the places and landscapes of her childhood experience. With time, these places and landscapes, by dint of being described, meditated upon, and revisited over and over in her imagination, would shape a kind of inner geography whose meanings she would never cease to explore.

To readers of *Street of Riches*, *The Road Past Altamont*, and *Enchantment and Sorrow*, this geography, steeped in nostalgia, is probably more mythical than real. Of the Deschambault Street of her childhood, Gabrielle says, "Was it the street that made me in its image or was it I who made it in mine?"[25] Here, the real and the imagined are indistinguishable.

The focal point, of course, is the house that Léon built in 1905 and which changed little throughout Gabrielle's childhood. In the Roy household, as in French-Canadian families generally, almost all communal activities took place in the big kitchen, which was adorned with a photograph of Pope Benedict XV and, over the sewing machine, a picture of the Holy Family. Upstairs, Gabrielle occupied the bedroom overlooking the street, but very early took up the habit of spending long spells in the attic, where, when still very little as Adèle tells it, "she held conversations with characters out of her imagination."[26] Later the attic, with its dormer, would become the schoolgirl's retreat, a place for reading and daydreaming. She would immerse herself in her sisters' old school textbooks, stored there by her mother, or books from the parish library, "all of which," she would say later with some exaggeration, she "had read by the age of twelve."[27] Another important part of the house was the big covered verandah, which ran all the way across the front and the west side, and was bordered by flowering shrubs. Here, in rocking chairs lined up facing the street, the family would pass the long summer evenings watching the sun go down and exchanging chitchat with the neighbours.

For years the neighbours were few and far between, for the area was slow to develop. In 1911, according to *Henderson's Winnipeg Directory*, there were still only five houses on Deschambault Street, four (including the Roys') built on the north side, so that across the street there were uncultivated fields from where the voices of frogs rose at night. One had the impression of being "at the edge of the vast, ancient prairie."[28] This is where the child discovered the immense Manitoba skies that would draw such lyricism later from the novelist.

> My childhood love is the silent sky of the prairie, fitting the soft, level earth as perfectly as the bell cover on a plate, the sky that could shut one in, but which, by the height of its dome, invites us to take flight, to fly to freedom.[29]

While she learned very early to feel at home with the vast landscapes of prairie and sky as contemplated from outside St-Boniface or in the country of her maternal grandparents, this was not where Gabrielle most liked to be as a child. Her preference leaned rather to two closer spots that belonged to her familiar world of everyday life and games.

The first was the yard around the house. With its high wooden fence all around and its apple trees, the yard soon became "her own tiny kingdom which she peopled with fairies, dwarfs, giants, princes and princesses."[30] In summer, the little girl would spend long hours there, playing and making believe. After she began going to school she would organize costumed performances, acting out playlets of her own conception with her friends, in the manner of those given at the convent.

The second of these favourite spots, and even more fascinating in the child's eyes, was a small wood at the end of Deschambault Street on the east side beyond the Canadian Northern Railway tracks. Through its middle ran a small tributary of the Red River called the Seine River. To this wood, only a hundred yards or so from the house, Gabrielle went often on excursions with other schoolchildren from the neighbourhood or with Clémence. Once there, she could play to her heart's content at being La Vérendrye, Tom Sawyer, or Robinson Crusoe, and the illusion, she would say later, could last "for weeks on end."[31] But best of all was when she went to the wood by herself, for then she knew the pleasure – the bliss – of finding herself in a world that was hers alone.

> There was a clump of friendly little old oak trees. All gnarled, they seemed to me, like a bunch of kindly old men meeting as friends to talk over things that were older still. In time I joined their circle. And this little parcel of countryside, better than anything afterwards, offered me the pure delights of solitude – a bird singing in some hiding place, or lobed foliage parting to show a patch of clear sky, all, it seemed, especially for the watching, listening child.[32]

This grove of oaks was among the jewels of Gabrielle's personal geography, as shown by the number of times it figures throughout the span of her work, not only in *Street of Riches* and *The Road Past Altamont*[33] but beginning in 1940 with one of her very first stories in *La Revue moderne*,[34] and continuing through to the autobiographical works she wrote near the end of her life. Two years before her death, in a letter to Clémence, she was still talking about "the little Seine which I so loved as a child, and to which in those days we would walk hand in hand, you and I."[35]

Such fascination for the wood of her childhood connects with an important element of Gabrielle's imagery and psychology. Located in almost virgin Nature and at the same time close by her mother's house, offering both escape and refuge, this place – like the attic in the paternal dwelling or her grandmother's bench-bed in which she loved to spend the night – brought the little girl a feeling of total well-being: a harmonious mix of freedom and security; freedom without danger and security without restrictions.

The house, the yard, the banks of the little Seine: the microcosm in which Gabrielle lived was a tranquil, protected world, the more tranquil in that an absence of conflict and a kind of general amenity was characteristic of the society around her, in the child's eyes at least. The people living on Deschambault and the neighbouring streets (Desautels, Desmeurons) were almost entirely French-Canadian Catholics whose background and principles differed little from those of the Roy family. Of the eleven houses on Deschambault Street in 1919, for example, Belgians lived in one, an English-speaking family in another, and an Italian lady[36] briefly in a third, newly built house next door to the Roys; the eight others were occupied by families with names as familiar as Bourgeault, Rémillard, Verville, Lavallée, Laflamme, and Bernier, while on the neighbouring streets the names were Prudhomme, Doucet, Pelletier, Couture, Brunet, and Ferland.[37] All these people knew each other, rubbed shoulders on a daily basis, went to pay their respects to the dead in the neighbouring houses, and everyone knew pretty well what was going on behind all the neighbours' doors. At the corner of Desmeurons Street, next door to the Roys on the west side, lived the "Tombstone Gauthiers," so named because the father, Joseph, made memorial stones. The children, Louis-Philippe, Claire, Raymond, and Thérèse, were best friends to Gabrielle, who was older than they and called the signals in their games together.

Beyond Deschambault Street, the same social and cultural homogeneity prevailed in practically all of St-Boniface, or at least the northern part, centred on the cathedral, the Grey Nuns' hospital, some teaching institutions, and a large number of houses occupied by religious congregations. Life was calm and orderly, "much the way it was in a small town in Quebec" in the same period.[38] St-Boniface was still a kind of ghetto, and Franco-Manitobans were still targets of discrimination, which became increasingly pronounced from 1916 on, but for the child Gabrielle, surrounded by caring adults and stepping outside her immediate milieu only to visit her maternal grandparents, whose surroundings were even more peaceful than St-Boniface, the hostility of the outside world remained distant, as if unreal. Nothing occurred to breach this "impression of security" which was, Gabrielle would say later, "what I remember best about the early years of my life in St-Boniface, [...] the security brought to life by having a past sustained by stories, by memories, and a proven moral and social order."

> I remember that you could hear a convent or chapel bell ringing almost all the time in one corner of the city or another. [...] There were always children walking two by two on the sidewalks of our city, it seems to me, led by nuns whose rosaries would chink as they walked. While over the sluggish brown waters of the Red River flew the call of the cathedral bells, gulls [...] flew practically among the cemetery's tombs, which crowded almost down to the river's banks. [...] I liked [...] having them come all the way to the middle of a continent to bring us a feeling of open sea, a kind of island complex. For it was as though we of St-Boniface really were on an island, rather alone in an ocean of prairie and surrounded by the unknown on every side.[39]

The collision with the unknown finally happened, and St-Boniface came to look like what it was, a suburb of Winnipeg where a humiliated minority lived, inward-turned in its efforts to escape the threat of its disappearance. But these discoveries and the resulting contradictory urges came later. For the time being, the little girl felt safe among her people, protected by the language and religion she had received from her parents and shared with her entire community. The feeling of insularity, living on "a little island of natives lost in some faraway sea,"[40] was another manifestation of the peace and security that surrounded *Petite Misère*'s childhood and underlay her early experiences as "an only child."

As increasing age took her further away from it, Gabrielle Roy's childhood world of Deschambault Street would become for her a kind of ideal, even a model of paradise. As her life unfolded, she would keep trying to rebuild that familiar framework around her, combining rural and urban life, situated on the fringes of society without being totally cut off from it, a framework in which she could feel entirely free and alone and at the same time benefit from the proximity and friendship of others. Such in any event was each of her favourite places: Epping Forest on the outskirts of London, the village of Rawdon not far from Montreal, Saint-Germain-en-Laye near Paris, and the little village of Petite-Rivière-Saint-François in Quebec. Both town and country, apart from the world and in contact with it, all these places where she felt happy and fulfilled as an adult would in a way be repetitions of the little street of her childhood.

CHAPTER 3

The Last Family Picture

The Three Sons • Anna • Adèle
Clémence and Bernadette
Mélina's Bereavements • Léon's First Death

anuary 1912. A handsome, rather formal picture in a standing frame taken to mark Léon and Mélina's twenty-fifth wedding anniversary shows the Roy family in all its finery. Gabrielle, then going on three, appropriately appears at front and centre. Her mouth slightly open, she seems surprised by the photographer's antics. She is wearing a starched dress and little black boots, her cheeks are full and her arms chubby. Her eyes are wide and fixed on the lens.

To her right is her father. He is thin, bony-faced, and blue-eyed. In his stiffly formal jacket and with his balding head, walrus moustache, and a faraway, seemingly anxious expression in his eyes, he looks his age (sixty-one). Head bent slightly to the side and arms propped on the arms of his chair, he appears stooped and frail.

To Gabrielle's left, her mother, aged forty-four, positively dominates the picture. A good-looking woman, she is tall and full-figured and sits very erect, her hair thick, parted in the middle, and pulled up and back in a roll high at each side, with volume ("puffed" in the terminology of the day). Her dress of dark-coloured, striped material with intricate working at the neckline, wrists, and waist emphasizes her matronly figure and slender white hands, which she holds genteelly crossed on her lap. Her eyes are partly hidden by half-lowered eyelids, which accentuates their oval shape. Hers is the image of a self-assured, determined woman in full control of her own life and the lives of the others in the photograph.

These three are in front and are seated: Léon in a large upholstered armchair, Mélina on a straight-backed chair, and Gabrielle on a small stool that is out of sight. Standing behind them are the other children, arranged according to age. In their best bib and tucker, coiffed with care, they all look mild-mannered and well-behaved. Gathered thus, the group has all the appearances of the typical large, fine family: healthy, prosperous, and obedient to the benevolent authority of the parents; in short, happy and perfectly united.

The reality, however, was very different. Behind the ideal, conventional image, discontent, strife, and anxiety were already at work and would intensify over the ensuing years. The expressions are calm, yet every one of these individuals already bore or would soon bear his or her share of pain, revolt, or resentment; every one, or almost, would be cause for tears, anger, or disappointment on the part of the parents, whose fine family was soon to be a scene of moral and emotional ruin, a kind of wasteland.

The ensuing years were in fact a time of dispersal. A normal process to be sure, considering the ages of the children, but it was accompanied by bitterness, frustration, and disagreements of every kind, often taking on the colours of failure. The Roy dispersal was more like a family disintegration than the broadening, the opening of family space resulting from the departure of Luzina's children in *Where Nests the Water Hen*.

The Three Sons

One child is already missing from the picture, the eldest son, Joseph, who had not taken the trouble to come for the occasion. Truth to tell, Jos, as he was called, had long since stopped coming to St-Boniface or even giving any sign of life whatever. He had gone to live permanently in Dollard, where he was soon to marry Julia Marquis (in 1914). His father saw him occasionally in the course of his travels, and then it was to lecture him, recommend that he drink with more moderation, and lend him money, whose repayment he would then wait for in vain. A few years later, Jos abandoned his farm and set off "to see some new country, squandering several hundred *piastres* drinking with chance friends" and neglecting his obligations as husband and father.[1] Around 1920 he found a job as a grain buyer, which he kept for a time before beginning again to drift about Canada and the United States like a hobo. From the moment he moved to Saskatchewan in 1906, the eldest son became increasingly estranged from his family. He simply faded from sight in their universe.

There remained the two other sons, Rodolphe and Germain, both of whom appear in the picture. Rodolphe, at the far right, rests both hands on the back of Mélina's chair, as if asserting that he is – and will remain – "the mother's favourite son,"[2] the child who is most like her and can always charm her with his gaiety, thoughtful gestures, and cajolery. In 1912, "Rado" was going on fourteen. He had been a boarder at the Juniorat de la Sainte-Famille run by the Oblates and was soon to enter the Collège de Saint-Boniface, a Jesuit institution. He remained there only a few months, however, and abandoned his studies for good in 1913, to the extreme displeasure of Léon, who, after failing to educate Joseph, had expected to do better with his second son. After a spell at Dollard, where he found many "opportunities for sinning" as Adèle puts it,[3] Rodolphe returned to Manitoba, where until his mid-twenties he led the life of a small-time jobholder and ne'er-do-well that foreshadowed his later instability and degradation. Though he would willingly give money to his parents and his goddaughter, Gabrielle, and came to see them fairly regularly and was quick to contribute to the upkeep of the house, he was an unpredictable, frivolous individual who could never really be counted on.

Germain for his part was still too young at the time of this photograph to give cause for worry. He too would attend junior college and then classical college, but at seventeen he ran away for a brief spell and now and then would pilfer money from his father. When he had completed his next-to-last year of classical college in 1923, he took off for Saskatchewan, where he obtained a teaching certificate and became a schoolteacher at Dollard and later South Fork. Although he was not a real source of concern for his parents, to them and the rest of the family he was always remote and secretive. Like Joseph, he would steadily drift away from them.

All three boys had problems with alcohol, and all escaped the family orbit – deserted it, so to speak. First Joseph, then Rodolphe, then Germain could hardly wait to get out of the house and away to somewhere distant. To varying degrees, all three seem to have been weaklings, incapable either of filling their father's shoes or standing up to him.

For will and vitality, we must look then to the girls, especially the two eldest, Anna and Adèle, whose intelligence, determination, and strength of character were already making themselves felt, running sharply counter to their parents' expectations and ideals.

Anna

In the 1912 photograph, Anna looks like a young girl, with her George Sand hairstyle and a very simple dress with a white choke-collar gimp. She has in fact been married nearly four years already, and has just given birth to her third son. In her eyes and the fold of her mouth can be read a hint of melancholy, a wounded or resigned expression that clouds her face and makes her look a little sad. Perhaps she senses her youth to be irretrievably lost.

Anna's story cannot fail to strike one as rather cruel. In her teens, she was considered an imaginative and sensitive girl, a gifted pianist with a taste for lovely things and fine living. She was driven by a kind of inner fire, a craving for glamour and happiness that brings to mind the young Emma Bovary. At the convent she was something of a rebel, but her determination won the respect of both her classmates and the nuns who kept trying to reform her. One thing already seemed certain to her: she was not going to end up like other women; she was going to be free, fulfilled, happy, and lead the comfortable life of plenty she was sure she had a right to.

After obtaining her teacher's certificate, Anna left for a time to teach in rural schools at Fannystelle and Dunrea, but the life was too austere for her liking. There now remained only one solution: she must find a man ready to love her and give her a life of ease, and marry him without further ado. The happy man she chose was Albert Painchaud. Despite her father's vociferous objections, despite her mother's warnings and those of her friends, Anna married Painchaud on 18 August 1908 at the age of nineteen. Neither Léon nor Mélina attended their eldest daughter's wedding, which took place in the cathedral on a Tuesday morning, in the strictest privacy.[4] Adèle wrote later:

> Anna imagined that the marriage would assure her an easier and pleasanter life. She would become free, rid of the tutelage of her parents, annoying restraints and stupid conventions. She would have her very own house, a warm, attractive home with every modern comfort, lovely golden oak furniture, and the rest in keeping.[5]

But disillusionment soon followed. Although she had announced to Adèle that she would "arrange not to have [children]"[6] so as to remain free to travel and amuse herself as she chose, the young bride discovered very shortly after the wedding that she was pregnant, and her first son, Fernand, came into the world on 2 June 1909, less than three months after the birth of his aunt Gabrielle. Albert Painchaud decided then to settle in Saskatchewan, where Anna joined him soon after. There for a number of years she lived a harsh pioneer life, far from the amenities and social life she had dreamed of. In 1910 and 1911 she gave birth to two more children, Paul and Gilles, after which, at twenty-three, she renounced childbearing for good.

For her marriage was not at all what she had hoped for. Like Azarius in *The Tin Flute*, Albert was a joiner-carpenter by trade, but circumstances obliged him to engage in a variety of occupations and led him into all manner of misadventure, with the result that the family's existence was unstable and often precarious. Though a good man and totally devoted to his wife, he had neither the ambition, nor the sensitivity, nor the means to deliver what Anna desired; she was too strong, too demanding, and too passionate a woman for him. Unsatisfied, she would flee the conjugal roof with increasing frequency to spend time in the place she had been so impatient to leave – her mother's house. She was there with her three children in January 1917 while Albert, who had sold his farm at Dollard, was moving the family's goods and chattels, this time to Montmartre, Saskatchewan. Still hoping to improve her life, Anna took a course in typing and stenography while in St-Boniface and then found herself a job, which she kept until the following summer. Then she rejoined her husband. In the autumn of 1921 she left again, this time for Montreal, where she stayed with Adèle. Meanwhile, doubtless hoping to keep her close to home, Albert at last built her the house of her dreams, the biggest and finest in the village of Montmartre. Everyone kept wondering how Anna and her husband could afford such luxury. The answer came one night in 1926 when the Painchaud house burned to the ground, after which the family moved to St-Boniface with, so the gossips said, the insurance money in their pockets.

Anna, Albert, and the children then lived in the house on Deschambault Street, where there were memorable altercations with Léon. Next, Albert left for California and did not return for eighteen months. Anna was aging and discovering slowly that the brand of happiness she so coveted was not to be hers. Her flights from home became less and less frequent, and she confined herself to the modest existence that was her lot and that, she now knew, would be her lot for the rest of her days. The determined young girl of yesteryear was turning into a

disillusioned and embittered woman in whose nature increasingly negative and destructive characteristics were becoming apparent. At thirty-
five, Anna already resembled the wounded creature of whom Gabrielle
would say later, thinking of Chekhov's *The Three Sisters*, "I often remember seeing her stand motionless at a window, gazing out but seeing
nothing, as though knowing she'd been destined for better things and it
was now too late."[7]

Adèle

Between Anna and Adèle, who since the death of Agnès was the second
daughter of the family, there were many similarities of character. Their
stories too are alike in the tormented, rather pathetic quality of their
lives. But there was a major difference between the two: Adèle would
never resign herself to her lot.[8]

"I never liked my face," she would confide later. "When I was little,
people used to call me 'la Gadelle' because of my round, red face [like a
redcurrant] and my big nose."[9] Yet in the 1912 photograph, she is a tall,
rather pretty girl by no means lacking in grace or presence. She would
turn nineteen in a few days and was about to begin her last semester of
studies before becoming a teacher. In her eyes and bearing can be read
pride, determination, and a defiant nature which were soon to translate
into concrete acts and launch her on a lifelong course of turbulence. It all
began in adolescence, it seems, when she discovered what her mother's
life consisted of, and the lives of most other middle-class Franco-
Manitoban women, and decided, as Anna had earlier, that this was not for
her. Thus the young Domitilde (Adèle's alter ego in her book *Le Pain de
chez nous*), when her mother has declared herself to be happy, replies:

> I can't understand how a married woman could be. She has a master she
> must bow to and whose bad temper she must endure. Take you, poor
> *moudra*, you've had a big family, you scrimp and save from one year to the
> next, and you're the butt of the tantrums Father throws all the time. [...]
> The wife is her husband's slave and does herself in bearing children.[10]

As long as she was dependent on her parents, Adèle was in no position to realize her desire for freedom and, even after obtaining her
teacher's certificate, despite occasional spats and some demonstrations

of "impertinent conduct,"[11] continued to behave like the obedient girl her parents wished her to be. True enough, even far away from St-Boniface she was still in the family sphere of influence, since she was teaching first in the convent school run by the Chanoinesses régulières des Cinq Plaies at St-Alphonse (where her father had settled when he first came to Manitoba) and then the following year in the village of her birth, at the École Théobald de Saint-Léon. Through the local *curé* and the Landry family (Adèle boarded for a time at her uncle Zénon's and then at her uncle Excide's), Léon and Mélina were able to maintain constant surveillance over their daughter's life and conduct.

However, this all changed in 1914 when a first turning point came. Since Adèle had just turned twenty-one, she could now openly reject her parents' tutelage and take her life into her own hands. Against Léon's advice she enrolled in a correspondence course with a view to obtaining a bachelor of arts degree, as a man might do. By dint of patience and "despite taunts from vulgar and ignorant people, hindrances, and obstacles sown in [her] path,"[12] she finally obtained her degree twenty years later, in 1934.

But 1914 was when she decided to break away and at last start fending for herself. She set out for the West, set out for freedom.

The West and freedom were called Dollard. There she was reunited with Joseph and Anna and at once landed a job at the village school. She was determined to live as she pleased and realize her ambitions, her cultural ambitions in particular. But "the village, newly built, was a-bubble. The population, composed of immigrants from France, the United States, and Quebec, formed a strange, motley conglomeration thirsting for pleasure."[13] Far from resisting temptation, the young woman made the most of the distance from her parents, as Anna and Rodolphe were also doing at this time, and flung herself into whatever this new and different milieu had to offer: dancing, alcohol, opportunities for all manner of dissipation, and love. As she said primly many years later, "My resolutions were swept away and I let myself go. Yes, I did some unwise things, some crazy things."[14]

This excerpt from one of her unpublished manuscripts is the only allusion in all of Adèle's immense autobiographical production to what was certainly one of the most "crazy things" she did in her life, the most secret in any event – her marriage, which was celebrated that first winter in Dollard.[15] Of the bridegroom nothing is known except that his name was Edward Marrin, he lived in Regina, and is thought to have been the scion of a prominent Winnipeg business family. It is also known that Adèle's decision was the despair of her parents, who, as soon as they learned of it, did everything in their power to prevent the marriage. Léon's intervention having achieved nothing, Mélina herself boarded the train and went to Dollard to dissuade her daughter, taking Gabrielle with her. The child, then five, would have lasting memories of this hurried journey through the prairies and the mysteries of love.[16]

The union was a short-lived folly; it seems to have lasted only a few weeks. According to family legend, which stresses Adèle's difficult nature, the hapless Marrin jumped out the window and took off, unable to stand any more.[17] Certainly, Adèle was not a woman to knuckle under meekly to a husband or settle for the narrow confines of conjugal life. Her passion must have cooled very quickly, whereupon she doubtless realized that the marriage, and the man she had chosen, were not at all to her liking or in accord with her ideals in culture, refinement, and freedom. Whatever the explanation, the whole affair caused quite a scandal. Adèle even had her teaching permit cancelled by the authorities and was obliged to leave Dollard in haste. She then went to Regina, where she succeeded in being taken on as a nurse's aid by the Grey Nuns, hoping, once her training was completed, to be sent to wartime Europe. For her, Europe was the motherland of intelligence and refinement; she had long dreamed of going there and would continue to dream of it all her life.

Her hope was not realized, however, and alone once more, she was obliged to turn again to teaching for employment. Early in 1916, she left Saskatchewan for Alberta, where she had obtained a teaching permit. Then began years of constant moves from place to place, taking her to increasingly remote villages in the Canadian West. "Adèle's hardship villages,"[18] as the family termed them, had names like Taber, or Legal, or Morinville, and their common characteristic was that they were all light-years away from the civilized world and refined way of life in which Adèle aspired to a place. In 1919, fed up with being unable to live "in a milieu favourable to [her] aspirations,"[19] she decided at the age of twenty-six to give up teaching and try her luck in the East. So she left for Montreal, where she became an office worker. In her spare time she continued her own education, haunting Saint-Sulpice Library, taking courses at the Monument National, reading, going to the theatre, devoting herself to culture and pursuits of the mind.

But this was a short period. After barely three years, lo and behold she was assailed by the last thing she expected: loneliness. Although her mother came to visit her in the summer of 1921, followed by Anna in October, Adèle felt increasingly alone in Montreal, where she had not been able to make friends. She hated her job more every day and remained a perpetual outsider in a city where she felt she would never shake off her immigrant status. So she returned to St-Boniface in July 1922, only to set out again immediately for Alberta and the same peregrinations from one remote settlement to another. Over the next five years, her postings were at Villeneuve, Beaumont, Bordeaux, Thérien, Foisy, Duvernay – each stay as brief as the last, as gruelling, as unrewarding. The men she met and sometimes took as lovers invariably let her down; there was even a priest who offered to share his life with her: "You'll confess to me," he proposed, "I'll confess to God; it could last a lifetime."[20] In her eyes, all the children she taught were equally lazy, deceitful, and bad-mannered. At each posting it was the same story: either she quarrelled with her neighbours or the school authorities and was dismissed, or she was dissatisfied with the place and people and decided to go elsewhere, to some other village that soon turned out to be equally hostile or disappointing.

A strange creature, constantly uprooting, rebelling, falling out with those around her, incapable of finding peace. In *Enchantment and Sorrow*, Gabrielle interprets Adèle's destiny as being a long quest for love, a quest continually frustrated, continually begun over.

> My poor sister! I realize now that she craved affection and longed to be understood and accepted, but everything she did seemed designed to rebuff affection. I've often wondered if people like Adèle are incapable of reaching out to others because there's no love in their lives, or whether their inability to reach out has kept love at bay.[21]

And Gabrielle adds, "One would have said she never could punish herself enough for having strayed into love in her tender and vulnerable youth."[22] But in Adèle's misadventures, as in Anna's, there was another and perhaps more important dimension, her refusal to accept the limits imposed by her sex and birth milieu, her need to pull herself up, improve her lot, accede to better things than those which society and her education had destined for her. Feeling that they deserved and were worth more than what their condition offered drove both Anna and Adèle, each in her own way, in their actions if not thoughts, to rise up against the model before their eyes, meaning essentially against everything their family and the mother who had raised them stood for: the modest, docile, and well-ordered life, the frugality, the day-to-day monotony, the submission, humiliation even, and all one's desires unsatisfied – in this sense, both Adèle and Anna were rebel daughters.

They were, in fact, their youngest sister's direct precursors. Gabrielle followed the same course as they. In her, as soon as she was old enough to express such things, we find the same dissatisfaction, the same aspiration to freedom and self-betterment, the same rejection of her mother's world, the same fierce compulsion to break away from her family and make her own life. But the similarities linking the temperament and destiny of the three sisters only reveals more brutally the pathetic quality of the elder sisters' lives, for where the youngest triumphed beyond all expectations, Anna and Adèle knew only the bitterness of failure.

Clémence and Bernadette

We return to the family portrait of January 1912. Two of the group, at the left of the photograph, remain to be considered. Their faces are remarkably similar, but the impression of similarity owes most to the way they are dressed and coiffed, for two more different people could hardly be imagined.

First Clémence, who resembles the description of her written later by her sister Adèle: thick, jet-black hair, dark, deep-set eyes, small, pointed nose. It had already been noted for some years that "Coumence," as she was called familiarly, was not like other children. She was less quick-witted, more indolent by temperament, and her behaviour was often odd and inexplicable; for example, her spells of excessive modesty, her terrors and sudden fits of crying, and the nervous breakdowns she was subject to, brought on by overexcitement, obstinacy, or melancholia. Then there were times when things she said and did seemed just too right, too lucid, as though someone else were speaking or acting through her.[23] What the source of her trouble was, no one knew exactly. It could have been a severe fever she had caught when very young,[24] or perhaps a trauma resulting from the advances of a confessor;[25] hypotheses and explanations were never clear, and medicine in those days knew of no remedy for her condition. One thing was certain, however, and it broke Mélina's heart: Clémence could not and doubtless would never be able to fend for herself.

Already she was repeating years at school. One year she landed in the same class as Bernadette, who was two years younger than she. Then the nuns wanted no more of her, and so at fifteen she left the convent without even completing sixth grade. It was about a year and a half after this event that the photograph of January 1912 was taken.

By this time, Clémence hardly ever left the house. Mélina had her do household chores and tend the youngest children. But this "Cinderella" role, as she would call it,[26] only made her more unhappy and unpredictable. One night in 1914, she ran away from home for the first time, obliging her parents to notify the police. She was found in the small hours of the morning, prostrated in the middle of a city park, and a doctor had to be called to bring her home. She was then placed with relatives in Somerset for four months, after which she went with Adèle to Dollard. She returned home several weeks later. In 1917, she left again with Adèle, this time for Morinville, north of Edmonton. The two sisters had trouble getting along, however, and after several months Clémence came back to St-Boniface to resume her household chores and her boredom. The ensuing years were particularly difficult; there was another serious breakdown followed by an internment in a sanatorium. Then in October 1922 she ran away and was gone for four days, during which, Mélina wrote to a relative, "we suffered [. . .] all that can be suffered on this earth."[27]

It would seem that Clémence's condition stabilized subsequently, or else her family finally accepted and became accustomed to it as something that neither she nor they could do anything about. She lived with her parents as both a perpetual child and maid of all work, inspiring sometimes solicitude, sometimes impatience and barely concealed contempt. She would be Mélina's cross to be borne to the very end, and at the same time the most loving and most faithful of her daughters.

"I was very dark-haired," Clémence would write to Gabrielle. "As dark as Bernadette was blonde when she was little."[28] Bernadette, by comparison with Clémence and even with Anna and Adèle, held a very special place in the family. Whereas her sisters brought worry and heartbreak to their mother, "Dédette," as Gabrielle called her, or "Bédette," as she was to Adèle, was her parents' pride and joy. She was a model child, pious, pretty, brilliant in school, an accomplished musician, who loved nothing so much as elegance and delicacy in everything, be it needlework, diction, or good manners. Among the family members she was "like a princess,"[29] someone for whom life seemed to have reserved only the best.

At the time of the photograph, Bernadette had just turned fourteen. She was studying at the Académie Saint-Joseph, where she was the only daughter of the family attending since Clémence's expulsion and Adèle's departure for normal school. She remained another three years, until it was time for Gabrielle herself to be enrolled. Then after a year's apprenticeship at the normal school, she became a teacher like Anna and Adèle before her and, also like her two sisters, served her first year of employment in the Pembina Mountain district, at Somerset. However, she was luckier than Anna and Adèle in obtaining a position in St-Boniface on the staff of the Institut Provencher for the following year, beginning in the fall of 1917.

Mélina was delighted to have at least one of her children at home and old enough to earn a living, all the others having left and settled far away. Bernadette's presence and the board she paid her parents were a godsend in the difficult times that followed Léon's forced retirement. Alas, this fortunate arrangement lasted only two years. Having "no inclination toward young men"[30] or people in general, and little liking for domesticity, Bernadette discovered that she had a religious vocation, as did three of her dearest friends. During the summer of 1919, she announced that she had decided to join the Soeurs des Saints Noms de Jésus et de Marie, who sent her to their Hochelaga noviciate in Montreal. She emerged two years later after taking her temporary vows, an event attended by Adèle, who was living in Montreal, and Mélina, who came east for the occasion. Henceforth Dédette bore the name Sister Léon-de-la-Croix, a name she had chosen in honour of her father.[31]

Fortunately her first assignment returned her to St-Boniface as a teaching sister at the elementary level. She would remain at the Académie Saint-Joseph for six years, until 1927, when she too vanished to distant parts, the wilds of Northern Ontario. But even during those six years while she was living near her parents' house, she was no longer *la belle Dédette*, as her mother used to call her. She was now Sister Léon, a sacred person who must be shown the respect due her habit and status. She did not belong to her family any more but to her community, whose strict rules had virtually made a stranger of her.

Thus, Léon and Mélina lost yet another of their daughters, not to a man this time but to God, which, meritorious though it may have been, was no less painful. As good Christians, instead of grieving over it they must perforce see cause for joy in it and humbly raise thanks to Heaven.

Mélina's Bereavements

In the photograph of January 1912, Joseph alone is missing. If another family picture were taken in, say, 1920 or 1921, many more would be absent, with only two faces remaining to be photographed with the parents: Clémence's – more expressionless, more inscrutable no doubt – and Gabrielle's. All the others had by this time left and were fending for themselves, one in a village nearby (Rodolphe) and the rest scattered across the country, from Saskatchewan (Joseph, Anna, and Germain) to Montreal (Adèle and Bernadette). And of all of them, except perhaps Germain, it could be said that their personalities were by now defined and their respective destinies irrevocably sealed. Virtually nothing would happen to them in the future that had not been foreshadowed by what they had already lived and revealed of themselves, nothing that was not in some way a continuation or mere repetition.

In less than ten years, corresponding roughly to Gabrielle's first ten years of life, the large, fine family of Deschambault Street had fallen apart like a house of cards. Mélina, now in her mid-fifties, had seen her children leave one after the other, her maternal role slipping away, most of it at least, along with the joys, responsibilities, and authority that went with it. Now she was facing old age, the age of loneliness and retrenchment.

It was a loneliness made the more cruel by the loss of her own parents, both of whom died in the course of these same years.

Since leaving Pembina Mountain and coming to St-Boniface in 1897, Mélina had always remained very attached to her family and the scenes of her adolescence. Every summer while Léon was visiting his colonies, she and the children spent their summer vacation at the Landry grandparents' farm where she had grown up. They also went for New Year's Day and often at Easter, despite the four-hour train ride between Winnipeg and Somerset. These "rustications," as Adèle was to call them, would sometimes last several weeks and for the children were a time of delight when they would play with their cousins, eat delicious meals, and take excursions in the countryside. As for Mélina, besides the rest afforded by these breaks in the routine and minor harassments of city life, she found in her parents' home a freedom and security that brought back the happy days before her marriage, "something like her youthful joy,"[32] – like the emotion Rose-Anna feels in *The Tin Flute* when she thinks of her birthplace on the banks of the Richelieu River.

Pembina Mountain was also a return to good old rural Quebec, whose customs, worship, traditional dishes, furniture, and architecture, not to mention language, seemed preserved here, safe from all harm. Among these first-generation immigrants, assimilation had not yet begun to work, and in the house of Élie Landry and his wife, people lived as if they were still in St-Alphonse-de-Rodriguez, deep in the Laurentian Mountains. So completely that Gabrielle could take inspiration from her stays in the country to invoke the charm of the typical old-fashioned French-Canadian Christmas:

> I remember charming Christmases when as a little girl I would go and spend them in a small Pembina Mountain village. [. . .] If it's true that French Canadians put on a feast whenever their hospitality is brought into play, what can be said of those Christmas *réveillons* when all the things the housewife had been storing up frozen for weeks suddenly found their way to the table: golden, crunchy, grilled salt pork, goose, stuffed chicken, roasts of pork, beef and lamb, pies, cakes, maple sugar and syrup [. . .]. This was the way [Christmas] was celebrated before 1763. This is the way it is still celebrated this year.[33]

But Gabrielle was born too late to have first-hand knowledge of her Landry grandparents' world. She had to re-create it in her own mind from the stories told by her mother and sisters, for it came to an end while she was very young. Élie was the first to die, on 6 August 1912 at the age of seventy-seven. A photograph taken on the occasion of his golden wedding anniversary the previous summer shows him as a venerable old man with white beard and hair, holding a fine pommelled cane in his right hand, like a patriarch's sceptre. But really it was a blind man's cane, for Élie had lost his sight years earlier, which exposed him to all kinds of mishaps and accidents. One day he fell into a lake and very nearly drowned. Sometimes he would get lost between the house and the village and people would have to be sent out to find him. He left to his survivors, besides a fine farm and "a little sum [. . .] which was quite respectable,"[34] the memory of a kind, affectionate man, an incurable dreamer.

In comparison, Émilie was the incarnation of common sense and no nonsense. As an old woman she was generous and hospitable to be sure, but rather cantankerous. "Quarrelsome,"[35] authoritarian, and devout, she had a horror of disorder and lack of discipline. She had never really accepted her husband's adventurous bent or the exile he had led her into so far from Quebec, in what she called a "barbarous land" full of "foreigners."[36] In many ways she was like Madame Laplante in *The Tin Flute*,[37] and Mélina must often have felt the way Rose-Anna felt beside her mother: inferior, pitiful, showered with favours yet bereft of tenderness.

But the feature of Émilie's personality that emerges most forcefully is the tirelessness and extreme competence with which this powerful woman managed and brought order to the realities in her life. She baked the best bread, made the best-tasting jams, sewed like a dream; everything she touched turned as if by magic into order and beauty. She held the world in her hand, one might say. As Gabrielle wrote in 1970:

> If she lived now, amid the preoccupation with self-fulfillment for women, my grandmother would likely be director of some big business or heading up a Royal Commission on the status of women. In her day, her talents were fully occupied from dawn to dusk making soap or cloth or shoes. She also concocted herbal remedies, dyes for her cloth and splendid designs for her rugs.[38]

This "almighty grandmother" is Gabrielle's inspiration in *The Road Past Altamont* when she has the child Christine say to the old woman who has just made her a doll out of rags, "You're like God [. . .] You're just like God. You can make things out of nothing as he does."[39]

While she had not been there in time to know her grandfather Élie, Gabrielle remembered much about Émilie very well, her face and things "this proud woman" did and said. "My grandmother's tall figure hovers over my first memories like the grain elevators of the west,"[40] she writes. She came to know her grandmother first at Somerset, where the air was good and the food plentiful, and where Mélina had sent her in the summer of 1915 to recover from an illness. The widowed grandmother was then living in the village not far from the church, in a little house that had been built especially for her on the model of a Quebec house. Then in October 1916 the old woman came to live in the same house as her granddaughter on Deschambault Street. Or rather she came to die, for it was her last winter and she spent it ill and unable to look after herself, and accepting only grudgingly the care being lavished on her.[41] Émilie ended her "reign" on 7 March 1917. Her body was laid out in the parlour of the house in St-Boniface, then buried beside Élie's in the cemetery at Somerset. She was eighty-six. Gabrielle, who would soon be eight, knew her first bereavement.

But the pain of loss struck most cruelly at Mélina, who found herself orphaned and as it were without resort against the crumbling of things and the relentless progression of time. The children's departure, the disaffection that kept taking them further away, Marie-Agnès's accident, Clémence's illness, and now the death of her mother; all around her seemed to be disillusionment and grief.

Léon's First Death

These troubles were nothing, however, beside what struck the household in the autumn of 1915, the dominant event of all these years, the pivotal catastrophe. Léon was dismissed from his job.

Since he began working for the federal government, Léon had always carried out his duties conscientiously. Although he had had no increase in salary since 1903, his superiors were pleased with him, his diligence, the dedication he showed toward the colonists, and also no doubt his zeal come election time. Which was why, early in 1912, the immigration commissioner in Winnipeg, Bruce Walker, wrote this ringing panegyric to "Officer Roy's" work and character:

> I do not think there is in all the Department any one man to whom more credit is due for successful settlement of colonies in the West than to Officer Roy. He has been personally engaged in the settlement of every large party who have homesteaded in the West during the period of his employment, and I look upon him today as one of my most efficient and reliable officers, and indeed at critical times and in critical circumstances I have no hesitation in calling on him to assist me in difficult work, and I am glad to say on every occasion his services have not only been given cheerfully, but success has attended his efforts.

And Léon's boss concluded, "I am very glad, therefore, to emphasize my recommendation that a substantial increase should be given to Officer Roy."[42]

The intent of this letter was, presumably, not only to obtain a raise for a model employee but also to protect Léon from the possible if not probable dismissal awaiting him, as it awaited all federal civil servants appointed by the Liberal party. The federal election of the previous fall had ended fifteen years of rule by Wilfrid Laurier's government and brought Robert Borden's Conservatives to power. Since then, all jobs obtained through Liberal patronage were in jeopardy. One can easily imagine Léon's agitation and the intercessions he had been soliciting in his efforts to save his livelihood. This may explain the anxious air about him in the photograph of January 1912, which was taken as Commissioner Walker, himself a staunch Liberal, was preparing to write his letter in praise of Léon's merits to their superiors in Ottawa.

The increase in salary was not granted. The new minister of the Interior had his aide reply laconically that "no action would be taken,"[43] but at least Officer Roy had kept his job. His days were numbered, however; he knew this perfectly well, because he knew the rules of political favouritism all the better for having used them to his own benefit fifteen years earlier. He knew that Conservative party workers in St-Boniface and other Manitoba villages, many of whom had not forgotten his "betrayal" in 1896, were working hard to turn the tables on him, making requests of their organizers and members of Parliament similar to those that he himself had made of Laurier and Sifton – asking that the Liberal Roy be removed without delay and replaced with someone more "reliable" and "deserving."

The axe fell in the autumn of 1915. In Ottawa on October 7, a memorandum signed by the deputy minister of the Interior landed on the desk of W. D. Scott, superintendent of Immigration:

> Kindly issue instructions that the services of Leon Roy, Interpreter of the Immigration Department, Winnipeg, are to be discontinued.[44]

The news was transmitted to Winnipeg and announced officially to Léon a week later by Commissioner Walker. Immediately, Léon attempted to riposte by writing (or having someone write) a letter of protest, which the same Mr. Walker hastened to transmit to Ottawa:

> When a faithful servant has been employed for eighteen years and has given not only entire satisfaction but has devoted the best years of his life in giving others who have come to our country the ways and means of settlement, you will [not] be astonished if I say that I am not only surprised but cannot understand this action on the part of the Minister.
>
> I was appointed by Order in Council in 1897 in the position I occupied and if it is for the good of the country that I should be dismissed I have nothing to say, but I think that in justice I should have been given a longer

notice or else my salary should have been paid for six months. I am a poor man, advanced in age and with a family on my hands . . .[45]

Despite its pathetic tone, the plea received no reply. Léon next tried stirring up the press; he wrote a long letter to *La Liberté* in which he denounced "those who hinder colonization with party politics by having men discharged, without expressed reason, after 15 to 20 years of service."[46] A little later, Wilfrid Laurier, now Leader of the Opposition, raised the question himself in the Commons, attempting to have the department's decision reversed.[47] This too was to no avail, and the former civil servant had finally to accept the truth of the matter: he was no longer wanted and nothing or no one was going to give him back the job he had lost.

There was certainly something distasteful about Léon's dismissal, first in the absence of some clearly stated reason, which prevented him from launching any kind of official appeal. Second in the curt manner in which it was done, without any offer of compensation. Finally, according to Adèle and Gabrielle, it was done just as the federal government was about to offer its employees a retirement plan, to which Léon would normally have been entitled.[48]

Be all that as it may, there must have been some purely administrative considerations as well. It should be remembered that Léon had just turned sixty-five and was no longer able to expend himself for his colonists as before. The First World War had greatly slowed the rate of immigration too, and there was less and less need for the services of interpreters and agents like him. Above all, it was accepted political practice that, having been hired because he was a friend of the party in power, Léon should lose his job once that party was out of power. What is surprising is not that he was dismissed but that it took so long. Since the Conservatives were in power both in Ottawa and Winnipeg (where they had been the governing party since 1900), they had been in double control of patronage in Manitoba since 1911. Léon perhaps owed his four-year reprieve to high-placed support, namely from Monseigneur Adélard Langevin, archbishop of St-Boniface, to whom he had had occasion to render service in the past for the settlement of Catholic colonists from Quebec and Europe,[49] and who was a personal friend of the provincial premier, R. P. Roblin. Monseigneur Langevin had died in the autumn of 1915, however, while Roblin, who had been obliged to resign the previous May, had seen his party beaten by the Liberals of T. C. Norris in the provincial election of August 6. It could be that Conservative party stalwarts, looking for vengeance, had decided to take it out on the old Liberal Léon Roy.

Whatever the case, for Léon it was disaster. Overnight, everything he had built in twenty years collapsed. Not only was he stripped of the prestige and security attached to his status as a civil servant, but all he had given of himself was brusquely reduced to dust. True, he was no longer undertaking those long journeys through the West and those visits to colonies that had given him such delight in earlier days, but at least when he went to his office in Winnipeg or withdrew in the evening to his office at home to study his file cards, prepare his lists, and write his reports, he could still feel he played a part in building the country, modest though it might be. Now all of this was finished and suddenly he was again as bereft, as superfluous, as orphaned as when he had left St-Isidore in Quebec. Except that now he was an old man and the future was not going to come to his rescue.

This was the man, "having fallen low, his hopes fled," whom Gabrielle ultimately had for a father. She was six at the time of his dismissal and "began to be frightened by the aura of tragedy surrounding him."[50]

> I was the only one of his children who hadn't known him as a man of great plans, fine accomplishments, and profound hopes which gave life to his clear blue eyes. Or at least, I was so young I could only have had the most tenuous, most shadowy memories of him while he was still that way.[51]

Rather like Christine's father in *Street of Riches*, the Léon Gabrielle knew was a broken man, spent from ruminating his sense of failure, as if dead inside. "For with this letter [of dismissal], not only had he lost all confidence in what he was, in what he could do, he had lost the feeling of ever having been useful. This letter in a sense stripped him of all his achievements, and he kept on living only to bear the weight of this defeat upon his shoulders."[52] In his daughter's eyes, as no doubt in his own, he was only a shadow of the man he had been, someone who belonged to the past and the darkness, a kind of ghost.

"That Person All Unknown to Me"

*I*n a way, the very early years of Gabrielle's life escaped the confines of historical time. Although influenced by the prevailing family and social circumstances, these years are not so much a defined period in her biography as a kind of mythical space preceding her life properly speaking, a space that her adult mind, returning later to its own origins and rediscovering the first impressions demarcating it, would endow with significance and depict as the age of innocence and purest authenticity. Evoking this "singular childhood" was therefore Gabrielle the writer's way of enabling us to grasp certain images fundamental to her identity and imagination.

This Edenistic phase ended somewhere between 1915 and 1920, when the little girl was entering middle childhood and her life began to organize into more or less significant events capable of shaping it into a "destiny." The period beginning then and lasting until about 1928, corresponding to the end of childhood followed by the years of adolescence, was crucial in this process. Gabrielle's character acquired greater definition, her relationships with those around her intensified and became more complex, and through introspection and reflection on the world around she became more keenly aware of her condition in life, her desires, her dreams, and also her aversions. To be sure, as an adolescent she was not yet in a position to follow her inclinations or make her own choices, since her education was not yet complete and she was still under the thumb of her parents and educators. However, observing her attitudes and the changes taking place in her, we can recognize already in the Gabrielle Roy of this period some of the most characteristic traits of the woman she would become with maturity; the contours of her future character and life preferences are even now beginning to show.

The Schoolgirl

In September 1915, a month before Léon's dismissal, Gabrielle began her first year of school at the Académie Saint-Joseph, where her sisters had all received at least part of their schooling, often as boarders. Gabrielle herself would live at home for the twelve years she attended the school.

The Académie was founded in 1898 by the Soeurs des Saints Noms de Jésus et de Marie (Sisters of the Holy Names of Jesus and Mary), for whom it was also a convent, but when Gabrielle was a pupil it occupied a brand-new building, inaugurated in 1912. This building was located at the corner of Avenue de la Cathédrale and Desmeurons Street, very near the Roy house. There were thirty or so nuns teaching there and the school was attended by some eight hundred pupils, all girls, divided among roughly twenty classes covering first to twelfth grade.

When she began school, Gabrielle was six and a half, which was fairly advanced considering the ages of other children taught by Sister Albert de Messine (Marie-Rose Gariépy) in her Grade 1 class; many of the little girls were seven and some were fully eight, nine, or even ten.[1] Most had French names, for in 1915 the Académie was still a French school, in fact if not by right.

As regards religion, the regime introduced by the Laurier–Greenway agreement of 1896 allowed or rather tolerated religious instruction in the public schools of Manitoba providing the number of pupils warranted it – a condition easily met by the Académie Saint-Joseph – and providing the time spent teaching it was strictly limited. This second condition was by no means met. As in Quebec in those days, religion meant almost everything. Not only was a great deal of catechism and religious history taught, but secular subjects – history, geography, reading and writing, as well as activities today considered "extracurricular" – were also heavily laced with religious references and content. The Conservative government of Manitoba, led by R. P. Roblin, who was a close friend of the archbishop, cheerfully closed its eyes to this civil disobedience when not covertly encouraging it.

As regards language, the agreement of 1896 provided that "in schools attended by ten children [habitually] speaking French or a language other than English, instruction may be given in English and in the mother tongue, in accordance with the bilingual system."[2] This applied to the Académie, since in 1915 it was considered officially to be one of these bilingual schools. In fact, French was the dominant if not exclusive language at the school, thanks once again to government tolerance. This was why Gabrielle's sisters had been able to pursue virtually all their studies in French, much as if they had attended a convent in Quebec City or Trois-Rivières.

This was not altogether the case for Gabrielle. In 1915–1916, her first year of school, there occurred a major change in Manitoba's educational policy with the return to power of the Liberals under the leadership of T. C. Norris. Judging the English language to be threatened by the invasion of "foreign" languages and distrusting in particular the French-Canadian and German minorities who were suspected of harbouring only half-hearted loyalty to the British Empire, which was then at war, the Norris government decided to put an end to the bilingual system of education. With the Thornton Act passed into law in the spring of 1916, it forbade the teaching of any language other than English in the public schools of the province, except for a single hour at the beginning or end of a day. This new regime, of which Gabrielle was one of the first "beneficiaries," would remain officially in force in Manitoba for more than half a century.

The fresh onslaught by the enemies of *la race* raised a tempest in French-Canadian circles, with the civil and religious elite mobilizing to plan and launch the resistance. This resulted in the founding in June 1916 of the Association d'éducation des Canadiens français du Manitoba, whose activities, once in definitive form, would be extremely well organized and effective.

At the Académie Saint-Joseph, the nuns had little choice but to conform as best they could with the new rules. So they officially changed the language in which they taught and spent more time teaching English grammar and literature, but for all that did not stop teaching French to their French-speaking pupils, adding to the one permitted hour of class per day other, unpaid hours, and during regular periods cheerfully defying the law, convinced that they were combatting fanaticism and comfortable to have the blessing of the new archbishop of St-Boniface, Monseigneur Arthur Béliveau.[3]

The difficulties created by such a situation in the years immediately following the adoption of the anti-French law are not hard to imagine, particularly for little French-speaking children like Gabrielle who were just beginning school in an educational system in the throes of change. Confusion reigned in the classrooms and the quality of the teaching suffered. Furthermore, for children raised in an almost entirely French family environment, school became an environment that seemed largely foreign, if not hostile, making their adaptation even more difficult. From that point on throughout their early years of school, the children had to direct most of their efforts to learning English, since that was indispensable to following the official curriculum of the Department of Education, and also to passing the various examinations, which were all held in English.

In such circumstances, it is understandable if a child as brilliant and gifted as Gabrielle (later years proved this abundantly) should be a rather indolent student until Grade 6 or 7. She did not have to repeat any year, but showed little taste for studying, fairly often missed school, and was content with very average marks. School for her at this time was far from the stimulating environment it became later after she began to assert and distinguish herself so forcefully as an adolescent.

Petite Misère

But the political and educational context was not all. The child's indolence also had roots in much more intimate factors related to private or family experiences between about 1917 and 1922.

These years seem to have been so difficult for Gabrielle that we can consider it a period of real crisis. Besides what we know of her performance at school, there are many indications that from the age of eight or nine she had ceased to be a happy child and her early discovery of the world and of herself had not been achieved painlessly.

The first manifestations of crisis were physical disorders. Adèle was coming fairly regularly to St-Boniface at this time and remembers her visit of July 1917:

> [Gabrielle] was seven when her health turned for the worse. She lost her appetite, began to bite her nails, and grind her teeth while asleep. She complained of headaches and stomachaches. *La mère* took her to the doctor who, having examined her, announced that the poor little girl had worms. He prescribed medicines that would destroy them.[4]

Far from being transitory, these illnesses were only the first of a series spread over four or five years, during which the symptoms kept accumulating and diversifying; after "worms" came "measles, tonsillitis, earache, chest and head colds which weakened her constitution and upset her nervous system."[5] The child even contracted a case of jaundice, which necessitated a short stay in hospital. If it was not a sore throat, an uncontrollable cough, or an attack of tachycardia plaguing her, it was extreme fatigue and she would be forced to rest lying down for whole days, either on the sofa in the living room or, if it was summer, in the hammock her father had bought for her and hung between two columns of the verandah. Recalling this period of her childhood, Gabrielle later wrote the story titled "My Whooping Cough." In it, the narrator remembers that, "They [...] said that I weighed no more at eight than formerly when I was four."[6] "They" means the other family members, including Adèle, who when speaking of her visit in 1917 observes:

> [Gabrielle] no longer had the strength or desire to play with her companions. She felt an imperative need for calm and rest. In my memory I see her lying on the sofa, in the office adjoining the dining room, her head in the hollow of a bent arm, her stockings pulled down on her thin legs, and moaning like a little wounded animal. *Le père* would come into the room sometimes and look at her, shaking his head.[7]

Everything happened as though the little girl were constantly ill and never managed to recover. However, this chronic weakness, together with the diversity of symptoms and the indeterminate nature of her illness, suggests something more general, something not only caused by physical deficiency but also denoting psychological or emotional problems in the order of depression.

Adèle herself, beyond noting that Gabrielle always "looked sickly, with those dark rings under her eyes, her thin body, and her skinny legs,"[8] stresses her petulance, her tears, her constant recriminations, and the gloom in which she seemed to enclose herself. "*La Misère*," she wrote, "had a morbid need of affection. [...] She considered herself unhappy and seemed to be begging others to take pity on her."[9]

In Adèle's eyes, this behaviour was just an expression of her little sister's bad-tempered nature, and at this time Gabrielle was simply doing already what she would do later, feigning unhappiness and bewailing it in order to draw attention and devotion from others. But in her moaning and groaning, sulking, and gloominess, as in her recurrent illnesses, one can just as well see signs of some real psychological distress, or at least some inner crisis.

Although the exact nature and causes of this childhood crisis are difficult to determine, we can gain some insight by recalling two "true little events" from this time that throw light on the child's behaviour and attitudes. The first was being given the nickname *Petite Misère* (appropriately translated by Harry Binsse as "Little Miss Misery"), an event that Gabrielle, in a confidence imparted in 1973, attributes to precisely this period of her childhood, contradicting both Adèle's version and her own fictional one in *Street of Riches*, which place it much earlier. This 1973 document would appear the more reliable in that it is the only version that is frankly autobiographical. Adèle could be right, and her father could indeed have invented the name at Gabrielle's birth, but the following story shows that, if so, Gabrielle had not really become conscious of it before the age of eight or nine. Joan Hind-Smith, who heard the story from Gabrielle's own mouth, reports it in these words:

> One afternoon, as her father turned into the walk of his home, he found [Gabrielle, then about eight years old,] crying and struggling with an old board which had been left by workmen who were tearing up the wooden sidewalk on Rue Deschambault in order to replace it with cement. The other children in the neighbourhood had snatched up the rest of the planks and had run off to make playhouses. Léon Roy, at the sight of his weak and pitiful Gabrielle, immediately nicknamed her "Petite Misère" – Little Miserable One. She was crying because only one board had been left for her, and to make up for this he made her a playhouse himself, in the backyard. Nevertheless, the nickname "Petite Misère" stuck, and it secretly angered her. She did not intend to be miserable – like him.[10]

"You didn't much like that nickname," Clémence reminded her in 1981.[11] Although expressing affectionate compassion on her father's part, the words *Petite Misère* were nonetheless perceived by Gabrielle at the time as a condemnation, marking her out as a burden and dooming her to misery. Identified with the opposite of joy, *La Misère* or *Misère*, as she was also called, could see only a kind of rejection in the nickname, a way of isolating her and denying her any worth.[12] This feeling could have been reinforced in the course of these same years by her older sister Bernadette's entering religion; the event that filled the parents with pride and joy and made Dédette the centre of attention and the family's favourite child for several months looked in the child Gabrielle's mind like yet another proof of her own unimportance, and of the exclusion she felt to be hanging over her.

Nothing, however, sheds more light on Gabrielle's state of mind and the significance she attached to her nickname *Petite Misère* than a second event that bears examination. This was her discovery of the particular circumstances of her birth. At about this time her sister Anna, who claimed to have the information from Rodolphe, Gabrielle's godfather, told her one day that when she was born, *le père*, her father, flew into a great rage and cursed Heaven for having saddled him with another child to feed and raise when he was so old and poor. In other words, Gabrielle learned abruptly that her birth had been an infliction for her family and that, far from being greeted with joy and love, she had been only "a child of duty," like Christine in *Street of Riches*, who says, "My father wanted no part of me. No one wanted any part of me. I should not have come into the world."[13]

Gabrielle continued to believe this story about her own birth, which she heard when she was eight or nine, for much of her life. It was only around 1970 that Rodolphe, who was then near death, set the facts straight: when Gabrielle was born, Léon was not at home but in Saskatchewan among the Doukhobors, from where he returned only six weeks later. The melodramatic scene of paternal ire had therefore been just a spiteful invention on Anna's part. Adèle, who heard the facts from Rodolphe, urged him to write to his goddaughter himself to put an end to the legend. Gabrielle then confided to Adèle:

> Rodolphe's letter restoring the truth about my birth has lifted a weight from my heart that has lain heavily on it for years. God grant that he's telling the truth this time and thank you a hundred thousand times for having obtained this letter, which doesn't make me love our father more – I always loved though perhaps feared him when I was young – but has sweetened the memories I have of him a bit.[14]

At the time, however, in a period when Gabrielle was still a child and her sense of herself was just beginning to crystallize, Anna's "revelation" came as a shock that left her dejected and confused. On her visit in the summer of 1917, Adèle found her in a state of decline, morally and physically. The child bewailed "that her birth, being undesired, should never have happened, that she was one too many in the family."[15] There were the same protestations three years later when Gabrielle talked in Adèle's presence about being "an unhealthy, unwanted, and neglected girl living between two old people who [squabble] all the time."[16]

That there was a degree of morose pleasure in this attitude, as Adèle thinks, is beyond question. Still, the child did have reasons for being disconsolate. It is far from reassuring to be seen by others as a frail, pitiable creature derisively nicknamed *Petite Misère*, to be told that one had not been wanted and is superfluous in the world. These experiences could not help but create or confirm in the child, initially at least, a sense of fragility about herself, if not unworthiness, making her want both to shrink from sight and to turn inward in solitude, in dreamy abstraction or despondency. The "only child," having once enjoyed everyone's attention and caresses, now all at once perceived herself as a child who was alone, superfluous in some way, and deprived of love.

This childhood drama does much to explain an important aspect of Gabrielle's childhood and adolescence – her extremely difficult relationship with her father. In both the "Petite Misère" and "unwelcome birth" scenarios, he was the principal protagonist. The little girl's surliness was directed above all at him. At this time Léon was a man broken by his recent troubles and left ill-tempered and bitter. He would retire to his "office" or sit smoking his pipe by the fire, ruminating his resentments, hardly ever saying a word to anyone, and seeming to have ceased to live. And if he had a word to say, it was to complain about the shortage of money, the hard times, and his children's ingratitude. He and Mélina had become more than ever strangers to one another, bound together now only by their constant quarrels. Having "unlearned the art of the caress," sunk "in an aching spiritual solitude," as Adèle puts it,[17] in Gabrielle's eyes Léon seemed like a distant, cantankerous old man incapable of love and hostile to any kind of happiness.

Later in life, Gabrielle would return to this negative image that she had retained of her father from her childhood. Or rather she would round it out and soften it with other, more touching images like those of the "rhubarb pie" and the "glass song" in *Street of Riches*, the hospital visit in *Enchantment and Sorrow*, or the gardener lovingly tending his plants. Thus in 1960, replying to one of Bernadette's "summer letters," she would recall "Papa [. . .] with his love of roses":

Poor old soul, nowadays when I picture him he's almost always in his little garden, tending his roses; or digging in a small flowerbed behind the house and finding an earthworm and holding it out to a robin following on his heels.[18]

Sweet though these reminiscences may be, they would in no way change the fact that the earliest images Gabrielle retained of her father, those that were most lasting and emotionally charged, would always be of a distant, uncommunicative man who was as good as absent from his daughter's personal life. In 1942, she declared to Adèle, "No, no! [. . .] for me childhood was not the age of happiness," and for this she laid the blame on her father; the thought of him always aroused "an unreasoned antipathy, even a submerged, unremitting rancour" in her.[19] She might well superimpose more appealing or lovable evocations over these bitter memories in her writings, but they were never more than re-creations in afterthought, products of an inner reconciliation that only the passage of years and Léon's death might have brought about. During the second part of her childhood and throughout her adolescence, which was all the while she was living with him, Gabrielle's attitude to her father remained tense, if not hostile. She felt she had been judged and rejected by him, and he in return decried her bad behaviour.

As for affinities within the family, the Deschambault Street household was divided into two camps. On the one side was a solitary, brooding Léon, supported nevertheless by the oldest of his children who were still at least a bit close to the family: Adèle, Anna, and, to a lesser extent, Rodolphe, who pitied their father and shared (or understood) his outlook on life, his fatalism, his need for frugality, his worries. On the other side were Gabrielle and her mother. Adèle, Anna, and Rodolphe, considering *Petite Misère* to be "spoiled, [. . .] temperamental, ridiculously demanding,"[20] and given to taking undue advantage of her mother's weaknesses, judged her behaviour harshly.

Between mother and daughter, the ties of dependency and near symbiosis that had formed in the course of Gabrielle's earliest childhood remained in place, now stronger than ever. Whether in compensation for her own loneliness as a more-or-less abandoned wife and mother or because she had the impression that the little girl really lacked affection, Mélina became Gabrielle's accomplice and almost her willing victim. Contrary to Adèle's and Léon's advice, she "understood" *Misère*'s indispositions and tantrums and would endeavour to soothe them. She was constantly trying to please her and make life easier for her. In order to give Gabrielle what she wanted, she sometimes spent money really foolishly, considering the tight budget the family was then living on. "When she wanted something," Adèle writes, "the child would redouble her wheedlings in order to get it. If *la mère* refused, she [Gabrielle] could always manage to change her wavering will with sighs and tears. Then *la mère* would shake her head and say, 'What can I do? She's sick.'"[21]

Alone with her mother against everyone else, Gabrielle saw herself increasingly as a pariah in the family. Hence no doubt her melancholy, her fussiness, her constant illnesses, and her indolence at school. Hence also, hence above all, the feeling – or delusion – that took shape in her mind in the course of this troubled period to the effect that since her father and siblings had not wanted her and called her *Petite Misère*, she did not entirely belong to them and must therefore make her life without them, even in defiance of them and all they represented. The rebelliousness and kind of rejection of family solidarity that were soon to be distinguishing features of Gabrielle Roy's youth may perhaps have found one of their basic psychological sources here.

A Crisis Resolved

The crisis that began when Gabrielle was about eight seems to have continued until she was at least eleven or twelve. As often happens, the events that brought it to an end at the same time marked its climax.

Misère's state of health, having deteriorated steadily since 1917, soon worsened to the point of seriously compromising her studies. In 1920–1921, the school administration's records show that she missed sixteen out of eighty school days in the first semester and fifty-four out of one hundred and twenty in the second. These absences were due to appendicitis, which began in the autumn of 1920. She had an operation in the spring of 1921,[22] which did not stop her from being promoted at the end of Grade 6. The following year, however, she did not go to school at all, so that her whole school year was lost.[23] It was not until September 1922 that she could return to the Académie, in Grade 7, a year behind her former classmates. Considering that the school was closed almost all autumn 1918 on account of the Spanish flu,[24] she was now considerably behind in her education.

Why did Gabrielle not set foot in school for the whole of the school year 1921–1922? In *Enchantment and Sorrow*, we find this laconic (or guarded) allusion: "Another illness [. . .] kept me at home for several months and made me lose a school year."[25] What this "other illness" was and how or why it began has been impossible to ascertain. It may have been a depressive reaction to her mother's prolonged absence in Quebec to attend Bernadette's religious profession, or there may have been imbalances and anxieties brought on by a difficult onset of menses. (Gabrielle was then going on thirteen.)

This second hypothesis would concur with what certain of Gabrielle's unpublished writings hint about her first experience of puberty. On this subject she never confided anything openly, any more than on most other subjects of the kind. However, certain pages of the "saga" based on her mother's life which she would begin to write many years later treat precisely of the teenage Éveline's discovery of the physical encumbrances related to being a woman. Éveline views her first menstruation as a disenchantment and humiliation:

> Now, from time to time, stabbing pains passed through her tender little body. And thoughts too passed like a pain through her head. Why had the body she used to have, free, slim and smooth, which knew no fetters, been snatched from her? [. . .] She perceived [. . .] everywhere barriers to her childhood games, and her spirit, which had lived in full light of day in liberty, free as a bird, rebelled.
>
> Ah, if this was what being a woman meant, well then, she did not want it. At this price, never would she want it, do you hear?[26]

Éveline discovers that "being a woman meant you were supposed to take second place in life"[27] and put up with weakness and pain. It is impossible to know how much this episode is based on stories told by Mélina, who, like other women of her generation and milieu, was extremely reticent when it came to talking about sex. It is more likely a transposition of Gabrielle's own experience, as hinted by this passage from *Enchantment and Sorrow*:

> Since I was now "a big girl" as she put it, [Maman] decided to enlighten me on the facts, or as I think she said, much more appropriately, the "mysteries" of life. She was so ill at ease I could hardly understand a word of what she was trying to tell me, except that being a woman was so humiliating it made you want to die.[28]

Whatever the deep-lying cause, these two years of lethargy (that of the appendectomy and that of the "other illness") marked what was clearly a turning point or, rather, an irreversible transition in young Gabrielle's life and discovery of herself. Transition meaning the end of one phase and the beginning of another: a break, a shift. On the one hand, the hospitalization and illness could still be ascribed to the depressive syndrome of the preceding years as its continuation and aggravation, but on the other, they signalled a deliverance: the absolute end to childhood and the birth of a new being, meaning a new body, yes, but also a new identity and will that were now no longer assigned to the girl by her family but by herself to herself, as if her life from now on depended on no one else.

It is not an exaggeration to give so much significance to this beginning of adolescence which, as Gabrielle put it, "left such an indelible mark on my life."[29] *Enchantment and Sorrow*, the sweeping work in which she related all of what she had lived and been, begins precisely with this period when at the age of twelve or thirteen she opened herself to the world around her and in a way became responsible for herself and the direction her life would take. As if it were here, in the climate and events of this age, that she was to find the true source of her destiny, as well as the very first face in which she might truly recognize herself.

The change proved to be radical, no doubt about it. Between the delicate, sulky, self-absorbed little girl of the previous years and the active, resolute adolescent embarking on the second half of her studies after an absence of nearly two years, the contrast could hardly be more total. To be sure, she continued to be afraid of her father, to feel resentful toward him and complain about him; to be sure, she still experienced periods of melancholy and intense nervousness, to the point of needing a doctor's care. She did not turn into a happy, blithe young girl overnight, but she was certainly not the same *Petite Misère* she had been before. On the contrary, she was now brimming with energy and determination; so intense was the will in her to succeed and express herself that it seems to have changed her completely. Things were happening as though her problematical relationship with her father and sense of being superfluous, which until now she had endured passively like a curse, were suddenly transforming into a burning need for affirmation and autonomy, fuelled and validated both at once by her discovery of her own power.

The Prizewinner

The first and most striking sign of this transformation was the change in Gabrielle's school results in the year following her return to the Académie. "I must have been about fourteen," the narrator in *Enchantment and Sorrow* recalls, "when I began to immerse myself in my schoolwork the way one enters a cloister. [. . .] At the end of that year I came first in my class for the first time in my life."[30] The exploit, which occurred in 1923–1924 when Gabrielle was in Grade 8, was repeated thereafter every year but one until she graduated from the Académie Saint-Joseph in 1928.

School records preserved at the Manitoba Provincial Archives have provided Gabrielle's marks in the provincial examinations for Grade 9 and Grade 11.[31] In the first case, they were 60 per cent in drawing, 74 and 89 per cent in "general science," and 94 per cent in history, which was the second best mark in all of Manitoba (where there were approximately 2,700 pupils at this level). At the end of this year moreover, Gabrielle was the only one in her class to be promoted "with honours."[32] For Grade 11, at the end of which she won the *prix de succès général*, or general proficiency prize, which carried a purse of five dollars, "the gift of Monsieur l'avocat Joseph Bernier,"[33] her results read as follows: 77 per cent in history, 72 per cent in algebra, 58 per cent in geometry, and 89 per cent in physics; as for English literature, composition, and spelling, they were 84 per cent, 52 per cent, and 100 per cent respectively. For a proper appreciation of these marks it should be remembered that all these examinations were taken – and the greater part of the teaching was given – in English. The only exception was French literature and composition, whose teaching the law allowed in classes at the secondary level (French being considered a "second language"). In these subjects in Grade 11, Gabrielle obtained a mark of 88 per cent. To the Department of Education, then, she had an excellent record, and at the end of Grade 12 it won her a Manitoba lieutenant-governor's medal, one of twenty-eight awarded to the best students in the province.[34]

The Académie Saint-Joseph, officially a creature of the Department of Education, had another equally and perhaps even more important connection through the Association d'éducation des Canadiens français du Manitoba (AECFM). In the early 1920s, as Gabrielle was beginning her secondary schooling, the association had become a well-structured and powerful organization with extensive backing from all levels of the Franco-Manitoban population, which supported it voluntarily by

participating in its activities and contributing to its fund-raising campaigns. Gabrielle's father willingly shelled out his annual one-dollar
membership fee and was even on several occasions one of the St-Boniface
delegates to the association's convention.[35]

Its ultimate purpose being to assure French "survival" in Manitoba,
the AECFM was concerned with anything to do with the "national
defence" of French Canadians. Its role was similar to that played in
Quebec in this period by the Société Saint-Jean-Baptiste (SSJB), which
was its model and ally. But the fight waged by the AECFM, as its name
implies, was more focused than that of the SSJB, since it was carried on
principally although not exclusively in education, where the goal was to
counteract the effects of the Thornton Act. To this end, its leaders
worked out a number of strategies for the supervision and support of
schools and teachers, which soon turned the association into virtually a
parallel department of education exercising control over all the French
Catholic schools in Manitoba through mobilization of local community
leaders, the clergy, and teachers.

One of the first and most effective of the association's strategies was
the creation of an unofficial French curriculum alongside the State-
imposed English school curriculum covering the entire duration of
studies. It was copied from the curricula in effect in Quebec and used the
same textbooks. It was officially an extracurricular activity and its teachers gave their time free of charge outside their normal hours of work. In
practice, however, the teaching of French and religion continued to
occupy a central place in the lives of French-speaking pupils and teachers alike, so that the AECFM program appears to have been treated as
compulsory, with many regular hours being devoted to it.

Strictly speaking this practice was illegal and had to be kept secret.
The Department of Education, which was perfectly aware of the situation, every now and then made a point of taking steps to counter the
influence of the AECFM by trying to put a stop to its activities in the
schools, either because "fanatical" voters had complained or some
inspector had wanted to show more rigour or dedication to duty than
the rest. Thus during the year 1923–1924, the keeper of the annals of the
Académie Saint-Joseph noted that there had been more fuss and bother
than usual and that discretion was considered appropriate: when the
school was investigated by several English school commissioners, the
archbishop asked the nuns to stop the saying of prayers temporarily
before and after classes.[36] Gabrielle recalled with amusement the

atmosphere of transgression surrounding the teaching of French and the subterfuge deployed by the teachers to foil the vigilance of inspectors.

> If at the convent we were celebrating the visit of some Church dignitary, red carpets would be laid on the floor of the big reception hall, ferns would be placed on pedestals, and portrait photographs of the archbishops of the West would be prominently displayed on the walls all around us. All day long we would speak the language of survival, and of the French-Canadian cause. A while later, another celebration would bring us a visit from some gentlemen from the Manitoba Board of Education. Then the principal, *la mère directrice*, would have the pictures of archbishops taken down; the Fathers of Confederation would take their place; we would have learned some very decorous compliments for the occasion, appropriate songs; all that day there would be nothing but British allegiance, loyalty to our sovereign, and a Canada stretching from sea to sea. The gentlemen from the Board of Education would leave enchanted, bowing low to our *mère directrice* and calling her *Madame*.[37]

These memories, recalled in a humorous rather than indignant vein, leave the impression that the "persecution" was not really as bad as all that. In fact, the government's policing of education generally remained discreet and anti-French "raids" were exceptional, at least in the schools of St-Boniface, where French and Catholic teaching went on in relative tranquillity, even benefiting from a surfeit of fervour generated by the official ban laid on it.

It must be said that the nuns at the Académie refrained from stooping to proselytism. Their English-speaking Catholic pupils, of whom there were more and more after 1916, did all their studies in English; the only ones who were expected to follow the AECFM program were children of French-Canadian families, among them Gabrielle Roy, who, more than any other, would turn out to be the pride of the school and the joy of her teachers.

To ensure application of its curriculum and "stimulate the love and study of our language,"[38] the association held a major Manitoba-wide contest every year. For contestants in the lower grades, there was a series of questions on subjects taught in French; those in more advanced grades wrote an essay on a specified subject.[39] The contest was held on a Saturday in May and the results were announced several weeks later in the weekly *La Liberté*, the Franco-Manitoban community's principal organ of information. Each summer the page given over to the contest stood as a kind of French-Manitoban honour roll. And each summer from 1924 to 1928, Gabrielle's name appeared at the top of the list, together with the mark she had obtained and the name of the prize she had won for her first place among all the French-speaking students in the province.

Up to Grade 10 the prize consisted of a medal. Gabrielle's first medal, given by the superintendent of public instruction of the province of Quebec, was awarded to her at the age of fifteen for the Grade 8 contest, which she won with a mark of 92 per cent, compared with a meagre 72 per cent for her nearest rival. The following year it was the gold medal of the Fédération des femmes canadiennes-françaises, awarded to the top contestant in Grade 9, which she won with a mark of 98 per cent.[40] Then, in June 1926, a mark of 93 per cent won her the "Médaille d'or de France," awarded by the French government to the winner in Grade 10.[41]

In the two following contests, those for Grades 11 and 12, she again ranked first in all of Manitoba, which demanded greater effort on her part because the few students who pursued their studies that far were among the hardest-working and most gifted. Gabrielle's marks now were close to perfection: 97 per cent in 1927 and 99 per cent in 1928.[42] At these levels the prize awarded by the association was less symbolic. Instead of a medal, it consisted of a sum of money that was fairly appreciable for the time: $50 for Grade 11, the gift of the Société Saint-Jean-Baptiste of Montreal, and $100 for Grade 12, given by the association itself.

Outside the annual contest run by the AECFM, there was plenty of opportunity for the students to compete together and win distinction. Here again, Gabrielle's triumphs came one after the other. In the spring of 1927, she won the laurels for her school in a speech contest organized by the association in conjunction with the *Winnipeg Free Press*, for which the subject was "what Canada has accomplished in sixty years of Confederation."[43] At the Académie, the most prestigious prizes were for studies in religion. Each year during May, the "month of Mary," a big ceremony was held in the assembly hall, in the course of which the prizewinners in each grade, wearing pale blue dresses and flowers in their hair, paraded before the parents and a goodly contingent of clergy assembled for the coronation of the "Queen of the May." This title was bestowed on the girl in Grade 12 who had obtained the best marks in catechism and religious history. The prizewinners in Grades 9, 10, and 11 were her "maids of honour." On this day, Gabrielle was usually the one

Above: Charles Roy and Marcellina Morin, Gabrielle Roy's paternal grandparents.
Below: Élie Landry and Émilie Jeansonne, her maternal grandparents.
(NLC NL-19162)

The Landry grandparents' golden wedding anniversary, summer 1911.
(NLC NL-19164)

The house on Deschambault Street, around 1910. (NLC NL-18232)

Family photograph, around 1901. *From left to right*: Clémence, Anna, Mélina, Adèle, Agnès, Joseph. *In front*: Bernadette. (NLC NL-19156)

Gabrielle, 18 months, and Bernadette, 12. (NAC PA-186952)

Adèle, 21, Gabrielle, 5, and Bernadette, 16. (NLC NL-19146)

The last family photograph, January 1912. *Front, left to right*: Léon, Gabrielle, Germain, Mélina. *Rear*: Bernadette, Clémence, Adèle, Anna, Rodolphe. (NAC PA-186947)

Three generations: Émilie, the grandmother, Mélina, the mother, and Anna, the daughter, 1916. (NAC PA-186949)

Gabrielle, around 1920, with her father, an adult relative, and three unidentified younger children in front of the house on Deschambault Street. (NLC NL-19166)

Mélina, Sister Léon-de-la-Croix (Bernadette), and Gabrielle, around 1925. (NAC PA-186957)

Gabrielle (*centre, front*) and her fellow graduates of the Académie Saint-Joseph, 1928. (NAC PA-186958)

Gabrielle at 20.
(NAC PA-186955)

Provencher School----1931---- Gr. 1
Gabrielle Roy

Gabrielle and her class of "beginners" at the Institut Provencher, 1931.
(Frères Marianistes, St-Boniface)

The cast of *Les Soeurs Guédonec*, performed by the Cercle Molière, 1936. *Front, left to right*: Pauline Boutal, the Sourisseau and Deniset children, Gabrielle Roy. *Rear*: Arthur Boutal, Élisa Houde, Joseph Plante. (Archives du Cercle Molière)

Paula Sumner and her first child.
(NLC NL-19149)

Gabrielle on vacation, around 1935.
(NLC NL-19144)

who won the distinctions,[44] and in May 1928 she was awarded the highest honour as "Queen of the May," together with a medal given by the archbishop.[45]

And so every time there was a prizegiving at the Académie, Gabrielle Roy's name was among those of the winners. But these successes that made her the darling of her teachers and the envy of her classmates were achieved only at the price of persistent hard work. "At fifteen," she wrote later, "I was a little old woman always buried in my books."[46]

The author of *Enchantment and Sorrow* attributes this persistency and craving for honours to her wanting at this time to please her mother, give her the support she was able to give,[47] and console her in the difficult life that was her lot. "And then [...] came the thought that if I was going to repay Maman for the endless sacrifices she'd imposed on herself, nothing less than dazzling success on my part would do"; "I'd have to [...] always come first in French and English and all the other subjects, win medals and other kinds of prizes, and keep bringing her trophies."[48]

These altruistic motives attributed by Gabrielle to herself in hindsight were doubtless at play, but that was certainly not all. "Coming first made me giddy," she says.[49] In the schoolgirl's determination and goals she set for herself, there was also fierce ambition, a will to assert herself and wrest recognition and admiration from others, meaning her teachers and classmates but also, and perhaps especially, her father and the rest of her family. Instead of coming out as contrariness and disobedience, the adolescent rebellion in her was taking the form of obsession with success, allowing her to prove beyond question to others and to herself that her place in the world was unique and she had not been born in vain.

In the winner of the AECFM prize, in the "Queen of the May," there was *Petite Misère* getting her own back.

The Education of a Dutiful Young Girl

Besides these early opportunities for making her mark and winning recognition, Gabrielle's years at the Académie Saint-Joseph brought her the best possible education a teenaged girl with her background could have in those days. The Department of Education considered the Académie to be one of the top girls' schools in all Manitoba. Beginning in 1925, the headmistress was Sister Luc d'Antioche, née Delphine

Beuglet, who was to turn it into an institution of the first order. In 1929 it obtained the title of "Collegiate Institute" and in 1936 an official affiliation with the University of Manitoba, giving it the right to grant the degree of bachelor of arts. At this public school, which in principle was open to children of all social strata, the Soeurs des Saints Noms de Jésus et de Marie provided the same kind of teaching and guidance received by the upper-class girls who attended their Outremont convent school in Montreal, which had been founded in 1905. True enough, moral and religious instruction was the major priority, with its panoply of prayers, retreats, compulsory sacraments, and devotional celebrations, and it is also true that patriotism was *de rigueur*, a fiercely traditionalist brand of patriotism consisting primarily of mistrust – sometimes even intolerance – of anything not *pure laine* French Canadian and Catholic. In the spring of 1919 in the annals of the Académie, for example, during the serious worker demonstrations then rocking the capital of Manitoba, we find this brief mention: "Alluding to the deplorable strike now going on in Winnipeg, Mgr [Béliveau] said that the cause is simply a deficiency of Christian spirit."[50]

The nuns who were preparing the girls for their roles as wives and mothers were convinced they were educating women destined for their society's elite. They placed a great deal of emphasis on the cultural and artistic education of their pupils, in both regular teaching and what today are considered extracurricular activities. All the girls took music, for instance. Like her sisters, Gabrielle learned to play the piano. When she reached Grade 7 she took an examination held "under the supervision of the Conservatoire national de musique affiliated with the Université de Montréal," and passed it "satisfactorily."[51] She joined the school choir and continued her piano lessons until the end of her studies, despite unnoteworthy aptitude. All her life thereafter she would sit at the piano and play with pleasure whenever the opportunity arose.

More than music, however, it was drama and elocution that fired her enthusiasm, perhaps because these activities were partly the responsibility of Sister Léon-de-la-Croix, her sister Bernadette, who, as a staff member at the Académie until 1927, was expected to inculcate in the girls the arts of voice intonation, corporeal expression, memorization, and perfect diction. For girls with talent there were plenty of opportunities to perform, the school year being punctuated with ceremonies and celebrations that included plays attended assiduously by all the prominent ecclesiastics, notables, and "benefactors" of St-Boniface.

Gabrielle was already known for her vivacious speech delivery, making her an admired performer. Shortly before Christmas 1925, the editor of *La Liberté* reported on a celebration in honour of the archbishop as follows: "It is always a pleasure to go to the Académie. The children are so well trained and everything exudes such a peaceful, tranquil air that it is always restful to step inside the establishment." On this occasion, a message of greeting was read and then the girls performed a religious play entitled *L'Âme de Thérèse*; in the first intermission, a girl gave a brief piano recital, and in the second, "Mlle Roy [delivered] a humorous piece, to the delight of the audience."[52] Two years later, on the occasion of a similar event, Gabrielle drew warm applause from the audience with a recitation "in charming fashion" of *Le Tisonier de ma mère* by Father Zacharie Lacasse, an early missionary to Manitoba.[53] Besides a pretty face and an excellent memory, she had a keen sense of intonation and expressive gesture. Among her schoolmates she was considered to be an actress of promising talent.

As for her school subjects, the education that Gabrielle received at the Académie Saint-Joseph may have contained "a hodgepodge of useless knowledge"[54] and plenty of precepts she would judge harshly later on, yet it distinguished itself royally on one point: bilingualism. "We were more or less English in algebra, geometry, the sciences, and Canadian history, but French in Quebec history, French literature, and particularly history of religion."[55] This bilingualism, requiring the student to become highly competent in both English and French, would have an impact on the future novelist's literary initiation, which she would emphasize herself in her autobiographical writings.

Our French literature textbooks acquainted us with Veuillot and Montalembert, pages and pages of them, and very little else; practically nothing of Zola, Flaubert, Maupassant, even Balzac. [. . .] The doors to English literature, however, were open wide and gave us access to its greatest minds. I'd soon read Thomas Hardy, George Eliot, the Brontë sisters, Jane Austen. I knew Keats, Shelley, Byron, and the Lake poets, and adored them.[56]

This was why she would say, "for a long time I thought that French literature was a pale thing beside that of England."[57] There was an exception, however: Alphonse Daudet, whom she loved so passionately she learned *Les Lettres de mon moulin* by heart. This discovery, a high point in her early literary and dramatic experience, she owed to Sister Marie-Diomède (Georgina Laberge), of whom she said later, "I think she showed me more about what is beautiful than any other teacher, and helped me choose my career by giving me the encouragement I needed."[58]

But in general the French authors inspired only indifference in her. French literature as taught by the nuns and the AECFM was heavily impregnated with conservatism and marked by clerical censure. High-minded writers, expurgated texts, almost total ignorance of modern works, a more or less apologetic view of literary thought and writing were *de rigueur*, while in English literature the State curriculum, while not exactly avant-garde, was nevertheless more liberal.

Gabrielle owed her appreciation and knowledge of English authors principally to another of her Grade 12 teachers, Sister Maxima (M.-A. Bellemare), who "was always very good to me. [. . .] Her love of beauty turned her instinctively towards Keats, one of the purest of English poets, and she used to read him with a warmth and affection that brought out his wistfulness and musicality."[59] But it was Shakespeare that Gabrielle liked best, Shakespeare whom she had studied since Grade 8 and read in the original English. A celebrated passage in *Enchantment and Sorrow* recalls her enthralment at a performance of *The Merchant of Venice* at the Walker Theatre in Winnipeg:

> In the highest balcony, leaning over the rail towards the actors – who from that height looked very small – I could barely catch the words, which for me were pretty obscure anyway, yet I was spellbound.[60]

In Gabrielle's memory, this event occurred while she was attending the Académie Saint-Joseph, but in fact the only performance of *The Merchant of Venice* at the Walker Theatre by the Stratford-upon-Avon Festival Company, which was on a North American tour, took place in the autumn of 1928, on Wednesday, October 24, a matinée.[61] At this point Gabrielle had already left the Académie and begun her studies at the normal school.

Whatever the exact date, this experience had a major impact on her. In the immediate aftermath, it incited her to read and memorize Shakespeare's other great plays; and she continued throughout her life to reread and quote from *Macbeth, Hamlet, King Lear,* and *The Tempest.* But the truth is that it was not only this work or this author in particular that was revealed to her on this occasion, it was also the very power of art

and literature in themselves. "All question of French or English or forbidden or imposed language disappeared. There was only a language that
transcended languages, like that of music."[62] In *The Hidden Mountain*,
Pierre Cadorai would experience the same entrancement: "The world
of art – for want of a better word – was vast, it encompassed almost the
whole of man: his boredom, his thoughts, his dreams, his suffering, the
sad joys, the summits, the depths . . ."[63]

It is no small thing for a writer to have read Shakespeare rather than
Racine, Keats rather than François Coppée. Although she said little about
the influence of specific books on her, and much of the reading that
influenced her most profoundly came at a later time, Gabrielle certainly
derived models, references, and a literary culture from her years of schooling that were rather different from those of other French-Canadian
writers of her generation, who had almost all passed through the mould
of the old-time classical education. The result was that in the literary
milieu she would join ten or fifteen years later, this knowledge she had
inherited from her bilingual schooling made her an oddity to some extent.

For the time being, however, while she was attending the Académie
Saint-Joseph as a girl of fifteen, sixteen, up to nineteen in her last year,
Gabrielle was nothing if not the model student. The evidence is not only
in her scholastic achievements but her entire behaviour as a dutiful, conscientious girl who was polite with her teachers and quick to comply
with all they expected of her.

Her classmates considered her gifted certainly, but also serious and
hard-working, always with her nose in her books and rarely partaking of
their group activities. Some were closer to her than others, like Denise
Rocan, Thérèse Goulet, Rita Guilbert, and Kathleen O'Neil, but it seems
a best friend of the kind girls of this age often have, a constant companion with whom one shares secrets and confidences and to whom one is
bound by a passionate, almost amorous connivance, she did not have.
Proud, sure of herself, often mischievous in public and, as she herself
recalls, even at times "bit of a show-off,"[64] she preferred her own company and most of the time kept her distance.

We know little about her love life in this period. Two or three of the
stories in *Street of Riches* depict Christine as an adolescent wakening
gradually to matters of the heart: her quickly repressed interest in jewellery and make-up, her first male conquest, the kiss stolen by a cousin
in the midst of a snowstorm. All very tame stuff, in short. Yet, according
to Adèle, Gabrielle had plenty of suitors who showered her with gifts

and kept asking her out with such ardour that her sisters considered her "a flirt, with [her] blue-green eyes and [her] honeyed smile."[65]

It is true that Gabrielle was a strikingly lovely girl. Her piercing eyes, slightly dusky skin, auburn hair cut short in the latest fashion, her fetching dresses, and the little hat with the names of her favourite authors embroidered on it were ample to captivate the boys of the two neighbouring schools, the Institut Provencher and, better still, the prestigious Collège de Saint-Boniface. It seems there was much coquetry, and plenty of flirtations, titillations, and beaus of an evening or a week, but she is not known to have had any suitor or heartthrob in the least serious. Here again, she kept her distance and seemed even then to be holding back from love, showing a resistance or distrust that, far from fading with time, became increasingly pronounced. In her adolescent years, this attitude no doubt owed much to the example of her older sisters Anna and Adèle, in whom she watched passion and marriage turn quickly to misery and disillusionment. But there was something else in this fear of love – the desire to keep herself free and available, not for the right man to make her life with but for a life of her own, for the moment when she could finally take wing on her own.

At Pembina Mountain

For if there was one thing that ruled Gabrielle's existence at this time – as with many adolescents – it was preoccupation with her own person and her own destiny, the need not so much to know herself but to forge an image of herself that would at one and the same time set her apart, reassure her, and fire her imagination. Thus in *Street of Riches*, the adolescent Christine spends long hours in the attic, sitting on the floor "in front of a Buddha, where I burned incense to myself." Alone with observances that her mother calls her "mumbo jumbo," she looks at herself in introspection, passionately seeking the face of "that person all unknown to me who would one day be I."[66]

Nothing gave more encouragement to this seeking, this contemplation of herself and "the road of [her] future,"[67] than her vacations in the country with her mother's family. Mélina's younger brother Excide had a farm in the Pembina Mountain region between Cardinal and St-Léon. After the death of the Landry grandparents, this was where Mélina spent the Christmas vacation and part of the summer, first with her children and then just with Gabrielle from about 1920 on. Léon would stay in St-Boniface minding his own small business and brooding, with Clémence for company unless Clémence had escaped and gone to stay with Anna or Adèle.

For Mélina, these spells at Excide's, as before at her parents' house, were periods of respite. Far from her husband, far from the worries of their daily lives, she rediscovered her memories with the surroundings in which she had once been happy. Excide's house, perched on a small rise overlooking an old, dried-up lake and surrounded with groves of trees through which one could glimpse the open prairie, was warmly hospitable and comfortable, with its two floors, its big verandah, and the attractive balcony above. Here, everything spoke a familiar language to Mélina. Her other brother Zénon lived in the neighbourhood with his second wife, Anna Fortier, whom he had married after the death of his first, Virginie Rocheleau. The Landry parents' graves were close by in the little Somerset cemetery. Mélina knew the people, the places, the customs; she was at home. But the difference between now and the way things had been when she came and stayed at her mother's was that when she arrived at Excide's each summer it was not to rest but to work, and work hard. For Excide needed her, especially after 1922 when his wife, Luzina, died. Luzina's daughters Éliane and then Léa, promoted to mistresses of the house before the age of twenty, filled in for her as best they could. Mélina helped with both the household chores and the work in the fields. In return, she and her daughter were housed and fed. She was in short a hired hand.

For Gabrielle, however, these summer vacations were pure delight, as she would recount later in a chapter of *Enchantment and Sorrow*. First there were the people: two women, both incarnations of kindness in Gabrielle's mind, her aunt, "the gentle, tender-hearted Luzina,"[68] and her cousin Éliane ("My dear, my very dear friend," Gabrielle wrote to Éliane, "I love you the way I cherish those who truly love me"[69]); her uncle, whom she regarded with the admiration and affection she could not feel for her father; and most of all Philippe, Cléophas, and Léa, cousins to whom she felt far closer than to her own brothers and sisters. Her real family was here, a loving, peaceful family in which she felt she belonged, if only because the children were her age and their father was twenty-five years younger than her own.[70]

She also found happiness on these vacations in the landscapes around her: a little grove of trees with the wind at play, an unexpected hill, a dirt road blowing dust, and the open space of the prairie as far as the eye could see. She never tired of exploring these places filled with her family's history, of looking at them from every angle, hearing their music, pursuing the countless daydreams they aroused in her. For the future novelist, this Pembina Mountain country was rather like Illiers-Combray for Proust; the object of inexhaustible fascination, a reservoir of memories, images, and characters to which she would keep returning in her writing.

There was another and perhaps more important reason why these summers in the country meant so much to Gabrielle as an adolescent. She was free here as she could never be in St-Boniface. Free of course from any thought of school, but free also of her family, her father, her sisters, of the bickering and unease that had become the common lot of all the inhabitants of the house on Deschambault Street. Nothing symbolizes this freedom better than the picture in *Enchantment and Sorrow* of the girl on horseback, hair flying in the wind, leaving her uncle's farm and riding through the surrounding fields and villages until sundown.

At Pembina Mountain, Gabrielle was free above all in her thoughts and dreams, free to focus them on what fascinated her more than all else: herself, her desires, her plans, the felicity and fame awaiting her. It was to these endless musings on her future life and person that her long rides invariably led her. Sometimes she would go to St-Léon to visit her aunt Luzina's old mother, where she would ask, "Tell me my fortune with your cards, Mémère Major [. . .]. Tell me what's in the future for me."[71] Sometimes she would guide her mount toward a small rise from where one could discover "such a vast expanse of sky and land it made me feel the world was mine," and she said to herself, "I'[ll] find happiness some day."[72] The narrator of *Children of My Heart* remembers these impassioned thoughts on gazing at the Pembina landscape:

> Like all great, free spaces, what it inspired in us must have been that dream-like but unshakeable confidence in life and what we will become, the face that will be ours in time.[73]

Throughout these summers at Excide's, Gabrielle was continuing the quest she had begun in her attic in St-Boniface where she had spent long afternoons lost "in confident euphoria, dreaming about the future,"[74] and, like Christine in *Street of Riches*, she would wonder, "What [shall] I be later? . . . What [shall] I do with my life?"[75] These were questions she would continue to ask herself for some time yet, but already they contained their own answers. She was going to be *someone*. She was going to have the life she would make for herself, and it was going to be a great and beautiful life, incomparably greater and more beautiful than she would normally be destined for.

Very early in fact, an idea, a desire implanted itself in her, something that would be a constant throughout her youth, if not throughout her life: the need to better herself, break free, attain a unique, exemplary existence and destiny brimming with beauty and nobility. True, ambition is the appanage of adolescence and every young man or woman expects to find wonders in store before encountering the world as it really is, but in Gabrielle the desire became so urgent in the course of her early years that it turned into a real obsession, the only thing that ruled her thoughts and behaviour. Everything in her strained toward this ideal image that kept beckoning yet escaping her grasp, an image that was both herself and someone else, another self she knew nothing about as yet, except that she was a better, happier self and infinitely worthy of admiration. This was what Adèle would call, unkindly, Gabrielle's "fantasies."

This desire to better herself worked in two ways, opposite and complementary both at once. On the one hand, it instilled self-assurance and nourished her desire to succeed. If she devoted herself so entirely to studying and needed so badly to come first in everything, it was for that "person all unknown" out there who kept calling her and whom she would not become without constant effort to distinguish herself, raise herself above others and the self she was at present. Her prizes, medals, honours beyond counting, she collected less as proof of her worth at the time than as early signs of the unique destiny she was projecting toward with every fibre of her being.

On the other hand, this desire for betterment was also a rejection. It was *Petite Misère* standing tall to rebuff not only her father's pity but the entire world into which she was born, a world dominated this time by the ultimate figure of veneration: her mother.

Gabrielle's Second Birth

Gabrielle's universe in her teens consisted essentially of two things: her immediate social setting of Catholic, French-Canadian St-Boniface; and her family, represented (epitomized in fact) by the presence of Mélina, who was soon to be sixty. In Gabrielle's eyes, the symbolic link between her mother and the Franco-Manitoban society was very close, to the point where they were virtually blended. It was Mélina with her stories who initiated Gabrielle to the history of French Manitoba, and beyond this to her entire past as a French Canadian. And it was because of these two enfolding presences, her mother's and the St-Boniface community's, that Gabrielle had thus far felt so protected, as if in the middle of an island of kindness and safety that protected her from all danger.

For the adolescent Gabrielle, becoming aware of belonging to her community meant also discovering her mother, looking at her with new eyes and repositioning herself or, rather, positioning the image she had begun to make of herself in relation to all that Mélina represented. It is with this in mind that we should read the first two chapters of *Enchantment and Sorrow*, in which the action takes place at the time of Gabrielle's adolescence and recounts what we might call her second birth, her true birth as a separate and autonomous individual. Chapter One begins with this all-important question: "When did it first dawn on me ..."

> When did it first dawn on me that I was one of those people destined to be treated as inferiors in their own country?[76]

When the original French edition, *La détresse et l'enchantement*, was published posthumously in 1984, what was immediately observed in these first two chapters – with some surprise, given Gabrielle's known political convictions – was a belated stand in support of French-Canadian nationalist claims. Less widely perceived, yet equally striking, was how large Mélina's presence looms in these "political" pages. It is Mélina who leads the humiliating expedition to Eaton's in Winnipeg, and from Mélina's mouth in Chapter Two that Gabrielle hears of the endless succession of hardships and the homelessness suffered by her people before she was born. At this particular time in her life, she not only discovers that "there [is] no cure for the misfortune of being French Canadian"[77] and that Franco-Manitobans are a second-class, scorned minority community, she also becomes aware especially of the wretched and humiliating condition of her own mother and her own family, who thereupon cease to look like the protective cocoon they have been to her throughout her childhood and become a ferment of misery, a barrier, a threat to her own happiness.

All this emerges clearly from the story Gabrielle tells of another scene from her teen years, a little later than those she recalls at the beginning of *Enchantment and Sorrow* but bearing the same significance. This time the event takes place in the summer when she was fifteen or sixteen, in 1924 or 1925. One day when Mélina has left to go shopping in Winnipeg, Gabrielle, who has stayed behind at home alone, begins suddenly to worry. "I had the curious feeling that in a way I had lost sight of her and perhaps I didn't really know her very well. This must have been the first time in my life that I thought of her not just as my mother but as a human being – by nature always somewhat inscrutable – with a mysterious life of her own, perhaps full of secrets and unsuspected things." At the corner of the street, where she has gone to wait for her mother, Gabrielle finally sees her get off the streetcar and receives an unforgettable shock from the sight.

> She was coming home emptyhanded. But much more than her empty hands, it was her face that stunned me when I raised my eyes to it. [. . .] Sad, absent, dejected, the admission one makes to oneself sometimes, thinking oneself alone, that one can take no more of so many struggles, so much suffering, so little understanding. [. . .]
>
> She did not see me as I went toward her, still smiling in spite of all as though I could tear her away from her life as from a bad dream. And in the fine fabric of her face, the fragile material that records everything about life, I could see with increasing clarity the marks of endless calculations aimed at bringing grace to our lives, and an old yearning, dimly seen through the figures, for another life, another world, and even, I do believe, the still-fresh humiliation of having been sent packing once again for asking to be served in French, for not knowing English, or simply for being what she was, a stubborn old French Canadian who was being inconvenient. Also a touch of weariness and discouragement that robbed me of whatever courage I might have had, accustomed as I was to taking mine from hers. Unable to stand it any longer, I rushed to her, calling to her for help rather than joyously as I had planned. [. . .]
>
> We never spoke, she and I, of this perhaps the most significant meeting of our lives. It may have been enough, long before I had notice of it myself, to launch me on a life of writing.[78]

It is not certain that this scene really took place, or the one in Chapter Two of *Enchantment and Sorrow* for that matter. But this is of little importance. What counts is the inner experience they reveal, which

Gabrielle Roy the seasoned novelist condenses into specific "events" on specific dates, although in reality it may have been a slower, more haphazard occurrence, more like a progressive transformation spread out over the whole of her adolescence. Distilling out the essentials, one could liken this experience to a kind of weaning whereby the child, whose whole life and identity have until now been inseparable from the mother's, becomes detached from her and can now *see* her, together with the whole community she represents. See their suffering to be sure, but also their prostration and the inferiority that clings to them incurably.

For Gabrielle, this realization and the emotion it stirred in her marked her emergence from the maternal universe, the moment at which, "for the first time," she began considering herself a person apart, separate, and distinct, and took charge of herself. When she discovered "for the first time" the true face of her mother and the true nature of the community she belonged to, Gabrielle was discovering not only who she was and where she had come from, but also who she wanted to be and where she wanted to go. From then on, one thing seemed clear: she would not be like her mother, she would not be "one of those people destined to be treated as inferiors" by being Franco-Manitoban. Whatever the cost, she would escape that accursed destiny.

Her resolution – inadmissable to herself – not to accept for herself the same plight as her mother and her community, which in a sense meant preparing herself to betray them, is not presented as bluntly as this in Gabrielle's autobiographical writings. She remembers it more as a feeling that, far from leading her to deny her people, drove her to take their humiliation upon herself and to act in such a way as to end it. In Chapter Two of *Enchantment and Sorrow*, after reporting the long story her mother has told her, the narrator adds, "It was then, I believe I remember correctly, that I resolved in the depths of my soul to make good for her."

> Maman [...] scolded herself for having talked to me so long [...]. I was near the end of my strength but my head was still full of my little plan to make good for her. I'd make good for my father, too, and my Beaumont relatives and my St-Jacques-l'Achigan relatives and my Connecticut ancestors before them. I was far away in the past discovering the hardship of my forebears, and from this I drew the will to place one foot after the other.[79]

There is no question that knowing about "the hardship of [her] forebears" provoked rebellion in the girl's mind and spurred her desire to get ahead, to better herself. Less certain is the selfless purpose assigned to this rebellion in hindsight by the woman in old age: saving her people, taking on herself the mission of making good for them. Reverting to the context of those years, the kind of social or national conscience attributed by the narrator of *Enchantment and Sorrow* to herself as the source of her filial and ethnic devotion seems hard to believe, or anachronistic in any event. This "tragic," or at least painful, perception of the French-Canadian condition that became common currency in Quiet Revolution Quebec has little in common with the nationalist ideology that inspired oratory and teaching in the period when Gabrielle was going to school. In contrast, the earlier ideology, full of the heroism of the French-Canadian people and their "providential mission," extolled the superiority of the "chosen race"; what it had in view was not "making good," not a break with a long past of humiliation and hardship, but "survival" of what had always been, an era of glory and grandeur. Gabrielle's own brother Germain wrote as follows at about this time in an address that the newspaper *La Liberté* deemed worthy of space in its pages:

> There comes to us a rightful pride in being French Canadians, in being the descendants of this generous people so quick with enthusiasm, so imbued with ideals, of a people which has always soldiered for the good, unceasingly taken up the cause of the weak and oppressed, constantly dreamed of defending the great interests of Christ and humanity.
>
> The study of our history stirs in us a fervent gratitude toward our ancestors [. . .] who fought to ensure us more freedom, more equality, more justice. They have left us a prosperous country and a rich treasure of examples, our "blessed heritage" which we should set our hearts on preserving intact.[80]

It would be surprising if Gabrielle, the nuns' model pupil at the Académie Saint-Joseph, had not herself been indoctrinated to a certain degree with the same convictions, she who, at seventeen, received an honourable mention for her entry in the *La Liberté* essay contest on the theme "Would you like to set sail on the adventure of French survival?"[81]

So there is reason for doubting that the "political awakening" experienced by the adolescent Gabrielle was just as it was supposedly reconstituted by the autobiographical texts of later life, whose intent was not only to tell the story of the narrator's youth but to justify it, redeem it by attributing to it after the fact a significance that perhaps it did not have

at the time. What seems more likely in the context of the day is that
Gabrielle, far from assigning herself the task of making good for her
people and working for their "liberation," as might be said today, discovered how heavily her belonging weighed on her and how urgent it
was, if she were ever to become the ideal person she dreamed of, to free
herself of her family and patriotic duty and throw off "the hardship of
[her] forebears," to have no further part of it.

It was not only or mostly her mother's sufferings and the political
inferiority of Franco-Manitobans that angered the young Gabrielle, and
not this that she decided to fight; it was the resulting inferiority for
herself and the obstacles to her own flowering raised by belonging to her
family and community. To make good for her mother, fine, but first and
foremost not to be like her mother or her people, and to make good in
defiance of them if need be: this was the more or less conscious resolution that formed in the girl's mind and that in a way was to govern the
next fifteen or twenty years of her life.

In the closing pages of "The Governor's Ball," Part One of *Enchantment
and Sorrow*, Gabrielle recognizes this feeling when she was leaving
Manitoba at the age of twenty-eight. Remembering the look her mother
had given her on the station platform, she writes:

> It was clear now that I wasn't leaving so I could make good for her, as it had
> pleased me to believe. Dear heaven, it was really so I'd be free of her, wasn't
> it? Free of her and the family woes clustered about her, in her keeping.
>
> [. . .] Then, at the end of the platform, there appeared a little crowd
> from the past, dressed in black. There were my forebears, the Landrys
> and the Roys too, the Connecticut expatriates, their ancestors who'd
> been deported from Acadia, their descendants repatriated to St-Jacques-
> l'Achigan, my St-Alphonse-de-Rodriguez relatives and those at Beaumont,
> even my Savonarola grandfather whom I had time to recognize beside
> Marcelline, his eyes dark and smouldering as in his photograph . . . the
> terrible exodus my mother had introduced me to one day. . . .
>
> Can I deny finding in my heart that perhaps I'd always wanted to break
> the chain, escape from my poor dispossessed people?[82]

The narrator situates this moment of realization at the very end of the
period of her Manitoba youth; it was like a sudden illumination flashing
through her thoughts. But the need "to save myself,"[83] and to that end
"to break the chain," to "be free of" her mother and her community, had

taken shape much earlier, at the beginning of her adolescence, in fact, and since then had kept haunting her, driving her in various ways to reject her condition and assert her freedom. In Gabrielle's attitudes and desires and the things she did, the breakaway that came in 1937 had been long in preparation.

In *The Tin Flute*, there is a scene that perhaps speaks volumes on this subject. Rose-Anna stops one day at the Five and Ten where Florentine works, and Florentine suddenly has the impression she is seeing her mother as she has never seen her before:

> Rose-Anna had only to turn up now in the blaze of this bazaar for Florentine to see her clearly at last, with her poor smile and timid manner that gave away her intention to take up as little room as possible.
>
> Florentine was stunned. [. . .] She now perceived her mother's life as a long, grey voyage which she, Florentine, would never make; and today, in a way, they were saying good-bye to each other.[84]

Breaking away from her mother and the people of Saint-Henri, rejecting for herself their bleak destiny, this is the deep-seated desire that governs Florentine's entire youth; this too is the case with Elsa, the heroine of *Windflower*, who also is haunted by determination not to repeat in her own life the confining life of her mother, Winnie, or of her people in general.

There is certainly a measure of ingratitude and delusion in this strong desire to break natural ties. Later, Anna and Adèle would voice sharp criticism of Gabrielle's behaviour, accusing her of having advanced herself to the detriment of her own family. But getting away from people may also be the best way of discovering the things that bind us to them. When Florentine suddenly perceives Rose-Anna's wretched existence and realizes that it can never be her own, "in that moment she knew that she loved her mother."[85]

A Stranger and a Princess

In fact, Gabrielle distanced herself relatively little from her family and community in this period. She learned English, to be sure, as all Manitoban schoolchildren were forced to do; she even learned it with more conviction and resolve than most young people of her age, and this in itself distanced her from her mother, who in twenty-five years in St-Boniface had never succeeded in mastering the majority language. In the context of French Manitoba in those years, English was the language of things foreign, of Protestants, of "the opposite camp," and thus represented a kind of forbidden ground, but was also by the same token the language of openness, liberation, the future, the language of the real world, in contrast to French, which symbolized protection certainly, but also inertia inside "the fortress."[86]

For the adolescent Gabrielle, willingly learning English and insisting on speaking and writing it as well as she could was one way of detaching herself from the loyalties pulling at her. Otherwise, she continued to know little in general about the world outside her community, whose growing marginality was making it more and more timorous and inward-turned.[87] Associating with young immigrants, reading Slavic and American writers, the pull of the East, a taste for fine things, all this was yet to come. For the time being there was no apparent change in Gabrielle's style of life; she studied hard, went to church, and was obedient to her parents.

Inside, however, she was a different person and it showed in her attitude toward her family, an attitude that displayed "a kind of selfishness," as she herself called it much later.[88] She was a stranger and a princess in her parents' house. She continued to feel rejected by her father, who was now in his seventies, and did not feel at ease with the family atmosphere, where quarrels, fault-finding, frustrations, and a kind of gloom seem to have become permanent features. Closeted in the attic or deep in her books, she behaved most of the time as though this world were no concern of hers.

It must be said that life was far from rosy in the house on Deschambault Street since Léon had lost his job. Outside Bernadette's infrequent leaves and Rodolphe's breezing in and out – Rodolphe, "when he was sober, was brilliant, charming, full of mischief, and very funny"[89] – it was always the same dreary, glum routine, the same cheerlessness now coupled with this perpetual worry over money.

Material insecurity and obsession with frugality had succeeded the past's relative comfort. In order to make ends meet, the family scrimped and saved and turned to all kinds of expedients. Léon tried to put his knowledge of agronomy to account. On a municipal lot beside the Seine, he grew vegetables that he sold at the market. For a time he even tried his hand at growing mushrooms in the cellar of the house. The family also had some chickens and a cow, which was kept in a shed at the bottom of the yard and taken to graze in neighbouring fields.[90] As in the days at Mariopolis and Somerset, Léon went into retail business; in 1924 he opened a small grocery, but the business turned sour and he was obliged to sell again at a loss almost immediately. As for Mélina, she did her bit amply; besides taking care of the house she took in sewing, made quilts that she sold in the neighbourhood, minded babies at her house, and washed and mended linen for the Oblates in exchange for Germain's board at the junior college. She constantly worked at keeping expenses down and had her farmer brothers send baskets of meat and vegetables from Pembina Mountain.

Since the parents now had only two of their children at home, Clémence and Gabrielle, the house was judged too big and expensive to run, so it was decided to make it produce some revenue. In 1918, Léon sold one of his pieces of land in Saskatchewan in order to pay for the installation of hot-water central heating, making it possible to take in nieces from the country or short-term boarders, some of whom turned out to be pleasant and others downright irksome.

This said, the family's living conditions were not so dreadful. Difficult, no doubt, but still a long way from poverty; the Roys were not in truly dire straits, despite what Gabrielle and even Adèle were to write later. They were no worse off than their neighbours or most households in St-Boniface. It was later that real poverty struck, after Léon's death and during the Depression, when Mélina found herself with virtually nothing.

For the time being, during Gabrielle's adolescence, the family was far from destitute. Although Léon was no longer earning a salary, he had his house, which he mortgaged around 1920, and a little money he had put aside when he sold his land in Dollard and some lots near his house on Deschambault Street.[91] This nest egg enabled him to transact in a small way now and then and remain active despite all. For even without a steady job he continued to dabble in business ventures and tried to maintain a certain status in the community of St-Boniface. Thus in the autumn of 1916, a year after his dismissal, he was one of a group of citizens who, with a view to "forming a Canadian parish," went on an exploratory expedition in the Fisher Branch region between Lake Winnipeg and Lake Manitoba.[92] *Henderson's Directory*, which had been recording his occupation as "French interpreter," identified him in 1917 as a "grain buyer," then "rancher" in 1924, and "grocer" the following year. Not until 1927 was Léon Roy (then seventy-seven) listed as "retired."

Léon was clearly not so hard up that in 1923 he could not make a donation of ten dollars for the reconstruction of the recently burned Collège de Saint-Boniface, which made him one of the more generous subscribers.[93] As for money coming in, while not abundant it was not totally lacking. Besides the board paid by lodgers, there was money sent regularly by Adèle, plus sums from Rodolphe, which were substantial if often uncertain. And then, the children were able to stay in school; Germain went to classical college until his next-to-last year, while Gabrielle attended the Académie Saint-Joseph until she was nineteen. This was a privilege enjoyed by very few girls in the neighbourhood, most of whom had to leave school after sixth or seventh grade to become waitresses, or maids, or salesgirls in the Five and Tens of Winnipeg.

So the family's impecuniousness was relative, which made it no less real or easier to live with, but certainly less serious. Léon and Mélina, having for years been accustomed to a certain financial comfort or at least the security brought by the stability of Léon's job and steady growth of their assets, felt debased. The threat of material degradation together with worry to see themselves aging made them frugal and anxious, even pusillanimous. On this subject, Gabrielle confided to Joan Hind-Smith, "We were the genteel poor. [. . .] Poverty is perhaps hardest for middle-class people who fight through it to keep up a certain 'rank.'"[94] It was not really being poor that caused her father's ill temper and created such a morose atmosphere in the house, it was mourning for a time past and feeling he had lost so much.

Money was a real obsession in the Roy household. It was constantly being counted, lent and borrowed between siblings, envied in another's hands, and endlessly quarrelled over. And in the midst of it all, Gabrielle behaved as if she were a princess untouched by any material care whatever, intent on her studies, intent on finding herself, intent on her resolve to have the best in life, and convinced that it was her right. Pretty dresses, hats, fine shoes, a riding habit, she persuaded her mother to give her whatever she wanted,[95] to the indignation of her sisters, who were scandalized by the extravagance. The first falling-out between Adèle and Gabrielle occurred at this time. From the far-off village where she was teaching, Adèle would often write to her goddaughter and Gabrielle would reply with "little letters in which her story-telling talent showed already."[96] One day Adèle slipped some money in the envelope, telling Gabrielle to use it to buy gifts for the other family members, particularly some new slippers for her father. But Léon, when reading Adèle's letter to Gabrielle – a rather frequent practice with him, apparently – discovered that Gabrielle had kept the money for herself. Adèle, outraged when informed, immediately stopped corresponding with Gabrielle. Since the letters of this period have been lost, there is no way to confirm the truth of this, but given Gabrielle's attitude with the family and her position in it at that point, it does not seem unlikely.

Gabrielle's position in the family was still very much a singular one, that of an "only" and adored child on whom the mother heaped all her indulgence. While Mélina's attitude to poor Clémence was constant worry mixed with impatience and scolding, Gabrielle seemed to her the consolation for all her troubles, because she was younger and because her intelligence, beauty, ambitions, even her demands exerted an influence on her mother that was almost hypnotic. Clémence was treated more or less as a servant, cooking and doing household chores, while Gabrielle was free to go about the business of being a gifted student and distinguished young lady, reviewing her homework, brushing her hair, putting a clean collar on her convent uniform. . . . She was not even expected to make her own bed or put her clothes away; her mother or Clémence took care of such things. Even less was she expected to sew, do dishes or spring cleaning, or prepare meals, all of which it was near compulsory for teenage girls of the day to learn to do and which Gabrielle for her part would not hear of, regarding such tasks uninteresting and a waste of her time. A housewifely occupation simply did not appeal to her, any more than marriage and maternity, for which most of her girlfriends were feverishly preparing. She was being summoned by other dreams, other ambitions, other ideals.

The Voice of the Pools

The young Gabrielle's urge to write made its first appearance in this context and at about this time.

From what the novelist confided in an interview later, she was ten or twelve when the urge first came upon her, which would be about when she made up her mind to be an industrious and brilliant student. At this early age, she seems to have written "a play which contained a villain, a hero, and a murder," and which she and her friends presented several summers running in the yard behind the house, with a big tree as scenery. As to her first fiction, here is what she said shortly before her death:

One day I remember when I was only about 12 years old, I bought a note-book. In it, I wrote in big letters on the first page, "Un Roman de Gabrielle Roy en 12 chapitres." My mother found it, and when she read what I had written in it, she threw it into the fire. [. . .] I had described my uncles from the country with their big moustaches. My mother thought I was being disrespectful. She didn't realize, as I did at so early an age, that artistic works can be born of ordinary events from the lives of ordinary people.[97]

Did these early efforts really occur, or are they part of the lore that every artist, even every person, entertains about his or her own begin-nings? There is no way to be sure, but there is no reason to doubt them either. Were they followed by other, similar attempts? Here again, one can only conjecture, but it does seem that around the age of sixteen Gabrielle began to want to be a writer.

Her success in school in French composition was enough to convince her that she had talent. Her compositions not only received the best marks, they were considered little masterpieces that the nuns read aloud in class, holding them up as examples to other pupils. Her pen won her public recognition too. Besides the composition prizes she won year after year from the AECFM, she came second in a major contest held in 1923 by *Le Devoir* of Montreal, and in the same contest the year follow-ing, when she was sixteen, her name figured again in the *Tableau d'hon-neur*, the competition's roll of honour.[98]

While successes of this kind could only encourage her penchant for literature, it is not at all certain that her vocation as a writer was evident at this time. It is true that Christine, the narrator in *Street of Riches*, is sixteen when she decides that her life will be devoted to writing. In her explicitly autobiographical writings, however, Gabrielle generally situ-ates her decision (to the extent that an event and date can be pin-pointed) much later, around the end of her twenties, if not later. Until then writing was undoubtedly there, but as one inclination, one urge among all those driving her, all of them more or less confusedly express-ing her one and only fundamental aspiration that was still without form or precise objective – to outdo herself, achieve by whatever means the highest goal, the most complete realization of herself. This way, she would be loved and admired as she felt she had never been. Would this success be brought to her by the theatre? By literature? By her scholastic achievement? By something else? The girl with "the large, anxious eyes [looking] far away towards the vast unknown called life" did not know as yet.[99] All she knew, and she knew it for a certainty, was that it would happen, not through the usual channels that her classmates were preparing to take, that her mother and sisters had taken before her and wished her to take as well, but through channels of her own.

"I wanted to write," Christine says, "as one feels the need to love, to be loved."[100] It is the comparison in this sentence that expresses the essential. In the adolescent Gabrielle, the need to write came second, a means rather than a true goal, which is much less clear-cut, as her life over the next ten years and throughout Part One of *Enchantment and Sorrow* would show. Adolescence was when she began to stir, when her thoughts and energies, breaking with her assigned condition and milieu, turned toward the future, toward "this other myself"[101] who kept haunting her but whose face and condition she could not yet see. This was when there appeared in her not the art of writing in the exacting sense that she later gave it but the ambition and inclination that would lead her to writing.

This is not at all to say that the urge born in the girl who hears "the voice of the pools" calling was pure fantasy, but it would be a mistake to go looking for a fixed, precise plan in this period. Gabrielle Roy was by no means a child prodigy or seven-year-old poet. Undoubtedly she thought a lot about writing and was attracted by it from an early age, but her desire to write remained an adolescent desire that was still vague and buried among other, more urgent desires. It was later that she would choose her true vocation as a writer, and she would do it knowingly and of her own volition.

CHAPTER 5

*R*eal Life Is Elsewhere

" *I* was late growing up," we are told in *Enchantment and Sorrow.*[1] Growing up; that is, reaching that age of restlessness, of self-expression when one expends oneself without counting the cost, the age of one's first real breaks with things familiar and one's first choices of some consequence.

Gabrielle Roy reached this phase during her twenties, when she became freer to do as she wished and the still vaguely defined goal she had set herself began to beckon with increasing urgency. Her feeling of un-belonging and the dream of betterment that had appeared during her adolescence were now translatable into acts, plans, decisions, inspired by an impatience leading her to reject the constraints of her milieu and look for another way of living, another way of being more in tune with her desires and the huge and growing ambition that had taken hold of her.

The decade following the completion of her schooling with the nuns was a time of great, even feverish, activity during which, along with her progressive emancipation, there evolved the psychological and material conditions that enabled Gabrielle to take the step that was both the end and the culmination of the period, her departure from Manitoba for good in the autumn of 1937.

The Death of a Pioneer

"Pioneer dies." This was the heading with which the *Manitoba Free Press* of 22 February 1929 announced the death of Léon Roy two days previously.[2] By a coincidence that may not have been purely symbolic, this new period in Gabrielle's life opened in mourning for her father. The old man, hospitalized some time earlier, had insisted on returning home to die surrounded by his family, which was the custom and considered right and proper. Mélina, Clémence, and Gabrielle were at his bedside, as well as *Tante* Rosalie and Yvonne, Joseph's eldest daughter, who was then living in the house on Deschambault Street.

This old-style, public death is the subject of one of the loveliest passages in *Enchantment and Sorrow*, if only in the poignancy of the remorse that transfuses the whole piece. "I hadn't thought I'd loved my father so deeply," the narrator writes. But now it was too late. "My grief lay in seeing no possibility of making amends. My relationship to my father would remain for ever as it was when death separated us. Nothing could ever be added, taken back, corrected, or wiped away. [. . .] The lost opportunity [could never] be recaptured."[3]

Does this retrospective emotion in the writer correspond to what the nineteen-year-old girl really felt in the presence of her father's remains? Did remorse for her strained relations with the dead man, for the scant affection she had shown him, come upon her then or only later, perhaps even in the last years of her life when she had begun to write her memoirs? One certainty is that Léon had to die and Gabrielle had to be freed of his presence before she could feel both this remorse and the filial piety expressed in the autobiography.

At the time, her behaviour seems to have been less virtuous. Not once, when she knew he was dying, did Gabrielle go to see her father in the hospital; she had too much work, she explains in the same passage in *Enchantment and Sorrow*. But Adèle, who had come running immediately from her faraway Alberta, presents a more cynical version in her own recollections:

> Before leaving the house to go to the station, I asked Clem [Clémence],
>
>   "So what's *La Misère* doing? *Le père* wants so much for her to go and see him at the hospital."
>
>   "She's skating with her friends at the college rink. You know she doesn't bother her head much about *le père*."[4]

However much Gabrielle may have wept on her father's grave and publicly displayed her mourning as related in *Enchantment and Sorrow*, it does not appear that she was overly affected by the departure of the father who had invented the nickname *Petite Misère*, whose brooding presence, in her adolescent mind, had stood as a constant reproach for her birth and a barrier to her happiness. Léon's death was a liberation in short, but her alienation seemed so irreversible that many years would have to pass before she made peace in her mind with the man who had sired her, so insurmountably remote she seemed to feel from him.

She did not know how much her own destiny would begin to resemble her father's before too long. Eight years later she would abandon the country of her birth, put her family and friends out of mind, and go to the other side of the world to try her luck. Surely this voluntary exile was in a way a repetition of the one in her father's life a half century earlier. With advancing age, Gabrielle would place increasing value in being a daughter of immigrants. Most often she would emphasize the maternal side of her heritage, and the history of the Landrys (or the part that came through in Mélina's stories at any rate) showed only the luminous side of migration, seen as an undertaking inspired by dreams, courage, and the desire for freedom, as a progression, an opening, a broadening of the person and the world around. Beside this positive, even idyllic image, Léon's life history reflects a very different aspect of the immigrant experience and psychology in which emigration is seen to be at root a solitary destiny, a break with one's group in which one moves away, abandons the country of one's birth and turns one's attention elsewhere. Gabrielle may have felt infinitely closer to her mother, she may later have thought of herself most as one of "Mélina's children,"[5] but in her behaviour and the direction she gave to her life she was as much, if not more, Léon's daughter.

The funeral was held in St-Boniface Cathedral, and then *le père* was buried in the cemetery beside his much-loved child Marie-Agnès. Neither Joseph nor Rodolphe was there. The only son who took the trouble to be present, to everyone's great surprise, was Germain, who had not set foot in the house for years. He had come from South Fork in Saskatchewan, where he was a schoolteacher. The girls were all present except for Adèle, who had been there but had had to leave to return to Duvernay. Sister Léon, who was then at a posting in Kenora in Northern Ontario, arrived the day before the ceremony; she had not been given permission to come earlier to witness her father's last moments.

To Earn My Living

When Léon died, Gabrielle had been studying at the Provincial Normal School in Winnipeg since the previous September. If on leaving the

Académie Saint-Joseph she had decided to embrace a teaching career, it was because everything was pointing her in this direction and she had little choice.

All her sisters had been teachers before her, as their parents had wished, particularly Mélina, who saw in this "a profession noble, lady-like and highly respectable,"[6] the best situation to which a well-brought-up young lady of slender means could aspire. Which was true. Among the few occupations open to young women of the day, teaching was without doubt one of the most advantageous. Restricted to the best educated, it carried undeniable social prestige and allowed a certain degree of intellectual life. The working conditions were by no means to be disdained either, particularly compared to those of factory workers, domestic help, office workers, and saleswomen, for it should be remembered that this was Manitoba. Whereas in Quebec in those days the lot of teachers verged on pure and simple exploitation, it was different in a province where the educational system was secular and directly controlled by the State. Primary school teaching could still be called a women's employment ghetto, but at least the hiring of teachers was not completely arbitrary and the pay, while not substantial, was still decent.

Gabrielle's decision could also be explained by another factor. In June 1928, she had won first prize of a hundred dollars in the Association d'éducation's provincewide contest. However, the rules stipulated that the money could be collected only on condition that the winner became a schoolteacher committed to serving the cause of French and its teaching in Manitoba. And to prevent any circumvention, the cheque was not made out to the prizewinner but to the Department of Education; the money covered his or her registration fee at the Provincial Normal School.[7]

It would be an exaggeration therefore to speak of teaching as a "vocation" for Gabrielle Roy. To the young woman who set out one September morning in 1928 for the imposing building on William Avenue,[8] getting her teacher's certificate was simply the most convenient way of earning her living, of achieving financial independence and hence her freedom.

Since the Thornton Act had forced the closing of the old École normale de Saint-Boniface, where Anna, Adèle, and Bernadette had obtained their certificates, attending the Provincial Normal School in Winnipeg was the obligatory course for any young woman wanting to become a teacher in Manitoba. This was a fiercely English and non-confessional institution; the few French-Canadian students who dared venture into its halls adapted with great difficulty and were made to feel like foreigners or inferiors.[9] Not only was the instruction given entirely in English but a good many of the teachers were Scots (McIntosh, McKim, McLeod, McIntyre), who were known among Franco-Manitobans for anti-French fanaticism. The students were required furthermore to do two practicums in the city's elementary schools, where all the classes were English; they were hardly ever sent to St-Boniface or a French village. Not surprisingly under these conditions, francophone candidates were rare and hard-pressed to succeed. For the year 1928–1929, of some five hundred students completing their "First Class" course of study, only five had French names. Gabrielle was the only one of these whose graduation recommendation by the school authorities was "unconditional"; three of her francophone classmates were among the twenty-two whose recommendation was "conditional" and the last was one of the six who were not recommended.[10]

Which is to say that Gabrielle did rather well. Short of succeeding as brilliantly as she had at the Académie Saint-Joseph, she nevertheless obtained excellent marks, including B+'s in Reading, Speaking, School Management, and Physical Education, and A's in Writing, Seatwork, and Pedagogy, this last given by the school principal, Dr. W. A. McIntyre, to whom the narrator of *Enchantment and Sorrow* later rendered grateful homage.[11] In sum, she finished the year with a score of twenty-four points, which placed her thirteenth in her class.

This success is attributable to her aptitude and hard work, but also to her knowledge of English, which she kept striving to perfect and which enabled her to integrate into this foreign environment far more easily than the other francophones. Instead of remaining on the defensive, she took pleasure in mixing with her English-speaking classmates and found such favour with them they soon forgot her difference and thought of her as one of them, seeing her as "a curly-haired little spit-fire – a dreamer – and the poet among us, with a weakness for the Unattainable."[12] Here we see another indicator of the ambition and will to succeed that were driving Gabrielle since she had glimpsed "the hard, solitary path"[13] she must travel to reach her salvation. To better herself, to be in a position to make her dreams come true, she must at any price overcome this first external obstacle, she must win on "the enemy's" home turf,[14] and to do this she must not let herself be boxed in by limitations imposed by what she was or by allegiance to her milieu. "All I was trying to do, [...] was get good marks," she wrote later. "I was working hardest on my English accent [. . .] and I lost sight of my father's suffering image."[15]

On 27 June 1929, three months after her twentieth birthday, Gabrielle Roy received her First Class Teacher's Certificate from the Department of Education, authorizing her to teach at the elementary school level.[16]

On this date she had, in fact, already been teaching for a month. The school in the Métis village of Marchand had found itself without a teacher, and Gabrielle, in view of her good marks at normal school, had succeeded in being sent there as a substitute for the final weeks of the school year. And so, as she said later, "I'd no sooner finished my studies [than] I was back in school."[17] Marchand, roughly fifty miles southeast of Winnipeg, was a desolate, impoverished little hamlet. Here, Gabrielle took charge of her very first school, which, like all country schools, was attended by children at levels ranging from Grade 1 to Grade 8.

It was here on her first day of class that there occurred an episode whose memory returned nearly half a century later when the novelist was writing *Enchanted Summer*.[18] A little girl by the name of Yolande Chartrand did not answer roll call. Gabrielle learned that she had just died of tuberculosis. As soon as school was out, she led her pupils to the little girl's house. Finding no one beside the child's body, the children and their teacher undertook to cover it with rose petals. This picture of "The Dead Child," one of the most striking in all of Gabrielle Roy's works, has special significance in its connection with this particular moment in her life. Separated from her mother for the first time and venturing alone into a world that has left her "terrified," here in "this mournful setting," [. . .] "one of the most lifeless vistas I've ever seen," in a way, as the child she has been, the young teacher also dies.[19]

Cardinal

The real severance, however, came in the course of the following year. After spending the summer in St-Boniface Gabrielle arrived in the village of Cardinal in mid-August 1929. She would not see her family again for ten months. "The year I spent there was one of the most important in my life," she writes in *Enchantment and Sorrow*.[20] Elsewhere she confides, "Another experience as rich, profound, and moving I have never known. Even my writer's life sometimes seems pale beside those days."[21]

Days of exhilaration and freedom, days of inner peace and full possession of herself. Perhaps for the first time since her early adolescence Gabrielle felt relieved, delivered of the tension that had been goading her always to want more, to rise above herself and those around her. Far from St-Boniface, far from the constant battles to win recognition and admiration, here she was as if on vacation from herself, or rather from "that person all unknown" who haunted her and kept pushing her toward the future. For a time, living in the present was enough and she had a feeling that was new to her and would rarely come again, of being in her appointed place, quietly doing what she was meant to be doing.

Today abandoned, Cardinal was then a community of some thirty houses, scattered on either side of the railway station. Christine, the heroine of *Street of Riches*, goes to this "red village" to earn her living.[22] And this same "western" backdrop, nearly half a century after Gabrielle's own stay there, inspired the settings of the two final stories of *Children of My Heart*:

> From the school windows I could see the bleak railway station, like all those built at the time, with its grain elevator, its water tank, a caboose that had been sitting on the ground for years. Everything was painted in that hateful oxblood colour that had no life or sparkle [. . .]. The main street predominated, of course, treeless and too wide, where nearly always the only thing moving was the wind, a melancholy dirt road, plaintive and dusty like the main streets of almost all the villages of the Canadian West in the first year of the Great Depression.[23]

The young woman would occasionally know boredom in this forsaken corner where there was practically no entertainment and nothing ever happened, but at least she was in familiar territory. Located between Notre-Dame-de-Lourdes and Somerset in the region called Pembina Mountain, it was part of the region where she had spent her summer vacations as a child and adolescent. Here she rediscovered the vistas she loved and the countryside of her maternal uncles, Zénon, Calixte, and, most of all, Excide, whose house she visited nearly every weekend and where she was treated like a queen. Her cousins Philippe and Cléophas courted her almost openly; Léa, who had replaced Éliane as mistress of the house and whom Gabrielle for this reason called *ma châtelaine*,[24] adored her and exchanged with her the prolific confidences

common to their age. Together, all the cousins did the rounds of the
parties and boisterously celebrated their youth.

But Gabrielle had other reasons for being happy. First, her job was
not a temporary engagement as at Marchand; here she was holding
down a real teacher's posting with a salary to match: $1,100 for the year.
She had likely obtained it the way nearly all French-Canadian Catholic
teachers obtained jobs in those days, through what must be called "valid
favouritism." Although Manitoba law prescribed uniform teaching curricula to be supervised by inspectors appointed by the State and provided
for strict control of training and certification of teachers, it left local
school commissions free to choose the staff for their schools themselves.
This was one of the technicalities used by the Association d'éducation des
Canadiens français du Manitoba – despite having no official status – to
exert its influence on linguistic and religious education in a French-
Canadian milieu. In municipalities where francophones were in the
majority, it sufficed to pack the school councils in order to change the
entire educational environment and ensure the recruitment of teachers
capable of truly serving "the cause." This influence was so far-reaching
that a newly graduated teacher in search of employment applied not to
the school commissions but to the association, which thus controlled the
placing of virtually all francophone teaching personnel in the province.

There could be other considerations too. In the St-Louis school district in which Cardinal was located, the sons of Grandfather Élie Landry
were prominent men respected by their fellow citizens, and their
influence on the local economic and political scene was considerable. It
is not surprising therefore that fifteen years earlier Mélina's older
daughters had been able to obtain their first teaching jobs in this same
region; Adèle had begun her career at St-Alphonse and St-Léon, and
Bernadette, before becoming a nun, had spent her first year of teaching
at Somerset. Now it was Gabrielle's turn to benefit from her uncles' protection and get herself a job in her maternal family's home region.

Gabrielle's job was even more interesting than those Adèle and
Bernadette had had. While they had taught in "big" villages where the
schools were large enough to be run by nuns, Cardinal had only a little
country school where the teacher was alone and so enjoyed a wide
margin of freedom in the organization of her work as well as in her
personal life.

When she arrived, Gabrielle took a room with board with a family in
the village. But the family moved away after a few weeks and so the

young woman soon found herself alone in the house. She asked one of the boys at the school to come and sleep at the house to protect her and tend the fire. Finding this situation less than proper, the father of one of the girls asked the general-store owner, Madame Château, whose daughter Aline was a pupil, to rent the teacher a room. This room was over the store, and this, when spring arrived, was where the children came to fetch Gabrielle every morning to take her to school.[25]

In the whole red-painted village, says the text of *Street of Riches*, "only the school had any individuality; it was all white."[26] This school, which bore the name "Saint-Louis A," was a small wooden building built next door to the church. It was attended by forty children, twenty boys and twenty girls, their ages ranging from five to fourteen. Some of them lived right in the village but most came from the surrounding quarter sections where their parents had farms. Gabrielle's class register, preserved at the Manitoba Archives, mentions certain of the names in *Children of My Heart*. There are three Badiou children, Marcel, Lucienne, and Aimé, two Du Pasquiers, Aurèle and Robert, one little Lachapelle, three Toutants, four Cenerinis,[27] but none has the first name Médéric or surname Eymard, like the hero of Part III of *Children of My Heart*.[28]

To her still-living pupils, Gabrielle Roy has left an unforgettable memory, which a reading of *Children of My Heart* in French or English must have made especially sweet. The young teacher put into practice the precepts of modern pedagogy instilled in her by Dr. McIntyre: light-handed discipline, affectionate relations with the children, a great deal of time for games, picnics, stories, and demonstration lessons. And so when little Aimé Badiou had been inattentive, Gabrielle had him come to her home after school and as punishment stuffed him with candies she had bought at Madame Château's. In class, Marcel Lancelot recalls, she was like "a butterfly," full of gaiety and thoughtfulness, always ready to listen to a child, to stroke this one's cheek, that one's hair, trying to hold the attention of all with simple words and kindnesses of every sort. The children, for whom school had been a synonym for boredom and forbiddance, could not get over it.

It is true that their new teacher was only twenty, that she was pretty and filled with enthusiasm. She skied and rode horseback and took long walks in the country. She gladly accepted invitations from their parents to meals and took an interest in the lives of her pupils outside school. But most of all, Mademoiselle Roy was not yet embittered by routine and disappointment; for her, teaching still had all the beauty and richness of first experience. New in this career, she saw her craft as the installation, outside the workaday world, of a space both open and protected in which teacher and children commune in the same innocence, the same happy state of security and wonder, a kind of reciprocal seduction joining them "by virtue of the most mysterious possessive force in existence, one that sometimes even surpasses the bond of blood."[29] Much later Gabrielle said, "We formed something like a little cooperative of mutual help, charity, and love,"[30] a feeling that is echoed in *Street of Riches* by what Christine feels standing before her pupils:

> I did not fully realize it yet – often our joys are slow in coming home to us – but I was living through one of the rarest happinesses of my life. Was not all the world a child? Were we not at the day's morning? . . .[31]

From a literary viewpoint, this year, or rather the memory of this year, was to be very significant for Gabrielle Roy. We know how important a place in her work would be occupied by the school as theme and the teacher as character, both of which she raised practically to the status of myth, particulary in Part II of *Where Nests the Water Hen* and in the stories of *Children of My Heart*. In the novelist's imagination, school was not primarily the large urban institution like the one she herself had attended or the other where she spent most of her teaching career; it was the little country or village school, isolated, lost in a vast, untamed expanse, where the miracle of education can come about with a maximum of poetry and purity. The model, the ideal of every school for Gabrielle, would always be this school at Cardinal where, however briefly, she had been this heroine, this humanist figure par excellence, a schoolteacher in the midst of a wilderness.

However, the relaxed pedagogy practised by the young woman did not meet with everyone's approval. In one of his periodic reports to the secretariat of the Association d'éducation, the Notre-Dame-de-Lourdes parish representative, one of whose tasks was to supervise the teacher, "complains that Mlle Roy does not teach enough French and that the children do not have lessons to take home."[32] Whatever the real implications of this note, it does suggest that Gabrielle, even in this early period, was hardly the ardent activist the association hoped to find in each of the teachers under its "jurisdiction." Linguistic and religious zeal, bold actions to advance "the cause," none of this was her style. Never would she feel caught up in these battles, either now or in later years.

It must be said that in the community she found herself in, the patriotic struggle appeared less urgent and rather different than in St-Boniface. At Notre-Dame-de-Lourdes and Cardinal, French Canadians by birth, meaning those born in Quebec or descended from Québécois, were not alone in the French-speaking population, which comprised as well a large proportion of French, Belgian, and Swiss immigrants.[33] Many of Gabrielle's pupils came from families whose parents or grandparents were born in Europe and had only recently immigrated to Manitoba. Such were the Badious, Lancelots, Vigiers, and Du Pasquiers. These families, some of whom were of French bourgeois or even aristocratic stock brought down in the world by the advent of the Third Republic, were less haunted by fear of assimilation and less obligated by patriotic feeling than the French-Canadian families. They were also different in their customs, their sensibilities, and their speech. So much so that the two communities mixed little and there was even a certain animosity between them.

Gabrielle appeared to be something of a turncoat to the French Canadians in fact, for nothing delighted her more than associating with French people from France and finding herself in a kind of "Europe in miniature."[34] She felt that when she was with these people, when she watched her language to make it as good as theirs, she was closer to that better, finer, freer life that was her fondest aspiration. She went often to spend an evening at the Badiou or Lancelot farm, where there was only one subject of conversation all evening long: France, its landscapes, its history, its artists, its matchless splendour. How far away St-Boniface seemed, and her mother's house and the whole little world she had been born into!

At the Lancelots lived a young man who was to become her first beau. His name was Jean Coulpier. He too was French. He was rumoured to be the son of a well-heeled family, an ex-banker who had come to Canada for a change of scene, like his compatriot Louis Hémon. Jean was greatly smitten with Gabrielle. They were often seen together in the village, arm in arm, or walking the little section roads. Barely five or six years later, in one of her first published stories,[35] Gabrielle imagined a young city woman by the name of Noëlla nostalgically remembering the time she spent as a teacher in the "Pembina region which has a harshness, a ruggedness about it, yet is infinitely appealing." Noëlla has a suitor, Jean, who is "an incurable dreamer" and wants to keep her forever by his side. The young woman however, incapable of finding satisfaction in "this disheartening countryside," has only one desire: to go back to the city.

"Give your mare a bit of the whip," she said to Jean on the way to the station, [...] "I'm all impatient to catch my train and go back to the lively, vibrant city, to swim in its swift, strong current. Ah, that's the life, the good life!"

Even though Gabrielle loved her pupils and her occupation, even though her time at Cardinal brought her contentment she had never known before, this "vacation," this relaxation of her yearning for farther fields could not last. Soon "that person all unknown" made her presence felt again, tugging her away from the present, away from this happy place; once again, she wrote later, "I peered into the obscurity ahead of me, trying to catch a glimpse of the life awaiting me."[36] In one of the few surviving letters from that year, in which the themes of enchantment and sorrow inextricably mingled can already be discerned, the young woman confides in her cousin Léa:

> It's true that I'm pretty mercurial. One fine morning I'll bewail my lot and beat my breast without end for all of humanity and then, come evening of that very day perhaps, I'll find everything around me good and beautiful. Light and shadows, gaiety and melancholia, smiles and tears, I'm one or the other, but deep inside forever caught up with a great, beautiful, unrelenting dream.[37]

A dream that forbade her to sit still, that on the contrary demanded that she move and seek adventure. "I would travel," says the narrator of *Children of My Heart*, "travel a lot [...]. I would visit far countries, cities, incomparable palaces. I saw myself reaching a high future from which I would look back with some commiseration toward the awkward little country teacher I had been."[38]

L'Institut Provencher

But before launching on distant voyages, the first hurdle was to leave Cardinal and get back to St-Boniface. Gabrielle had never really wanted to teach in the country. As early as June 1929, from her little school at Marchand, she had submitted an official application to the St-Boniface School Commission in hope of getting a job in the city. After being turned down she tried twice again during her year at Cardinal. The arguments she presented to *Messieurs les Commissaires* were the same each time: she had studied at the Académie Saint-Joseph, her achievements in the AECFM competitions "attest to the work I have accomplished," she had received "an excellent report" on leaving normal school, and most of all, "my mother is a widow and property-owner in St-Boniface having paid taxes for over twenty years."[39]

The last of these letters was dated 14 May 1930. On the following June 20, the secretary of the St-Boniface School Commission, Louis Bétournay, wrote her this reply: "There will be room for another teacher at Provencher School next September, and our school commission is prepared to engage you at that time on the conditions of service and remuneration set forth in its bylaws."[40]

We can picture Gabrielle's delight. No sooner said than done, like Noëlla, she left her school at Cardinal, her cousins, and Jean and his love behind, and went up to St-Boniface to "the life, the good life" awaiting her.

Gabrielle had been extraordinarily lucky to land a job at "l'Institut collégial Provencher" at this moment. Since the beginning of the Depression, school commissions had been subjected to such draconian budgetary cuts that teachers both male and female were in oversupply and had no end of trouble being hired and paid. In Gabrielle's own family this was the predicament not only for Adèle but also Germain and his new bride, Antonia Houde, who were experienced teachers. For a young teacher like Gabrielle, getting herself any job was therefore a kind of privilege; getting herself this job at Provencher was close to miraculous.

At the time this was the only French-speaking school in St-Boniface that accepted lay teachers; there were less than twenty of them and needless to say they were the cream of the crop. To be taken on at Provencher, the Department of Education's certificate was far from the only condition. The candidate had to be perfectly bilingual, single, a graduate of the Académie Saint-Joseph, and live in St-Boniface. But even fulfilling these requirements was no guarantee, for an additional, indeed the paramount, requirement was the personal approval of Brother Joseph Fink, the principal, who had the last word in the selection of his teachers.[41]

Gabrielle fulfilled all these requirements and, besides, the scholastic milieu of St-Boniface remembered her as a brilliant and extremely studious girl, one of the best students the Académie Saint-Joseph had ever had. Less than two years earlier at a ceremony organized by the nuns, Brother Fink had with his own hands presented her with the lieutenant-governor's medal she had won for her excellent marks. Being taken into the fold at Provencher, for the prizewinning student and "Queen of the May," was simply one more reward added to all the others she had received for her determination, hard work, and aptitude.

In the fall of 1930, Gabrielle was therefore in a position many other teachers envied her for. She was only twenty and here she was practically at the peak of a teaching career. Compared with Cardinal, Provencher was a kind of paradise. The pay was lower on account of the Depression, true enough. From $1,000 annually in 1931–1932, it dropped to $922 the following year and remained there until 1937. Still, this was much better than the pay received by Quebec teachers.[42] Gabrielle would keep this position and this salary throughout the years of the Great Depression, when unemployment was very severe in the western provinces, more severe than in other parts of Canada. In such a context of underemployment and depressed prices, one counted oneself extremely fortunate to have an assured income, even a small one.

But there were other, equally valuable advantages to working at Provencher. First, Gabrielle could live with her mother in the house on Deschambault Street. The school, at the corner of Avenue de la Cathédrale and Saint-Jean-Baptiste Street, was only a few minutes' walk away. At home she had the run of a big, comfortable house that she could call her own, where food was put on the table, her washing was done for her, and she could do as she liked, stay out late at night, have friends in, or retire to the privacy of her room if the spirit moved her.

She would have had a hard time finding a situation like Provencher elsewhere. Her colleagues were mostly young, single, educated if not cultivated, and she had known them since childhood or adolescence when they were all attending the Académie Saint-Joseph together. Their names were Renée Deniset, Valentine Couture, Marie-Rose Beaulieu, Antoinette Baril, Gratia Fortin, Berthe and Anna Marion, Gertrude Kelly, Denise Rocan.[43] With them, Gabrielle shared her experiences, her thoughts, and a good deal of her leisure time.

She felt very close to Léonie Guyot, who taught Grade 3. Although the same age as Gabrielle, Léonie was "with more experience."[44] Born in Fannystelle of a Savoyard father and a French-Canadian mother, she had begun teaching at seventeen, first in country schools then at Provencher where she began in September 1931, a year after Gabrielle. She was both attractive and intelligent. Besides her teaching talents she had great distinction in manner and speech, a flair for music and drama, and extensive literary knowledge.[45] She and Gabrielle very quickly became fast friends.

They spent breaks together, visited one another, and attended various professional and social functions together. In the spring of 1933 for instance, on an evening organized by "Le Cercle d'études Marie-Rose" of the Académie Saint-Joseph, of which Gabrielle was then secretary, they each read an argument on the theme "Is Country Life Better than City Life?" Léonie defended the city and Gabrielle the country;[46] the editor of *La Liberté* wrote, "the spirited and humorous manner [in which the speakers] treated this serious question elicited general hilarity many times over."[47] A few days later Léonie gave a talk to the local chapter of the Association d'éducation and it was Gabrielle who presented her, as she did the following year at a teachers' convention of which she was chairman and at which Léonie spoke on "social education."[48] Although they were drawn together initially by their occupation, their relationship rested primarily on mutual admiration and affection. Thus when Léonie lost her mother in April 1937, Gabrielle wrote her a note full of thoughtful concern, displaying already the art of the letter of consolation of which the novelist's correspondence in years to come contains so many examples:

Mon petit,

Last night I went late and stood outside your house. It was plunged in darkness and the wind wept all around. I didn't dare knock at your door. And yet I did so want to see you and weep all alone with you, in a small dark corner of the big empty living room.

[...] Your mother will always be by your side, helping you. You'll see. It won't be as cruel as you think it's going to be right now, because she'll never be far away and her spirit will never leave you. Very often people we've loved are closer to us in death than in life, especially noble people like your mother.[49]

Professionally, the Institut Provencher was one of the best schools in which a Franco-Manitoban teacher could hope to work. Founded in 1907, it was attended by approximately a thousand pupils, all boys, ranging from Grade 1 to Grade 12. The female teachers had charge of *les petites classes*, or elementary grades, while *les grandes classes* at the secondary level were still the domain of the Marianist brothers who ran the institution. At their head, Brother Joseph Fink, a widely renowned educator of whom Gabrielle draws a flattering portrait in *Enchantment and Sorrow*,[50] played his role with a masterful hand; when he died in 1935 he was succeeded by Brother Joseph H. Bruns. As a public school,

Provencher did not enjoy the same prestige as its neighbour institutions, the Collège de Saint-Boniface, a secondary classical establishment for boys run by the Jesuits, and the Académie Saint-Joseph for girls, but to the extent that practically all the male children of St-Boniface passed through it, if only for their elementary education, the school and its staff had an important place in the cultural and social life of the city. It was also highly regarded by the inspectors of the Department of Education, who considered it an excellent school where the teachers were competent and well supervised, the curriculum was respected, and the Union Jack was properly "up and in good condition."[51]

The clientele of Provencher comprised both little French Canadians and children of other origins. In principle, all of them were subject to the same pedagogical regime, but in practice the francophones were grouped in separate classes to enable them to receive teaching that, although officially English, was in fact bilingual and in which the French curriculum, illicit though it was, occupied a substantial place. This type of segregation was practised especially in the early grades. Thus in Grade 1 there were at least two "receiving classes," one consisting of French-Canadian children and the other of pupils from other ethnic and linguistic groups.

Valentine Couture was the teacher for the first of these groups and Gabrielle had charge of the non-francophones, which meant that she taught only in English, in compliance with the law. Of her class, usually forty or so little boys ranging in age between five and nine, she remarked later that it was "a class of children representing nearly all the nations on earth, most of whom knew no more English than they did French."[52] In fact, the class lists show that at least two-thirds of her pupils had English and Irish surnames or given names; the boys of Italian, German, Slavic, or Flemish origin were numerous, but clearly in the minority (there were a few French Canadians too). Here again, we find certain names familiar to readers of *Children of My Heart*: Vincento [Rinella], Clare [Atkins], William Demetrioff, Walter Demetrioff, Tony Tascona, Nikolaï [Susick].[53]

Standing before such a big class and teaching entirely in English was certainly a major challenge for the young Gabrielle, but the work was not as hard as it had been at Marchand and at Cardinal. Instead of pupils at different levels, Gabrielle now had a class composed entirely of "beginners," and so it remained each year,[54] which relieved her of preparing a new curriculum every year and left her more free time.

Brother Fink had good reason to be pleased with his choice. Although Gabrielle had little experience, she proved to be a conscientious and sensitive teacher with a gift for engaging the boys' interest. As at Cardinal, her method depended on kindness and openness, and she succeeded in imposing her authority without being rough or raising her voice, unlike certain of her colleagues. "She was very lovely and very generous," recalls the painter Tony Tascona, who was her pupil in 1932 and 1933. "She did everything she could to help the poor children at the school. She must have spent half her pay helping them."[55] Recounting the facts sixty years later, and influenced as others have been by what he may have read in *Children of My Heart*, the former schoolboy is no doubt exaggerating. Be that as it may, the Institut Provencher did receive a large number of children from underprivileged circles and families reduced to difficult circumstances by the Depression, and the teachers expressed compassion in different ways. On occasion, Gabrielle would take one of her pupils home with her so that her mother could mend a piece of clothing or give him something to eat.

The photographs of Gabrielle's class, taken faithfully each year before the main entrance of the school,[56] show motley troops of urchins assembled with a young woman whose air is both gentle and detached, a half-smile on her lips. She gives the impression of watching over them as if they were her own children. But at the same time there is something about her which is not theirs; her mind – or her heart – is not entirely with them. Gabrielle's experience at Provencher was in no way comparable to what she had known at Cardinal. However much better her working and living conditions may have been, the intensity of her commitment was not the same. That feeling of communion, that kind of mystique inspired in her by her role as country teacher, had given way to a more down-to-earth, practical view of her occupation. She taught as best she could, she performed her appointed task with irreproachable professional conscience, but it no longer fired her enthusiasm. Teaching had become her livelihood. Her real vocation, her real interests, lay elsewhere.

The First Published Pieces

Among the advantages of Gabrielle's job at the Institut Provencher, one of the most valuable was that it allowed her time to do things other than teach. She went out, amused herself, launched into all kinds of activities, in other words took advantage of being a city dweller, and young, attractive, full of energy, and completely independent.

The years of her youth in St-Boniface were exhilarating in many ways, but were also years of tension and hard work. For if Gabrielle was "burning the candle at both ends," wasting her strength and not listening to reason, as her mother kept scolding her,[57] it was not only for her own amusement and indulgence in her youth but also because the urge to reach that greater happiness she had been dreaming of since her teen years was stronger than ever. Earlier, the dream had made her a model student and then a model teacher, but now that she was in a position to take charge of her adult life, her impatience and ambition redoubled. There was no question of making do with what her teaching position offered – an occupation, a salary, a niche for life. In her mind the job at Provencher was no more than a launching pad, a temporary base from which to take flight toward her true goal, which was elsewhere and much higher. There was not a moment to lose; the time had passed for static contemplation of the future. She must act, work, apply herself now to create the "person all unknown" that she must become.

Some time would need to pass before this passion would crystallize around literature to the exclusion of all else. For the time being, all the while she was at Provencher and even a bit beyond, Gabrielle remained faithful to both her teenage loves: writing and the theatre, which between them had become real roads to salvation. But of the two it was the theatre that most caught her fancy, and to this we return later in this chapter. It was the theatre, she believed, that would take her where she wanted to go.

Not that she neglected writing or failed to devote a considerable share of her energy to it. In her early thirties literature was not yet the one central occupation to which the young woman had decided to give herself body and soul, but it was already far more than the adolescent's childish and largely inconsequential enthralment that had stirred the strange message from "the voice of the pools." Although she had still made no real decision about it, her desire to write, to become a writer, was already a plan, no doubt a plan among others but one serious enough to require acts, behaviour, and a mode of life in which literature held an increasingly important place.

How important may be gauged from a recollection by Thérèse Goulet. Thérèse had known Gabrielle at the Académie Saint-Joseph and her brother Maurice had rented the second floor of the Roy house as lodging for his small family. She came from time to time to mind her brother's children and Gabrielle would spend the evening with her. The two young women would browse in Maurice's library and talk about their dreams for the future. "We would ordinarily finish the evening with something to eat and after dessert there would invariably be some reading aloud, poetry, part of a play, etc." Then Gabrielle would read Thérèse one of her "little compositions" in progress.

> I remember very specially the draft of an essay vigorously entitled "Great North Wind." My friend had wanted to wait for the ideal moment to read it to me. She chose in fact one of those harsh winter evenings when the wind was whistling and blowing both at once. [. . .] She asked me to criticize it. Impossible task. I found it altogether perfect.[58]

Then Gabrielle talked about her plan. "I'm going to write," she declared. In order to do so, she was ready, she said, to work tooth and nail, to take advantage of every experience that "puts one in touch with life," and to brave "the rocky climb of a difficult and unrewarding career."

This resolution showed first in a profusion of reading. Gabrielle had been a devourer of books since childhood, but now that she could please herself and literature appeared to be one of her possible life choices, her reading became more fervent and freer, meaning more varied and modern. This at least is what may be deduced from remarks by family members and close friends as well as more or less specific indications here and there in her earliest writings and correspondence. She was always very reticent on this subject in any direct way. "A novelist of the spoken word," as André Belleau would say,[59] she was not among those writers who attach great importance to the formative influence of other writers and invoke it in their work. Reconstituting a list of her readings in this period would therefore be a delicate and necessarily speculative operation.

What appears obvious, however, is that her reading was done mostly in English. She still read Alphonse Daudet, adored *Le Pêcheur d'Islande* by Loti, and, it seems, immersed herself in Balzac's novels. Like everyone else, she also undoubtedly read the many serial novels and other colourful tales that appeared in the newspapers and magazines of the day. But her favourite authors, like most of her discoveries, came to her in the language of Shakespeare, which was natural considering the context she lived in. Devoid of a public library, St-Boniface had only a small parish library bursting at the seams with religious books but offering in the guise of literature only a few nineteenth-century Canadian books in French and some sentimental and right-minded little novels imported from France.[60] The only French "bookstore," if it could be called that, was L'Étienne, the forerunner of the shop presided over by Gérard Bessette's *The Bookseller*, lacking only Hervé Jodoin and his "caphar-naum."[61] In Winnipeg, on the other hand, the market for literary books in English, both originals and translations, was much more open to modern productions.

Gabrielle not only continued to read the English classics and learn Shakespeare by heart but was also making the acquaintance of new authors no one had talked about at school, from Edgar Allan Poe to Lewis Carroll, from Robert Louis Stevenson and Elizabeth Barrett Browning to Somerset Maugham, Edgar Wallace, and Agatha Christie. At the same time she was discovering modern American literature, particularly novelists of the new social realism then at its zenith: Hemingway, Steinbeck, and Erskine Caldwell.

However, her great discovery was the literature of northern Europe, to which she was introduced by her immigrant friends and which she read in English translation. It is not verifiable that it was during these years and not later in her career that she first read the Slavic and Scandinavian authors to whom she would remain attached all her life and with whom she would always feel an aesthetic and moral fellowship – Gogol, Turgenev, Tolstoy, Ibsen, Pär Lagerkvist, Sigrid Undset, and several others. It is certain, however, that her attraction to the Nordic lit-erary space dates from this period, just as it is certain that the Nordic space and sensitivity were revealed to her through a text that would forever remain a beacon for her, an ultimate model – *The Steppe* by Chekhov, which she read during these years, if not slightly earlier, in a state of utter dazzlement.[62]

The influence of these readings on Gabrielle Roy's style and inspira-tion would not be felt until much later. For the moment, they served mostly to give Gabrielle comfort in her plans and a picture of the uni-verse she hoped to enter. She kept trying to write throughout these years with redoubled passion. "I'd scribble page after page," she would recall in *Enchantment and Sorrow*. "I had stories of a kind crowding into my head [. . .]. I'd plunge this way and that, into humour, realism, mystery, and horror in the manner of Edgar Allen Poe."[63]

This was where part of her salary went. She bought a portable type-writer and enrolled in a literary composition course given in Winnipeg by Mrs. Lillian Beynon Thomas. This journalist and woman of letters had played a major role in the feminist and social movement in prewar Manitoba and after her retirement was giving lessons in creative writing, focusing principally on the short story and playwriting, fields in which she herself enjoyed an enviable reputation.[64] From her studies with Mrs. Thomas, which were entirely in English, Gabrielle remarked later that she obtained better understanding of "the art of defining characters."[65]

Another sign of the seriousness of her commitment to literature was her desire to publish, which led her to dispatch a great many manuscripts to various papers and periodicals, if her sister Anna is to be believed.[66] Finally the great day arrived. To the astonishment of family members, a first text by Gabrielle Roy, along with her photograph, appeared early in the year 1934 in the columns of The Free Press, one of the two Winnipeg English dailies. For several months, the paper had been running a contest calling for short stories of very limited length. The prizewinning story, published on 11 January 1934, was "The Jarvis Murder Case," a detective story in which, for a sum of ten dollars, the murderer admits his crime to the narrator-investigator.

Gabrielle was twenty-four when she thus "officially" entered the literary scene.[67] But her first published text had nothing in common with what was to become her manner of writing as a novelist and story writer; although it was a clever and nicely written tale, it could have been composed by anyone on the literary entertainment page of any minor-city paper. This said, "The Jarvis Murder Case" did have at least one precursory feature: it was a prizewinner, heralding the long parade to the podium that Gabrielle Roy's career turned out to be.

There is nothing surprising about this first text being written in English. As we have seen, Gabrielle did most of her reading in English at this time, and it was in English that she had taken her creative writing lessons with Mrs. Thomas. She would continue to write in English throughout the 1930s and published at least one more English text, in the Toronto Star Weekly in December 1936. This is a fairly long, humorous story titled "Jean-Baptiste Takes a Wife," which evokes the unpretentious French-Canadian society of Pembina Mountain and draws extensively on playwriting techniques.

Two more stories of hers were published not long after this, in French this time, in the Montreal magazine Le Samedi: "La grotte de la mort," an Amerindian legend or pseudo-legend about the sad fate of a young Ojibway woman in love with a white man, and "Cent pour cent d'amour."

Neither French nor English appeared to be the only language of literary expression to the young woman at this time; she was simply an artist groping, hesitating, and until she found her own niche, leaving no stone unturned, which she would continue to do for some years yet. She kept trying this and that in terms of genre and inspiration, passing from detective yarns to social caricature to love stories and even descriptive poetry, judging by the title of the piece she recited to Thérèse Goulet, and also moved freely between French and English, unable yet to settle down. What was important at this time was not so much what she wrote but the mere fact of writing, of finishing her texts, seeing them published; it all amounted to escaping her anonymous little teacher's life and bringing what she knew she could do to realization.

But for her at this point, literature was still only one road among others. And not the surest or shortest way to her destination either, compared to another road then open to her, by which success looked more tangible and more immediate – the stage.

The Excitement of the Stage

"Our city," Gabrielle wrote later, "was a fervent lover of music, pageants, shows."[68] And, indeed, perusing the chronicles of the period, one is amazed to find how busy the cultural life of St-Boniface was at this time, particularly in winter, for all its limited population and small-town atmosphere. In spite of – or because of – the Depression, not a week went by without a song recital, a recreational evening, a dramatic presentation, a band concert, or a card party with poetry readings and musical pieces. These events would take place in one of the schools of the city or, for a larger-scale production like an opera or a play such as was organized at least once every year, in one of the Winnipeg theatres. The Walker was huge and well equipped, "Winnipeg's most English [theatre]"; the Dominion was "smaller, more intimate."[69] The reviews were always rhapsodic, qualifying the most modest event as memorable or an exemplary illustration of national genius. And it seems the audiences never failed to turn up to applaud the actors, musicians, orators, and other artists, all of them amateurs to be sure, but fired with ardour that gave lustre to the talents of some and made up for the shortcomings of others.

A fine example of this fervour was the great student debate organized in the autumn of 1935 on a particularly controversial theme at that moment: "The Vote for Women: Is It or Is It Not Acceptable?" To defend the negative, two representatives of l'Université de Montréal had come all the way to Manitoba, Paul Dumas, a medical student, and Gérard Cournoyer, a law student. Opposing them on the positive side were two of the most brilliant students at the Collège de Saint-Boniface, Georges Ramaekers and Marcel Carbotte. After an enormous buildup that made the front page of *La Liberté*, the event took place amid great pomp on Tuesday, November 21 in the assembly hall of the Institut Provencher, to which flocked a large and distinguished audience. In the next week's edition, another front-page story reports that the judges were unable to choose a winning side and therefore declared a draw. But the evening, writes the journalist, "will count among the best intellectual and artistic enjoyments we shall be given to remember."[70]

A city as fond of theatricals and entertainment was particularly fertile ground for Gabrielle. Since her years at the Académie Saint-Joseph if not longer, she had loved drama and had kept honing her talent. She was not lacking in aptitude; while she did not have a big voice, her inflection and timing were all there, as well as her sense of mimicry and expressive gesture. Her physical presence as a young lead served her well too; she was delicate and vibrant, gifted with charm and vivacity to which her penetrating gaze added fire. But most astonishing of all was her memory, which she seems to have inherited from her mother and had been developing for years, so that she could effortlessly retain pages and pages of text, French or English. And then, she had *le feu sacré* as the saying goes: she was truly inspired. Performing in public, drawing laughter or emotion from an audience, using one's stage presence to bring to people one does not know the pleasure of loving or hating imaginary beings, and being admired for this little quarter-hour of illusion and beauty, seemed to her one of the most precious things to which she could aspire.

Already during her year at Cardinal (one evening in April when there had been a card party and showing of the film *Rin-tin-tin* in the Notre-Dame-de-Lourdes parish hall), she had stood before the audience "to deliver the short story *Les trois messes basses* by Alphonse Daudet, which was a resounding success."[71] But it was in St-Boniface that her "career" took off. For a time she performed solo, principally "declaiming" small selections, some of which were from her own pen. Thus on 6 January 1931, at a choral concert directed by Marius Benoist, she filled the intermission reciting a story titled "Le marchand de sable est passé."[72] Two months later

she gave another solo performance during a school commission celebration, reciting "La chanteuse." That year and the two following, her
name figured regularly on the recreational programs of a variety of
meetings, benefit evenings, bridges, and musical teas held under the
patronage of diverse organizations like the Cercle ouvrier, the Anciennes
of the Académie Saint-Joseph, the Fédération des femmes canadiennes-
françaises du Manitoba, and others.[73] Judging by the large number of invitations she received, or at least the frequency of her fees, Mademoiselle
Roy's "declamations" were very popular with St-Boniface audiences.

But the dramatic art is difficult to practise alone. Gabrielle joined
groups. Most groups that formed at this time were *ad hoc* affairs organized for a single production and dissolved as soon as it was over. This was
the case, among others, with the troupes that specialized in tours
through the villages of French Manitoba, most often with backing from
a local organization like the Association d'éducation, the Collège de
Saint-Boniface, or the paper *La Liberté* taking the opportunity to
advance "the cause" in the farthest corners and recruit workers, benefactors, and subscribers among the good people drawn to the performances. These tours took place in summer and gathered young people of
varied talents, actors, musicians, clowns, and other entertainers, who
would set out every evening from St-Boniface laden with their equipment, bound for a village where an improvised stage would have been set
up for them. In *Enchantment and Sorrow*, Gabrielle tells of one of these
tours she joined, in 1934 or 1935, together with Fernand Tellier, Gilles
Guyot, Marc Meunier, and several others.[74] Her own turn was as a stand-
up comic, which demanded verve, humour, a sense of narrative effect,
and prodigious memory.

As fun and relaxed as it was, this kind of theatre – popular, spontaneous theatre, close to burlesque and the country fair show – was no
more than a summer diversion for Gabrielle. It amused her and enabled
her to continue to act when the artistic life of St-Boniface was at a stand-
still, but it was not really what she expected of the theatrical experience
which in her mind should be more serious, more refined, an experience
that took her away from ordinary life and language and lifted her into a
world of beauty and fulfilment, to which only true art can give access.
This "noble" conception of theatre was precisely the inspiration behind
the Cercle Molière troupe, which she joined as soon as she had returned
to St-Boniface from Cardinal and was on staff at the Institut Provencher,
late in 1930 or early in 1931.

The Cercle Molière had been founded in 1925 by Louis-Philippe Gagnon, bookseller, Raymond Bernier, civil servant, and André Castelain de la Lande, a French teacher of Belgian origin who was its artistic director until 1928. It was directed subsequently by Arthur Boutal, a journalist and printer by trade, and his wife, Pauline, née LeGoff, an artist and fashion designer. In the 1930s, when Gabrielle Roy was a member, they built it into a well-organized, dynamic, first-rate troupe. The Cercle was beloved by Franco-Manitobans and known across Canada.[75] It was an amateur troupe but the stagecraft it practised was highly polished and disciplined. The plays presented were not always masterpieces; beside *L'Arlésienne* by Alphonse Daudet, which met with great success in 1928, there were many boulevard comedies like *Chut! voilà la bonne* by Albert Acremant (1926), *Popaul et Virginie* by Alfred Machard (1929), and *Le Train fantôme* by H. D. Erlanger (1932). These plays by the authors most highly regarded by Parisian audiences were considered the last word in chic French taste, however. And the productions were impeccable, for Arthur Boutal left nothing to chance, insisting on methodical choice of actors, long rehearsal time, care over visual elements such as make-up and scenery, and so on. He demanded perfect diction and physical bearing from his actors and instilled in them scrupulous respect for the text and stage direction. In short, as observed by Armand LaFlèche who was at the heart of Franco-Manitoban theatrical life in those years, this was a far cry from the improvisation and nonchalance of the itinerant troupes. The Cercle Molière, he wrote, offered "a brand of theatre and techniques that were more modern, with a better understanding of French theatrical customs, a scenic ambiance, a colour, a stylization barely known before, and finally a diction and wit that was more French than Canadian, it is true, but stimulating and indispensable."[76] In its own way the Cercle played a role in the theatre movement of the period that was analogous to that which would soon be played in Quebec by other amateur troupes like the Compagnons de Saint-Laurent (founded in 1937) or the Paraboliers du roi (1939), without sharing the religious orientation that marked these two. It gave a generation of young artists an opportunity to study a more polished brand of dramatic art and benefit from training at a semi-professional level.

Taking part in the activities of the Cercle demanded a great deal of time. Rehearsals in preparation for the annual production were held three times a week in various parts of the city (in an abandoned warehouse, the basement of the cathedral, or even, as in 1935–1936, in

Gabrielle's classroom at the Institut Provencher). They began in autumn and continued until the end of winter when the single performance (sometimes two) of the chosen play would take place, usually in a theatre in Winnipeg. In addition, members were expected to attend monthly meetings to discuss the Cercle's affairs and take turns presenting their own solo numbers. And this was without counting less formal events – evening gatherings, receptions, group suppers. Belonging to the Cercle Molière meant spending most of one's leisure time in the wonderful world of the stage and literature where "there was an air of excitement about everything,"[77] as Gabrielle would say later.

And so the young woman took her membership in the group very seriously. Although at first she had no role in the annual play she was a vigorous presence at meetings. As early as January 1931 she presented two recitations to the assembled members.[78] The following May she was elected "organizer" for the 1932–1933 season. In this post she had responsibility under the bylaws of the Cercle for "the preparation of a program of literary, dramatic, or musical events to be given at all monthly meetings of members," a duty she fulfilled very well indeed, judging by the minutes preserved in the archives of La Société historique de Saint-Boniface.[79] Finally, her name is mentioned in connection with the meeting of 20 October 1934, when she presented the recreational portion consisting of two comic numbers; the second of these, which she played in company with Fabiola Gosselin and the sisters Renée and Thérèse Deniset, was a parody of the convent-girl tableaus in which she herself had played parts when she was a pupil of the nuns at the Académie Saint-Joseph. The audience split their sides laughing.

Gabrielle had taken the decisive step. She had taken the stage. Better still, she had tasted success. Not personal success, but success for the whole troupe, which would soon know its first real triumph with a play in which Gabrielle was making her début: *Blanchette* by Eugène Brieux. This Breton melodrama in three acts tells the eternal story of the little peasant girl whose parents have been at pains to educate her and who, beguiled by the attractions of the city, begins to build castles in the sky and leaves her family for Paris, where she finds nothing but disappointment and disillusion. Chastened, she comes home, begs her father's pardon, and marries the neighbour's son.

This play was the Cercle Molière's choice for 1933–1934. Arthur Boutal was the director and his wife, Pauline, was the set designer. The cast

featured Suzanne Hubicki (née LeGoff, sister of Pauline Boutal) in the
title role, with Arthur Boutal and Élisa Houde playing the father and
mother of Blanchette. The other roles are episodic. Gabrielle played Lucie
Galoux, an aristocratic girl. The performance took place on Thursday,
30 November 1933, at the Dominion Theatre, to enthusiastic acclaim as
always, with "a special mention for Mlle Gabrielle Roy, [who was] very
much at ease, very appealing."[80]

If the Cercle Molière had decided, contrary to usual practice, to
perform its play in the autumn rather than spring, it was because it
intended to take part in the brand-new Dominion Drama Festival,
which had just been created in Ottawa under the distinguished patronage of Lord Bessborough, the governor general of Canada. Following
this première performance, rehearsals therefore continued all winter in
preparation for the regional selection, which was held in Winnipeg in
March 1934. The troupe played Act 2 of *Blanchette* and placed second
behind an English-speaking troupe from Selkirk.[81] Since the national
contest was bilingual however, this second place qualified the Cercle
Molière for the national finals, which were to take place in the federal
capital toward the end of April.

The actors were beside themselves with joy. But money had to be
raised for the journey to Ottawa. A fund-raising campaign was launched.
Gabrielle, like the other members of the troupe, summoned up her
energy. She attended a card party organized by English-speaking ladies of
Winnipeg at the Corona Hotel and played her role as Lucie Galoux in a
special performance of *Blanchette* at the Institut Provencher.[82] At last the
great day arrived. Gabrielle obtained a week's leave from the school
commission[83] and the whole troupe boarded the train for Ottawa.

Several days later the news was blazoned across the front page of
La Liberté: "The Cercle Molière wins the trophy for French plays!" The
actors from St-Boniface had won the francophone section of the contest
hands down, ahead of three troupes from the country's East, La Rampe
(Ottawa), the Cercle dramatique des étudiants de Laval (Quebec City),
and the French section of the Montreal Repertory Theatre. The drama
critic for *La Presse* of Montreal, Jean Béraud, may not have been overly
impressed by the Manitoba troupe's performance, except for Arthur
Boutal's acting which he found excellent, but St-Boniface was ecstatic.
While the city's social set gave one reception after another in honour of
the prizewinners, the editorialist of *La Liberté*, Donatien Frémont, who

generally paid little attention to such frivolous things, pulled out all the stops with a vibrant article to hail "the Ottawa triumph," whose glory would redound to "the whole French element of Manitoba."[84]

While the *Blanchette* triumph reflected on Gabrielle, her personal part in it was not large. Still, the success spurred her enthusiasm and encouraged her to work all the harder to earn herself a place in the troupe. The following year the Cercle mounted a play by Émile Augier and Jules Sandeau, *Le Gendre de M. Poirier*, directed by Denys Goulet. Gabrielle was given a bigger role this time, that of Antoinette, Marquise de Presles, in which Louis-Philippe Gagnon, one of the founders of the Cercle Molière and now a drama critic, judged her "pleasing, spontaneous, much more the marquise than the daughter of Monsieur Poirier, very natural in her movements (which were as varied as one could wish) and in the dialogue." Mlle Roy, he added, had achieved "a very fine interpretation and we have not seen this confidence and flexibility before in her."[85] But the play was a damp squib in the national drama festival – it did not even get beyond the regional selection, which took place at the Dominion Theatre on 2 February 1935.

Truth to tell, this play had been too hastily prepared and insufficiently rehearsed. The troupe entered the contest again the following year (1936) with another Breton play, *Les Soeurs Guédonec* by Jean-Jacques Bernard, "a dramatic comedy in which two peasant women – tightfisted spinsters – meet up with some mischievous orphans and discover a deep maternal love."[86] The director was Arthur Boutal. Gabrielle this time played the title role of one of the Guédonec sisters, Maryvonne; the other, Marie-Jeanne, was played by Élisa Houde.[87] And the miracle happened as it had two years earlier, only for Gabrielle the excitement now was even greater than the first time.

To begin with, the play took first prize in Winnipeg, where it was presented on 22 February 1936. The local reviewers waxed rhapsodic: "Mme Houde and M[lle] Roy, in the leading roles," wrote Denys Goulet, "played with a naturalness and restraint that confirm their talents as intelligent, consistently sensitive, and extremely diligent actresses."[88] The ritual began again: feverish activity as the big day approached, fund-raising, an additional performance at Provencher, and the troupe's departure for Ottawa,[89] where the actors were billeted with supporters.

The gala evening was held on Saturday, 25 April 1936. All of political and diplomatic Ottawa was there, including Prime Minister Mackenzie King, who stepped on the hem of the evening dress of the little green-eyed actress all agog to be there, and courteously begged her to excuse him. That evening Gabrielle tasted all the magic of "the governor's ball" that Mélina had missed years before.

In French, besides Act III of *Les Soeurs Guédonec*, there were three plays in competition: *Topaze* by Marcel Pagnol, Act I of which was being presented by the Conservatoire national de musique de Québec, *Il était une bergère* by André Rivoire, played by the Théâtre-École de Montréal, and *L'Indienne* by Laurette Larocque-Auger, a Canadian creation rendered by the students of the École de musique et de déclamation de l'Université d'Ottawa. This last author's path (or that of her pseudonyms Claire Richard and Jean Desprez) would cross Gabrielle's many times over in the years to come. On this occasion it was Gabrielle who won the day: once again the prize for the best French play went to the troupe from St-Boniface, to the great displeasure of some of the Québécois, who considered that Arthur Boutal, a "Parisian," should not have the right to direct plays entered in the contest.[90] To the Cercle Molière also went the prize for the best actress in French, awarded not to Gabrielle Roy nor to Élisa Houde but to Pauline Boutal for her performance in the role of Madame LeCahu.

For Gabrielle, who had just turned twenty-seven, this victory was unquestionably the high point of her career as an actress. It not only brought her the sense of accomplishment she had been dreaming of for some years and toward which she had been working tirelessly but it also helped confirm her conviction that the stage was a life that suited her, that her talent was real, and that she might well hope to reach the high goal she yearned for by this route.

And yet she was not the troupe's most gifted actress, and certainly not "the star of the Cercle Molière," as she was depicted a decade later by a Parisian columnist.[91] Her beauty attracted attention undoubtedly and made her an appealing ingénue; she was also hard-working and enthusiastic. But she did not have that stage presence, or verisimilitude, or above all the impeccable diction that distinguished other actresses of the group such as Pauline Boutal, Suzanne LeGoff, or Élisa Houde, all of them older than she and more experienced. This said, Gabrielle had her youth and great confidence in her own talent to her benefit. She knew that with persistence and the proper training she could overcome her limitations and become a very good actress.

She also had an advantage over her comrades of Le Cercle Molière in being the only one active in English theatre as well. In the early 1930s, she had taken courses in English diction at the Jean Campbell School of Speech and Dramatic Arts in Winnipeg; her name figured on the program of a recital given on 11 March 1932 at the Winnipeg Welsh Church by the students of Mrs. Campbell, during which she, the only francophone among some twenty young performers, accompanied at the piano by "Digby Tomlinson, Blind Pianist," presented a story titled "Angels."[92] Several months later, at a soirée of the Fédération des femmes canadiennes-françaises, one of her two recitations was in English, titled "Impersonation."[93]

Subsequently she increased her involvement in English theatre. In 1935, she belonged to the amateur troupe the Winnipeg Little Theatre, which was more or less the English equivalent of the Cercle Molière. Founded in 1921 on the model of the Hart House Theatre in Toronto, which gave rise across Canada to what was known as the "Little Theatre Movement," this company enjoyed the active protection of Lady Margaret Tupper, niece of the lieutenant-governor of Manitoba and herself an actress. Directed by John Craig, who was as impelling a leader as Arthur Boutal with the St-Boniface troupe, the group played the best classic and modern English repertoire, from Shakespeare to George Bernard Shaw, from Oscar Wilde to Coward and Galsworthy, as well as American plays (O'Neill) and translations of foreign works (Rostand, Maeterlinck, Ibsen, Pirandello).[94]

Gabrielle had supporting roles in two productions, in April 1935 and in January 1937. In the first she played the part of Elizabeth Rimplegar in *Three-Cornered Moon* by Gertrude Tonkonogy, a New York comedy in three acts already popularized by the movie of the same name. On this occasion Arthur Boutal, at a meeting of the Cercle Molière, "encouraged the members to go and hear Mlle Gabrielle Roy [. . .] who has made her début with 'The Little Theatre' at the Dominion."[95] By 1937 it seems that Gabrielle was no longer a member of the Cercle Molière, as if, after the success of *Les Soeurs Guédonec*, she had decided to concentrate exclusively on her career in English.[96] On January 29 and 30 of that year she appeared in another comedy in three acts, *The Man with a Load of Mischief* by Ashley Dukes, which was performed at the Winnipeg Orpheum Theatre.[97] In both cases her performances received warm praise from the critics.[98]

Gabrielle for her part felt that things were going very nicely for her, since her spell at the Little Theatre, like her experience at the Cercle Molière, was playing a crucial role in the new direction she was about to give her life. "I had some success as a small town actress," she wrote later to a friend, "and I fancied myself gifted with great histrionic possibilities."[99] This had a direct bearing on the major decision with which these years culminated for her: to leave teaching and try her luck at a career on the stage.

In a text she wrote near the end of her life, Gabrielle recalls her experience as a member of "that little group of impassioned amateurs," the Cercle Molière, with much gratitude. The theatre gave the opportunity, she says, "to step outside our own limits and enter a magic world where we're allowed to change our lives and destinies."[100]

To step outside her own limits, to change her life and destiny. This indeed was the young teacher's biggest preoccupation during these years and no doubt the principal reason for her attachment to the theatrical world. For the theatre made it possible for her to step outside her own limits and escape her own life not only in the play of dramatic illusion but also in a real and immediate way, enabling her to live in a rich and stimulating world where she felt fulfilled in her desire for culture, elegance, and refinement, and where she had the opportunity to develop her talents and prepare for the future awaiting her. With all this, why would she not love the theatre? Why would she not wish for the theatre, the best thing in her life, to become her whole life?

A Small-Town Girl's Emancipation

Rather like Blanchette in the play by Brieux, the Gabrielle of this period could never be content with what was brought to (and imposed on) her by being a schoolteacher and belonging to a modest suburban Winnipeg family that had once enjoyed a certain notability but since Léon's death had lost standing and quickly dropped into run-of-the-mill obscurity. Since this turn of fortune the young woman had had one single desire, one strategy: to escape the confines of her condition and thereafter live the life of freedom and fulfilment she felt she was destined for.

Socially, this meant raising herself above the class she was born into and carving a place for herself in the city's better social circles. St-Boniface was a minuscule, marginal, and rather inward-looking society but like any other it had its elite groups, in particular a small, secular elite composed of educated people, wealthy or less so, who by their modes of life and thought held themselves to be not only more refined and elegant but more "modern," more "open," more "daring" than ordinary folk. These people formed what some called the "intellectual class" of St-Boniface, the small and distinguished ranks of artists, readers of books, lovers of culture, good taste, and beauty. They were travellers or had travelled, knew the world, followed the fashions of the moment, prided themselves on being avant-garde, and felt entirely in tune with their time. They did not necessarily regard ordinary people with contempt; they simply knew that they were better. Toward the lower orders they either bent a solicitous eye, educated them, and strove to raise them to their own level, or maintained a lofty disinterest and cared not a whit what people thought. They were different, they were liberated, and they were happy.

At this time the Cercle Molière was central to the life of this elite, who identified with it, supported its activities, and were the first to take credit for its successes. Arthur and Pauline Boutal enjoyed immense prestige, and for Gabrielle her association with them was not only a way of perfecting her dramatic skills but also, and more importantly, a means of social and personal advancement. The Boutals' lifestyle, their cultivation, their sensitive and open minds, the purity of their language, everything about them answered her need for distinction and beauty. From time to time, as she would recount later, she would have occasion to attend "one of those exquisite light suppers that one only expected to have at 'The Peninsula.'"

> This was the name I had given to the curious little property the Boutals owned, which was bordered on three sides by the winding Seine River and hidden from view besides by tangled bushes and overgrown weeds, as if in the country. This couple brought to their orbit unerring good taste, a cultivated mode of living, and ardour in their work . . . [101]

Admired qualities all in sharp contrast with the usual smalltime mediocrity and with Gabrielle's ordinary existence both at Provencher and at home on Deschambault Street. In their presence she could forget the "[incurable] misfortune" of being "one of those people destined to be treated as inferiors."[102]

Arthur and Pauline Boutal were French. He was born at Seyches in the *département* of Lot-et-Garonne in southwestern France and grew up at Angoulême; she was a native of Brittany. In this also they were typical of the small St-Boniface circle they moved in, for its cosmopolitanism was one of its most striking features. Recent immigrants were especially numerous and active in this "intellectual class," in which one sought less to be identified as French, Belgian, Ukrainian, or Italian than to maintain or re-create forms of European-style sociability hinging on art, culture, and the sharing of a certain graceful and civilized behaviour. Within the group, this attitude created a climate of openness, tolerance, even an "intercultural" kind of solidarity which may not have been perfect but was in contrast to the homogeneity of the French-Canadian society of St-Boniface at this time and the degree of mistrust levelled by its members at "foreigners."

The dominant figures in this group were people born and raised in France like the Boutals, or in Belgium, or their offspring. These immigrants were fairly numerous in St-Boniface, Cardinal, and Notre-Dame-de-Lourdes. They were – and felt – different to Franco-Manitobans of Quebec ancestry, from whom they were distinguished not only by their accent but also by their general educational level, lifestyle, and interest in things artistic.[103] It was no wonder that so many members of the Cercle Molière were French: Élisa Houde, née Charlet,[104] Henri Pinvidic, Marius Maire, Gilles Guyot, the Sourisseau children, Jean de la Vignette, Alain LeGoff, brother of Pauline Boutal, and their sisters Christiane and Suzanne. The same held in a number of other cultural organizations in the city: Joseph Vermander, of Belgian origin, was leader of the Fanfare La Vérendrye, the brass band; Donatien Frémont, editor-in-chief of *La Liberté*, was a Breton who had come from Saskatchewan in 1923; as for Marius Benoist, who reigned over the musical life of the city as both orchestra and choir conductor, he himself was not French but his wife's family were, as well as a number of his musicians.

Gabrielle took to this milieu like a fish to water. In Cardinal many of the French people she used to visit had been former middle-class city dwellers or even descendants of aristocrats, but became farmers when they came to Canada. Here in town, the French people she was fortunate enough to associate with were civilized, cultivated; their manners, their sensitivity, their patterns of life and thought retained the imprint of the European education they had received and continued to value. She who belonged to a community so provincial and rough-hewn could have asked for nothing better than to share their penchant for the theatre, literature, and social events.

It is not surprising therefore that her best friends were French. One of these was Léonie Guyot of course, and another was Renée Deniset, a young woman to whom she felt very close at this time and who was the daughter of one of the most prominent St-Boniface families. The father, François Deniset, had come from Besançon with a sizeable fortune in real estate, had married a French Canadian, the daughter of a senator and sister of a member of Parliament. They lived on Provencher Avenue in a sumptuous house frequented by streams of visitors, with young men circling close about their three daughters. The eldest, Thérèse, was then embarking on a singing career that was soon to take her to Europe; in April 1935 she had already scored a resounding success in Winnipeg in the title role of Gounod's *Mireille*, produced and directed by Marius Benoist at the Dominion Theatre. (Gabrielle and Renée had participated as make-up artists under Pauline Boutal's direction.[105]) Jacqueline, the youngest daughter, also possessed a lovely voice and was preparing to leave for Montreal, where she was to marry Jean Benoist, the brother of Marius. Renée, less musically gifted than her sisters, was a teacher at the Institut Provencher.[106]

But the friendship between Renée and Gabrielle had little to do with the occupation they shared. They would see each other at meetings of the Cercle Molière, of which Renée too was a member, and whenever else there was an opportunity to be together and enjoy each other's company. There were plenty of opportunities. In winter, it was cross-country skiing or skating parties. In summer, there was tennis, bicycling, or camping, as in the summer of 1935 when *La Liberté* announced, "Mlles Renée Deniset and Gabrielle Roy are spending the week at les Chutes des Sept Soeurs."[107] But what they enjoyed most were the parties. There was a dinner at the Hôtel Saint-Charles during the Christmas vacation 1935 for instance, given by Jeanne Galliot, daughter of a French physician from Lourdes then visiting St-Boniface.[108] They went together to luncheons, engagement parties, teas, and other festivities, each time mingling with convivial, distinguished St-Boniface society.

But the best parties were the ones they threw themselves. Renée was an accomplished hostess and made sure that readers of *La Liberté* knew it. In December 1934 for example they were apprised that she had given "an impromptu soirée in honour of Mme Pierre de Saint-Denis," and the following August that she had graciously invited a small group of friends to her home, including the flower of St-Boniface youth.[109] Gabrielle was often involved. She helped Renée write the invitations and prepare the evening's program when there was to be music and dancing. On the day of the party, while Renée was getting her parents' house ready, Gabrielle would bring dishes prepared by her mother and Clémence. Together, they would greet the guests as they alighted from their cars, and as the evening progressed would liven it in manners worthy of the best of hostesses. Among the young women in long dresses escorted by beaus in white tie and tails, Gabrielle was a striking figure. Not only was she among the most attractive, with her impeccably tasteful dress complimenting the coppery brown of her hair, discreet make-up enhancing her grey-green eyes, and face lit up by a smile that was somehow engaging and distant both at once, but she was also the most spritely and vivacious of all the girls present. As she moved from group to group, she would be mischievous one minute and serious the next; she was always ready to laugh, sing, or discuss, and never tired of dancing. The men adored her, the women thought her amusing and nice – except the ones whose beaus she stole. Renée's sister Thérèse was one of these, and held it against Gabrielle for many years.

Attending these parties was another close friend of Gabrielle's who, while not European French, also belonged to a prominent St-Boniface family. Her name was Paula Sumner. She was the granddaughter of Louis-Arthur Prudhomme, former member of Parliament, former judge, former president of the Association d'éducation, historian, member of the Royal Society of Canada – a man of considerable stature. Paula, five years younger than Gabrielle, wore her caste status like a mantle. Since she was safe from want she had no gainful occupation and led a life that social engagements, travel, and philanthropic and cultural activities sufficed to fill. Tall and beautiful, she was considered a "blue blood," a bit eccentric, even snooty, in a different class, no doubt because of her flawless speech, her always exquisite clothes and grooming, and, of course, the family she belonged to.

Paula attended activities of the Cercle Molière and, it seems, it was there that she and Gabrielle became friends. The relationship was so close that of all the friends from this period, Paula was one of the few that Gabrielle kept in contact with long after she left St-Boniface. In 1955, she was still saying, "[Paula's] friendship is one of the most precious things I have ever had in my life."[110]

What the basis of this friendship was is difficult to tell in the absence of first-hand information from persons close to Paula, and since correspondence between the two women was not kept. We can only imagine that this intelligent, cultivated young woman of St-Boniface high society, who had no ties and to whom life seemed to have given everything, was for Gabrielle both a model and a kind of alter ego. No doubt they were drawn together by the same tastes, attitudes, and ways of seeing things; no doubt they shared the same inability to identify with the community around them and dreamed of the same betterment, the same marvels, the same "elsewhere" in which they imagined real life to exist.

For Paula, change came soon. In the summer of 1937, for the first time ever, France sent a consul to Winnipeg.[111] His name was Henri Bougearel. Throughout St-Boniface, and particularly the little circle that Gabrielle and her friends moved in, the event stirred great excitement; the diplomat was not only the embodiment of France, of distinction itself in other words, but was reputed to be himself a highly cultivated man. He had been the cultural attaché at the consulate in Montreal for four years. But there was more: he was as handsome as a god, forty years old, and a bachelor. Paula's great conquest was precisely this Monsieur Henri Bougearel, whom she married a few years later. Becoming a consul's wife, perchance someday an ambassador's, entering the prestigious world of diplomacy, and the French one at that, what more spectacular achievement could a young woman dream of?

Paula's wedding took place in Montreal in 1943, at almost the same time as Renée Deniset's to an Irishman in Ottawa, where Renée had gone to work during the war. But all the while they were still in St-Boniface, the three friends – for Renée was also close to Paula – simply lived their young lives and thought about their future. Gabrielle in any event thought about hers constantly and with even more determination than during her adolescence. She may have been well into her twenties and well ensconced in her occupation, but she was certainly not going to come into line, settle down, give up wanting to become what she had always wanted to be, although she had no idea what that was except that this "me that didn't yet exist"[112] was going to be completely different and infinitely preferable to her present self.

Which is to say that the future for her did not hinge on marriage. Marrying would mean not only tying herself to a man and a family – tying herself down and knuckling under – but also giving up her job at the Institut Provencher and losing all independence and all chance of realizing her ambitions. And so, like the heroine of one of her very early stories, "[she aspired] to celibacy with the same tenacity as others to marriage."[113]

Not that she was lacking suitors, far from it. Because she was physically attractive, as contemporary photographs show, and at the same time brilliant, witty, and adventurous, men jostled to win her favour. None succeeded in holding her very long, however. Those with the least chance were the young French Canadians, whom she considered rather uncouth and narrow in outlook. The young men who did become in the least close to her were all, like her girlfriends, involved in the theatre or other arts.

This was the case with Bohdan Hubicki, for example, whose brother Taras, Suzanne LeGoff's husband and hence Pauline Boutal's brother-in-law, was a teacher of music who enjoyed great respect in the small St-Boniface milieu. Ukrainian in origin, Bohdan was a blond young man of delicate physique who was possessed by a single passion – the violin – which he played with consummate skill at soirées of the Cercle Molière among other occasions. He and Gabrielle, Léonie Guyot recalls, "had something in common. Both having artistic temperaments, they had the same tastes"[114] and the same dreams. But Bohdan was even more impatient than Gabrielle; though penniless he left shortly for England, where he intended to continue his musical education and pursue a career.

Apart from Bohdan there was Clelio Ritagliati, the son of Italian immigrants, also a violinist, who also left for England in 1936. But neither Bohdan nor Clelio had been a steady boyfriend for Gabrielle it seems, though both would no doubt have eagerly accepted the role. To her they were simply male friends who were a little closer than the rest, whose sensitivity, preoccupations, and ambitions were in harmony with hers. And besides, they were well-mannered, cultivated young gentlemen who were charmed by her, believed in her talent, and encouraged her to give her all to it.

With other beaus however she did not necessarily feel the same affinities. For a time she was seeing one whose surname was Brooke, of Winnipeg, dashingly handsome (the "matinée idol" type according to Léonie) but rather pretentious. The flirtation was over after a couple of dates.[115] Her relationship with Guy Chauvière, which began in 1935, lasted somewhat longer. Guy was French. He was a secondary school teacher, a tall young man of genteel bearing, a year older than Gabrielle, and his mother, Éva Chauvière, was very active with the Cercle Molière. He was slightly lame in the right leg, which inclined him to be a little shy, but he was cultivated, spoke elegantly and flawlessly, and, having inherited his parents' beautiful manners, treated Gabrielle with impeccable courtesy. He not only escorted her to social events but they often talked on the phone, went to the theatre or the movies together, or simply spent the evening at Guy's parents', where Gabrielle was enchanted with the French distinction and good taste reigning there.

But Guy had no illusions. He could see that Gabrielle would never be his. She was too demanding, too single-minded in her desire for success, and too headstrong for him to have a chance of marrying her. "She wanted everything," he recalled many years later. "I don't know in what way, but she wasn't happy. You could feel it. My mother knew it. Everyone knew it. She wasn't happy."[116]

Not happy, meaning continually dissatisfied, restless, haunted by her fierce desire for a different life, a different world. This was why her loves never lasted very long, if indeed these relationships in which her heart never seems to have been committed can be called "loves." There is no question that she enjoyed beguiling, and allowed many young men to keep company with her, but she tied herself to none of them in any serious way whatever and made no promises whatever. Nor does it seem that she had any as a lover. As to that, she behaved like any well-brought-up young woman of her era: she was controlled, modest, and refrained from any sexual relationship before marriage. This chastity probably did not take great resolve on her part, being both the price and the guarantee of her present freedom and future flowering.

Her flightiness was bound to irritate Adèle and Anna, who, out of spite perhaps, saw in it another proof of their sister's selfishness. "Pretty and in the prime of her youth," Adèle writes in one of her charges against Gabrielle, "she was pleasing to young men of her age. Caressing and wheedling as soon as a friend was keeping company with her, she would smile and simper, brushing gently against him. Many was the poor and serious friend who, after one or two coaxings from the fair maiden, wisely drifted away, judging that he did not have the means to satisfy the demanding tastes of a gold-digger."[117]

In point of fact, if some of Gabrielle's swains took fright over her ambition and "demanding tastes," most of the time it was she who lost interest and stopped going out with them after a few weeks or months. And so, showered with masculine admiration, she nevertheless remained inaccessible, virgin, and free of any attachment. "I seemed to inspire [love] then as naturally as I breathed," she would write later, "[but] I wasn't yet letting myself be caught."[118]

Adèle's ill-temper over her younger sister's behaviour is understandable. It reflects the opinion shared by most of Gabrielle's family members who were watching her slip away from them, turn increasingly away from their world, their values, their customs, their moral precepts, and particularly from their conception of what a young woman of her age and condition should be.

To Adèle, the people Cad associated with, particularly the Boutals, had less than a desirable influence on her (Cad was Gabrielle's nickname, short for *cadette*, meaning "youngest"). "These emigrants," she writes, "showed a certain pity for the French Canadians who were producing many children without concerning themselves over their education. On contact with these 'intellectuals' who made so much of their culture, Gabrielle felt a certain embarrassment to think of her parents"[119] and began to regret if not despise the milieu she had been born into.

And it is true that much in the life that Gabrielle led during these years estranged her from her family and community. She not only spent a good part of her life in English, writing in English and performing in English drama, she spent a great deal of time in Winnipeg, seeking the company of immigrants and steering clear of the Deschambault Street neighbourhood. She had only French or "foreign" boyfriends, rejected the idea of marriage, and thought only of her own pleasure. As for her girlfriends, she chose them from the ranks of high society and with them indulged in activities normally restricted to the rich – sports, camping, theatre, and other frivolities that ordinary folk cared nothing for, especially in this period of depression and troubles of all kinds.

But what Adèle did not know was that Gabrielle's emancipation – or rebellion – ran much deeper than its non-conformist manifestations showed. It can be said in fact that during this period the young woman was steadily moving away from the world she had come from, a world that to her seemed small, backward, stifling. She ceased to recognize her place in it, no longer felt at home in it, and all she was really doing now was seeking to detach herself from it in order to assert her own individuality.

This can be seen for example in the perfunctory enthusiasm she showed over national and religious solidarity. As a teacher, as a winner of the Association d'éducation's prizes, in principle she ought to have given an example and devoted herself generously to "the cause." But all this left her cold. She did attend the annual conventions of the Association d'éducation and the meetings of the Fédération des institutrices catholiques – not to do so might have attracted serious professional vexations – but her participation remained purely passive and the fiery speeches over the urgency for "Manitobans of the French race," as Lionel Groulx proclaimed them at the time, to "close ranks around their church spires," to "cling to the soil"[120] and defy all the threats of the modern world, these not only ceased to move her, they soon seemed to her to be the very expression of the narrowness of mind that she longed to flee.

For the time being, she refrained from parading her dissidence for she valued her reputation, meaning her job. But in private, with her friends of the Cercle Molière or with Renée and Paula, she made light-hearted fun of the patriotic preachifying and fear of foreigners. And later when she was free to speak she would willingly return to this atmosphere of hatred and intolerance in which she claimed to have been brought up. We were taught, she confided to a correspondent in 1946, "that although English and protestant people might go to heaven by some indirect route, it wasn't right for us to mix with them."[121] "Our life was an inward-looking one," writes the narrator of *Enchantment and Sorrow* in a similar vein, "which led almost inescapably to a kind of withering. [. . .] Sometimes you'd have thought we were living in some walled enclosure during the wars of religion, Albi withstanding the Saracens, or some other luckless medieval city under siege behind a bulwark of prohibitions, portcullises, and interdicts."[122]

As other young artists and intellectuals were doing in the same period in Quebec, with the ground-breaking magazine *La Relève* then flourishing, she dissociated herself from the old, conservative, more-or-less xenophobic nationalism that was as dominant at the time in the social, religious, and scholastic institutions of Manitoba as in those of Quebec, if not more so. She did it out of conviction, because to her this xenophobia seemed contrary to the ideal of fraternity and understanding that was forming in her through contact with her pupils and her anglophone, Ukrainian, and French friends, an ideal that was to find expression in her future works. But she did it also out of her own personal need for freedom in opposition to the control claimed over her, as over all individuals especially the women, by the hypersensitive little society to which she belonged.

This indifference, even disdain, that the "survival" cause inspired in her also increasingly characterized her attitude toward religion. She was prevented of course by the context, appearances, and her dependence on the St-Boniface school authorities from openly showing herself to be agnostic or a non-practising Catholic; she had to teach religion to the Catholic children in her class every day from 3:30 to 4 P.M., on a volunteer basis, as did all her colleagues at the Institut Provencher, and this seemed to her in Léonie Guyot's recollection to be "inane, not to say besotting."[123] Without discussing it with anyone, she abandoned the faith of her childhood fairly early, "disgusted," as she confided before long to Adèle, "by the conception that most people, very often Church people, have of God." No one, she added, had "succeeded in giving me an image of God that rose above the mediocre"; all that had been inculcated in her, she continued, was "terror of God, or if you like, lack of faith in the certainty that God loves me for myself."[124] How could she not feel in "revolt," as she says in *Enchantment and Sorrow*, "against a dogmatic attitude that saw evil in everything, laid claim to sole possession of the truth, and, if it could, would have denied us any communication whatever with a generous human disparity."[125] Closer to her heart seemed the ideas of Jean-Jacques Rousseau whom she read in private, discovering that she shared his spirit of tolerance and mysticism centred on oneness with nature and love for one's fellow men – readings that gave her a reputation even among her friends as a "free-thinker."

From an ideological point of view, Gabrielle therefore nourished ideas that were fairly advanced for her era and milieu, without always daring to acknowledge them publicly. According to one chronicler, one of her friends was Grace Woodsworth, daughter of the founder of the new Co-operative Commonwealth Federation party (CCF), whose socialist leanings she shared for the most part.[126] Although unconfirmed, this does not appear at all impossible, considering the overall climate of those years and the young Gabrielle's nature, inclined toward bold, "modern" conceptions. The leftist ideas that engendered suspicion in the small, traditionalist world of her origin were, in Winnipeg and the circles she now moved in, ideas that were very widely held in this era of the Great Depression and the New Deal. And Gabrielle's own nephew, Paul Painchaud, openly declared himself a communist, which did nothing to improve the bad-apple reputation he shared with his two brothers.

But while politics and social questions mattered to the Gabrielle Roy of this period, they do not seem to have been really major preoccupations. What mattered most to her, what guided her behaviour, her thoughts, her desires, was closer to the bone: her personal liberation and her own salvation.

A Depression-Era Family

Before he died in February 1929, Léon Roy had not made a will, since he had practically nothing left to his name except an insurance policy for $825, which Mélina collected. The house – which he had placed in his wife's name several years earlier – remained encumbered with a mortgage of $1,200. The insurance money together with a gift of some $500 from Adèle served to pay off this mortgage, so that the widowed Mélina found herself both a property owner and penniless,[127] with Clémence unable to earn her own living and dependent on her.

At first she managed to get by. The house now being too big, she had her son-in-law Albert Painchaud turn the upper floor into a separate apartment that she could rent. In fact the idea had come mostly from Anna and Albert, who moved into the new apartment themselves. They lived there until 1934, sometimes snaffling part of the ground floor as well when their sons were home. Subsequently, according to *Henderson's Guide*, the tenants were named Defoort, Gillespie, and DeCrane, unless these were simply boarders taken in by Mélina to bring in some monthly cash. Mélina also continued to take in washing and sewing, and Rodolphe and Adèle sent her a little money from time to time. Finally there was Gabrielle, who, since she had been teaching at Provencher, paid $25 of the $100 she earned each month for her bed and board.

But neither Mélina nor Clémence really saw much of the money Gabrielle turned over or benefited personally from it, for Gabrielle was a demanding boarder. In exchange for her money the house had to be kept worthy of the society with whom she kept company. It was Mélina who paid for the telephone subscription, restored the furniture, and kept the house clean and attractive so that Gabrielle might properly receive her guests and suitors. In December 1933 for example, one read in *La Liberté*:

> M. and Mme Arthur Boutal gave a charming reception on Saturday evening at the home of Mlle Gabrielle Roy, 375 Deschambault Street, in honour of the artists who took part in the performance of "Blanchette." A succulent supper was served.[128]

One can easily imagine the roles assigned to Mélina and Clémence in the course of this "charming reception" and "succulent supper," they who had never attended a single performance of the Cercle Molière and must have felt thoroughly intimidated by Gabrielle's distinguished friends.

Gabrielle was in truth not exactly the soul of generosity. She scrupulously paid her share, but she must not be asked to do more. During the summer months, for example, since she was earning nothing she gave nothing, so that Mélina was obliged to abandon the house until autumn and go to work at Excide's farm with Clémence. The fact is that Gabrielle spent a lot of money. Besides her dresses, a fur coat, her sporting equipment, and all her activities and amusements, she treated herself to vacations, sometimes by a lake, as in 1935 with Renée Deniset, sometimes in Quebec, where she went at least twice in the course of these years.

The first of these trips took place in the summer of 1932.[129] She left about mid-July and drove with cousins across the roughly fifteen hundred miles to the region of her mother's birth, where at last she discovered the landscapes her mother had been telling her about since her childhood. From this first contact with Quebec and the Québécois she would say in *Enchantment and Sorrow* that she was left disappointed and rather embittered;[130] she returned after two months, announcing to *La Liberté* that when in Montreal she had seized the opportunity "to take elocution lessons."[131] As for the second trip, it took place two years later in the spring of 1934, when, after the triumph of *Blanchette* at the drama festival in Ottawa, "Mlle Gabrielle Roy and M. Henri Pinvidic [were] prolonging their sojourns in the East in order to visit relatives and friends."[132]

Gabrielle, in short, had too many needs to go "throwing her money down a bottomless pit."[133] And besides, once she had made up her mind to leave Manitoba she had to save a small portion of her salary each month in preparation for that event. All of which made her look pretty stingy to her family. So when Antonia, Germain's wife, informed Mélina of her intention to choose Gabrielle as godmother to her first child, Mélina replied, "You know, Gabrielle's not the giving kind. You'd do better to take Anna."

Yet Mélina was not complaining. Gabrielle was perhaps not open-handed with her and Clémence, and may have been demanding and sometimes even ill-tempered or capricious, but at least she had stayed and was helping Mélina endure her solitude. Between mother and daughter, the relations were not always easy. Mélina would often scold Gabrielle for the exhausting pace of her life, her untidiness, and her ideas and behaviour that were so inappropriate for a well-brought-up young woman. Gabrielle would retort acerbically, hurling accusations of her own, as Léon used to do, about the older woman's concealments and fixations. Yet none of this prevented Mélina from feeling closer to Gabrielle than to any other of her daughters. The beauty, exuberance, even the ambition of the youngest fascinated her, as if in Gabrielle she were rediscovering her own youth, as if in her life she were finding compensation for her own. There was no one among her children and close relatives – not Anna, or her daughter-in-law Antonia, or Léontine, her grandson Fernand's wife, or her sister Rosalie whom she visited regularly – who could entertain her as Gabrielle could, who could make her laugh loud and long and lead her into all kinds of conversations, imaginings, and foolery that made her forget her age. Occasionally Gabrielle would even come and sit on her mother's knee to tease her and be petted like a child. Such behaviour, such complicity between mother and daughter were bound to scandalize Adèle, in whose eyes Mélina was a venerable sixty-year-old to whom devotion and respect was owed. The narrator of *Enchantment and Sorrow* writes:

> My older sisters used to resent it. "Maman will give her anything," they used to say. "Maman's soft on her." Yet it wasn't exactly that. The truth is that she was old and I was young; I'd become the sunshine of her old age, so to speak.[134]

That Mélina had a tendency to give in to her daughter over everything, that she felt incapable of correcting her and imposing her authority, is understandable. Gabrielle was not a child any longer, she was earning her own living, she was paying her board and lodging. How, and invoking what, might Mélina claim still to have some kind of power over her? And besides, had she ever had such power? Gabrielle had always been her little darling, her special child, her pride and joy. The other children were long gone by the time they were as old as Gabrielle was now, and here was Gabrielle still at her mother's side. Surely she, Mélina, was the one who should express her gratitude and submission.

From the moment she came back to live in her mother's house, Gabrielle resumed the position that had been hers since adolescence, that of stranger and princess, a position more evident and uncontested than ever since her father's demise. A stranger because she no longer belonged to her family; her pastimes, friendships, dreams, ways of life and thought, all estranged her from Deschambault Street, where she came now only to eat, sleep, and retire to her room. If she wished, she could have lived there without paying attention to anyone else, like an ordinary boarder. But this boarder was also the princess of the house. As a daughter of major age and provider, she had nothing to answer for and was dependent on no one, while the others, meaning her mother and Clémence, lived as it were under her thumb, if not at her beck and call. It was she who made the decisions, it was around her needs that domestic activities were organized. Neither Mélina nor Clémence had any choice but to bow to her wishes, her plans, even her moods and caprices. Pity the princess, on the other hand, who must preside over a dark and melancholy house between a grumbling forty-year-old and an old crone who spends her days rocking in the kitchen.

As the Depression dragged on and its effects were felt more keenly in the house on Deschambault Street, Gabrielle's position became more difficult. It did not take many years for her mother's slender financial resources to dwindle to virtually nothing. Because of unemployment, boarders and tenants were few and far between, and those there were had monumental difficulty paying what they owed. Anna herself, whose husband and sons were out of work, spaced out her payments. Rodolphe and Adèle, also grappling with the troubles of the period, were now sending practically nothing home. Rodolphe lost the station master's job he had finally landed and returned to St-Boniface, where he became something of a vagrant, squandering what little he earned on drink and gambling. Adèle continued her wandering, although more and more often finding herself short of money. After her father's death, she tried her chance a second time in Montreal as an office worker, but the beginning of the Depression forced her back to the West almost immediately to resume her teaching career in the far-flung villages of Alberta: Durlingville, St-Paul-des-Métis, Beaumont, Charron, and finally Tangent, a minuscule village in the Peace River Valley where she settled in 1935. She did have a job but working conditions for rural teachers were worsening year by year. Adèle, who had a university degree, earned barely enough to live on. And she was not the only one affected; Germain and his wife, Antonia, were also hard-pressed, both being obliged to teach in schools in the back of beyond and make do with starvation pay, when they were not offered just food and lodging in return for their services. In the context of financial support, the two remaining children are hardly worth even mentioning. Bernadette, who had been sent by her community to Kenora in northern Ontario in 1927, was transferred in

1935 to the almost equally remote Keewatin, where she was appointed superior of the convent. She was hardly ever given permission to come home any longer, and in any event possessed nothing. Joseph finally was still as absent as ever; it was heard that he had lost everything and had joined the hordes of ambulant unemployed wandering about the country, hopping CPR freight trains and terrorizing town councillors.

In short, Mélina could not depend on anyone any more. Her situation was becoming close to desperate. She could no longer keep up with tax payments on the house and was obliged to take in people on relief in order to discharge part of the debt owing to the municipality. More than ever she would pare every expenditure, scratch for every opportunity to earn a few cents, invent ways of " 'plugging holes,' borrowing here to pay there, running hither and thither, a plug here and a patch there," never thinking of anything but money, we are told in *Enchantment and Sorrow*, the "debts, taxes, compound interest, the vicious circle holding us tighter and tighter in its grasp."[135]

For Gabrielle there was an aspect to the situation that was intolerable. Undoubtedly she was distressed by the material difficulties her mother had to contend with, if only because they poisoned the atmosphere in the house, but this was not the worst of the matter. The fact was that Gabrielle was directly threatened by these difficulties, not in terms of poverty, since she still had her own job and her own salary, but in terms of responsibility, meaning the obligation to take upon herself her mother's maintenance and household expenses. Her salary, which held at close to $100 a month throughout these years, would suffice to feed and clothe her, her mother, and Clémence, and cover the cost of taxes, heating, and repairs to the house. But for this she would have to double or triple the amount of her monthly board and consequently give up putting aside a portion as savings; in other words, give up her independence, her unfettered youth, and worst of all what she had her heart most set on – her plans, her future, the real life awaiting her out there, elsewhere.

This was a sacrifice, a negation of herself and her dreams that she could never bring herself to accept. Which was why the pressure of Mélina's financial problems, far from causing her to rethink her plans, had the effect of hardening them, underscoring their urgency. "It was during these difficult years," she would write, "that I began to think only about taking flight."[136] In other words there seemed to be a direct connection between Mélina's increasing hardship and Gabrielle's increasingly stronger and more irresistible desire to escape. As if now she must not just fulfil herself, but at the same time flee the responsibilities that her mother's old age and poverty risked imposing on her.

And so she had only to cut the last bonds and free herself for good. Her decision was made: she was leaving for Europe.

Before an account of the various happenings arising from this decision, we should pause briefly to examine an unusual situation: a young woman with all the advantages – education, occupation, income – refuses her indigent old mother the support that she alone is able to give her. In a sense, Gabrielle's whole life was gambled in this refusal, this act of severance that was as courageous as it was ruthless. For without it, without this filial disloyalty, what would have become of her? Could she have been the woman and writer she became? Some years later Gabrielle would say, "A writer must be prepared to sacrifice everything on earth that gets in the way of his learning and his work and his thinking and imagination."[137]

But in another respect, neither the woman nor the writer would ever get over the tearing away by which she made her selfish choice. At the time, Gabrielle thought only of her deliverance and rebirth in fulfilment of herself. But her mother, the memory of her abandoned mother, would begin one day to torment her to the point of invading not only her life and thoughts and awareness of herself, but even her writing, which thereupon became a long effort at redemption, reparation of the past, which is as good as to say a neverending effort, because the past, of course, cannot be repaired. But then, neither can it be left unrepaired.

Fly! Oh, to Fly Away!

Gabrielle's urge to leave St-Boniface had long been with her. One might say even that it had been the major constant of her youth. Beginning in adolescence, when she became aware of the conditions of her mother's life and, more broadly, conditions for her "poor dispossessed people,"[138] this urge crept unrecognized into her and began to goad her; wanting to make good for her people, or wanting to escape their hold on her, already what this really meant was wanting to leave them. Then when she reached adulthood and began earning her own living, the idea, while still distant and improbable-seeming at first, gradually took form, became plan, then resolution, then real obsession. "I couldn't help it," she would write, "it was like a mania driving me to tear myself away."[139]

To leave, tear herself away, indeed. But where to go? This question Gabrielle did not even put to herself, no more than any young French Canadian drawn by the arts or intellectual pursuits in those days. It would be Europe of course, it would be France, the land of culture and beauty, the land of theatre and literature, beautiful language, and joy in the good things of life – the land of the Boutals and all their distinguished St-Boniface friends. This was what Gabrielle explained to Rex Desmarchais some years later, recalling "the particular situation we were in, a number of my companions, both men and women, and I myself," in the 1930s in Manitoba:

> Teaching and the theatre in particular opened horizons on culture and most especially literature for us. On the other hand, we realized clearly that the poor cultural milieux existing in the Canadian West were totally inadequate to allow us full development of our faculties, our intellectual, literary, and artistic possibilities. We yearned ardently for the abundant living waters springing from the fountainheads in Europe, in France. A journey, a sojourn across the Atlantic was more than a dream for us, it was an obsession![140]

Gabrielle realized very early that this sojourn in Europe was an indispensable condition of her artistic training as an actress or writer, and equally early made up her mind that that was where she would go. With a view to this journey, which she thought about constantly, she began to put aside a little money, "penny by penny,"[141] beginning in her very first year of teaching. Her whole being was in tension, expectation of the great adventure to come. Theatrical activities, writing, socializing with the city's small artistic community, not letting herself be caught in love, all these were ways of making her departure for Europe both possible and necessary. For this departure, which she thought of as the fulfilment of "the curious dreams that had driven me for years to achieve something I couldn't identify, that would allow me to be myself,"[142] this departure was her hope, her escape to that other life, to that other self, to "a thousand possibilities" that were "all ahead, almost all of them intact,"[143] and were calling to her as they were to Christine in "The Road Past Altamont." And failing to answer the call would mean throwing her life away.

For years the young woman had been content to hear the call without being able to answer. But time passed and her impatience grew, as well as her distaste for her present life and her fear of being imprisoned in it forever. And so, as with the narrator of *Children of My Heart*, "the thought of being chained for a lifetime to [her] teacher's desk" soon filled her with a kind of "horror."[144]

> And the future descended on me, making all my years to come resemble this one day. I could see myself in twenty, thirty years, still in the same place, worn down by my task, the very image of the "oldest" of my present colleagues whom I found so pitiful.[145]

More broadly, everything about her life in St-Boniface began to weigh on her, in a way detaching itself from her and seeming stagnant and meaningless. Thirty years later in a very beautiful passage in "The Road Past Altamont," a story in which she felt she had conveyed "the essential truth" about this period of her life,[146] she would re-create the feeling that gripped her then and made her more impatient than ever for the time when she could leave at last. Christine, the narrator, hears a voice inside her saying, "Why do you put off going? Sooner or later you'll have to do it. . . ."

> I was tempted to ask, "Who are you who pursues me so?" but I did not dare, for I knew that this foreign being within me, who was quite insensitive, if need be, to the sorrow he would cause to me and to others, was also myself. [. . .]
>
> I walked in our town and it had become as insubstantial and pale to my eyes as a cinema town. The houses on either side of the street were of papier maché, the streets themselves empty, for when passers-by brushed against me, I seemed scarcely to hear them come and realize that they had faces. When it snowed, I seemed scarcely to be aware that snow fell on me. I myself, moreover, was filled with a kind of emptiness, if it may be so expressed.
>
> Sometimes a strange question arose from within me, as if from the bottom of a well: What are you doing here? Then I would cast my eyes around me. I would try to attach myself to something, familiar to me yesterday, in this world that was fleeing from me. [. . .] The thought, seemingly so trivial and yet disturbing, accompanied me everywhere: This is over. This is no longer your place. Now you are a stranger here.[147]

Gabrielle made her final decision, it seems, early in 1936, shortly before her twenty-seventh birthday. She still did not know exactly when she was going to leave, but one thing was certain: she was going to Europe and she was going as soon as possible.

As soon as possible meant as soon as she had put together enough money, made the necessary arrangements, and done the best she could to leave her mother and Clémence no longer dependent on her and able to manage in her absence.

The first thing to be done was to part with the old house on Deschambault Street which, the narrator of *Enchantment and Sorrow* would say later, "used to suck us dry,"[148] for it cost dearly and no longer earned anything. Mélina was reluctant; after all, this house contained all her memories and was the one home port to which her scattered children returned from time to time from the four corners of the country. Soon however, she had no choice. The backlog of unpaid taxes had grown to such a point that during the summer of 1935 the municipality ordered the sale of the house, to be concluded by 29 April 1936, as Gabrielle was returning from Ottawa, still flushed with the drama festival victory of *Les Soeurs Guédonec*. The sale price was $2,842; of this, over $1,000 went directly to the municipality so that the buyer, Frédéric Saint-Germain, paid Mélina only $1,800, or $150 down and $200 per year at 5 per cent interest, which amounted to a little less than $18 a month for eight years. The transaction also provided that Mélina could occupy the second floor of the house for a monthly rental of $20.[149]

May 1 was moving day. Mélina had to sell off the furniture that would not fit in the three-room apartment. Anna, now living in Winnipeg, bagged the piano for $50, which she paid at the rate of $4 a month. For Gabrielle these arrangements were fairly satisfactory. True, Mélina was losing her big house, her verandah, her yard, and her flowers, and at sixty-nine years of age would have to go up and down the narrow stairs to the second floor every day in order to go to mass or to Anna's or Rosalie's. But at least she was out of debt and could count on small monthly receipts, which should suffice.

With the coming of summer, as usual Gabrielle suspended her board payments. While her mother and Clémence were at Pembina Mountain, where they stayed until the end of October, since the harvesting and threshing season was the busiest at the farm, Gabrielle decided to go to Camperville, a remote village on the fringes of Lake Winnipegosis where her cousin Éliane lived. Éliane, the eldest daughter of Gabrielle's uncle Excide, had been married to Laurent Jubinville since 1925 and had six children. Gabrielle gave lessons to the four oldest in exchange for bed and board. In her free time she roamed the neighbourhood or wrote little stories inspired by Amerindian legends, as she had been doing for some time. Two known texts from this period are of this genre: the first is "La grotte de la mort" which was published in 1936; the other, titled "La légende du cerf ancien," remained unpublished during Gabrielle's lifetime. Although she worked at this latter story during her stay in Europe, the idea and first draft probably date from this summer at Camperville, a village in a region largely populated by Métis and Amerindians.[150]

The memory of these weeks of calm in the bosom of nature, made bright by the friendship of Éliane and her children, would emerge more powerfully a dozen years later in *Where Nests the Water Hen*. "I spent a sweet, dreamy summer there," we read in *Enchantment and Sorrow*, "at peace with myself and untroubled by my plans for the future, just content with the moment, which hasn't always been the case."[151]

But as with her first year of teaching at Cardinal when she also found herself in the same orbit as Éliane and Léa and her other Landry cousins, the Camperville moment of grace was short lived. In September Gabrielle returned to St-Boniface and her job at the Institut Provencher and immediately began again to prepare feverishly for her departure for Europe. To fatten her nest egg she saved more, spent less, sold some personal effects, and recruited students to whom she gave private lessons in elocution.[152]

In November however, disaster struck. Mélina, returning from a visit to Aunt Rosalie, fell and fractured a hip. The accident placed Gabrielle's journey in jeopardy. The hospital, the operation, the medications, the care – what was it all going to cost? Would Mélina be left a cripple? Would someone have to be paid to take care of her for the rest of her life? Luckily nothing of the sort came to pass. Pleading her case with Doctor Andrew Mackinnon, the orthopaedist who treated Mélina, Gabrielle obtained his permission to defer payment of his fee at least until her return from Europe. This debt was well and truly paid, but six years later, in 1942.[153] Mélina's state of health improved rapidly, besides; she returned home from the hospital about 15 November 1936[154] and was released from her body cast shortly before Christmas, which she spent quietly at the little apartment on Deschambault Street. Gabrielle and Clémence were with her, as well as Anna and Léontine, Fernand's wife, who came to visit. "It was a bit like other years gone by when we were all together again," the convalescent wrote; life these days seemed very hard and cheerless, she said, but added, "it only makes us sad and opens up old wounds to talk about our dear memories that are buried for ever, beneath the snows of the past."[155]

When she wrote this letter to Adèle the old woman was already beginning to walk again unassisted. In another few weeks her recovery would be complete. Gabrielle sighed with relief; her departure was not in jeopardy after all.

The expenses entailed by the accident had nevertheless eaten considerably into the small sum that Mélina had received on the sale of her house. By good fortune, she was soon to turn seventy and would become eligible for the government old-age pension. At this time the pension was not automatically granted once a person reached the designated age. To have the right to it one also had to prove genuine need; in other words, that one had no personal property or source of income, and nobody to count on in one's family.

At the Manitoba Provincial Archives, there is a declaration dated 11 January 1937 in which Mélina, who signs herself "Emelie" Roy, in order to comply with the law describes her state of destitution at that time.[156] The total value of her possessions amounted to $184, consisting of $150 worth of furniture, $25 on deposit with the Banque Canadienne Nationale in St-Boniface, and $9 in bank notes and small change in her purse. The sum she received monthly from Fred Saint-Germain served to pay her rent. As for help from her children, it was negligible, practically non-existent. Apart from Gabrielle, "schoolteacher and elocution teacher," who paid her mother $25 per month for ten months, none of them were in a position to give anything whatever, as demonstrated by the recitation of the states of their adversity. Jos: "on relief, no income." Anna: "no income, 3 children, husband not working." Adèle: "married, teacher, earning barely enough to live." Rodolphe: "address unknown, single, unemployed, no income." Germain: "married, one child, address unknown, teacher, income not deemed sufficient to contribute."

On 9 February 1937, the day she turned seventy, Mélina began receiving a monthly pension of $10.44 from the government.[157] It was not enough, of course, and if some way were not found of reducing expenses further, Gabrielle was going to have to continue paying her an allowance. The solution was to give up the apartment on Deschambault Street, which was going to be too big anyway once Gabrielle had left for Europe, and find less expensive lodging for Mélina and Clémence. Mélina announced to Monsieur Saint-Germain that she would leave

375 Deschambault Street for good in the month of June. Now Gabrielle could officially request a leave of absence from the school commission.

> Sirs,
>
> So that I may realize my plan to spend a year in Europe studying drama and French diction, I would be most obliged if you would grant me a year's leave of absence.
>
> I submit this plan to you [. . .] with the certainty that you will see in it not only my intention to pursue my personal development, but also my hope of acquiring knowledge which may serve the development of drama at our school.
>
> [. . .] I ask you however to consider that I could not put this plan into execution without the assurance of being able to resume my position on my return, with the benefits presently attached thereto. In granting me this privilege, you would be according me a much valued mark of appreciation for which I would be deeply grateful and of which I would strive to remain worthy.[158]

The reply arrived ten days later: Mademoiselle Roy could leave in peace, for her position would be waiting for her in September 1938, "as if you had never been away."[159]

When vacation time came, Mélina sold her few remaining pieces of furniture to a second-hand dealer and left for her brother Excide's to take up her "hired hand" functions. She stayed there all summer. In October, when they returned to St-Boniface, she and Clémence moved into the two small rooms in the house belonging to Madame Agnès Jacques at 335 Langevin Street where Mélina would live out her days.

The summer of 1937 was therefore the last that Gabrielle spent in Manitoba before leaving for France at the end of August. Hoping to top up her savings during the weeks remaining, she obtained a remote district summer school from the Department of Education. The pay was good: $5 a day plus free room and board. The school was not far from the village of Meadow Portage in the Waterhen School District, some three hundred miles north of Winnipeg between lakes Manitoba and Winnipegosis.

Knowing nothing about the remote corner where she was going to spend the summer, she boarded the train at the beginning of July for Rorketon. There she was to meet her friend Joseph Vermander who was working as a postal inspector and was going to drive her to a point close to her school, which was on a wild island called "Ranch-à-Jeannotte" in "a curious region [. . .], a low plain consisting mostly of muskeg, a mixture of earth and water; a region covered with rushes, lakes, and rivers, and inhabited by countless birds. [. . .] I was the one, I think, who first called it the Little Water Hen country."[160]

Joseph Jeannotte, the owner of the island, grazed animals there, and they were tended by his uncle, Monsieur Côté, who lived on the island with his wife and seven children, the youngest of whom was Alice, who was two. Gabrielle was the third teacher to come here during this summer.[161] There were seven pupils attending the school, four Côté children and three Métis living nearby. This sojourn – which Gabrielle recounted later many times – passed much as had that of the previous summer at Camperville: Gabrielle taught school, went swimming, took long walks by the river, and "scribbled."[162] Her hosts, however, were less endearing and attentive than Éliane and her family, so that during the five or six weeks she spent in their company she had many days of "boredom and depression."[163]

Her mind, it must be said, was totally absorbed by the great adventure ahead of her. Returning to St-Boniface in mid-August, she stayed with the Misses Muller, some relatives of Joseph Vermander, and busied herself with final preparations for her departure. Her savings totalled about $1,000, some of which she spent to pay for the train and boat tickets she had reserved before leaving for Meadow Portage. They were one-way tickets, so that she could be sure of having enough money to live on in Europe for about a year. While waiting to receive her passport (which was to be issued to her in Montreal on 31 August 1937[164]), Gabrielle cast about for people who could inform her on the best ways to manage in Paris and London. One of these, Professor Jones of the French Department at the University of Manitoba, gave her the name of one of his students, whom Gabrielle immediately contacted by letter. There was also "the wardrobe trunk" to be bought and filled with clothes, books, some of her texts no doubt, and of course the medals she had won at the Académie Saint-Joseph, which she could always sell in case of need.

But these concerns were nothing in comparison with the raking-over she was given by her family and community during the final weeks before her departure. No one could understand why she was going; a hare-brained idea, said some; youthful folly, said others; pure and simple betrayal, said others still. However insistently Gabrielle repeated that she was going to Europe to study, to perfect the dramatic art that had already won her many instances of praise right here in St-Boniface and in Winnipeg, and that she had every intention of returning to take up a stage and radio career, nevertheless the tongues waxed harsh. What the devil was she going to be doing there, said some, and where was her money coming from? It was inconceivable in those days of unemployment to leave a steady, well-paid job and go off into the blue like that, especially if one was a young woman alone without either a woman companion or a husband. Who did she take herself for, said others; did she think it was as easy as that to succeed where others had failed? What vanity, what ingratitude; how could she go and leave her poor, sick old mother like that!

The harshest attacks of all came from her own family, as she recalled later in *Enchantment and Sorrow*.[165] "You're leaving us!" Clémence flung at her, while Anna made fun of her pretensions and warned that she was in for disappointments. As for Adèle, who was spending that summer in Manitoba, she was the most outraged; she accused Gabrielle, as she continued to do later, of evading her responsibilities as the youngest daughter, and letting herself be dazzled "by the mirage of a brilliant artistic career which [was going to] shower hundreds of thousands of dollars into her greedy hands."[166]

Bernadette, who was then teaching temporarily at the Académie Saint-Joseph, was the only one to offer comfort to her young sister and encourage her in her plans, for which Gabrielle was still thanking her six years later. "At a moment when I was feeling so alone, so bereft that life no longer seemed to have any purpose or direction, this was what you were to me, my big sister."[167]

As for Mélina, she did not understand why Gabrielle was so determined to go to Europe, but having protested and waged "a tenacious fight"[168] to keep her from going, in the end resigned herself and even, perhaps, accepted it. She went so far as to travel from Somerset (where Adèle had come to visit her and try to set her against Gabrielle) to St-Boniface to spend the night with her youngest daughter before her departure. The next day she went with her to the station. In a beautiful scene in *Enchantment and Sorrow* (which Adèle dismisses as pure invention),[169] Gabrielle recalls that night, which she and her mother spent together in the same bed, and during which they came to their ultimate reconciliation.

On the evening of 29 August 1937,[170] a little troupe of friends from the Cercle Molière, the Little Theatre, and the Institut Provencher gathered at the station to say goodbye to the traveller. At this moment no one, not they, nor Mélina, nor Gabrielle herself knew that she was leaving for good.

The following week there appeared this item in *La Liberté*:

Mlle Gabrielle Roy of Saint-Boniface left Monday evening for Paris, where she will study drama at le théâtre de l'Atelier, under the direction of Charles Dullin. Mlle Roy has already acquired an enviable reputation on our local stages. She was a member of Le Cercle Molière and twice went to Ottawa to compete for the national festival. We wish her bon voyage and much success in her studies.[171]

CHAPTER 6

Adventure

*I*t has been said that Gabrielle Roy's departure for Europe at twenty-eight years of age was the first act of her life as a writer, a severance that would determine her entire career, and which, in a way, she would never get over. But seen in a broader perspective, this departure was less a severance in itself than a continuation or consummation of an event that psychologically had already occurred much earlier. Flying the family nest, getting away from St-Boniface, undertaking the voyage to Europe, all of it was a pursuit of those "expanded horizons,"[1] the full realization of herself that had been her obsession since adolescence and the major preoccupation of her final years of teaching and theatrical experience in St-Boniface.

The voyage to Europe for any young Canadian or American of the period with the slightest artistic or intellectual inclinations was a rite of passage in his or her worldly and cultural apprenticeship. No one could pretend to be a real painter, writer, actor, or intellectual, no one could claim to be "cultivated," without having made an Atlantic crossing and discovery of "the Old Countries." This initiation was especially crucial for young French Canadians; only Europe could deliver them from the limitations and provincialism of their native milieu; only Europe could give them a direct access to the thinking, forms, and works of the most advanced modern culture; only Europe could offer them, intellectually, morally, or even sexually, their first, honest-to-goodness experience of freedom.

Gabrielle Roy was no exception. At the same moment as she, or very nearly, other young people of her age, among them Jean Desprez, André Laurendeau, and Alfred Pellan, were taking the requisite trail and doing their studies in Europe. There was nothing very original about the itinerary followed by the young Manitoban: London, Paris, Provence – a ritual path trodden by all travellers from North America, be they tourists, apprentice writers, or rich newlyweds.

This said, Gabrielle's European sojourn was to play a crucial role in her personal evolution. Separated not only from her family but also from her occupation and the community that had structured her life thus far, obliged now to depend solely on her own devices, she had necessarily to define herself at last and decide in a concrete way what path she was going to follow.

But Gabrielle was unaware of all this on the late summer day in 1937 when, after stepping off the train in Montreal,[2] she discovered the tiny third-class cabin in which she was to make the Atlantic crossing. She may have been fired, as she told Rex Desmarchais some years later, "with an invincible confidence in life, [with] ardent desire to see the marvels of Europe and drink liberally at the very source of knowledge and beauty,"[3] but she did not know what was ahead of her. She left for Europe intending to complete her training as an actress and returned a writer. She left St-Boniface for a year and it took her eight to fulfil her dreams. Eight years of constant peregrinations and tireless work, eight years of hunting out the least opportunity to get ahead and battling everything that might hold her back. Eight years of adventure that would be like a long campaign of conquest, both of her own identity and recognition from others.

This period, beginning with her departure for Europe and ending with the publication of *Bonheur d'occasion* and its translation, *The Tin Flute*, appears to have been the most hectic perhaps of Gabrielle's entire life. It was a period of relentless activity, revealing as never before the fierce will driving her to better herself, to make a place for herself, to succeed whatever the cost. Will, ambition, but also courage, determination, mettle, rejection of half-measures, and above all a craving for freedom and accomplishment – these traits emerge strongly in Gabrielle in her European and Montreal years, which is perhaps why, looking back, these years would seem to her to have been the most intense and exhilarating of her life.

A Student Abroad

Gabrielle's European sojourn lasted twenty months, from the autumn of 1937 until the spring of 1939. We know a good deal about its principal events through Part Two of *Enchantment and Sorrow*, titled "A Bird Knows Its Song," the whole of which is devoted to it. The following pages are therefore confined to an overview, but with attention to the various traces to be found in other texts or documents of the period.

Having boarded ship in Montreal, the traveller disembarked in London but stayed only a few days before continuing directly to Paris, for her intention, as she had told *La Liberté* shortly before leaving St-Boniface, was to attend the classes in dramatic art given by Charles Dullin, the director of the Théâtre de l'Atelier; classes at the École nouvelle du comédien (the official name of the school of the Théâtre de l'Atelier) were beginning that autumn on October 15.

In the French capital Gabrielle was met by the former student of Professor Jones she had been in touch with during the winter. This young woman's name, which the narrator of *Enchantment and Sorrow* cannot remember, remains unknown. Before Gabrielle's arrival in Paris, this "compatriot" had found her a boarding house, whose address has also slipped the autobiographer's memory. It was, in fact, number 13, square Port-Royal in the XIIIe arrondissement. This small *square* – the term is an anglicism that rhymes with "star" and is bestowed by the French on certain residential squares in Paris – has a single access through an iron gate off the rue de la Santé and is surrounded by a series of nine-storey buildings, all of similar design. Number 13 is at the far end and the apartment that belonged to Madame Andrée Jouve,[4] where Gabrielle boarded, was on the seventh floor. It was a fairly affluent apartment, serviced with hot water and an elevator and situated in a quiet and very respectable neighbourhood, of which many inhabitants were doctors and personnel attached to nearby hospitals (Cochin, Val-de-Grâce, Sainte-Anne); the theatre district and Saint-Germain-des-Près were perhaps rather distant, but the boulevard Montparnasse and the jardin du Luxembourg were just a step away. In short, Gabrielle could not fault this boarding house, which was indeed "grand" as boarding houses go.[5]

Shortly after her arrival, some of her personal effects that she had left in the basement of the building were stolen, including her prize medals, according to *Enchantment and Sorrow*. The Paris police record shows that the burglars, three adolescents, were apprehended almost immediately and that Gabrielle was not the only victim of the break-in; there were at least six or seven complainants, all of whom lived at number 11 or 13 square Port-Royal. Madame Jouve was not one of the group.[6] The record mentions the disappearance of "a fur coat," but says nothing about Gabrielle's medals.

Gabrielle had meanwhile embarked on her personal program of study, though without much success. As planned, she had gone to see Charles Dullin, who was then playing *Volpone* by the English dramatist Ben Jonson, in a French adaptation by Jules Romains of the German adaptation by Stefan Zweig.[7] This initiative came to naught, for Gabrielle was so intimidated she turned and fled before learning whether the master would or would not accept her as his student. In compensation she saw as many plays as possible, at the Théâtre de l'Athénée, where she admired Louis Jouvet in *Électre* by Giraudoux, at the Comédie-Française, where they were playing *Cyrano*, and elsewhere. After a few weeks, in a new attempt at studying seriously, she went to the Théâtre des Mathurins, run by Georges and Ludmila Pitoëff. In *Enchantment and Sorrow* she recounts this visit as following a performance of *The Seagull* by Chekhov which had particularly moved her. But this is not possible, for *The Seagull* (played in French as *La Mouette*) would not be presented until the winter of 1939 and Gabrielle did not see it until then, when she was passing through Paris on her way back from Provence. In the autumn of 1937 the Pitoëffs were indeed rehearsing *La Sauvage* by Jean Anouilh, as is stated in *Enchantment and Sorrow*, but what was currently being played at the Théâtre des Mathurins was *Celui qui reçoit des gifles* by Léonide Andreieff, which was replaced in mid-November by *L'Échange* by Paul Claudel.[8]

Here too, and despite her admiration for Ludmila, Gabrielle soon dropped her lessons in dramatic art. Not that she had suddenly become indifferent to drama; it was Paris she was not getting along with. To be sure, she admired the beauties of the city and was roaming it as a starry-eyed tourist, but there was nothing holding her here. Nothing and no one. In these years of the Popular Front, Paris may well have been at the peak of its vitality and influence, it may have been a gathering place for the most celebrated artists and writers, a-buzz with debate and manifestations of every kind, the intellectual centre of the universe as H. R. Lottman would have it,[9] but Gabrielle felt alone and foreign and, as she would say later, "too frightened by the city"[10] to benefit from it and try to fit into it. She decided to leave almost as soon as she arrived. Her first stay in Paris, after all those dreams of it, had lasted less than two months.

London in comparison was bound to appeal to her, not so much the city itself as the fact that she had friends there who were delighted to gather her up and see to her every need. Bohdan Hubicki, the violinist friend from Winnipeg who had come to England to study and make his career, had been writing her since September, pressing her to come and join him. There were other acquaintances in London too, like the actors Margot Syme and her husband Robert Christie who had played in Winnipeg before coming to England, and Clelio Ritagliati, the other young violinist whom Gabrielle had known in Manitoba. And she soon made new friends as well. Her education and youth in Manitoba, as well as her familiarity with the English language and culture, made London's life and environment more "natural," more accessible than France and Paris had been. The result was that she hardly felt out of place at all in London, almost at home in this city that, until the quite recent Statute of Westminster (1931), had been the true capital of Canada, and in the world Gabrielle came from still remained the most powerful cultural pole.

And then, London was as much a theatrical mecca as Paris, where the student might pursue her training perhaps even more advantageously than in the French capital. The minute she arrived in November she buckled down to the task. With Bohdan's guidance she enrolled in a major theatrical school, the very official and very famous Guildhall School of Music and Drama on John Carpenter Street near Blackfriars Bridge. Her registration card shows that she took three courses: dramatic art (with Miss Rorke), elocution (with Mr. Ridley), and stage make-up.[11] She also performed in one of the plays prepared that year by the students.[12] The teaching at the Guildhall, she soon wrote to her friend Léonie, was "very academic in style, very traditional. [...] But that doesn't prevent it from being a marvellous place to study music or the technique of drama. It's the best academy of the kind, I believe sincerely, not only in London but in all of Europe."[13] She also took private lessons from Madame Alice Gachet, "a French lady of vast experience" established in London, whose pedagogical talents were valued by the leading actors of the day such as Charles Laughton and Vivien Leigh; with her, Gabrielle worked in French.[14]

The ex-schoolteacher worked very hard at learning to become an actress. The theatre looked to her more than ever to be her true vocation. Whether it would bring her fame, whether it would lead her to the opulent life she dreamed of, she did not know. She was sure, however, that it was going to be the source of her livelihood. In February she even wrote to the St-Boniface School Commission, of which she was still an employee on leave of absence, asking for the creation, specifically for her, of a post for the teaching of "phonetics, diction, and practical courses in dramatic art" in the schools of her native city. The proposal was rejected out of hand by the commissioners, no doubt with raised eyebrows.[15]

The drama student settled in Fulham, a district in the west of London and slightly outside the centre, where the price of a room was reasonable and from where she could easily reach Piccadilly Circus, Trafalgar Square, and the theatre district. To get to the school she would often get off the Underground at Charing Cross and walk the rest of the way along the Thames embankments. Her first room, which Bohdan had found for her, was at 71 Winchendon Road.[16] But she was mortally lonely and depressed there and soon moved, with Bohdan's help again, to another boarding house not far away but in a more lively neighbourhood, at 106 Lillie Road.[17] Here, her landlady, Gladys Pryce, and her husband, Geoffrey, took an immediate liking to Gabrielle and made "[her] life very pleasant,"[18] treating her practically like one of the family.

As she had done in Paris, once she was settled in London she began systematically visiting the city and its environs, armed with her small camera. She was particulary drawn by the Thames embankments and scenes of surviving rusticity, such as Gladys's cabin opposite Hampton Court, Greenwich, and the old mill at Wimbledon.[19]

But she soon stopped being just a tourist and began to live like a real student, independently, happily, meeting people, going out and about to all kinds of activities. At the school she struck up a friendship with a fellow student by the name of Phyllis, who took her home one day for Sunday dinner with her family. She and Phyllis saw a great many plays together. Soon after arriving in London, Gabrielle also began going often to Canada House on Trafalgar Square, where Vincent Massey was the High Commissioner at the time. There, Canadian students could meet, avail themselves of the various services at their disposal, and exchange useful addresses.[20] It was through this connection that, introduced by Clelio, she used to visit the Hampstead home of Mrs. Ellis, who entertained Canadian students studying in London and plied them with apple pie so that they would feel "more at home." But soon she was frequenting another salon, Lady Frances Ryder's in South Kensington, introduced by her friend Bohdan. Lady Frances's flat was in Sloane Square near Cadogan Gardens. There, every day except Saturday, overseas students who were subjects of His Majesty were invited for tea; they could play ping-pong or badminton, converse, and eat as much as they wished, while ladies, all of them distinguished and charming, would move about attending to them, cajoling them, offering them theatre or concert tickets and doing whatever they could to make them feel at home in England. As Gabrielle wrote at this time:

> You have to have lived alone in London during one of these dreary, depressing winters, in one of these humble little boarding house rooms so aptly called "digs" in the local slang, to appreciate the salutary influence of a home where, whoever you are, rich, poor, young, old, from New Zealand, South Africa, Canada, you are warmly welcomed, received into the great family of the Empire, treated not as a passing visitor but as a cousin, a very dear and long awaited cousin.[21]

The most coveted privileges open to Sloane Square habitués were the invitations to weekends and even longer sojourns in the country as guests of aristocrats soft-heartedly inclined toward foreign students. On this score, Gabrielle was particularly favoured by Lady Frances, "my favourite benefactress and saint," as she described her to Léonie.[22] In her autobiography she writes of invitations to stay in the country that she received through Lady Frances and accepted, first from a Lady Curre at Itton Court in Monmouthshire (Wales), and then from a Miss Shaw at Bridport[23] in Dorset on the English Channel. According to *Enchantment and Sorrow*, this second visit occurred in November 1938; however, she was already talking of this visit to Miss Shaw in two articles published in July and August of the same year, which leads one to suppose that her peregrinations through the English countryside, from one upscale homestead to another, from one protectress to another, took place in fact the previous spring during the Easter holidays, thus during her first year in Europe.[24]

All this first year was a relatively happy period for Gabrielle. She did have spells of gloom and discouragement, particularly during the Christmas holidays, but generally her frame of mind was that of an active young woman brimming with energy and pleased with the experience of life she was having. She was seeing the sights, getting around the country,[25] taking advantage of every opportunity for discovery, and most of all enjoying to the full the most precious thing these experiences offered: freedom.

Total freedom, without any interference or supervision, without explanations or by-your-leaves to offer anyone, a degree of freedom Gabrielle had never known and that enabled her in this year 1937–1938 to complete her personal emancipation, shake off all that still stamped her as a dutiful, submissive little small-town girl, the product of the strait-laced milieu of St-Boniface.

First she stopped going to church or practising the religion that for her, even while at Provencher, had been no more than an obligation imposed by the surrounding conformity. In this respect, she was no different from many other French Canadians of the period for whom Europe offered the opportunity to break with the religious obligations of their native society. The worthy priests of French Canada were right to look darkly upon the trip to Europe as threatening to the faith of their flocks.

Threatening to their faith and to their chastity. For Europe was also, was above all, the place of consummate moral perdition: carnal sin. Here again, Gabrielle was no exception. It was in England, at the age of twenty-eight, that she had her first sexual experience.

From Love to Literature

Captivating, even seductive, Gabrielle had always been, and she had never been short of suitors, whom she had always kept carefully at bay. One who knew something about this was poor Bohdan, who was truly devoted to her. His was an adoration in which friendship was the sublimation of passion – a friendship made the more complete, the more protective, by the extent to which the passion dared not avow itself, as if the young man realized instinctively that the only way to win Gabrielle's affection was never to touch her or propose anything beyond utter devotion. But Bohdan was probably not alone in this during these years. At the Guildhall, in the drawing rooms of Sloane Square, even on her own street, many men fell under her spell; like the Welsh baritone who invited her to that grand social event at the Austrian ambassador's in London; like David, the young New Zealander with whom she went on a week's trip by car through the southwest of England as far as Land's End;[26] like the young Parisian with whom she attended the performance of *The Seagull*; and like all the rejected suitors littering "the trail of broken hearts" in Provence.[27] But Gabrielle also broke hearts among women. Phyllis, Gladys, Lady Frances, Miss Shaw, later Esther and Ruby, all had a kind of veneration for her, yet not one could keep her entirely to herself for more than a few months. This charm she exercised over people, this power she possessed for attracting their friendship or love, and for turning them into devoted protectors in almost every case, was one of the great "laws" of Gabrielle's life. We have seen it at work with her mother, her educators, and friends in her childhood and youth; we are seeing it at work again in Europe; and so it will be even in the last years of her life.

Yet before coming to England Gabrielle had never felt passion or experienced physical love. Her charm had devastated the men around her but not one of them had ever possessed her heart and body. Modesty, inhibition, frigidity, who can say? On this score, Gabrielle was not much different to most girls of her background, who, on pain of scandal and undying remorse, remained virgins until they married. And so her liaison with Stephen, her "first lover,"[28] was one of the high points of her time in Europe. The ultimate sign of her liberation.

It is not necessary here to recapitulate this episode in detail, since its ups and downs are related at length in *Enchantment and Sorrow*, which is the only available source of information on the matter. We shall recall simply that the meeting took place at Lady Frances's flat in the spring of 1938,[29] that Gabrielle and Stephen became lovers almost immediately, and that the relationship lasted at most a matter of weeks, until mid-summer approximately. In certain respects, the story is like "some far-fetched novel."[30] A Canadian of Ukrainian origin like Bohdan Hubicki, Stephen (whose family name remains a mystery) was a secret agent serving an organization dedicated to combatting Soviet domination in the Ukraine, which meant, in those years prior to the German-Soviet Nonaggression Pact, that he was an ally of the Nazis. The situation was forcing him to lead a double life ill-suited to love: he had frequently to be away, his attitude had to remain guarded, and he was unable to commit himself totally to the relationship. This kind of behaviour soon provoked thorough discontent in Gabrielle, who wanted nothing less than "to be loved exclusively, with an undivided love."[31]

These at least were the reasons the narrator of *Enchantment and Sorrow* would give forty years later to explain the breakup with Stephen. But there was probably more to it than that. There may have been political reasons as well. It does seem that Gabrielle had rather leftist opinions at this time; four years later she admitted to her sister Adèle the sympathy she had conceived while in London for the thinking of Hewlett Johnson, the Marxist and anti-fascist Anglican cleric known as the Red Dean,[32] and this thinking was hardly compatible with Stephen's anti-Soviet alignment.

Still, ideological disagreement alone was surely not enough to cool a passion as hot, as sensual as that between these two lovers. Their breakup was perhaps due more to the sheer intensity of this passion, this "electrifying attraction"[33] that had flung them together and to which neither was ready to yield entirely or irrevocably. Stephen, certainly, would not commit himself, and he did not have Bohdan's protective and submissive attitude toward Gabrielle. But Gabrielle did not give herself totally either. From what she reveals in her autobiography, she lived this adventure both as an exhilarating discovery and a terrible inner conflict, divided, torn as she was between a passion that ravished her senses and loss of her self-possession, a "bondage"[34] that she did not want and could not accept. Surrendering to Stephen, giving way to this love, would mean losing not only her independence but most of all control of her life; it would place at risk everything she had worked so long and hard for, her career plans, her drive for personal achievement, her success and fame to come. It would mean betraying "that person all unknown" in her who kept demanding to come forth and have the world at her feet.

In the circumstances, love was under a kind of interdict for Gabrielle as much as for Stephen, and their mutual love-at-first-sight was bound to burn out. Much later Gabrielle would say that because of this liaison, "I was long in mortal fear of the thing called love; perhaps I always shall be."[35] But this mortal fear came upon her only afterwards. We shall see that her breakup with Stephen was not the end of her experience with love.

For the time being, what is most interesting is the coincidence between the end of the love affair with Stephen and the moment of Gabrielle's decision to become a writer. According to the account in *Enchantment and Sorrow*, it was as if she had detached herself from Stephen in order to enable herself to begin to write, or as if breaking up with her lover had been what led her to turn to literature. And so it would seem that renunciation of love and investment in literature went hand in hand, like two sides of one and the same event, or of one and the same revelation.

From the information in *Enchantment and Sorrow* we can assign a precise time to this event, the summer of 1938, and an equally precise place, the village of Upshire in the county of Essex, just outside London to the northeast on the edge of Epping Forest. It was here that Gabrielle had come by chance upon the house of Esther Perfect and her father in the course of a bus trip. The house, on the outskirts of the village, was one of a group of row houses called Century Cottages; it was a modest dwelling at one end of the row and had a little garden overlooking a broad vista of rolling countryside not unlike that of Pembina Mountain.[36] "It was all I could possibly desire,"[37] Gabrielle would say: a place that was secluded and yet close to the city, where she felt at peace, freed of the usual daily routine, and able to do without Stephen. She was received there by two gentle, pious, unpretentious people who lavished their affection and care on her. It was something like her uncle Excide's farm when she was at Cardinal, like her cousin Éliane's house at Camperville, or the enchanted surroundings at La Petite-Poule-d'Eau. Century Cottages seemed like something out of this world, an oasis of happiness and peace where she could quietly give way to her fondest wishes without having to fight for anything or prove anything, just *tout entière à l'écoute et à la jouissance de soi-même*, as Jean-Jacques Rousseau would say, undividedly listening to and revelling in herself.

The weeks she spent at Esther's were among the happiest of her whole stay in England. It was as if all of a sudden she were back in her sheltered, pampered childhood that was untainted by any conflict. To the young woman come to find refuge under her roof, Esther offered everything a mother can offer: she fed her, cared for her, relieved her of domestic chores, bringing her consolation and love all the while. But Esther went one better than Mélina: she never opposed Gabrielle in any way, never admonished her over anything, and above all never expected anything in return for her care. Gabrielle had no need to feel guilty toward her, or responsible for her, or obliged to live up to her expectations. Furthermore, Esther the virginal, Esther the angelic, was the goddess of a world from which men, or at least the roughness and demands of men, had vanished. For Esther's father, William Perfect, the seventy-year-old gardener, the white-bearded widower, never as much as raised his voice. Unobtrusive, never grumbling, he was barely distinguishable from the flowers and birds among which he spent his life. His role, one would say, was simply to keep Esther company and reflect her infinite maternal kindness.

The portrait of Esther Perfect and her father in *Enchantment and Sorrow* probably does not correspond to the whole truth. In writing it, Gabrielle likely drew on more than her memories of the summer of 1938; involved as well are very certainly elements inspired by later stays in Upshire, in 1949 and 1963. Esther the character as she appears in *Enchantment and Sorrow* is substantially outlined in an abundant correspondence documenting these visits. Also, the anecdote of the book of

pressed flowers that Gabrielle supposedly began to assemble on her first
visit to the Perfects' did not in fact occur until 1949. But these anachro-
nisms matter little. What is important is that the autobiographer chose
to place under Esther's sign and influence the story of the event that
started it all: her decision to become a writer.

It was in the idyllic atmosphere of the house at Upshire, if we are to
believe *Enchantment and Sorrow*, that Gabrielle finally discovered that
writing was her vocation and decided henceforth to devote her life to it.
In her writerly awareness she would always remember this ideal period
fondly, even nostalgically, as if she considered it an exemplary image of
what writing is: a shelter from the world; and what it needs: quieted passions, total availability, and obliviousness to all material preoccupations
– conditions that can be made possible only by the presence of some
kindly and protective, discreet and yet utterly devoted figure. Inwardly
for Gabrielle, writing would always mean, would always demand a re-
enactment of this initial scene, a symbolic return at least to Esther's protective, magical world.

But there was another circumstance behind this conversion to
writing whose influence should not be overlooked: Gabrielle had some
texts accepted for publication by a Parisian newspaper. As we have seen,
she had been making attempts at writing for some years and had had at
least four pieces published in Canadian periodicals before coming to
Europe, but she did not think these important enough to be persuaded
of her own gifts and consider that she should turn to literature rather
than the stage. Writing was still secondary for her, a kind of hobby.
However, it took on a different complexion when during this summer of
1938 recognition came not from Montreal, Toronto, or Winnipeg but
from none other than Paris, which to every French Canadian of the day
(and even to this day) was the centre of the literary world. If the editor
of a French publication, who received manuscripts from all over, judged
her texts worthy of being printed and then read by the world's most
demanding and cultivated readership, her talent must be real and she
could devote herself to writing with every chance of success.

The name of the paper in question was *Je suis partout*.[38] Founded in
1930, this "great weekly about life worldwide," as it termed itself, was one
of the best known of Parisian periodicals, with a circulation of fifty
thousand copies. The narrator of *Enchantment and Sorrow* does not
mention the paper's name, saying that she knew it "only through having
bought an occasional issue in London."[39] Politically it was a rightist

paper, even extreme rightist; it was considered to be the "young off-shoot" of Charles Maurras's *Action française* and its editorial line expressed the ultranationalist opinions of its prime movers, Robert Brasillach and Lucien Rebatet. *Je suis partout* was vociferously pro-Franco and anti-Communist; it was even one of the most eloquent tribunes of fascist radicalism in interbellum France.

People have been surprised that Gabrielle Roy should be associated with such a publication, but they too often forget that when she sent in her articles, *Je suis partout* was not the openly anti-Semitic, collaborationist, even informer-sympathizer paper it became during the Occupation (and which brought about its closure after the Liberation in August 1944). It was certainly a politically committed, openly reactionary paper, but to its readers of the day there was more to it than its ideological posturing. It was also and just as much a general interest weekly that gave a great deal of space to literature and even, through Brasillach's influence, to "avant-garde literature." Some of the best pens of the day were at home in its pages: André Bellesort, Pierre Drieu La Rochelle, Marcel Jouhandeau, Jean de La Varende, Thierry Maulnier, Henry de Montherlant, Claude Roy, Henri Troyat, and many others. For a young author like Gabrielle Roy, who was completely unknown and belonged to no "network," appearing in such a publication was close to miraculous; it was hard to imagine more powerful encouragement, more dazzling confirmation of her potential.

And yet the miracle was not as great as all that. For several years, *Je suis partout* had been taking an interest in French Canada, a "prolific and faithful people" on whom the paper had published an article by Robert de Roquebrune in November 1937. In January 1938, this interest, sustained by the ideological capital that Brasillach and his friends were counting on making out of it, brought about the inauguration of a "Canada" page because, the editors wrote, "this admirable country where the French tradition is preserved in so proud and pure a fashion should be better known to the French. . . ." The make-up of this page, which appeared very irregularly, was placed in the hands of the Québécois Dostaler O'Leary, then a journalist at the Montreal paper *La Patrie*, who was the theoretician of a conservative and anti-democratic French-Canadian independentism.

It was for this Canadian page that three articles by Gabrielle Roy were accepted. They appeared in the issues of *Je suis partout* of 21 October and 30 December 1938 and 18 August 1939. The first, titled "Les derniers nomades," was a portrait – an unflattering one – of the Saulteux of the Canadian West; the second, "Noëls canadiens-français," was an evocation of old-time French-Manitoban Christmases; and the third, "Comment nous sommes restés français au Manitoba," explained to French readers how French Manitobans had stayed French. There is nothing worth noting about these texts in themselves except their rather clumsy style and a certain ideological naïveté. Still, they are important by reason of the role they played that summer of 1938 in Gabrielle's turn toward a writing career.

In the pages of her autobiography that tell of her decision to write, she stresses the fact that it was in French that she chose to write:

> For a time I had thought it might be a good thing to write in English; I had tried with some success and I was torn. Then suddenly there could no longer be any hesitation. The words coming to my lips and from the point of my pen were French, from my lineage, my ancestral bonds. They rose to my soul like the pure waters of a spring filtering through layers of rock and hidden obstacles.[40]

A startling fact, perhaps. Gabrielle had not only been living in London for several months but had received all her education in English and at this point most of the literature she was reading was still in English. And yet she chose to write in French. She would recognize later that French, being her mother tongue, was easier to handle than English, and that to become an English writer she would have had to work "very, very hard."[41] Another explanation would come to light in one of the last interviews she granted, not long before her death:

> I soon discovered that one couldn't write in two languages at the same time. I just wasn't the same person in English that I was in French. When I wrote in English, I was less serious. *L'anglais me donnait un ton frivole.* In St. Boniface we had an accent when we spoke English and we had a little difficulty expressing ourselves. *Alors, on s'attendait que nous soyons "funny".* On the other hand, French is the language of my heart. In French, I was able to express my deepest and most profound thoughts and feelings.[42]

This said, she did not on the spot give up all thought of writing in English, as can be seen from at least one unpublished manuscript that goes back perhaps to this period or the years immediately following her

At Oxford, 1938. (NLC NL-19178)

In Kew Gardens (London), 1938. (NLC NL-19167)

Esther and William Perfect in their garden at Upshire. (Photo taken by Gabrielle Roy; NLC NL-19171)

At Prats-de-Mollo, 1938. (NLC NL-19151)

From *La Revue populaire*, October 1939 (Larose photo). The caption, translated from French, reads:

"A number of readers have written enquiring as to the background of Mlle Gabrielle Roy, whose excellent article on Canada House in London we published in the August issue of *La Revue Populaire*. Mlle Gabrielle Roy, a French Canadian, was born in St-Boniface, Manitoba. Her first contributions were to the *Toronto Star Weekly*, the *Winnipeg Free Press*, and the Winnipeg Catholic publication the *North West Review*, as well as *La Liberté*, which is edited by Monsieur Donatien Frémont. The major Parisian weekly *Je Suis Partout* has also published several of her articles on Canada. . . . A dramatic artist as well as a journalist, Mlle Roy has also performed at the Ottawa Drama Festival with the Cercle Molière of Winnipeg. After studying dramatic art with Mme Alice Gachet in England and in France, Mlle Roy returned to Canada in April 1939. Since then she has been contributing to a variety of Montreal newspapers and magazines. On radio she plays the role of *Colette d'Avril* in the daily Radio-Canada program *Vie de Famille*, and also performs in *Miss Trent's Children*."

Aboard the *Marie-Louise*
at Port-Daniel, 1940.
(NLC NL-17532)

On assignment among the Montagnais of Sept-Îles, 1941. (NLC NL-19172)

Family reunion at the "Villa Antoinette," Tangent (Alberta), summer 1941. *Front, left to right*: Anna and Clémence. *Rear*: Mélina and Adèle. (NLC NL-19174)

Mélina in California, May 1939. (F. Ricard coll.)

At Adèle's, Tangent
(Alberta), 1942.
(NLC NL-17530)

In St-Boniface, after Mélina's death, summer 1943. *Front, left to right*: Clémence, Anna, and Gabrielle. *Rear*: Aunt Rosalie and Adèle. (Photo taken by Blanche, Rosalie's daughter; NLC NL-19173)

Henri Girard. (F. Ricard coll.)

At Rawdon, winter 1943 or 1944.
(NLC NL-18616)

Henri Girard at Rawdon, around 1944.
(F. Ricard coll.)

At a party at the Frelighsburg farm of Premier Adelard Godbout, 1942. (NLC NL-19152)

Henri Girard and Gabrielle at a party at the Frelighsburg farm of Premier Adelard Godbout, 1942. (NLC NL-19153)

On assignment to
research log driving,
1945. (NLC NL-19148)

With Saint-Henri children, 1945. (Conrad Poirier photo; NLC NL-19150)

return to Canada.[43] However, it was in French that she wrote all her major works to come.

For the moment, writing was meeting not only her inner needs; there was also a question of living from it, or making something from it at least, for after ten months in Europe the money she had brought with her was beginning to run out. Encouraged by the acceptance of her texts by *Je suis partout*, she began to send others to Canadian publications in hope that they too would earn her a little money. And things went not so badly. The weekly paper *La Liberté* of St-Boniface accepted four "Lettres de Londres," which appeared between 27 July and 21 December 1938, while *Le Devoir* of Montreal and the *Northwest Review* of Winnipeg each published an article. All these are short, topical articles or sketches based on Gabrielle's experiences in England. Their literary value is very limited.

Having pieces published strengthened the young woman's resolve and convinced her that she could live by her pen if she wished. In any case, it was at this moment that she decided to try her luck and stay an extra year in Europe, as she announced to the St-Boniface School Commission in a letter on 23 July 1938. Although her request arrived a little late, the commission immediately granted her a renewal of her leave of absence.[44]

But writing meant not just doing potboiler travelogues. More than anything, Gabrielle wanted to prove herself as a storyteller and writer of fiction. So she returned to her inspiration of earlier years and began again to write stories. Most went into the wastebasket or remained unpublished, but we can imagine that a number of the stories she published after settling in Montreal were written or at least begun here in Upshire, in the little room overlooking the downs where, nestled in her pillows, she would write for long hours with her portable typewriter on her knees, and with Esther downstairs trying to make as little noise as possible while washing up after breakfast.[45]

Homeward Bound

Having given up her room on Lillie Road, Gabrielle stayed at Century Cottages until the end of August. Then after a day trip to the Malvern Drama Festival in Worcestershire, where she saw a performance of George Bernard Shaw's *Saint Joan*, she returned to London and took a new room even farther from the city centre, in a house owned by people by the name of Norton, at No. 4 Sutton Lane, Chiswick. Bereft – or relieved – without Stephen, Gabrielle resumed her activities of the previous winter, going here and there with Phyllis, Bohdan, or David, meeting other Canadians at Canada House, taking afternoon tea at Lady Frances's, and perhaps spending more weekends in the country with the rural gentry. Her social life was well filled and there were plenty of beaus. "I collect two or three a week," she wrote to Léonie. "I do wish you were here. How you'd chuckle at the hundreds of funny little obsessions the English have."[46] In her free time she enjoyed her favourite walks along the Thames embankments, in Strand-on-the-Green, and in the botanical gardens at Kew which was across the river from where she was staying.

And yet there was not the same exhilaration as the previous year. To begin with, there was the international situation; the threat of war was creating great uncertainty, particularly for foreign nationals. The atmosphere was tense. And now that she had turned to literature, Gabrielle sensed that there was less reason for being in England. Her studies in dramatic art were less enticing. In early autumn, she signed up for workshops at an experimental little theatre, but very soon stopped going to them and did not return to the Guildhall or to her private lessons with Madame Gachet. In fact dramatic arts hardly interested her at all any more, and her faith in her future as an actress was rapidly fading. In *Enchantment and Sorrow* she recounts that it was then, toward the end of 1938 or at the very beginning of 1939, that she decided to give up the stage altogether. Or, rather, that the decision was forced on her for reasons of health. A doctor, she says, told her that she did not have either the physical constitution or the respiratory strength for a career on the stage. According to Adèle's reporting of what Gabrielle told her in 1942, her sister's decision was owing to the fact that her voice was judged unsuitable for radio, and her diction too flawed.[47]

Whichever the case, all indicates that she did at this time give up what had been one of her most cherished ambitions. The thrill of the stage that she had experienced with the Cercle Molière and the Little Theatre, the hope she had conceived of becoming a great actress and winning fame and fortune, all of this suddenly burned out, or at least dropped back to second place behind what now looked like her true vocation.

Why stay in London, then, where life was so expensive? Her financial reserves were melting away alarmingly. Should she go back to Upshire and spend more happy days under Esther's wing? She considered this, but the Perfects were not able to take her in. She decided then to be back in Canada for Christmas. At least, so she announced to her friends and family, judging by an item in *La Liberté*: "Mlle Gabrielle Roy, after studying dramatic art and French elocution in London and Paris for a year and a half, is to return soon to St-Boniface."[48]

At the last minute she changed her mind, or rather she decided to indulge in a last vacation before heading home. She decided to go where rich English people liked to go, to the Midi, the South of France, both because she needed warmth and sunshine to help her recover from her respiratory problems and because, since reading Daudet, the region appealed to her as "the great dream of [her] youth."[49] She would spend almost all the money she had left on this trip, augmented by loans, especially from Bohdan and a London friend, Connie Smith, and perhaps Lady Frances.

She left for Nice in early January 1938. From the moment of arrival, she was dazzled: "Everything was flooded with light."[50] And Provence amply fulfilled its promise. For three months the traveller lived in a state of continuous enthralment, nurtured by the charm of the countryside, the friendliness of the people, and a feeling of freedom, a total lightness of being as if all in her was relaxed, as if she no longer had memories or cares, as if, after eighteen months of struggling against herself, suddenly nothing existed outside the pleasure of being there under the sun, blending with the beauty of things around her. Some forty years later, she would write:

> I don't know if I've ever been as happy as in those three months I spent wandering with a pack on my back from St-Tropez to Ramatuelle, from Ramatuelle to Agay or Mouans-Sartoux, from the little Maures mountain range to the rocky inlets and rounded coves of the sea, intoxicated by the smells, the light, the heat, the people's gaiety, their tartness too sometimes [. . .] During these few months I must have been as if without a care, without a future, without ties, perhaps without a country other than that for which our hearts yearn innocently, in none but the pure and radiant clarity of the sky.[51]

She spent the first four or five weeks with Ruby Cronk of Toronto, whom she had met during the Channel crossing. They roamed the countryside together, Côte-d'Azur, Bouches-du-Rhône, Camargue, Languedoc. They had no itinerary except what took their fancy at the moment or as chance meetings suggested. They walked or rode bicycles, took a *micheline* or a bus, and sometimes waited by the side of the road for a good Samaritan to come along and take them aboard. They would stop for the night at a little village inn and might stay a few days if they liked the way they were received and the country around looked promising.[52]

But Ruby eventually went home. Gabrielle then went to stay at Castries, between Nîmes and Montpellier, in a family boarding house kept by two elderly ladies, Madame Paulet-Cassan and her sister Thérèse, where the two travellers had spent several days the previous month.[53] Here, Gabrielle found the same ambiance as at Century Cottages: a place in the country yet not too isolated, the possibility, if she wished, to go walking in the neighbourhood or withdraw into a solitude in which women under the spell of her charm lavished her with pamperings and affection, everything she needed, in short, to turn again to her little type-writer and start writing stories and articles, which she put away in her baggage to take back with her to Canada.[54]

Going back to Canada was a move she could not put off any longer. At the end of March, after celebrating her thirtieth birthday, she left Castries and before heading north went to Perpignan, and from there to Prats-de-Mollo-la-Preste, a town in the western Pyrenees three miles from the Spanish border. After the three idyllic months she had just spent, reality here was brutal. In Spain, General Franco's armies had taken Barcelona in January and now had just entered Madrid; with the civil war nearing its end, the republican partisans had been routed and were fleeing reprisals by seeking refuge in villages across the border in France. At Prats-de-Mollo, the horror had reached a peak and Gabrielle joined in the relief work as best she could for a few days. But she was also there as a budding journalist, to see war at close hand and denounce it. She took photographs, learned how things had been and were now for the refugees, wrote an article sympathetic to the republicans, and sent it to *La Presse* in Montreal, which never printed it.[55]

The time had come to leave. Before taking the boat for Canada she went to say her goodbyes. On the way to England, she stopped for a few days in Paris to see Madame Jouve and go to the theatre (this was when she saw *The Seagull* at the Pitoëffs' theatre). Once in London, she wrote a line to Stephen, who did not reply. She may have gone out one last time with her friend Bohdan, whom she would never see again, for he died the following year in a German air raid, after having married an English musician. Finally, she spent her very last days in Europe in Upshire with

Esther. She boarded ship in Liverpool at the beginning of April 1939. Hitler's tanks entered Warsaw five months later.

"I felt I had failed in everything," the narrator of *Enchantment and Sorrow* writes, "love, drama, writing. Yes, in everything."[56] It is true that she was returning to the land of her birth without having achieved the goal she had so long been striving toward. Neither fame nor fortune were within reach and she had no idea what was to become of her. Still, two things at least had changed. First, she had succeeded in living alone for nearly two years; her emancipation and callow youth were well and truly over. Next, she had begun to see where her vocation lay; not in theatre as she had thought, but in literature. She had not yet produced anything of much worth, but it was here that an opening might lie.

The final pages of *Enchantment and Sorrow* relate Gabrielle's arrival in Montreal and the dilemma she had to face. Would she return to St-Boniface and go back to her job at the Institut Provencher, as reason and her filial duty would have her do? Or should she not use the momentum she had built up, keep steering toward her dreams, and try her luck in Montreal? On the one hand, there were those repeated appeals from Mélina, who longed for her daughter's return and wanted her by her side to lighten her old age. But on the other, there was this irrepressible, still unsatisfied urge to escape her insignificant destiny and at long last reach those "expanded horizons" that were taking so long to get to, and that she could not give up striving for.

After some reflection her mind was made up. It had been made up long ago, in fact, ever since the day when as a girl she had resolved to reject the life her mother and her people were preparing for her. She would not go back to Provencher, she would stay in Montreal to give herself another year or two, as she wrote then to Mélina.[57] And so she chose once again to pursue her own adventure, setting aside her duty of loyalty.

> I was suddenly seeing that I could now no longer live, breathe, much less write, in the rarefied atmosphere of French life in my native province. [. . .] Without for the time being suspecting how strong a bond would tie me to this city, I stayed. And I threw myself into writing in exactly the way one throws oneself into water without knowing yet how to swim.[58]

One thinks here of what Marthe Robert writes about Robinson Crusoe's "rejection of his family," when, in defiance of his parents, he decides "to succeed by taking risks [. . .], with no other baggage than self-confidence and the will to *arrive*": "having wished to become nobody's son he becomes in fact completely orphaned, completely alone, the innocent self-begetter in a kingdom of complete solitude."[59]

Starting Out in Montreal

The island of Montreal has little in common with Defoe's hero's island. We would need to think more of Rastignac, another orphan by choice, or Jean Lévesque, an authentic orphan, as a model for Gabrielle Roy in these years just beginning. This time she was in the lion's den and there was no way out. She was going to need all her energy and determination to get herself known, command attention, find the necessary means of earning a living first of all, but also make a place for herself, a leading place if possible, in a milieu in which no one knew her and everyone wanted a piece of the cake. Gabrielle would say late in life that her Montreal years had been particularly hard. "Melancholy, loneliness, almost indigence were my only companions";[60] and yet she would depict these years as "tremendously exhilarating, [. . .] the most wonderful years of my life."[61]

When the train let her off at Windsor Station in the spring of 1939[62] Gabrielle had hardly a cent left to her name. Opposite the bus terminus on Stanley Street, south of Dorchester (Boulevard René-Lévesque today), she found a seedy, minuscule room for $3 a week, "the most horrid little room imaginable except in a prison."[63] Fortunately she soon received the funds accumulated in her pension account from the Manitoba school authorities in response to her letter of resignation. This came to perhaps $100, which was not much, but it did take care of the immediate future and afford her a more suitable room. The one she found this time, thanks to Pat Cossak, a friend who worked at Windsor Station, was farther west on Dorchester Street, on the south side in a sector of Westmount that was like the country in the city, as the new arrival described it in a short text from this period:

> You'd think you had just come upon the antiquated heart of some sleepy small town. All is placid and serene. The hundred-year-old trees that flood this corner of Montreal with shade vie together to link their boughs and form a peaceful avenue that gives shelter to houses with quiet façades. [. . .] But best of all on this peaceful Dorchester Street is a big house with

tiers of gables and cornices in which, high up facing the street, is a row of three identical little windows; three enchanting little windows, each made, you'd think, especially to frame a young and pensive face. . . .[64]

Gabrielle would spend all her years in Montreal in this part of the city, where life went on entirely in English and where she found somewhat the same atmosphere she had known and loved in London. But her new room, although less wretched than its predecessor, was on the top floor and had the disadvantage in summer of becoming "a real furnace, beneath its white-hot roof."[65]

It was shortly after this move, it seems, that she met George Wilkinson, a former United Church minister turned labour leader in Newfoundland during the Depression and living for some years now in Montreal, where he had continued to be active in leftist circles.[66] He was a man of forty-four years of age who had studied in the best universities but had been left fearful if not unbalanced by his experiences with the Newfoundland police. According to Ben-Z. Shek, on the strength of information from a friend of Wilkinson now deceased, he and Gabrielle were lovers, even "engaged," and lived together for a time. This is not impossible, but seems unlikely considering the nature of a boarding house like Gabrielle's at this time. "Living together" might simply mean that she and Wilkinson were boarders in the same house, no more and no less. Whatever the case, it is virtually certain that Gabrielle did know Wilkinson,[67] but also that if she was his mistress their liaison did not last beyond the summer or autumn of 1939 since, as we shall see, she then made a new friend – or lover – who was to become much more important in her life.

For the moment, in the course of these first months in Montreal, one thing was paramount for her: to place her texts, get herself known in the literary and journalistic milieu, and immediately begin the long climb of her career as a writer. However, since she needed money and had no help to fall back on, unlike classical college graduates, priests, and children of well-heeled families, she had only one choice, to become a "poor ink-slinger"[68] – a freelance journalist earning small fees.

She launched her campaign the minute she arrived. Armed with her articles published in *Je suis partout* and several Canadian publications, she made the rounds of editors' offices.[69] At the weekly *Le Jour*, founded a year and a half earlier by Jean-Charles Harvey, the sensationalist author of *Les Demi-civilisés* (1934), the assistant editor Émile-Charles Hamel proposed that she write articles for the women's page, which

Gabrielle accepted with alacrity despite a frugal fee: $3 per "paper" of four or five pages each.

And so there appeared in *Le Jour* of Saturday, 6 May 1939, on page 7, an article bearing Gabrielle Roy's name and entitled "Amusante hospitalité." In light tone, it depicts everyday life in a smart-set English country house as seen by a visiting Canadian student. Like a number of those that followed, it was likely written in Europe when Gabrielle was accumulating material with a view to coming home. Its publication inaugurated Gabrielle's journalistic career in Montreal, a career which was to last six years and quite quickly achieve appreciable success. There was a period of learning and trial and error while she was virtually unknown and had to sell her texts wherever she could, gradually compelling recognition of her name, although this did not last more than a year or two. By the end of 1941, in the penpushing circles of Montreal, she had become a relatively well-known journalist and story writer with a style pleasing to mass market readers and magazine editors, so that her texts were published readily, her fees were increasing, and she was able to live from her work.

But in 1939 this was still in the future. Throughout the summer, while the journalistic community was working at half-speed on account of the summer vacations, she had no choice but to take her article every week to *Le Jour* on Ste-Catherine Street not far from St-Denis Street. From May 20 to August 19, she missed only one issue of the paper.[70] Her contributions became rather less regular after this but continued until March 1940. Altogether she provided over thirty texts to Jean-Charles Harvey's weekly.[71]

Le Jour was considered one of the most avant-garde papers of the day.[72] Politically and ideologically, the ferocious liberalism and anti-nationalism of its editor and publisher, even socialism on the part of some of its writers, was in sharp variance with the generally ultra-conservative if not reactionary agendas then in favour with the majority of francophone intellectuals. The same held in art and literature, where *Le Jour*'s contributors, while not being exactly avant-garde, nevertheless rejected the prevailing conformity and traditionalism and advocated what one might call genuine modernism. These contributors were different in the quality of their writing, their independence of mind, and even their relatively marginal position in the literary milieu of the day, whether they belonged to the new generation, like Jean-Paul Lemieux (born in 1904), Jean-Jules Richard (1911), Émile-Charles Hamel (1914),

Yves Thériault (1915), Réal Benoit (1916), Paul Toupin (1918), and Gilles Hénault (1920), or were established authors like Alfred DesRochers, Jovette Bernier, Jean Narrache, Jean-Aubert Loranger, and Louis Dantin, the paper's head literary critic. Although its circulation was not large (around ten thousand copies), *Le Jour*, in contrast to a magazine like *La Relève*, was an immediate introduction to the world of journalism, combative rather than informative journalism undoubtedly, but an atmosphere in which pressure was constant; a contributor had to write fast, have style, and be able to interest a wide public and sense the spirit of the moment. For a beginning journalist it was excellent schooling.

This said, Gabrielle's position at *Le Jour* was rather peripheral. She was in sympathy with the ideas of Harvey and his team, but her role with the paper was not at all political. Confined to the women's page, her articles had no pretence other than to entertain her readers in an amusing and original way. Any subject would do, as long as it offered a certain degree of absurdity. Sometimes the writer would recall her travels in France and England, sometimes present little vignettes of life in Montreal, sometimes offer totally fictional little stories;[73] in all cases, the only thing that mattered was to be amusing, unpredictable, and never to dabble in anything serious or depart from a tone of light conversation. And so it seems rather much to draw from these writings composed in haste for the purpose of entertaining and with purely potboiling intent ("only platitudes,"[74] Gabrielle would say later) some vision of the world or articulate political thought. In fact, the only interesting thing about them if any is the rudimentary skill or professionalism they display – the beginning of a certain style and a certain humour that will reappear, refined and more skilfully handled, in the seasoned writer's short stories and even some of her books.

As for Gabrielle's relationship with the group of journalists, writers, and intellectuals who gravitated about Jean-Charles Harvey, practically nothing is known of it. Only Gilles Hénault, much later, would remember having been there at the same time as she. George Wilkinson was writing articles for *Le Jour* and she was seeing him, of course. Beyond this, her social life was like that of all immigrants newly arrived in a strange town who have no choice in the beginning but to socialize with the only people they know; for her, these were her fellow Manitobans.

In Montreal at this time, there was a small, quite active Franco-Manitoban community, composed mostly of young people of Gabrielle's age who had left their province on account of the Depression and had come to look for work in Quebec, where they made efforts to keep in touch with one another, saw each other regularly, and helped each other out as best they could. One of their meeting places was the boarding house run by the Benoist sisters on Jeanne-Mance Street, where Gabrielle was in the habit of eating in company with other francophones transplanted like her to Montreal. One she used to see there in particular was the younger sister of Renée Deniset, Jacqueline, who had left St-Boniface in 1937 to become secretary to Émile Couture, himself a childhood friend of Gabrielle's and now superintendent of colonization for Canadian National Railways. Soon she would also rediscover Louis Gauthier, her neighbour on Deschambault Street as a boy. He was now an architect, a graduate of Columbia University, working for the federal government and living in Montreal. Being better off than Gabrielle, now and then Louis would take her to a movie, a restaurant, or a concert on the mountain. Although she did not regularly attend Franco-Manitoban gatherings, Gabrielle did go as a matter of principle at times. She was present at a Christmas party that Émile Couture held at his home in St-Lambert, and in January 1942 she even attended an official reception held by the Association des Anciens du Manitoba on the occasion of a visit to Montreal by the prelate of St-Boniface, Monseigneur W. L. Jubinville.

While this kind of company could be a refuge on days of loneliness and discouragement, and could be turned to if need be for help, a connection, or a loan of a few dollars, Gabrielle had no intention of getting trapped in it, of attaching too much importance to being Franco-Manitoban. She was in Montreal not to perpetuate her past but to distance herself from it, escape her origins, build her own identity in some way, relying only on her own resources and her unshakable confidence in her lucky star.

A Happy Encounter

Besides her column in *Le Jour*, the budding journalist did succeed in selling a couple of texts here and there in the few months following her return to Canada, one to *La Revue populaire* and another to *Paysana*. But none of this was really of any consequence or brought in enough money to meet her needs. This was to change when, around midsummer, her efforts took her to the offices of *La Revue moderne* on Notre-Dame Street East.[75]

Founded in 1919 by Madeleine (a pseudonym for Anne-Marie Gleason-Huguenin), over the years this monthly had become one of the most popular and financially successful of French-Canadian magazines, until internal strife almost brought about its disappearance in 1938. When Gabrielle appeared on its doorstep it had just been bought by the young, dynamic Roland Beaudry, who undertook a sweeping overhaul of the magazine, giving it a more attractive cover, a new team, and above all stronger editorial direction in what had always been the backbone of the publication, its literary content. This literary content was essentially mass-appeal literature addressing a readership as broad as possible and composed very largely of women. What this readership was looking for was not stylistic prowess but escape, psychological analysis, and the titillations of love. In this genre, the *pièce de résistance* of every issue of *La Revue moderne* was the "complete novel" by a popular French author of the kind typified by the ineffable works of Delly and Magali, chronicling the amorous tribulations of pure and romantic young girls assailed by every imaginable adversity, battles between depraved evildoers and handsome rescuers, kisses by the seaside at sunset, dialogue dripping with "intensity," exotic settings (Europe and North Africa), and the final triumph of love, luck, and virtue.

La Revue moderne's new owner held to a proven formula by continuing to publish these "complete novels" but took a bolder step in deciding to include in the magazine a certain number of stories by Canadian authors. In order to attract these authors and celebrate the magazine's relaunching, a major competition was announced in May 1939. For the best story published in the magazine in the course of the year to come, a prize of $500 would be awarded – a tidy sum for the day in those circles.

The efforts to revamp *La Revue moderne* bore fruit; its circulation rose rapidly from 31,000 copies in 1940 to 70,000 in 1943 which, according to the magazine's management, could easily have been surpassed had it not been for government restrictions on paper. Roland Beaudry was not alone responsible for this success, however. Equally if not more important was the role of the literary editor, Henri Girard.

A fascinating figure, this Girard. Rather mysterious besides. There are few people who even remember him today, and hardly anyone has written a word about him. And yet this was a remarkable man, a great intellectual whose keen, cultivated mind was open to the most advanced thinking and artistic developments. He was a free thinker, which perhaps explains the oblivion into which his name has fallen, along with the names of others whose lives and thinking were out of step with the intellectual conformity of prewar Quebec. Thus we have only very fragmentary information about him, although sufficient to give us an idea of his personality and the considerable role he played in the career and personal evolution of Gabrielle Roy.

Girard was born in Montreal on 1 January 1900. He began to publish articles as an art critic in the late 1920s in *La Revue moderne*, which at the time was run by Robert Choquette, then by Jean Bruchési. An habitué of the Saturday gatherings organized by Albert Pelletier, publisher of the magazine *Les Idées*, he subsequently became a journalist at the daily paper *Le Canada*, where he was an associate of Olivar Asselin.

Ideologically, Girard was what one would call a left-wing liberal; although not a member of a left-wing party, his leanings were socialist and anti-Fascist. In 1937 he and Edmond Turcotte, the editor of *Le Canada*, were among the few Montrealers present at André Malraux' speech in favour of the Spanish republicans. He also took part in protest meetings that were called when Maurice Duplessis's government tried to muzzle left-wing opposition with the adoption of the so-called padlock law, meetings that consequently drew the ire of stiff-necked conservatives.

But Girard was first and foremost interested in art and literature. For *Le Canada* he wrote articles on painting, architecture, drama, and poetry, each time as an advocate of renewal and modernization. Among others he celebrated Saint-Denys Garneau's *Regards et Jeux dans l'espace* when the book appeared in 1937.[76] As an art critic he was close to Gérard Morrisset, John Lyman, Robert Ayre, and their kind, who were following the changes going on in painting in Montreal with a sympathetic eye and doing the groundwork for acceptance of the modernist upheavals that were to follow, triggered by the war and the immediate postwar ferment. Paul-Émile Borduas quotes Henri Girard, alongside Maurice Gagnon and Marcel Parizeau, as one of his allies in his differences with the École du meuble, and in 1948 Girard was one of the few commentators to speak out in favour of the groundbreaking manifesto *Le Refus global*.[77] His positions on aesthetics and literature were marked by sound eclecticism; while opposed to academic attitudes and open and amenable to new movements, he was wary of audacity for its own sake and remained attached to what he considered the great eternal values of art and literature: harmony, equilibrium, beauty – values which to him were entirely reconcilable with innovation and modernity.[78]

Henri Girard did not write a book, but his articles demonstrate great stylistic mastery. Like his friend Gérard Dagenais (whom we shall meet shortly), he knew his language to perfection and was considered an authority on the subject. So *La Revue moderne* could not have recruited a better literary editor. Girard held this position from May 1939 until June 1942. As such, he was responsible for the quality of the texts published and especially for the choice of stories to appear in each issue. His ideas on this were forthright: the readers must be given "all the literature possible and, particularly, all the *Canadian* literature possible."[79] Canadian literature in general had a poor reputation with the magazine's readership. "Our literature," wrote one columnist, "is not a whole lot of fun. Our writers generally are [so] solemn and severe, you'd say they were constantly bearing the fate of the world on their shoulders. They love to lay out pretentious paragraphs oozing tedium."[80] One of Girard's goals was to break down this association of Canadian literature with platitude. To this end, he urged authors to abandon the old, conventional plots, shake off the old stiffness, and be more "modern." He wrote in 1940:

> There is literature and literature. We are not casting a slur, it goes without saying, against those upon whom fate or fortune has smiled and who can only contemplate the ultimate in literature, but we have believed and still believe that people of more humble tastes, like you and ourselves, have the right to read works that are interesting to them and afford them hours of pleasure.[81]

This "interesting" literature was not necessarily facile literature according to Girard; he had in mind works "that show real, live characters in action" and "accurately describe today's Canadian society." He was by no means preaching literary revolution; *La Revue moderne* was an unmistakably commercial publication and not at all avant-garde, although it did in its own way illustrate and encourage the dissemination in French Canada of a new, more contemporary, more accessible taste, an urban taste more in tune with the expectations of readers of the day who adored movies, popular songs, and "fridolinades," musicals featuring Gratien Gelinas as "Fridolin." Under Girard's guidance, this was the spirit in which *La Revue moderne*, in each issue, published four or five stories by authors as well regarded as Robert Choquette, Ringuet, or

Alain Grandbois, but also by young, still unknown writers whose names might have been Adrienne Choquette, Germaine Guèvremont, Claire Richard, or Gabrielle Roy.

When Gabrielle appeared before Henri Girard, her timing was perfect. The magazine needed manuscripts, and those the newcomer was submitting appealed immediately to the literary editor who, in the August 1939 issue, hastened to announce to his readers that a first story by Mademoiselle Gabrielle Roy would be published "next month." "La conversion des O'Connor" received favoured treatment; it was announced on the cover, commented upon on the introductory page, and figured first in the block of five stories contained in the issue.

Yet it is not an outstanding text. In the O'Connor household there is concern over the absence of Lizzie, the mother, who in fact has only taken off temporarily on a shopping binge, a fleeting show of rebellion against her condition as woman of all work. She is soon gripped by remorse and returns to the fold, where her husband and children have come to realize all that they owe her. What took Girard's fancy in this story was no doubt its lightness of tone, the liveliness of the narration, the skilful blend of humour and emotion, in short, all the characteristics of the pleasant, witty mass-market literature that the management of La Revue moderne was looking for.

But Henri Girard was not won only by Gabrielle's texts. He was equally if not more taken by the beauty, the vivacity, the self-confidence, the entire person of this young woman with the "green-grey eyes [that] look squarely into yours," he was to say, "[expressing] both an intense curiosity and the calm strength of intelligence."[82] In a word, he was smitten. And Gabrielle did not rebuff him.

Between the beautiful stranger and the solemn literary editor there developed a privileged relationship that lasted seven years. Everything worked to draw them together, beginning with their need for affection. Henri was married, but unhappily; his wife – a shrew, he complained – hated him and made his life miserable. And Gabrielle was like a lost bird, all alone in Montreal with no one to alight on. They confided in one another and discovered that they had the same sensitivity, the same taste for refinement, art, the beauties of nature. They shared the same ideals and had similar opinions on politics, social justice, and morality.

Gabrielle had several reasons for being enchanted. First there was Henri's sweet, tender personality; he was not very handsome, was on the plump side, but he had a heart of gold, never raised his voice, and

emanated infinite kindness. Then there was his immense culture, his
mastery of the French language, and his knowledge of contemporary literature. And finally there was his experience. Since he was ten years
older than she and had been moving in the journalistic and intellectual
circles of Montreal for over ten years, he knew everyone, journalists,
publishers, artists, politicians. He had friends and acquaintances everywhere, knew at which doors to knock, and had an unerring grasp of the
tacit rules governing journalistic and political circles. He was a powerful
man in other words, or one who knew how to win the ear of the powerful, which to a beginner like Gabrielle could only add to his charm.

In return, was there ever a pupil more winsome and promising than
Gabrielle? Henri had seen it at first sight. This young woman had everything she needed for success – talent, beauty, determination. The bond of
affection between them was inextricably entangled with no less strong a
bond of dependence and protection. Henri would be Gabrielle's mentor,
would take her career in hand and be her literary adviser and friend.

As a starter, he made the author of "La conversion des O'Connor" a
regular contributor to *La Revue moderne*; in the year 1939–1940, a text
by Gabrielle Roy appeared in every issue but two. In October, it was
"Le monde à l'envers," a story featuring a young woman in love and her
lady-killer husband. In November Girard reprinted the article titled
"Londres à Land's End," which Gabrielle had given a year earlier to the
Manitoban paper *La Liberté*, embellished this time with photographs
taken by the author. Then it was back to stories: "Cendrillon '40"
appeared in February 1940, followed by "Une histoire d'amour" in
March and then "Roi de coeur" in April. These texts are all in the same
touching, often sentimental vein, there is a lot of dialogue, the situations
are colourful, and curiously the characters are never French Canadians,
even when the action is set in or near Montreal. Broadly speaking this is
superficial, competently constructed literature. However two stories do
stand out somewhat: "Gérard le pirate" (May 1940), in which Gabrielle
clearly uses memories of her childhood in St-Boniface, and "Bonne à
marier" (June), which is the French version of "Jean-Baptiste Takes a
Wife," a comedy of rural life published in the *Toronto Star Weekly* three
years earlier.[83]

For each article published Gabrielle received $12, meaning that she
could double the monthly income she was then making from her contributions to *Le Jour*. Girard's generosity was demonstrated even more
significantly when "Le conversion des O'Connor" won *La Revue moderne*'s

short-story contest. A minor disappointment, however – there were two winners and Gabrielle had to share the $500 prize with another of the magazine's habituées, Claire Richard, alias Jean Desprez, or Laurette Larocque-Auger by her real name, whose story "Le coeur de Nadine" appeared in the January 1940 issue. The texts had, of course, been properly evaluated by a jury that was prestigious, impartial . . . and well advised.

But *La Revue moderne* was not all, and Gabrielle could not go very far with the small fees and the little prestige the magazine was affording her. She must do more, she must do better, and to this end must broaden her plan of attack. With the help of her new friend she set out to diversify her activities and penetrate other areas likely to increase her earnings and make her talent more widely recognized.

The Mike and the Boards

As if publicly announcing her arrival on the Montreal scene, Gabrielle had her photograph taken by Larose, one of the most highly regarded studios in town. The picture was printed in large size in the October 1939 issue of *La Revue populaire*. It shows a lovely young woman with a shy but dignified expression, whose bright eyes, natural hairdo, and broad smile seem to be sending the world a message of happiness and confidence. Under the picture are detailed the beautiful newcomer's background and qualifications: her birth in St-Boniface, membership in the Cercle Molière, studies in Europe, articles in *Je suis partout*.

It is also stated here that Mademoiselle Gabrielle Roy is a radio artist. Although she had discovered as she was ending her studies in Europe that she was not cut out for the stage, once settled in Montreal she was trying to turn her experience in dramatic art to account, if only to round out her monthly earnings. The prime source of employment for actors in those days was radio, which by now had achieved the status of mass media and was beginning its first golden age, the age of serialized fictional dramas or "soap operas." Thus it was that in the autumn of 1939, Gabrielle, perhaps through the good offices of Henri Girard, who had many friends at Radio-Canada and himself figured in public affairs programs, obtained an episodic role in the serialized radio play *Vie de famille* by Henry Deyglun.[84] Sponsored by Procter & Gamble, this daily program was in its second season and was so popular with the public that the periodical *Radiomonde* began publishing a print version of it in

December 1939. The character Gabrielle played and would continue to play until the end of the season was a sensitive young girl by the name of "Colette Avril." Among the other actors were Marthe Thierry, Nicole Germain, Guy Mauffette, Mimi d'Estée (wife of Deyglun), Jacques Auger (husband of Jean Desprez), and Marthe Nadeau, with whom Gabrielle developed a close friendship.

In the course of this season, 1939–1940, the former student at the Guildhall School of Music and Drama also took part in the activities of the Montreal Repertory Theatre (MRT).[85] This English-language troupe, founded in 1929 by Martha Allan, had quickly created a French section whose dynamism and distinction were then at their peak under the direction of Mario Duliani, greatly pleasing both theatregoers and the press, with the weekly Le Jour and Henri Girard's La Revue moderne in the vanguard. In the autumn of 1939, the MRT French section, renamed "Mont-Royal Théâtre français," announced its establishment in the Salle Saint-Sulpice on St-Denis Street and the arrival of new members, including the well-known actors Fred Barry, Albert Duquesne, and Marthe Thierry, and a newcomer, Gabrielle Roy.[86] Joining the Montreal theatrical circle, Gabrielle was reacquainting herself with a milieu and individuals she had known some years earlier in Ottawa at the Dominion Drama Festival.

Gabrielle Roy's name does not appear in the cast listing for any play, however. Her part was at a different level: writing. One of the MRT's missions had always been to encourage local playwriting, which was sorely in need of it. Thus in the autumn of 1939, aiming to stimulate creation and recruit new authors, the company announced a major competition for Canadian one-act plays. In the course of 1940, there would be four "galas" at each of which four plays would be presented, the best of which would be performed at a final gala. The jury to select the grand prize-winner was composed of Doctor Roméo Boucher, the journalist Louis Francoeur, and the novelist Philippe Panneton; cash prizes would be awarded to the competitors at the end of each gala and the grand prizewinner would receive an additional sum of $200.

Since the days of the Académie Saint-Joseph, Gabrielle had been accustomed to competitions. She submitted a play in one act and three scenes entitled La Femme de Patrick.[87] This is a stage adaptation of her first short story published in La Revue moderne, "La conversion des O'Connor," which had enjoyed "a great success."[88] The play was presented at the Salle Saint-Sulpice on Sunday, 2 June 1940, at the second "gala of unpublished French-Canadian plays"; Mario Duliani was the director; two of the actors were Paul Guèvremont and Pierre Dagenais.[89] The competing authors were all known by pseudonyms, as the artistic style of the day required. The other plays were *Comédienne* by Pierre Dutaut, *Lacets, crayons* by Pierre Andray and Carl Robert, and *Toto* by Jean Desprez, which won the first prize of the evening. Gabrielle's came third, bringing her a consolation prize of $15. Despite this, *La Femme de Patrick* received rather favourable press. "A lively comedy," wrote the *Le Jour*'s critic; "this is real theatre, with a strong note of originality and great personality," proclaimed *Le Canada*'s; as for the commentator in *Radiomonde*, Jean Desprez herself, she found that "the author has not sufficiently freed herself of the *short-story* form," and ascribed the play's failure to inadequate preparation by some of the actors.[90] Even so, the evening was such a success that the four plays were presented again several days later; and finally *La Femme de Patrick* was broadcast on June 15 over the radio station CKAC.[91] As for the grand prize, it was won by an unknown by the name of Gérard Bessette, who was just twenty years old, for *Hasard*, a verse play in which the action takes place in a bookstore.

This experience seems to have brought Gabrielle Roy's theatrical career to an end. During these years she did make some further attempts at playwriting but not much came of them. In her personal archives, there is the manuscript of "a radio play in four acts" titled "Oui, made-moiselle Line"[92] which probably dates from this time but was never performed. In February 1941 on the radio show *Je me souviens* she gave a dramatized adaptation of one of her stories previously published in *La Revue moderne*.[93] Finally, dating from 1942 (or 1943 at the latest), there is a play inspired by the Canadian West that remains unpublished.[94] That is all. Otherwise, Gabrielle's presence on radio was limited to a number of readings of her published stories by professional actors, which enabled her to reach a wider audience and increase her earnings from royalties somewhat.[95] In short, her career as an actress and playwright did not last beyond her very early years in Montreal, during which she was doing anything and everything to survive and get herself known.

Now drama for her was only something to fall back on. What interested her was literature, and in the circumstances literature meant journalism. An opportunity arose at this point that would allow her to drop the piecemeal commitments and the scramble for fees and really concentrate on writing as her chosen occupation.

A Seaside Vacation

In June 1940, Gabrielle Roy joined *Le Bulletin des agriculteurs* where soon, and for the five years to follow, she had a steady job, a steady income, readers who were both attentive and more varied than those she had previously had (who had been almost exclusively women), and a superlative training ground for writing – everything she needed in order to become a writer. After two years of wandering in Europe, after another year in Montreal while trying to carve a place for herself in the artistic and literary world, at last she was getting somewhere – she was going to be able to live by her pen, stop worrying about tomorrow, and give herself entirely to her calling. Being taken on at *Le Bulletin* was Gabrielle's first real breakthrough, her first recognition, and the event that steered her conclusively into writing. "I owe it to the intelligent understanding and generosity of the publishers of *Le Bulletin des agriculteurs*," she confided a few years later to Rex Desmarchais, "that I had the time and freedom to write my novel, *Bonheur d'occasion*."[96]

But how did she land this job when hardly anyone knew her and she, at this point, knew nothing about *Le Bulletin des agriculteurs*, which was published in Montreal but distributed exclusively in the rural areas of Quebec? In her interviews and later recollections, Gabrielle attributed the credit sometimes to helpful friends[97] but more often to her own personal initiative.[98] In reality, it seems that once again it was Henri Girard who played the decisive role by persuading René Soulard, the editor-in-chief of *Le Bulletin*, to hire his protégée.

In order to understand Girard's intervention, and more broadly the development of Gabrielle Roy's career in journalism, we must pause at the particular context of these wartime years.[99] The press in Montreal, like book publishing, was going through a phase of very vigorous expansion, owing both to the local economic recovery and the fact that there was no longer a supply of periodicals and books from France. The result, for the papers, magazines, and innumerable publishers springing up in Montreal, was unprecedented prosperity, enabling them to increase their production and circulation (despite paper rationing), diversify and liberalize their content while freeing themselves of church influence, and substantially increase their staffs. A young woman hoping to make a career in journalism and literature and arriving in Montreal around 1940 could hardly have chosen a better place and time; papers and periodicals were flourishing as never before, and more than ever before were in need of authors and high-quality texts.

La Revue moderne was a case in point, as we have seen; so was *Le Bulletin des agriculteurs*.[100] This monthly had been in existence since 1918, but its golden age came truly during the Second World War. Its circulation kept climbing, from 63,000 copies in 1939 to 145,000 in 1948. Its editorial content was transformed; although it remained a specialized periodical focusing on agricultural questions, its coverage broadened as its almost entirely rural readers, influenced by the war, the generalization of radio, and the rise of urbanization, became more receptive to a broader and more varied range of interests. A good proportion of each issue was thus devoted to "novels and stories" like those abounding in other periodicals of the period, filled with fine thoughts and exciting adventures. There was also the "Père Bougonneux" column authored by Valdombre (Claude-Henri Grignon), plus a range of articles on local and European current events. *Le Bulletin* was, in short, in the same situation as other weeklies and monthlies; it needed new blood and new material, meaning contributors who were as talented and original as possible.

For an understanding of the path taken by Gabrielle during the war, another factor besides this heyday for the press in general must be taken into account, and that is the political one. When Gabrielle arrived in Montreal in April 1939, Quebec was still governed by Maurice Duplessis's Union Nationale, but Adélard Godbout and the Liberals took power in the election of the following October 25 and kept it until August 1944. Since the Liberal party was re-elected in Ottawa in 1940, throughout these five years the Liberals therefore had power at both levels of government, and exerted even more direct influence over the political, economic, and ideological life of the country in that the promulgation of the War Measures Act in September 1939 gave the State virtually absolute powers of intervention and control. In Quebec, this situation partially explains the exceptional nature of government action during the war years, which turned the period into a kind of foretaste of the Quiet Revolution; there was the grant of woman suffrage in 1940, the compulsory education act in 1942, greater union recognition in 1944, and, in the same year, partial nationalization of electricity and the creation of Hydro-Québec.

In the world in which Gabrielle moved, the change of political regime had marked effects. It gave an enormous charge of energy to the press of Liberal allegiance, for whom the three years of the first Duplessis government had been a harsh exile in the wilderness. Overnight, the strength and visibility of papers and magazines close to the Liberal party burgeoned, thanks to the political and financial support coming their way from the men in power. Gabrielle, from the moment of her arrival in Montreal, had the good fortune – or the instinct – to get herself into this vigorously expanding network, first at *Le Jour*, then at *La Revue moderne*, whose new publisher Roland Beaudry was a well-known Liberal. As was Henri Girard, moreover, whose past at *Le Canada* and ties with Edmond Turcotte had made him known amply as one of the most convinced and reliably Liberal journalists in Montreal.

For Henri, helping Gabrielle meant above all using his contacts in the Liberal network for his young friend's benefit. There were influential Liberals all over in literary and journalistic circles, at Radio-Canada, at *La Revue populaire*, and at *Le Bulletin des agriculteurs*, whose owner was Arthur Fontaine, secretary and bagman of the Liberal party (a single organization federally and provincially in those days) and whose editor-in-chief, René Soulard, had known Girard when working for *Le Canada*. Moreover, *Le Bulletin*, as an agricultural publication, enjoyed special favour in the eyes of Premier Godbout, who was himself an agronomist. When Gabrielle appeared at the paper's offices, preceded by her friend's recommendation, the doors opened as if by magic. Not only was Monsieur Soulard anxious to receive her texts, but although she had never done any reporting either in *Le Bulletin* or elsewhere he agreed to her proposal that she go and spend part of the summer, all expenses paid, in a place already well known and about which even an experienced reporter would have trouble finding anything new to say, a place that in fact was a vacation area: the Gaspé.

Gabrielle would say later, "I had been dreaming of the Gaspé without knowing it; without ever having set eyes on it, I dreamed about it anyway, the way one dreams of Easter Island without knowing it either."[101] And so, glad to leave her mansard now that the dog days were turning it into a sweatbox, she took the train to Matapédia and from there the small local railway that winds its way along the Baie des Chaleurs to the town of Gaspé. On the way she decided to get off at Port-Daniel, where, not far outside the village, she rented a room in a house belonging to a fishing couple, Bertha and Irving McKenzie.

And as at Upshire, it was magical. This white house on the seashore, this room with its huge window, this landscape filled with light and the cries of birds gave the traveller the feeling of suddenly being at home "in a country never seen before, but [finding it] the way I had pined for it, and deep in my heart hoped for it to be. Thus there exist lands corresponding exactly to our least explainable dreams."[102] The McKenzies took to her with total affection, as Esther had done, and asked only to make her happy, responding to her smallest wants, seeing to her comfort and tranquillity, and for a pittance providing her with one of the havens of peace and safety for which she felt so great a need. For the next fifteen years, Gabrielle would return often to spend part of the summer at Port-Daniel with these two souls who in a way had replaced Esther and her father – part parents, part servants. During this first sojourn of the summer of 1940, she went for long walks and discovered the countryside. For the article she had promised *Le Bulletin des agriculteurs*, she went to Gaspé and from there to Rivière-aux-Renards and Grande-Vallée to gather information on the economics of fishing and the newly founded Pêcheurs unis movement. At Port-Daniel, she went out fishing with Irving or with Père Élias Langlois, an old sea dog she made friends with and who took her out on his *goélette* christened *Marie-Louise*. But mostly she busied herself reading and writing, to the point where to the villagers she became "the story-maker."[103]

When she returned to Montreal she had in her baggage at least two stories inspired by the Gaspesian setting. One, "Les petits pas de Caroline," is a humorous romance about a hardened bachelor who takes refuge in the Gaspé only to find love there. This was the first text by Gabrielle Roy to appear in *Le Bulletin des agriculteurs*, in October 1940. The second of the two, "La dernière pêche," would appear in *La Revue moderne* of November and was a melodrama on the death of an old fisherman by the name of Mathias Langlois. Four or five other stories that remain unpublished may also have been written during this summer or one of the following summers at Port-Daniel.[104] As to the investigative report *Le Bulletin* had sent her for, it was published in the November issue under the title "La belle aventure de la Gaspésie." Accompanied by photographs probably taken by Gabrielle herself, it is a carefully written, well-documented text whose content bears no resemblance to the usual stereotypes. In contrast to the tourist-trade blurb commonly churned out on the Gaspé, the journalist presents the picture of a region progressing by leaps and bounds and which is taking its social and economic modernization in hand, thanks to the cooperative movement and – partisan politics obliging – the enlightened aid of the State.

So that autumn Gabrielle's career as a "penpusher" was launched and
thereafter she no longer had to struggle to be published. In September
an article on Manitoba appeared in *La Revue populaire* and she resumed
her contributions to *La Revue moderne*, where, although interrupted
since May, her pieces continued to be much appreciated. Besides "La
dernière pêche," five of her stories were published by Henri Girard during
the season 1940–1941. Their themes and styles are varied. "Un Noël en
route" (December 1940) takes place in a countryside of Manitoban inspiration and recounts a difficult reunion between a vagabond and his
mother, from whom he has been separated for years. For others, the
writer uses Montreal as a setting to evoke the complicated love story of
an adolescent ("Avantage pour," October 1940), or the modest existence
of freelance artists ("À O.K.K.O.," April 1941). In "La sonate à l'aurore"
(March 1941), which she wrote after learning the news of the tragic death
of her friend Bohdan, she imagines the death in the London blitz of two
young musicians in love. Finally, "Six pilules par jour" (July 1941) and
"Embobeliné" (October 1941), which were in sequence, remind one
rather of the radio series by Robert Choquette, *La Pension Velder*, which
was all the rage at the time. The action takes place in the boarding-house
setting that Gabrielle knew well, with relations between unmarried
boarders developing into intrigues both comical and bittersweet.

Still, it was above all joining *Le Bulletin des agriculteurs* that was the
pivotal event for her. Initially, not counting the report on the Gaspé, *Le
Bulletin* received her as a short-story writer, publishing two more stories
in quick succession after "Les petits pas de Caroline" under the pseudonym "Aline Lubac." The first, titled "Le joli miracle" (December 1940), is
a Montreal variation on Puccini's *La Bohème*, in which a young art
student, Éric, meets Loubka, a pianist who adores Chekhov:

Opening [*The Seagull*] at random, she fell upon this passage in which
Trigorin says, "What is there splendid about my life? I am haunted day
and night by one persistent thought: I ought to be writing, I ought to be
writing, I ought . . . I have scarcely finished one novel when, for some
reason, I must begin writing another, then a third, and after the third a
fourth. I write incessantly, post haste, and I can't write in any other way."

Dramatic artists, painters, musicians, Loubka thought, are all subject
to a similar law, but they are dependent. A dramatic artist depends on
other artists, on the ambiance of a theatre and a special atmosphere to

communicate his creation; a painter can do nothing without colours; a musician nothing without the instrument he knows. As far as that goes, only the writer is independent. A pen and a sheet of paper is the most he needs to give form to his thought.

The other story, "La fuite de Sally," which appeared in *Le Bulletin* of January 1941, is a London story featuring a young woman whose husband, a young painter "with a gentle Slavic face," refuses to go with her on a walk in Epping Forest, where they have been before. Sally leaves alone and rediscovers "a small cottage of pink stone with a long thatched roof," where a little hunchbacked woman invites her into the garden and serves her a delicious tea among the bees and flowers.

All these texts were more or less repudiated later by Gabrielle. "[I] don't recognize myself at all in it any more," she would say about one of them in 1973. "The effect it has on me is strange. It's exactly as though I were reading another author's text."[105] It is true that most of these early stories, especially those for *La Revue moderne*, are graceless and immature. Yet they are not entirely devoid of interest. Besides illustrating the tenacity and passion for writing that was driving their author, they show a nice command of the conventions and procedures of mass-market literature. Since she knew her readers well, she not only knew how to give them what they wanted, which was sentimentality, light humour, escape, but one could say she did it with skill, spirit, and gaiety. This sensitivity to the tastes and expectations of readers was certainly one of the factors in the success of *Bonheur d'occasion*, whose style in certain ways is not so far from mass-market literature.[106] And since she was drawing most of her subjects from her own experience, the apprentice writer was gradually becoming accustomed to turning her life into stories, fables – into writing. Getting the knack.

And then, something not to be sneezed at, these texts were earning her money, so that late in 1940 she was able to escape her little room under the roof and – on advice from her friend Pat Cossak – move to a much more comfortable boarding house where she felt that "compared to what I'd had before I was in the lap of luxury."[107] The house, vanished today, was located not far from where she had been living, but on the north side of Dorchester Street, at No. 4059.[108] The landlady, Miss McLean, took an immediate liking to her and lavished her with small attentions. Except for a couple by the name of French, the boarders were all single; besides Pat Cossak there were Solange, and Gertrude, and Miss

Finley, and still others, and Gabrielle was soon on the best of terms with all of them. The journalist would be on the road a good deal, but Miss McLean's house would be her home port until 1943.

Discovering a City

The stories that Gabrielle published in her first two or three years after returning from Europe were one facet of her writer's apprenticeship, but these stylistic exercises, these less than totally successful attempts at finding her voice and giving form to stories with substance from a literary point of view, were not nearly as valuable a learning experience as the other activity that was soon absorbing her almost entirely – investigative reporting.

"It was around the end of 1940," Gabrielle was to say, "that I became attached permanently to *Le Bulletin des agriculteurs*."[109] The originality and stylistic merit of her article on the Gaspé had drawn attention and convinced the paper's management that Monsieur Girard's friend had the stuff to become an excellent contributor. She was therefore offered attractive conditions: total freedom in the choice of her subjects, a commitment to publish her articles regularly, and more substantial compensation together with payment of her travelling and living expenses while away gathering material.

Her first articles, those she began preparing in the course of the autumn of 1940 and which were published at intervals through the next year, are rather innocuous. Their subjects are almost exclusively agricultural – the end of the seigneurial regime, the modernization of farms, the operation of a college for young farmers sponsored by the provincial government, the story of a farm machinery manufacturer, the Quebec agricultural exhibition[110] – and there is nothing very special about the writing, except abundant use of the pronoun "I" and rather forced application of certain techniques little used in journalism, such as personification, repetition, and anticipatory dreams.

But this gawkiness was short-lived. Over the winter of 1941, while beginning a major investigative project on the city of Montreal, which was preparing to celebrate the 300th anniversary of its founding, the journalist honed her own style, mode of research, point of view, and even the very original and characteristic manner of writing that were to mark her production of years to come. From this investigation resulted four articles that appeared between June and September 1941 and are worth noting on several counts.

First, these articles are presented as a continued series and have a common title, *Tout Montréal*. This idea of a "series," a succession of texts devoted to a single subject, would become Gabrielle's preferred format for her contributions to *Le Bulletin des agriculteurs*. The advantage is that this format, a bit like the serial novel in fiction, helps to maintain and stimulate readers' interest from one issue to the next, and also allows the journalist all the necessary space to enlarge on the subject, probe it, treat it from various angles, and modulate it at will. In their structuring, the articles composing *Tout Montréal* are a foretaste of what was to be Gabrielle's "method" in all her investigative articles: a mixture of facts – historical, statistical, and other, gathered in the course of investigation both on site and through library research – and a strong element of subjective input, which sometimes takes the form of an autobiographical account of her own discovery of her subject and sometimes shows through lyricism or irony, but always involves and even requires a literary type of writing in which the utmost care is given to verbal invention, to imagery, to composition – in short, to the production of a text in which form is as important as content.

But most noteworthy of all in these articles is the vision of Montreal that they offer, a broad, complete vision that embraces the city in all its topographical, socio-economic, and human diversity. The first article, titled "Les deux Saint-Laurent" (June 1941), is constructed in two sections, two crossings, as it were. First, following St-Laurent Boulevard, the reader discovers the neighbourhoods of the old port, Ville-Marie, Chinatown, the streetcar terminus on Craig Street, Place Jacques-Cartier, Bonsecours Market. Then the direction of movement changes to the course of the St. Lawrence River, westward from the port as far as Lachine, passing through Verdun, Pointe-Saint-Charles, and Ville LaSalle. In her next article, "Est-Ouest" (July), the journalist takes the great arteries running westward from Bout-de-l'île to Westmount. Along Notre-Dame, Ste-Catherine, and Sherbrooke streets, she explores the district of Hochelaga, the Botanical Gardens, the streets around the Carré Saint-Louis, and the department stores of the west end. Under the title "Du port aux banques" (August), the third article concentrates on the most active, most vibrant parts of the city where there is also the greatest contrast. Here are evoked first the industrial districts of the centre-south, then St. James Street, the district of financial institutions and great trading companies. Finally, "Après trois cent ans" (September) recalls the history of Montreal and attempts to identify the great cultural traits that distinguish the city. Of the four articles in the series, this is probably the least successful, perhaps because it is more synthetic and necessarily more abstract, contrasting with the descriptive wealth of the preceding three which teem with details and in which the journalist shows herself fascinated by the vortex of multiple, unexpected, and contradictory sensations that create the fabric of urban existence.

Another positive quality of this picture of Montreal is its astonishing modernity. Modernity of language, dominated by nouns and nominal constructions with strong imagery and extremely precise vocabulary, but also modernity of perception and judgment. This is light-years from the stained-glass image generally affixed to Montreal in French-Canadian speeches and texts of the period, in which the same stereotypes are perpetually recycled: "the mystic city," "the world's second French city," "the city of a hundred and fifty spires," and so on.[111] Gabrielle's Montreal, in comparison, is a city of constant movement, of exchange and juxtaposition of opposites. It is a place impossible to summarize, so that only its physical presence can be grasped in the constant disorder, noise, and vibration emanating from it and making it something like the epitome of modern life.

Gabrielle's freshness of perception about Montreal undoubtedly owes something to her outsider status at the time she was producing these articles. But her "progressive" ideological attitudes certainly had something to do with it too, making her sensitive to aspects the traditionalist view generally overlooked, including the whimsically baroque style of Montreal's architecture, the ethnic diversity of a number of neighbourhoods, and the inequality of social and economic conditions in which the population lived.

For us, however, this series of articles is significant above all in that it directly and immediately provided the groundwork for an event of major importance: the discovery of Montreal by the author of *Bonheur d'occasion* (*The Tin Flute*), the discovery of the real world that, with an expansion here and a change there, would provide the foundation on which the fictional world of the novel would be built. Although the working-class districts are not the central focus of the articles, their place in them is not insignificant either. Even in the first, the journalist speaks of the houses of the poor in the southwest of the city, "with their rags drying in the dust and their captive swarm of children cavorting between grimy walls, where one can hear the plaintive voice of the people, fretting, striving, suffering." Then in Pointe-St-Charles, she sees "the city's great junkyard [and its] miserable village of shanty-dwellers who have built their huts from wreckage, in the cramped space between a breath of fresh air and the poisonous stench of the place. Wretched pariahs, living on refuse among billions of flies and the dances of rats, they have turned their backs to the city and see only the river flowing by, majestic and serene." This place and this spectacle will be found again in *The Tin Flute*.[112]

It is the third article that depicts the working-class neighbourhoods of the portside and the banks of the Lachine Canal most strongly, settings already steeped in certain characteristics that the writer will soon be exploring and incarnating with genuinely fictional characters and situations. Here, a long quotation begs to be heard:

> A termite population lives in the heart of the great industrial furnace. The minute their eyes seek escape they encounter factory chimneys. Their horizon is grimy and hemmed in on all sides [. . .].
>
> Their churches have taken on a coal-like hue. Their schoolyards open onto miasmas. Their playgrounds vie for minute spaces with factory yards.
>
> The *faubourg* Saint-Henri sees so many trains go through! Incessantly the locomotives roar. Incessantly the safety barriers fall and rise again. Incessantly the express trains thunder by: the Ocean Limited, the Maritime Express, the Transcontinental, the New York Central. The little wooden houses tremble on their foundations; the lowly dishes rattle, and human voices rise above the din to carry on conversation at a screech. In the inner courtyards, the washing is already black before it's dry. And nighttime, endlessly jostled by the shuddering of wheels, endlessly torn by the hiss of steam and the crunch of ballast, keeps no true rest for exhausted working men and women. [. . .]
>
> You have to have been on Saint-Antoine Street outside Imperial Tobacco at noon when the lunchtime whistle goes. Swarms of working girls in smocks escape and head for home or the cart that sells French fries and hotdogs. A bag of fries, a soft drink bought at the little corner store, and that's it for a quick pick-me-up, balancing on one foot or against a wall, jigging, chattering, already thinking only of what they're going to do with their evening. Quick! Quick! Quick! Already they don't know how to slow down. At five o'clock they'll run and put up their hair in curlers, paint their nails, eat on the fly. Then they'll be off to an evening of fun.[113]

This text, in which the atmosphere and colour of *The Tin Flute* are already visible – and even the silhouette of Florentine Lacasse – was published in August 1941. It is impossible to say when it was written, or especially when the discovery it records was made. Holding to what Gabrielle herself had to say about this on various occasions, she first went to the Saint-Henri district in 1940 or 1941 (and therefore shortly before the publication of these articles on Montreal). It is certain in any case that this first incursion happened in late spring or early summer, not long after she settled in Montreal.

At this time she was living in Westmount, in a neighbourhood that was both quiet and village-like, a reassuringly familiar atmosphere, so she felt not too much out of water. Westmount also had the advantage of being close to downtown, where the papers, periodicals, and radio studios were concentrated. At first, since she knew Montreal hardly at all, she rarely left the immediate vicinity of her boarding house except to take her articles to *Le Jour*, *La Revue moderne*, or *Le Bulletin*, whose offices were in the Drummond Building at the corner of Peel and Ste-Catherine streets. In her free time she would go to read and relax in Westmount Park which was not far from home and in which was located the public library, where she was a frequent visitor. Her longest walks took her mostly northward along the shaded streets on the side of the mountain or the pathways of Mount Royal Park, or else up to "that kind of farm that the Soeurs de la Congrégation de Notre-Dame had beside their convent, occupying a rectangle enclosed by four street corners, where I would often go to walk in the evening, greeting the farmer who, there on the verandah of a real little country house, would be smoking his pipe and rocking his chair in the middle of the field of turnips and sweet corn."[114]

But soon her walks were casting wider. Since she lived at the top of a hill separating Westmount from the districts to the south, "on the borderline of the poor and the rich,"[115] she decided one day to turn her steps down the hill. What drew her first was the Lachine Canal, along which she would go sometimes to take the cool of the evening when it was hot. Then she discovered the banks of the river which thereafter became the customary destination of her walks – "my personal Ganges" she later called the river.[116] She would take the bus across Verdun into Ville LaSalle and spend long afternoons stretched out beside the water in a small, quiet bay at the bottom of the embankment along LaSalle Boulevard.

As for the district of Saint-Henri – which is to say, the square of the same name and the streets around it – she would state later that she had gone there "by pure chance, by whim if you will," in the course of one of her walks.

> Usually, I chose as the goal of my walks the pretty avenues of Westmount and the side of the mountain. One day, [. . .] I went down toward the south of Atwater Street, I turned west along Saint-Antoine Street a bit and found myself quite unexpectedly in the very heart of Saint-Henri. What can I tell you? How can I express the feeling I suddenly had? It was like a thunderbolt striking lovers; it was a revelation, an illumination![117]

Was it really chance that took her there, was it "boredom" and the simple need of "human warmth," as she would confide much later in another of her interviews?[118] This is possible, but it is also possible that she went to Saint-Henri as she went to other parts of the city, as a journalist gathering information and impressions for the articles that *Le Bulletin des agriculteurs* wished to publish in connection with the tricentenary of Montreal.

Whatever the case, she was electrified. The reasons are multiple and probably unfathomable. Let us simply recall those that she recalled herself, often with several years' hindsight. The character of the district first, the picturesque intensity of its life, the difficult conditions faced by its families of both workers and unemployed, the stifling ambiance in such sharp contrast with the continual, shrieking passage of trains and ships, all this sociological reality had the stuff to arouse the interest of the journalist and the "indignation"[119] of the woman of the left, as shown by the *Tout Montréal* articles. But for the Franco-Manitoban who had been living for nearly three years among English-speaking people – first in London, then Westmount – Saint-Henri was also the rediscovery of her own language and the people she was descended from. Like St-Boniface next door to Winnipeg, this village in the bosom of a city was the gathering of a people confined to a kind of ghetto on the fringe of the modern world and modern prosperity, looked down on, become almost outsiders in their own country, people with tortured speech and a mentality and customs ill-suited to the urban context, a society showing still more pathetically than St-Boniface its ravaged but living face, showing its suffering to be sure, but also its profound, its quintessential humanity. Discovering Saint-Henri, the narrator of *Enchantment and Sorrow* would say, was discovering a "feeling of having come home, of oneness with my people, whom my mother had taught me to know and love in my childhood."[120]

But there is another, perhaps more determinant reason to explain Gabrielle's fascination for the setting and people of Saint-Henri in her early years in Montreal, a reason that drew her back again and again. Here she could see, if not immediately at least very shortly, an extraordinary wealth of material for her writing.

We shall return later to the writing of *Bonheur d'occasion*. It is enough to say for the moment that the beginnings of this book were directly tied to the discovery made one spring evening by a fledgling journalist, a few steps from where she lived, of a wide world whose reality and beauty were there before her very nose, and which no one else had yet seen.

The Peregrinations of a Journalist

Summer 1941. When her articles on Montreal began appearing in *Le Bulletin des agriculteurs* Gabrielle was again in the Gaspé, where she had come to rest at the McKenzies' as she had the previous year. And, as she had the previous year, she wrote, perhaps polishing her final two articles on Montreal or putting the final touches to "Embobeliné," the story *La Revue moderne* was to publish that October. Perhaps too she was working on this new story that was to become *Bonheur d'occasion*.

Around mid-July, after leaving Port-Daniel, she took the ferry from Rimouski to spend two or three weeks at Sept-Îles on the North Shore in order to prepare two articles for *Le Bulletin* for that autumn. The first of these, titled "La côte de tous les vents" (October 1941), is a portrait of several villages and outposts of a region still at the pioneer stage, set in a magnificent landscape but socially and economically dominated by monopolies; here, the journalist writes, "capital reigns as absolute master."[121] The second article, "Heureux les nomades" (November), speaks with great sensitivity of the contradictory lives of the Montagnais, who are submissive and apathetic when settled temporarily on their reserve at Sept-Îles, but proud and independent in their hunting lands of the back country.

These two articles – this "mini-series" – marked a new stage in Gabrielle's journalistic apprenticeship. They display the same attention to reality and the same sense of description so magnificently illustrated in the *Tout Montréal* series. But here the physical and social environment, although still very present, becomes as well a background against which one or several individuals emerge, to whom the journalist assigns special places, treating them like real characters, meaning both heroes and types. As heroes, they are strongly singularized, with detailed physical and character portraits (sometimes supported by a photograph), recall of their background, portrayal of their gestures, words, and particularly the emotions that stir them even in silence. As types, what is stressed is their exemplary value: they are seen as representatives, either as belonging to a particular group or in the effect on them of widespread phenomena that the journalist wishes to make understood. Gabrielle would henceforth use this technique of the representative portrait in almost all her articles, a technique illustrated in these two articles on the North Shore by her evocation of the aged Héliodore Vigneault, mariner by trade, who incarnates the hopes and virtues of the settlers of the Letellier range, and of the newly elected chief of the reserve, Sylvestre McKenzie, a symbol of the droll impassiveness of the Montagnais people.

In September 1941, after her spells in the Gaspé and on the North Shore, Gabrielle adopted the pattern of life she would follow for nearly four years until the publication of *Bonheur d'occasion*. Intended to reconcile the need to eat and the demands of the journalistic trade with her writerly ambitions, this pattern – this discipline, rather – consisted of dividing her existence into two distinct phases repeated each year: on the one hand, travelling and adventure; on the other, retreat and writing. The first phase generally took place in late summer or the course of the autumn. For several weeks or months the journalist would travel, investigate, conduct interviews and research; in short, roam the world and gather her material. Then come winter she would return home and devote herself entirely to writing her articles for the *Le Bulletin* and, as soon as she had some free time, to writing stories and, before long, her novel.

Although shorter, the travelling season was, of course, the more eventful. Here we see a Gabrielle brimming with energy, setting forth on all the highways of Quebec and Canada, and beyond the highways to the byways, visiting the remotest corners, meeting all kinds of people, undaunted by bad roads or bad weather, eating and sleeping every night in a different place, lonely inns, humble peasant cottages, construction cabins, everywhere eager to see new things, discover people, store up acquaintances and notes for her future writings. She would set out always alone with as little baggage as possible so as to be completely free to move around and available for all the unexpected encounters, exchanges, and friendships that travelling can bring. It was the exciting, turbulent life of the "great reporter," a trade that very few French-Canadian journalists practised in those days with anything like as much effectiveness or passion.

Among these reporters, Gabrielle was certainly one of the few women. Feminine journalism was almost always confined to personal or domestic matters – food, fashion, psychology, education, care of the body, and so on. Serious things, meaning politics, economics, social questions, and the wide, wide world, were the prerogative of men. This was the way it was at *Le Bulletin des agriculteurs* in the period when Gabrielle was a contributor. A number of women signed with pretty pseudonyms (Madeleine, Alice Ber, Lise Printemps, Simone d'Alençon) the columns that made up the section headed "Votre domaine, Madame," and occasionally women's names appeared among the authors of the "Romans et nouvelles," but as soon as one turned to the serious part of the magazine, the "Articles d'intérêt" and other more meaty stuff, one was in strictly masculine territory dominated by specialists and thinkers like Louis Francoeur, Roger Duhamel, Georges Langlois, Alphonse Proulx, and the very liberal Abbé Arthur Maheux, who each month paternally addressed "*À toi, mon cher habitant*" the fruit of his cogitations on the state of the nation. The only woman whose name figured in this section of the magazine and who occasionally figured on the cover, the only woman whose articles were considered on a par with those of masculine contributors, was Gabrielle Roy. It is true that, unlike Madeleine or Alice Ber (Jeanne Grisé-Allard), she was single and so could take the liberty of leaping the fence around "Votre domaine, Madame." This made her one of the liberators of women's journalism in Quebec, along with a few other educated single women from outside the province, like Marcelle Barthe, whom Gabrielle had known years before in amateur theatrical circles and became reacquainted with at Radio-Canada, and Judith Jasmin, with whom she was in contact at this time and became friends with after the publication of *Bonheur d'occasion*.

Gabrielle Roy's journalism was different from that practised by most of her masculine colleagues, however, at least in the periodical print domain. Rare indeed were the real reporters who ventured far from their editorial offices, out to encounter people and situations, laying themselves open to the disorder and the unexpected out there in the world.

In this Gabrielle was a rather unique case, working "American style," so to speak, somewhat as Ernest Hemingway had done, or as the likes of Steinbeck or Dos Passos were doing at about the same time as she.

Her first campaign, her first "outing," Gabrielle conducted in Montreal itself to write her four articles of the summer of 1941. Not counting her Sept-Îles trip (which was a side-trip, strictly speaking), she undertook her second outing late that summer when, on Henri Girard's suggestion or that of management at Le Bulletin, she decided to follow a group of Magdalen Islanders leaving home to be resettled in the Abitibi region.

Colonization had been one of the "solutions" favoured by the State for the economic distress of the Depression, particularly after the adoption of the Vautrin Plan in 1934. Although by 1941 the Depression was a thing of the past, it was still believed in many government backrooms that the best cure for poverty was a return to the land. Which was why, in view of the fish marketing problems then being faced by Magdalen Island fishermen, the provincial government was offering to relocate some fifteen families to the other end of the province, to Nepawa Island in Lake Abitibi, where they would receive free land and allowances necessary for their settlement. The operation, as was right and proper, was accompanied by a major publicity campaign.[122]

Good reporter that she was, Gabrielle went to accompany the "Madelinots" to their new home. Did she go to the Islands, make the crossing with them by boat to Pictou in Nova Scotia, then take the train with them to Quebec City? Although probable, this is impossible to confirm. It is certain that she was with them when they arrived in Quebec City and during their brief stay there, and took the train for La Sarre at the same time as they. After a journey of four days, she was still with them as they drove to Lake Abitibi and took the ferry to Nepawa Island, where the group landed in the middle of the night.

She stayed in Abitibi for two or three weeks, sleeping a night in one township, the next in another, sometimes turning up alone at a family's house, sometimes guided by a civil servant whom she asked to show her everything, "the beautiful, the less beautiful, and the most depressing."[123] She took an interest in all to do with the lives and lot of the colonists. She entered their houses, ate at their tables, helped with their work of (mechanized) land clearing, contemplated with them the bleak, magnificent landscape around them, heard their homesick sighs, their recriminations, and their expressions of confidence and hope.

Based on this investigation, she wrote a series of seven articles titled

Ici l'Abitibi, which were published sequentially from November 1941 to May 1942. The impression one gets from them might be called moderate realism. The descriptions of the countryside, which is seen as both beautiful and often inhospitable, like the stories of the lives of the colonists, in which the advantages of new beginnings must be weighed against material and moral difficulties of every kind, are a marriage of lucidity and compassion. But here again the contrast is striking between what the journalist saw and what the conservative ideology of the period projected as idealist visions of colonization. One realizes this when comparing Gabrielle's articles with a book like *L'Abatis* by Félix-Antoine-Savard, which was published in 1943 and bears on the same subject: in the reporter's articles we have the down-to-earth and precise approach of the journalist; in the book we have the priest's, the aesthete's, and the propagandist's.

It is hard to read Gabrielle's articles as a plea in favour of colonization and a return to the land. Particularly in the early articles of the series one can see the fascination she has for certain ideas or themes tied to the opening of the new colonies – migration, foundation, solidarity, as well as a vision of "Christian socialism" in which, while "[borrowing] much from the Soviets, [. . .] there is [respect for] the right of small property and [. . .] individual initiative."[124] But the further the investigation progresses the more problematical the optimism becomes, yielding soon to hints of disillusionment. The series ends with two articles on the neighbouring small towns of the region, La Sarre, Amos, and Duparquet, as though the journalist had realized that it was they, the lumbering and gold-mining towns, not the new townships so painfully cleared for farming, that represented the real Abitibi.

From this series of articles there also emerges a fine gallery of characters: a Galician by the name of Sup and his seven sons; the Pomerleau brothers of the Villemontel range; Wolfrid Hannurkeski, the solitary and tenacious Finn; Azade Poirier, the old fisherman converted to colonist, and his daughter, the tiny Rose, who shines like a pearl in this grey, harsh setting.[125] There are also portraits of the principal "officials" of the colony: Louis Simard, the indefatigable district manager, who reminds us of Léon Roy among his colonists; Abbé L., in whom, Gabrielle writes, "I recognized the country priest of Bernanos, living among the poor and himself as poor as they";[126] and Mademoiselle Estelle, the schoolteacher, who is like a twin sister to the young woman who turned up one morning in September 1929 to take over her school

in a remote Manitoba village called Cardinal. Titled "Pitié pour les institutrices!," this fifth article of the series was both a denunciation of the
conditions imposed on rural teachers in Quebec in those days and by
the same token a kind of manifesto in favour of the school reform that
the Godbout government was then embarking on, against the will of the
most conservative elements of the clergy and episcopate.

Over the months while her Abitibi articles were appearing, Gabrielle
published only one short story, "La grande voyageuse," in *La Revue
moderne* of May 1942. In this story with "premonitory" overtones, after
the death of their mother a group of daughters must jointly care for
their sister, an awkward old maid by the name of "Bédette." This was the
last of Gabrielle's contributions to the magazine under Henri Girard's
direction, for Girard left his job to return to the daily *Le Canada*. Not
surprisingly, *Le Canada* retained Gabrielle's services not long after.

During the summer of 1942, Gabrielle was preparing another investigative tour with a view to writing a new series of articles. This time she
turned to the land of her origin, the Canadian West, where she had not
set foot since leaving for Europe five years earlier. However, the project
was going to entail rather considerable expenses that *Le Bulletin* could
not assume alone and therefore needed the intervention of other spon-
sors. One of them turned out to be *Le Canada*, which decided to send
Gabrielle as a special envoy to Dawson Creek in British Columbia to
cover the building of a highway to Alaska, begun by the United States to
thwart the Japanese advance in the Aleutians. Besides the support of
these two newspapers, the journalist received a free pass from Canadian
National Railways, which saw the publication of a series of articles on the
new regions of the West as excellent publicity for its colonization department, whose superintendent was Gabrielle's friend Émile Couture.[127]

The tour was to last nearly four months. At the beginning of July
Gabrielle was in St-Boniface, from where she immediately set out westward. Her first stop was a few miles from Winnipeg in the village of Élie
where her cousin Belle lived, the daughter of her uncle Édouard Roy.
Not far from Élie she visited the Hutterite colony of Iberville. She then
boarded the train for Saskatchewan and travelled the province from
south to north, stopping first near Regina with the Doukhobors at
Kamsack. Then she went to the Rosthern region north of Saskatoon,
where there was a colony of Mennonites who were "the third and last of
the groups of mystics" she was interested in,[128] and finally to the vicinity
of Ridgedale and Edenbridge, east of Prince Albert, where some recently

arrived European Jewish colonists were living. From there she went west to Alberta via North Battleford, visiting the colony of Good Soil not far from the border near St. Walburg, where Czech refugees driven from Sudetenland by the Munich agreements had come to restart their lives. Next she spent a few days at Mundare just east of Edmonton, in a region populated mostly by Ukrainians, before continuing north-westward to the Peace River district between Grande Prairie and Lesser Slave Lake, where a number of French-Canadian colonists had settled around the villages of Tangent and Falher. Finally, on October 28 she was at Dawson Creek, from where she travelled by truck to Fort St. John to observe the construction in progress on the new highway that was to lead to Fairbanks in Alaska. She returned to Quebec early in November.

Such was the itinerary, pieced together from the articles that she based on this long tour (part investigative reporting, part travelogue) and that appeared between the autumn of 1942 and the spring of 1943. In *Le Canada*, after the story on the Alaska Highway, they consisted of a series of four articles titled *Regards sur l'Ouest* and, in *Le Bulletin des agriculteurs*, a new series published under the collective title *Peuples du Canada* (translated later as *Peoples of Canada*).

This series, consisting of seven articles, found Gabrielle at the peak of her journalistic prowess, in full possession of her art. Here she handles and combines more effectively than ever before the various aspects of writing that go to make a good story: narration, description, portraiture, reminiscence, essay. For each "people" she meets, each religious sect or ethnic group, she tries to give the reader all the information needed for both an accurate and lively picture of the human reality represented by that community. Historical background, religious or cultural explanations, demographic, geographic, or economic statistics combine with the journalist's personal experience with these people: the way they treated her, their conversation, her meetings with this one and that among them, and always the sense of brotherhood that has transcended the differences of language and culture and allowed her to feel like one of the family among them, one of the great human family.

These texts are ideologically important. They are Gabrielle Roy's first complete and unequivocal expression of a vision of the world with which she would tend to identify increasingly. It is not an easy vision to describe in a nutshell, for she had no program or systematic doctrine, not a real ideology in the usual sense of the word, just a body of feelings, ideas, and opinions – a sensitivity if you will. Broadly speaking, a vision

that could be called an idealist or liberal socialism that, without preaching class struggle or revolution, deplored the ills and misdeeds of capitalism and believed in the possibility of establishing a more just, more
equal, freer, and above all more fraternal society in which divisions of all
kinds – economic, cultural, and national – would yield to a universal
harmony founded on a sharing of collective wealth and respect of
differences. To this end, any movement working to the benefit of this
harmonization and this humanization of relationships was deserving of
support, be it unionism, cooperatives, the lightening of work through
mechanization of manual labour, democratization of teaching, or the
struggle against the exploitation of women. But what was essential lay
less in changes to rules and structures than the implantation of a new
morality and a new social sense: that is, the conversion of each individual
and each community to the values of mutual aid and solidarity, out of
which could emerge the society of the future, a society that would be the
opposite of the torn, fratricidal world seen in the horrible spectacle of war.

In Gabrielle this vision of the world took form during her Manitoban
youth through her contacts with her Winnipeg friends, spurred by her
rebellion against the narrow-mindedness of her home community,
then consolidated in Montreal when she was associating with people in
the "extreme" liberal milieus of *Le Jour* and Henri Girard's entourage.
The *Peoples of Canada* series, even more than the Abitibi series, was
steeped in this secular faith, this wager on the advent of universal fraternity and solidarity.

On this was based the central motif of these articles, which had
already been there in previous articles and would become an important
element in the novelist's future work, the motif of the colony, or the little
community of migrants who have turned their backs on the vicissitudes
of the past and gathered in a remote yet Edenesque spot in the back of
beyond to start anew in friendship and joy, beginning the human adventure over again from new foundations.

This myth of the colony, in which it is not unreasonable to see a
transposition of "Robinson Crusoe" fantasies that Gabrielle had entertained as a child, inspired another ideological trait to be noted in these
articles – Gabrielle Roy's own special conception of Canada, which she
acquired perhaps from her father and which will be found in a number
of her writings to come. Here, Canada appears as one huge colony, the
ideal country for new beginnings and mutual understanding. In this

country as the journalist portrays it, all the inhabitants are immigrants; all for whatever reason are fleeing the past and striving to build a better future, and all in this sense are brothers. Inequalities, national rivalries, power relationships are reduced to the minimum; not only is there "room for all minorities"[129] but it is precisely the minorities, with the concord reigning among them, that make Canada the forerunner of future humanity.

This being so, it is significant that among the different "peoples" of the Canadian West that she studies, Gabrielle pays no attention at all to the British, who after all are the majority. It is as though the group did not fit the image she had of the country, as though the dominance of the British prevented them from being part of this mosaic of small isolated communities that to her mind Canada consisted of. The real Canadians in her eyes were the Mennonites, the Hutterites, the Doukhobors, and all the other unfortunates come from elsewhere to rural areas to form little pockets where mutual aid and hope of a better world shone brightly.

Also among these groups were the French Canadians, who are the subject of the last article of the series. Not the French Canadians of Quebec but those who had abandoned their province and come to the Canadian West to found colonies and mingle with the other minority groups. Freed of constraints, "left to their own devices," these French Canadians had rediscovered here what they had lost in Quebec, their spirit of initiative, their courage, their tolerance toward others. Here, wrote the journalist, "the more a French Canadian is isolated, [. . .] the more enterprising he shows himself to be."

> He awakens to venturesomeness. A love of space, of plenty of elbow room, replaces his passion for those "Thirty Acres." His pressing desire to possess all of his country has driven him to the West, and keeps him here. His country extends from one ocean to the other. [. . .] He is more mystical already, I would say, than his brother in Quebec. His eyes are open to the immensity of Canada. [. . .] Our people are friendly people. [. . .] And voyaging, new horizons, contact with all races teaches them much about friendship. [. . .] Wherever French Canadians live as neighbours to Ruthenians, Galicians, Sudetens, and Doukhobors, they show themselves to be their friends. [. . .] In short, what the French Canadian likes best is all the great variety his new life offers him. He is perhaps already more simply Canadian than French Canadian.[130]

The Western French Canadian in other words was a new improved French Canadian, a precursor. Like Edmond de Nevers, who in the late nineteenth century saw in the Franco-Americans of New England the forerunners of the great future for which the French Canadian people were destined,[131] Gabrielle Roy, far from reiterating the nationalists' tired old refrain about the fate of "our severed brothers" and calling for the sacrosanct "survival," portrays the francophones of the West, particularly the impoverished Peace River colonists, as the vanguard of their people, engaged in building a regenerated, fraternal, open society called Canada.

While she was always fairly discreet, expressing such ideas gave Gabrielle's articles polemical implications that, considered in their context, should not be underestimated. At the time they were being published in *Le Bulletin des agriculteurs* and *Le Canada*, Quebec was just emerging from the tempestuous debate aroused by the federal conscription plebiscite of April 1942, and political passions were still simmering. Gabrielle never took a position explicitly on this question, but celebrating Canada as she did in these articles, praising the greatness and ethnic diversity of the country that had just voted massively against the feelings of the majority in Quebec, or getting emotional over the lot of the Alaska Highway workers "who have sacrificed their love of country for an even greater idea," was just a slightly roundabout way of indicating which side she was on. Similarly, when she praised the French Canadians of the West for their bilingualism and noted that those of them who refused to speak English were "doomed to slavery," and that "the biggest boon to the French Canadians of the West [was] perhaps to have obliged their children to learn English,"[132] the journalist, consciously or not, was taking sides in a controversy dividing public opinion in Quebec. Implicitly, she was lining up behind T. D. Bouchard, Jean-Charles Harvey, and other *rouges* who were advocating early teaching of English in Quebec schools, to the great displeasure of the nationalists. Considering that the latter represented the thinking of the clear majority among the francophone elite, Gabrielle's liberal opinions may seem courageously contentious, and in a way they were indeed that. It should not be forgotten, however, that in the context of the war effort, these opinions were in full conformity with the official line of thought promoted by the Liberal governments of Quebec and Canada, especially the latter, through its powerful tools of propaganda and censorship.

For us today however, what is of greatest value in the articles brought back by the journalist from this western tour is all the raw material in images, ideas, and impressions they contained, and which would nourish the work of the novelist in years to come. Gabrielle may have been born in the West and lived there for many years, but she really discovered it and conceived a vision of it that would re-emerge later in her work only in the course of this tour. The places, scenes, faces, and people presented as real "facts" observed in the process of reporting would be transformed through aesthetic contemplation and language into clearly literary motifs charged with new beauty and new meaning. In the second article of the *Peoples of Canada* series for example, the journalist speaks of a Caucasian woman by the name of Masha who grows flowers in a remote corner of Saskatchewan, and tells of visiting her during her stay among the Doukhobors; in the following article she writes of the death of an old Mennonite who was a slave to her husband and whose name is Martha. How can one fail to see in this the source, or one of the sources, of *Garden in the Wind*? Later in her tour she describes attending a Ukrainian festival that is a direct foretaste of one of the chapters of *Where Nests the Water Hen*, and then, "On the threshold of his café [she sees] the figure to be found in every town and hamlet of the West, the man who always seems bored but never discouraged [. . .]: the Chinese restaurant-keeper"; while this restaurateur bears the hackneyed name of Charlie, he might have been called Sam Lee Wong.[133] Elsewhere still, she is moved by "the weary face of Annie, the young waitress" in Dawson Creek, in whom it is difficult not to recognize the twin sister of Nina, the little nomad in *The Hidden Mountain*.[134]

These similarities are not immediately apparent, to be sure. In the harvest of images she stored away in the course of this tour through the West, Gabrielle did not know then what a treasure she was bringing back with her. All that counted at the time was her journalist's work, the articles she had to write, the truth to be conveyed as best she could. And yet as we can clearly see today, it was through this work, which in appearance had very little to do with literary "creation" and took less imagination than hard work, less daring than patience, that the novelist really learned her craft. Recalling Hemingway's beginnings, Milan Kundera notes that in his time (and it was still true in Gabrielle Roy's time) journalism did not consist primarily of writing editorials and having opinions on everything; "in those days, being a journalist meant getting closer to reality than anyone else, exploring all its hidden crannies, getting one's hands grimy with it."[135] Being a journalist, and especially a reporter as Gabrielle was during these years, meant above all looking, listening, understanding, getting behind or beneath the ready-made images, the preformed judgments. It meant being interested in the facts, in the people, in real life rather than the theories, diagrams, and other fictions that stand for real life.

While it trained her eye and honed her skill in handling people, reporting also gave Gabrielle the opportunity to practise a new kind of writing, more direct, more restrained, less intent on effects and stylistic prettiness, more down-to-earth than the writing in most of her stories of this time. It was a matter of using words and sentences to demonstrate rather than surprise, of staying in the wings of the world's stage instead of presuming to be the star attraction. This said, her journalistic style was not in the least cold and technical. On the contrary, its great virtue – with which she brought a renewal to the entire journalistic genre of her time and society – was not to deny emotion or subjectivity but, keeping it well under control, to use it as a supplementary and even indispensable means of seeing and explaining what she saw. Thus, when one reads *Tout Montréal, Peoples of Canada*, or any of the other major feature series that she wrote for *Le Bulletin des agriculteurs* between 1941 and 1945, one is given a particularly gripping picture of things as they were in those days, and also witnessing the birth of a voice, a manner of thought, a writer's universe.

Gathering About a Loved One's Remains

Gabrielle's grand tour of the summer and autumn of 1942 was not dictated entirely by professional imperatives. It was also an opportunity for her to return to the scenes of her youth and be reunited with her family, or at least re-establish the contact that had been lost since her departure in 1937 and not exactly restored by her decision to give up her teaching job in St-Boniface permanently.

For a long time, and particularly during her first years in Montreal, Gabrielle had borne a grudge against her family and her sisters in particular, who, she would say later, "had refused to give me a word of encouragement in the hour [. . .] I so needed it" and "had warned me long in advance that I'd have only myself to blame on the day I came down off my high horse and had to pay the price of quitting my job."[136] All she felt toward them, or her brothers for that matter, was bitterness and resentment. She owed nothing to anyone, she considered, and expected nothing in return.

Even with her mother, things had been far from simple. Gabrielle would certainly never have disowned her, would never have burned her bridges with her, but Mélina's messages insisting that she come back to Manitoba, repeating that she was expected, asking to know the date of her return, provoked as much if not more impatience in her as feelings of guilt. Why was she being badgered this way when all she wanted was one thing, to be free of the past, to depend on no one but herself and move ahead without ties, without obligations until the victory that would surely come one day if she could attain her one and only goal? What did she need from brothers and sisters and an old mother who wanted only to have her back there beside her, the way things used to be long ago?

She had seen her mother about eighteen months after her return from Europe. It was in Montreal, in early autumn 1940. Despite her advanced age, Mélina had begun to travel. In the spring of 1939 when Gabrielle was arriving in Montreal and settling into her first boarding house on Stanley Street, Mélina was in California, where she had gone to join her brother Moïse, who had moved there because his wife, Thérèse Généreux, suffered from asthma. Thérèse had died several years later, and now Moïse was dying. Heeding only her sense of duty, Mélina had hurried to be with him as soon as she heard the news, but Moïse had died before she stepped off the bus at her destination.[137] She stayed more than two months by the Pacific Ocean among her nephews and nieces. The following year, the old woman set out again, this time on a long tour that lasted over a year and took her all over the country, visiting one of her children after another. She went to Kingston, Ontario, where Rodolphe was pursuing his military training, to Hoey, Saskatchewan, to help Germain's wife, Antonia, who was then pregnant with her second daughter, and finally to Tangent in Alberta to spend the summer with Adèle.

Worried about Gabrielle, Mélina then decided to go to Montreal, where she had not been since 1921. Gabrielle rented a room for her mother on the ground floor of the boarding house she herself was living in. However, the two women hardly saw each other during the two or three weeks of Mélina's stay, for Gabrielle was very busy with her radio work and Mélina was often absent visiting members of her family or attending to her devotions at Notre-Dame-du-Bon-Secours Church or St. Joseph's Oratory. Besides, when they did see each other, more often than not they quarrelled. Over several days Mélina had seen, heard, and surmised enough to have grave doubts about her daughter's virtue, and to feel justified in scolding her. A man was coming regularly to Gabrielle's room and leaving at unseemly hours. On Sundays Gabrielle did not go to mass, and she smoked too. "I know now," Mélina declared once back in St-Boniface, "I know where Gabrielle gets her success, and I'd rather die before seeing her triumph."[138] The two women had not parted on very good terms, and her mother's visit had done nothing to make Gabrielle want to patch things up between them.

But time, as always, eases wounds. Toward the end of 1941 Anna, the eldest sister, began writing to Gabrielle to give her news, and gradually the link was re-established. Less nervous now about her career, which was finally taking a healthy turn since she had been with *Le Bulletin des agriculteurs*, Gabrielle began to feel the burden of her solitude and rediscover her attachment to her family. Not to the point of forgetting the spitefulness of the past or being inclined to give up her independence, but at least she lowered her guard, her resentment softened, and she was ready to see those she had left behind.

The new contact was made late in the summer of 1942, during her tour of the West. The itinerary she followed through the colonies of Saskatchewan and Alberta eventually led to her sister Adèle's in Tangent, in the Peace River district of Alberta. Adèle had settled there in 1935 as a schoolteacher. As usual her relations with the *curé* of the parish and the parents of her pupils soon deteriorated, so that in 1939 she decided to retire from teaching and become a farmer on land she had bought from a colonist two years earlier.[139] She had named her house – her cabin, to be truthful – "Villa Antoinette" and furnished it so as to make it propitious for works of the mind and "the cult of memory": a desk, a small bookcase, an upright piano, photographs of parents and ancestors, portraits of great men, and, in the midst of all, an engraved representation of Death. Although the space in it was minimal, the house quickly became a vacation spot for the women of the family. Anna came first, spending five weeks there in the summer of 1940, alone with Adèle. Then the following year there was a big family reunion, with Mélina coming to complete her pan-Canadian tour, accompanied by Clémence. The two women stayed at Tangent through the summer; Anna joined them in mid-August, and until early autumn mother and daughters lived an interlude of loving tenderness together. Gabrielle, whose hurly-burly journalist's life left her practically no respite, envied them this happy time from afar, having read a long epistle from Anna.[140]

A year later, on 22 August 1942, here she was herself arriving at

Tangent. Wearing high heels and "a tailored suit in a large black-and-white chequered tartan" as Adèle recalls,[141] she looked in a bad way, thin, depressed, completely exhausted by the six-or seven-week tour she had just completed, often in gruelling conditions. But her stay at the Villa Antoinette put her back on her feet. Between the two sisters, who had not seen each other for ten years, the meeting of minds was perfect. In the evening by the light of an oil lamp, they would tell each other what had been happening in their lives over recent years, and Gabrielle opened her heart to Adèle. She talked about herself, her childhood, the lack of affection she had suffered, and her father's severity toward her. She talked about Henri Girard, the support he gave her, and their blighted relationship. And during the day, while Adèle was at her school (for she had returned to teaching the previous March), Gabrielle busied herself with her writing. She wrote her articles with the help of notes and photographs accumulated in the course of her tour, interspersing her work sessions with walks in the surrounding countryside, conversations with the colonists, or shopping expeditions to the village – a hamlet where there were "two stores kept by French Canadians [and] a sparse population comprised of a large percentage of Ukrainians and Poles,"[142] Tangent having been founded in 1928 by colonists named Purcha and Yaramko. It was Tangent and its region that furnished Gabrielle with the material for her four articles for *Le Canada* titled *Regards sur l'Ouest*, as well as the last article of the *Peoples of Canada* series, in which Adèle appears, unnamed but portrayed as the very model of the cultivated schoolmistress who is totally devoted to her calling.

Gabrielle was enjoying herself, in short, and making the most of this interlude of peace and friendship in her tumultuous life.[143] By October 14, the day of her departure for Dawson Creek, she had put on weight, regained her self-confidence, and had almost finished her articles for the *Le Bulletin*. She had probably also begun some fictional texts.

Her tour of family visits was not yet over, however. Several weeks later, on her way back to Montreal, she stopped off in St-Boniface for four days at her mother's, in the little apartment on Langevin Street.[144] We do not know much about this meeting, except that the prodigal daughter regaled Mélina for hours with stories of her journalistic adventures and literary successes, and this time the contact between the two women seems to have been entirely warm. In any case, they would write to each other often in the succeeding months, and in none of her letters did Mélina find fault with Gabrielle over anything.

And so, reconciled with Adèle and with her mother, and having seen Anna and Clémence for the first time in five years, and possibly Germain and Antonia as well,[145] Gabrielle returned to Miss McLean's shortly before Christmas 1942 with her heart, mind, and body restored to health and composure.

She spent the Christmas and New Year's holidays in Montreal, then in February left for Rawdon, as she had the year before and would continue to do in years to follow. This village, which she had discovered during the winter of 1942, offered her the ideal setting in which she liked to live and work. It also had the advantage of being not too far from Montreal, where she often needed to go on business. Rawdon was a pleasant, peaceful village; there were little tree-lined streets, comfortable, elegant houses, a gently British ambiance, polite, discreet inhabitants, all the things that Gabrielle loved about the pretty corner of Westmount she had lived in since 1939. To which were added two more not inconsiderable advantages: the cost of living was not nearly as high as in Montreal, and the nature all around offered opportunities for long outings, skiing in winter and bicycling or walking in summer. Gabrielle would often push northward as far as the hills of St-Alphonse-de-Rodriguez, where her mother was born. With time, this proximity would count increasingly in the attachment she felt for Rawdon.[146]

But what really attached her to this village and brought her back time after time was the comfort she found there. The house in which she took a room belonged to an Irish couple, Charlie Tinkler and his wife. It was "a big wooden house in gingerbread style" with an enormous garden at the side running down to the river, and it stood at the corner of 9th Avenue and Lake Morgan Road. For $10 a week, Gabrielle had a huge, clean, bright room on the second floor, alas not very well heated, but she could have her meals served to her there at the hours she wanted them, and could type as much as she liked in her bed with her little portable typewriter on her knees. Contrary to the way things were in Montreal, where Miss McLean pampered her, certainly, but where she had to share the house with ten other people, here she was the only boarder and so received the undivided attention of the owners of the house. Charlie and his wife were captivated as soon as they saw Gabrielle, by her vivacity, her laughing eyes, and that fragility, that way she had of giving herself over to you, putting herself in your hands, so to speak, like a bird fallen on your doorstep. As she had with her mother long ago, as she had at Esther's, and at Port-Daniel with the McKenzies,

Gabrielle felt loved. Without understanding much about it, the old couple respected her work and did all possible to enable her to devote herself to it in peace, lavishing attentions on her, making sure not to disturb her, and adoring her as if she were their own child. "They too," she would write later, "my little old people in Rawdon, in my years of constantly moving about, when everywhere I could have been just someone passing through, in their own way made me a kind of home."[147]

That winter of 1943, here she was once again in her writing haven at Rawdon. She was putting the last touches to her final articles on the West before turning them in to *Le Bulletin des agriculteurs*, and most of the time also working on stories and the manuscript of a novel she had started.

But soon her peace of mind was troubled by bad news about her mother. One cold February morning Mélina had suffered a heart attack in the middle of mass at St-Boniface Cathedral; with great difficulty, she had been brought home. She was better, certainly, thanks to care from Clémence, who was living with her, and from Anna and Aunt Rosalie, who came almost every day. Still, in view of her advanced age the doctor feared the worst and had had the last rites administered.

Where she was, Gabrielle could do nothing except write. The only correspondence between her and her mother in our possession dates from this period. It consists of thirteen letters from Mélina, written between 7 March and 19 June 1943. There were at least as many from Gabrielle, but only one has survived, and that because Mélina used the back of it to write one of her own. Bedridden, using a pencil, the old woman recounts the small details of her daily life and gives news of her other children. There is a lot about money, small sums she has received from this one or that, about her savings, her intention to invest in building a little house in Somerset, a plan that, of course, was never realized. Gabrielle sends her $10 at the beginning of every month, "to help you put meat in the stew-pot."[148] She also sends magazines, chocolate, "*laurier de saint Antoine*," and even, at her mother's request, "crossants, a kind of donut I liked a lot when I was in Montreal, they didn't cost much and they were good."[149] One day when Gabrielle has sent her some maple syrup, she writes, "If you can spare a few dollars that would suit me much better, but if you're short don't send anything."[150] She asks her daughter several times when she is going to come and see her. "I'll be mighty pleased," she writes on May 10, "the day you arrive in St-Boniface, that's to say, at home"; and on the 30th of the same month, "I'm still looking for another letter from you, telling me you should be arriving soon."

At the beginning of April, Gabrielle left Rawdon and returned to Montreal, where she took her room at Miss McLean's again. But there was far too much to do to allow her to go on another western trip, particularly since at this point her professional situation was improving by leaps and bounds. Whereas at first her fee for an article in *Le Bulletin* had been only $15, as for any fledgling journalist, it rose to $30, then $50, and before long $100 and even $150. And with her stories on the West in *Le Canada* further enhancing her reputation, the managers of *Le Bulletin* (and perhaps the Liberal bigwigs) were anxious to try to bind her to them even more closely. In May 1943, they offered her a breathtaking contract: for an undertaking to give *Le Bulletin* at least eight texts a year, she would receive a salary of $275 a month, twelve months a year.[151] It was like striking gold. Financially, she would have no further worries; only four years after giving up her teaching job, she was earning three times what she had been earning then. At last her efforts were paying off; at last she could tell herself she had almost reached "the mountain-top," as she wrote to her mother on the day of her thirty-fourth birthday.

Her mother, out there in St-Boniface, continued to decline. In June, when Gabrielle sent her (unchanged) monthly $10, Mélina sent her last letter: Thank you for the money, she writes, "it's already a lot I don't need any more keep it for yourself and when I'm dead if you've got any left you can look after Clémence." Then she talks about the story that Gabrielle has just published in *Le Bulletin des agriculteurs*. "I've just received la grande Berthe and read it. I think it's the best thing you've written, the best of your life."[152] Exactly one week later a telegram arrived at Miss McLean's: "Maman died 10 this morning. Funeral Tuesday. Come if possible. Germain."[153] That evening Gabrielle took the train for St-Boniface, her eyes swollen from crying.

At the end of her life, Gabrielle devoted her very last work, which was to be a sequel to *Enchantment and Sorrow* and which she did not have time to finish, to recounting – to remembering – this episode. In it, we find the narrator on the train, at night, haggard and sobbing uncontrollably, rehashing in her mind the events of the past months when, she says, working like a galley-slave, all she wanted was "as quickly as I could, to scrape together the money I needed to come back to Manitoba and attend to Maman and have her given the best care possible," eager as well "to bring back to her the reason to be proud of me that I'd gone to the end of the earth to find for her, at the price of so much effort."[154] It was during this journey, she adds, that she discovered the privileged relationship that would ever after attach her so strongly to her mother, the mother who had died so far away while she, Gabrielle, was not there, to tell the truth had never been there.

> During that night of June 1943, somewhere in an Ontario forest, there began between my mother and me that singular exchange of voices in which I alone received her confidences through the silence, or rather that long inexhaustible quest for someone departed which can end only with our own end, since it is never any other way but through our own experience that we can know that person's, through our own illness know her cruel illness, through our own melancholy know her unquenchable melancholy, through our own death her last lonely moments. And so it is always too late to make known to someone we love how well we understand her and the poor life she has led, discovering some detail about it we never noticed before.[155]

As the train bore her toward Manitoba, did Gabrielle really have such a clear awareness of this inner conversion going on in her? No one can know of course. But in a sense she would pursue this "exchange of voices," this endless healing of the silence between the daughter and her dead mother, throughout all of her *oeuvre* to come.

Gabrielle arrived in Winnipeg on Monday morning and went straight to the Coutu funeral parlour, which Mélina had chosen herself "because it [was] cheaper." On the coffin was an immense spray of carnations sent by *Le Bulletin des agriculteurs*. For two days she received the usual condolences and heard all about her mother's dying moments from Clémence. On Wednesday morning, just before the coffin was closed, Bernadette disentangled the worn old rosary from the dead woman's fingers and gave it to Gabrielle as a keepsake. The funeral mass was celebrated in the cathedral, from where the procession, when it emerged shortly, did not have far to go to the cemetery just outside the door. Behind the coffin carried by Mélina's two brothers, Excide and Zénon, walked first (it was the rule) the ladies of religious organizations to which the deceased had belonged. Then came the bereaved children; this was their first family reunion since Léon's death fourteen years earlier, and it was to be their last.

Germain, who was forty-one, was at the time teaching at Mossbank in Saskatchewan, where he was a sergeant in the Royal Canadian Air Force; his second daughter, Yolande, was two and a half. It was he, the youngest son, who led the funeral procession, for the two others were absent, they whom a dyspeptic Anna called "complete drunken bums."[156] Joseph, the eldest at fifty-six and now a grandfather, had made only a flying visit two months earlier to see his sick mother, leaving again almost immediately for Dollard, where he was working in the grain trade. He had not communicated further with anyone. Rodolphe, who was going on forty-four, had been saved momentarily from his decadence by the war. Enrolled in the army since 1940, he had been having part of his pay sent to his mother. He too had seen her for the last time in April during his two weeks' leave, which he had spent with her, making her laugh and trying to wheedle money out of her. Since then he had been sent to England to prepare for combat.[157]

It was therefore mostly a procession of women following the coffin, a procession of Mélina's daughters: Clémence and Anna, who lived in St-Boniface, Gabrielle, who had come from Montreal, and Bernadette, who had obtained a last-minute permission and was resentful that her superiors at the Kenora convent had not allowed her to come sooner. The only one missing was Adèle, but this was because the journey from faraway Tangent took forever. It was decided therefore, pending her arrival, not to bury the body that day but to put it in a tiny charnel house; as soon as she arrived by train that evening, Adèle went there with Anna, had the coffin opened by the sacristan, and prayed before the "dear face" of the loved one. The next morning, beneath a radiant sky, Mélina's body was committed to the earth beside those of Léon and the two Agnèses.

Germain and Sister Léon had to leave as soon as the ceremonies were over. Gabrielle and Adèle stayed on for a time at Anna's, where Clémence joined them.[158] The house was located on River Road in St-Vital, just south of St-Boniface. It was a big house that Albert Painchaud, Anna's husband, had built four years earlier with the help of his sons. To please his wife and at long last give her the beautiful dwelling she had dreamed of having through all the thirty years of their marriage, Albert had bought a lot beside the Red River without telling Anna, which had so vexed her that she had not spoken to him for six months. The result was that the house, built without her advice, was impressive on the outside, all white with bright blue trim, but poorly thought out and impractical inside. Anna, however, had ended up making the best of it and ruled over the domain unreservedly. For many years "La Painchaudière," as the house and big garden on the river were pompously called, was the closest thing that Gabrielle and her sisters had to a family home.

Here, this early summer of 1943, the four orphan girls gathered to share their grief and confide in one another. Anna was still dissatisfied with her life and now was guilt-ridden for not having been enough help to her mother in the last months of her illness. But she herself, who would soon be fifty-five, was beginning to have health problems; two or three years later she would have her first operation for cancer. Adèle had sold her farm at Tangent and was regretting it already; at fifty years of age she had little idea where or what to turn to next. Finally, she would leave for the Peace River district once again that summer and resume teaching in other far-flung villages: Volin, Codessa. Gabrielle, who was a bundle of torment and affliction, sought consolation in long walks beside the river or in the neighbouring woods. Of the four sisters, only Clémence made no complaint, yet it was she who had most to complain about. With Mélina gone, here she was at forty-seven, more dependent than ever before and with nothing ahead of her. She who could not manage on her own and had never in her life learned anything other than serving, doing housework, and waiting passively for others to settle the most minor details of her existence, who was going to care for her now? There was no question of Anna taking her in; Clémence's ways and chattering got on her nerves too much. There was no question of it either for Adèle, or Gabrielle, or Bernadette. For the moment, Madame Jacques agreed to let her stay on alone in the little two-room apartment on Langevin Street, but this could not last for ever, the sisters knew well. Just as they knew, without admitting it to themselves, that Clémence would henceforth be the cross that all of them would have to bear. "Maman left her to us," Gabrielle wrote after returning to Montreal, "[...] so we'd know that it's good to make sacrifices."[159]

Occasionally, Aunt Rosalie would come and pass the time of day with her nieces, mingling her grief with theirs, for she had always been very close to her older sister and she too felt rather orphaned. Some photographs taken by Blanche, Rosalie's daughter, shows the five women at one of these gatherings. Looking at them, one is struck by how much Adèle, Clémence, and Anna are alike, all of them unlovely with their severe hairdos and dowdy clothes, and in the contrast between their own

228 GABRIELLE ROY ◆ A LIFE

appearance and the modern, distinguished style given Gabrielle by her well-cut attire, over-the-shoulder leather handbag, make-up, and airily coiffed hair. Everything about her says that she comes from elsewhere, from the big city, from a world light-years away from that of her mother and sisters.

A Blighted Love

It was not long before the harmony among the sisters turned sour. They began to quarrel over trifles. Gabrielle left La Painchaudière at the beginning of July, in a hurry to escape a climate that reminded her of the altercations of years gone by.

Still, these few days beside the remains of their mother had brought Gabrielle closer to her sisters. Set apart from them by age as much as by temperament, having practically wiped them out of her life when they had left home, and even more since she herself had left, here she was belatedly discovering all that united her with them despite the years of mutual silence and unawareness that had been keeping her apart. It was as though Cad, the kid sister, to compensate her loss now that she was an orphan, now that it was too late, was feeling the need to rejoin the family circle and become the daughter and sister she had worked so hard to cease being.

In the months following her return to Quebec, Gabrielle began to write to each of her sisters, and soon there was a web woven among them centred on "the little body that had been our mother."[160] She wrote to Anna, she wrote to Clémence, and her first letter to Bernadette is dated 15 September 1943. Her longest letters of all she wrote to Adèle, letters filled with remorse toward Mélina. On September 16 she confided:

> Lord, how I would have loved to be with her in her last years and give her, who asked so little, give her all, all those things she must have desired. It's sterile to indulge in such reflections, I know, but what can I do, I live with them constantly. This then is the real regret: not having been kind enough, affectionate enough, tender enough. This is the worst, the most crushing of regrets.[161]

Six months later, the same "sterile" regret continued to haunt her. Again she confided to Adèle:

I understand our poor mother's grief, you know, her supreme heartache when she had to leave her house on Deschambault Street. She put on a jaunty air, yes, but what a wound must have opened in her at that moment. If only you knew how often I've thought about that day and how many times I've chastised myself over this.

Poor little, brave little woman! All her heart was in this great, simple duty: the family, the home. Once it was destroyed, she never stopped trying to remake it [...], clinging to everything she had been able to save from disaster and collecting it round her [...]: yellowed portrait photos, stoups, primitive little pictures, all the small treasures she still had in the little apartment on Langevin Street when she died.

I can admit to you that it was the sight of these poor little relics of the past that made me cry the most real, the most bitter tears of my life.[162]

This return to the family fold did not last, however, and a great deal more time would have to pass, with many more quarrels, many more reconciliations, and many more quarrels again, before life would bring Gabrielle to feel truly attached and indebted to her sisters. For the moment she was far too caught up in her work and too much in need of her independence to be weighed down with remorse and fidelity to the past. Nine months after the letter immediately above, she was saying firmly to Adèle: "Do write me again, it gives me a lot of comfort, but avoid, please, reminding me how much grief I may have caused Maman, because I already suffer quite enough over that."[163]

When she returned from St-Boniface in midsummer 1943, she left again at once for the Gaspé so as to spend the rest of the summer at the McKenzies'. There, says the sequel to *Enchantment and Sorrow*, she wrote and wrote with more inspiration and determination than ever, in a second state that was her own way, perhaps, of escaping her grief ("As soon as I emerged from work, I would begin again to suffer for being of this world"[164]), or of living with it for the rest of her life. One night in a raging storm, in spite of Bertha McKenzie's warnings, she went out for a walk on the beach. Having taken refuge at the back of a cave, she spent hours in contemplation of the tempestuous sea, enthralled, like Chateaubriand's René, by the fury of the wind and waves "endlessly bewailing the sorrow of the world."

Around the middle of the night I came home chilled and wet to the bone, for a cold, heavy rain had begun to fall, and hurting from head to foot, yet curiously, mysteriously delivered, as if the bitterness at least had been lifted from me ... But really, I'm still at a loss to understand how I emerged from that night, if not at peace, at least willing to live in this world.[165]

In September she returned to Montreal, but briefly, for she no longer had a fixed address there. Since her new contract with *Le Bulletin des agriculteurs* assured her an income that was more than comfortable, together with complete freedom of movement, she had decided to reorganize her life around the only thing that was important to her: writing. For that, the Rawdon retreat was all she needed, and this was where she had decided to make her domicile from then on. Among the reasons she may have had for the choice were the comfort and care she found in the house of "little Mother Tinkler," as she called her amiably. But there was also the fact that the ambiance of Montreal, where the cost of living was horrendously expensive, did not lend itself to work: "The war is making itself felt increasingly on this overpopulated city, which has become almost hysterical. Really, people are crazy, you know, crazy with sorrow, bewilderment, guilt, and anxiety."[166] The open air, good food, and peacefulness of Rawdon were better for her fragile nerves and the preservation of her health, which at the time, she said, was "a battle rejoined each day."[167]

On her way to the Gaspé in July she had therefore stopped briefly in Westmount to give notice to Miss McLean that she would not be keeping her room any longer. Thereafter, whenever she needed to come to Montreal, she would not stay long and would put up at a hotel. It was always the same one, the Ford Hotel on Dorchester Boulevard between Mackay and Bishop streets, the building in which the Canadian Broadcasting Corporation would install its studios in 1953. The establishment offered long-term rentals if desired and was comfortable, well located, and very quiet. From the autumn of 1943 until she left Montreal for good in 1947, the Ford Hotel was Gabrielle's pied-à-terre in Montreal, but her principal residence throughout this period remained in Rawdon.

She did not much like city life and never would, whether in Montreal, Paris, or even Quebec City. Unlike those writers who need to feel a stirring of words and ideas around them, for whom urban vibrancy is a necessary stimulation, she was one of the "insular" kind who need solitude, discipline, concentration exclusively on themselves, and who work well only when cut off from the world, away from others so as to be closer to their own individualities and their own thoughts.

She therefore tended to stay away from Montreal as much as she could. There was hardly anyone to keep her in the city either, except the two people she was really fond of, Paula Sumner, the companion of her youth in Manitoba, and Henri Girard. But Paula, after living for some years in Montreal and marrying the diplomat Henri Bougearel there, left Canada in September 1943 for San José in Costa Rica, where her husband had been sent as chargé d'affaires by the French government. And so Gabrielle lost "the only woman friend I had in Montreal."[168] As for Henri Girard, he so adored Gabrielle, he so wanted her to be happy, and he himself had so little freedom that he dared not demand that she give up anything whatever for him, and especially not the solitude and peace that Rawdon offered her.

For the privileged relationship begun three or four years earlier between Gabrielle and Henri had kept deepening and unfolding to increasingly tender and exclusive feelings that gradually turned the mentor and his protégée into lovers. We know relatively little about the evolution of this love, given the scarcity of first-hand accounts and documents. All that remain are a few recollections of contemporaries and a few letters kept by Adèle, in whom Gabrielle had confided during her stay in Tangent in 1942 and who was the only one of the family to know of the relationship.

Scarce though they are, these indications allow us to surmise how deep this love became and the place it occupied in the lives of Gabrielle and Henri. In the first letter she wrote to Adèle after her mother's death and her stay at Port-Daniel in the summer of 1943, Gabrielle wrote, "I saw my friend on my return from the Gaspé and once again experienced the quality, so rare, so precious and delicate, of his friendship."[169] And to Henri himself, in a note sent the following May from Rawdon:

Cher fou de fou!

How long this beautiful Sunday has seemed without you. I've been looking for you everywhere among the trees, among the apple trees just beginning to flower and under our big willow where the wasps must have finished their building (luckier than we) because I no longer hear their buzzing.

[...] How I miss you! It's unimaginable, terrible, constant, limitless. [...] *Je t'embrasse tendrement.* G.[170]

To which Henri replied immediately, evoking "this torment wracking me day and night." For, he adds, "I live through hours of appalling disconsolation too. So often, an urge comes over me to drop everything and go to join you, right now, right now, to fly to you with the speed of thought, to be with you and hold you. [. . .] We two together once more, my love . . . we two together."[171]

They were very seldom together, however. They saw each other, as Gabrielle said, "only rarely, at very long intervals, and for very short minutes."[172] They met in Montreal when Gabrielle came on business, or in Rawdon, where Henri would come occasionally to spend a few days. But most of the time they were apart, because of Gabrielle's frequent travels and her determination to live outside Montreal, but also because Henri was a married man and could not or dared not break free. Much as he might promise ("The certainty is growing in me that I'm going to find the ploy and that it will let us live together in our joy and our truth, in full view of heaven and earth"[173]), the obstacle seemed insurmountable. "There's reason for separation according to the Church," Gabrielle wrote, "but his wife's a madwoman who hates her husband and has always made his life miserable but won't consider any solution that would set him free."[174] In any event, a separation would have cost a great deal of money, and Henri did not have any.

And so, added Gabrielle, "it's the tragedy of my life to have met the only man who suits me perfectly, who loves me without a shadow of selfishness, when he's not free according to some stupid social conventions."[175] But the situation, far from causing her to drift away from Henri, made her cherish him even more: "For if heartache comes to me from this blighted love, through this also come all consolation and all beauty and light."[176]

That Henri loved her "without a shadow of selfishness" seems indeed to have been the case. Gabrielle was young, she was beautiful, she was sensitive, talented, destined for all kinds of achievement, while he, aging, with a heart condition and an alcohol-ravaged liver, had only his failed marriage, his aborted artistic ambitions, and ahead of him a future of sameness, confined to the small, prosaic existence of editorial offices and radio studios. How could he not be dazzled by Gabrielle, marvelling that she should deign to pay attention to him, and accordingly ready to give her anything? This in any case is what seems to have been perceived by the few people who remember them together: Henri, head-over-heels in love, open-mouthed in admiration of her, like a starry-eyed adolescent, and Gabrielle, kind, certainly, but more detached, inattentive sometimes, and even a bit cold; in the couple, it was she who dominated and made the decisions.[177]

Were they lovers? To Adèle, both of them denied it. First Gabrielle, when at the end of 1944 she wrote, "You're wrong in supposing that my friend and I are linked in the physical sense of the word. Our friendship is purely moral, purely intellectual, and one of the most beautiful that can be in this world."[178] Then Henri, when he confided the same thing in his last letter to Adèle three years later.[179] In the opinion of others however, including Marcel Carbotte, Gabrielle's husband later, the relationship between Henri and Gabrielle had unquestionably been one between lovers, and their declarations to the contrary were merely to reassure Adèle. But one has to wonder whether Adèle, with all she had lived through herself, would really be as easily scandalized as all that. We shall probably never know the truth of the matter, which is perhaps not a vitally important truth anyway. It is entirely possible that Gabrielle and Henri, to borrow an expression from one of Gabrielle's short stories of this period, were linked only by a kind of "voluptuous chastity."[180]

What is more than probable in any event is that sexuality was less important for Gabrielle than the intellectual benefits of her relationship with Henri, who had a great deal of experience and taste in anything to do with art and literature, and was an initiator and guide for her in these realms. According to Adèle it was he, for example, who led Gabrielle to broaden her reading and discover among others the great French novelists, both classic and contemporary: Flaubert and Maupassant but also Mauriac, Gide, Proust, Giraudoux, Saint-Exupéry, and especially the authors of the prodigious *romans-fleuves* so popular in those years, Duhamel of *Salavin* (1920–1932) and *La Chronique des Pasquier* (1933–1945), and Martin du Gard of *Les Thibault* (1922–1940), a work that Gabrielle admired greatly.[181]

If he was a reading master, Henri was also a writing master, a kind of personal editor who followed Gabrielle's work, reassured and encouraged her, discussed her ideas or outlines with her, and read her manuscripts before publication. He would suggest changes, explain points of grammar and vocabulary, and help her give elegance and discipline to her style. Adèle, here again, remembers that when Gabrielle was writing her articles for *Le Bulletin des agriculteurs* at Tangent, she would hasten to send a copy to Henri, who would return it immediately by airmail, full of deletions, additions, and annotations; "improved" according to Adèle.[182]

It was also Henri who, when Gabrielle was in Montreal, steered her around socially. On her own initiative, almost the only people she saw were her Franco-Manitoban compatriots – Jacqueline Deniset, Émile Couture, Louis Gauthier, and a few others – and she did not see them often at that. Otherwise, she moved in the same circles as did Henri, who was considered an affable man and had a network of many friends and acquaintances.

There were two networks, in fact, one politico-journalistic and the other artistic, corresponding to Henri's two major spheres of activity. We have already seen Henri's role in Gabrielle's journalistic advancement. But Girard did not simply recommend his protégée to his newspaper- and magazine-owner friends, he also introduced her to the professional and political clubs. With him, Gabrielle used sometimes to attend the Press Club events at the Windsor Hotel, at which gathered lowly reporters and Montreal press barons alike. With him, she met the CBC people and the Wartime Information Commission people, she was a guest in the influential editor Edmond Turcotte's home, and even attended a big country party at Premier Adelard Godbout's farm at Frelighsburg, the only woman among all the editorialists, lawyers, and potbellied politicians who were the period's Liberal movers and shakers. It was in this milieu that Gabrielle met her future publisher, Gérard Dagenais, and her future business manager, Jean-Marie Nadeau, both of whom were friends of Girard.

Although as a journalist Henri was obliged to mix with the political crowd, his own interest went first to literary and artistic life. He was friends with a good many writers and particularly painters and art collectors among whom, once again, Gabrielle made friends and acquaintances. For example, it was Girard who introduced her to Jean Palardy and his wife, Jori Smith,[183] at whose studio on Sainte-Famille Street largely English-speaking writers and artists used to gather for evenings that were renowned. There were Frank and Marian Scott, Stanley Cosgrove, John Lyman, Philip Surrey, Mason Wade, P. K. Page, Ronald Everson, and the young Mavis Gallant, joined by the painters Adrien Hébert and Jean-Paul Lemieux. Also attending at times were Doctor Albert Jutras and his wife, the extravagantly whimsical Rachel Gauvreau, both of whom also frequented the group that included Borduas and Maurice Gagnon. Among the Palardy studio's habitués was another physician art collector, Paul Dumas, whose future wife, Lucienne Boucher, was a friend of Alain Grandbois and Alfred Pellan, and was also editor of the women's pages of *La Revue moderne*. In 1944, Paul Dumas published *Lyman* with Les Éditions de l'Arbre in the series "Art vivant," in which publication of a work by Girard was also expected.[184] This coterie, more or less all of whom were "returnees" from Europe, led a life that was hardly in step with conventional morality and cultivated the most advanced thinking of the day, whether in art, politics, or even theology.

The border between these networks, the politico-journalistic and the artistic, was by no means impenetrable. Both were part of what one might call the modernist and liberal groundswell for which wartime Montreal was particularly ripe, and which in the course of these years and some years to follow gave birth to the important literary and artistic revival that is part of recent history. Henri Girard, and Gabrielle through him, were part of this ferment; it was in this milieu that their friends and companions moved, and largely around modern art and literature that their life as a "couple" revolved.

These loose associations of Gabrielle's no doubt explain why it has been said that she was "communist" at this time. In fact, it seems she never was a real communist, meaning a party member, much less a party worker, activist, or placard-bearer. But there is no question at all that she was sympathetic to the communist ideal, or at least to certain of the causes defended by the communists in those days. Among the artists and intellectuals she associated with, all were more or less fellow travellers for whom communism (which, it should be remembered, was an officially "friendly" ideology since the U.S.S.R. had entered the war) was a means of moving society toward greater freedom and justice; but not the only means, just one among many. In the eyes of Jori Smith and Jean Palardy's entourage, it was socialism and the CCF that were on the right track. As far as Gabrielle was concerned, we have already seen in her *Peoples of Canada* articles (confirmed in her Quebec feature stories of 1944–1945 and even *The Tin Flute*) what her political positions were at this time. These positions clearly place her to the left of centre if by this one understands that she deplored the ill effects of capitalism, was in favour of greater social and economic justice, and was sensitive to the hardship and humiliation suffered by humble folk. It was in this spirit that she took an interest in the work of activists like Madeleine Parent and Charles Lipton. However, all this was fairly normal in the liberal circles that she and Girard moved in and was a far cry from calling for revolution and dictatorship of the proletariat.

But political and social struggles were certainly not uppermost among Gabrielle's preoccupations. Nor were her relationships with Henri's artist and writer friends. While they were her social contacts when she came to Montreal, and while she met them with pleasure and even went so far as to exchange correspondence with certain of them, she had no confidants or real friends among them. She did not make great efforts to attend their gatherings either, preferring to remain apart and spend most of her time on her work. And so when she gave up her room in Westmount and took up permanent residence at Mrs. Tinkler's, on balance she did not feel she was losing much.

Still, she had to leave Rawdon once in a while, if only to earn her living. Since her western tour in the autumn of 1942, she had not launched another investigative undertaking and had given nothing to *Le Bulletin des agriculteurs* for the whole summer of 1943. In the early autumn she submitted a short story, "La pension de vieillesse," which appeared in the November issue. It was time for her to rebuild her store of images and interviews in preparation for a new series of articles. As a follow-up to her series on the Canadian West, there was talk of her going to Louisiana, but the plan fell through. Instead, it was decided that she would prepare "a series of major articles on the different regions of our province, especially from the economic and social points of view."[185]

Entitled *Horizons du Québec*, this series began appearing in January 1944 and continued until May 1945. It was the last and the longest (twelve articles) of the series that Gabrielle wrote for *Le Bulletin*. It was also the least successful. It is not at all that the articles are uninteresting; as usual they are richly documented and well written; they are based on the journalist's personal experiences and give a lively sketch of Quebec at the time and its rapid transition to economic and social modernization. The problem lies rather in the series itself, its organization or composition. Reading the articles one after the other, one finds neither the unity of style nor the coalescent vision that had made *Tout Montréal, Ici l'Abitibi*, and *Peoples of Canada*. Stylistically, the strictly documentary tone of some of the articles – on industrial development in the Eastern Townships, for example – clashes with the far more imaginative, even poetic mood of certain others, especially on Charlevoix and the Gaspé. Furthermore, the division and sequence of subjects does not seem to follow any clear objective. Everything happens as though the journalist-writer – here more journalist than creative writer – had not really committed herself to her research, as though she had no plan or overall perspective to guide her investigations and had made do with accumulating articles and putting them together to make up a series to satisfy the terms of the contract she was being paid for.

Horizons du Québec was not in fact the result of a methodical investigative tour as all the preceding series had been. It was based on several short trips and sojourns in various parts of Quebec where Gabrielle went not only or necessarily for work but for her personal pleasure or on the suggestion of friends. And these trips never kept her away very long from Rawdon, where her real interests lay at the time.

At the very beginning of autumn 1943, for instance, she took advantage of an invitation from Jori Smith and Jean Palardy to their summer house at Petite-Rivière-Saint-François to pay brief visits to other parts of northern Quebec. She went first to the Lac-Saint-Jean district, where she admired the "prodigious" town of Arvida, took a cruise on the Saguenay River, and from there came back down to Charlevoix, where she visited the Île aux Coudres and the *goélette* shipyard at Petite-Rivière, which was the subject of a film Jean Palardy had just made for the National Film Board.[186] One evening in Baie-Saint-Paul, she called on the painter René Richard and his wife, Blanche, and returned several times subsequently to spend the evening. From this journey of two or three weeks she drew the first four articles of her series for the following winter, which she began writing in November as soon as she was back in Rawdon.

For her fifth article, which appeared in May 1944, she had no need to go anywhere, because it was about the Gaspé, and she limited herself to telling the story of a fishing trip she had taken the previous summer with her elderly friend Élias Langlois of Port-Daniel. Then when summer came she began again to "hunt for copy."[187] In June she spent a day with a market gardener on Île Jésus and went with him to Bonsecours Market; this yielded an article that reminds one a little of the *Tout Montréal* series.[188] Then she went to spend her 1944 summer vacation in the Sutton and Lake Memphramagog district, from where she made excursions to neighbouring towns and cities – Magog, Sherbrooke, Granby, and as far as Asbestos and Lac Mégantic in one direction, and Drummondville and Victoriaville in the other. Here again, combining work and pleasure, she took notes in anticipation of her articles for the following autumn and winter, then retreated peacefully to her Rawdon "Shangri-La."[189] As for the final two articles of the series, published respectively in April and May 1945, researching them did not require much travelling: they were about the lives of forestry workers, first in a lumber camp not far from Chertsey, between Rawdon and St-Donat, then on the L'Assomption River where Gabrielle joined a team of log-drivers in the vicinity of St-Côme, some twenty-five miles north of Rawdon.

Meanwhile, however, late in 1944, *Le Bulletin des agriculteurs* had put an end to the contract it had had with Gabrielle Roy since the spring of 1943. Not that the publishers were dissatisfied with her, it was just that *Le Bulletin*'s resources no longer allowed the payment of such high salaries, for the simple reason that the government at Quebec City had changed.[190] In the election of August 1944 Maurice Duplessis's Union Nationale had returned to power, meaning that the time of plenty was over for the entire liberal press. One may even wonder whether this event was not responsible for the change in tone observable between the first and last articles of Gabrielle's *Horizons du Québec* series. While those of the winter of 1944 are fairly strongly imbued with liberal and socialist ideology, those published after the fall of the Godbout government seem far tamer, as if the journalist (or her publishers) felt obliged to step warily in view of the new political climate. Whatever the case, *Le Bulletin* continued to publish Gabrielle's texts and consider her a regular contributor, but withdrew the favoured treatment she had been receiving for the past year and a half. Henceforth she was paid by the article, which if not a reduction in income (for the remuneration was still generous) meant at least a return to the freelance status and the relative precariousness that went with it.

"Profession: Authoress"

By the time she lost her comfortable job with *Le Bulletin des agriculteurs*, Gabrielle was no longer considering herself primarily a journalist in any case, if indeed journalism had ever been more for her than a way to earn a living. What attached her mostly to the trade was the money and the freedom it left her to devote herself to what for her was now the essential: her work as a creative writer.

This becomes particularly evident in the year 1943, when she moved permanently to Rawdon and had inscribed in her new passport, "profession, authoress."[191] It was as though a kind of turning point occurred at this moment, a new departure that would goad Gabrielle – she would soon be thirty-five – into redoubling her efforts to set aside all that had thus far succeeded in distracting or delaying her, and to focus her life on her plans of a literary nature.

We see this first in the short stories she gave *Le Bulletin des agriculteurs* in these years, for which she sometimes used a nom de plume – "Aline Lubac" or "Danny." Less numerous than those she published in *La Revue moderne*, these stories were distinctly more ambitious stylistically, in length (the magazine sometimes presented them as "complete novels"[192]), and especially in pursuit of originality in theme and composition that, while not always convincing in its results, was nevertheless showing more assertively than before. Two of these stories, "La grande Berthe" (June 1943) and "La pension de vieillesse" (November 1943), are based on peasant customs and mores among French Canadians of the West,[193] to which the theme of money and covetousness lends accents reminiscent of Balzac or Claude-Henri Grignon. Gabrielle's other stories of this period are of a newer kind, psychological tales in which the technique is intended to be more "modern," more daring, although today it appears rather clumsy and conventional. They are interesting mostly in the recurrence in varying modes of the same theme, the impossible or blighted love, a theme not unrelated to Gabrielle's own situation with her "dear friend." Thus in "La vieille fille" (February 1943), Solange, a forty-year-old schoolteacher, evokes her failed relationship with a man whose desire she has rebuffed out of distaste for the physical side of love. "François et Odine" (June 1944) on the other hand is a fable in which two young villagers, having discovered the horrors of conjugal life, choose to save their love by renouncing marriage and giving themselves freely to one another in the midst of Nature where "all living was loving. And all that was loving was found again. And all that was found again, taken, and given, was bursting with life."[194]

It is in the novella titled "Qui est Claudia?" (May 1945) that the meditation on love goes further and the autobiographical inspiration is most evident. This story portrays the self-examination of a thirty-year-old actress who "has obtained from the gods the gifts of intelligence and beauty, and the gift, rarer still, of eliciting love as one desires it." Alone before her mirror, Claudia remembers "the years, so difficult to endure, before fame fulfills the artist (and when you said the word 'fame,' already you were thinking of other words: wealth, princely fees, envy)"; then she sees again in her mind's eye the succession of liaisons she has had: Taras, the Ukrainian violinist, the sensual Georges, who came to an alcoholic end, Étienne, the only one who left her, and Harry, her current lover, older than she and slave to her slightest whim. Yet Claudia is not happy, for she is "the poorest of the poor among women: the one who has never been in love."[195]

All these stories have a laboured, artificial tone that makes them seem rather like writing exercises or questionably successful attempts at handling forms and subjects currently in vogue in the "commercial" literature of the day by an author who already has a certain public recognition. The texts are written hastily and without much care, unlike the work that was the major project, the major undertaking of these two or three years: *Bonheur d'occasion*.

While we know with certainty when the novel was finished – in early summer 1944 – we are less sure when it was begun. There is no exact documentation on this, either a manuscript or any clue in the letters that have been found. All we have are Gabrielle's own statements, most of them made late in life and lacking in clarity, even coherence. In her autobiographical texts, she allows it to be understood vaguely that the work began in 1941,[196] which corresponds to the date reported also by certain interviewers;[197] however, others have reported that it was 1942,[198] or even 1943.[199] What is certain is that the beginnings of *Bonheur d'occasion* came after her discovery of Saint-Henri, which could just as well have been in the spring of 1940 as 1941. All considered, we can conclude that she began writing her book in the spring of 1941, in her room at Miss McLean's, or in the summer of that same year during her second sojourn at Port-Daniel while she was finishing or had just finished her *Tout Montréal* articles.

There is the same uncertainty over the form in which the idea of *Bonheur d'occasion* first occurred to her. At times she speaks of a kind of illumination suddenly allowing her to see the entire edifice of her future novel even before she began to write it. "Suddenly, one day it was all there – characters, theme, meaning – as a huge, hazy mass, yet with a sort of coherence already."[200] At other times she talks about first having begun a short story, and only later, in the face of the unexpected dimensions the story gradually took on, having to resign herself to making a novel of it.[201] Between these two stories of the genesis, the contradiction is perhaps not quite complete; *Bonheur d'occasion* might well have begun as a short story, since this after all was the genre that Gabrielle the penpusher was then given to in order to earn a living, with a vision soon following of a much more substantial work than the one allowed or demanded by what she had already drafted.

How this transformation came about, how the initial illumination or idea for a short story turned into the outline of a novel, here again we can only indulge in conjecture, based on memories that Gabrielle would impart later. In a short English text from 1947, written at the time of the novel's publication as *The Tin Flute* in the United States,[202] and in "Le pays de *Bonheur d'occasion*," published in 1974, she speaks of the long "investigation" that preceded or accompanied the writing of her first drafts, meaning all the time she spent roaming the Saint-Henri district, exploring its humblest corners, walking its streets and squares, mixing with the people, waiting for workmen at the doors of factories, visiting lodgings for rent, snack bars, churches, etc.

> But I remember best the sounds of human voices on the warm night air, like a friendly buzzing. Feeble streetlamps at the corners of these short streets showed family or neighbourly groups sitting in circles on the sidewalk, or sometimes in the middle of the road. Each a small agora where life was discussed. First the rural scene they had left behind just yesterday because it no longer supported them and they hoped for better from the city. Next unemployment, a fact of life for one of every three families. Here, hardship was inexorable. Then came the war, which would probably straighten things out, it was said. From one little street to the next, you could hear the people breathe their sighs.[203]

In short Gabrielle was practising the same method as realistic and naturalistic novelists: observation, documentation, the gathering of detail straight from life. Living then on Dorchester Street, as soon as she had a free moment she would go down to Saint-Henri. "I went walking there I don't know how many times," she would say, "hundreds of times probably, at all hours of the day and even the night."[204] She went there in summer, she went there in winter, she went there in spring. Very often Henri went with her, both as bodyguard and note-taker. And so, she would say, "one day I found I had the germ of a novel on my hands"[205] – a body of material so rich, so dense, so full of narrative potential, and so laden with meaning, such a vast fictional universe in other words, that it would never fit inside a short story, even a novella. Thereafter, it had to become a novel.

Without questioning the accuracy of such an explanation, one cannot consider it the only one possible. Certainly, when Gabrielle embarked on writing *Bonheur d'occasion*, it was in response to the reality of Saint-

Henri, unemployment, and the war. But no doubt at this time she also had an urgent desire to write a novel, and a need to try her hand at something more meaty than the articles and short stories she was spreading about in publications of the day. She wanted badly to publish a book, a fine book that would bring her fame and prove to herself and others that she had not been wrong to get away from Manitoba, leaving her mother and sisters behind, because she was a real, honest-to-goodness writer.

She threw herself into writing her novel with a kind of frenzy, giving it every possible moment of freedom she could squeeze between the preparation and writing of her texts for *Le Bulletin des agriculteurs*. The progress of her manuscript became her principal if not her only preoccupation, for which she was prepared to sacrifice everything, social occasions, recreation, even her health if need be. Even her love life came second, or at least was now arranged around her work. Henri not only understood and accepted this but encouraged her, thus binding the bond between the two of them even more firmly. He admired "this exquisite genius of a woman"[206] whose "great strength [. . .] is never to disperse her energy" and for whom, he would say, "time is precious, not in the monetary sense but in the most profound sense of the realization of herself, this daughter of solitude."[207]

As almost always with first novels, this project that absorbed her so utterly, this *Bonheur d'occasion*, became for Gabrielle the receptacle for everything she was, everything she thought, everything that weighed on her and haunted her. She put what she knew of Saint-Henri and Westmount into it, certainly; she put her vision of the world into it, her moral and political ideas, and the stylistic skill brought to her by her reading as well as her experience as a journalist and author of popular literature. But she also put a great deal of her own life into it, her own personal memories and most private thoughts, without always intending to or even being aware of it. All is transposed, modified, metamorphosed, to be sure, and thus hidden from the sight of others and in part from her own as well, but the novel, realistic as it is, focused as it is on the external world, is no less charged with undeniable subjectivity. There is no doubt for example that the Lacasse family owes a great deal to Gabrielle's memories of her own family. Azarius is a carpenter like Albert Painchaud, Anna's husband; Eugène reminds us of Rodolphe, the attentive but dependent son; Rose-Anna of course is Mélina's twin sister. And how could we fail to see in Florentine, the girl with the "green eyes,"[208] or in the pair Jean Lévesque and Emmanuel Létourneau, partial

and tangled projections of Gabrielle herself, of her yearning for betterment, her idealism, and her problematical relationship with her birth
milieu.[209] While *Bonheur d'occasion* is a portrait of a period and a
society, it could also in a way be a self-portrait.

Gabrielle wrote at least two versions of her novel, perhaps more.[210] It
seems that the first, begun in Montreal or the Gaspé, was continued
intermittently until the spring of 1943, when Gabrielle was living at
Rawdon and Mélina, in St-Boniface, was suffering from the illness from
which she was soon to die. This version (which is lost today) consisted
of perhaps eight or nine hundred typed pages written directly on the
typewriter;[211] it was a first draft, written rapidly and without corrections.

On her return from Manitoba the following July after her mother's
death, Gabrielle took this "enormous manuscript" with her to Port-
Daniel and set to work again. Did she rework the existing version,
adding new pages? Did she immediately begin a second version? In any
case, early on the morning after her arrival she began to write more
feverishly than ever, as if her grief had increased her energy tenfold.

> I propped myself up in my bed with pillows at my back, my typewriter on
> my knees, and the tray close by on a night table, and set to work, typing a
> few lines, stopping to nibble at a piece of toast and drink a big draught of
> black coffee. I might have thought I was at Esther's, except that I was sur-
> rounded by water and now my heart wasn't in it. This is the way the days
> went by. I would go up to my room with my breakfast and begin at once
> to type, even before getting washed and combing my hair, would con-
> tinue until around noon, begin again about two and not stop until late
> afternoon. Not knowing who or what I was working for, or even where
> such strenuous effort was leading me, I was possessed by a will to arrive
> as fast as possible at some place I didn't know I was going to.[212]

In September she had to interrupt her work to return to Montreal
and resume her journalism. Perhaps she worked at the novel through the
autumn in her spare time. The fact is that when she moved back to
Rawdon toward the end of 1943, she had a complete version of her novel,
either the first version which she had returned to and finished, or the
second which she had begun at Port-Daniel the previous summer.

Now she began to rewrite it all. Chapter by chapter, she corrected,
trimmed, rearranged, rewrote sentences and scenes, this time trying for
overall concision in her narration. Henri once again brought his help

and advice to bear. "She thus reworked certain chapters six or seven times – and entirely," he wrote. At some point she deleted a long passage "because in her judgment it slowed down the pace of the narration." And yet, Girard added, "it was a particularly lighthearted chapter. The scene takes place at the home of Éveline, Boisvert's fiancée. The description of Éveline's brother rocking in the rocking chair while Boisvert woos the girl is one of the most screamingly funny things yet written in Canada."[213] Wherein probably lies the reason for the cut made by Gabrielle, who must have decided that this satire was not in keeping with the tone she wished to give Bonheur d'occasion, which was anything but "screamingly funny."

It would seem that she completed this new version around May or June 1944. Considering it final, she decided to have a clean copy typed by her friend Jacqueline Deniset, who was a secretary at Canadian National Railways. On the morning she arrived in Jacqueline's office, the latter recalls, she held her manuscript in both arms, "like a baby" and said as she handed it over, "Either nobody's going to notice it or it's going to be a hit." For her services, Gabrielle (who was then earning $250 a month) offered Jacqueline $25, but might, she said, give her more later if the book was a success. It was this clean copy – 499 pages in two black binders[214] – that Gabrielle submitted to the eventual publisher of Bonheur d'occasion, Gérard Dagenais.

At the age of forty-one, Gérard Dagenais was then at the peak of his career. Along with Bernard Valiquette, Robert Charbonneau, Claude Hurtubise, and a few others, he was one of a contingent of literary entrepreneurs who had seized on the favourable circumstances created in Quebec by the German occupation of France and the dampened Parisian publishing industry to go all out getting themselves into the publishing business. Their heyday would be brief, to be sure, and all would more or less go bankrupt when peace returned, but their activity and spin-off effects gave publishing and the literary movement in Montreal an impetus that was irreversible. In this group, Dagenais had something of a reputation for brashness. He had been trained in journalism in the thirties, had joined La Revue moderne in 1943, and was its literary editor for a brief period. Under the pen-name Albert Pascal he had published translations from English with a number of publishers. Early in 1944, therefore shortly before Gabrielle entrusted her manuscript to him, he founded his own publishing house, La Société des Éditions Pascal, and purchased the magazine Amérique française from Pierre

Baillargeon, its founder. This magazine was one of the literary publications whose emergence had also been furthered by the war.[215] The first
book published by Les Éditions Pascal, *Iberville le conquérant* by Guy
Frégault, appeared in the spring of 1944; it was followed in the same year
by a dozen other titles that were either reprints of French books (Pierre
Louÿs, Francis Carco, François Mauriac, Jacques Chardonne) or works of
established authors (Adrienne Maillet, Carl Dubuc, François Hertel).

Dagenais was a good friend of Henri Girard and it was most probably through Henri that Gabrielle made contact with the owner of Les
Éditions Pascal, who received the manuscript early in summer 1944.
"There was Gabrielle Roy before me," he would write later, "her curly
brown hair falling over her shoulders, her eyes very serious, eager, her air
by turns young, moody, lively, determined." He read the book "all at one
go, one Sunday" and was "delighted." "At last," he said to himself, "a good
realistic novel!"[216]

At the beginning of July, publisher, novelist, and mentor together
revised the text of the manuscript, making some minor last-minute
corrections. Then the contract was signed in Montreal on August 28; it
consisted of a single page stipulating that the work would appear
"about the end of October 1944 [. . .] printed in one volume," and that
the author would receive royalties of 10 per cent, against which an
advance of $100 would be payable on publication.[217] None of these terms
would be respected.

Although Gabrielle badgered Dagenais and declared herself "very
disappointed with the delay in the publication of my novel,"[218] delays
dragged on and on. In its February 1945 issue, *Amérique française* at last
announced publication of *Bonheur d'occasion*, "a major novel in two
volumes to appear together within a few days."[219] But the few days
turned into weeks, then months, and still the book did not appear. As for
the printing in two volumes, Gabrielle was exceedingly vexed and did
not resign herself to it with good grace, insisting that the two volumes be
presented and sold together "in a single package" and for a single price.[220]
When *Bonheur d'occasion* finally came off the presses at Therrien Frères
in June 1945, the pagination of the two volumes was continuous, but the
chapter numbers began at I in each volume.

A reader opening the first volume of Gabrielle Roy's first novel would
read on the first page this simple dedication: "To Mélina Roy."

CHAPTER 7

The Burden of Fame

*B*onheur d'occasion (*The Tin Flute*) was a major phenomenon in the history of Quebec and Canadian literature, a break with the past that the critics have commented on abundantly. A major phenomenon too, with even greater impact, in Gabrielle Roy's personal history, which the book's appearance literally divided in two.

This first book and especially its immense success marked both an end and a beginning. First, it was the end of the long road Gabrielle had travelled from the time of leaving Manitoba in 1937 through settling in Montreal two years later – or from even earlier still, when she began yearning as an adolescent to rise above the petty existence her community held in store for her and one day, whatever the cost, reach those "expanded horizons" for which she felt she was created. At last her efforts and ambitions were being crowned with success; at thirty-six years of age, here she was in the limelight, a real writer, here she was rich and famous.

A new period of her life now began that was to contrast sharply with the one just finished. Gabrielle's character remained the same – determined, independent, obsessed by a desire for accomplishment and a need for recognition – but the scene was to change. Having proven herself and overcome external obstacles – financial need, being unknown and dependent on her family and birth milieu – she must now continue her struggle on another and perhaps more exacting front: pursuing her work and destiny as a writer.

That she was a writer, the success of *Bonheur d'occasion* had incontestably shown. The onus was now on her not only to carry on being a writer but ever more and ever better, to the exclusion of all else. Broadly speaking, this was the preoccupation that dominated the entire second half of Gabrielle's life: to maintain the standard set by her first book and surpass this first one with more books, which in their accumulation would become part of and even the entire fabric of her life, to a point where eventually there would be nothing left of herself outside of them.

She entered the new territory gradually with the years. Before the change was complete, before Gabrielle's life became a kind of barrenland entirely given over to writing, there was a transition phase corresponding more or less to the seven or eight years following the publication of *Bonheur d'occasion*. During this period, whose focal point was a second sojourn in Europe between 1947 and 1950, the earlier struggle for social and professional betterment continued for a time, aided by the international success of her novel. Yet alongside the struggle, the conditions of Gabrielle's future life were progressively falling into place, with her marriage, difficulties with writing, health problems, and an increasingly pronounced tendency for reclusiveness.

Cinderella

It is hard for us today to imagine the magnitude of the financial and public-relations success of *Bonheur d'occasion* and its translation, *The Tin Flute*. In the context of Quebec and Canada, nothing like it had ever been seen. It was a kind of miracle worthy of Cinderella or any Hollywood success story. Almost overnight an obscure journalist with an obscure agricultural magazine became a real live princess; she was admired across the country, applauded abroad, fawned over by the public, hounded by reporters, honoured with prizes and distinctions, and (which did no harm at all) showered with money. The success of this book and its author was the first "American style" success in the history of Quebec and Canadian literature, and there has perhaps been no other to surpass it since.

Beyond the fact that the book appealed to the public at large as well as the mavens of "learned" literature and the critics, the striking thing about this success is how long it lasted (nearly three years) and how it crescendoed. It built up in waves. The first happened on the local scene, in Montreal, Quebec, and English Canada, where the book in the original French was already doing very well in the first year following its publication. Then the pace quickened when the American translation was announced in 1946, and quickened further month by month to reach a peak in the spring of 1947, by which time Gabrielle Roy was the most celebrated writer in the country. Finally, she was awarded the Prix Fémina in Paris in November 1947, confirming *Bonheur d'occasion* to be an international as well as a local success.

Before recounting these events in more detail, we must note the arrival on stage of a new character in the drama of Gabrielle's life, one who played a very important role in her spectacular début: Jean-Marie Nadeau.

Forty years old at the time, in 1945 Jean-Marie Nadeau was not yet in the pre-eminent position he was to hold during the decade to follow in the Liberal party of Quebec, of which he came to be one of the leading thinkers and, as such, one of the prime movers of the Quiet Revolution. He was already an important man, however; a brilliant jurist, teacher of political economics and history at the Université de Montréal, and ex-conservator of the Bibliothèque Saint-Sulpice, he was known as an avant-garde intellectual of Keynesian convictions with grand ideas for Canada and Quebec in the postwar era. It was Henri Girard who introduced him to Gabrielle at a party at former premier Adelard Godbout's in the summer of 1945. He and Girard were friends; they had known each other since the early 1930s when Nadeau, after studying in Europe, was active in the "progressive" magazine milieu in Montreal and was a contributor to Olivar Asselin's *L'Ordre*. During the war they had worked together at the newspaper *Le Canada* and at the international service of the CBC.[1]

A lawyer with an excellent reputation practising as senior partner in a law firm with his brother André, Nadeau had a thorough knowledge of copyright and publishing law and often served as legal adviser to his artist and intellectual friends. In September 1945, for a modest retainer and a commission of 10 per cent, he became Gabrielle Roy's "business manager," which is to say her solicitor and literary agent. Henceforth she left to him the negotiation and sometimes even the signing of her contracts, collection of her royalties, sale of her works abroad, her income tax business, and generally everything to do with the management of her rights and her money. Their professional relationship, which spanned some ten years, was never intimate but always correct if not cordial. But it was particularly between 1945 and 1950, while Gabrielle most needed his services, that Nadeau was most active on her behalf. The abundant archives show that he served her with noteworthy competence and honesty.[2]

In the beginning, the new novelist had called upon *Maître* Nadeau to help her resolve her problems with Les Éditions Pascal. *Bonheur d'occasion* appeared on bookstore shelves at the end of June 1945, selling for $3 for the two volumes. Although it was already summer, the critics sprang to action immediately, especially in the Montreal press of liberal tendency where, of course, Henri Girard had many friends. Thus, Émile-Charles Hamel, writing in *Le Jour*, drew his readers' attention to "one of the most true-to-life, boldest, and best written books published hitherto in Canada," and Jean Béraud in *La Presse*, René Garneau in *Le Canada*, and Berthelot Brunet in *La Nouvelle Relève* wrote similarly effusive reviews.[3] All the other critics very quickly fell into step and the praise rained liberally, all finding *Bonheur d'occasion* to be "a novel the like of which we had dared not hope to see in French Canada." Even the righteous *Le Devoir*, while noting that "the theme could have given many opportunities for scabrous scenes," complimented the writer "for having managed to treat it with great delicacy of touch" and thus given a book that, while not suitable for putting "in the hands of maidens and youths," was even so "not likely to shock much less scandalize people of experience."[4] Meanwhile, floods of letters were arriving from anonymous readers and others as prominent as Roger Lemelin, the author of the recent book *Les Plouffe*, who expressed to Gabrielle "all the admiration I feel for your stupendous work. I know whereof I speak, Mademoiselle"; Marcel Dugas: "You have written an admirable book, [...] the first great French-Canadian novel"; and Michelle Le Normand: "Not counting my husband's Les Opiniâtres [...], I don't know one Canadian novel you haven't beaten hollow."[5] The book was received almost unanimously with enthusiasm, and this success was soon being reflected in sales. By the end of summer, the first edition of some two thousand copies was almost sold out and demand was still running high.

The publisher, Gérard Dagenais, had neither the money nor the competence to handle a success of this magnitude. Relations between him and Gabrielle quickly deteriorated. The cheque for $100 that Les Éditions Pascal had issued her as an advance soon after the book's publication was refused several times by the bank for lack of funds. Then at the end of September when the first royalty payment of 10 per cent of sales came due as provided by the contract, Gabrielle received nothing despite her repeated requests. Dagenais was decidedly a poor payer.

Gabrielle lost no time. Determined to benefit as she should from the success she had been awaiting for so many years and which looked very promising indeed financially, she decided to take proceedings. It was for this that she approached Nadeau, who immediately took things in hand.

Since he and Dagenais were old acquaintances, the lawyer attempted first to obtain an out-of-court settlement, then threatened to have proceedings begun by another law firm. This dragged on until 1947. What Nadeau did immediately was have Dagenais give up his contract with Gabrielle and return her rights. A new agreement was signed to this effect on 18 October 1945, by which Gabrielle herself became the publisher of her novel. With a loan of $2,000 that Nadeau negotiated for her with the Banque Canadienne Nationale, she financed a second printing of *Bonheur d'occasion*, whose text was tidied of its printer's errors by Henri Girard and in which "Copyright 1945 by Société des Éditions Pascal enr." was replaced by "Copyright 1945 by Gabrielle Roy."[6] Under this agreement, Les Éditions Pascal, whose name still appeared on the book's cover, now did no more than distribute the book. The stock was kept on Fullum Street in the basement of Jean-Marie Nadeau's brother Georges's house, and Dagenais bought copies from Gabrielle to resell to bookstores.

This system was very profitable for Gabrielle. She had control of the merchandising of her book and was collecting about a third of the sale price after expenses instead of the usual 10 or 15 per cent, which enabled her to pay off her loan from the bank within a year. The reason was that sales were skyrocketing, stimulated by word of mouth and ecstatic commentary in the press and on radio. The second printing of four thousand copies was sold out by April 1946 and another three thousand copies were printed, still under the name of Les Éditions Pascal. A few months later, yet another printing had to be envisaged. However, like a number of other Montreal publishers that had sprung up in the exceptionally favourable circumstances created by the war and then with the return of peace had neither the working capital nor the backing to cope with a return to competition with the French, Les Éditions Pascal ceased operations in the course of the summer of 1946. In September, the fourth printing of *Bonheur d'occasion* was therefore entrusted to Les Éditions Beauchemin, under the same terms as those agreed upon with Dagenais: Gabrielle Roy was the publisher and Beauchemin, whose name now figured on the cover of the book, was the exclusive distributor to Canadian bookstores.

At this point, however, *Bonheur d'occasion* was already launched on a new career whose spectacular development would considerably enhance Gabrielle's reputation and the sales of her book at home in Quebec. The scene this time was abroad, first in the United States and then in France, but the master of ceremonies of all events was still Jean-Marie Nadeau, who admired *Bonheur d'occasion* immeasurably and believed it to be destined for a brilliant international career.

Surprisingly to us, Nadeau's first target for *Bonheur d'occasion*'s exportation was not France but the United States. This can be explained by the context of the period, when publishing in France had still not recovered from the Occupation and after five years of war the French presence had paled in Quebec. In the autumn of 1945, using as his selling point the immense popularity being enjoyed by the Montreal edition, Nadeau proposed the book to two New York publishers, Roy Publishers and Reynal & Hitchcock. It is difficult to know what had motivated his choice of the first of these two, but the second was one of the major New York literary houses. According to Gabrielle, it also happened that Miriam Chapin, the sister of one of the owners, Curtice Hitchcock, came often to Montreal to stay with friends who saw Gabrielle socially. Miriam had read the book and, profoundly moved, persuaded her brother to publish it.[7] On November 26, since there had been no response to his proposal, Nadeau resorted to an old agents's ploy: he sent telegrams to both publishers announcing that Miss Roy had received another offer and inviting them to submit theirs without delay. Roy Publishers declined; Reynal & Hitchcock asked for a week's delay, which Nadeau granted. On 4 December 1945, Curtice Hitchcock wrote to Nadeau: "We are enormously enthusiastic about the book and hope it will become one of the great successes of its season." The letter was accompanied by a contract (which Nadeau signed the same day) stipulating that the English translation, over which the author would have a right of approval, would be published before the month of June 1947. Gabrielle received an advance of $500.

Reynal & Hitchcock had some difficulty finding a translator. Nadeau and his client were obliged to wait impatiently until April to hear that the job would be done by Hannah Josephson, an American who had translated Aragon and Philippe Soupault. She set to work during the summer of 1946. For the near-untranslatable title as it stands in French, she considered "Bargain in Happiness" or "Bargain in Love," but knew that something less simpering and more striking would have to be found.

Over in France, not much was happening. Nadeau had not really looked for a publisher there before the spring of 1946, it must be admitted. For a time he thought about Gallimard but did not follow up the idea. Then Pierre Tisseyre of the Agence littéraire atlantique transmitted an offer from a Parisian house called La Jeune Parque. Before accepting,

Nadeau made inquiries of his European contacts, who telegraphed immediately: "New house created during Resistance. Credit question-able." He therefore left the offer unanswered, to the annoyance of La Jeune Parque: if Gabrielle Roy was going to be as picky as all that, they informed him, she could shift for herself making a name with the public in Paris. But Jean-Marie Nadeau was not born yesterday. Let's not be in any hurry, he advised Gabrielle, let's wait till the book's out in New York; we'll be better placed then to negotiate with the French publishers. By the end of November 1946, there was still nothing settled about a Paris edition of *Bonheur d'occasion*.

A Woman in Flight

Gabrielle may have left responsibility for all the wheeling and dealing over the book's fortunes to Nadeau, but this did not prevent her from closely following the various phases. As closely as her other activities permitted at any rate, for while *Bonheur d'occasion* was selling well and she had become a star on the local literary scene, life still had to go on. And she still had to write.

When her book came out in June 1945, she was at Mrs. Tinkler's in Rawdon. A month later she left on assignment for *Le Bulletin des agricul-teurs*, as she had every summer since 1940. This summer, in an extension of the series *Horizons du Québec*, whose last article had appeared in May, she was doing an investigative series on Quebec industry, which was then undergoing rapid expansion. She visited factories, descended into mines, had manufacturing procedures and the workings of machinery explained, questioned workers and bosses, and finally wrote three arti-cles that appeared in *Le Bulletin* of September, October, and November 1945. These articles are very thorough and quite technical, and were not only the last that Gabrielle wrote for *Le Bulletin des agriculteurs* but the last of her career as an investigative reporter, a career that had spanned six years and was remarkable for its truly exceptional productivity, par-ticularly when measured by today's standards.

This same summer, Gabrielle submitted a short story titled "Un vagabond frappe à notre porte" ("A Tramp at the Door") to Gérard Dagenais for the magazine *Amérique française*, which several months earlier had for the first time published a short story of hers, "La vallée Houdou" ("Hoodoo Valley"). These texts, similar in style and inspiration, appear to have arisen out of the same project, a book that Gabrielle seems to have begun working on after completing *Bonheur d'occasion* in the summer of 1944 and that was to have been called "Contes de la Plaine."[8] Besides "La vallée Houdou," which features a group of Doukhobor colonists, and "Un vagabond frappe à notre porte," whose characters are members of a French-Canadian prairie family, this book was to have contained a number of other stories of the Canadian West inspired by Gabrielle's summer tour of 1942 and her stay with her sister Adèle. This appears to be the case with "La lune des moissons," a naturalistic type of story from about this period that relates the violent and ironic tale of a family of immigrant farmers who tear each other to bits over sex and money. Whether this piece was to have figured in "Contes de la Plaine" is impossible to know, for the project fell by the wayside. The book was revived thirty years later in a different form, however, when Gabrielle assembled her collection of stories titled *Un jardin au bout du monde* (*Garden in the Wind*).

Once her reporting chores were over, Gabrielle would have liked to repair to Rawdon, which had become more or less her permanent residence, but had to spend almost all autumn 1945 in Montreal (she stayed at the Ford Hotel), kept there by her book, whose success was continuing and already turning her into a celebrity pursued by journalists, booksellers, librarians, and other "agents" of the small Montreal literary world. Her picture was appearing in newspapers and department store windows – a picture she had had taken the previous autumn at Dagenais's request by Annette Zarov, "one of the finest portrait photographers in Canada."[9] This time it was a celebrity photograph. Gone were the girlish face and manner still lingering in the one taken by Larose in 1939. Her features here are those of a mature woman, her lips and eyebrows perfectly traced, her long hair falling over her shoulders à la Rita Hayworth, her eyes grey-green and pensive. She was now a woman of great beauty, certainly, but marble-like, inaccessible, in the manner of those ethereal beings whose images adorned the lobbies of theatres and movie houses of the period, described so aptly by Roland Barthes.[10]

What is today called "promotion" made demands on Gabrielle with which she simply had to comply. In September 1945, for example, she granted an interview to Judith Jasmin on Radio-Canada; another interview had appeared in *The Gazette* several days earlier.[11] On November 1, she attended a supper organized in her honour by the Association des anciens du Manitoba at the Pennsylvania Hotel; Émile Couture spoke, followed by the distinguished critic Roger Duhamel.[12] "Publicity, it seems, is very necessary," she wrote in her correspondence. "And then, the public is insisting more and more on knowing the author of a book."

All this was "hard to bear," she added, and no doubt she felt it sincerely.[13] She nonetheless paid active attention to her business interests and was both amazed and delighted by the popularity of *Bonheur d'occasion* and all the praise from the critics. Had she not always aspired to renown, admiration from others, wealth? Far from having no interest in the success of her book, she was determined to reap especially its financial benefits and was jealous of her rights, constantly urging Nadeau to be tough in his negotiations and administration.

Eventually, however, all the excitement, all the things to be attended to, all the public attention became burdensome and affected her health, on which her past five or six years of strenuous activity had already taken a toll. Above all, this train of life was hampering her writing. When she was in Montreal she could no longer follow the strict routine she had set for herself since returning from Europe: an early rise, writing all morning until around one o'clock, going out for walks or drives or meeting people only in the afternoon, spending the evening reading or listening to music, and going early to bed. After these three months in Montreal, three months of excitement and dealings of one kind or another, she was longing more than ever for solitude and rest.

She therefore returned to Rawdon shortly before Christmas. But as if Rawdon were still not isolated enough, she decided to leave in the second half of January 1946 for somewhere much farther away, California, fully determined, as she wrote to Jean-Marie Nadeau, "not to give a single thought to my novel."[14] Why California? No doubt because it was so distant and she was sure of finding the peace she wanted and the sunshine she needed, but also because she had family there, the family that Mélina had gone to visit in 1939. The children of Uncle Moïse Landry had settled on the Pacific coast, some in Los Angeles, others at Vista in the vicinity of San Diego where their father's property was located. In answer to the question concerning the purpose of her visit when she requested her visa at the American consulate, Gabrielle answered, "to observe and study as a writer."[15] She arrived in Los Angeles by train very early in February. From there she went for a time to Laguna Beach, where she took a room at the Del Camino Hotel, then moved farther south and rented a cottage on the sea at Encinitas, not far from Vista. There she stayed until mid-April, from time to time seeing her cousins with whom she had had no contact since childhood, but insisting on being alone as much as possible to collect her wits and restore her inner peace while "trying to forget that I ever wrote Bonheur d'occasion." For "joy springs not from what is done but from what is to be done."[16]

This journey had all the earmarks of an escape. An escape from the public relations and social whirlwind created in Montreal by the success of *Bonheur d'occasion*, especially since the announcement of the contract with Reynal & Hitchcock, but also, it seems, an escape from the increasingly complicated turn her relationship with Henri Girard was taking. Nothing had changed for Gabrielle and Henri since they had become lovers (whether sexual or platonic). Although they could not live without one another, they had to be resigned to living apart, which increased their passion but left them chronically unsatisfied. This, at least, was how it was for Gabrielle when she wrote to Adèle in the autumn of 1945, when the hoopla over *Bonheur d'occasion* was at its peak and she felt "fulfilled in every way except real happiness."

> My dear Henri is doing not too badly, although to my unbearable chagrin, difficulties in his life I cannot banish, only ease a little. He is the most courageous and most upright soul I have ever in my life had the privilege of knowing. This to tell you how my life has been enriched and at the same time tried by my having met this man.[17]

To put an end to this insufferable situation, Gabrielle had imagined a solution: she and her friend would leave Quebec and go and settle with Adèle in the hinterland of Alberta, where, freed of Henri's wife, they might live their love in peace and tranquillity. On this idyllically romantic notion she opened her heart to Adèle as early as December 1944:

> I've dreamed sometimes that I'd go and live with you, and that my dear friend, Henri Girard, would come and join us to help with the gardening, husbanding, etc., while at certain hours of the day we would all work alone at our own writing, according to our penchants. I would live with you and him (with him in pure and simple friendship, because I could do without all the rest, on condition I could see him, talk to him sometimes). His health and mine would no doubt improve, because both of us are nervous wrecks.[18]

Did Gabrielle really take this idyllic Paul and Virginie dream seriously? In any event, she told Henri about it and he agreed with the idea, seeing it as the only possible solution for their thwarted love and perhaps the best way of keeping Gabrielle. And so the dream became a plan, and Henri decided to write to Adèle himself:

Mademoiselle et chère amie,

We have talked so much about you, Gabrielle and I, that you will probably allow me to consider you a friend. [...]

You, too, understand Gabrielle. You know that she has genius and has written an immortal book.

But this exquisite woman of genius will never be the author of one single book, as are most French-Canadian writers, including Claude-Henri Grignon. Which is why we have thought, she and I, of finding a nest under your roof, the ideal small romantic corner for effective work.

Please understand that we are in no way asking charity of you, or a refuge for our poverty, because Gabrielle and I, while both very limited in our means of subsistence, can live without holding out our hands to anyone. We are by no means poverty-stricken and, if God grants us life and health, will never be.

I understand therefore that we will establish a "modus vivendi" with you whereby all expenses pertaining to our living quarters would be shared equally. Except that in your absence Gabrielle and I would assume all day-to-day expenses.

I would be most appreciative if you would drop me a line about this.[19]

For her part, Gabrielle asked Adèle to say "[her] most eloquent prayers so that [they] might all be together soon."[20] From Tangent, Adèle replied to the lovebirds that she was prepared to take them in because, she said later, "knowledge and experience of love, its fleeting joys, its disappointments, its griefs, inclined me to be indulgent of human frailty."[21]

The plan was not followed through, however. Did Henri and Gabrielle quarrel? Did Henri's wife step in to prevent it? We will probably never know. "Unexpected things happened," Adèle wrote laconically, "and Gabrielle changed her mind."[22] Among these unexpected things, how could we fail to observe that less than a month after Henri's letter of 11 November 1945 to Adèle, Gabrielle learned that *Bonheur d'occasion* would be published in New York, with all the promise of fame and fortune that this implied? One may conceive that this news made the thought of holing up in Tangent, even with the man who loved her, a good deal less enticing. To be sure, this man had taken her under his wing at a time when, as a young beginner newly arrived in Montreal, she was in need of protection and counsel; to be sure, she was grateful to him, but her situation was not at all the same any more. She was famous, almost rich; she was on the brink of conquering the world. Was Henri still the man she needed? Was she prepared to give up everything in order to live with him? The novella entitled "La source au désert" dates probably from Gabrielle's sojourn in California or the following summer. This is not a very successful text from a literary point of view – the writing is stilted, the construction clumsy, the characters and their thoughts hard to believe – but it throws light on Gabrielle's state of mind at the time. It is the story of a physician, Vincent, who is hamstrung by an ill-matched marriage, and Anne, a young woman twelve years his junior who has been to Paris, Bruges, the Camargue. Vincent asks Anne to go away with him and she agrees, but at the last minute changes her mind because she knows that their love, not having been lived openly, is bound to fade. "And suddenly, Vincent, I foresaw our whole life shrinking from the sunshine, the pure air. Our life avoiding loved and respected faces. Our love hiding from the light, from fine, proven friendships. . . ."

Gabrielle had well and truly dropped the idea of an elopement to the wastelands of the Peace River. Instead she left abruptly for California, alone, and stayed out of the country for more than two months. Had she broken up with Henri? It would seem not, because their relationship continued after her return to Quebec. Far from going into a sulk, Henri continued to devote himself to his friend's career. In the spring or summer of 1946, it was to him that she entrusted the revision of the text for the third Montreal printing of *Bonheur d'occasion*, and he would again serve as messenger between her and Nadeau. In May 1947, he even published an article celebrating the new novelist in *La Revue moderne*.[23]

What Henri Girard did not suspect and Gabrielle herself perhaps did not dare admit to herself was that the more impetus *Bonheur d'occasion* gathered, the closer their love came to its end.

Annus mirabilis

And *Bonheur d'occasion* kept gathering impetus. In Quebec, sales were still increasing and soon there came the first honours: in June 1946,

Gabrielle received one of the prizes given by the Académie française for "services rendered abroad to the French language"; several months later, the newly created Académie canadienne-française, not to be out-done, awarded her its first medal. In those days, radio was a voracious consumer of novels and was hungering to broadcast an adaptation of *Bonheur d'occasion*. The Montreal station CKAC made an attractive pro-posal to Nadeau but Gabrielle turned it down because, she said, "I cannot give the necessary time to appraising and revising the texts" and because "I feel an extreme distaste for lending my name to a series of sponsored programs. Others do, I know, which is no discredit to them, but personally I cannot bring myself to do it."[24]

Soon, however, the praise and highest honours were coming from outside Quebec, propelling *Bonheur d'occasion* into the front rank of lit-erary and general news and bringing Gabrielle fame and fortune she would never have dared dream of.

It all began in the spring of 1946, when the book began to be noticed in English Canada, thanks to one of the most influential of Toronto critics, William Arthur Deacon, who had been a columnist with the *Globe and Mail* since 1922.[25] His attention had been drawn both by the stir in Montreal over *Bonheur d'occasion* and a letter from his friend Hugh MacLennan, whose novel, *Two Solitudes*, had been published in Toronto early in 1945. MacLennan was fired with enthusiasm: "Beyond any shade of doubt, it's the best novel of any large city ever done by a Canadian. [...] This book is every bit as good and valid as Dickens at his best, written with terrific verve and a command of Saint-Henri dialect which is literally magnificent."[26] Deacon, who had himself lived for many years in Manitoba, immediately wrote to Gabrielle asking for an interview. Gabrielle replied from Encinitas, giving her consent and sending him a copy of *Bonheur d'occasion* and a résumé of her life and career.[27] Since she was going to be passing through Toronto on her way back from California, Deacon and his wife, Sally Townsend, invited her to spend Easter weekend with them. The meeting was extremely cordial and the Deacons threw a little party attended by some neighbourhood writers: Jacob Markowitz, E. J. Pratt, Philip Child, Franklin McDowell. Gabrielle was also reacquainted with Margot Syme, an actress she had known ten years earlier at the Winnipeg Little Theatre. Margot was Sally's daughter by a previous marriage. Out of these few days, there developed a friendship between Deacon and Gabrielle that lasted over ten years, throughout which the *Globe and Mail*'s literary critic was an untiring champion of Gabrielle Roy and her works in the literary circles of English Canada.[28]

Although the translation of *Bonheur d'occasion*, *The Tin Flute*, was not yet finished and he did not read French, Deacon had effusive reviews of the novel published in his paper and in *Saturday Night* magazine in the spring of 1946.[29] He also made efforts to find a local publisher for *The Tin Flute*. As early as November 1945, before the contract with Reynal & Hitchcock was signed, Oxford University Press of Toronto made overtures, but Nadeau replied, "Miss Roy prefers to publish the translation of her book [. . .] through an American firm."[30] Other Toronto houses such as J. M. Dent & Sons, Collins, and Macmillan Canada showed interest subsequently, but the world rights now belonged to Reynal & Hitchcock, which posed a serious problem, Deacon pointed out, because if Canadian sales were handled directly by the New York publisher they would be considered "foreign" sales and Gabrielle would receive only "export royalties," or 50 per cent of normal royalties. Deacon then persuaded the prestigious house McClelland & Stewart to obtain the Canadian distribution rights and agree to pay Gabrielle the full percentage that would be owing to her, as if a separate contract were in force between them. Next, the same Deacon, for Gabrielle's own good, of course, tried to have her join the Canadian Authors Association, of which he was one of the prime movers. She declined politely.

Without questioning Deacon's good faith or disinterestedness, it must be said that *The Tin Flute* was grist for his mill. The *Globe and Mail* columnist was an ardent proponent of the new literary nationalism that had sprung up in English Canada in the 1930s and had received a powerful stimulus from the country's participation in the allied victory in the war.[31] With others, he was calling for the emergence of an "authentically Canadian" literature that would express before the world the realities and culture of contemporary Canada. *The Tin Flute*, like MacLennan's *Two Solitudes*, fit the bill perfectly. Not only was it strongly rooted in the local scene, its literary merit was recognized by all, including the Americans, who were about to publish it. And then, the author herself was sympathetic to this new nationalism and declared herself proud to be a Canadian and to have faith in a state of understanding between the two linguistic communities. "I too love Canada dearly. [. . .] I don't think that I would care to live in any other country," she wrote to Deacon. "To know each other across the language barrier, as you put it, has always been my aim and I am truly delighted to see more and more signs of better understanding between Canadians of French and English expression."[32]

So expectation had been created even before the book appeared in English Canada, and its success was practically guaranteed. Deacon had prepared the ground well, along with a few others, including that tireless observer of the Quebec literary scene, W. E. Collin.[33]

After her weekend at Bill and Sally's, Gabrielle hurried off to Montreal to prepare for her summer at Rawdon. She was not rich yet, but she did have some money from the sales of her own edition of *Bonheur d'occasion*. She considered buying a car and maybe a small house but soon gave up the idea. She could not go back to Mrs. Tinkler's because the establishment already had a full complement of boarders for the summer, and so decided to rent a cottage by the Ouareau River, where she moved in May. She spent all of the summer of 1946 and part of the autumn there, far from the tumult and yet close enough to Montreal to keep abreast of her business interests, whose management *Maître* Nadeau efficiently attended to.

Gabrielle's routine remained as always. She would write in the morning and in the afternoon go swimming or walk over to pass the time of day with the neighbourhood ladies who lived in a big house that had a verandah all around with a row of rocking chairs on it. One of these ladies agreed to keep house and cook for her, for Gabrielle, at thirty-seven years of age, was no better at domesticity than she had been in her youth. This woman, whose name was Thérèse, had a penchant for art and literature. Looking after the author of *Bonheur d'occasion* put her on cloud nine. One of her nephews, Gilles Constantineau, recalls that Gabrielle gave him her actress's make-up kit that summer, "sticks of theatrical make-up, pots of miscellaneous creams, wigs, brushes," etc.[34] Gabrielle must have acquired this material in the Cercle Molière or Guildhall School period and had been keeping it and dragging it around with her as if, although she had long given up the stage, she still envisaged the possibility of going back to it in case things failed to work out as she hoped.

Rested and refreshed, Gabrielle returned to Montreal in mid-autumn and settled in the Ford Hotel. In New York, the translation of the first volume of *Bonheur d'occasion* was finished in October, and of the second at the beginning of December. The title being considered now was "Borrowed Bliss." Peggy Hitchcock, the widow of Curtice (who had died suddenly in May 1946), came to Montreal to hand the manuscript personally to Gabrielle. Gabrielle only glanced at it for lack of time and because she had total confidence in the translator. She showed it to Hugh MacLennan, however, who told her that the translation was good, although some time later he told Bill Deacon that he found it rather mediocre.[35] It is true that it contains incongruities, due mostly to mis-understanding of Montreal's particularities, the most famous of which is the translation of *La poudrerie déchaîna* by "The powderworks exploded."[36] The sound of the local speech is not well conveyed, but all in all the translation is not bad. In any case, the English text unques-tionably reached a vast readership unfamiliar with the reality depicted by the book; in this sense it can be said that Hannah Josephson amply fulfilled her contract.

In the circumstances, what more could be said? Mere days after the translation was finished a sensational development occurred: John Beecroft, the head of the powerful Literary Guild of America, decided that Gabrielle Roy's novel would be his "Book of the Month" for the fol-lowing May.[37] On December 18, the day the contract was signed between the Literary Guild and Reynal & Hitchcock, a telegram arrived to announce the news to Gabrielle, who needed only an instant to realize that all of a sudden everything was going to be different for her. Up to now, *Bonheur d'occasion* had brought her a great deal: honours, renown throughout Quebec and a bit in Canada, promise of more than satisfac-tory publication in New York, and enough income to enable her to give up journalism and live – modestly – on her royalties. But all this was nothing compared to what lay before her now: her name across all of the United States, her book in the hands of millions of readers, and money – money in quantities she had never imagined having, even in her wildest dreams.

The Literary Guild – the oldest and most prestigious book club in the United States with its million members scattered throughout the country – was also the biggest and most widely known in the world. The criteria for choice of monthly featured books offered to members were without doubt primarily commercial, but aesthetic considerations were not nec-essarily or totally absent. Thus, among authors selected since 1927, while the likes of Pearl Buck and Daphne Du Maurier dominated, we find names as important as Aldous Huxley (October 1928), Maxim Gorki (April 1930), Selma Lagerlöf (January 1931), Gertrude Stein (September 1933), Stefan Zweig (February 1938), and Roger Martin du Gard (April 1939).[38] For an author or publisher, having one's name on the cover of a Book of the Month was clearly the ultimate seal of approval and literally meant a fortune. This was exactly what the contract of 18 December 1946 brought to Gabrielle Roy. Its numbers, for the period, were breathtaking: for an "estimated minimum requirement" of 600,000 copies, the Literary Guild would pay a sum of $93,000, to be divided equally between the publisher and author. A subsequent printing would raise this to 700,000 copies and the total royalties to some $110,000.

When the contract with the Literary Guild was signed, the title of the English version of the book was tentatively "For Richer, For Poorer." It was only during the winter of 1947 when the very last touches were being put before publication that the final choice of *The Tin Flute* was made. The tin flute, the cheap toy that Daniel receives as a gift in his hospital room, became a metonymic emblem for the entire novel, to which a catchy subtitle was added: *A Bitter-Sweet Love Story*.

This was the first time the Literary Guild had chosen a work as yet unpublished. Ordinarily, the club offered its members a book already proven through normal distribution channels. This time it was the reverse. In view of the prospects raised by the Guild selection, Reynal & Hitchcock decided to increase the size of its own edition destined for bookstores to 50,000 copies and to organize a big promotional campaign in New York for the launching, which was set for 21 April 1947, several days before the Guild members were to receive their copies by mail.[39] Gabrielle, who had been living in seclusion at Rawdon, was invited to go but was loath to. After much persuasion she relented, on condition that *Maître* Nadeau go with her. They took a plane to New York and stayed at the Algonquin Hotel on 44th Street. For five days Gabrielle submitted to the frenzy of publicists and reporters, book signings, interviews, cocktail parties, and other public-relations shindigs. An intoxicating experience, she wrote to Bill Deacon, but one which above all reinforced her determination to live far from the media hurly-burly and the social whirl. All this commotion tired her out and set her nerves on edge. She had the feeling that whatever she said was distorted by the journalists, and most of all it put her under unbearable pressure to be the centre of attention, as if that adulation and all those eyes were demanding that she keep outdoing herself in order not to disappoint. "I was paralyzed. It was no longer 'Do what you can.' It was 'Do better.'"[40]

And so she returned from New York more dead than alive. Instead of going back to Mrs. Tinkler's, she decided to go and stay for a while with Jacqueline Deniset and her husband, Jean Benoist, where she was sure of being well taken care of and could recover from her exhaustion. Their apartment was at the corner of Prince Arthur Street and Park Avenue. There for several days, Jacqueline recalls, Gabrielle seemed to be in a state of prostration: she had no appetite, could not sleep, bemoaned her existence, and otherwise talked about nothing but getting away to where no one could find her. Then one morning she began to feel a little better. "All I'm missing," she told Jacqueline, "is a husband."[41]

Cinderella may have had no Prince Charming, but in everything else she was fulfilled beyond all expectations. While *The Tin Flute* did no better than respectably with American critics and in American bookstores,[42] Canadians were delirious. The announcement of the Literary Guild selection and then the launching of the book in New York sent the press into paroxysms of excitement. Radio programs, newspapers, magazines, all recounted the episodes of the success story with awe, and all of them wanted interviews with the star of the moment. Only two interviews appeared, one in English, the other in French. Both are developed at length and both contributed to the creation of Gabrielle Roy's image as a person who was deeply private, sensitive, modest, and entirely devoted to her art and the well-being of mankind. The first was granted to Dorothy Duncan, the wife of Hugh MacLennan, for *Maclean's* magazine. The article appeared just as the book was coming out in New York. "It is the most complete, most intelligent article that anyone has written about me," Gabrielle wrote.[43] The second was conducted in March 1947 at the Rawdon Inn by the novelist Rex Desmarchais for *Le Bulletin des agriculteurs*, to which Gabrielle felt indebted. She instructed Francine Lacroix, Nadeau's secretary, to turn down all other requests for interviews.

Despite this, *Bonheur d'occasion* and its author were talked about everywhere and the critics were exultant. In Toronto especially, Joyce Marshall recalls, the success of *The Tin Flute* created a climate of feverish excitement and exhilaration that is difficult to imagine today. Bill Deacon, who had been waiting for a year for this, wrote two effusive articles in the *Globe and Mail*[44] and everyone rejoiced to see "the great Canadian novel" appear at last.[45] For this was the principal motif inspired by the adulation of Gabrielle Roy and her book; they demonstrated magnificently, if demonstration were needed, that the time of humility and dependence was over, that Canadian literature had come into its own and could have "universal" reach. This was also the feeling of a number of Quebec writers, for whom, as Roger Lemelin wrote, "The success of *Bonheur d'occasion* dispels any remaining doubt as to an existing market for French Canadian literature. [...] Poets, novelists, composers, painters, the road to fame lies ahead [. . .] now that the eyes of the intellectual world are turned towards French Canada. Thank you Gabrielle Roy."[46] As for Robert Charbonneau, who was just bringing out *La France et nous*, a collection of articles resulting from a polemic he had been waging since 1946 with Duhamel, Aragon, Mauriac, and other Parisian members of the Comité national des écrivains,[47] he sent a copy to Gabrielle Roy, whose novel seemed to him to illustrate perfectly the independence, originality, and "Americanness" of French-Canadian literature. Gabrielle replied, "I subscribe entirely to your point of view that Canadian literature will exist only to the extent that we remain ourselves, without inferiority complex as without false pride or incurable nostalgia for Paris."[48]

As might be expected, Gabrielle's immense celebrity – and the wealth she was imagined to possess – attracted an avalanche of letters, to which Francine Lacroix was instructed to reply politely but firmly. One cannot help but be touched by some of these letters, like those from French-Canadian expatriates in the United States who saw this brilliant success both as a vindication and a comfort.[49] Others are more addlepated: a reader in New Brunswick suggested that the author of *Bonheur d'occasion* "compose a novel that would master the unsuspected beauties of this province and make them known to the good people of Quebec";[50] another fan sought her investment in a safety device for trains he had invented; there was also a mother of thirteen children who wanted to move to Alberta and open a bakery and was asking the famous writer to finance it all for her.[51]

Aside from the Literary Guild selection, something else happened that spring to further nourish the news media and colour "Gabrielle's triumph" in truly fairy-tale hues. It was announced that *The Tin Flute* had been sold to Universal Pictures, one of the major Hollywood movie studios, for $75,000.

This had been in the making for over a year. In the contract signed with Reynal & Hitchcock, Nadeau had seen to it that Gabrielle, while ceding her film rights to her publisher, would nevertheless receive 90 per cent of the revenues deriving therefrom. In April 1946, on the advice of his friend, the fabulously successful French mystery writer Georges Simenon, he retained the services of Maximilian Becker, head of the New York firm AFG Literary Agency, to represent his client on the American and international market. During the four or five years that he was Gabrielle's agent, Becker successfully concluded a number of profitable sales, including a short story in the very with-it New York magazine *Mademoiselle* and translation rights to *Bonheur d'occasion* in Germany, Sweden, Spain, Denmark, Slovakia, Norway, and South America.[52] His efforts over film rights were slow to bear fruit, however. In Montreal meanwhile, the producer Paul L'Anglais made an offer in the autumn of 1946: $150 dollars for an option of one year. It was finally through another agency, Curtis Brown Ltd. of New York, who were working for Reynal & Hitchcock, that the deal with Universal-International Pictures was reached.

The producer immediately put a screenwriter to work turning the novel into a screenplay of 140 pages in which the action takes place in Montreal "in the winter of 1939."[53] Rumour had it that the role of Florentine was going to go to the magnificent Joan Fontaine. A year and a half later, however, Gabrielle learned that the film was not going to be made. "I'm not surprised," she wrote to Nadeau. "Unless the sense is completely changed, I can't imagine Hollywood wanting to present a work of this nature at a time when there's such a war psychosis reigning in the United States."[54] The Korean War was in the offing, in fact, as were Senator McCarthy's witch-hunts, but Universal's reasons for dropping the film were never specified. The upshot was that Gabrielle Roy collected some $67,000 for a film that was never made.

A Marriage of Convenience

On 2 June 1947, the day the contract with Universal Pictures was officially signed, Gabrielle was in Manitoba, where she had arrived a month earlier after her stay with Jacqueline Deniset.

She had been considering this trip since the autumn, when she learned that her sister Anna had undergone a serious operation for intestinal cancer, but the events of the winter and spring, the media maelstrom, and the trip to New York had forced her to keep postponing it. When she finally arrived in Winnipeg in early May, her aim was not only to bring support to Anna and reunite with her sisters, whom she had not seen since the death of their mother four years earlier, but to escape the tumult of the past months because, she said, "it has become extremely disagreeable for me to hear talk of Bonheur d'occasion."[55]

For two years the success of her book had monopolized her almost totally. It delighted her certainly, but it forced her to live in a state of nervous hyperactivity that she found hard to bear. The longer it went on, the more it aggravated the cyclothymic side of her temperament that brought either exhilaration, increasing her energy tenfold and intensifying her preoccupation with her public image and successful handling of her financial affairs, or plunged her into a state near depression. She felt she no longer had possession of herself, that she was squandering herself on obligations both boring and ineffectual, cheating herself and betraying her vocation as a writer. Success weighed on her like a kind of curse, like a threat to the continuation of her work if not to her personal equilibrium.

It seems she was not alone in suffering from the "best-seller syndrome." In 1947, shortly after *The Tin Flute* came out, Ross Lockridge, Jr., another first novelist, had his book selected by the Literary Guild and was gorged with money by Hollywood; three months later he was found in his garage, dead by suicide.[56] Fortunately Gabrielle did not reach this extreme end. Her response to the periodic crises of nervous collapse to which these two years of overstimulation drove her was escape. Escape to California during the winter of 1946, escape to Jacqueline Deniset's on her return from New York, escape finally to Manitoba, far from the media hysteria following the Literary Guild selection and the announcement of the contract with Universal Pictures.

But when one is as big a star as this, it is hard to remain incognito. "I had the disagreeable surprise as I got off the train," she wrote to Nadeau, "to be met by journalists and photographers who had heard, dear knows how, about my arrival."[57] In Winnipeg, people lapped up the smallest piece of news about the diminutive Manitoban who had sprung so suddenly to national pre-eminence, and the *Tribune* and the *Free Press* kept up a steady stream of praise for the author and her book.[58] Over in St-Boniface, the reception was more restrained, however. While *Bonheur d'occasion* had received a glowing review from the Jesuit Albert LeGrand shortly after its publication, public opinion generally considered it a work of questionable morality; it was also found to be pessimistic and too crudely realistic.[59] Soon there appeared a harshly critical article in *La Liberté et le Patriote*, signed "Marie-Reine," accusing Gabrielle Roy of not "writing as a Christian" and of shamelessly exhibiting evil.[60] While in Montreal the Franco-Manitobans "in exile" were celebrating their compatriot,[61] many in Gabrielle's home town continued to resent her leaving the bosom of the community and becoming famous after "deserting" her people.

Gabrielle paid little attention to this resentment. She had not come to Manitoba to jubilate but to rest and write. She spent May and June with Anna and Albert at St-Vital. Anna had been suffering from an early form of intestinal cancer since 1944, but the operation she had just undergone seemed to have been successful and she had come home to La Painchaudière, where her convalescence was progressing well; she had begun again to read, write her long epistles, and smoke like a chimney. On the other hand Clémence was not doing well at all. Gabrielle found her, she wrote to Nadeau, "in such a pitiful state of health that I immediately put her in hospital for a complete examination [. . .] because she has come to a point of extreme debility."[62] Indeed, since "poor Mother left me all alone on earth,"[63] as Clémence put it in her first letter to Gabrielle, her psychological health had deteriorated progressively. She lived alone in the small room that Madame Jacques rented her in the house on Langevin Street where Mélina had ended her days. Anna came to see her once in a long while, but mostly it was Aunt Rosalie who attended to her as best she could. Entirely dependent, all but prostrated, living in isolation, almost abandoned by everyone, Clémence, now over fifty, had less and less desire to live and was letting herself sink into a melancholia that seemed incurable. Gabrielle briefly considered taking her in with her but could not face it. And so with help from Bernadette and Aunt Rosalie, she set about arranging for her sister to enter a home. By September of that year, the problem was resolved and Clémence was admitted to the Joan of Arc Home in the north end of Winnipeg; a fee of $50 would be paid monthly by Jean-Marie Nadeau on Gabrielle's behalf.

These worries apart, Gabrielle's stay at La Painchaudière soon brought her the calm and relaxation she had come in search of. She took the opportunity to get back to writing. She had done practically none for a year except for one short story, "Dead Leaves," which was appearing just at this time in *Maclean's* magazine of Toronto, in both French and English versions. It is the story of a small-time Montreal accountant by the name of Constantin Simoneau who is obsessed by debts he has incurred to have himself treated medically, and who works so hard to pay off these debts that he ruins his health permanently. Along the same lines as this text, during this spring and summer of 1947 Gabrielle wrote another short story titled "Sécurité," whose hero, Ernest Boismenu, can think of nothing but insuring himself against all possible risks, including his own eternal damnation. It was probably also during this period that she began other stories that, like the previous two, are "sequels" to

Bonheur d'occasion with their Montreal setting and a certain social critique, and are also precursors of *Alexandre Chenevert* by reason of the type of characters they feature, the themes they treat, and their ironical or satirical tone. This is the case, for example, with "La justice en Danaca et ailleurs," a rather clumsy fable that derides postwar fiscal policies, and certain texts that remain unpublished or were abandoned, like "Un homme de principes ou Le bon Sèbe" and "Le nihiliste," both portraits of more or less seedy journalists,[64] and "Les trois Mac," a story featuring another character by the name of Boismenu who is much like the hero of "Sécurité."[65]

It was also while she was at Anna's that Gabrielle began writing the acceptance speech she would give on the occasion of her induction into the French section of the Royal Society of Canada, to which, although she was the author of only one book, she had been elected by the members of the section the previous April. According to custom, she would have had to consent to have her candidature presented, a move instigated perhaps by Jean-Marie Nadeau, himself a member of the French section of the society since 1946. Nevertheless, when Gabrielle was informed of her election, she at once warned the secretary, Séraphin Marion, that her availability was going to be limited. "Since I agreed to apply for admission to your illustrious assembly, the conditions of my life have greatly changed. It is important for me now to travel and isolate myself. It is even very unlikely that I will be able to attend meetings of the Society for some years."[66] The reply was that this did not matter; all that was asked of her was that she attend the presentation ceremony and give a speech on the occasion. The date was set for 27 September.

She spent a good part of the summer polishing the text of this speech, which was of major importance in her eyes because with it she would be entering the world of "great" literature. Having conquered the vast mass-market readership and the journalists, she knew that she would now have to win over this other more refined, more distinguished readership of scholars and authentic academicians. Accordingly she experienced some difficulty composing these few pages, as her correspondence that summer reveals; she sought the tone, the ideas, the turn of phrase that would be the worthiest and noblest possible. Finally she settled on a novelist's solution, imagining a "return to Saint-Henri," revisiting the characters of *Bonheur d'occasion* as they have become since the end of the war, and expressing her views on the current state of the society, the economy, and politics. It is one of the most openly leftist texts Gabrielle Roy ever wrote. She who herself was sitting on a veritable fortune at that moment was denouncing the inequalities born of unbridled capitalism, the heartlessness of "the system," the iniquitous lot inflicted on the poor and the dispossessed, and was calling for "a new social order based on the dignity of work and a just division of wealth," because "salvation in our social development lies in a constant broadening of human relationships."[67]

At La Painchaudière, however, human relationships and division of wealth were not going as smoothly as all that. At the beginning, everything was fine between Gabrielle and Anna. They were happy to be together, both relieved, one to be regaining her health, the other to have escaped her frantic existence of the past months, and they were getting along marvellously, spending hours together talking about this and that, recalling the past, promising each other always to stay close and united. Gabrielle was thoughtful of Anna, and Anna of Gabrielle. Aided by a short visit from Sister Léon, who came from Kenora especially to see her little sister, the climate remained unclouded for several weeks. But all too soon things began to go wrong, as they had four years earlier when "Mélina's daughters" had gathered in the same house on River Road after their mother's funeral. Two things helped spark the tinder.

First, one fine morning Adèle arrived from her far-away Alberta and moved in with her two sisters. Adèle was going through a difficult period. The previous year she had lost almost everything and been seriously injured in a fire in her house at Codessa. After several weeks in hospital, she had returned to live at Tangent, where Anna and Clémence had come to spend part of the summer of 1946 with her. Subsequently, seeing Gabrielle's success, she decided to give up teaching and devote herself entirely to "a literary and historical *oeuvre*."[68] However, since she still had to keep body and soul together, she had offered to come to Quebec and become Gabrielle's secretary-housekeeper, which suggestion Gabrielle quite simply ignored. And so it was a broken woman, stripped of virtually everything, who turned up at Anna's and faced Gabrielle at the peak of her triumph, swathed in glory, honours, and money, and not always hiding the adulation and favours coming her way.

Relations among the three sisters very quickly soured, as if, with Adèle present, Anna was at last finding a confidante and ally against Gabrielle, whom she accused of being insensitive, capricious, and superior with her. In fact, what Anna and Adèle were criticizing in Gabrielle was her lack of "generosity," meaning that she was not coming across with as much money as they might have hoped, and was not encouraging them

The author of *Bonheur
d'occasion* (*The Tin Flute*),
by Zarov, 1945.
(F. Ricard coll.)

An Eaton's window in Montreal, 1947. (NLC NL-19158)

Marcel Carbotte, around 1945. (NLC NL-19161)

Gabrielle and Marcel at Concarneau, 1948. (NLC NL-19175)

Gabrielle Roy by Jean-
Paul Lemieux, 1953.
(Bibliothèque municipale
Gabrielle Roy, Quebec
City)

The author of *Rue Deschambault* (*Street of Riches*), by Zarov, 1955. (NLC NL-19157)

Gabrielle Roy's summer cottage at Petite-Rivière-Saint-François, seen from the river side. (NLC NL-19137)

Petite-Rivière-Saint-François: overlooking the river through the "angel musicians." (NLC NL-19139)

Berthe Simard, summer 1957. (Photo taken by Gabrielle Roy; Berthe Simard coll.)

On *la track* at Petite-Rivière-Saint-François. (Berthe Simard photo; NLC NL-19140)

In Quebec City, 1959. (NLC NL-19143)

Marcel and Gabrielle in Greece, 1961. (NLC NL-18239)

in their own literary projects. For Anna, like Adèle, had taken it into her head to start writing; why might the same thing that was happening to Gabrielle not happen to her too? She had begun to write her memories of pioneer life at Dollard and was asking advice from Gabrielle, who was pretty cool to the whole idea and not showing much confidence in her sister's talents. As for the money, both women were astonished at Gabrielle's "stinginess"; had she not said years ago that if she had to work so hard and neglect her family as she did, it was so that one day, once she became a success, she could help them out and assure their well-being? So now that she was rich, what was she doing, where were the promised dollars, where were the gifts of money and other things? It is true that Gabrielle valued her newly earned, hard-earned money and was not freehanded with it; she did dole it out to Adèle or Anna from time to time, but so cautiously and in such limited amounts that the sisters felt they were receiving charity, which, far from softening the resentment they dared not express openly, only left it gnawing deeper.

This way, an atmosphere poisoned by greed, jealousy, frustration, and mutual suspicion was born between Gabrielle and her two sisters, an atmosphere whose effects would be felt cruelly in years to come. For the moment, Gabrielle lost little sleep over it. Anna and Adèle's attitude, their expectations of her, their spite, their manoeuvrings to get their hands on some of her wealth only made her the more comfortable with the total independence from her family that she made a point of displaying. She was too sure of herself, felt too different to her sisters, felt that her destiny was too superior to theirs for these attempts at manipulation to really hurt her and provoke anything more than a mixture of irritation and weariness.

The second event that changed the climate at La Painchaudière that same summer of 1947 and distanced Gabrielle even further from her two sisters was the intrusion of someone new, who was immediately considered an undesirable by Anna and Adèle: Marcel Carbotte.

The meeting happened shortly after Gabrielle arrived in Manitoba. In the face of "the round of invitations, requests for autographs, etc.," that had "begun again with a vengeance," the famous writer resolved, "in self-defence,"[69] not to let herself in for any public events at all. Out of kindness, however, or for old times' sake and probably out of pride too, she did go "on the spur of the moment to pay her respects to her former schoolteachers at the Académie Saint-Joseph," to whom she gave a little speech praising their devotion to the French language.[70] A few days later, a dinner in her honour was to take place at the Cercle Molière, whose president had written to her back in November 1945 to congratulate her "for the brilliant success of your novel."[71]

This same president now telephoned her with an invitation to come and see her comrades of yesteryear. Gabrielle began by saying no, but the president was so insistent and so kind, promising to come and fetch her by car himself and to bring her back the minute she indicated her wish to leave, that she had no choice but to accept.

This president's name was Marcel Carbotte. He was thirty-three, a bachelor, and a practising physician; his office, at 496 Aulneau Street, was one of the busiest in St-Boniface. He was a tall, handsome man with a deep, steady voice and was so filled with admiration and had so many gracious things to say to his guest that Gabrielle was immediately captivated. As was Marcel, who was enchanted by the beauty of this woman five years his senior; he was fascinated by her hair, her eyes, her delicate skin, but also her ease of manner, the aura of freedom about her entire person. Each, in short, had the feeling of discovering in the other that rare, that unique person who alone can fulfil one's most private needs. It was perhaps what one might call a bolt from the blue. On the way home from that dinner, Gabrielle wrote in a copy of *Bonheur d'occasion*, "to Doctor Marcel Carbotte, in happy memory of this evening."[72]

Marcel became a habitual visitor at La Painchaudière in the days and weeks that followed. He and Gabrielle spent long afternoons alone in the garden, sitting on the grass or out of sight in the summerhouse, talking, discovering interests, ideas, ambitions they had in common, and, recalls Yolande, Gabrielle's niece who was then seven, billing and cooing like a pair of turtledoves. But what Gabrielle liked best were their drives in Marcel's car, an old Man-Can that took them to places of her youth that she wanted to see again: the banks of the Red River, St-Norbert, prairie villages. One day they went as far as Pembina Mountain on a pilgrimage to Uncle Excide's farm and the little school at Cardinal. But for Gabrielle this world now belonged to the past. "All I got from it," she wrote to one of her friends in Montreal, "was a violent attack of boredom."[73]

A friendship thus developed between her and Marcel that before long turned into love. There was so much drawing them together. In the first place there was physical attraction, as their correspondence that summer shows, but because of their ages and Gabrielle's nature, the love between them was not entirely blind. For Marcel, Gabrielle's celebrity and status as a writer, a prestigious one at that, could of course only add to her charm. Her wealth did no harm either; had he not proclaimed loud and clear (said the gossips) that he would marry a rich woman? Still, he was not exactly poor himself; he had been practising medicine for six years and had put aside a good $10,000 in savings. But most of all, Gabrielle represented a breed of woman he had little chance of meeting in the small, provincial town of St-Boniface; a woman who had travelled and knew the world, a cultivated woman with an open mind who expected great things from life, from their life together.

It was rather similar for Gabrielle, who found in Marcel all the desirable things a woman of her kind might look for. Apart from his presence and proud bearing, apart from the social prestige and financial comfort that went with being a physician, he had the refinement, sensitivity, and culture associated in her eyes with people of the milieu she had always found fascinating and preferred to her own: that of francophones of recent European ancestry.

Marcel's father was born in Wallonia, in Belgium, and had immigrated to Canada in 1890 at the age of twenty. He returned to Belgium to marry a compatriot, Aline Scholtes, and brought her back to settle at Fry, Saskatchewan, where the couple had two daughters, Léona and Marthe, and one son, Marcel, who was born on 9 February 1914.[74] Marcel's childhood was spent first in *la petite Belgique* at Fry, where the customs and language of the Old Country were kept alive by the Belgian community, and then in Belgium, where his parents returned to live between 1923 and 1926. From this family background, Marcel had kept (and would always keep) the manners, lifestyle, and above all speech, meaning vocabulary and accent, that set him apart from the French Canadians around him and gave him that continental French flair Gabrielle liked so much.

Added to this was Marcel's love of art, literature, and the theatre, which he owed to his background and which his entire education had reinforced. When they returned from Belgium, his parents sent him as a boarder to the Collège de Saint-Boniface, where he was one of its most brilliant students. The purity of his elocution stood him in good stead in oratorical contests and theatrical performances, and with his writing talent he contributed regularly, from the fourth to the final year of his *cours classique*, to the "Page du collège" that the paper *La Liberté* published two or three times a year.[75] No doubt Gabrielle herself had heard of him and his accomplishments during the time she was teaching at the Institut Provencher.[76] When he graduated with a bachelor's degree in June 1934, Marcel wanted to become a doctor, but because of the Depression his parents could not afford to send him to university and so he came home to live with his family for two years. Then a doctor friend of his father's who had seen him perform on the stage offered to finance the rest of his education, enabling him to enroll at the Faculty of Medicine at Laval University in Quebec City, where he remained for five years before returning to establish a practice in St-Boniface in 1941. The practice had flourished and he had acquired a reputation as one of the best physicians in the city. His spare time was devoted to the passions of his youth, in particular the history of painting and architecture (about which he had considerable knowledge) and the theatre. He joined the Cercle Molière, where Pauline Boutal was now the director since the death of her husband, Arthur, and became a very active member of the group and one of its most popular actors. He was offered the presidency of the Cercle in 1944.[77]

In the world Gabrielle was to be living in henceforth, Marcel Carbotte would therefore make an ideal companion. He was the image of what she was yearning for: the friend, the human presence on whom she could depend daily and with whom she could share her anxieties as well as her joys. She would soon be forty; the solitude, austerity, and instability of the life she had been leading for ten years was beginning to weigh heavily. She needed to feel supported, comforted, protected by someone who would look after her, believe in her, and help her accomplish all she wanted and ought to accomplish in the years to come. "Unconsciously," she said later to Joan Hind-Smith, "I was looking for a true friend in the world. So was [Marcel], very likely – and this we became to one another."[78]

But did Gabrielle not already have this "true friend" in Henri Girard? Perhaps, but choosing Marcel in any case meant breaking off with Henri. Adèle, who had been the confidante of their love, could not believe that Gabrielle was casting Henri off so lightly and with so little remorse. The only explanation Gabrielle ever offered Adèle was this comment one day: "I didn't really love him, you know. [. . .] In the first place, he's nine years older than I am, he's a cardiac case, and then he doesn't appreciate the value of money."[79] Whether or not Gabrielle actually pronounced these words, this was not the whole story. The breakup with Henri came after a long period of vacillation, hesitation, if not progressive deterioration of their relationship, in Gabrielle's mind at least. There is no question that Henri loved her, he had proven this amply, ever since he had first counselled and guided her in the world of journalism and literature. Most recently, he was the one who had revised the text of *Bonheur d'occasion* in preparation for its publication in France.[80] There is no question either that she had loved Henri, she had told him so, she had even written as much to Adèle; not two years ago, she had been prepared to go and live in the boondocks with him. But what frustration this love entailed, what constant unfulfilment! For seven years, it had always been the same dead end: Henri was not free; Henri could not give himself completely to her. In the long run, the situation became harder and harder to bear and by slow degrees Gabrielle drifted away from him, a pattern that the events of the past year, the success of *Bonheur d'occasion*, the sudden wealth, the fame, only deepened and eventually made irreversible. Henri was no longer the man for her, the man she needed. Marcel, who offered her the same admiration and the same devotion, had a lot more going for him than Henri: his younger age, his looks, social standing, financial condition, and above all the fact that he was not tied down. It was these things no doubt that won Gabrielle's heart – and head. And besides giving her tenderness and protection and perhaps sensual satisfaction too, Marcel freed her of Henri for good, freed her from the grip of that love doomed to be eternally thwarted.

At the beginning of July, barely two months after they first met, Gabrielle and Marcel decided to get married at the end of August and leave together for France, where Marcel was to begin residencies in gynecology.

At La Painchaudière, the climate had not improved. Anna and Adèle, having an eye on Gabrielle's money, did not like *le beau* Marcel's presence one bit, or his tactics for "snaring" their sister, whom he "[besieged] relentlessly [, . . .] leaving her no way of escaping the entrapment" of his "prefabricated love."[81] Though they put on a pleasant face for the sake of appearances, they looked on him as something close to an embezzler. As for Gabrielle, she was being irresponsible, ready to hand over her wealth to a stranger and so depriving her own family of the fair share that should normally be their due.

To get away from this pettiness, escape the dog days, and finish her Royal Society acceptance speech in peace, perhaps also to give herself a last moment of reflection before her marriage, Gabrielle left St-Vital in mid-July and went to Kenora, just the other side of the Ontario border. Marcel drove her there, and on the way the lovebirds spent a weekend together on the shores of Lake of the Woods. Then Marcel went back to St-Boniface and Gabrielle stayed at the Kenricia Hotel. Apart from returning briefly to St-Boniface at Marcel's request to meet Father Émile Legault, who was visiting Manitoba, she remained at Kenora until early August, spending her time writing, reading (Bergson, Constantin-Weyer, Steinbeck), relaxing at the beach, going for walks, and visiting Sister Léon, whose convent was nearby. Marcel came for a weekend and met Bernadette, who, unlike Anna and Adèle, adored her future brother-in-law and appreciated his gentleness, refinement, and total devotion to Gabrielle; Marcel took an immediate, reciprocal liking to Dédette. This complicity between them lasted their whole lives.

As always when she was living in isolation, Gabrielle maintained a prolific correspondence. Almost every day, she wrote either to Jean-Marie Nadeau or Bill Deacon to discuss business matters, particularly money management, which was a major concern for her. Almost every day she wrote as well to her *Cher grand fou*, Marcel, who wrote back regularly. These letters from the summer of 1947 are interesting in that they throw light on the nature of the bond between the future spouses and the more or less explicit "pact" on which their relationship would depend. What is most immediately striking is the intensity of their passion, the desire that each has for the other and the wonder they experience over the simple fact of having met; these are love letters, in short.

But what is also striking, for Gabrielle especially, is the idealistic, sublimated nature of this love, which she sees first and foremost as enabling both of them to surpass themselves, raise themselves to new heights, spiritually, artistically, and morally. Evoking "the demands of the creative spirit," the "higher awareness of one's mission in life," she glimpses what "a life's work or career like yours and mine should be [...], offered entirely for the greater good of others."

> I have no doubt, dear Marcel, that with you I shall always be sensitive to the ills surrounding us and shall not lose the desire to fight them.
>
> [...] Since I've known you, I've become much more demanding of myself, to a point where this concern will either destroy me or raise me infinitely above myself, and then, dear, I shall owe it all to you.[82]

Marcel shared this romanticism, but expressed it with less exuberance, or at least with much more humility:

I consider you to be something so huge, *chère petite*, and I know myself to be so small that I don't always understand how I could be useful to you in the evolution of your genius, and if some day I manage to be no more than the lamp on your table, it will make me unspeakably happy.

"It's still marvellous when one thinks about it," he wrote in another letter, "that a little girl from Deschambault Street should have the mission of revealing her people to the world. Your people are proud of you, my dear love, and as for me I'd give you the Nobel Prize right off."[83] To which Gabrielle replied, "I don't deserve it yet, dear. [...] But with you to help and support me, who knows, perhaps some day I may happen to receive other honours! I would be proud and happy for it mostly because of you."[84]

Each of them thus had a clearly established role. Marcel's, said Gabrielle, was to "protect me," to "relieve me of my cares." She for her part owed herself entirely to her work, she was "the priestess of solitude, the lady of silence and liberty," she whom no hindrance must distract from her "mission," even when the "demon [...] of defection [paints] in such consoling colours a life totally detached from all bondage, all fetters, especially money, a life which could be wholly given to contemplation."[85]

This was the basis of their love from the outset, as conceived by both, and this was how it would remain, for better or for worse.

From Kenora, Gabrielle returned for a brief stay at La Painchaudière, that "jail,"[86] to see to the final preparations for her departure. Meanwhile, Marcel had asked his friend Abbé Antoine d'Eschambault, who was known as an outstanding artist and scholar, to bless their marriage.

The wedding took place on 30 August 1947 in Saint-Émile Chapel. There were no guests and no members of either Gabrielle's family or Marcel's present. As soon as the ceremony was over, the newlyweds jumped into Marcel's car and sped away due east.

Toward new triumphs for Gabrielle.

Success Story, Conclusion

Their destination was France. For Marcel's medical studies it would have been more appropriate to go to the United States, but since *Bonheur d'occasion* was to be published shortly in France, that was where the couple had chosen to live for a time.

Flashback. Jean-Marie Nadeau had been perspicacious when he advised Gabrielle not to accept the offer from the publisher La Jeune Parque, and to wait until things were under way in New York before choosing a Parisian publisher. On 20 December 1946, exactly two days after the signing of the agreement between Reynal & Hitchcock and the Literary Guild of America, René d'Uckermann, the editorial director of Librairie Ernest Flammarion, wrote to Gabrielle Roy to say that he had read and very much liked *Bonheur d'occasion* and would like to publish it in France. Flammarion, which had published *Trente arpents* by Ringuet in 1938, was one of the most highly regarded of French publishers; its "stable" included such prestigious authors as François Mauriac, André Maurois, and Maurice Genevoix. Then in March 1947, Éditions Bernard Grasset also rose to the bait, having in mind, of course, the success of *Maria Chapdelaine* by Louis Hémon, which the house had published in 1921, but by then the contract with Flammarion was already signed.

Contrary to d'Uckermann's wishes, Gabrielle kept the Canadian rights to her book, which she continued to market herself in association with Les Éditions Beauchemin, the licensed distributor of the novel since the autumn of 1946. However, she granted the French house a right of first refusal for the publication of her next two novels, becoming thus and for many years a "Flammarion author."

For d'Uckermann, there was no question of simply reproducing the Montreal edition. First of all, for commercial reasons he judged it necessary to give up the two-volume format, an idea that had Gabrielle's immediate approval. The text would need revising moreover, for while *Bonheur d'occasion* had been written in French, its language contained certain terms and turns of phrase and certain allusions to local realities that, if not "translated," might confuse or repel French readers. One of the house editors was therefore instructed to revise the text before sending it to the printer. This editor was André Thérive, who had been a literary columnist with the paper *Le Temps* from 1929–1942. Thérive had a certain knowledge of Canada for having been a frequent guest at Lucienne Boucher's mother's Parisian *salon*, where he had rubbed shoulders with Alain Grandbois, Marcel Dugas, and other Canadians.

Two lists prepared by Thérive were sent to Gabrielle for her approval; one proposed "corrections," the other "excisions" that had the effect of shortening the novel by roughly twenty pages. After submitting these lists to Henri Girard, Gabrielle returned them to d'Uckermann during April; she accepted the changes, except for those that to her affected the sense of what she had wanted to say. Altogether, the Flammarion edition does not significantly change the text of *Bonheur d'occasion*; it lightens it, even improves it in spots.

Flammarion would have liked the book to come out quickly, if possible in the spring of 1947, so as to reap the benefit of the fallout from the American edition. However, a number of snags, including a shortage of paper, forced postponement until the autumn.

Even before Flammarion showed its interest in *Bonheur d'occasion*, Quebec had received a visitor of note in the person of the Comtesse Jean de Pange, née Pauline de Broglie. This Parisian woman of letters, author of numerous novels, had long been interested in North America, where she had lectured on romanticism at Wellesley College, the distinguished women's university near Boston. But Madame de Pange's prestige stemmed above all from the fact that she was a member of the jury of the Prix Fémina, which was founded in 1904 and with the Goncourt was one of the most highly regarded and rewarding of prizes on the Parisian literary and journalistic scene. In February 1946 then, the Comtesse had been in Montreal and had read *Bonheur d'occasion*. Enchanted, she asked to meet the author, congratulated her, and, without promising anything, allowed her to understand that she might take her case in hand when the book was published in France, explaining to her that her chances would certainly be better if she were in France during the annual prizegiving season.[87] Gabrielle needed no further persuasion to yield to a wish she had been nurturing for some time, which was to see France again, to go there for a few years of writing and good living.

So it was that as soon as they were married the newlyweds' principal objective was to reach Paris in time for the publication of *Bonheur d'occasion*. Before boarding ship, they were to stop for a few days in Montreal, where Gabrielle had her speech to give on the occasion of her induction into the Royal Society, and would get her new passport (as Madame Carbotte), draw up her will (with Marcel and Clémence as beneficiaries), and see Jean-Marie Nadeau to settle a number of business matters left dangling by her four-month absence.

From St-Boniface, Marcel's car took them first to Toronto, where Gabrielle introduced her husband to Bill Deacon. They arrived in Montreal on September 7 or 8 and went to the Ford Hotel. On September 15 they were in Rawdon at Mrs. Tinkler's to pick up the things that Gabrielle had left there. Then several days later a party at Jori Smith and Jean Palardy's gave an opportunity to Gabrielle's friends, who were astonished to hear of her marriage, to meet the lucky bridegroom.

Henri Girard was not there, of course. But he had sent a present: *Choix de poèmes* by Francis Jammes, a copy published by Mercure de France in 1946, with this laconic inscription on the flyleaf: "*À Gabrielle Roy, au Dr Marcel Carbotte, tous mes voeux de bonheur, Henri Girard.*"[88] In fact, everything indicates that Gabrielle's marriage had sent Henri into a deep depression that lasted all that fall and obliged him to leave Montreal for a number of weeks. Several months later, when his period of mourning was virtually complete, he confessed to Adèle, who had just written him a consoling letter:

> You know, Adèle, her leaving very nearly killed me. I felt old and almost incapable of working. With Gabrielle gone, there was no reason to live. Just think that for seven years I gave this woman who was not my mistress the best of my heart and my mind. All that was fine in me, all that I had learned of aesthetic feeling in my youth I gave to her unselfishly and unreservedly.
>
> Please note that I regret none of it, Adèle. Like Mozart's master, I simply contributed to the evolution of a genius. A humble contribution of little importance all in all, but one which, at the time, was necessary in order for her work to become what it is.[89]

This self-effacement was not painless, however. "I try unsuccessfully to put all that relates to her out of my mind," he says in the same letter. "I use thousands of stratagems. But she is still there, present in my brain, and she keeps on torturing me."

How long did the torture last, and what became of Henri Girard after Gabrielle chose Marcel over him? This is a mystery. All we can presume is that the friendship, without ceasing completely, became very distant and episodic. From Paris, Gabrielle asked Nadeau once or twice for news of Henri, but not more. In 1949 she tried to send him a few of her recent manuscripts in order to have his opinion and advice, but it is not certain that he responded to her request.[90] Five years later when *Alexandre Chenevert* was published, there arrived this simple telegram: "Received Alexandre. Very moved. Henri."[91] From this moment on there is no further trace of him. Henri Girard simply disappeared.

It must be said that Gabrielle did nothing to prevent his disappearance. Not only did she not speak of Henri Girard or her relationship with him in any of her writings – even in her unpublished autobiographical texts – but shortly after her marriage and against Marcel's advice she destroyed all the letters she had received from him.[92]

If he was absent from the little celebration at the Palardys', he was equally absent from the ceremony held by the French section of the Royal Society on September 27 in the Salle de l'Ermitage.[93] The evening was in commemoration of the sixty-fifth anniversary of the society's founding and had been given an extra measure of grandeur: the ambassadors Georges Vanier and Pierre Dupuy were presiding and the celebrated violinist Arthur Leblanc was to perform the musical interlude. Many journalists crowded into the hall, mingling with everyone who was anyone in Montreal, plus expatriate Franco-Manitobans come to hear the speeches of the two new members, the linguist Léon Lorrain and the novelist Gabrielle Roy. But when Arthur Saint-Pierre began his opening address, there were murmurs of displeasure: Gabrielle Roy, the star of the evening, was not yet there. She did not arrive until an hour later, after Lorrain's speech, in time to hear her sponsor, the historian Gustave Lanctôt, pronounce his eulogy. "Madame," he declaimed in the customary style, "in the ten years that women have been admitted by the society, you are the first to cross the threshold of its literary sections. And you have crossed this threshold in triumph, having obtained the largest number of votes ever received." There followed a résumé of Gabrielle Roy's career and "contribution to our literature."[94] Then the member-elect approached the microphone. Despite her diminutive size, she looked more beautiful and more dignified than ever in her long black dress with white lace at the collar and cuffs and without jewellery except for a small clasp holding her hair at the back of her neck. Her voice was a little hoarse, but she used it with perfect intonation and emotion.

> I was hoping to put before you a subject which, in our pursuit of peace and justice, might have joined our flagging hearts in a moment of joy.
>
> But [pause] not long ago I returned to Saint-Henri. [...] I listened to people talking on the street corners, in the little shops, around the railway station, and in the market square. It was unbelievable, but the labourers, the workers of this neighbourhood, were making the same sour prediction as the financiers and captains of industry. [...] Saint-Henri was once again

telling me its tale of wasted human energies, wasted human hopes [. . .].
It's a funny thing [. . .] how it's always the workers who get the blame for
making prices rise, for upsetting the economy. What about those important people who are never seen and are so hard to imagine behind the high
walls of the spinning mills and factories of Saint-Henri, far beyond those
ramparts of smoke and steam and the rumbling of machinery? [. . .]
Everywhere I went, I found the same weariness of life. A society cannot for
so many years cast disdain upon its fundamental wealth – its workers and
natural resources – without sooner or later paying dearly for it. [. . .] Weary
as we are from striving toward a better society, a more just and intelligent
social order which we can only hope for once we have ceased our follies,
Rose-Anna's humble life and Emmanuel's unsung death, if they have
inspired us to carry on, will not have been entirely in vain.

The audience held its breath. Never before had anything like this
been heard at the generally starchy and tedious sessions of the learned
society, nothing as bold or as moving as this. The liberals, unionists,
and whoever passed as socialists, reformers, or leftist sympathizers in
Montreal could not get over hearing this famous writer – whose speech,
recorded, was radio-broadcast the next day by Radio-Canada – publicly
espouse their cause, they for whom the Duplessis government had been
making life miserable since returning to power three years earlier. The
Communists in particular, who had been delighted that Gabrielle Roy
was joining the Royal Society because they saw it as "a golden opportunity to denounce capitalism royally,"[95] had the speech taken down in
shorthand by one of their number and published it in *Combat*, their
weekly paper.

What none of these people knew, however, was that this speech was a
kind of testament. If it summed up the broad-based social thinking that
had inspired Gabrielle Roy during her years of journalism and while she
was writing her first novel, it was also a farewell, if not to this line of
thought itself, at least to her public expression of it. Never again would
she declare herself as explicitly on the problems of the moment. Whatever her ideological sympathies, she would henceforth refrain from
active involvement or any kind of commitment.

As soon as her speech was over, the heroine of the evening excused
herself and left the hall with Marcel, who had already loaded the car with
their luggage and provisions they had been advised to take with them in
order to cope with the rationing that was still in effect in France. That

very night they set out for New York. There, they embarked (with their car) aboard the *Fairisle*. The crossing was supposed to take nine days; it took twelve, mostly because of one superbly stormy night that they would remember with exhilaration for the rest of their lives.

From London, where the *Fairisle* landed, the travellers crossed the channel and arrived at Anvers. They spent eight days in Belgium visiting Marcel's family, with whom Gabrielle found little kindred spirit. Then to Paris. They arrived on October 23 and moved into a small apartment in the Hôtel Trianon Palace at 1bis rue de Vaugirard, a stone's throw from 27 rue Racine, the head office of Éditions Flammarion. The first days were difficult. Their hotel may have been in the heart of the literary quarter, and they may have encountered André Gide in person on rue Monsieur-le-Prince, but the lack of comfort, the cold, and the scarcity and excessive price of commodities had them homesick for Canada. "How," she wrote to Nadeau, "can workers and minor civil servants live in this city where things we consider necessities cost astronomical prices! In the presence of such great hardship, one can only seek and find a little comfort with a hideous feeling of guilt and embarrassment!"[96]

But Gabrielle and her husband had little time for wallowing in such feelings, caught up as they were with the whirl of *Bonheur d'occasion*'s launching. The book had arrived in the bookstores and on reviewers' desks two weeks before, on October 9, with a press release that began, "At the same time that the French public were beginning to see many Canadian soldiers among our liberators on our soil, literary circles were awakening to the revelation of the biggest best-seller of the war years in Canada." Gabrielle Roy's novel, it added, had "singular documentary value":

> While celebrated works have hitherto shown us the Canada of peasants, logcutters, and trappers, this one brings us into urban life in Montreal, into working-class neighbourhoods teeming with people much like those of American "suburbs," except for their language.

The publication of *Bonheur d'occasion* was therefore to be considered "an historic act [. . .] since its purpose is to show the national rootstock that an almost unknown corner of North America remains a little piece of France despite all."[97]

Friendship toward the Canadian "cousins" and gratitude owing to Canada for its part in the recent liberation of France, for the five or six weeks leading up to the autumn's awarding of literary prizes, would be the card that d'Uckermann and Madame de Pange would play for all they were worth in their press campaign and their lobbying of members of the Fémina jury. The *comtesse*, determined to see her protégée win, was sparing no effort. "She was my best ally and my main support," Gabrielle wrote in 1956. "This bubbling, intrepid, impetuous woman rushed hither and yon in Paris and crossed swords on my behalf in the faubourg Saint-Honoré and the faubourg Saint-Germain. She attacked the undecided, bore down on the recalcitrant and shook the indifferent. 'We've been talking long enough,' she said, 'about links of friendship and fraternity with our relatives in French Canada. It's time to do something about it.' "[98] As for d'Uckermann, whom Gabrielle was meeting for the first time ("He was a man whom I could see very much at home in the time of Louis XIV, polite in a way that is nonexistent now."[99]), he was mostly active in journalistic corridors and among critics friendly to Flammarion – a wily publisher and fiercely determined to achieve his goal.

Monday, 1 December 1947. At last the cabal by d'Uckermann and Madame de Pange bore fruit; on the third ballot, by eleven votes out of eighteen, the Prix Fémina was awarded to *Bonheur d'occasion*, which the ladies of the jury had chosen in preference to, among others, *Forêts de la nuit* by Jean-Louis Curtis (which would win the Prix Goncourt), *Cap de désespérance* by Jean Feuga, and *Gens de Mogador* by Élisabeth Barbier.[100]

Gabrielle, of course, was in seventh heaven. And Marcel too. The Fémina, recognition obtained in the very capital of French literature, was this not the ultimate recognition, the ultimate triumph that an author could aspire to? The media maelstrom began again with a vengeance; Gabrielle entered the fray head on. She who had been so shaken by her New York experience and had sworn never to let herself in for that again, who barely three months before leaving for Paris had declared to Nadeau, "I won't go along with any publicity over there,"[101] was once again caught up in the fire and fury of luncheons, courtesy visits, parties, and interviews. To each journalist she told the story of her birth in Manitoba, her years of obscurity as a freelance journalist, the "infinite patience" it had taken to write *Bonheur d'occasion*, and each was moved, captivated both by the story and the presence of (to quote one) "this young person whose austere prettiness no makeup softens, while her long chestnut hair gathered at the neck frees an intelligent forehead above unforgettable eyes." Another columnist, giving rein to outlandish imagery, noted "Immense, greenish eyes, smouldering with melancholy.

A mouth bound to the base of the diaphragm by slings belying an intrepid soul. A nobly chiseled nose. A luminous forehead." And a positively charming accent.[102]

Among Canadians living in Europe, the excitement reached an apogee. This was the first time a Canadian writer had won a major prize in Paris, drawing attention to Canada from the whole of France. It would be another twenty years before it happened again – the Prix Médicis to Marie-Claire Blais in 1966. The Canadian ambassador, Georges Vanier, who had been present when Gabrielle had given her speech to the Royal Society of Canada three months earlier, gave a big party in honour of the prizewinner. Among the guests was Father Pierre Teilhard de Chardin, whose books were yet to be published (and would be only after his death in 1955). Seeing his roman collar, Gabrielle was inclined to bridle, but the paleontologist-theologian's conversation soon won her over. As she recounted later:

> I watched him, fascinated, because he was speaking with a great many gestures as warmly expressive as his words, and suddenly I had the feeling I was living an hour of unique value in my life. I felt I was in the presence of one of those beings whose like appear in humanity once in a very long time, and who see things far, far ahead, things which perhaps all of us may see some day.[103]

Teilhard talked to her that evening about one of his favourite themes, the "Progress" of universal Consciousness, a theme to which, in the coming years, Gabrielle would attach great importance in her own thinking and writing.

Meanwhile, the Parisian critics had begun to pass judgment on *Bonheur d'occasion*. The verdict was lukewarm, if not negative. To be sure, the novel was found to have merit; to be sure, a few critics close to Les Éditions Flammarion like Paul Guth and Francis Ambrière had praise for it; to be sure, André Rousseaux, the pontif of *Figaro littéraire*, said he liked it,[104] but nowhere was there any real show of enthusiasm or strong feeling either for or against the author and her book. "We like to find a few high points that catch us off guard in a novel," wrote Thierry Maulnier, for example, "a few pages that imprint themselves so strongly in our memory that we can forget all the rest; I did not find these pages in *Bonheur d'occasion*."[105] The same reservations were expressed almost universally: Gabrielle Roy's novel was an honourable, interesting book, it was said, but no more; "a good populist novel, a work of observation rather than creation," written in "fluent style, even too fluent, but studded with picturesque and racy expressions."[106] Still, hardly anyone was surprised that such an ordinary book should have won the Fémina, because everyone knew it was mostly a matter of rewarding Canada. Thus Robert Kemp, in *Nouvelles littéraires*, admitted that the novel by Curtis was "better" but hastened to add, "the ladies of the Prix Fémina deserve absolution," because "being able to show our maternal tenderness to this great and beloved child of Normandy, our gratitude for its faithfulness and sacrifice, is such great pleasure that, who knows, I too might have voted with the majority."[107] "No doubt," Louis Barjon also recognized, "through Gabrielle Roy it was the heroic and fraternal Canada that the ladies of the Fémina wished to honour. We can only applaud them for this! . . . And conclude, a bit unkindly, that for the author of this honest book, such a success was a real *bonheur d'occasion*." Unkind conclusions were also drawn by others, like the columnist in *Carrefour* who let it be understood that the Fémina had been given to Gabrielle Roy because France needed Canadian wheat . . .[108]

Altogether the French critics, without being malicious, were rather cool to *Bonheur d'occasion*. No doubt they really did not understand Gabrielle Roy's novel, not only because they could not read it in its own context but also because the book did not fit the mould of what those critics at that particular time expected of a novel. There was misunderstanding all round: Paris gave *Bonheur d'occasion* a prize for the wrong reasons, and the critics judged the book negatively for another set of wrong reasons.[109]

This ambiguity was reflected in the commercial success of the book in the months following its publication. By June 1948, Flammarion had sold some 43,000 copies of *Bonheur d'occasion*. It was no doubt a respectable figure but far below what a publisher could expect from a "good" prizewinning novel. Subsequently, while Flammarion sold several hundred copies of the book each year on the Canadian market (in violation of one of the provisions of the contract), in France sales fell to almost nil and once the season of the Prix Fémina had passed *Bonheur d'occasion* and Gabrielle Roy sank almost immediately into oblivion.

Fleeting though it was, Gabrielle's Parisian triumph had great repercussions in Canada. In Montreal especially, it contributed to a renewal of popularity for the book and brought even more fame to its author. But public reaction was divided. On the one hand, there was rejoicing to see France recognize the existence and value of "our" literature, which was proof that this literature was at last achieving "universal" status,[110] while, on the other, there were those who, without admitting it, deplored the "pejorative" image of French Canada that Gabrielle Roy's novel was projecting to the whole world. In certain milieux, Robert Charbonneau would recall later, there was embarrassment that *Bonheur d'occasion* should "show us naked to foreigners" and make us look like "uncouth creatures."[111] In the district of Saint-Henri, this "feeling of mortification," this discontent, had for some time even been taking the form of open revolt, led by the parish priests Gauthier and Boileau. Boileau declared from his pulpit, "Saint-Henri is not made only of lanes, holes-in-the-wall, and hovels, and it is not true that its inhabitants are disorganized, disoriented, and in despair. This young woman, who came here from the salons of Westmount, has done us a very bad turn. [Her book] is pernicious propaganda."[112]

The denunciation had little effect, however, and *Bonheur d'occasion* continued its brilliant course in Canadian bookstores. In December 1947, the new printing bore on its cover the message "25,000 Copies Sold!" In English Canada, McClelland & Stewart sold nearly 14,000 copies of *The Tin Flute* between July 1947 and June 1948, and Bill Deacon made sure that the book won "the Governor General's Award for the best fiction of 1947";[113] in those days, only books published in English were eligible for the prize. And then, *Bonheur d'occasion* was beginning to be the subject of specialized critical studies; for the first time, a thesis was written on it, at the Université Laval, and critics soon began "rereading" it. These unspectacular developments had the effect of removing Gabrielle Roy's novel from currency and quietly installing it in another space, a local space indeed but one in which it was assured of endurance: it was now one of the "classics" of Canadian literature.[114]

Quiet Days in France

In Europe, meanwhile, Gabrielle was slowly recovering from her autumn in Paris. It had been an exciting time, but it had left her exhausted, her nerves raw. The wait for the jury's decision, the interviews, the social events, the few days of glory, and then the cool, condescending reviews had kept her in a state of tension for three months, affecting her morale and her health; she slept poorly, had the flu repeatedly, had no appetite, and was chronically tired. "I haven't been very well since arriving in Paris," she wrote to Jean-Marie Nadeau on 9 December 1947, "and all this excitement has hardly helped. All I want is to be alone where it's quiet. How hard it is to protect the only thing of value to me!"

As she had done in the winter of 1946 when she left for California, and then in the spring of 1947 when she took refuge at La Painchaudière, she decided when the Fémina furore was at its most intense to escape to a calmer place where she could gather herself and rebuild her strength. At Judith Jasmin's suggestion she chose Geneva, which, besides being distant, offered comforts that were very difficult to find in Paris in this immediately postwar period – properly equipped and heated housing, varied food, and functional public services, not to mention pure air and beautiful natural surroundings.

Early in January 1948, Marcel drove her to Geneva. He stayed with her for three days and then returned to Paris, where he was to begin his residency in gynecology and oncology at the Hôpital Broca, under Doctors Béclère and Moricard.

Gabrielle spent three weeks alone in Geneva, staying at the Hôtel de l'Écu. At first she sought to accomplish only one thing: clearing her mind, "distancing my thoughts from everything that reminds me of obligation" and "disappearing from the sight of men. Being the way I was before, unknown, owing nothing to anyone."[115] To her husband, who had undertaken to collect all the reviews and newspaper items about the Fémina in a scrapbook, she wrote:

> Above all, above all, *mon Marcel*, don't send me any articles in which I'm mentioned. You still don't realize that that's become intolerable to me! I have to go through a cure of my morale, and it takes depths of solitude and demands a degree of silence that you can't imagine.[116]

For relaxation, she would go to a movie or a concert or for a walk beside the lake. She made contact with an admirer who was a secretary at the Red Cross and obtained permission to consult the archives containing the records of thousands of real-life personal and family dramas during the Second World War, which for her represented "what I like best, the warm, bitter wave of what is human."[117]

She also took advantage of this sojourn to consult a physician recommended by Marcel, but Doctor Naville could find no cause for her health problems other than a "nervous disorder"; he recommended, as would

Doctor Hudon to Alexandre Chenevert, that she "completely give up all intellectual formulation – in other words, stop myself from thinking."[118]

But, she adds, "I don't know how to." For the principal goal of her escape, as always, was to free her mind in order to begin writing again, something that had become impossible in the constant whirl of Paris. Each morning she would sit, agonizingly, at her desk and wait. At first nothing would come, "but anyway," she said, "I must get back to the habit, that is essential."[119] Then, on January 23, after several days of feeling "in the deepest depths of discouragement," there was a spark. Her account of this experience is worth quoting because it illuminates well how what can be called the process of inspiration worked in her, and also because she very rarely wrote about such experiences in her correspondence. The process would occur in two phases. First, she would suddenly feel possessed, "visited" by an idea, a character, a voice that seemed to come from outside:

> Today, my angel, life looks different. [. . .] It's because you see, *mon chéri*, I'm suddenly feeling that divine creative emotion I've been deprived of so long returning in me. I don't yet want to shout it out loud so as not to scare off this fickle human feeling that's so infinitely more difficult to control than any other. However, I do receive visitors. How else can I define this sorcery of inner vision that allows one to see and know people one never knew before. And not only does one know them, but they arrive in one's mind each with a name, a face, and a life background, all tied up in a little bundle. This is what I call receiving visitors. [. . .] The mind in this is like a sorcerer's apprentice. At its whim – and without one's will having much to do with it – it sorts, assembles, and when the time comes delivers the story, the narrative to me, which I then have only to write.[120]

These words, "which I then have only to write," introduce the second phase of the process, the writing itself, meaning the writing down, the distillation, the wording of the "inner vision" given to her at first by a miracle, as it were. Two days after telling him about the "rapturous minutes" she had experienced, Gabrielle wrote to Marcel:

> Now [. . .] for all that I have the consolation of working in joy several hours a day. Not very long, you understand, for I have the impression that this joy is like oil in a lamp which has to be used with moderation, or I may find I've quickly used it all up. The moment of illumination [. . .],

that doesn't last, you know. It's very brief, very quickly fades back into life's routine. But often a flash like that, a single one, will have been enough to let me see the entire development of a book. After, well, after comes the daily job, often without much gusto, but at least by then I know more or less where I'm heading. What I have to do then is free the thought in the raw state from its gangue-matter, by the sweat of my brow give it the least prosaic form possible. How much effort, how many missteps too there will have been before coming to this point. Yet never would I dream of complaining of the hard work demanded by a character or an idea begging to be conveyed. I'm too happy, believe me, to have seized that tiny spark in the state of low spirits I was in.[121]

The "story" in question here was the rough draft of what would later become the first chapter of *Alexandre Chenevert*.[122] It was in similar terms that Gabrielle had described the genesis of *Bonheur d'occasion*, and it was in this same way – in two successive phases, "the illumination" and "the job" – that she would experience (and describe) the genesis of almost all her books. But in Gabrielle Roy's creative activity, there was and would always be a third phase, or rather a phase that both preceded and followed the other two, and that could be called the zero phase: the interminable, barren phase of non-inspiration. A stationary phase, to say the least, which she lived through (and always would) as if it were a kind of death, something that was necessary, she knew, but so hard to endure. "What blackness I have been through to get where I am," she wrote in a letter of January 23. "My eyes are brimfull of tears from it, for in the darkness I had kept asking for this light with doggedness and single-mindedness close to desperation." This alteration between light and darkness, between wandering in the desert and the joy of her work was what henceforth would rule Gabrielle's existence, her movements from place to place, her relationships with others, and even her physical and psychological equilibrium.

"My health," she wrote to Nadeau on the same day that she sent the second of her letters to Marcel quoted above, "has benefited greatly from my stay in Switzerland. I'm feeling very well."[123] Then the next day she informed her husband of her intention not to return to Paris until her work was "well under way."[124] But Marcel was lonesome. Although he went out with his friends and swatted at his medical books, he missed his "little Gaby" terribly; "I have no words to describe how intensely I pine for you," he wrote her.[125] This was the first time they had been separated since their marriage. Still, frustrating though it was, the distance brought home to them how deeply they felt for one another. Not a day passed without a letter from Geneva crossing another from Paris, each bearing tender words and affection. Their separation brought them closer, in fact. "See how I am," Gabrielle wrote, "where I was carping at you a hundred times a day over nothing, now all I can remember are the good things there are to admire in you. How I love you!"[126] Then, two weeks later, "I love you, my Marcel, *mon fol amant*, so much that sometimes it frightens me. Never before you was I bound by any bonds, save those of destiny, which are so cruel, so inexorable, but against which it is fruitless to struggle."[127]

Whatever "delicious chain of slavery" Gabrielle felt bound by to Marcel ("dear Marcel, who overcame my fierce love of freedom"[128]), those other bonds, "those of destiny," remained unbroken. As much as by love, perhaps more, she still felt bound by what had been haunting her since her youth, those "expanded horizons," that "person all unknown to me," that duty of betterment and beautification that melded with the pursuit of her work. And to her, this fealty came before the one she owed Marcel or, at least, the love she and Marcel shared could not be built outside of it or in opposition to it, but must be dedicated to its furtherance, and be enriched thereby. This was the substance of the "pact" that their marriage had sealed. When Marcel complained of being abandoned, she consoled him, but he had to accept the "sacrifices" that her work imposed, as did she herself. Toward the end of her Geneva sojourn, she wrote:

> *Pauvre enfant*, how your unhappiness hurts me and how I wish I could keep you from suffering so! I too, you know, have been so melancholy I haven't known where to turn for some relief. And yet I will have to leave you alone a few other times, go into isolation to search my thoughts. Again submit myself from time to time to this trial of solitude at whose end I've seen the road I'm to take. Oh, if you only knew what a single story, a single minute of inspiration often costs in denial of oneself and painful sacrifices.[129]

When Gabrielle returned to Paris on 9 February 1948, the dust raised by the Fémina had pretty well settled. At last she could experience, as she said later, "the happiness of existing very simply, very humanly, among the good people of Paris."[130] Between Marcel and Gabrielle, despite sudden mood swings and the minor irritations of daily life, there was almost perfect harmony, as if they were finally on their honeymoon, five months after their wedding. The small material problems of their first days in France were now in the past. Not only were food parcels arriving regularly from North America, sent by Jean-Marie Nadeau, Judith Jasmin, Jack McClelland, or Max Becker, but their living quarters were far more pleasant. While Gabrielle was in Switzerland, Marcel had left the Trianon Palace and moved them not far away to the Lutétia, one of the most comfortable (and most expensive) hotels on the left bank.

Gabrielle's finances were in good shape. In two years, thanks to the Literary Guild and the Hollywood contract, plus royalties on sales of *Bonheur d'occasion* and *The Tin Flute*, she had earned over $100,000. In the spring of 1948, she had $7,000 in her Montreal bank account and $75,000 with her New York publisher.[131] That year she was greatly preoccupied with money matters and corresponded voluminously with Nadeau on the subject because she was frightened to death of being fleeced of her money through income tax. After numerous consultations with civil servants and accountants unaccustomed to dealing with writers, Nadeau devised a satisfactory arrangement involving income spreading. Beginning in 1948 and for the six years following, the publisher Harcourt Brace & Co. (which absorbed Reynal & Hitchcock in 1948) would pay Gabrielle Roy an annuity of $15,000 per year, and only this sum would be taxable, added to her other current receipts. Until 1954 at least, Gabrielle was thus assured a more than satisfactory income.[132]

This said, while she lived a life of ease she shrank from throwing her money around and watched her business interests with an eagle eye. Toward her family she showed generosity that was both real and measured. She kept her promise to her mother, paying a monthly board of $50 for Clémence's upkeep. She also made substantial donations to Bernadette's community from time to time, and helped pay medical school fees for her niece Lucille, Germain's elder daughter. She sent small sums to a few friends as well. But she did not take kindly to having her arm twisted or her gifts taken for granted. During this winter of 1948, a particularly nasty squabble erupted between Gabrielle and Anna, which was worsened on both sides by accumulated frustrations and many things the two sisters had held back from saying the previous summer while Gabrielle was staying at La Painchaudière. It was set off by a trivial error: Anna had taken the liberty of removing Clémence from the Joan of Arc Home, "where [Clémence] was dying of boredom and loneliness,"[133] and placing her again in a private home with a Madame Baune, where the board was more expensive. To meet this expense, Anna had written directly to Nadeau to have him send more money. Incensed, Gabrielle protested with an inflammatory letter:

> It's easy to be generous with other people's money. I know better than anyone else what my resources and expenses are, and exactly what I can afford to give Clémence. [. . .] It would be exceeding strange to have my beloved family, after preventing me from working out my own life – remember all the discouraging words, all the unfair faultfinding – turn round now and tell me what I have to do. I know very well what I have to do. [. . .] Your minds are made up that I'm wallowing in the goods of this world and probably that I'm an egotistical monster too. I've been hurt by that for so long I ought to be toughened up by now. [134]

Anna replied immediately with an exceptionally splenetic epistle:

> Listen, Gabrielle, you've become famous, you've been fawned over more than enough; you're probably some kind of genius; people have let you see so much of the glamour of it all; you mustn't think you're a deity who can't be touched. [. . .] Keep your pennies, *ma petite*, make quite sure of that; you may try to pull the wool over our eyes, but we understand you better than you think. [. . .] You're a celebrity who's different; when you say you've got certain virtues, you believe it yourself; you're a person who stupifies, who mystifies, who fools a lot of people. [. . .] You should have been hurt a long time ago, when you were little, then today you'd have a gentler, more understanding turn of mind. In a word, you'd be someone who's a bit less boorish and spoiled.[135]

Feeding on spite and jealousy, Anna's fury had no bounds. It spilled over into her letters to Adèle: "Don't let yourself be sucked in by [Gabrielle's] weepy talk, she's rich enough to pay her debts, rich enough to pay her share generously. Stinginess she's got by the bale; heart, she hasn't even got one as big as a hazelnut."[136] They sounded like Cinderella's stepsisters. "Anyway," Anna pursued, cranking herself up another notch, "before we die maybe we'll see all this tinsel turn to ashes and dust. [. . .] Almighty God, let you and I write just as well, or better than she! That would be our vengeance!"[137]

The storm soon abated, and the two women returned to better feelings toward one another. In the years to come, Gabrielle continued to send Anna small sums of money and correspond with her occasionally, and even saw her a number of times. There would never again be the same intimacy between them, however, until Anna was near death fifteen years later beneath the sunny sky of Arizona.

These spats did not mar the quiet happiness that Gabrielle and her husband found in their life in Paris, once the Fémina maelstrom had passed. Far from family and relieved of professional obligations, they were like students or wealthy vacationing foreigners in the most beautiful city in the world. At the Lutétia, for the equivalent of $16 a day, they occupied two large adjoining rooms where they could take all their meals. They lived there for five months until the summer of 1948, at which point they had first envisaged returning to Canada. But the time had passed so quickly since their arrival and they were enjoying France so much that they decided to stay another year. Besides, Marcel had completed only six or seven months' residency at Broca and would have to stay longer in order to obtain his specialist's certification there. And then, once this second year had passed, they decided to stay yet another year until the autumn of 1950, despite what Gabrielle had announced to Jean-Marie Nadeau.[138]

They did not stay all this time in Paris. In October 1948, for reasons of economy but also because Gabrielle wanted to be closer to the country, they moved to the western outskirts of the capital, to Saint-Germain-en-Laye, where they had found a boarding house that suited them perfectly and would be their home for their last two years in Europe.

Number 31 Rue Anne-Baratin, a stone's throw from the *château royal* of Saint-Germain-en-Laye and its park, was a large, handsome, upscale three-storey house surrounded by a garden and provided with every comfort. A wealthier version of Balzac's *pension Vauquer*, the Villa Dauphine was divided into six or seven small apartments occupied by people of a certain age and no less certain fortune, who dined together every evening around a huge oval table and then moved into the living room, where they would chat politely or play a hand of bridge before going to bed. There was Madame Racault, Madame Mille, Monsieur Barbe and his sister Madame Joly, and the very well-read Madame d'Aumale, who made a gift to Gabrielle of a great black and red cape that the duke her grandfather had worn. The landlady was Madame Isoré, whose portrait Gabrielle sketched in words for a friend: "an elderly, most distinguished Madame, full of little bows, fine compliments, flattering little comments, and as sharp as a nail when it comes to business."[139] For about a thousand francs a day each (old francs, in other words about two dollars) Marcel and Gabrielle had two adjoining rooms, their meals, and a bell for calling Irène, the maid.[140]

For Marcel, living outside of Paris was not very convenient, since he had to drive all the way to his hospital in the XIIIth arrondissement every day. But he did not complain because Gabrielle adored Saint-Germain-en-Laye, revelling in both the comfortable living and the proximity of the state park, where she would go often on entrancing walks, "especially at twilight, the hour of in-between" which she so loved.[141] To her, Saint-Germain was in a way another Upshire. "[I have] all the things I like here," she wrote to a friend, "the park a step away, a few refined people I can talk to, books, a beautiful setting and the interesting atmosphere of a small, rather provincial town, [. . .] yet it's very close to Paris."[142]

She might not set foot in Paris for a week or two. But she did like being able to go there so easily when the spirit moved her, to go window shopping or stroll in the parks or along the *quais*, or most often to the theatre, in which Ludmila Pitoëff's former student was still keenly interested and which attracted her and her husband regularly to the centre of the city. They saw productions of Sartre, Giraudoux, Claudel, Molière. Visiting museums and exhibitions was not Gabrielle's favourite pastime, however, while Marcel was both enthusiastic and well informed about them; to these, Marcel went alone or with friends.

Despite Gabrielle's need of isolation and her distaste for socializing, she and Marcel readily made some lasting friendships during their years in France. Not many among the French, however; they dined at René d'Uckermann's from time to time, or met with Marcel's medical colleagues or superiors, but this was all. Their circle was made up mostly of Canadians – diplomats, artists, and writers who happened to be in Paris. Some of these were primarily Marcel's friends, like Paul Beaulieu and his wife, Simone, who lent Marcel their apartment in Neuilly during the summer of 1948 before the move to Saint-Germain-en-Laye; this was the case also with Jean Rousseau, who had been Marcel's classmate at the Université Laval, and especially Jean Soucy, Jean-Paul Lemieux's former student, who had come to complete his training as a painter in the Parisian *académies*. The Carbottes, as people were beginning to call them, also saw the journalist Marcelle Barthe and the Canadian ambassador and his wife, Georges and Pauline Vanier, as well as Fulgence Charpentier, a Canadian embassy employee who used to come to the Villa Dauphine and fill them in on the latest Parisian goings-on.[143] As for Gabrielle, she was reunited with her old friend Paula Bougearel, who had recently returned to France with her children and her mother. She also became close friends with Jeanne Lapointe, a teacher of literature at the Université Laval whom she had met at a Canadian embassy reception at the time of the Fémina; the two women saw each other fairly regularly during the year 1947–1948 which Jeanne spent in France. The following year it was Cécile Chabot (recently elected to the Royal Society of Canada), who came to Paris for a period of two years; she and Gabrielle, after meeting by chance at an exhibition of works by Simone Beaulieu, became very close friends. One weekend Gabrielle would go to Cécile's in Paris and the next weekend Cécile would come to Saint-Germain to spend the afternoon with Gabrielle. Cécile, a poetess, painter, and aquarellist, was a tiny woman with an angelic air and the heart of a child; her sensitivity, her love of nature, her diffidence, her ingenuousness about people and life, everything about her matched the characteristics of the type of woman Gabrielle felt most drawn to, women like Esther Perfect, Bernadette, and later Berthe Simard and Adrienne Choquette, women who were both reassuring and fragile, incapable of malice, bitterness or envy, and who were the very image of innocence and kindness. Women in whom she found, idealized, the memory of her mother and the projection of her own identity, one of the identities she imagined for herself. There was a bond forged between Cécile and Gabrielle during these Parisian years that never weakened.

While she appreciated her quiet life in Saint-Germain, Gabrielle loved nothing better than going for long drives with Marcel. There was hardly a weekend when they did not set off, alone or with a friend, to explore some corner of the countryside around Paris, the Île-de-France or adjoining areas, dazzled by the gentleness of the nature and the "elegance of form, colour, [the] works of art"[144] all around them. Then as soon as Marcel could take a few days off, they would go a little farther afield. In 1948 they spent the Easter vacation in Normandy, where Gabrielle wanted to be by the sea and visit "certain small villages immortalized by Proust: Balbec among others."[145] For Christmas and New Year's they went to Provence, where, having felt "the need to revisit earlier scenes of happiness," Gabrielle experienced the same enchantment as when she had been there ten years earlier with Ruby. Before returning to Paris, she insisted on making a detour through Castries to see Madame Paulet-Cassan and introduce her husband to her.[146]

The following year was equally busy. In April 1949, since Marcel's mother was visiting in Belgium, this was where they went, bringing Cécile Chabot with them. After a few days with Marcel's family not far from Brussels, they visited Bruges, Gand, Anvers, then pushed on as far as Amsterdam. A few months later, Gabrielle and Marcel went to spend the month of July in Basses-Pyrénées. "It is so pleasant," she wrote, "to be among people who can still enjoy themselves in all innocence."[147] For Christmas and New Year's Day, they went to Alsace, to Paula's, once again with Cécile; Paula was now living in Strasbourg, where her husband had been appointed to the very recently founded Council of Europe.

Although they travelled together, Gabrielle and Marcel did not travel in the same way. While Marcel, his nose in a guidebook, would seek out churches, monuments, and museums and stop often to buy stacks of postcards, Gabrielle would contemplate the landscapes and want to know about the rural people of the region; it was through these things, she said, that France provoked the strongest emotions in her, not artistic emotions, "which are of a different order, since in part they address one's intelligence, but sweeping impressions elicited by Nature allied to particular types of humanity."[148] From this interest followed her attachment to France's wilder regions, the Camargue or the coast of Brittany for instance, about which she wrote several texts whose manner could be described as midway between poetic travelogue and the feature article she had written so often in years gone by.[149]

The Second Book

These day trips and short excursions with Marcel were almost always spells of relaxation for Gabrielle that allowed her to leave her writing chore temporarily. The spells had to be brief, however, or there were soon feelings of guilt, for ever since the publication of *Bonheur d'occasion* she had had one single preoccupation – and occupation – which was writing another book. This was what all the journalists asked about; this was what everyone, publishers, critics, readers expected of her; and this was what she herself aspired to with every ounce of her being – to prove to herself and others that, as Henri Girard had predicted, she was not "a one-book author" like so many other Canadian writers.

This pressure was directly proportionate to the high renown brought her by her first book, and it never left her, at times inspiring "a guilty feeling of not deserving all I have,"[150] at times driving her to work like a galley slave, and to crippling anxiety. "Never have I been able to work on demand," she wrote to Marcel in January 1948. "At such times I have been paralyzed by the distress I have felt. And this feeling of demand I feel on contact with almost everyone."[151] To which Marcel replied, "There's something out of kilter in you, my dear love, which you must recognize and put straight. Remember how Étienne Gilson said to you [. . .], "There's no hurry, take your time, Madame, there are too many bad books dashed off by people who in fact have plenty of talent."[152]

But there was nothing for it. The more time passed, the more cruelly she was gripped by the urgency of producing this second book that was expected of her, this and the fear that it would not measure up to the first. She had decided to move to Europe and to stay there as long as she did mostly to give herself every chance of adequately meeting this demand weighing on her, in hope that this "exile" at the wellspring of French art and literature would be more favourable to the pursuit of her work and career than returning to Canada after the Fémina. Her entire life, whether at the Lutétia or the Villa Dauphine, was organized around writing. Every morning from the time she rose until around noon, her thoughts clear and her body rested, she would sit at her desk and type a few pages; these hours were sacred. All the rest, friendships, correspondence, going for walks, was put off until the afternoon and evening. She had established this routine when she was first in Europe and had followed it faithfully since, and would maintain it throughout her life.

Yet strict as it was, this daily ritual was not enough to bring her the freedom and total availability of mind that she needed to make sufficient headway in her work. Try as she might to reserve her mornings, the sounds of the world outside, minor worries, telephone calls, appointments, and other obligations of a social nature prevented her from concentrating as completely as she would like. And then there was Marcel, whose comings and goings, moods, and mere presence sometimes came into conflict with the "professional" demands placed on his wife and interfered with her concentration. And so during these three years in France, Gabrielle kept up the habit she had acquired when she was a journalist of arranging at least one period a year that would be exclusively hers, hers to give totally to her writing. For this she had to be alone far from the city, far from the fuss and bother of daily life and all familiar company, in some remote spot where she would have nothing to do but meditate, examine her thoughts, letting herself live one day at a time, body and mind rested, contemplating nature and forgetting everything beyond the essential: her writer's vocation.

Although the Geneva sojourn of January 1948 was one illustration, it was usually in summer that Gabrielle treated herself to (or imposed upon herself) these periods of "widowhood," which were a cross between studious retreats and vacations and could last as long as several weeks. In June 1948, for example, she left for Concarneau in Finistère. If she had chosen Brittany, it was because she hoped to find in this maritime setting and ragged coastline (reminding her of the Gaspé) the fertile ambiance she had known at Port-Daniel while she was writing *Bonheur d'occasion*. She stayed not far from the beach at the Hôtel de Cornouailles, an establishment that was more than comfortable and full of retired English, Belgian, and Swiss people, with whom she was polite but distant. It took only a few days to establish her timetable, which she summarized as follows for her *cher grand Marcel*, who was spending the summer in Paris:

> Breakfast between 8 and 9 o'clock; work or semblance of work until twelve, twelve-thirty; short walk in the town of Concarneau or on the beach; lunch; letter to my Marcel, then, if it's sunny, a long stroll on the sand; otherwise, Gaby leaves on another walk thinking of you; then in late afternoon I allow myself an hour or two of reading. Finally I dine around 8 o'clock, stay outside a few minutes, then go to my room and to bed around half past ten.[153]

Her daily letters to her husband are filled with affection, considerate admonitions, loving words, but also the need to reassure him and persuade him to accept their separation. To "a kind of grudge against my need for solitude, or rather, a kind of gloomy reproach" that she perceives in Marcel's letters, she replies at once, "But dear, you might as well reproach me for needing to eat, breathe, think. I want so badly for you to be completely of one mind with me, that is, in agreement even about the demands that are harsh and cause us to suffer." And she reminds him of the unspoken pact that must continue to bind them. "From time to time, I really will have to get away, to ask this sacrifice of you, but it will never be without pain or without my loving you more for the generosity of your heart."[154] It was she, always, who decided how long their separation would last, depending on the dictates of her work. On July 3 she wrote to Marcel, who was complaining of loneliness:

> *Cheri*, I beg you, don't grieve so. After all, I may not stay here all summer. Consider now a separation of 2 or 3 weeks, then after that we'll see. I've felt so low these last few days that I very nearly called you to ask you to come and get me, but sooner or later I would have been ashamed for it. So I'm going to try and stay a while.[155]

Two weeks later, after he had asked her to set a date for her return, she replied:

> Right now, I can't confirm to you that I'll be ready to leave by August 20. It all depends on the work I'll have got done by then. I may manage it, but I doubt it. And this time I'm determined not to interrupt my work as long as it hasn't progressed enough so I can stop worrying about interruptions and the bother of moving.[156]

In the end, she stayed alone at the Hôtel de Cornouailles until 28 August, when Marcel came to join her. They spent the first two weeks of September visiting the environs and discovering the local customs, attending in particular the "pardon" of Saint-Anne-la-Palud. As she left for Paris, Gabrielle bore away an enchanted memory of her sojourn of nearly three months in Brittany. "I've loved Concarneau," she told Jeanne Lapointe, "as few places in the world. [. . .] It's one of those wild little spots [. . .] where one imagines being able to live happily without wanting anything, poor fools that we are."[157]

This contentment was above all the product of the rest and unwinding her vacation had afforded her, for her writing had hardly progressed at all. Indeed, it had only taken a few days of solitude for her to rediscover the "pure and delightful emotion" of being able to write "with a facility I had long since lost,"[158] but this had yielded only two little stories inspired by life at the hotel, plus a heavily symbolic evocation of the Île de Sein, off the Pointe du Raz to the west of Concarneau.[159] None of these texts really amounted to anything, and the second book that was to follow *Bonheur d'occasion* was still not begun.

Not only was the second book not begun, but during this summer in Brittany Gabrielle abandoned a novel that it seems she had started working on at Rawdon early in 1947, if not earlier, in the period of

"Contes de la Plaine." This project was to be a vast panorama in the form of a "saga" relating the story of Gabrielle's own parents, and through them of the French-Canadian immigrants who left Quebec at the end of the nineteenth century to go west and settle on the new farmlands of Manitoba. The story features François Hébert, his wife Domitilde, nicknamed "Bobonne," and their children, the youngest of whom, Évangéline (or Line or Lina), is still an adolescent at the time of the great departure for the West and soon becomes the leading character in the plot. After falling madly in love with Donald McGillivray, a young Scot she meets during the journey, Line resigns herself to marrying Édouard Tessier, himself a colonist and a Liberal party worker.[160] Gabrielle had been working on this project steadily since she had been in France, stopping only to write brief texts here and there (when she was in Geneva, for example), but always coming back to it before long, resuming her documentary research[161] and drafting hundreds of pages. They were pages that did not satisfy her, however; she was not finding the tone, the form, the style that was right for a work whose intent was perhaps too ambitious or too ill-defined, hovering between sociohistorical novel and educational narrative, between the portrait of an entire collectivity and the inner adventure of a young woman in search of herself. Try as Gabrielle might, the project was going nowhere, and soon after arriving at Concarneau she decided to "put off till later the work so long under way."[162]

Back in Paris at the end of September and established in her new surroundings at Saint-Germain-en-Laye the month following, she still had no second book in sight. Manuscripts, yes: the story she had written in Switzerland the winter before, a few stories she had brought with her from Canada, several chapters of the "saga," her texts from Brittany. But nothing in all this seemed likely to end up as a book. She would have to look for something else. During that autumn of 1948, she began a somewhat outlandish project of which today there remain three short-story manuscripts that are complete in themselves and yet related: "Le déluge," "La première femme," and "Dieu."[163] Halfway between paleontological fantasy and biblical imitation, they present a fictional reconstitution of the origins of humanity in overblown, clumsy style, a fable in which violence is pitted against the instinct of solidarity, pain against love, submission against rebellion. For us today, the only interest in these texts is that they illustrate the state of aesthetic disarray in which the author of *Bonheur d'occasion* was then floundering, except that something else shows through as well, a little-known aspect of her thinking

and sensitivity at this time: an extremely pessimistic view of the feminine condition and the relationship between the sexes. The second of
these stories in particular shows a new Eve, in the guise of "Grunhilde,"
becoming aware at the dawn of time that the eternal fate of woman will
be submission to the brutish desire of man, condemnation to physical
sex, therefore to procreation, therefore to suffering.

> Her wild heart was not yet muddled by tenderness and pity. Her mind did
> not perceive many things, but this much it had grasped: pain was perpet-
> uated by love. Therein was the venom, the tyranny, the poison. In love.[164]

Written rapidly, these texts too stayed in the bottom drawer, for
Gabrielle no doubt considered them too crude, too preachy, or too
unpoetic to be worth the trouble of reworking them or pressing ahead
with the project underlying them. In the months that followed she tried
again, writing two more short stories, inspired this time by her trip to
Belgium with Marcel,[165] without finding any more promising idea for a
possible second book. Added to the anxiety of seeing time slip away from
her – she turned forty that spring – these successive dead ends gradually
undermined her morale. "I have often been discouraged lately," she
wrote to Bill Deacon in April 1949, "seeing how little work I have accomplished."[166] As usual, her health suffered; it was enough for her writing
to fail her to bring back the gastric troubles, the sore throats, the insomnia, the whole "host of small demons that make life hard for me."[167]

This was likely her state of mind when, in May or June 1949, one of
her little car trips with Marcel and some friends (among whom were
Paula Bougearel and Cécile Chabot) took her to Chartres, where the
stained-glass windows that had been removed for safekeeping for the
duration of the war had just been reinstalled in the cathedral. This visit
revived an impression of the year before, in this same square before the
cathedral, with Marcel and Jeanne Lapointe.[168] That day there had
sprung to her memory an incongruous image, to say the least, in that
exceedingly civilized site: the image of the Little Water Hen and its vast,
virgin Nature, this wilderness at the end of the earth where, as a young
teacher, she had spent several weeks a dozen years earlier. "And at once
there arose within me a kind of soft, poetic regret for this island where I
had known such utter boredom."[169]

In her account of this in 1956 (in which she seems to blend her memories of her 1948 and 1949 excursions to Chartres), Gabrielle attributes

the start of the process leading to her second, eagerly awaited book, *La Petite Poule d'Eau* (*Where Nests the Water Hen*), to this sudden memory, this kind of "illumination." She would spend all of her second year in Europe writing it.

As decisive as the Chartres illumination may have been, there were other circumstances behind the genesis of this book that bear mentioning. One was the suggestion made by André Rousseaux in his admiring review of *Bonheur d'occasion* that Gabrielle Roy might write a book about her early teaching days on the Canadian prairies. Then there had been Gabrielle's conversations with Marcel about the Water Hen district, which Marcel knew well for having practised there as a young doctor at Sainte-Rose-du-Lac before establishing his practice in St-Boniface. In the summer of 1947, shortly before their marriage, it seems they had returned there together by car, and Marcel had introduced an old friend and former patient to Gabrielle, Father Antoine-Marie de Lykochine, a Russian count turned Capuchin missionary who had settled at Toutes-Aides in 1940; in the village the father was admired for his polyglot talents and the assistance he afforded his Métis parishioners in their dealings with the Winnipeg fur merchants.[170]

This said, the Chartres illumination was without question an important moment of crystallization in which Gabrielle all of a sudden saw the broad outlines and central significance of the book to be, as she would do with almost all her books. In her later account of this episode, she attaches this significance to the historical context of her sojourn in France:

> Perhaps the times were propitious for such nostalgia. In Europe, in the postwar period, I had seen the traces of the horrendous suffering and evil inflicted on each other by the older nations. And my fancy, to relax, to be able to hope, found its pleasure in returning to the land of the Petite-Poule-d'Eau, a place intact, as if only just emerged from the Creator's dream. There, I thought, the chances of the human species are still almost untrammelled. There, if they wished, men could perhaps make a fresh start.[171]

Such an interpretation is certainly a fair one. In this period marked by the foundation of the United Nations and collective soul-searching over the causes of the Second World War, Gabrielle was greatly preoccupied, as were many artists and intellectuals, by the future of humanity and the fate of civilization. This is borne out by her acceptance speech to the

Royal Society of Canada, her interest in Teilhard de Chardin's ideas, her unpublished stories of the autumn of 1948, and many passages in her letters. Still, the Chartres illumination also had significance of another, more personal and immediate order that cannot be overlooked; that is, the pressing situation of a novelist sorely in need of a second book.

The Little Water Hen memory indeed arrived like a miracle to untangle Gabrielle's increasingly difficult "professional" situation, offering her an opportunity to escape the pressure paralysing her and get back to writing. And so the evocation of this "place intact, as if only just emerged from the Creator's dream" might bring salvation to "the human species," but in addition and especially to the novelist herself who, thanks to this image of her own past in surroundings she had known herself, could at long last "relax, [. . .] cope," and "perhaps make a fresh start."

A kind of backtracking underlay this new beginning, then. Through memory and imagination, Gabrielle's mind turned away from the present and shook free of the "demand" obliging her to follow up on *Bonheur d'occasion*. Falling back on the memory of the Little Water Hen she had formed when she was not yet the author of *Bonheur d'occasion*, when all for her was still freedom and promise for the future, and when "[her] chances [were] still almost untrammelled," she rediscovered an availability of mind that not only enabled her to write her second book but to write it as though it were her first. This was the only way if she were to continue to write: detach herself completely from *Bonheur d'occasion*, put it behind her and look to a totally different universe. In other words, write not in sequel to the first book, as she had more or less been trying to do, but *counter* to it, imagining a world, characters, even a form, that would be the exact opposite of all that *Bonheur d'occasion* would lead one to expect. Social realism would be replaced by dreaminess and Utopia, the present by the past, the urban setting by the great unspoiled outdoors, suffering by happiness, social and ethnic inequalities by harmony and fraternity, the Lacasse family by the family of Luzina and Hyppolyte Tousignant. *La Petite Poule d'Eau* was therefore to be a kind of mirror-image of *Bonheur d'occasion*, an anti-*Bonheur d'occasion*, a work in which an author finally breaks free of the celebrity her first book had brought her.

Gabrielle began writing this second book during the summer of 1949, it seems, with a facility she had not experienced for ages. There was no shortage of material. First, of course, there were the memories of her summer of 1937 at "Jeannotte's ranch" with the Côtés. But mingling with these memories were soon other images like them that filled in the gaps, like those from the summer of 1936 at Camperville with her cousin Éliane's family, or even from the days when as a child and then adolescent she used to spend her vacations at her uncle Excide's farm. And then there were Marcel's knowledge and memories retained from his own spell in the Water Hen district, which he communicated to her generously. All the while she was writing *La Petite Poule d'Eau*, Gabrielle could count on help and advice from her husband, who followed the progress of the manuscript closely and felt personally involved in the creation of the book, which is acknowledged by the dedication "To Marcel."

There were also more literary reasons for the ease with which the writing of *La Petite Poule d'Eau* went. After the toil of the tight structure demanded of her by *Bonheur d'occasion*, Gabrielle was here experimenting with a new, more flexible, looser form than that of the classic novel: a sequence of stories complete in themselves and each independent of the others, yet linked by the same theme, the same space and the return of the same characters, and most of all by a tone and point of view in common. After the "documentary" style of *Bonheur d'occasion*, *La Petite Poule d'Eau* was also the discovery of a new vision of people and things, a vision filled with poetry, emotion, and gentle irony, through which Gabrielle was able to reconnect with things she had loved in her youth, in particular Chekhov as he appeared through "The Steppe," an influence which is nowhere as visible as in this book.

By midsummer the first story, "Les vacances de Luzina," was finished. From then on, Gabrielle had one idea in mind and that was to withdraw alone to write more of her book. After taking a short vacation with Marcel at Ascain, she chose to return to where her writing career had begun, Upshire in England, at her friend Esther Perfect's.[172] She arrived there on August 14 and stayed until October 13. The village and house had not changed except that the effects of the war had made life there a bit less easy, what with the rationing and difficulties in obtaining supplies, and the fact that Esther and her father were now really quite poor. However, the money that Gabrielle paid them for her board was a help and made them even more attentive to her. Otherwise there were the same charming, felicitous, peaceful surroundings in which one had "the feeling of living outside of any particular period and in an atmosphere which the horror of our century has spared."[173]

At the beginning of her stay at Upshire, Gabrielle was trying only to rest and regain her health; she ate "like a horse," took walks in the country, reread Wordsworth, went botanizing with Esther, did embroidery, took photographs, went to London from time to time to visit museums or see her old friend Connie Smith, and most of all let herself be lulled, as she had years before, by the beauty and tranquillity of the place. "My stay here," she wrote to Marcel when she had been there a week, "is bringing me the greatest relaxation. It would be really impossible, I think, not to be soothed by this village gently slumbering on the flank of memories and the forest, and above all by the unfailing patience of those who are giving me shelter."[174]

For Upshire, besides being an "oasis of happiness in the raging sea of life,"[175] offered something that neither Geneva nor Concarneau had and that for Gabrielle was more precious than anything else: a tenderly devoted person giving her all that a mother can give – affection, care, admiration, protection – and doing it with infinite tact. Such indeed was the angelic Esther, whom Gabrielle described in these terms to Marcel:

> What a delightful character this Esther is. [...] She's something like Cécile Chabot, without the talent perhaps, but with the same romantic outlook, too sweet, naïve, verging on mawkishness yet always far from it by reason of an ingenuousness, a perfect innocence of the soul. [...] Esther, I believe, is one of those rare people who continue to see daily life with eyes unjaded by its beauty and keep receiving joy from it. I marvel at how, having lived in this little village, she can still appreciate its sweet harmony, observes each flower as she passes, and still feels joy to see a cloud floating in the sky. [...] The poor child has refused once and for all [...] to see the ugliness and malice of the world and she peoples the universe with her own charity and her own forthrightness.[176]

In this idyllic ambiance, Gabrielle was soon writing again. If only to reassure Marcel and soothe him in his loneliness, she kept him informed of her progress. On 29 August, she wrote, "I don't dare talk to you yet about the work I've done and which would be discouraging for me to show to you in its present state, but I've gained a little confidence. . . ." A week later the news was better: "I'm working now every morning with a bit less difficulty, and nothing would make me as happy as to have something to show you when I leave Upshire." At last, on September 20, she announced to him that she had "a long story under way that would go with Les Vacances de Luzina ['Luzina Takes a Holiday']," warning him at the same time that he had better not expect her back soon: "I'd like to finish a first draft of it before closing my bags and leaving Upshire," she said, "because I'd like to keep up the pace of the narration and not risk jeopardizing it with the least change in my present routine."

This long story was either "The School on the Little Water Hen," in which appears the character Mademoiselle Côté, the little schoolmistress in whom, Gabrielle would say later, "some readers have thought they recognized me,"[177] or "The Capuchin from Toutes-Aides," the last of the three stories that would make up the book.[178] Whichever it was, when Gabrielle returned to Saint-Germain-en-Laye around the middle of October, her work had passed the point of no return; this time the second book was well and truly under way.

From la Ville lumière to Ville LaSalle

Gabrielle spent her last autumn and winter in Europe finishing *La Petite Poule d'Eau*, revising and completing the drafts she had written at Saint-Germain and Upshire between June and October 1949. The last page of the final manuscript – and of the published book – is dated "May 1950, Saint-Germain-en-Laye." Now at long last she could submit her new book to René d'Uckermann, the head of Flammarion, who replied immediately, "*La Petite Poule d'Eau* is an excellent book, destined to become a classic."[179] She also sent the manuscript to Jean-Marie Nadeau, asking him to transmit it to Les Éditions Beauchemin and to Eugene Reynal, the former boss at Reynal & Hitchcock and now officially her editor at Harcourt Brace.

With the book finished, Gabrielle and Marcel had no further reason to stay in Europe, particularly since Marcel's studies were coming to an end and he must think about establishing a practice. Besides, even though there was no shortage of money, it seemed to Gabrielle that the time had come to trim back her train of life so as not to use up all her savings; the money saved was going to come in useful after 1954, the fateful last year of payments from the United States. Gabrielle's health was also worrying her; she felt "almost continually tired" and soon was found to have "a small goitre and all the signs of hyperthyroidism,"[180] which meant an operation might be necessary. And then there was homesickness; like many expatriates who after a long absence tend to idealize the people and places they have left behind, Gabrielle began dreaming about "how incomparably beautiful, youthful, and dynamic life is in Canada" and discovering "affection for many things we never knew we loved" before they were lost to sight.[181] The writing of *La Petite Poule d'Eau* had been nourished by this homesickness for Canada, and in turn reinforced it.

The return home was set for the end of summer 1950. In June, while Marcel stayed at the Villa Dauphine alone, busy with packing and trying to sell their old car, Gabrielle left Paris again for a final sojourn of work alone, this time in the little village of Lyons-la-Forêt in Upper Normandy, where she took a room at the Hôtel de la Licorne. What she wrote there and how long she stayed is impossible to know, for only two of her letters are on record, dated June 20 and 21. However, a quarrel – whose cause we do not know – seems to have erupted between her and Marcel, causing her to return abruptly to Paris and leaving both of them with a bitter memory of "that nasty Lyons-la-Forêt business."[182]

In mid-August Gabrielle was at the Villa Dauphine, overseeing final preparations for leaving. "I beg you not to give word of my arrival in any way," she wrote to Nadeau. "I insist absolutely on living a very secluded life, which I need most urgently to do, moreover."[183] She and Marcel left Saint-Germain for good on August 25 or 26. They went first to London to the Mayfair Hotel for a few days of sightseeing and shopping, then to Liverpool to board the liner *Ascania*, which docked in Montreal on 15 September 1950.

As with many others returning from Europe, Gabrielle's first reaction was one of shock. "There are a lot of things that hurt," she wrote to Cécile Chabot, who was still in Paris. "The Canadian speech seems hideous to one who has become accustomed to the beautiful French speech. The advertising is abominable."[184] The Canadian newspapers exasperated her. This feeling of dislocation would lessen, to be sure, but she would continue to read *Le Figaro littéraire*, *La Revue de Paris*, or *Nouvelles littéraires*, and her speech would for many years keep the slightly clipped accent she had acquired during her three years in France.

The first thing for her and Marcel to do was find somewhere to live. When they were in Europe they had talked several times of wanting to live in an "old farmhouse" at Rawdon, where they would be alone, far from everything, enjoying a cloudless, peaceful happiness; there Gabrielle imagined "my quilts, my braided rug, a Quebec stove, shelves for our books, geraniums in pots, an old-time rocking chair, and [it would be] the loveliest haven you could wish for."[185] It was only a dream, of course, the "Robinson Crusoe" dream of solitude and escape that

Gabrielle would keep on cherishing all her life. Although she had often allowed herself to bask in this dream from the mists of her childhood, she had never truly realized it; another, equally pressing need prevented it, her need for public admiration and the presence of someone to take care of her. Besides, there was Marcel. There was no question, after three years of specialization in France, of his going and burying himself in the country. But which city should he choose? For a time he considered Quebec City, where he had studied and where he still had contacts, but Gabrielle's friends were in Montreal and were urging her to stay there. Judith Jasmin was the most insistent, as well as Jori Smith and Jean Palardy, who threw a little party to celebrate the Carbottes' return and show their desire to see them stay. Albert Jutras and Paul Dumas, themselves physicians, persuaded Marcel that he could obtain a post in one of the region's major hospitals. Finally the decision was made: it would be Montreal.

But Gabrielle hated the idea of settling in the city, in the midst of all the traffic and hordes of people. She must have a calmer, more secluded place, closer to nature. As she had done in Paris, she took Marcel to the suburbs, more specifically to Ville LaSalle, which she remembered fondly from the time when as a young writer still hungry for fame she would come to relax on hot summer days, walking along the riverbank and resting in the little bay not far from the Lachine rapids. It was here at the edge of the town that she and Marcel found an apartment that suited them, at No. 5 Alepin Street. The brand-new neighbourhood was peopled by middle-class households attracted to the suburbs by the postwar economic explosion; small, single-family houses and duplexes were springing up like mushrooms, yet there was still almost a rural feel to life on account of the trees, the neighbouring farmland, and most of all the river flowing by. Monsieur Hamel's house, where the Carbottes became tenants, consisted of the ground floor occupied by the owner and his family and two four-room apartments upstairs complete with a bathroom each, central heating, and all the modern conveniences. Gabrielle and Marcel rented the apartment on the left; its only attraction was that it overlooked the river, which could be seen and heard at all times and whose bank could be reached by crossing LaSalle Boulevard, a stone's throw away.

Gabrielle appreciated the charm of the place and had made up her mind to take full advantage of it. Once they had moved at the beginning of October, she began again with pleasure to take long walks. She and

Marcel used to go for drives in the vicinity. The material conditions in which she was obliged to live, however, were "far from the cosseted, protected life I led at the [Villa] Dauphine," as she wrote to her friend Cécile. The humdrum grind of daily existence did not agree with her. She was living for the first time in her own apartment and had neither liking nor aptitude for the thousand little chores it takes to do for oneself. She would have to have help. Before leaving Europe she had made plans to bring back Irène, the little maid at the Villa Dauphine, but Irène had been made pregnant by the cook and the plans had fallen through. As for finding someone locally, in those days of the baby boom and full employment it looked well nigh impossible. In the meantime, Marcel did the cooking and housekeeping, which was not so difficult because they did not have much furniture and ate frugally.

All through that autumn, Gabrielle was not in very good health. Doctor Dumas, whom she consulted soon after returning from Europe, diagnosed such a state of weakness that he recommended complete rest. This only reinforced her tendency to reclusiveness and withdrawal into her own shell. Her friends would invite her out or suggest they come and see her, but she would always decline, offering as excuse her health problems and the necessity, if she were to have enough energy for her work, to give up everything else, meaning virtually all social life.

There was no shortage of work. The publication of *La Petite Poule d'Eau* was scheduled for that autumn, preceded by its string of tedious but necessary chores: revising the manuscript, correcting the galleys, checking the page proofs, and so on, all things which Gabrielle had to do in haste, badgered by Monsieur Issalys, the publisher at Les Editions Beauchemin, who wanted the book to come off the presses as soon as possible. But he wanted it so because Gabrielle herself wanted it; for patriotic reasons she insisted that at all costs *La Petite Poule d'Eau* should come out in Montreal before appearing in France.

It would be useful to recall the contractual terms governing the publication of Gabrielle Roy's books in French at this time. Under the contract signed in 1947 for the publication of *Bonheur d'occasion*, Flammarion had a right of first refusal over the author's next two novels. However, since *La Petite Poule d'Eau* was not considered a novel but "a collection of three stories," it was agreed that Flammarion would publish the book but still have its right of refusal over the Gabrielle Roy's next two books. Also under the 1947 contract, Flammarion's rights applied only outside Canada, while the author retained all her rights within the country, so in Canada she could have the book published by whomever she wished. Which is what she did in the autumn of 1950, signing a separate contract for the Canadian edition of *La Petite Poule d'Eau* with La Librairie Beauchemin of Montreal. Several reasons justified the choice: Beauchemin had been (and continued to be) the exclusive distributor of *Bonheur d'occasion* in Canada, had an existing business relationship with Flammarion, and was one of the few secular publishing houses in Quebec that were still active and financially sound despite the low point then being experienced in the Quebec publishing industry. These arrangements allowing dual publication of Gabrielle Roy's works in France and Canada would thenceforth apply to all of her books in French up to and including *La Rivière sans repos* (1970) (*Windflower*, 1970).

As far as *La Petite Poule d'Eau* was concerned, René d'Uckermann had given Gabrielle Roy to understand that it would be desirable for its Parisian publication to be as early as possible in the autumn of 1950, hence the haste with which Beauchemin was obliged to work. However, there was one delay after another and the Flammarion edition did not appear until 24 May 1951, six months after the Beauchemin edition. In France the book went almost unnoticed, receiving only cursory or slightly condescending comment. Sales were not more than a few thousand copies.

In Quebec, however, the critics were waiting impatiently; much was expected of the author of *Bonheur d'occasion*. But the general impression made by *La Petite Poule d'Eau* was one of disappointment. There were some enthusiastic commentators, especially among the righteous-minded who were overjoyed to read at long last in this era of moral and intellectual turpitude "one of the most wholesome works," in contrast to "the hopeless pessimism of fashionable novels" and widespread "acceptance of man's debasement";[186] Andrée Maillet, for her part, regarded Gabrielle Roy's book as "the masterpiece, the first, the incontestable masterpiece of our literature, [. . .] the first book produced by us, our people, our country [. . .] to equal certain of the great works of universal literature."[187] Overall, however, opinions were much more restrained, not to say negative. Several of the important critics, like Guy Sylvestre, Gilles Marcotte, and Julia Richer, without being scathing as was one by the name of Harry Bernard, allowed their disappointment to show.[188] Marcotte, while he liked the character Luzina, declared that *La Petite Poule d'Eau* was "nothing to compare with the revelation that *Bonheur d'occasion* was for us" and hoped the future would bring "a more important work." There was the same lack of enthusiasm from Sylvestre: "While in *Bonheur d'occasion* the interest of a fictional nature properly speaking was great, the content of the stories in *La Petite Poule d'Eau* is very weak, the plot nonexistent, and the analysis of feelings pretty sparse all told." The critics were nonplussed by the book's architecture, not knowing what to call it, and by its style, which seemed clumsy to them. Altogether, the prestige which the publication and success of *Bonheur d'occasion* had brought to Gabrielle Roy seemed to have been somewhat undermined. "*La Petite Poule d'Eau*," Guy Sylvestre concluded, "clearly reveals to us the limitations and merits of a talent which is one of the greatest we have discovered among us. Gabrielle Roy is not a great writer but [. . .] one of the most honest story tellers we have and certainly one of those rare Canadian writers who does not leave us indifferent."

For all the critics' polite phrases and circumlocutions, Gabrielle clearly saw the misunderstanding and coolness with which her book was received in French-Canadian literary circles.[189] And she was wounded by it, in her pride as in her need for recognition and success. Probably not unrelated to the bitterness she felt was the sudden aggravation of her state of health. Around the end of November, the "small goitre" that a doctor in Saint-Germain had diagnosed the previous spring began to degenerate so quickly that she had to undergo a thyroidectomy. The operation kept her in hospital for two weeks and left her weak, reduced to total passivity, and heavy-headed from the many medications she was supposed to take. "I have no reflexes any more, nothing left in my head," she wrote to Jeanne Lapointe.[190] To her translator, who came to visit her, she gave "an impression of bone-weariness, of someone who is beginning once more to be alive after a long and exhausting trouble, but someone still deeply in need of rest."[191]

In hope of speeding her convalescence, she spent the first two weeks of January at Lac Guindon in the Laurentians, at an establishment called the "Villa du Soleil." She returned in a more peaceful frame of mind and ready to get back to work. But despite the tranquillity and the closeness of the river, Ville LaSalle did not lend itself to writing. Like it or not, Gabrielle had to continue to attend to *La Petite Poule d'Eau*, read the reviews appearing, grant an interview here and there, and stay almost constantly in contact with Jean-Marie Nadeau. She also had to move about socially and see some friends and acquaintances. One day she received a visit from Ringuet, who came to interview her for an article he had promised the magazine *Flammes*, the bulletin of Les Éditions

Flammarion. Gabrielle, whose face looked "pain-racked," was reserved, as if distrustful with him. "[She] evades the question," he wrote. "I know of no one more secretive, who is a worse enemy to herself."[192] The reason was that she was overawed by her interviewer, a man of great culture and celebrated author of *Trente arpents*: "[He] always intimidates me a bit," she confided to Marcel. "I can't be natural and relaxed with him."[193]

It was a very different Gabrielle that Judith Jasmin found at this time. The two women had known each other for five or six years and had much in common, their tastes and ideas, but also their experience of the stage and in radio and journalism in Montreal. Before Gabrielle's marriage they had been in the habit of seeing and telephoning each other regularly, and when Gabrielle left for Europe Judith had remained one of the privileged points of contact between the Villa Dauphine and Montreal. They were always happy to be together, although their meetings were few and far between because of Gabrielle's ungregarious temperament and Judith's many occupations. They did see each other at the home of Jean-Marie Nadeau, who regularly invited clients and friends for evenings of discussion among people with progressive ideas. Less often, Judith would come to Alepin Street and spend a few hours with Gabrielle and Marcel. The atmosphere would be all relaxation and confidence. "Gabrielle would take her place in her rocking chair," Judith recalls, "and start telling stories endlessly; she's a born story-teller. Sentences always correct, complete, perfectly balanced. She speaks the way she writes and doesn't make any insipid, disconnected conversation, the kind that's called 'small talk.' When Gabrielle talks it's always interesting; what you get is a little story that's complete, filled with light humour, which you don't dare interrupt."[194]

Judith was one of the few visitors allowed into the apartment in Ville LaSalle. With two cats but still no maid, Gabrielle virtually never had guests – or went out. She was not really writing at all any more; her efforts were thwarted by business to be attended to and chronic fatigue. Marcel's morale was not in top shape either. Contrary to the prospects that had been held out to him, he still had found no job in Montreal and the chance of finding one seemed increasingly dim. He therefore continued to be financially dependent on Gabrielle while waiting desperately for a door, somewhere, to open for him. It affected his mood. Sometimes edgy, sometimes despondent, he was often ill-tempered, prowling about the apartment like a caged tiger. It hurt Gabrielle to see him this way and she would try to comfort him. "But above all don't get discouraged; as long as you have courage, I will too. [. . .] If we have to, we'll go somewhere else. It's a great big world and somewhere, certainly, there must be a place for both of us to earn our living. I'm by no means discouraged by all this, believe me, I'm still convinced that we're quite simply passing through a long period of bad luck – but after that the sun will shine for us."[195] The same day as this umpteenth letter of encouragement to Marcel, she sent another to Jeanne Lapointe, whose tone was very different: "None of the plans we've made have worked out [. . .]. It's enough to make us think we're not wanted anywhere. My heart is broken by the disappointments Marcel has had to suffer since our return."[196]

Gabrielle wrote these letters from the Gaspé, where she spent the summer of 1951. Since she could not manage either to rest or work in the apartment in Ville LaSalle, she had decided to take a vacation, without Marcel or anyone, to try and concentrate and begin seriously to write again. As two years before when she went back to Upshire, she was returning to one of her beloved pieces of paradise from days gone by, the house of Bertha and Irving McKenzie in Port-Daniel.

Rediscovering with emotion "my little room with its rocking chair, the big desk and my two windows open to the daisies, the trees, and the blue of the sea in the distance,"[197] she resumed her trusty old routine: walks in the neighbouring countryside, swimming in the sea, knitting, reading (Gide especially), and writing letters daily to Marcel who, alone in Montreal, vainly continued his job-hunting, no longer daring to complain of being separated from his wife. "I'm glad," she confided to him shortly after her arrival, "that you can now understand that solitude, although for me it's a bitter penitence, is nevertheless useful to me from time to time. It only strengthens my affection for you in any case."[198]

In no time the vacationer felt that her "poor carcase"[199] was recovering and at last she could get back into her work. Less than she would have liked, however, for she still had to attend to *La Petite Poule d'Eau*, whose English translation was about to appear.

At Harcourt Brace, the manuscript had been accepted even before the book appeared in French. Since Hannah Josephson, who had translated *The Tin Flute,* was not available, the publishers had turned to Harry Lorin Binsse, who already had to his credit the translation of *Sous le soleil de Satan* by Georges Bernanos. Binsse was a Canadian, the son of an "immensely rich" mother and owner of "a magnificent dwelling in La Malbaie," which he soon converted into a restaurant in order to defray expenses having to do with his prodigious need of alcohol. He would be Gabrielle Roy's translator until the early 1960s. Gabrielle appreciated his great competence and amiably eccentric personality. The translation, titled *Where Nests the Water Hen*, was ready in the spring of 1951. Gabrielle reviewed it during the summer and the book was published the following October. Here again there was dual publication, in New York under the Harcourt Brace name and in Toronto by McClelland & Stewart, which did not have the rights but bought the books from Harcourt Brace and paid the royalties directly to Gabrielle Roy, the same arrangement that had been negotiated with Reynal & Hitchcock for *The Tin Flute*.

When he had agreed to publish *Where Nests the Water Hen*, Eugene Reynal had made a point of warning Gabrielle and Jean-Marie Nadeau that the "particular form" of the book might present "a marketing hurdle,"[200] and they should perhaps not count on the book being a best-seller. This foresight proved correct. Although the book received abundant and sympathetic commentary, particularly in cities of "the American heartland," although it was admired by conservative reviewers who saw in it "a refreshing, invigorating breeze" in a literary era "when so often only sin and crime and fear and utter sordidness are presented as being 'true to life' and achieve best-seller rating,"[201] sales of *Where Nests the Water Hen* did not take off. Two months after publication, they stagnated at a little over four thousand copies for the whole of the United States. Which is as good as saying the book was a failure.

Fortunately it was not quite the same story in English Canada. Although sales were not immediately very satisfactory there either, the critics were more favourable than they had been in Quebec the previous year. The loose structure was less disturbing and most of all there was more sensitivity to the Canadian nature of the work. This "Canadianness" of *Where Nests the Water Hen*, which was picked up by some American critics, including Sterling North,[202] provided ammunition for the defenders of a "specifically Canadian culture," which the Massey Commission (whose report was tabled in 1951) was at this time trying to define and promote. In their vanguard was Gabrielle's good friend Bill Deacon, who was once again eulogizing "our little genius from St. Boniface." This book, he declared in the *Globe and Mail*, expresses the Canadian soul better than any other: "No other writer of first rate talents has attempted to recreate for us the life of our remotest frontier. [...] Nowhere else has the literary pioneer reached and recorded the pioneer of the soil." The same national fibre resonated with W. E. Collin, who had read the book in French and saw in it "a picture of the stock out of which will proceed the Canada that is to be."[203]

Alexandre Chenevert's Calvary

We return to Port-Daniel and Gabrielle's vacation in the summer of 1951. She was there for a rest, but first and foremost to write. As usual it took some time to get down to it, the more so since getting settled in Ville LaSalle, her operation, and Marcel's problems had kept her from writing for close to a year. "The forge," as she said, had "had time to cool down."[204]

And yet soon she managed, laboriously, to get back to work. On July 11, nearly three weeks after arriving at the McKenzies', she asked Marcel to send her "150 to 200 sheets of typewriter paper." Two days later, she was able to announce that the forge was relit:

> I'm working a bit every day. Nothing very remarkable yet. Still, I've reason not to be too displeased if I consider how rusty I was. I've taken up the story of my dear, my poor Alexandre Chenevert again.[205]

This dear, poor character, this lowly Montreal cashier, had come to her for the first time while she was in Geneva in January 1948. He had been inspired, she recounted later, by the sight of a line of foreigners queuing up outside a government bureau in Paris in the autumn of 1947.[206] But the idea of featuring a simple, ordinary man whose brain is bombarded by a constant flood of modern information, whose conscience is racked by the suffering in the world and who ruins his life by trying to make it a greater or more nearly perfect life than it is, this idea goes back to the early months of 1947 or even earlier. So this character had been on her mind in one way or another for at least four years. "I'm mistaken perhaps about the interest there may be in such a person who is so little unlike so many others," she confided to Marcel, "but I love him and that is enough for me."[207] It was Marcel, moreover, who had urged her at this time to make him into a novel. For over a year after returning from Geneva she had continued to work at this novel, spending whole weeks at it, leaving it aside then returning to it, but always unsuccessfully. Then had come *La Petite Poule d'Eau*, relieving her for a time of this character who would not come to life. But *La Petite Poule d'Eau* could only be an interlude. Some day, she knew, Alexandre Chenevert would come knocking at her door again and there would be no escaping him any longer, for she was bound to him not only by love but also, as she said later, "a sense of duty."[208]

The duty of finishing what she had begun? Perhaps, although around this time she had not flinched from abandoning a good many other texts she had begun. Why was she so attached to this project? Why was it so special that she had to keep returning to it or else feel guilt for having betrayed a trust? Although there are probably no answers to these questions, two or three things deserve attention. One is that with time the character Alexandre Chenevert became a kind of emissary with a twofold mission for Gabrielle. First, he had a "message" to convey, for this, it should be remembered, was a period of "engaged" literature; the novel of the day, Gabrielle declared in 1948, should "be rooted in its era and espouse its tragic problems."[209] This to her was one of the essentially significant things about the novel she wanted to write; it was to express a vision of the world, an interrogation – both deeply anxious and ironical – on the condition of contemporary man, along the lines inspired by her own reflections and readings of recent years (Gide, Camus, Sartre, Saint-Exupéry). More deeply still, however, Alexandre Chenevert occupied her imagination so persistently that he became a kind of alter ego for her, a character increasingly less fictional and less detached from her, someone whose role was in a way to gather in and objectivize all that she was living and feeling: her low spirits, insomnia, experience of illness, her religious worries, her anxious relationship with money, and especially that back-and-forth pendulum, that constantly being torn between the need to love others and the need to escape them, between the feeling of her own importance and her own smallness, between confidence and unworthiness, between the enchantment of being what she was and the sorrow of not being really that. No other of her characters thus far had been – and no other thereafter would be – as close to her, as intimately entwined with her own thinking and her own life.

For Gabrielle, it was not only that these bonds prevented her from turning her back on Alexandre Chenevert, there was also the fact that in the eyes of the world, as in her own, she still had an "order" to fill, a follow-up to *Bonheur d'occasion* to produce, meaning another book both up to scratch with the one that had made her famous and more or less directly in the same vein. *La Petite Poule d'Eau* had been a temporary escape, freeing her of the obligation for the time being without letting her off. She still owed her readers, her critics, and her publishers a real "second book," a book as good as the first. This book therefore had to be a novel in the usual sense of the term, meaning a story of sufficient length in which believable action develops in a coherent and sustained manner. Moreover, this novel, like *Bonheur d'occasion*, would in some way need to be a picture of a real, contemporary milieu based on direct observation, so that readers might recognize their own familiar world and identify with the characters.

Whether she liked it or not, everything conspired to make her the prisoner of her poor Alexandre Chenevert. And she worked at his story as if she were a prisoner, a slave chained to a task she had not chosen but was forbidden to give up. "It took me longer to write this than any other work," she would confide later; "[I] had not enjoyed writing it."[210] Apart from the first chapter, for which the *conte* she had begun in Geneva in 1948 provided the first draft, almost all of it gave her trouble, the construction, the dialogue, the descriptions, traps she kept falling into. She felt she was becoming mired, losing her way. When she left Port-Daniel in August 1951, the fire was perhaps relit in the forge, but the novel had advanced hardly at all.

Back in Ville LaSalle, she spent the autumn labouring over her manuscript. The atmosphere had much improved in the little apartment on Alepin Street. After having for a time considered establishing a practice in St-Jérôme north of Montreal, Marcel had finally obtained a post at the Hôpital de la Miséricorde. It was not what he had dreamed of ("the Hôtel-Dieu or nothing," he had said when he arrived in Montreal), but at least he had something to occupy his days and provide for his needs; Gabrielle was "greatly relieved to see him at work at last and so much happier."[211] To cap this turn of fortune, a domestic arrived on their doorstep in the person of Connie Smith, the London friend whom Gabrielle had brought to Canada especially to take her into service.

Unfortunately, this favourable combination of circumstances did not last. In January Marcel left for Quebec City, where the Hôpital Saint-Sacrement was offering him a much more attractive post than the one he had at La Miséricorde; he would be able to concentrate on his speciality, practise surgery, and do a little teaching and research. He and Gabrielle agreed not to move until the spring, however, so as to be sure that Marcel was well ensconced and content with his new job. In the meantime, they would have to live apart. Marcel rented a room from Madame Chassé, who ran a boarding establishment in the Château Saint-Louis, an apartment building in the Upper Town of Quebec City; Gabrielle stayed in Ville LaSalle with Connie. But at this point a quarrel broke out between the two women; Connie, who was homesick in Canada, demanded a raise, Gabrielle refused, and so Connie decided to go back to England, leaving on February 3 aboard a cargo ship. Her employer paid her passage. They had known one another for nearly fifteen years and now all was over between them.

And so Gabrielle was alone in the little suburban apartment. The only company she had left was Ki-Min, the remaining cat, a grey, which she soon had to get rid of. Cécile Chabot, now home from Europe, would come now and then for a bit of a chat. Doctor Jasmin and his wife, neighbours with whom Gabrielle was on good terms, would invite her sometimes to come and listen to recorded music with them (*Boris Godunov*, Ravel, Corelli, Mozart's *Requiem*). Occasionally she would go as far as St-Lambert on the far side of the river, where her old friend Jacqueline Deniset was now living; one evening she went to see a documentary film on the Inuit at the Collège de Saint-Laurent. She also had occasion to go and meet Jori Smith and Jean Palardy, Philippe Panneton and his wife, or the diplomat Jean Désy and his wife; but social events put her in such a state of "mental overstimulation" that she felt she had to avoid them. "It's not fun," she said to Marcel. "I like to see certain people, but it seems I ought to adapt myself to my temperament and not force it to serve me as it does not wish."[212]

Physically she was in a lamentable state. "I have rarely been as weak and exhausted as at present." Her liver was giving her trouble, she had palpitations, and she had no appetite, not to speak of colds, insomnia, and "this relentless weariness" that hardly ever left her,[213] despite – or perhaps because of – the numerous injections she was receiving and all the medications she kept trying. Although Marcel wrote her that he was happy with his work at the Hôpital Saint-Sacrement, that all was going well for him, that he was "preparing to make a happier life for [her] than in the past,"[214] her melancholy seemed incurable. "For a few days it seems to me I'm beginning to climb the hill, then down I come again."[215]

Was it working too hard at her *Alexandre Chenevert* manuscript that had dragged her down to such physical and moral prostration? Was it discouragement to see nothing come of all her effort? Whatever the case, she wrote nothing that winter. "I have completely abandoned all intellectual work for nearly two months," she confided to Marcel on February 21. "Let's hope that under this heap of ashes accumulated on my head I'll find a little flame still alive one day."

She knew there was only one way to emerge from her torpor, the way that had always worked so well for her before, as it did too for poor Alexandre Chenevert: a retreat, seclusion far from the city, away from the traffic of men and ideas in a peaceful solitude that alone could afford her concentration and inspiration. She had been longing since January "to leave for a little sojourn elsewhere than here, where I'm too dispir-ited and find myself constantly thinking the same thoughts."[216] And so as soon as April came she hastened to leave Ville LaSalle, not to join Marcel in Quebec City but to return to her haven of years past – Rawdon, the house and care of "little Mother Tink," the contentment of being back amid Nature at last, alone with herself, "away from all the complexity of life that exhausts one's nerves."[217]

Exhausts one's nerves and keeps one from writing. Now more than ever she was feeling an urgent need to get back to work, all the more since d'Uckermann was becoming impatient. Gabrielle had spoken to him of her novel in progress and in reply he was pressing her to make haste: "You must publish [this new book] with less lapse of time than you allowed between *Bonheur d'occasion* and *La Petite Poule d'Eau*. Readers need these repeated reminders so that an author's name becomes graven in their memories, and this is how [that author's] reputation is established."[218] There was no time to lose, she knew this. Six months later, the *Alexandre Chenevert* manuscript was practically finished.

Marcel hardly saw his wife during these six months, except for June, which she spent in Quebec City. Gabrielle was leading a real rover's life, going from one "hermitage" to another, hauling along her little typewriter and her manuscripts, and writing, writing, with a constancy and determination reminiscent of her days of journalism, before the *Bonheur d'occasion* triumph.

But it was at Rawdon that the ball began to roll. She had been there barely a week before she announced to Marcel:

> I'm working a bit; not too badly perhaps; it's hard for me to judge. Anyway, I hope it will all get organized in the end, I mean these successive drafts that I've put on paper and that up to now haven't seemed to hold together so well. It seems to me there's a slight improvement. But let's not

talk too much about it! How many times I've driven off marvellous possibilities by shouting too soon that I'd got it![219]

Then, two days later:

Alexandre Chenevert is emerging from limbo. Will I really manage to
finish this book some day! Sometimes I think it's possible; sometimes I
doubt it. Really, it's as absurd to launch on such an undertaking as to set
out on foot around the world. Yet I could not avoid doing it.[220]

Her work at this time consisted of revising the "successive drafts" she
had already written, transforming them into chapters, and writing them
anew so as to set the character well in place and build a credible narrative. By the end of May, after six weeks of deletions, additions, and intensive writing, she had in hand the first two parts of her novel.

There remained the third, which she knew was going to be "the
hardest."[221] Before tackling it she gave herself a month of respite, which
she spent with Marcel in their new apartment in Quebec City. Then she
left again at the end of June. First she went to Montreal, where there were
some business matters to settle with Nadeau; while there she visited
Bernadette, who was at the Côte-Sainte-Catherine convent for a spell, and
saw Cécile Chabot. Then she took the train for Port-Daniel, arriving on
the morning of July 1.

She was there until the middle of August, staying as always with the
McKenzies and partaking of her usual vacationer's activities – sunbathing,
walking, bicycling, and fishing excursions. This time the period of physical conditioning was very brief. By July 5 she had taken up the manuscript
she had interrupted on leaving Rawdon and begun work on it again, in
hope, she told Marcel, of "having a reasonably good summer."

It would in fact be "a magnificent summer," blessed by the gods, "the
most beautiful I have ever known on any coast."[222] The weather was
perfect, she felt a physical and moral well-being she had not known for
some years, and her peripatetic life, without ties or responsibilities, gave
her a feeling of such buoyancy that one would have said she was back in
the heyday of her youth, before fame, before marriage, when all she had
to care about was freedom, availability, full possession of herself and a
grip on the world awaiting her. To Jeanne Lapointe, she wrote, "I assure
you, dear Jeanne, that there is something good about this existence. [...]
It has taught me (necessarily) to give up big furniture and voluminous

possessions. [. . .] I think I'll never be able to make myself live like other people now, I mean with pots and pans, a stove and sofas. [. . .] I tell you, I've lived too long on the roads. The beautiful roads."[223]

As a consequence – or the cause – of the "idyllic" summer, the writing of *Alexandre Chenevert* progressed much faster than Gabrielle had foreseen. Each morning in her room, where Bertha brought her her coffee, she patiently "[tried] to unwind the reel."[224] By early August she was able to announce proudly to Marcel that the heavy work was done:

> I've advanced my work quite a bit. I'm so impatient to have you read it. Right now I'm putting a hand to the chapters that seem to me the weakest. There's still an enormous amount to do, but at least I've finished all the framing of the work, put up the building. What remains to be done now is inside – and I feel sort of relieved, surprised too, after such strenuous efforts, to have reached this stage despite all.[225]

With the hardest part behind her, there was still much to do before the novel could take its final form. Gabrielle devoted her last weeks in the Gaspé to this work of polishing and finishing, but could not quite achieve all she had set out to. "In the alchemist's back room," she wrote to Jeanne Lapointe, "I have transformed, slightly refined a few substances, but I'm still far from pure gold."[226] Then, since the weather was turning cool at Port-Daniel, she announced to Marcel that instead of rejoining him she was going back to Rawdon so as, she hoped, to finish a few more chapters there.

At this point, Marcel was in Boston. The previous winter, shortly after establishing his practice in Quebec City, he had been offered a residency in oncology and cytology at Vincent Memorial Hospital, a Harvard University affiliate, with the understanding that he might receive an American grant. He had liked the idea and so had Gabrielle. Since there were delays with the grant, Gabrielle advanced him the necessary money and he arrived in Boston on August 1, intending to stay several months. Gabrielle told him she would come to join him after her vacation in the Gaspé and then, as we have seen, decided first to spend several weeks at Rawdon in order to work on *Alexandre Chenevert*, loath to break her daily writing routine and risk jeopardizing everything so well launched at Port-Daniel by returning too soon to her ordinary life.

Although Marcel protested that once again they were going to be apart on their wedding anniversary, she waited until she had finished her work before leaving for Boston. For this she extended her stay at Mrs. Tinkler's until the middle of October, when at last she had a first complete version of her novel that she was reasonably satisfied with. Then she was able to go and join her husband, whom she had not seen for almost four months.

Having learned in the meantime that he would not be getting his grant after all, Marcel had decided to shorten his stay at Vincent Memorial. Gabrielle spent the last two weeks of October with him in a stylish furnished apartment on Commonwealth Avenue, not far from Copley Square. They returned to Quebec City by car early the following month after a side trip to Cape Cod and New York.

When she arrived at the Château Saint-Louis, Gabrielle was buoyant. She felt she was at the end of the long ordeal; after five years of patience, meditation, and laborious writing, she had at last succeeded in giving birth to her dear, poor Alexandre Chenevert. This, at least, was what she thought when, after the New Year's Day holiday of 1953, she went to Montreal for a fortnight to have her manuscript typed by Jacqueline Deniset, the same friend who had typed *Bonheur d'occasion*.

But she was not yet out of the woods. Unable to judge her book with any accuracy after so much effort and reworking, she gave copies of the typescript to a few people close to her. Cécile said she was bowled over by the central character, as Jacqueline had been while typing the text. Marcel suggested corrections of a medical nature. However, Jeanne Lapointe, who had experience with manuscripts and a very keen literary sense, was much more restrained. She suggested to Gabrielle that the manuscript had great merit, but its construction and style needed reworking. Pencil in hand like the teacher of literature she was, she crossed out or underlined all that seemed superfluous to her, as well as awkward sentences, laboured metaphors, sentimental formulations, and even a whole chapter that takes place at Christmas.[227] Decidedly, Alexandre was putting up dogged resistance to his birth.

Gabrielle was devastated at first. But at the point her novel had reached, there could be no question of abandoning it, so she had no choice but to get back to work and repair at least the weaknesses that Jeanne had detected. In order to work with her mind at peace, she returned once more to Rawdon and settled in at Mother Tinkler's in mid-April 1953, armed with her manuscript. At first as always, things dragged. "I strain like a dog toward a roast of beef," she told Marcel. "[. . .] My brain feels empty after the sustained effort I put in every morning from eight o'clock till noon. It's been drudgery getting myself going, you've no idea, real drudgery! A nasty business. Now, things are beginning to hum a bit." She wrote this letter on May 1. The next day she asked Jeanne Lapointe to join her for two days of work together. Jeanne's suggestions, she confided to Marcel, were "infinitely valuable and advantageous to me."[228] A new version of the book was at last ready in the second week of May. Before returning to Quebec City, Gabrielle had the text typed locally by a typist who gave her headaches but whose work was presentable enough that she was able to submit it a few weeks later to her publishers in Montreal, Paris, and New York. This time, *Alexandre Chenevert* was well and truly finished.

"Today is a day of celebration," René d'Uckermann wrote immediately to Gabrielle. "I have just received the manuscript of *Alexandre Chenevert*."[229] As for Eugene Reynal, he announced his decision to publish the book but warned once again that its success was not at all assured, for "the grimness of the story culminating in Alexander's suffering and death [. . .] may prove too stark to appeal to the general reader"; he advised Gabrielle "not to set [her] sales expectations too high."[230] *Alexandre Chenevert* was published in Montreal by Beauchemin in March 1954, and in Paris by Flammarion the following month under the title *Alexandre Chenevert, caissier*. The English translation by Harry Binsse, titled *The Cashier*, did not appear until a year and a half later, in October 1955; as usual, Harcourt Brace of New York was the publisher and printed copies in the name of McClelland & Stewart for Canadian distribution.

The book was received in more or less the same way that *La Petite Poule d'Eau* and *Where Nests the Water Hen* had been three years earlier, or perhaps even more coolly. In Paris, a few critics close to Flammarion lauded its "human truthfulness" and the "universality" of the central character,[231] but the reading public did not follow their lead and the novel, with its author, quickly sank into silence. It was the same in the United States, where the reviews were good, but sales barely exceeded 2,500 copies,[232] while in English Canada the book drew only scant interest from both critics and readers. It was in Quebec where the book sold well (Beauchemin's sales were 5,000 copies in three months) and where the critics were harshest. "There was a fine subject for a short story there," wrote Jean Béraud, the columnist for *La Presse*, "a moving character study of a hundred pages; the book has 373." In *Le Devoir*, Gilles Marcotte could not hide his disappointment: "From the rich polyphony of *Bonheur d'occasion* to the little two-note clarinette solo of *Alexandre Chenevert*, the distance is great"; the book, Marcotte added, "was not written with the joy of authentic creations"; it gave an "impression of artifice" and toil. His opinion was echoed by most of the critics.[233]

Gabrielle, of course, was hurt by the negative judgments in the Montreal press. To defend herself, she attributed them to reasons of ideology; the critics understood nothing of what she was trying to convey, she told her friend Bill Deacon.

> I begin to see that this chord I'm always trying to touch – this theme of human love regardless of nationality, of religion, of tongue, this essential truth doesn't mean much to my people and although I know the necessity of patience, I'm a little sick at heart, sometimes. How can people be so blind to the one truth we should learn as we live, the one truth that matters![234]

The rift between Gabrielle and the Quebec critics that had appeared with the publication of *La Petite Poule d'Eau* had simply deepened, regardless of the fact that *Alexandre Chenevert* was a completely different work. These journalists and commentators did accord Gabrielle Roy special attention and very great respect and continued to consider her one of the best local writers. But for most of them she was above all the author of *Bonheur d'occasion*, and any new book of hers must meet the expectations created by this first novel that had made her famous eight years earlier.

CHAPTER 8

"Writing, As If It's Your Very Reason for Living"

An Incident at Tangent
Years of Respite • A Peripatetic Bride
The Hermitage at Petite-Rivière-Saint-François
The Saga of Writing • A World of Women
Gabrielle and Her Sisters • Winter Migrations
The Grande Dame of Literature, or The Ambiguities of Fame
Secrets • After the Storm • Elegy to Bernadette

From the moment Gabrielle moved to Quebec City, her life entered a new phase that one might be inclined to call maturity, since it was a phase of stability and concentration, revealing certain aspects of her personality and work of which there had been suggestions in previous periods but which became fully evident at this time. The reason is that the landscape was now different, as when a mighty river, having raged across its valley, at last finds the space it needs to flow freely and exist only of itself in a world and time that are its own.

This rather ponderous metaphor seeks to convey the fact that the period of battle and feverish activity was over for Gabrielle Roy. At forty-five, she could tell herself that she had realized the dreams of her youth, at least the dreams of a material and professional nature: a writer she had become; fame she had achieved in profusion; money had rained upon her in greater quantity than she had ever imagined. As for love, although this had not really been part of her dreams, she had known it or in any case had inspired it in many others, women and men, friends and protectors, and one of them, Marcel, had pledged his life to her.

All this she had won through steely independence and determination, which for fifteen or twenty years had kept her constantly on the go. All this time, there had been only one thought in her head: to act, work, expend herself without counting the cost in order to increase her chances of success, prove her worth, and make a place for herself, the first place if possible, in the world she had chosen to move in. From Manitoba in her twenties all the way to postwar Paris, her life had borne all the marks of a fight whose aim was conquest, full of bustle and ups and downs, movement from place to place, breakups, strategies, and endless activity. This was the time that was now over. Beginning in the mid-1950s,

Gabrielle's life began to move at a different, much slower, steadier, and less frenetic pace than the one she had been setting hitherto. Notable events were less frequent, and in any case less spectacular; there were few external changes and those there were were never drastic or sudden. Her life gradually took on the peacefulness, the more or less repetitiveness characteristic of middle age, once the battles have ceased and are supplanted by a certain detachment, a certain immobility produced by a combination of resignation, wisdom, and self-possession.

From this point on, the biographer has fewer pivotal "happenings" to pinpoint, fewer "bends in the road," fewer "scenes" to report. It is no longer so much a question of following the unfolding of a story or relating what the subject did as evoking the atmosphere, the colour of her existence, endeavouring to distinguish the gradual changes that, close to imperceptible though they may have been, were nonetheless real and profound. For while Gabrielle Roy's life became less exciting as she advanced in age, as with most of us, it would be wrong to say that nothing more of importance happened. On the contrary, this period beginning in 1953 and continuing until her death was the richest of her life and certainly the most valuable for us since it was the period of her fullest accomplishment as a writer.

Herein is the principal reason for the slowdown that appears to be the feature of this period. Practically nothing in Gabrielle's life from now on was not tied to this single occupation, writing, an epic quest and yet one that is hard to recount. Now that she had succeeded in becoming a writer, it was as though henceforth she were nothing but a writer, and in the most absolute sense of the term: someone who breathes, thinks, suffers, and feels joy only in and through writing, someone whose desires, emotions, cares, whose very identity is in every way bound up with the books that are born of her imagination, the books that alone can give her the sense of her worth and existence.

Gabrielle's life had long since been centred on her vocation as a writer, but until now that vocation had been strongly remindful of Balzac's character Rastignac, the country boy come to conquer Paris: it drove her to action, translated into an all-consuming ambition. Now that this was over, there was another phase beginning, not necessarily happier or less intense but certainly more concentrated, simpler, and turned in on writing to the exclusion of all else. In her own way, the Gabrielle Roy of this period makes one think more and more of Flaubert as Marthe Robert sees him, the artist who is utterly dedicated to his work and finds in his art a sensuousness and fulfilment superior to anything the material world and human beings could offer him. But as Robert points out – and the life of Gabrielle Roy bears out – this sensuousness is at the same time an asceticism that demands discipline, strict observance, and virtually total abstinence from all else. Ordinary existence, everyday acts, relationships with others including intimate relationships, all must not only arrange themselves tidily around writing but be of lesser importance, always taking a back seat to it. Even if his works address all men, the writer lives in a closed universe in which he appears turned solely toward himself in a kind of "narcissistic ecstasy," but in which, when all is said and done, he is only a slave subject to the implacable law of his work, to which, Marthe Robert adds, he makes "the expiatory sacrifice [...] of his own life, dedicated entirely to his own writing or, as it were, converted into writing, positively consumed by pen and ink."[1]

Gabrielle did not conform to this model as perfectly as Flaubert or Proust, but she undeniably had strong leanings toward it. For her too, writing became the only task, the only law that ruled her existence, her thoughts, her relationships with others. A total writer she was perhaps not, but that and only that was what she aspired constantly to be. Not first of all a woman, wife, spouse, friend, sister, or citizen, but a writer, along with all that this meant in terms of demands she made on others, her own freedom, and selfishness if necessary, but also a sense of grandeur and obligation to give of herself. For her conception of writing and the role of the writer, which originated in her years of journalism and here differs sharply from the Flaubertian view, was that of a kind of missionary heroism. To her, the writer is not the world's subverter but its consolidator and should not confront men with their own worthlessness but reveal to them the beauty and gravity of their existence, thereby bringing them closer to one another, to brotherly feelings.

In Gabrielle's eyes, the writer's narcissism, his need for withdrawal and independence, his unavailability to others and the obsession leading him to attend to his own person and his own work with callous disregard for all other calls on his attention, are justified by a higher altruism that consists of offering oneself and one's work for the happiness and progress of humanity. In a letter as early as 1947, she explains to Marcel this rule of what we might call her artist's moral code:

We must accustom people [...] to accepting our conditions when they are not dictated either by selfishness or pedantry but by the requirements of the creative mind or the higher awareness of one's mission in life. Thus, men may be given infinitely more than the pleasure of one evening, one meeting, one interview, which are mighty insignificant pleasures when one thinks about it in terms of a lifework or a career [. . .] offered entirely for the greater good of others.[2]

One had to "be far from men in order to truly love them," she said on another occasion.[3] An artist's duty of compassion and solidarity requires him to remain apart, that he attend only to himself and his work and not allow himself to be distracted by the noise of the world, the constraints of belonging, and concrete affections. When you write, "you cut yourself off from the world, you're like a convict in solitary confinement."[4]

In the decades that she had left to live, Gabrielle Roy's sole ambition was to write and remain worthy of her writer's vocation. From this would come her joys and her torments.

An Incident at Tangent

Alexandre Chenevert was not yet out when another book began to beckon the novelist, a book that among other things signalled the beginning of the retreat inside herself and the re-examination of her own destiny that was to be the major tendency in her work from then on. This book was *Rue Deschambault*, translated by Harry Binsse as *Street of Riches*.

Gabrielle confided later to Gérard Bessette that the idea for this book had come to her while she was "reluctantly" writing a speech she was to give in the spring of 1954.[5] This text, titled "Souvenirs du Manitoba," having prompted the woman in middle age to return to her childhood and youth in St-Boniface, seems to have opened the floodgates to a whole series of images and faces buried in her memory, all of which, from the vantage point of such distance, appeared to her to be imbued with both the poetry and the inner truth she had been seeking.

But the speech of 1954 was no doubt not the only thing that triggered this project. At the root of *Rue Deschambault*, and the speech too perhaps, there was another, slightly earlier event of which Gabrielle never spoke but which her sister Adèle talks about in several of her writings.

We go back to the autumn of 1953. The National Film Board, or perhaps it was Radio-Canada, invited Gabrielle to prepare a screenplay inspired by the region of her birth;[6] for this purpose she was offered a trip to the West in addition to a fee of several hundred dollars. Having accepted, the place Gabrielle chose to go was where she had been so happy some ten years before, on her tour to research and begin writing her *Peoples of Canada* articles – to Tangent in the hinterland of Alberta, to her sister Adèle's, where she hoped to find peace and quiet for writing, and countryside to stimulate her imagination.

This was the first time she had crossed Canada by plane; the experience reminded her of Saint-Exupéry, of course.[7] The first days at Tangent went well. The two sisters told each other about their lives in recent years. In the daytime when Adèle was working in the fields, Gabrielle explored the region and began the screenplay she had been commissioned to write. Titled, "Le plus beau blé du monde ou La mère Zurka,"[8] it is a portrait of a Polish immigrant by the name of Marissa who recalls her youth in the land of her birth, her marriage to Stepan, a thieving, violent-tempered alcoholic, their arrival in the Peace River district, and their up-and-down existence as colonists, now prosperous, now wretchedly poor, in this region both magnificent and poignantly remote. The text, which anticipates certain passages of the story "Un jardin au bout du monde" ("Garden in the Wind"), was never finished, and the film never made.

At Tangent, however, there occurred an incident that did not seem to have serious consequences at first but turned out to have terrible long-term repercussions. Since Adèle had left teaching and was living the life of a pioneer, she had been obsessed by the idea of writing, an obsession that she shared with Anna. In fact, a story of Anna's was to be published by the Toronto magazine *Chatelaine* in 1955[9] but caused no stir and opened no doors for her. Even more than Anna, who was a married woman after all, Adèle was determined to become a writer; that is, by dint of study and sacrifice to win recognition from a wide readership and earn a great deal of money, like Gabrielle. One has to be impressed by the similarities between the two sisters: both were pursuing the same ambition, the same ideal, and were doing it with the same tooth-and-nail obstinacy. Gabrielle was younger, had had the benefit of favourable conditions, and success had come to her quickly, but Adèle, who was going on sixty and had unshakeable self-confidence, saw no reason why similar good fortune should not be granted her as well.

She had been working for some years on a manuscript to which she had just put the finishing touches. This was *Le Pain de chez nous*, which recounts the past of her own family, from her parents' move to

St-Boniface (in 1897) until her mother's death (in 1943). The story, which Adèle refused to present as a "made-up novel," purports to be strictly historical, albeit "[enhanced] by poetic truth."[10] This historical exactitude, however, does not prevent the author from settling her accounts and sometimes passing harsh judgment on the deeds or nature of her characters, all of them easily identifiable to anyone the least familiar with Adèle's family. The father's name is Charles-Léonce Morin, the mother's is Mélanie, and the children, ten in number, are named Alonzo (Joseph), Léona (Anna), Domitilde (Adèle), Agatha (Agnès), Prudence (Clémence), Bédine (Bernadette), Robert (Rodolphe), Valmor (Germain), Marie-Agatha (Marie-Agnès), and Gaétane, the youngest, nicknamed *La Petite Misère*.

In the spring of 1953, Adèle had succeeded in placing her manuscript with a Montreal publisher owned by the Dominican Fathers, Éditions du Lévrier,[11] which agreed to publish it for Adèle for $750, provided that "the name of the Roy family shall appear as signature to this work," for the good fathers saw clearly that the book had no other interest than that arising from the "revelations" it contained concerning the famous author of *Bonheur d'occasion*. Adèle did not shrink from playing this card. "My sister Gabrielle," she wrote to her publisher during the summer of 1953, "has just finished a new novel which Messieurs Beauchemin will be publishing shortly [this was *Alexandre Chenevert*]. Would it not be a good opportunity to launch my *Pain de chez nous* before the end of the year?"

Had this suggestion hastened matters? Perhaps. The fact remains that in the closing days of September 1953 while Gabrielle was at Tangent, Adèle received the first proofs of her book from Montreal. About what happened then we have only Adèle's version, which she repeated countless times thereafter in her writings, always attributing the same hateful role to Gabrielle. One day, it seems, Gabrielle read the proofs against Adèle's wishes and then did everything possible to denigrate the work and discourage her sister from publishing the book.

> She went through the 193 pages of my manuscript in less than two hours, ravaging my literary garden, trampling my most brilliant flowers, without any thought for my feelings, without any delicacy, without the least generosity! According to her judgment, what she called "the reader's point of view," my book was not worth much. She dashed my hopes. What was the good of publishing it? Why not destroy it instead? Had I worked all

those years in vain? All my efforts, all my toil and trouble to honour the memory of my dear parents, all of it in vain![12]

Adèle had counted so much on support from Cad; this broke her heart and devastated her self-respect.

Why did Gabrielle behave this way? Why, instead of making her reputation and connections work to Adèle's advantage, was she so dead set against her sister's book? Trying to answer this question would be entering a psychological quagmire in which it would be hard not to lose one's footing.

According to Adèle, it was first and foremost out of bitterness toward their dead father, whose memory Le Pain de chez nous honoured, that Gabrielle showed such spitefulness. This seems unlikely, considering the fact that "Souvenirs du Manitoba" and Rue Deschambault, which were written not long after, offer a rather positive image of the paternal figure. In any case, Adèle does not say anywhere that Gabrielle openly confessed this supposed hatred of their father; she saw it rather as the "subconscious" motive behind Gabrielle's criticisms, which in themselves were primarily literary criticisms. Where Gabrielle was finding fault in fact was with Adèle's clumsiness, awkward style, and, sadly, lack of artistic training. This was what she had already written to her the previous spring after Adèle had sent her the first chapter of her manuscript:

> It's not with gladness of heart, you can be sure, that I'm warning you not to get your [literary] hopes up. [...] Your manuscript shows real talent in places. How can I put it to you: I have the impression that if you had started to write works of the imagination when you were young, if you had lived in a more enlightened milieu, and finally if you had had the opportunities I had, you would have benefited just as much as I and you might today have a solid craft and be successful at it.[13]

Granted, addressed to an elderly lady for whom writing was a way of getting the better of the triviality and harshness of her life, these words were not exactly models of tact or consideration, but they spoke the truth for all that, such a brutal truth that Adèle could not accept it and had no choice but to attribute the message to unacknowledgeable motives on Gabrielle's part.

Is this to say that Gabrielle was totally disinterested, and that her opposition to Le Pain de chez nous was for purely aesthetic reasons? To believe this, we would have to forget the picture of Gabrielle that Adèle's story was presenting to her eventual readers, a picture that was unflattering, to say the least. Gaétane is a child and then young woman who is difficult and capricious, a monster of selfishness and conceit who has no pity for her parents and no interest in anything but her own ambitions. It would certainly not have been of any advantage to Gabrielle Roy, known and respected by the public as she was, to allow such disparaging tales about her early life to be spread around. This said, one wonders what drove Adèle to write and want to publish this attack on her younger sister. At this point Gabrielle had done nothing to her that could justify any kind of retaliation, had neither done her any wrong nor refused her anything whatever. At least not intentionally. Adèle, however, could not abide Gabrielle's success; knowing as she believed she knew her younger sister's true nature, she told herself that Gabrielle's talent, her fame, her money were embezzled, obtained through false pretences, the more so since she, Adèle, who deserved so much, had received nothing. In plain words this is called jealousy, and jealousy almost always ends up poisoning the entire existence of the person entertaining it, as we shall see.

The incident did not leave much immediately apparent trace. Adèle swallowed her humiliation and Gabrielle left Tangent pleased with her stay. From Edmonton, she wrote to Adèle before boarding the plane, "I have brought away such a beautiful memory of these ten days with you that I would gladly begin the trip all over again, tiring though it might be, if it were to be redone. [. . .] I haven't told you enough how much I love you and admire you for the long, hard struggle you're carrying on."[14] As far as can be seen, neither one suspected the drama that was soon to come between them for good.

Despite Gabrielle's objurgations, Le Pain de chez nous was published in March 1954. Adèle published under her baptismal name, Marie-Anna A. Roy, which she would use thenceforth for all her writings and for purposes of record came to replace the name by which she had always been known in the family. Although her publisher promoted the book by stressing that Marie-Anna was "the sister of Gabrielle Roy," the book was not a success. Instead of attributing this to the mediocrity of her text, Adèle blamed the failure sometimes on evildoings on Gabrielle's part, sometimes on Gabrielle's failure to lift a finger to promote her poor sister's book despite her influence in literary and journalistic circles. But there was worse. According to Adèle, Gabrielle's attitude had its source in the dark design spawned in her mind on reading the proofs of *Le Pain de chez nous*, which was to use her sister's material herself. The "proof" burst into view shortly afterward with the publication of *Rue Deschambault*, which was nothing else, Adèle declared, than "a shameless piracy of my work,"[15] a kind of plagiarism. "Reading her *Rue Deschambault*, I understood why Cad was so set against my *Pain de chez nous*. When she came to stay with me she had already started work on her book. She took good care not to breathe a word of it to me, but she took advantage of reading my novel in order to fill out her own stories!"[16] Thus, in Adèle's eyes, to the insult she had suffered when Gabrielle was at Tangent was added the injury, two years later, of seeing herself robbed of her work, which was not only failing to earn her anything like what she had expected but was serving to bolster her sister's fame and fortune, surely the last straw in unfairness. "The publication of *Rue Deschambault* struck me like a dagger in my heart!"[17] she wrote. From then on, her resentment and jealousy knew no bounds; getting back at Gabrielle, pursuing her relentlessly with her diatribes and what has to be called hatred, sinking her talons into her as into a prey, this became the great, perhaps the only passion in her life, to be pursued even beyond the grave.

Yet one only needs to read the two books one after the other to see the absurdity of the plagiarism theory. True, the milieu in both books is much the same, necessarily since the two sisters were drawing their inspiration from their family past. And true, a reading of *Le Pain de chez nous* could have played a role in the birth of *Rue Deschambault*; it could even have been determinant; every writer is subject to this kind of influence. Beyond this, however, it would be hard to imagine two more different books, in tone, atmosphere, construction, the arts of characterization, place description, suggestion of thoughts and emotions, and above all in approach, Adèle's being realistic and documentary and Gabrielle's, while largely autobiographical, remaining much freer and more imaginative. Aesthetically speaking, the dull, monotonous narration of *Le Pain de chez nous* and its laboured ideological cant are a far cry from the sensitive writing and entirely inner climate of *Rue Deschambault*, whose refreshing originality, far from suffering in comparison with Adèle's book, only looks the more striking for it.

When she wrote *Rue Deschambault*, Gabrielle was picking up the threads of her Manitoban past, but also in a way the threads of the "saga" project she had begun to work on after the publication of *Bonheur d'occasion*; this was a theme and these were characters that had been part of her universe for some years.[18] Moreover, the structure of the work enabled her to write in a form she had been practising since the beginning – the short story – which was far more natural to her than the classic novel, as demonstrated by the long ordeal of *Alexandre Chenevert*.

All these reasons probably explain the ease and speed with which *Rue Deschambault* came to realization. It would seem that Gabrielle set to work on it in the spring of 1954 during a brief stay at Port-au-Persil, where she had gone to escape the publicity over the publication of *Alexandre Chenevert* and to rest from the fatigue and dejection in which she had been vegetating since the beginning of the year. A few weeks later she interrupted the writing of the book to attend the annual meeting of the Royal Society of Canada, for which she had prepared a speech titled "Souvenirs du Manitoba." This was the first time she had taken part in an activity of the society since her election to it in 1947. The meeting of 1954 was being held in Winnipeg, and the journey was an opportunity to see family members she had not seen for nearly seven years, as well as to steep herself once again in the landscapes and memories from which the writing of *Rue Deschambault* had drawn.

The speech was delivered on May 31 at the university; notable among those in the audience were Frank Scott and Jean-Charles Falardeau. Immediately afterward Gabrielle retired to La Painchaudière, where Anna, whose health was a little better, was once again gathering Mélina's daughters. She had brought Clémence and Adèle, who were living together; two months earlier Adèle had left Tangent for good and had moved for a time to St-Boniface. She and Gabrielle were seeing each other for the last time in their lives. Anna also brought Sister Léon, who, after two decades of good and loyal service in the wilds of Northern Ontario, had been repatriated by her community five years earlier to the Académie Saint-Joseph. As usual the conversation was lively. Gabrielle and her sisters reviewed at length their memories of their beloved *moudra* and the old yellow house and the days of youth for all of them, before life had parted them. Gabrielle also took advantage of her trip to Manitoba to become better acquainted with Marcel's younger sister, Léona, and her husband, Arthur Corriveau. Although she and her sister-in-law did not find a common wavelength between them, she went with Léona and Arthur on long drives and was happy to revisit places from her past. One afternoon they took her to Somerset in the Pembina Mountain district, where nostalgically she rediscovered Uncle Excide's farm and memories of those glorious vacations of long ago. Then they pressed on as far as Cardinal, where Marcel Lancelot, Gabrielle's former pupil and now the teacher, met her at the door of the school; Gabrielle went in, sat at her old teacher's desk, put her chin in her hands and gazed at the empty classroom, saying nothing, remembering.

Once home from Manitoba, Gabrielle went to spend most of the summer 1954 in Baie-Saint-Paul, at the Auberge Belle-Plage. In her little room on the third floor, she typed a few pages of her manuscript each morning. The first story she finished was "My Aunt Thérésina Veilleux," inspired by her memories of her uncle Moïse Landry and his wife, the delicate Thérèse, who had died twenty years earlier by the Pacific Ocean. Other stories followed the first without predetermined order, just haphazardly as her crowding memories ordained. Then, as she said later, "I saw that I had a work, that I might have a work,"[19] a collection with enough coherence and unity to make a book that would hold together. The unifying thread of this book is the childhood of Christine, the heroine and narrator, who gradually discovers herself and the world around her from her early childhood through to the end of adolescence. Around this thread, Gabrielle organized the stories she had already written, wrote some new ones that seemed necessary for balance in the structure and theme, and set aside those whose tenor no longer seemed to suit the spirit of the work. This was the case with "Ma vache," a little story written in the same period as those in *Rue Deschambault* but published separately some dozen years later in a periodical.

In November 1954 the manuscript was finished and sent to Flammarion. René d'Uckermann expressed delight with it, although he doubted it could become a best-seller "because we're in a period where you have to make a racket to attract attention."[20] Nevertheless, although the original contract was expiring with this book, he not only agreed to publish it but insisted that Gabrielle commit herself to submitting her next manuscript to him, which she agreed to do. Unlike what had happened with *La Petite Poule d'Eau* and *Alexandre Chenevert*, this time it was the Parisian edition that appeared first, in September 1955. The Beauchemin edition followed a month later, produced in great haste with a cover bearing a drawing by Gabrielle and Marcel's friend Jean Soucy. As for the English translation, Denver Lindley, Gabrielle Roy's new editor at Harcourt Brace, was anxious not to give it to Harry Binsse, who had taken so long with the translation of *Alexandre Chenevert* he had tried everyone's patience. A translator by the name of Leclercq was found, but his work was so poor that the job was given back to Binsse, who as usual took his time. The book, entitled *Street of Riches*, did not appear until October 1957 in New York, and under the McClelland & Stewart imprint in Toronto.

Years of Respite

In the broad picture of critical attitudes to Gabrielle Roy and her work, the reception given *Rue Deschambault* and *Street of Riches* marked a turning point. It can be said that with this book the author's position in the literary community and market finally reached an equilibrium. Since this position would vary little in the next ten or twenty years, it is worthwhile pausing briefly to examine it.

First of all, the fortunes of *Rue Deschambault* in France and *Street of Riches* in the United States confirmed what had been suggested by the lack of enthusiasm for *La Petite Poule d'Eau* and *Alexandre Chenevert* and their translations: Gabrielle Roy was not – or was no longer, if she had ever been – an author with an international readership and reputation. Those few French and American critics who took an interest in her greeted her new book with lavish compliments,[21] but they were not numerous and were mostly of very marginal influence. Clearly, in France and the United States, Gabrielle Roy was now only a minor writer whose work moved the tender-hearted and the friends of Canada, but appeared out of step and lightweight in the literary scene of the hour. This was reflected in the sales figures: in eight months, Flammarion was hard-pressed to sell some three thousand copies of *Rue Deschambault*, many of them undoubtedly on the Canadian market, despite the contractual ban on such sales. In the United States, a year after publication, *Street of Riches* had not even sold five hundred copies, leaving aside the three or four thousand distributed to members of the Catholic Digest Book Club, a pale competitor of the Literary Guild of America. Obviously Gabrielle Roy's renown in Europe and the United States had not outlasted the short-lived international success of *Bonheur d'occasion* and *The Tin Flute*. A few other of her books would still appear in Paris and New York after *Rue Deschambault* and *Street of Riches*, as well as some foreign-language translations in other publishing centres,[22] but her days on the world literary scene were numbered.

However, the more Gabrielle Roy's name and marketing clout faded abroad, the more firmly entrenched they became in Quebec and Canada. One could say that international oblivion was offset by a kind of corresponding "repatriation" or Canadianization of her work, since its importance and value appeared to be considered increasingly priceless and unquestionable in both Montreal and Toronto. This enthusiasm, largely due to the cultural nationalism then flourishing in Canadian intellectual and political circles, found voice in the chorus of praise with which the publication of *Rue Deschambault* was hailed in the local press. From Montreal to Quebec City, from René Garneau to Rita Leclerc, from *Le Petit Journal* to *L'Action catholique*, everyone rejoiced at the "remarkable unity of construction and tone," the "flawless perfection of style," the "admirable restraint," and above all, as Gilles Marcotte put it, that "generous faculty of sympathy" illuminating each of the stories, each of the characters in *Rue Deschambault*.[23] In the bookstores of Quebec, it sold very well: Beauchemin's first five thousand copies sold out in three months and there were two new printings in 1956.

On the English side, sales of *Street of Riches* were slower: around three thousand copies in a year. The critics, however, were every bit as enthusiastic as their French counterparts. In the *Montreal Star*, the *Gazette*, the *Globe and Mail*, the university magazines, everywhere *Street of Riches* met with admiration from the book reviewers.[24]

The striking thing about the reception given *Rue Deschambault* and its translation by the Canadian critics is not so much the unanimity of praise as the absence or at most the secondary nature of references to *Bonheur d'occasion* or *The Tin Flute*. When *La Petite Poule d'Eau* and *Alexandre Chenevert* and their translations were published, the commentators had reacted to the expectations Gabrielle Roy's first book had led them to conceive, hence the mixed surprise, disappointment, and even lack of understanding expressed in a good number of their verdicts. This time *Bonheur d'occasion* had not been forgotten, but, as one critic observed, Gabrielle Roy was no longer thought of as the author of that book and no other.[25] She now had a body of work, was now a writer in the full sense of the term, a writer whose "art [. . .] is always in progress" and gives "proof of a talent which gains in depth as it diversifies," a writer who "has attained the point of development where her style is nothing more or less than her own individuality."[26] All this put the author of *Rue Deschambault* in a class by herself among Quebec writers. "Half of [this book]," Guy Sylvestre declared, "is worth more than the whole of most books published hereabouts," where, he added, "there is perhaps no one who can write as well, without apparent effort, without affectation, without fakery" as Gabrielle Roy; no one, chimed in Pierre de Grandpré, "who has so authentic a vocation for writing."[27]

The success of *Rue Deschambault* was soon being reflected in more or less official distinctions. In the autumn of 1956 the Société Saint-Jean-Baptiste awarded her the Prix Ludger-Duvernay, which at the time in Quebec was one of the most prestigious literary honours, as attested by the list of winners since its creation in 1944: Lionel Groulx, Germaine Guèvremont, Robert Charbonneau, Alain Grandbois, Léo-Paul Desrosiers . . . At the ceremony on December 12 at the Windsor Hotel in Montreal, Roger Duhamel, the chairman of the jury,[28] spoke in praise of the winner, who then gave a speech recounting in half-ironic, half-emotional tone "How I Received the Fémina." Other honours came from English Canada. Late in 1955 Gabrielle Roy was named one of the "Women of the Year" by the Canadian Press, along with Maureen Forrester, Charlotte Whitton (the mayor of Ottawa), and the swimmer Marilyn Bell. The following year in Toronto there appeared a school edition of *La Petite Poule d'Eau*. Having the very authentically "Canadian" work of Gabrielle Roy read by every schoolchild in the country had been a pet project long nurtured by Bill Deacon; first he caught the interest of Jack McClelland at McClelland & Stewart, then of officials in education departments, then of the publishers Clarke Irwin, who in 1956 published an edition comprising the French text of the first two parts of the novel together with an introduction and notes in English. On another plane, the first scholarly studies of Gabrielle Roy's body of work began to appear in English-Canadian literary magazines.[29] Finally, in 1957, *Street of Riches* won the Governor General's Award for Fiction, ten years after the same award had been won by *The Tin Flute*; it was the first time a writer had received this honour more than once.

Rue Deschambault was, in short, Gabrielle Roy's second triumph. A less spectacular one than *Bonheur d'occasion*, less resounding but perhaps more solid and lasting in that, with this fourth book, the author was emerging from the shadow of *Bonheur d'occasion*, engaging the critics (and readers), despite their initial reservations, with a style, a form, a world that had nothing in common with her first book and would henceforth define her own unique, irreplaceable voice. It was not a final victory, to be sure, and there would still be many fluctuations in

Gabrielle Roy's critical and commercial fortunes, but none of this would jeopardize the privileged status that was now hers. For the rest of her life, Gabrielle Roy would remain one of the undeniably leading authors of Quebec and Canadian literature.

How much effect did this new favour with the critics and readers have on Gabrielle's personal life? Can we consider it responsible for the relative peacefulness of her existence apparent in those years? This is hard to say. There is no question that this period of her life, between 1953 and the early 1960s, was one of the most tranquil and harmonious she had ever known, even considering that it coincided with what was then called "the turn of life." There were no major conflicts, no tensions, just a period of peace and enjoyment of her own person and meditations – things revealed in the lovely photograph taken in 1955 by Zarov for the launching of *Rue Deschambault*, which for many years was the only image of herself that Gabrielle allowed in circulation. There is a world of difference between the smiling star portrayed in the 1945 picture taken by the same photographer and the calmly, pensively beautiful woman shown here; the face is angular – ageless one could say – the hair drawn to the back of the neck, the lips in repose, the eyes far away and filled with both gravity and kindliness.

As we have seen, it was only in 1952 when she returned from Boston that Gabrielle moved to Quebec City. She and Marcel lived at the Château Saint-Louis, a large, upscale apartment building on the south side of Grande-Allée. The neighbourhood was a delight, close to the Plains of Abraham and Old Quebec, and the almost bucolic tranquillity of its streets reminded Gabrielle of the corner of Westmount she so loved. The St. Lawrence River below was always spectacular and always changing. And Marcel's office was only a step away on Rue St-Cyrille (boulevard René-Lévesque today). At first Gabrielle and her husband rented two rooms from Madame Chassé, where Marcel had boarded when he arrived in Quebec City. After a while they moved into a small apartment of their own on the seventh floor, and then in 1963 into a larger one on the third, where they lived for the rest of their days. This was a beautiful six-room apartment at the southwest corner of the building, whose huge living room overlooked the Plains of Abraham and the river. Since Gabrielle still had no taste whatever for domesticity and both she and Marcel were very busy with their work, they hired a maid to do the housework and took their meals at restaurants or in the dining room that Madame Chassé ran on the ground floor of the building. In this way, the life they led was lacking in neither comfort nor amenities.

The fact is that, without being really rich, they were now enjoying perfectly comfortable incomes. For Marcel the lean years were over; he had acquired a clientele and his fees were those of a specialist. Gabrielle continued until 1954 to receive $15,000 per year from her American publisher. Subsequently the amount of her royalties diminished considerably: in 1955, they dropped by half, then fell to less than $3,000 in the following years.[30] Fortunately the money she had been able to invest since 1947 was bringing in interest and dividends of about $1,200 a year. This sudden drop in her income was cause for anxiety at first. "I have the impression," she wrote to Jean-Marie Nadeau, "that I must begin all over again on another scale, since I do not expect any more windfalls like *Bonheur d'occasion*."[31] She soon adapted to her new regime, however, and far from suffering from it even found a kind of contentment in it, for the drop in income forced her into – and gave her an excuse for – leading the kind of life she wanted, with a minimum of comfort undoubtedly, but without a binding excess of luxury or possessions. She loathed spending money, hated debt like the plague, and was simply not cut out for prodigality. She had few needs. She went out very little, did not drink, dressed simply, borrowed the books she wanted to read from friends instead of buying them, and wrote at a tiny little desk in her bedroom, using the old portable typewriter she had bought in the days when she was a schoolteacher.

Until this time, two of her major annual disbursements, apart from income tax, had been money she sent to her sisters and Jean-Marie Nadeau's fees. Now that her income was falling off, it was here that she would have to cut back. She would certainly continue to pay for Clémence's room and board, but to Bernadette she now sent only a few dollars once in a while, and sometimes also to Adèle and Anna. As for *Maître* Nadeau, she soon announced a reduction of his power of attorney: he would continue to look after her contracts and deal with the income tax authorities, but henceforth she would attend to other things herself (replying to requests for rights and permissions, official letters, management of her investments, and so on). Her contacts with him thenceforth became less frequent, to the point where in November 1957 he wrote: "I have the impression that your thoughtfulness keeps you from ending the power of attorney you entrusted to me a good many years ago, and which I have tried to fulfill as best, or as least poorly, possible. I want you to feel perfectly at ease and can assure you that for my part the high regard I have always had for you will change not one whit, even if you should ask me to return the files that belong to you." To which she replied immediately: "I have no intention whatever of ending the power of attorney I entrusted you with, and I am still grateful to you for your advice and the way in which you take care of my business matters."[32] But in fact she no longer needed him. Since she published nothing for six years after *Rue Deschambault*, there were no contracts to negotiate; the only contact between the writer and the lawyer had been a few letters at income-tax declaration time. On 5 October 1960 when Jean-Marie Nadeau was killed in a car accident, he and Gabrielle had not seen each other for over two years.

And so, "modest and ordinary"[33] though it may have been, Gabrielle's income from the mid-1950s on sufficed amply to assure her what she valued most: her freedom. Not only did she not have to depend financially on her husband, but she was earning enough not to have to scratch constantly for money. She did keep meticulous account of what was due her and insisted on receiving it, but she never did anything purely to increase her earnings, feeling that her writer's conscience forbade it. When Radio-Canada, which was already broadcasting adaptations of Roger Lemelin's *Les Plouffes* and Germaine Guèvremont's *Le Survenant*, proposed to do similarly with *Bonheur d'occasion* for a weekly fee of $250, which would have doubled Gabrielle's income, she turned the offer down because, she said, "I would have to be actively involved myself for it to be well done – and I would rather use my time doing something new."[34]

In Quebec City, Gabrielle adapted gradually to her new environment. Just as she had done in Paris, then in Montreal after her return, she firmly turned aside advances from journalists and avoided public appearances. In literary circles, she had only polite and rare meetings with fellow writers like Alain Grandbois, Roger Lemelin, or Anne Hébert (when Hébert was visiting the country). At first it was mostly her Montreal friends she continued to see, which brought her often to the big city for brief sojourns, particularly in autumn and winter. She would stay either in her old familiar neighbourhood, at the Laurentian Hotel on Dominion Square, or not far from the Université de Montréal at Cécile Chabot's in an apartment on Stirling Avenue that Cécile shared with her sister Thérèse and their mother. Gabrielle loved to stay with them because the three women smothered her with attention. For a while she even thought of renting a room in the neighbourhood where she might stay occasionally and have the benefit of the friendship and all the "spoiling" that Cécile and her mother lavished on her.[35] Cécile was Gabrielle's dearest friend at this time, the one in whom Gabrielle had total confidence and whose well-being was of as much concern to Gabrielle as if she were her own sister.

> Ma Cécile,
>
> [. . .] I dreamed about you last night, and that is no surprise because I think about you almost constantly and intensely; so much that it seems to me you must have felt something by telepathy because you had the kindness, the thoughtfulness to write to me. [. . .] Chère enfant, such a fragile you, what is the mysterious source of your strength? Through you in any case I have learned many things and keep on learning.[36]

During her stays in Montreal, Gabrielle would also see some people she had known in the good old days, like Jean Palardy and Jori Smith, Albert and Rachel Jutras, Ringuet and France, his new wife. She also had opportunities to have dinner at Chambly, where her friend Jacqueline Deniset now lived. And she never left again for Quebec City without spending part of an evening with Judith Jasmin, to whom she still felt very close. Judith was the only person who ever succeeded in extracting Gabrielle from her retreat and persuading her to appear once in a while in public. Thus it was by her good offices that Gabrielle agreed to give a speech at the Ritz-Carlton in the autumn of 1955 to the members of the Alliance française[37] ("[the] overall impression," Gabrielle wrote afterward to Cécile, "was of a crowd of well-dressed apes"[38]).

Besides seeing her friends, Gabrielle would take advantage of her little excursions to Montreal to do some shopping, go to the theatre or the movies, see Guy Boulizon, publisher of Les Editions Beauchemin, or consult her physician, Doctor Dumas. She was still experiencing periods of great fatigue, even depression, especially when winter arrived, and she would complain often in her letters of any number of minor discomforts that indisposed her and provided excuses for refusing this or that engagement, but there was nothing serious in any of it. As she approached fifty, her constitution was still sound and she could still find the energy to do whatever she really needed or wanted to do. As to the rest, she wrote to Adèle, "I'm not doing badly at all, providing I live at slow speed,"[39] which was the speed of her entire existence during these years.

After a while, the shuttling between Quebec City and Montreal became less frequent because with time Gabrielle gradually made herself a new life in her adopted city. When she arrived, she had practically no friends there aside from Jeanne Lapointe. The two women had been brought together by the preparation of the manuscript of *Alexandre Chenevert* and continued to see each other after for a year or two. Then their contacts became less frequent and eventually ceased. Gabrielle did not entirely subscribe to Jeanne's literary thinking or sensitivity. Early in 1954, Jeanne had Gabrielle read a long article she had prepared for the magazine *Cité Libre* in which she had written an appreciation of Québécois literature and writers. In it she had praised Gabrielle Roy, but had spoken of the regrettably "slow pace" of *Bonheur d'occasion* and the deplorably "humanitarian sentimentality" of *La Petite Poule d'Eau*, while extolling the writings of the new star of the hour, Anne Hébert, who had just published successively *Le Torrent* (1950) and *Le Tombeau des Rois* (1953).[40] In her letter of reply, Gabrielle is polite to Jeanne but cannot hide "that frosty impression" she has been given by the article and the harsh judgments in it. And, without naming him, she pleads the case for her beloved Alexandre Chenevert:

> It seems to me nevertheless that any character who succeeds in stepping outside a book, living his own life, remaining alive in our minds long after the reading, should in himself be a marvel to us. Especially if the character is insipid, dull, run-of-the-mill, for I should think it much more difficult to create a character of the ordinary, everyday kind than to describe a person who is exceptional.[41]

In the period when Gabrielle and Jeanne were cooling to one another, a new feminine friendship was given to Gabrielle, a double friendship this time that was to last the rest of her life. One day around the end of 1953, Cécile Chabot wanted to send a package to Gabrielle and gave it to one of her friends, Madeleine Chassé, who worked in Montreal but went every weekend to Quebec City. This lady's friend, Madeleine Bergeron, delivered the package to the Château Saint-Louis and invited Gabrielle to visit with the two of them. The three women hit it off beautifully and immediately. They were very soon telephoning each other several times a week and meeting often for shared activities, so that Gabrielle could only thank Cécile for having brought her together with "the Madeleines," as she had already taken to calling them, who had "become in so short a time the kind of friends I've wanted all my life."[42]

Interesting women, these two, whose lifestyle, thinking, and interests were out of step with the current feminine models in the Quebec of those days. Both had remained unmarried and they had chosen to live together as much for convenience as by choice. Madeleine Chassé was eight years older than Gabrielle; she was the daughter of journalists (her father had founded a small paper, *L'Avant-garde*, and her mother had been manager of a major paper, *L'Événement*) and was herself a career secretary. Madeleine Bergeron was six years younger than Gabrielle. A native of Quebec City, she did volunteer social service and since 1947 had been running the Cardinal Villeneuve School for the physically handicapped in Ste-Foy.

In Madeleine Chassé, Gabrielle found a competent and devoted secretary. Their collaboration began in the autumn of 1954 with the typing of the *Rue Deschambault* manuscript. Since Gabrielle's usual typist, Jacqueline Deniset, was about to have a baby, Madeleine Chassé took over. She continued for seven years to do a variety of jobs for Gabrielle. Madeleine Bergeron, for her part, loved to drive and having soon discovered how much Gabrielle loved to go for drives would invite her almost every week for an afternoon in the country. With no itinerary other than Gabrielle's inspiration or whim, the three of them would take off without any particular goal along some secondary road, turning down some crossroad, stopping to walk on some footpath for an hour or two; they liked nothing better than to feel they were far away from everything, until the approach of night brought them back to home and reality. For Gabrielle these little tripartite excursions were always festive occasions.

There would be clouds at times over the friendship between Gabrielle and the Madeleines, but until the very end the Madeleines would remain obliging and attentive to their friend's needs, anxious to share her good days and bring cheer to the bad ones.

A Peripatetic Bride

Although he saw a certain amount of the Madeleines and sometimes joined in the activities of the little "community" – meals, New Year's festivities, snowshoeing excursions in winter, sojourns in the country in summer – Marcel was increasingly leading his own life. Setting up his practice, his job at the hospital, his professional contacts, in short everything to do with his work kept him very busy, especially during his first two or three years in Quebec City, where he immediately felt far more at home than in Montreal.

He quite quickly made a group of friends with whom he shared his taste for the arts. Two of them became especially close, Cyrias Ouellet, a former contributor to the magazine *Regards*, and the painter Jean Soucy, with whom Marcel spent much of his free time and who introduced him to painting, both in watercolours and oils, at which the student proved to be fairly competent. Marcel and his companions would go off together on excursions, most often to the Île d'Orléans, to go swimming, cycling, and painting from nature.

Between Gabrielle and Marcel, the ardour of the first years had already passed, replaced by a kind of friendly agreement that had them living together without really being a married couple, at least in the usual sense. Until they moved to Quebec City their union had rested partly on a certain mutual dependence, Marcel "protecting" Gabrielle and providing some of her material comfort (transportation, moving house, and so on), and she meeting most of their expenses. But the situation had changed. Marcel was now earning his own living very nicely, and Gabrielle, since the barrage of attention from the public had slackened and she had broadened her circle of friends, was no longer needing the same protection from Marcel. The result was that they did without each other more readily and tended to lead separate lives, as if there were no longer much in common between them.

They had no children and there was no question, had never been any question of their having any, despite complaints from Marcel's mother, who had remarried and was now Madame Dordu and lived in Repentigny, a suburb of Montreal. She and Gabrielle had never much liked each other. Madame Dordu criticized her daughter-in-law for not being a good wife and depriving her son of offspring, to which Gabrielle retorted, "But who's told you I'm the one who can't?"[43] In fact, the absence of children was part of the initial pact between her and Marcel. "My children are my books," Gabrielle used to say. Their sexual relationship was indeed not very active. Nor had it ever been, except perhaps in the first summer just before their marriage when Marcel had gone to join Gabrielle in Kenora, then for a few months following. The passion had soon faded. From the time of their arrival at the Hôtel Lutétia, then in all the boarding houses and all the apartments they had occupied since, Gabrielle had insisted on having her own bedroom and sleeping alone in it. Were they were lovers beyond the initial period of their marriage, were they still after the move to Quebec City, and would they continue to be throughout their thirty-five years of life together? The answer seems clearly to be no.

And it seems clear that this distance, originally at least, was Gabrielle's doing, with her reservations about love inspired both by her temperament and the memory of her initiation with Stephen. It frightened her to let herself go, yield body and soul, simply forget herself; it seemed like a threat, or like the opposite of what she had been seeking ever since first becoming aware of herself; namely her freedom, full control of her being and life, refusal to submit to anyone so as to remain entirely available for the fulfilment of her own self, which was the only thing she wanted. This attitude to sexuality, this fear mixed with distaste, is expressed most directly in certain of the texts she was working on in this particular period between the mid-1950s and late 1960s, especially in two novels or draft novels that have remained unpublished, "La Saga d'Éveline" and "Baldur." Both of them unfinished and perhaps unfinishable (possibly for this reason, in part), these texts show women for whom carnal love and procreation are experienced as a kind of degradation, at least a subjugation and debasement of their lives that can lead only to suffering and death. A sublimation or distortion of libido? Probably. But this "virginity," this frigidity, like it or not, was one of the sources of Gabrielle's creativity, one of the wellsprings of her work.

Distant in their intimate relationships, Marcel and Gabrielle were no less so in their professional activities. Here again, during their stay in Europe and the year following their return, there had been a brief period of collaboration. Gabrielle was taking a genuine interest in her husband's studies and profession, and shared and encouraged his taste for the arts, and Marcel was following Gabrielle's literary efforts, reading and commenting on the new stories she showed him (he helped when she was writing *La Petite Poule d'Eau*, it will be recalled). Very soon, however, this harmonious state of affairs gave way not to indifference but a kind of detachment or distance on the part of each with respect to the work and interests of the other. The break came during the writing of *Alexandre Chenevert*, when Gabrielle called on her husband for information of a medical nature. Marcel would say later, "I made remarks that Gabrielle didn't like (mind you, she took account of them). I said to myself at that point, I'll stick to my medicine and Gabrielle to her writing, and that was the end of it." Marcel indeed continued to read, and love, everything his wife published, but never again, from the early 1950s on, would he read a text of hers during its writing or intervene in any way in her work in progress, and never again would she ask him to. In this way a wall was raised between them that neither sought to cross. Gabrielle not only had nothing to do with Marcel's career any more, she ceased to take any real interest in his passion for art, conceiving even a certain irritation for his habit of buying and collecting antique furniture, pictures, and others things of value; to her, all that was only "waste" and clutter so that Marcel, if he was to keep buying as he wished, had to hide his purchases from her. Instead of bringing his finds back to the apartment, he would stack them in his office or in the homes of complicitous friends.

The social life they shared was therefore rather limited. Not that the doors of the better social circles of Quebec City were not open to them; hosts and hostesses could ask nothing better than to have the great novelist and her husband cross their thresholds. Once in a while, Gabrielle and Marcel did attend a dinner or other social evening together at the home of some physician, academic, or celebrated artist, but these occasions were rare. Not as rare as social events in their own home, however, for the Carbottes never gave parties; they were not equipped for it, either in furniture, dishes and cutlery, or sense of hospitality. Socializing was just too taxing for Gabrielle. The moment she found herself in a group, she would feel such an obligation to shine, to capture everyone's attention with her conversation and storytelling (in which she excelled, for she was still a good actress) that these sessions would leave her tired and nervous to the point where she would need days to recover, meaning as many days lost to her work. And so, while she enjoyed meeting privately with a few friends, she shrank from social events of the kind that Marcel would gladly attend.

In their everyday life their relationship was often tense. Both being edgy by nature they had spats over trifles; the least vexation, the least domestic inconvenience would make them anxious and irritable and they would say things they would regret afterward. This said, their flare-ups and quarrels were rarely serious and reconciliation was never long to follow. Except once it seems, in the summer of 1954, when Gabrielle was on vacation in Baie-Saint-Paul. For some reason she and Marcel had such a bitter domestic fight that she decided to leave alone for Port-Daniel without seeing her husband again or telling him she was going.

"I think destiny has perhaps spoken,"[44] she wrote to Madeleine Bergeron. Distance brought her around, however. A few days after arriving in the Gaspé, she wrote to Marcel:

> As for what happened between us before I left, I hope you realize that very often our words exceed our thoughts. I said some horrible things to you that I'm sorry for, that I'll always be sorry for – and no doubt also I'll always remember certain words you said to me. They contained enough truth to hurt a great deal, for a long time; but were they entirely true! That's what I don't know myself![45]

Gabrielle finally returned like a good wife to Quebec City, and Marcel went with her to Baie-Saint-Paul for the end of her vacation. This storm, like the others, passed without causing irreparable damage, but shaken this way their relationship gradually changed to the distant, friendly rather than loving compact that had them living to the end as partners bonded to one another by conjugal inevitability as much as by any deeply felt attachment.

This episode illustrates what appears since the beginning to have been a constant in their marriage – the contrast between the difficulty they had living together in the reality of day-to-day existence and the tenderness they felt for one another as soon as they were apart, out of each other's sight, with their relationship carried on through letters and telephone conversations. Every time, it was the same scenario. Gabrielle would barely have left the Château Saint-Louis, where the couple had great trouble spending a day without walking on each other's toes and snapping or snarling at each other, before she was writing Marcel to tell him she was sorry about their quarrels, that his health worried her, that he ought to do this or that to keep himself busy, and that she was thinking of him and valued him. "I shall have no peace of mind as long as I have no good news from you. My dear Marcel, for pity's sake don't refuse me all confidence as if I were a stranger. Let's forget what's past and cultivate a better present. [. . .] Something very fine that still could exist between us would be total openness, and confidence."[46]

They would continue to be apart often and sometimes for fairly long periods. It was always Gabrielle who determined these separations; it was she who left and she who chose the moment of reunion. Since the day they met it had always been thus. At regular intervals she needed to be alone, to get away, and then nothing could hold her back. In the early years Marcel endured these periods of enforced solitude with difficulty; he was lonely and sometimes even protested timidly. With time, however, he became accustomed to his wife's absences; he not only stopped grumbling but began to manage very well on his own, taking advantage of these spells of freedom to indulge his taste for social events, his artistic activities with his friends, and his penchant for loafing and a certain slovenliness in his attire and around the house.

In the course of the first few years following their move to Quebec City, Gabrielle took three trips of some length. Although she was at pains during this period to reduce expenses to a minimum, those occasioned by her vacations and her need for movement were not affected, because in her mind these were professional expenses. Three times, then, she left for distant parts without Marcel, although she kept in almost constant touch with him through a great many letters.

The first two trips took place in the same year, in 1955. In the spring she went to France, where she stayed a little over two months. When she arrived in Paris she went to the Grand Hôtel du Louvre, not far from the Palais-Royal, and stayed the whole month of May, going out and seeing friends. She saw Jean-Paul Lemieux and his wife, whom she met by chance at the theatre, briefly saw Anne Hébert just back from Florence, lunched at the home of René Garneau, cultural attaché at the Canadian embassy, spent an afternoon with the boarders at the Villa Dauphine at Saint-Germain-en-Laye, and received Monsieur d'Uckermann, who was bringing her the proofs of *Rue Deschambault* to correct. But best of all she was reunited with Paula Bougearel, whom she had not seen since 1949 and who was now living in the French capital with her two children and her husband, the latter having been posted there recently from Strasbourg. Enchanted to be seeing one another and each as intoxicated as the other with "the excitement of Paris," the two friends arranged to meet as often they could, to go to the theatre, the cinema (they saw *La Strada* in particular, which Gabrielle found "incomparably poetic"), the museums, or shopping.[47] It was during this stay that Gabrielle discovered the Orangerie and the Louvre, which had never attracted her before, despite Marcel's urgings. She visited them several times in a state of wonderment, a foreglimpse of that experienced by Pierre Cadorai, the hero of *La Montagne secrète* (*The Hidden Mountain*).

At the beginning of June the two women left Paris for Brittany, where Gabrielle had been dreaming of returning since her marvellous summer of 1948 at Concarneau. This time she and Paula went to the gulf of

Morbihan, to an inn, the Hôtel Boris, whose proprietor's name was Monsieur Le Bonniec.[48] Gabrielle was delighted with everything. She told Bernadette, "I have all the things I love here: a little fishing village, very old and very picturesque; prairies covered with yellow-flowered broom, whose brightness seems to be throwing light towards the rather grey sky [...] and most of all the ever-present sound of sea."[49] Paula was the ideal companion. She and Gabrielle went for long walks together on the beach, talked to the local people, went on excursions to Quiberon, Vannes, and as far as Belle-Isle, happy to feel so close and so in tune with one another. But after ten days Paula had to leave. Alone now, Gabrielle spent her days reading and sunbathing, but her heart was no longer in it, so she returned to Paris, where she booked into a more modest hotel, the Lutèce, in the Sixth Arrondissement. Paula once again took her under her wing, "running from the other end of Paris every day to visit me."[50] They forgot their age together, they were once again the laughing, sparkling young women of St-Boniface days.

It was time to think of returning to Canada, but first Gabrielle was planning another visit, to England this time, with "my old friends the Perfects,"[51] whom she had not seen since the autumn of 1949. Soon all was arranged: she would leave for London on July 12 after undergoing a minor emergency operation for haemorrhoids in an upscale clinic in Neuilly, where she experienced the benefits of pentothal. "I had a feeling of total well-being," she wrote to Marcel.

> Never have I had such a sensation of lightness, of confidence and also of unity. You know, that feeling of doubling, of being two people at once and in conflict, well, there was nothing left of that. It seemed to me that I was really just one single person, in the most perfect harmony.[52]

Her convalescence was barely over, however, when she received some news that obliged her to forgo her trip to Upshire and take a plane immediately for Dorval. Marcel had suffered a heart attack and was in hospital.

It was not very serious, she was informed when she arrived in Quebec City. So little cause for concern in fact that Marcel was able to leave the hospital after a few days. And Gabrielle left again in mid-August for another trip alone, leaving Marcel to rest in Baie-Saint-Paul. This time she took the train for Saskatchewan, where she spent two or three weeks in Dollard, the same Dollard where Léon Roy in years gone by had bought land and wanted to settle his children.

The only one who had settled there permanently was Joseph, the eldest son, whom Gabrielle had completely lost sight of for thirty years but whom she had wanted to see again before it was too late, because he was said to be very ill. His lungs burned by wheat dust, soon to be seventy, still inclined to the bottle but turned tender and nostalgic with the passage of years, Jos, who spoke only English now, led a poor, withdrawn existence with his wife, Julia, who ran the local telephone exchange out of her house. Their children had all left home long since. From the very first days Gabrielle and her sister-in-law, despite the difference in their ages, discovered a friendship that included Jos, an old man with "a most considerate soul [. . .] for all his rather rough manner," as Gabrielle would say later.[53]

But this journey was to represent much more for her than a reunion with a distant brother. She was rediscovering here the whole world of her father, and beyond that a whole landscape she thought she had forgotten. She wrote to Marcel:

> I saw Papa's old farmland. It's so beautiful! Magnificent wheat, a beautiful golden spread with small buttes here and there, in the distance, the Cypress Hills. It seems my father cherished this land like the light of his eyes! I would like to have it belong to us again. I was five years old, I think, when I came here, and I used to think I didn't remember anything about it; and yet as I listen and observe, fragments of the past come back to me, like pieces of a dream.[54]

The prairie, the sky, the horizon, the colours of the setting sun, "the primitive beauty and feeling of infinity that reigns in this countryside," all "this nearly painful immensity"[55] impressed themselves on her and cast an enchantment on her that she tried to express later with the great descriptions in "Garden in the Wind" and "Where Will You Go, Sam Lee Wong?" Every day, tirelessly, she explored the surroundings of the village, visited the farms and ranches, walked in the fields of wheat, climbed the hills, travelled the deserted and dusty little section roads, watched the grain elevators being unloaded. It all fascinated her, she wanted to see everything, learn about everything, as if she had returned at last to the true land of her birth. For a few days she accompanied Department of Agriculture officials on their inspection rounds of the region, once again storing up images, anecdotes, and information on all kinds of things, as in the days when she was a journalist.

People too attracted her. With Julia she visited a number of neighbours, like the simple, good-natured Smouillat, a solitary old Basque, or
the Cadorais, a family of Bretons whom Gabrielle's father had helped
settle many years before.[56] They told her their story, their troubles and
their attachment to this countryside. Sometimes she would walk the
single rustic street of the tiny hamlet, where "it's the image of frontier
life, particularly on Saturday night when the farmers come to the village
to do their shopping."

> The tavern fills; people walk about on the wooden sidewalks or meet in
> the store. You hear the accents of several countries, and while there is
> gaiety, a kind of melancholy still permeates all this, perhaps the bleakness
> of lands as yet unformed and lumpish.[57]

It does not seem that Gabrielle wrote anything at all during her stay at
Dollard, except for her letters to Marcel and a few friends. She was too
taken up with her discovery of the place, too enthralled by the images
jostling around her and inside of her. But for all that, this journey was one
of the most successful of her life. Like her major investigative tour for the
Peoples of Canada series thirteen years earlier, it was to prove important
in her evolution as a writer, bringing enrichment and clarity to her vision
of the Canadian West, and thereby to the compass her work would give
later to what, in her eyes, was a shining example of the human condition.

She did not write anything either during the third and last journey
she took in this period, and yet this journey too had repercussions on her
work, in particular in the genesis of the book she would begin writing
shortly, *La Montagne secrète* (*The Hidden Mountain*). In the winter of
1957, about a year and a half after coming back from Saskatchewan, she
left Marcel behind again and set off for several weeks, southward this
time. She went with the painter René Richard and his wife, Blanche,
whom she had known for many years but to whom she had grown closer
in the past two or three. They were to drive all the way down the east of
the continent to the Gulf of Mexico.

The travellers left Quebec City on February 14. On the 16th they were
in Westford, Connecticut, where René and Blanche were visiting friends.
Four days later, thanks to turnpikes that gave them "the sensation [of
navigating] in one of H. G. Wells's fantastic landscapes,"[58] they finally
arrived in the Carolinas, where for the first time Gabrielle discovered the
world of American blacks.

It's a heartbreaking sight. Here and there, wretched fields of cotton or sugar cane, whitish soil, and the wooden huts of the Negroes [. . .] They, the Negroes, when you meet them on the road or see them sitting on their front stoop, turn away their eyes as if they think they don't have the right to look you in the face. [. . .] Same desolation, same resignation everywhere. Nowhere around here do they seem to feel at home. I'd like to be able to stop in their milieu a while, win their confidence perhaps and get to know them better.[59]

But René and Blanche had a single obsession and that was to arrive as quickly as possible at the seaside. This the travellers finally did on February 26 when they came to the Island of Santa Rosa, a suburb of Pensacola, and settled in a resort called Gulf Breeze. Gabrielle rented a motel room with a patio and the Richards another room with a kitchenette. With Blanche there to prepare the meals and attend to their material needs, Gabrielle and René, as conscientious artists, soaked up the landscape, one accumulating notes and the other sketches with which to nourish their future works. They were intrigued by the vegetation, especially the great oaks "with their pendulant mosses like heads of hair" that "in the evening, or under a slightly darkened sky, take on a rather macabre air."[60] Gabrielle would remember this image later when writing her story "L'arbre." But neither she nor René liked the signs of American civilization. "What God put here remains great and beautiful," Gabrielle wrote; "what man has put here – except perhaps the ancient Spanish – remains vulgar, of poor quality. It's always the same story really, on our continent: man disfigures Nature and marks his passage with huts."[61]

After two weeks of idleness, for a change of scene the vacationers took a trip to New Orleans. While the Richards found the urban hurly-burly too nerve-racking and decided to stay in a village on the outskirts, Gabrielle took a hotel room on St. Charles Avenue in the city centre. She stayed there alone for three or four days, walking, exploring, observing all around her, and "finally [understanding] the enormity of the black problem in the South of the United States."[62] Her letters to Marcel teem with descriptions and notations of every kind, as if she was determined not to forget and was trying to store up as much information as possible, using the method she had used before when walking the neighbourhood of Saint-Henri, hunting for details for Bonheur d'occasion. During one of her exploratory walks, she discovered the old St. Louis

Cemetery, a relic of the ancient multi-ethnic and cultivated society of New Orleans. "As I was walking there," she told Marcel, "I made the acquaintance of a Creole, half Negro, half French, a very interesting woman, who told me a bit about her own life and the brilliant life of days gone by in the Vieux Carré,"[63] in the same way that the elderly Inès, who would recount her memories to Elsa, the heroine of *Windflower*, would be met by Elsa in the old cemetery at Fort Chimo.

The three travellers returned to Gulf Breeze on March 14 and prolonged their stay until the end of the month. Gabrielle and René often had conversations that continued far into the night; she talked to him about her art, her quest for the perfect work; he talked to her about his manner of working, told her about episodes of his past life, his wanderings in the Far North, his discovery of painting, his studies in Paris.[64] When she returned to Quebec City that spring, Gabrielle had ample material for her next book.

Other than these three journeys, there was also a brief family visit to Manitoba in the summer of 1958. Having learned of her sister Anna's poor state of health, Gabrielle decided to go to La Painchaudière to give her some help, as she had done eleven years earlier. This time she stayed only two short weeks, because Anna was not as ill as had been thought. Besides seeing Clémence and Bernadette as usual, as well as Germain and Antonia, she spent some time driving around Pembina Mountain with Anna and Albert, and went with her old friend Jos Vermander up to the Little Water Hen district, where she had not set foot since the summer of 1937.

The Hermitage at Petite-Rivière-Saint-François

Aside from the letters she sent almost daily to Marcel and a few others, Gabrielle wrote virtually not at all when travelling, as she was kept so busy with meeting people, the landscapes to be seen, the discoveries, the enjoyment of the world around her. She did not write much either in Quebec City, where business matters, her friends, her conjugal life, the whole domestic routine kept her from concentrating. In fact there was no possibility of writing for her without complete calm and isolation. "Creative work is slow sometimes, often lunatic," she wrote to Cécile Chabot. "It likes freedom, independence, and the feeling that it has all the time it needs for itself; on the other hand, as you know, it has modest tastes and could blossom in a hut better than a palace, if in that hut there were peace for the mind."[65] And even more, it might be added, if in that hut, or not far away, there were someone devoted, unobtrusive, and able to provide her with the well-being and affection she needed to feel sheltered from the world, relieved of all cares, and free to immerse herself entirely in her thoughts. Writing remained tied to the "Upshire complex," meaning to the conditions in which it initially came to her at Century Cottages far from everything, in the protected and peaceful, idyllic, as if amniotic ambiance created around the young artist by that inviting landscape, and Esther's presence.

Gabrielle had succeeded in re-creating this ambiance subsequently at Port-Daniel and then at Rawdon, where her need for peace and quiet and her urge to write had kept bringing her back for ten or fifteen years. But with time these places began to lose their power and no longer brought her such happiness. In July 1954 when her quarrel with Marcel made her want to escape, her instinct drove her to take refuge at Port-Daniel in the kindly house of her friends the McKenzies where she had felt so at home before when writing *Bonheur d'occasion* and *Alexandre Chenevert*. But the charm was not working any more. The place was still beautiful, but it was more and more desolate. "The mine swallows up the men and the women are left to stay alone; the houses deteriorate quickly; the fishing boats stranded on their sides in the little bays seem to be dying. This is what is becoming of this countryside I've so loved."[66] The loner was soon lonesome, and barely three weeks after her arrival she ended her "exile."[67] She would never again return to Port-Daniel.

As for Rawdon, where she spent several weeks in the spring of 1953 in order to finish the manuscript of *Alexandre Chenevert*, she returned there once again in March 1959, driven by the hope of "getting something going [. . .], in the stillness and stimulus of the air which, morally or physically, is going to put new life into me."[68] But Mrs. Tinkler was no longer of this world and Gabrielle had to stay at the Rawdon Inn, where the treatment she received, well intentioned though it was, could not compare with what she was used to from "little Mother Tink." This brief sojourn, once again, was the last; she would never return to this village where, since 1942, she had been so happy and had written so many pages.

If she abandoned her habitual refuges, it was also because since coming to live in Quebec City she had discovered – or rediscovered, having already been there in her reporting days – a region close by: Charlevoix. She stayed there for the first time in June 1953. Shortly after finishing their work on *Alexandre Chenevert*, she and Jeanne Lapointe took a vacation together. They went first to Laterrière near Chicoutimi, to the house of a friend of Jeanne's, Marie Dubuc, the daughter of the wealthy industrialist J.-E.-A. Dubuc; Marie received them in the huge domain she occupied with "her companion and associate," a certain Thalia.[69] From there, Jeanne and Gabrielle travelled down to Port-au-Persil, a resort between La Malbaie and Tadoussac. They stayed at the Hôtel Port-au-Persil, where a small colony of artists and intellectuals were vacationing. There was the journalist Marcelle Barthe, accompanied by her beau of the moment, a Slav by the name of Vodanovitch. Also Jean-Paul Lemieux and his wife, Madeleine, who had been summering at Port-au-Persil for fifteen years and with whom Gabrielle became better acquainted during this time. Once Jeanne had left, she and the Lemieux went out together almost every day on excursions in the environs, to go fishing, or simply for posing sessions on the shore of the river; Jean-Paul had begun a portrait of Gabrielle, which meant that Gabrielle had to stay sitting on a rock for hours. At the end of that summer, Marcel bought the painting and hung it in the apartment in the Château Saint-Louis.[70]

At Port-au-Persil the weather may have been magnificent, the friends charming, and the little inn most pleasant thanks to the good-heartedness and culinary talents of Madame Bouchard, but Gabrielle soon felt guilty not to be working. "Vacations like this, with people around me, are perhaps good and useful this year," she wrote to Marcel, "but not for too long, I think. It's a strain for me always to have people around. I suddenly feel a great painful need to be alone with that inner being in us which is so monopolizing and demanding."[71]

In other words, this was not the place that suited her for writing. Except in winter perhaps, when the vacationers were gone and she could have all the time she wanted to rest and be alone; twice she returned for brief stays, in March 1954 and February 1956. For Gabrielle's summer retreats, however, Port-au-Persil was quickly supplanted by Baie-Saint-Paul, which she discovered through Madeleine Bergeron and where she immediately felt in friendly country. It was in 1954 – the summer of her flight to Port-Daniel – that she first came with the two Madeleines to spend her summer vacation at Baie-Saint-Paul. She worked all that summer on *Rue Deschambault*. She liked the place so much she returned for a brief stay the following year, between her return from France and her departure for Saskatchewan. In fact it was not so much Baie-Saint-Paul that attracted her as the hotel she stayed at, the Belle-Plage, outside the village by the water's edge, at the mouth of the Rivière du Gouffre. Madame Gravel, the innkeeper, was a marvellous cook. Here Gabrielle could be at ease to write, be alone when she wished, and when she wished enjoy the presence of her dear friends the Madeleines, and their car. At Baie-Saint-Paul lived also René Richard, with whom she never tired of conversing for entire evenings. In other words, there was everything here to make her as happy as she had been in years gone by at Rawdon, Concarneau, or Port-Daniel.

Captivated by the charm of Charlevoix and the mildness of its summer, Gabrielle decided in 1956 to rent a little house that her old friend Jori Smith owned not far from Baie-Saint-Paul, at Petite-Rivière-Saint-François. It was beyond the village by the dirt road that crossed the plateau called La Grande-Pointe, a little old two-storey farmhouse with a garden planted with willows. There was no direct view of the river, but all one had to do was go down one's front steps, cross the road, and look over the top of the cliff to have at one's feet a breathtaking view of sea, islands, mountains, and sky vaster here than anywhere else on the Charlevoix coast.

Gabrielle moved in at the beginning of June. In spite of persistent bad weather she appreciated the peacefulness and beauty of the spot, occupying her days with reading, playing the piano, stoking the fire in the stove, and walking in the neighbourhood. Any time she could she would visit the Richards for a spell in the evening. Their friendship thus strengthened and deepened. In July Marcel came to spend his vacation with her, while the Madeleines spent theirs as usual at Baie-Saint-Paul and Cécile Chabot also came to spend some time at Petite-Rivière in a neighbouring house. And thus the summer passed, pleasantly and peacefully as Gabrielle wished it to.

Soon, however, Jori turned up and moved into the house with Gabrielle. At first all went well and the two old friends enjoyed being together again. But Jori was going through a difficult period and had trouble always being in good humour. As Gabrielle explained to one of their common acquaintances, "at the moment she's upset and even tortured because she's not getting what she would like to get on her own as an artist. And you can imagine how painful that is. I have felt this way and in these moments have wanted to flee the whole world, even my dearest friends."[72] It could also be that Jori took umbrage at Gabrielle's constant presence, Gabrielle's brilliant career reminding her how unsatisfying her own had been. And then, her marriage was not going well; she and Jean were preparing to separate, which they would do the following year. In any case, at the end of September Gabrielle left Jori in the house and took refuge in the Auberge Baie-Saint-Paul, where the proprietor, Madame Rémillard, received her "as if I were a princess of the blood."[73] In return, the boarder oversaw the homework of the son of the house, young Gil, a future Quebec government cabinet minister.

But for Gabrielle the big event of this summer of 1956, and perhaps one of the most important reasons she became so attached to Petite-Rivière, was meeting a new friend, Berthe Simard.

La Grande-Pointe was in a way the fiefdom of the Simard family, which had been there since the late seventeenth century. Liguori, Berthe's father, belonged to the tenth generation.[74] He had conveyed his worldly goods – the old house, outbuildings and land extending from the river to the base of the mountain – to his son Aimé, who was now the head of the clan. They were in no way rich at the Simards', but they were in no way poor either; woodcutting in winter, the sugar bush in spring, market gardening and eel fishing in summer, then apple picking in autumn provided an adequate living for the family, in which there were only two children, Jean-Noël and Louisette, for Aimé had been prematurely widowed. It was Berthe, Aimé's younger sister, who had inherited the absent wife and mother's role. Having looked after her aged parents and with much care and affection nursed her sister Marie-Anne, who had died of tuberculosis at the age of thirty-two, Berthe, remaining unmarried, had taken over the care of her brother and her nephew and niece as if they were her own children. A tiny woman, energetic and dainty at the same time, gracious and as lively as a little bird, it was she who did the cooking and housekeeping, grew the vegetables and flowers, and also saw to the needs of Abbé Victor, her other brother, who had become a priest. She was vestal caregiver and servant to the whole family, in other words. But her lot was far from a burden to her. Giving of herself, feeling useful to others, untiring activity and the fervour of her religious faith, plus a profound love of nature, brought her contentment that reflected in her entire person, glowing in her eyes, her manner, her gestures, and every one of her words.

The meeting took place near the end of June. Until then Berthe had not dared approach the famous writer, out of shyness as much as fear of disturbing her. But one day, on the advice of Jean Palardy, she called at the little house with some wild strawberries and a bouquet of wildflowers.

Enchanted, Gabrielle received her kindly and the two women immediately felt drawn to one another, as if after years of waiting they had finally found each other and discovered a bond of friendship that seemed to Gabrielle like "a kind of miracle." "Real friendship in this world is such a rare and difficult thing to find," she would write soon to Berthe. "I feel unbelievably fortunate to have you for a friend."[75]

Berthe's presence, together with the happiness of this first summer at Petite-Rivière-Saint-François, led Gabrielle to take a step the following spring that she never would have expected of herself. She became a property owner. On 7 May 1957, before Notary Jean-J. Girard of Quebec City, for $5,000 cash she purchased a cottage that a man by the name of André Laberge had built on a piece of land acquired seven years earlier from Aimé Simard. Gabrielle's new property was a little closer to the village than the Palardys', almost opposite the Simard house, on the south side of the road, hence just at the edge of the cliff. The cottage was modest, a single storey covered in white asbestos shingle, and without a foundation; besides a single room running the whole length of the side facing the river, there were two small bedrooms, a kitchen, and a garage. But its situation, the huge garden surrounding it, and the view it offered were magnificent. As Gabrielle explained to her sister Bernadette, "the view is one of the most beautiful in the world."

> From the top of a small cliff we overlook the river where it's very wide; on one side there's a line of lovely hills, and below us lies Île-aux-Coudres, about midway between the two shores. Behind, we have a high mountain covered with maples and birches almost to its peak. A marvellous sight![76]

The new property owner moved in shortly after her trip to the Gulf of Mexico with the Richards, in June 1957. From then on she came to Petite-Rivière-Saint-François faithfully every year, from the end of spring until the beginning of autumn, for the twenty-five remaining years of her life. Thus a quarter, even half of Gabrielle Roy's life henceforth would be spent here, near this remote village in this flimsy, rather comfortless little house perched on the cliff, where for all that it was "the first time in my life that I've had my own home";[77] it was, she would tell her sister-in-law, Antonia, as though this house were "the only real refuge I've had in my wandering life since Deschambault Street."[78]

In the first two or three years there was much to be done getting the little house and the garden in order. One of the first priorities was the installation of a two-seater lawn swing not far from the house. Gabrielle loved to sit in it to read, write, or talk to the rare visitors she had. As for furnishings, landscaping, and upkeep of the grounds, these things were mostly Marcel's domain. With his unerring taste and the pleasure he took in these tasks, carpets, armoires, and other antique furniture soon arrived to embellish the interior of the house, while outside, around a gradually cleared and levelled lawn there appeared masses of flowers, hedges, and several attractive clumps of trees – birches, poplars, and spruces. Marcel tended with particular affection three or four thujas standing in a close little group at the edge of the cliff, profiled against the sky, which used to sing in the wind; Gabrielle called them "her angel musicians."

But Marcel was not there very often. He only came on weekends (unless some emergency or work overload kept him in Quebec City) and during his two or three weeks of vacation in July. The rest of the time Gabrielle was alone, entirely occupied with herself and her work, like Robinson Crusoe on his island. In the first summers, she settled on a routine and living habits that were to change hardly at all. Like the routine she had adopted in all her other refuges, this one had a single raison d'être and a single goal: to allow her to write. For this, she must not only have peace and quiet but also total freedom. Along with relative comfort and pleasant company within reach, if she wished it, she needed to be alone when she wanted, avoid all fatigue, and not be under any obligation or constraint that might interfere with her work. Petite-Rivière offered her all this.

There was the housekeeping, the meals, the washing, and so forth, but fortunately there was someone to do these things for her. At the beginning it was a distant cousin on her mother's side, Rose Soumis, who came from Montreal to spend the summer with her as a maid of all work. Then, from about 1960 on, this role fell to Berthe Simard, who literally took upon herself the upkeep and well-being of "Madame Carbotte" as she called her politely, and who did so with both satisfaction and devotion. In March or April, having been lonesome for her friend all winter, Berthe would set to work spring cleaning and preparing the house for the great day of Gabrielle's arrival. Then all summer long she would clean the house, do the washing, and very often prepare the light meals that Gabrielle usually ate at noon. Since she drove a car, Berthe also took charge of the shopping in the village or Baie-Saint-Paul. Sometimes she and Gabrielle would take off in the afternoon on one of the drives that Gabrielle so loved, along the winding secondary roads of the back country. If there was some plumbing or carpentry to be done, it was Berthe who did it, because she was very good with her hands, or she called on Aimé or Jean-Noël. Finally, when autumn came and it was time for Gabrielle to go back to her "*Cachot* Saint-Louis" as she called it,[79] she would give Berthe a cheque for $200 or $300 and ask her to close up the house and bed everything down for the winter.

But Berthe's helping hand did not stop there. Constantly present and available yet wise enough to keep her distance and never intrude, she was the ideal companion who could listen, admire, commiserate, without expecting anything in return except Gabrielle's friendship and happiness. Almost all the time that Gabrielle did not devote to her writing or reading she spent with Berthe; at any hour of the afternoon or evening she would hurry to the old house for a bit of talk or just for a rest and some company. But their best times of all were the long walks they used to take almost every day, in good weather and bad alike, sometimes south to the end of the road across the plateau, sometimes (which Gabrielle liked most because to her it was "the very image of freedom"[80]) along *la track*, the old railway track that wound its way along the foot of the plateau between the tidal flats and the cliff. As if they were children again, they would hop from one railway tie to the next, play at being tightrope walkers while holding each other's hands, or just walk along the ballast, sometimes laughing, sometimes serious, marvelling over everything they came across, wildflowers, birds, groundhogs, or frogs. One of Berthe's cats or dogs would almost always tag along and, as Gabrielle reminded Berthe, would be surprised by their behaviour. For Gabrielle these hours were the sweetest; "and yet," she said, "nothing happens . . . nothing but the silence, the sounds, the breathing of infinity, without which everything else we get is worth nothing."[81] Time seemed suspended, all the troubles and pain went away, all that was left was the feeling – the illusion – of departure, movement, a possible new beginning for everything. When they got home, Berthe would invite Gabrielle to have supper with her and Aimé, and after to spend the evening with them, sitting on the verandah or, when it was cold, in the big kitchen with the big wood stove purring. Gabrielle would be happy.

Aside from Berthe and her immediate family, the hermit of Petite-Rivière-Saint-François did not see many people. A little neighbourly and courteous exchange with Jori, a visit to the Richards', an afternoon now and then with the Madeleines while they were on vacation at Baie-Saint-Paul or Les Éboulements, or with some other friend passing through,

was the extent of her social life. When Marcel came to join her, then the
Carbottes did accept invitations to dine or spend an evening with one or
other of the distinguished vacationers in the region. It might be with
Jean-Paul and Madeleine Lemieux, who moved to Île-aux-Coudres in
1957, or Jean Palmer, wife of the president of Canadian Celanese, who had
a house at Les Éboulements, or at Marie Dubuc's on Île d'Orléans, or at
Jori Smith's; Jori loved nothing better than organizing parties, giving La
Grande-Pointe "a sort of inhabited look, like a very, very select resort."[82]
At other times there would be a gathering at a house in Pointe-au-Pic
belonging to the lawyer Pierre Boutin and his wife, Simone, or with
Yvette and Jean Sénécal, friends of the Madeleines who gave magnificent
dinners. It was at the Sénécals' property at Les Éboulements one day, in
the small lake in the middle of the property, that Gabrielle touched some
trout in the icy water with her hand. Never was this happy company
invited to the Carbottes', however, for here as at Quebec City, Gabrielle
neither could nor had any desire to entertain. Yet she did not dislike the
gatherings, would be the gaiest and most charming of guests, in fact; she
hardly drank at all but loved to eat, particularly desserts, and never had
to be coaxed to take the floor, launching into a story that would have
everyone listening, such was her skill with dramatic effect, gesture, surprise, and humour.

These events were not very frequent, however, and Gabrielle was
most often impatient for Marcel to go back to Quebec City so she could
return to the solitude and peacefulness of her retreat with its day-to-
day routine. A retreat and routine focused very much on reading as
well as writing, for Gabrielle was still a voracious reader of books, as she
had been when she was young. Although she returned time and again to
her favourite authors (especially Teilhard de Chardin, Saint-Exupéry,
Colette, and Camus, along with Selma Lagerlöf, Katherine Mansfield,
and Virginia Woolf), she also read current Parisian authors (Roger
Peyrefitte, Paul Guth, Romain Gary, Jean Giono, François Mauriac), the
autumn's literary prizewinners, the works of her generation's French-
Canadian writers (André Langevin, Yves Thériault, Claire France, Anne
Hébert, André Giroux, Léo-Paul Desrosiers, Alain Grandbois, Germaine
Guèvremont), and classics of fiction (Kafka, Dos Passos). Aragon's *Les
Cloches de Bâle* impressed her deeply on account of Clara, who struck
her as the model of the new woman. She liked the style of General de
Gaulle, whose *Mémoires de guerre* reminded her of Chateaubriand and
Sainte-Beuve. But one of her great fascinations was still Proust's *À la*

Recherche du temps perdu (*Remembrance of Things Past*); she owned an edition printed in Montreal in 1945 in which, pencil in hand, she kept seeking lessons in writing and sensitivity.[83]

She did most of her reading in the afternoon and evening. As at all her other favoured refuges, however, the most important part of the day at Petite-Rivière was the morning, which was the time for writing. Almost every day she would get up, sit at the little desk she had had placed in front of the window overlooking the river, and there until noon would concentrate totally on her work. No one must disturb her in the course of these inviolable hours, not even Berthe, who not only scrupulously respected her wish but also acted as her sentry, making sure that nothing and no one invaded her neighbour's peace and quiet.

The Saga of Writing

Summertime at Petite-Rivière-Saint-François thus became Gabrielle's season of choice for writing, and so it would remain for the rest of her life. All her books after *La Montagne secrète* (*The Hidden Mountain*) would be written in the little house above the river, during the blessed period between May and October. The rest of the year, while she was in Quebec City or travelling, she rarely managed to do any work at all, but it hardly mattered since she knew that summer would return, and with it that long space of unencumbered time and peace when all her occupations and all her acts turned on this one felicity: a morning of writing from dawn till midday, in the most beautiful setting in the world, with loving souls nearby.

Some days went almost entirely to the prolific correspondence she maintained, to which she attached great importance and devoted much care. Unlike so many other writers, Gabrielle did not keep a personal diary; she had no notebooks relating to her work either, except those in which she sometimes noted quotations drawn from her readings.[84] Their role is filled in a way by all those letters she wrote almost daily to her friends and members of her family, in which the immediacy of her life is reflected through its changing course with its major and minor cares, its joys, moods, expectations, and disappointments, as well as the most commonplace and most exalted thoughts that passed through her mind. This is of no small significance. Instead of committing her reflections to a diary or notebooks for her own use, Gabrielle addressed them always to

others, as if her awareness and entire being, in order to express themselves, needed to reach out to someone, externalize, have an effect on
another person and be understood, loved, or admired by that person.
Strictly speaking then, there was no such thing as private writing, or at
least there was no difference between writing for herself and writing with
others in mind; for her, writing always meant writing *to* someone.

Gabrielle wrote letters all the time, winter and summer alike and
wherever she happened to be. Rarely a day went by when she did not
mail at least one. When she was at Petite-Rivière-Saint-François, however,
her morning writing sessions were less taken up with correspondence
than creation – work on her manuscripts – which she considered both a
chore and a pleasure to which she applied herself with such diligence
that all other concerns were thrust to the background, for in her eyes it
was her work that gave value, even meaning to her life.

There were periods when it all seemed easy; images would come, sentences would flow, the manuscript would progress rapidly, as if all she
had to do was let it unfold by itself, capture on paper a movement, a
story, and characters springing fully formed from the hidden depths of
her imagination. This is likely how she wrote almost all her books,
apart from *Alexandre Chenevert* (*The Cashier*) and perhaps *La Route
d'Altamont* (*The Road Past Altamont*): in the space of a few months, in
the course of a densely concentrated writing campaign, for the duration
burning with a kind of intense inner fire. To Judith Jasmin, who asked
whether she wrote every day, she replied:

> No, not every day. I'm cyclical. I'll work ardently for several months. In
> these lovely peaks which are peaks of exaltation, everything, everything is
> visible to me, everything is close, everything is precious. And I lose no
> time getting it all under cover.[85]

"Next," she said, "come the other times, spells of a bit of melancholy,
perhaps; [. . .] it all seems empty; [. . .] it's hard to live through." The
reason was that these moments of grace, these high periods were necessarily infrequent and above all unforeseeable. However, she could
not simply sit and wait for them because this would mean risking not
being ready when they materialized. And so, she explained further, "I
try to arrange things so as always to be available at times when I'll feel
like working, when I'll be able to begin working." In other words, even
when she did not feel much inspiration and writing was not coming

easily, she did not change her habits; she faithfully set aside her mornings, reread what she had written, and kept herself free to resume work at any moment.

Inevitably, this discipline made her rather unsociable and often made her look to others and even to her family and close friends as entirely self-absorbed, reclusive, and still more, selfish. And it is true that she hardly ever invited anyone to Petite-Rivière; when people came to visit she would arrange for them not to stay too long, and to lodge and eat elsewhere than in her house so as not to have to look after them herself, which would have obliged her to give up her routine and her own comfort. The reason, however, was that the pursuit of her work involved demands of discipline, even austerity, that were incompatible with the ordinary obligations of life in society. She used to like to say that it is by denying himself to others and even his family that an artist can best connect with them and show his love for them.

Judging from the fact that in the fifteen years following the appearance of *Rue Deschambault* Gabrielle Roy published only two books, *La Montagne secrète* and *La Route d'Altamont*, one could suppose that she was writing less. In reality, although she completed only two works, this was a very active period in which she began or reactivated a great many projects, working sometimes on only one at a time and at other times on two or more at once.

While most of the unpublished manuscripts that have been preserved are undated, there are several that can reasonably be assumed to have been written in this period of roughly 1955 to 1970. This is the case, for example, with several stories like "Le vieux Prince," "La maison au bord de la mer," and "La petite faïence bleue," which were likely rough-drafted around 1955.[86] This is also the case with a longer manuscript, probably a planned novel, whose principal character is a Ukrainian woman by the name of "Madame Lund." In its setting (the Canadian West) as well as its themes (immigration, the loneliness of a married woman, gardens), this novel, to which she did not give a title, seems to belong to the same series as "La lune des moissons" (which appeared in *La Revue moderne* of September 1947) and "Le plus beau blé du monde," the screenplay she wrote in 1953. This was the series that was inspired by Gabrielle's sojourns at Tangent and that, after many transformations, would evolve into the story "Un jardin au bout du monde," published in 1975.

It was perhaps this novel about Madame Lund that Gabrielle was working on during her first summer in her house at Petite-Rivière-Saint-

François. "I don't yet dare raise my voice to cheer what I'm doing at the moment," she wrote on July 17 to her friends the Madeleines. "Still, my work is perhaps a bit better in the last few days. [...] For you two [...] I want so much to finish a book you'll perhaps be a bit pleased with. That is all I ask because, it's true, that really is all I can give."[87] Once she was back in Quebec City, however, she was less sure of the value of her new manuscript. "I've worked a great deal this summer," she confided to Bernadette, "but so far I'm not too pleased with what I've done. Perhaps when I take it up again later I'll manage to make something not too bad of it."[88] She had worked long and hard indeed, since there were some hundred typed and annotated pages of the manuscript; yet the first draft, in which the story ends with the death of the heroine and therefore seems complete, remains the only version of the novel, which Gabrielle set aside and never returned to.

This said, there is no way of verifying that the book to which Gabrielle alluded in correspondence during the summer of 1957 was indeed the novel about Madame Lund, which dates from this period but perhaps not from precisely this summer. It could just as well have been the other project that returned often to haunt her, the major Manitoban "saga" she had begun ten years or so before, shortly after the publication of *Bonheur d'occasion*, and abandoned in 1948 after pages and pages of attempts that led nowhere. In any event she took up her old saga manuscripts and set to work once again, trying to give this work she had pondered so long a content and form that would at last satisfy her. No doubt she was prompted partly by the publication of *Rue Deschambault*, of which the saga, inspired by her own mother's story, was a kind of continuation or expansion in time and space as well as psychologically. She was certainly devoting a great deal of effort and time to this draft novel, judging by the number and variety of manuscripts of the saga that she wrote in this period.[89]

First of all she tried to continue the story of Éveline (the heroine's name had previously been "Évangéline") from the point where she had broken off years before. Thus materialized a dozen chapters of a novel in the third person relating the family and conjugal life of Éveline and Édouard in St-Boniface, of which one episode is about an invitation to a ball at the lieutenant governor's mansion. But in the course of this second phase of the writing, the work had less to do with the story itself than the form and type of narration best suited to the story. This is why most of the manuscripts simply repeat characters and events already there in the previous version, such as the Hébert family (sometimes called Langelier), the journey from Quebec to the West, settlement on the prairie, young Éveline's waverings between her two suitors, and her marriage to Édouard. Discontented with the type of narration she had been using – a conventional, linear, third-person mode – Gabrielle began to explore other avenues that might convey the significance she wanted to give her book more sensitively. For example, she dropped the realistic perspective in favour of more poetic, more intimate writing; some of the most important events in Éveline's life were now brought around to her own point of view, as if she herself were recounting them, and recounting them to an "I" whose presence remains timid but who, seeming to designate Éveline's daughter, is reminiscent of the "I" of *Street of Riches*. Instead of holding to the traditional novel divided into chapters, Gabrielle also tried out a looser, more open construction with the story divided into a series of related but independent episodes, each forming a kind of novella. Thus we see the appearance, sometimes in more than one version, of new texts with evocative titles: "Un soir dans la plaine," "La caravane en détresse," "La photographie de famille," "Les conversations sur la galerie." While the content of these texts relates to this or that episode of what was previously a continuous story, it is now divided into separate entities, all related and yet each complete in itself, and together having a natural unity. In short, things were happening as though the saga project was breaking down, fragmenting and trans-forming into a work of a completely different kind, no doubt a less ambitious one than the great historical novel Gabrielle had dreamed of at the outset, but more true to the style and approach that henceforth would increasingly be the unique characteristic of her writing.

Still, the time and effort she put into pursuing and reworking her project resulted in nothing satisfactory at this moment, and once again there were hundreds of pages left in boxes, with no thought in her mind of publishing them. Was she discouraged? Disappointed rather, and resigned in a way. "I've not accomplished much over these last years," she wrote to her friend Cécile in October 1959:

> Of course I've worked, and a lot, even. However, none of all I've begun or even advanced a fair way seems to me to have been worth the effort. I think all in all that no worthwhile artistic work can come of our effort alone – however heroic. So a good part – almost all – of a work realized is simply given to us.[90]

What was this gift, this sudden and mysterious inspiration that was the source of works – and that came to her in the months following this letter, turned her away from the saga that was going nowhere and suddenly made her undertake a new and completely different book from all its predecessors – which this time was to make it all the way to publication? Unfortunately this question must remain unanswered. What is certain is that the grace accorded her was powerful enough that hardly more than a year after this letter to Cécile Chabot she was writing in a very different vein to her new friend Joyce Marshall.

> I am glad to report that *The Mountain* – and this, very simply, may be the title – as far as I'm concerned is now finished. That is – imperfect as it may be – I feel that I cannot do much more for it. Like a parent, a grown-up child, I suppose, however different it may be from the ideal child, I have to release it . . .[91]

She would therefore have written *La Montagne secrète*, for this was the book in question, in very little time. In fact the spadework was done by the end of summer 1960; all that remained were corrections throughout and changes to certain passages, and these too were done by the time Gabrielle announced to Joyce that her manuscript was now ready.

> By the way, I profited a great deal by your keen advice, given last summer, and strengthened a weak part of the story. This being done led me of course to discover other weak spots which I likewise scaffolded. I rather like this part of the business. Now I feel somehow like a builder, reaching to this beam, giving it a prop, rushing to this corner, lightening a screw, hammering here, hammering there. At last, looking upward, downward, left and right, I feel that the place is safe. At least there are not great fissures, no bad holes. Somehow the place, the building – call it what you like – stands on its own. And the strange thing is that it does not now seem possible to tear it down, even if you should be the only one to know about this secret building.[92]

The speed with which Gabrielle wrote this novel may be explained, at least partially, by the wealth of material available to her, which naturally she owed to her relationship with René Richard, who for so many years had been "telling her the tales of his travels," and whose paintings and drawings she admired, especially a self-portrait that Marcel had introduced her to.[93] And she recognized her debt to him by dedicating her book "To R. R., painter, trapper, devotee of the great North, whose lovely tales made me aware of the Mackenzie and Ungava." But the sources of *La Montagne secrète* were just as much if not more Gabrielle's own experiences, especially her memories of Europe, the old ones like her wide-eyed discovery of Provence and more recent ones like the revelation of the Louvre during her trip of 1955. Also central to the novel, there returns a theme that had been haunting her for over twenty years: deer hunting. This theme appears in one of her very first texts, "La légende du cerf ancien," which she wrote in 1938 and remained unpublished in her lifetime.[94] Above all, *La montagne secrète* was an opportunity for her to investigate, allegorically and through the existential adventure of a fictional painter, the spiritual adventure of every artist and thereby her own life and her own vocation as a writer. She proposes an image of this life and this vocation that is at once heroic and austere, in which love and nature reign, along with solitude and the sacrifice of human affections dictated by the superior demands of art and beauty. In this sense *La Montagne secrète* is a thinly veiled self-portrait; in the face of Pierre, Gabrielle Roy is in fact painting her own as she sees it or wishes it to be, that of the ideal being who in her mind is the artist utterly devoted to his work to the exclusion of all other demands, and whom that work at one and the same time devours and sanctifies.

René d'Uckermann had the manuscript on his desk by the end of September 1960. Seven months later he still had not responded, although since the publication of *Rue Deschambault* he had been putting constant pressure on Gabrielle not to allow "too much time to pass between one book and another" because "you must maintain contact with the [reading] public."[95] In October 1961, when the Canadian edition of *La Montagne secrète* was published by Beauchemin, there had still been no reaction from Flammarion. The contract was not signed until April 1962 and the book appeared in Paris only six months later, almost simultaneously with the English translation by Harry Binsse, *The Hidden Mountain*, which was published by Harcourt Brace and McClelland & Stewart late in 1962.

At this point Gabrielle was already busy writing another book. Or rather, she had returned to her saga, which she had therefore set aside only temporarily, long enough to write *La Montagne secrète*. Unwilling to give up this idea of a major book inspired by her mother's life, she plunged back into it and worked with a vengeance, determined this time not to abandon the subject before making something worthwhile of it.

Out of this third phase of the writing of the saga came perhaps the novella titled *De quoi t'ennuies-tu, Éveline?*,[96] whose approach recalls somewhat "La photographie de famille" and "Les conversations sur la galerie," and which recounts another of Éveline's adventures, this time in her old age, "when she no longer expected any great surprises, either for her heart or mind."[97] However, once she had finished the first draft Gabrielle immediately lost interest in this manuscript, which thereupon went to join all the others in some bottom drawer.

Now, instead of prolonging her heroine's story by creating new episodes, she decided to begin it all again from the beginning, no doubt to have done with it once and for all. This time she returned to the conventional form of linear narration in the third person, divided into chapters, but making Éveline the principal character of the story and her learning experiences as a woman the theme around which the high points of the narration are organized. Thus begins the umpteenth version of the saga,[98] which opens with Éveline's birth at St-Alphonse-de-Rodriguez and tells the story of the Langelier family's journey to the West as far as St-Léonard-des-Plaines, where the protagonists choose land to clear for a farm and Éveline announces her decision to go and study at a convent. Here the story breaks off. It did little good to have a clean copy of the 125 pages or so that she had finished typed, for once again she never managed to bring this manuscript to completion and abandoned it, this time for good. Never again after the mid-1960s would she attempt to return to it. Her noble family saga, this great monument she had dreamed so long of raising to her mother's memory, she failed after all to bring forth. And after twenty years of reflection and successive drafts there was still no finished book. All that is left of the saga project is a sprawling abandoned worksite littered with discontinued manuscripts, shadowy characters, and story fragments, frozen forever in a limbo of incompletion.

This said, "La Saga d'Éveline" had not been undertaken and worked at so long in vain. When Gabrielle turned her back on it for good she had begun another book that, as different as it may have been from the original project, was still a continuation, a reclamation of the wreckage, so to speak. This book was *La Route d'Altamont*, a novel haunted, like the saga, by the face and life of the mother, but whose focus shifts from mother to daughter, from Éveline to Christine, from biographical to *auto*biographical mode told in the first person.

Nothing better illustrates this change than the evolution of the title story, "La Route d'Altamont" ("The Road Past Altamont"), which relates the separation of mother and daughter. It seems that Gabrielle wrote an initial version in the late 1950s in the course of her efforts over the saga, since the mother's first name was Line and the narration was in the third person. When she returned to this text around 1962, she made various changes (first-person narration, an improved plot line, a different point of view), which not only brought Christine to the forefront but turned an event that previously took place in the mother's life into an episode that henceforth marked a turning point in Christine's, who now became the narrator and heroine of the tale. In this same period Gabrielle also revived another story she had begun writing in the late 1950s in the aftermath of *Rue Deschambault*, and which had been published in 1960 in the very first issue of the magazine *Châtelaine* (French language) under the title "Grand-mère et la poupée" ("Grandmother and the Doll"). Adding two additional parts to this first version and changing the title to "Ma grand-mère toute-puissante" ("My Almighty Grandmother"), she lengthened the story considerably and here too broadened its significance.

Other similar stories built more or less around the same themes – Christine's youth, the mother's old age – continued to appear in the early 1960s. An example is "Ma cousine économe" ("Sister Finance"), published in 1962;[99] another is an ambitious story of which Gabrielle wrote four or five versions at this time without managing to finish it, the tale of a woman called Gilberte who, through the various phases of her life, rediscovers the ties that have bound her and her sisters to their *moudra*, who is now dead.[100] Further examples are two other stories written in the course of these same years, "Le déménagement" ("The Move") and "Le vieillard et l'enfant" ("The Old Man and the Child"), the latter very likely written before 1963 since in that year Gabrielle adapted it for a screenplay titled "Le phare dans la plaine" or "Un jour au Grand Lac Winnipeg."[101] It is these two that, along with "Ma grand-mère toute-puissante" and the new version of "La Route d'Altamont," make up the "series of longish stories"[102] to which she gave the overall title *La Route d'Altamont* and whose termination she announced to Jack McClelland, her Toronto publisher, in the early days of 1965, adding that she "would like to wait a bit longer before I decide what to do with them."[103]

The original manuscripts of *La Route d'Altamont*, it should be noted, like those of other stories written or rough-drafted in the same period, are handwritten, contrary to Gabrielle's long-standing practice; she had been an unconditional devotee of the typewriter. The reason was that typing was giving her backaches. She had to give up her old portable typewriter therefore and settle on a new way of working, which she would keep to from then on until the end. For the first draft she would write by hand, sitting at a little desk, in an armchair (this was her favourite), a rocking chair, or even her lawn swing with her manuscript on her knees. Most often this manuscript was a simple, cheap school notebook, and she would write in it with a ballpoint pen as fast as possible, without any previous plan or notes, throwing onto the paper everything that came into her mind, crossing out little but using the margins and the backs of the pages liberally and rewriting certain passages two or three times. "What is important at this time," she said, "is to grasp life. I become nervous rather easily. Everything has to happen quickly. Take from the left, take from the right. Grasp a moving thing and try to safeguard its mobility in spite of the writing's fetters."[104] Then using this first draft she would immediately write a second, still by hand, on the following pages or in another notebook; she might write two or three drafts of a single text this way. When she finally felt her story had reached more or less final form, she would read it to a few people close to her, and taking account of their reactions, correct it again as needed, then put the notebook aside awaiting her return to Quebec City. There, come autumn, she would have the manuscript typed by a secretary, annotate and amend the text again, have a new clean copy typed, check it again, and at last send it to her publishers. A final correction would take place on the first and sometimes the second set of proofs. These revisions and corrections – "all the rigmarole involved in publishing, all the time it wastes, all the fatigue it brings"[105] – Gabrielle endured as a necessary evil; she complained about them, but always saw to them with meticulous care.

Although finished at the beginning of 1965, *La Route d'Altamont* was not published until around the middle of the following year. For the domestic edition Gabrielle hardly knew who to turn to. She wrote to a friend:

Beauchemin have been most unpredictable lately, changing head almost every month, and I'm sorry, of course, for I have long been attached to this old and, at one time, very fine publishing firm. I suppose that I will have to look elsewhere, but certainly not in Pierre Tisseyre's direction, for, although he does sell books, and is a good businessman, I suppose, he is not at all what I would consider a friend of books and authors. I would rather go with Claude Hurtubise of HMH who, little by little, is winning the best and most serious authors of French Canada.[106]

HMH was then the house that published Yves Thériault, Jacques Ferron, Alain Grandbois, Anne Hébert, and a number of others. And so it was there, under the "L'Arbre" imprint, that *La Route d'Altamont* was published in 1966. The Paris edition followed about a year later; Étienne Lalou, the new literary director at Flammarion, would have liked Gabrielle to replace "Le déménagement" with a text "that would match the rest better in depth,"[107] but this idea was not followed through and the Paris edition of *La Route d'Altamont* was an exact reproduction of the Montreal edition.

As regards the publication in English, two new facts deserve mention. The first is the new role played by the publishers McClelland & Stewart Inc. of Toronto and particularly its publisher, Jack McClelland, whom Gabrielle considered a friend and who, since the death of Jean-Marie Nadeau, had been increasingly often serving as her adviser and literary agent. Until now, M&S had been only a kind of subcontractor for the New York house Harcourt Brace, with whom Gabrielle used to deal first and with whom she signed her contracts. This time she not only had separate contracts with the two publishers but she dealt first and almost exclusively with McClelland and it was through him that her arrangements were concluded with Harcourt Brace. One of the first effects of this change, this "Canadianization" of Gabrielle Roy's works in English, was the dismissal of Harry Binsse, her regular translator since *Where Nests the Water Hen*. Gabrielle had always appreciated his competence, but she had long been criticizing him for being "a terrible procrastinator,"[108] being exasperatingly slow with his work. Gabrielle suggested that Joyce Marshall be called upon to replace him; Joyce had translated "Grandmother and the Doll" in 1960. Since she had become one of Gabrielle's friends over the previous six or seven years, Gabrielle entrusted the manuscript of *La Route d'Altamont* to her even before it was published in French and collaborated in the work of translation subsequently, so that *The Road Past Altamont* was on the bookstore shelves in Toronto and New York as early as autumn 1966, barely six months after publication of the original version by HMH.

A World of Women

While for Gabrielle the summers at Petite-Rivière-Saint-François were favoured periods of peace and happiness, when the chills of October came it was time to leave her refuge and head back to the city where professional chores and social obligations were waiting. Where Marcel was also waiting, the husband she felt close to as an old, inseparable companion, and distant from as someone she had trouble understanding, and who she felt was no longer giving her the solicitude and affection she needed.

But returning to Quebec City also meant rejoining a whole circle of friendships. The two Madeleines were there, faithful as ever and still tirelessly attentive. There was a falling out in 1961, however, when Madeleine Chassé announced to Gabrielle that she could no longer be her secretary because Madeleine Bergeron had asked her to work for her at Cardinal Villeneuve. The resulting coolness was short-lived, but Gabrielle was never again as close to the Madeleines as she had been before.

It was at this same time that Gabrielle came to know the woman who was perhaps to be the dearest friend of her mature years, Adrienne Choquette. Adrienne, a writer of some notoriety (she had won the Prix Athanase-David in 1954 for *La nuit ne dort pas*), was six years younger than Gabrielle and like Gabrielle had had a career as a journalist. Having practised journalism in Quebec City since 1948, she was currently editor of the magazine *Terre et Foyer*. In 1961, when she published *Laure Clouet*, a short novel expressing in restrained fashion a simmering revolt against the oppression and outdated values of the past, Gabrielle telephoned her to express her admiration. Thus began a friendship between the two women that kept deepening as they discovered how much their outlook on life, their sensitivity and tastes, even their political and social thinking coincided. With her unassuming manner, gentleness, congenial nature, altruism, piety, and the kind of candour conveyed by her person and speech, "Drienne," as Gabrielle called her affectionately, resembled all the women Gabrielle had loved this much, women both fragile and protective, who seemed immune from everything and therefore innocent and pure, and who for all that had a richer, closer relationship with the world than ordinary mortals. With Adrienne, who was as admiring, devoted, and obliging as Berthe or Esther, Gabrielle enjoyed as well a literary complicity that was under no shadow of any feeling of competition or envy.

Adrienne lived with Medjé Vézina, who had been the editor and publisher of *Terre et Foyer* for thirty years and was known in poetic circles for her one collection of poems published in 1934, *Chaque heure a son visage*. Both saw a good deal of Simone Bussières, whom they had met through the Quebec City branch of the Société des écrivains canadiens and was herself a novelist but primarily a "pedagogical writer,"[109] radio hostess, and soon-to-be publisher. In 1964, Simone moved to Notre-Dame-des-Laurentides north of Quebec City, far out in the country. When the time came for Adrienne to retire four years later, she and Medjé had a house built beside Simone's. This became a frequent destination for Gabrielle (and sometimes Marcel). Gabrielle loved this countryside of gentle hills and sparse forest, which she called "the tundra," and loved to find herself in the midst of this little community of friends where she was welcome any time she wanted to come, either for dinner and an evening of talk by the fire or a relaxing afternoon, in summer cooling off by the pool, in winter roaming the countryside on snowshoes, cross-country skis, or Simone's snowmobile.

Among Adrienne, Medjé, and Gabrielle, the harmony seemed perfect, but between Gabrielle and Simone, a woman of another stamp – energetic, self-assured – there was little meeting of minds. Simone perhaps bore a certain grudge against Gabrielle, who had not liked Simone's novel, *L'Héritier* (1951);[110] she may have been a bit resentful that Gabrielle had won Adrienne's affection. Although she admired Gabrielle's work and skill as a raconteuse, she did not like her ways or her personality.

Another habituée at Notre-Dame-des-Laurentides was the poetess Alice Lemieux-Lévesque, with whom Gabrielle was soon fast friends as well. After making her mark in the 1920s with two little books titled *Heures effeuillées* (1926) and *Poèmes* (1929), Alice had lived for years in France and the United States and had published nothing more until 1962, when, on her return to Quebec City, she published *Silences*, then five further collections of passionate but outdated poetry. The friendship between the two women was particularly close between 1967 and 1971. Alice, who lived with a friend by the name of Jacqueline, had a lively, sparkling temperament, full of gaiety and humour: "Your voice," Gabrielle wrote to her, "sometimes rings in my life like the song of an affectionate little bird reaching a hermit in his cell. And how it cheers the hermit's heart!"[111] She so enjoyed Alice's company that when she felt depressed she would sometimes telephone to ask her to come over by taxi, at Gabrielle's expense of course. And "M'Alice," as her friends used to call her, would hurry to the Château Saint-Louis to bring cheer to the poor hermit.

The Madeleines and the Notre-Dame-des-Laurentides group were Gabrielle's closest circle of friends; these were the people she saw most often, though her meetings with them could hardly be called frequent. There was another circle in Montreal where Gabrielle continued to go at least once or twice a year for business and shopping but also for a few days of rest at Cécile Chabot's or Jacqueline Deniset's. With Judith Jasmin, on the other hand, the meetings became rarer, Judith being too taken up with her many activities and displaying political positions that may have appeared too radical for her friend. From time to time Gabrielle would take advantage of her sojourns in Montreal to renew contacts with old acquaintances like Françoise Loranger, Réginald Boisvert, the journalist Lucette Robert, or the novelist Germaine Guèvremont, whom she had met in 1960 at a party at Cécile's. The two novelists subsequently exchanged a number a letters and met two or three times, either at Germaine's house at Le Chenal du Moine, a village near Sorel on the south shore downriver from Montreal, or in Quebec City. In September 1967 they spent four days together on the Île-aux-Coudres, where Germaine was with "her good friend Louis Pelletier."[112] The following year Gabrielle went to Sorel for Germaine's funeral, then agreed to write the eulogy "Germaine Guèvremont, 1900–1968" for the publications of the Royal Society of Canada. Evoking confidences made to her by the deceased, she stressed the degree to which Germaine Guèvremont, over the years "when for the benefit of television she was obliged to neglect what is properly called writing, suffered from a feeling of constant guilt, tormented by the thought of not having accomplished all she should have."

At the beginning of the 1960s, another writer friend entered Gabrielle's life. This was Joyce Marshall, a native of Montreal who had moved to Toronto some years since. Joyce had made herself known through two novels published in the United States[113] and was making her living as a freelancer in English-Canadian literary publishing and broadcasting. It was through Madeleine Chassé, who was a friend of hers, that she first made contact with Gabrielle and met her at the Château Saint-Louis in June 1959. Although her hostess declined to grant her the radio interview she had come to ask for, Joyce left enchanted. She wrote in her diary:

She is frail but gay, simple and warm, tiny with a tortured dark face, a very deep voice and wonderful light eyes. We liked each other and I feel much happier for this liking. I know so few writers. And Gabrielle doesn't want to talk about her work, any more than I want to talk about mine. A wonderful basis for a friendship – the knowledge, though not the discussion, of shared problems.[114]

Letters followed and a meeting of minds developed that was to last over twenty years. And yet their meetings were rare: in 1960 and 1967, when Joyce came to spend some time at Petite-Rivière-Saint-François, and in 1969, when Gabrielle made a brief trip to Toronto. Still, letters and telephone calls enabled them to keep each other abreast of what they were doing and thinking; and their thinking was similar on almost all subjects, whether literature, philosophy, or politics. Joyce had Gabrielle reading most of the major English-Canadian authors of the period, especially the novelists Ethel Wilson and Margaret Laurence. But it was on Gabrielle's work that their friendship rested above all, and would continue to. Joyce helped Gabrielle with the writing of *La Montagne secrète*, then became her translator in 1966 with *The Road Past Altamont*. From then on their friendship was inextricably mixed with their professional relations. The correspondence between the two women is filled with linguistic considerations and discussions of this or that point of translation; in these things Gabrielle was almost fanatically careful and perfectionist. Furthermore, since she virtually never went to Toronto where she had important literary interests, she tended to consider Joyce as her "antenna" and messenger in the Queen City, not only for her translations but also for her relationships with McClelland & Stewart and the publishing and journalistic milieu in general.

When one tries to reconstruct Gabrielle's entourage during her mature years, whether in Quebec City, Montreal, or Petite-Rivière-Saint-François, one is struck by the fact that her world was peopled almost entirely by women – rather like the gynaeceum of her childhood. They were widowed like Simone, or separated like Alice, or like most of them had simply never married (Berthe, Cécile, Adrienne, Joyce, the Madeleines) and lived alone or in pairs, without husbands or permanent male companions. Gabrielle for her part was married, but the distance that kept widening between her and Marcel and the fact that they were spending more and more time apart had the effect that a man, that men in general, no longer had any place in Gabrielle's everyday world. The days of "the trail of broken hearts," the days of Stephen and Henri, were well and truly past.

This was no hardship for Gabrielle. Her need for comforting and affection was answered best by the company she found in these feminine presences. "Unfailingly, one of us must needs support the other," she wrote to Alice, "and it's beautiful, very beautiful that it should be so – I mean this constant need of one another that exists among us, this appeal for help that at least is not sent out in vain."[115] It was perhaps she who benefited most from this solidarity, for all these women orbiting about her, or almost all, admired and cajoled her, were ready to serve her in any way, came running the moment she crooked a finger, and were awestruck to have her as a friend. But was Gabrielle really their friend? Did she really feel toward any one of these women the deep desire to give of herself, the unselfishness, and above all the concern for perfect equality that makes for true friendship?

She did not see a great deal of them in any event, preferring to telephone them or, even better, write to them. It is true that even past the age of fifty she continued often to be away from Quebec City. Every summer she was at Petite-Rivière, where the cottage was not very inviting to visitors; on the rare occasions when Cécile, Adrienne, Simone, and the others came, they had to bring a picnic with them. And when autumn arrived and Gabrielle returned to the Château Saint-Louis, she could not wait to get on the move again, as if her apartment, as beautifully as Marcel had decorated it with paintings and antique furniture, were a prison to her.

In the first few years after she bought the cottage she still took seaside vacations at the beginning and end of the season. In June 1960 she spent ten days at Cape Cod with Marie Dubuc's niece Thérèse, who was unmarried like her aunt and had a house near Provincetown. Two years later it was Percé she chose for a rest period; Marcel drove her there in mid-August and left again almost immediately. She stayed there alone for three weeks, hunting for agates on the beach in company with Léo-Paul Desrosiers and his wife, and sunbathing,[116] trying either to forget her quarrels with her husband, or patch things up with him by letter. "I've thought about the two of us," she wrote him, "with sadness and great desire that we may manage finally to live together as friends."[117] She returned to Quebec City on August 31, a day too late to celebrate their fifteenth wedding anniversary.

This period was also marked by other, more major trips. During the single year 1961 Gabrielle took three. In the spring she flew to Manitoba to research an article on the province of her birth that *Maclean's* had commissioned her to write. But, she said, "it was not only for this article that I let myself be persuaded to undertake this trip. The impressions I'll bring back could be useful for my next novel";[118] she was then writing "La Saga d'Éveline" and perhaps the stories of *La Route d'Altamont*. Once arrived, she began conscientiously carrying out her journalist's duties, as in her days with *Le Bulletin des agriculteurs*. She interviewed Premier Duff Roblin, visited the Winnipeg Grain Exchange, gathered statistics on the distribution of ethnic and linguistic groups (which statistics led her to be rather pessimistic about the future of Franco-Manitobans). She blended these facts with images she had gathered three years before during her tour of villages of the south and the Little Water Hen, adding, of course, her old, original knowledge of the province of her birth. "Will I even be able to see Manitoba as it really is today?" wondered the sometime journalist. "I'm not sure. I have so many memories, and, as we know, they can be stronger than reality."[119] The article – Gabrielle Roy's last of a documentary nature – appeared a year later, in July 1962.

When she had completed her investigative work, the traveller, who was staying at the Fort Gary Hotel, barely had time left to see members of her family. She had arranged for her visit to St-Boniface to coincide with the ceremony at which Yolande, Germain's younger daughter, was to receive her nursing certificate. Sadly, the celebrations gave way to tragedy when Germain was critically injured in an accident on the highway leading to St-Boniface. Gabrielle visited him in the hospital and succeeded in speaking to him one last time. When he died on May 21 she had already taken the plane back to Quebec City.

Germain was the second of her brothers to die in five years. Jos, whom she had seen in 1955 during her visit to Saskatchewan, had died in November 1956 of emphysema. Germain had just turned fifty-nine. He had got through the Depression rather well in spite of his unstable temperament and weakness for drink. After being an instructor in the Royal Canadian Air Force during and after the war, he returned to teach in St-Boniface (where his pupils nicknamed him "German King") and then on the Saulteux reserve at Pine Falls, where his wife, Antonia, also had a well-paying job as a teacher. Gabrielle and he were never very close, even though he was the youngest of her brothers and therefore the closest in age. She was not much affected by his death, except by the grief it caused Antonia and Yolande, for whom she felt great fondness.

Less than three months after returning from Manitoba, she received a new *invitation au voyage* she could not resist. A geologist acquaintance suggested that she accompany him to the Far North of Quebec, where she had never been but whose awe-inspiring landscapes she had imagined while writing *La Montagne secrète*, complete now for six or seven months and about to appear. The journey lasted a week. The travellers took off from Roberval and put down at Fort Chimo (Kuujjuaq today), a village on the Koksoak River not far from Ungava Bay. The villagers were both Inuit families and whites from the South. Gabrielle did her reporter's investigating; she visited various sites, observed the people, questioned missionaries and government agents, and took notes. There resulted a thirty-page text titled "Voyage en Ungava," which she originally intended to publish but eventually stayed in her bottom drawer;[120] perhaps she envisaged extracting a good deal more from this experience than just an article.

"Voyage en Ungava" was indeed a direct precursor of *La Rivière sans repos* (*Windflower*), the "Eskimo" novel she would begin to write six or seven years later and would publish in 1970. It contains in the form of field observations most of the elements that, reinvested and transformed by the imagination and rearranged around the adventures of fictional characters, would provide the settings and plots of this novel and the three stories she wrote to accompany it. In "Voyage en Ungava," the traveller tells of a movie showing at the Catholic mission, a visit to the abandoned cemetery of old Fort Chimo, transportation of the sick to hospitals in the South, installation of a telephone in an old man's tent. ... The entire narration is marked by Gabrielle's concern over the consequences of the cultural shock being experienced by the aboriginals on contact with white civilization and modern technology. One day when she goes to old Fort Chimo, she sees something that leaves a strong impression on her imagination:

Wandering [...] from lifeless hut to empty hut, we finally found one with life. Entering, we see a young mother carefully combing the hair of the most beautiful child in the world. The mother herself is only half Eskimo. From what father, what Scot perhaps, does she have that smooth forehead, those fine features? And who gave that enchanting child his curly hair, of which the mother, coiling it around her fingers, is so clearly proud

– perhaps the only unhurtful gift the white race has made to her? But she is reserved, unsmiling while we are there, often turning her eyes to the window, not knowing what attitude to take, seeming obsessed by something which to herself is beyond understanding.

"This motion literally haunted me," Gabrielle would say. "It was the source, so to speak, of *La rivière sans repos*."[121] But what is most interesting is to see how this picture, in becoming literary material, would take on enrichment and modify in the writer's mind. In interviews about *La Rivière sans repos* and *Windflower*, every time she spoke of her trip to Ungava she would recall this scene with the mother and child but without ever saying that the mother was of mixed blood, only the child; and the child would not only have curly hair, he became a kind of blond, blue-eyed cherub.[122] In other words, if memory is the instigator and nourisher of fiction, fiction in return changes the memories on which it depends. Thus literature in a way ends up transforming life itself.

Gabrielle was barely back from Ungava before she was packing again for another trip, the third in less than four months. This time she left with Marcel, who was going to attend a medical convention in Vienna from 4 to 8 September 1961. With the convention over, they flew to Athens for three weeks of sightseeing in Greece and around the Agean Sea. They travelled with a group by bus, went on a cruise, in short did the classic tourist itinerary: Delphi, Epidauris, Olympia, the Cyclades, Crete, Istanbul. At Lindos on the island of Rhodes, Gabrielle found a landscape in which she felt she would like to live, "among the bougainvillaeas and the women all in black seen against the whitest walls in the world, and the little interior gardens made of simple pebbles arranged with such grace that they compose exquisite mosaics."[123] Having bought their presents, they stopped in Paris for barely a week and returned to Quebec City on October 2. This was their last trip together. Henceforth each of them would go alone, when and where they liked.

Two years after the trip to Greece, Gabrielle left for another two-month tour in Europe, while Marcel stayed at the Château Saint-Louis and took care of the move to their new apartment. This tour was entirely one of nostalgic rediscovery. At fifty-four, Gabrielle was retracing her steps of twenty-five years earlier when she first went to Europe. She arrived in London on 5 August 1963 and was there for three weeks, staying first at the Stafford Hotel on St. James Place, then at the Cadogan Hotel on Sloane Street next door to the house where she had attended

Lady Frances Ryder's receptions. On the very first day, she met a girl from Sweden, "a beautiful blonde young woman, as are seen in that country,"[124] a journalist by trade who also was in England on vacation. She wrote to Adrienne:

> I've made a very charming friend, a Swedish girl, blonde and sweet enough to eat. It was by the loveliest of chances that I came across her, in Trafalgar Square among the pigeons. Since I thought she had a pleasant face, it was she I approached to ask directions. She didn't know any more than I did; so we helped each other, first to get to Piccadilly, next to find a decent restaurant, after that to do the museums, and so on. That's the way it's been for ten days now, and I think it's going to be hard for us to part.[125]

Siv Heiderberg – this was the young woman's name – had a very limited knowledge of English. She attached herself to Gabrielle "like a little dog."[126] Gabrielle walked the city tirelessly with her, "spurred on," she told Berthe, "by curiosity and a desire to revisit neighbourhoods, monuments, and parks [...] that I'd known long ago."[127] She also visited the museums, fascinated once again by Rembrandt, Hobbema, and especially *Giovanni Arnolfini and His Bride* by Van Eyck, a painting "which comes to my mind almost every day of my life."[128] Finally she went to spend a few days with Esther, kind Esther with her "beautiful, blue-green, smiling yet sad eyes." The region was now urbanized, Century Cottages "falling into ruins."[129] Father Perfect was no longer of this world, but Esther "doesn't seem to have aged a bit since the last time I saw her. [...] It is true," the visitor observed, "that she has an ageless face, which has never been young and perhaps will never be old."[130] After bringing back the sweet memories of yesteryear together, the two women parted, never to see one another again.

From Upshire Gabrielle went off to Paris, where she arrived on August 26. She took a room at the Lutèce. Here again, in spite of bad weather she spent most of her time walking, seeing movies and exhibitions, marvelling at the "fairy-like spectacle" of the Place de la Concorde lit up at night, rediscovering "a bit of the happiness I had to be living in Paris."[131] Twice she went to Saint-Germain-en-Laye to see old friends again and go with them to visit the neighbouring countryside where she had so loved to go for drives with Marcel years before. In Paris she saw Anne Hébert, who was also at the Lutèce, and especially Julie Simard, a nurse who was working in the same hospital as Marcel. Julie did not leave Gabrielle's side, ate with her every evening, and watched over her well-being like a mother.

Weary of the cold, overcast weather, Gabrielle persuaded Julie to travel with her to the Midi, where she wanted to go at all cost before returning to Canada. They left Paris on September 7. The next day after a stop in Les Baux-de-Provence, they were in St-Rémy, where they were staying at the Hôtel Glanum until the 12th. They went for long walks in the environs, basking at last in fine weather. Next they spent a brief spell in Avignon and returned to Paris on the 15th. Gabrielle flew back to Montreal ten days later after walking about the city some more and meeting the people she had not had time to see before.

This voyage steeped in nostalgia had happened more in memory than in space, as though Gabrielle had wanted to recapitulate her past. London, Paris, Provence; with the approach of old age, a woman retraces the footsteps of the woman she was, as if to come full circle, see one last time what she knows is forever lost, her youth, her innocence, her freedom. This in truth was Gabrielle's last real voyage. After 1963 she would no longer set out on the highways and byways of the world in quest of landscapes and people to be discovered or rediscovered. These days were now over for her. Which does not mean that she was going to stay put, quite the contrary. Until the end of the 1960s, until her late sixties, not a year went by when she did not leave Quebec for at least a few weeks, even a month or two, but these were not trips or voyages properly speaking but simply more or less prolonged sojourns in this or that place, where she would stay pretty well put once arrived. These sojourns were determined either by family duties or the need to flee the rigours of winter and seek a climate more favourable to her health and work.

Gabrielle and Her Sisters

In January 1964, barely four months after her European tour, Gabrielle was summoned by family necessities for the first time since her mother's death to travel afar, to Phoenix, Arizona, where her eldest sister Anna was dying.

Anna's hitherto colourless life had over the past two or three years taken a pathetic and accelerating turn for the worse. Too old to continue maintaining La Painchaudière, she and her husband had sold the house in February 1961 after living in it for over twenty years. Albert Painchaud died eight months later and Anna found herself a widow at age seventy-three. Then began a period of restless wandering that ended only with her death. She lived first with her eldest son, Fernand, and his wife, Léontine, in their St-Boniface apartment. Together they all went to spend the winter in California with the children and grandchildren of Anna's late uncle, Moïse Landry. When she returned in March 1962, Anna left for Marmora, Ontario, to stay with her second son, Paul, and his wife, Malvina. She was there four or five months and then took off for Montreal, where she lived for a time with Adèle before heading next for Pennsylvania to join her third and last son, Gilles, and his wife, Béatrix. There was soon discord between mother and daughter-in-law, however, and Anna returned to St-Boniface for Christmas. She left again in January 1963 for another stay in Marmora, from where she pushed on to a spot on the Ottawa River where Adèle had rented a small cottage. She was back in St-Boniface in March but a month later was setting out on a new expedition, this time on a mission to the West Coast with Bernadette to aid their sick and alcoholic brother Rodolphe. Back once again in Manitoba, she took a room at the Marion Hotel, long enough to catch her breath. The intestinal cancer from which she had suffered for twenty years and had obliged her to undergo two or three operations – and which she had always overcome before – now struck her cruelly. Thin and in pain, she nevertheless undertook another trip in October, to Phoenix. It would be her last.

Fernand and Léontine had been living in Phoenix for a year, having reached their fifties and flown the harsh climate of Manitoba for this paradisian region. Fernand had found a modest job at a dog-racing track and bought a mobile home at the Blue Skies Trailer Park, where living was comfortable and inexpensive. When he learned that his mother did not have long to live, he went in his car and brought her home for the winter so that she might enjoy the sun and warmth of Arizona in the time she had left.

On December 26 she had to be hospitalized. Alerted by Fernand, Gabrielle arrived on 10 January 1964. From the minute she stepped off the plane she marvelled at the splendour of the place, this landscape filled with sky, this light, this heat, all this exuberant vegetation in the midst of the desert. A beauty the more poignant for its cruel contrast with the emaciated body of the dying woman, who from day to day kept losing ground and knew, despite the morphine, that she was going to depart without having had her rightful share of happiness. Visiting her every day, Gabrielle learned to know her sister better. "I know now that she was consumed by a need to love and be loved, and that something was preventing her from letting herself go in response to this need. Poor soul, life must have caused her such pain."[132] Anna died on the morning of January 19; it was a Sunday and the weather was radiant.

Gabrielle stayed in Phoenix for the burial, which took place on Tuesday. The sky was magnificent once again, and the body was lowered into the grave amid an orgy of colour and beauty, as Gabrielle described later in one of the loveliest passages in *Enchantment and Sorrow*:

> Everywhere, not so far from this miraculous oasis, it must have been winter. Here it was perpetual spring. The cemetery was a profusion of giant poinsettias, hibiscus, and clusters of vivid red jacaranda. Insects buzzed merrily, flitting from clump to clump. [. . .] On a branch of a paloverde a mockingbird sang as though his heart would burst, the "gentle bird of youth" so beloved of southerners, and no wonder, once you've heard it sing.[133]

A dramatic little episode followed Anna's death, when the family learned of the contents of the will she had made in August 1962 while visiting Adèle. She had bequeathed what little she possessed to charities, leaving only modest monthly allowances to her sons that they could not pass on to anyone; of the three, it was Fernand who received the smallest allowance, although it was he, with Léontine, who had been the most devoted and attentive to his mother, and who lived "practically in poverty."[134]

Anna's death was an important moment in Gabrielle's life. Not that the bereavement affected her terribly; Anna was twenty years her senior and they had little in common. However, the event marked the beginning of a two-fold conversion in Gabrielle. It set in motion an inner development whose culmination would be reached several years later on the occasion of another death, Bernadette's. This first was a conversion in the strict, religious sense of the term. In Phoenix, seeing Anna eaten away by cancer, for the first time since seeing her father die thirty-five years before, Gabrielle was placed before the concrete reality of dying and death. Seven years later she would say that this experience played a decisive role in her return to the faith (although we find no mention of this in her letters of 1964 or 1965). "Anna," she would say, "did not seem to entertain any hope of an afterlife. At least, her eyes let it be understood and I could not bear it. This life that was ending cut me to the quick. I could not accept that for Anna whom we'd loved, who had had a place among us, who had lived her life with joys and sorrows, everything was going to end. That tomorrow there would be nothing left of her."[135]

It had been thirty years since Gabrielle had abandoned all religious practice. If she returned to it around 1964, it was not only because of Anna's death, but also an intellectual evolution influenced by her readings of the works of Teilhard de Chardin and the renewal brought to Catholicism by the Council of Vatican II (1962–1965). In the years following, she began again to go to mass and receive the sacraments, but she was by no means conventionally devout. Her religion remained very personal and undemonstrative, her most fervent prayers destined less for God and the saints of the official Church than her own "little saints," Mélina, Anna, and soon Bernadette.

The other conversion that Anna's death led to or precipitated was Gabrielle's return to the family fold that she had so badly wanted to escape, beginning in her youth. Although she had remained in contact with her people at intervals after leaving Manitoba, sending a little money from time to time and visiting occasionally, this tenuous tie had always been a burden and, she believed, was no longer genuinely part of the woman she had become, alone and far from her family as she was, and even in spite of her family. During her brief stay at La Painchaudière in 1958, what she had felt in the presence of Anna, Clémence, Bernadette, and the others was above all this feeling of alienation. "You have no idea," she wrote at the time to Marcel, "what an ordeal it is for me to be reunited with my family. I'm constantly invaded by the feeling that I'm a foreigner in their midst, as if we no longer had anything in common but such a pale, distant resemblance that it seems like a dream."[136]

But now it was as though Anna's illness and death had placed Gabrielle squarely before the prospect of her own solitude, and she suddenly rediscovered her dependence on her family, her place in it, and her need for the presence and support of her sisters. Now that Anna was gone, she felt more orphaned than after her mother's death when she had been young still, caught up in her ambitions and desires and unable really to measure the void in which she could be left by this loss. Her vision was clearer this time.

Poor, tragic Anna, she had to die to make us realize that since Maman's death she had in a way taken her place, become in turn the nucleus, the centre and soul of the family. Now there's no one left to really hold us together, and for all the affection we have for each other, it's not entirely the same thing. A piece of the cement that held us together has dropped away.[137]

But was it only a feeling of loss that affected Gabrielle? Was there not also, was there not above all, fear? Not so much fear of finding herself alone – that was something she had always wanted – but fear of seeing her past catch up with her, her old failing and her old guilt toward her mother, from which Anna's presence had until now protected her. This fear now had a name and a face: Clémence, the ailing sister whom Mélina, when she died, had left alone in the world, and whom Gabrielle had promised to take care of. Since their mother's death, Anna had taken Clémence's care on herself. Gabrielle paid the small fees necessary for her upkeep, but it was Anna and Albert who visited her, saw to her well-being, dispensed the care she needed, and took all the relevant responsibilities, the poor woman being incapable of managing her own life. Gabrielle had been able to feel she was doing her duty to her mother, since Clémence lacked for nothing. But what was going to happen now that Anna was no longer there? Who would take up the torch and fulfil the promises made to Mélina?

In principle it should have been Adèle, who was now the oldest in the family, but Adèle had neither the lifestyle nor the aptitudes to become Clémence's guardian. Since selling her farm at Tangent in 1955 she had wandered from here to there without anywhere to settle down. After teaching for three years, once again among the Métis of Manitoba, and having self-published a strongly autobiographical "novel of the Far North of Canada" entitled *Valcourt ou la Dernière Étape*, she retired from teaching in 1959 and went to spend two years in Europe. After this she settled in Montreal, where she lived in conditions close to abject poverty, devoting her time to genealogical research and her manuscripts, which she copied and recopied tirelessly on her small typewriter. None of these manuscripts would be published before 1969 when, again at her own expense, she had printed an historical study titled *La Montagne Pembina au temps des colons*, followed in 1970 by *Les Visages du vieux Saint-Boniface*. How could Adèle, so unsettled and so bereft, look after poor Clémence? Besides, the two of them were far too different temperamentally to get along. In 1954 they had already tried unsuccessfully to live together. They would try again in 1966, when Adèle suggested that Clémence move into her apartment – Clémence was all for it. But

Clémence was so slow, so apathetic, and Adèle so bustling and full of energy, so rough too, that their ménage did not last even two months. Clémence came out of that cohabitation worse off than before.

As for Rodolphe, no one dared consider him to care for his sick sister. He lived in British Columbia, was always penniless, and lived in a kind of slum. And how could he be counted on? After his illness of 1963, the owners of a motel in Powell River had hired him as a night watchman. "I hope," Anna wrote before she died, "that he won't do something to disappoint them and open their eyes about him."[138] For Rodolphe, everyone knew, kept bad company and drank and played cards like a man possessed.

That left Bernadette. Although she was no longer young – sixty-six when Anna died – Sister Léon was in the best position to take over Anna's role with Clémence. In 1950 she had returned to the Académie Saint-Joseph to teach diction and dramatic art, giving her an opportunity to spend several summers in Quebec City taking courses. She used to write dramatic sketches herself, and maintained the best of relations with Pauline Boutal and others of the Cercle Molière. Since Gabrielle had been making a career in literature, a complicity had developed between them although they rarely saw each other. Bernadette had left the family house in 1919 and had not known Gabrielle in her teen years or as a young woman as had Anna and Adèle, and so had nothing to hold against her. On the contrary, she felt only pride and admiration for her youngest sister, congratulated her on each success, genuinely wished for her happiness, and kept a scrapbook of articles, interviews, the least little item that appeared about her. Understandably, Gabrielle felt a very special tenderness for "Dédette." Of her four sisters, she felt, Dédette was the only one who understood and really loved her, the only one who, far from raising any kind of resistance to her, gave her total devotion and returned an image of herself that corresponded to the best of what she was and wished to be. Between the two sisters, the nun and the artist, despite the difference in age a true friendship was thus created, nourished by regular correspondence and founded on shared sensitivity and values: a love of nature, a taste for art, faith in idealization, and veneration of their dead mother.

Anticipating Anna's death, Gabrielle pulled out all the stops to have Bernadette agree to take Clémence under her wing. When Anna had gone East, she wrote:

I've just received a rather laconic letter from Clémence. She misses Anna, I think. Luckily she still has you. She tells me about your visits with an artless joy that lets me sense how much they mean to her. Poor little Clémence, how often my heart aches to think of the way she lives, her curious lot in life.[139]

Looking after Clémence, protecting her, making her happy, she let Bernadette understand, was not only remaining faithful to Mélina and soothing her worries, "if it's true that she can still worry,"[140] it was also making Gabrielle happy by relieving her of this worry gnawing at her – this responsibility hanging over her – and therefore deserved her deepest gratitude. For, she kept reminding her elder sister, "I would [...] give anything for Clémence to be happy in life – as happy as she can be."[141]

And so, beginning in 1964 it was Bernadette who saw to Clémence's care and well-being, while Gabrielle sent her encouragement with her letters and dispatches of money from afar. Bernadette could not take her sister into the convent with her, but thanks to the help and influence of her community she arranged for her to live in good establishments where she could visit her often. Under Anna's reign, beginning in the mid-1950s, Clémence had spent most of her life as a boarder in a home run by the Soeurs de la Présentation on Taché Avenue. In the spring of 1965 when Clémence was preparing to celebrate her seventieth birthday, Bernadette succeeded in placing her in a residence for the elderly in the village of Ste-Anne-des-Chênes, over sixty miles southeast of Winnipeg. The place was out of the way but pleasant, the establishment comfortable, and the staff competent, but Clémence was very soon lonesome and began to decline, so that Bernadette, now freer in her movements because of greater flexibility in her community's rules, had constantly to be running to her to entertain and comfort her.

It was during this summer of 1965 that Gabrielle, wanting both to give a lift to Clémence's morale and repay Bernadette for her efforts, decided to bring them both to Petite-Rivière-Saint-François for three weeks of vacation with her and Marcel. Arriving in mid-July, the two visitors settled into the little house that Gabrielle had rented for them from Jean-Noël Simard, Berthe's nephew. This little house was right next door to the "big" Simard house, so that Berthe could keep an eye on Bernadette and Clémence and take care of them while Gabrielle was working – which she continued to do every morning as was her habit. In the afternoons they would go for walks, or down to the tidal flats by the river, or for drives in Marcel's car, to Île-aux-Coudres or the villages around about. After the meal (often prepared by Berthe), they would spend the evening on the verandah, laughing and talking.

Bernadette and Clémence were in seventh heaven. The landscape, the weather (magnificent), the birds, the pretty little house, Berthe's kindness, Marcel's presence, everything was a festival for them and enchanted them. Clémence, wearing a hat and white gloves, never tired of stroking the animals and gathering enormous bouquets of wildflowers, while Sister Léon, wearing her coif, would sit for long spells at the top of the cliff, working with birchbark and gazing at the river and the islands. These almost seventy-year-olds were like two enthralled, excited little girls enjoying the sweetness and beauty of the world for the first time in their lives. One morning from her window, Jori Smith saw Clémence giving a hug to some trees at the side of the road.

For Gabrielle, these days of sharing would remain one of the most memorable times of her life. "I think we three sisters [. . .] made a kind of small masterpiece of this time together,"[142] she would write. Then and there, she had some difficulty adapting to having her sisters around, she knew them so little really and had not lived with them for so many, many years; and so there were moments when she became irritated and "flew off the handle" with them rather harshly. But their joy invariably reflected on her and excited her too; seeing Clémence and Bernadette so happy, and especially seeing them happy because of her, because she had seen fit to receive them and give them a little of her time, this much was enough to gratify her, let her feel better about herself by assuring her, in a way, of her own kindness.

Between her and Bernadette, the memory of this enchanted summer would remain like a beacon, the symbol not only of their communion but also, through their solicitude for Clémence, of the faithfulness binding them to "our little mother Mélina."[143] "Oh, if only this beautiful thing can happen to us once again in our lives!" Gabrielle's letters then kept saying to her *chère petite soeur*. Year after year the *petite soeur* kept hoping, and year after year Gabrielle kept putting off the invitation. Thus during the winter of 1969 she wrote to Bernadette, "As for this summer, my poor child, I'm still quite unable to make a decision, owing to a climate of uncertainty and a lot of other reasons"; but, she added soon, "if the trip can't be arranged for this summer, you mustn't get discouraged, but hope it will be possible next summer."[144] But the next summer Bernadette would be dead, without ever again having set eyes on "the sea" at Petite-Rivière-Saint-François.

Winter Migrations

Much as Gabrielle loved her summers at Petite-Rivière, the winters at Quebec City were difficult. She did adore the snowstorms; the spectacle of snow gusting about on the Plains of Abraham exhilarated her, and on snowy, blustery days she liked nothing better than to take the ferry to Lévis and stand on deck in the full fury of the elements. Now and then she would spend an afternoon with the Madeleines at Mont Sainte-Anne or go for a few days to Notre-Dame-des-Laurentides to take the fresh air and go on snowshoeing expeditions in "the tundra." However, the flu, bronchitis, sore throats, and other respiratory ailments that assailed her with the arrival of real winter weather sooner or later obliged her to stay indoors and brought her to a state close to depression. At these times she came to be a mere shadow of her normal self, crippled with weariness and ennui, incapable of the smallest effort, and each day longing for the return of spring.

The older she became, the less well her health and morale withstood these forced shut-in periods. Beginning in the mid-1960s, she therefore tried to spend the worst of the winter under more clement skies where she could find mild weather and air neither too dry nor too humid for her fragile lungs. She did not want luxury or entertainment. What she had to have was peace and quiet, a comfortable place to stay, and surroundings where she could walk all she liked. But the place and the climate were not all. She also needed a friendly presence, not too far away but not too close, someone who, while respecting her privacy, would see to her material needs, would help or comfort her if called upon, and without asking too much in return make her feel loved and protected. The ideal would be the same as ever in other words – to recreate the free yet warm ambiance she had enjoyed at Century Cottages with Esther, at Rawdon with Mother Tinkler, at Port-Daniel in the McKenzie house, and still enjoyed every summer, thanks to Berthe, at Petite-Rivière-Saint-François.

She would find such ideal conditions very rarely in the course of her winter migrations. The first of these took place in February and March 1966 when, reassured over arrangements for Clémence, she left to stay for a time in her beloved Provence, in Draguignan, a town in the back country of the Côte d'Azur. Her old friend Paula was living there now after several years in Durban, South Africa, Henri Bougearel's final posting in his diplomatic career. Gabrielle had not seen Paula since their summer vacation in Brittany in 1955, when they were alone, just the two of them, as in the days of their youth. This time the whole family was there – Henri, the three children, Monique, Alain, and Claude (Marcel and Gabrielle's godson, whom Gabrielle had seen briefly in Paris in 1963 and who was now eighteen), and also Madame Sumner, Paula's mother. At first Gabrielle found much pleasure in their company. She would spend long evenings in endless "gab sessions" with them,[145] then go back to her hotel. In the afternoons, she would go for walks in the surrounding country or for short excursions in the Renault 4L that she had rented and that Paula drove. The countryside was magnificent and flooded with sunlight.

But after a few weeks, things began to deteriorate. The more Gabrielle saw of the Bougearels, the less they hid their troubles – the difficulty they were having re-adapting to France, their shortage of money, their worrisome children, and the gloom that they never managed to throw off. "It's a bit the atmosphere of *The Glass Menagerie*," Gabrielle wrote. "I have the impression that they're all getting to be more or less schizophrenic. Everything with them is a problem or becomes a problem, and the worst is that when you watch them at it you get to be like them."[146] Soon Paula could stand it no longer and had to be hospitalized, the victim of a depression brewing for years. And so Gabrielle, having come to Provence "to take it easy in the sunshine and in idleness,"[147] found herself helping out her friend and her friend's family, which she did for a few days before escaping to Nice for her final week before returning to Canada. The picture she brought away of Paula – the tall, beautiful, radiant Paula of yesteryear – was one of a broken woman, abandoned to her own devices and her own melancholy in a far corner of a third-rate mental clinic.

The winter after this she stayed in Quebec City, where she was working on a text she had been commissioned to write for the World Exhibition of 1967. The following December, however, she yielded to an invitation from Cécile Chabot and her mother to go with them to Florida. They were so good to her on her visits to Montreal that she was sure of having plenty of attention, even being spoiled, throughout her vacation. The three women arrived in Miami soon after Christmas,

finding Cécile's sister Thérèse already there. But Gabrielle hated everything about the city; "everywhere," she wrote to Berthe, "there's pressure,
crowding, confusion, noise."[148] Then as if by a miracle there arrived a
message from Marie Dubuc, whom Gabrielle had known years before at
Laterrière and seen from time to time in Quebec City. Marie, who was
spending the winter at New Smyrna Beach, a resort on the coast farther
north near Daytona, was announcing that she had found an attractive,
inexpensive oceanfront motel and was inviting Gabrielle to come and
join her and her friend Clara. Without a minute's hesitation, Gabrielle
left the Chabot ladies behind in Miami and took the bus for New
Smyrna, where she arrived on January 5, dead tired but soon reinvigo-
rated by the beauty and peacefulness of the new surroundings.

She stayed over two months, totally happy and relaxed. Everything
there filled her with contentment. The climate, the vegetation, the sea
breeze of "Smyrne," as she called it in French, made her feel she was in
one of the world's most beautiful and secluded little corners, almost the
equal of Petite-Rivière-Saint-François. And the beach – "this beach so
soft on the feet, pure to the eyes, gentle to the soul," where she would go
down every morning to watch the terns and take a long walk, alone, "*en
sauvageonne*," with "a peacefulness and joie de vivre in my heart I had
almost forgotten."[149] Gone were the health problems, the fits of coughing, the sleepless nights one after another; "I haven't felt so much at ease
in a place for a long time,"[150] she wrote to Bernadette. Marie took her for
drives and walks in the nearby woods, helped her with her shopping and
meals, and introduced her to Canadians on vacation on the coast, always
taking care not to disturb her and never making her feel under any obligation whatever. In the middle of February Marie also organized a little
weeklong trip for her with Colette Palardy, Jean's sister, through the
Everglades to Key West; Gabrielle returned enchanted.

How could she not write in such a paradise? Five days after her
arrival she announced to Marcel, "I'm trying to train myself to work at
least an hour or two in the morning. As always it's hard to get going."
Ten days later: "It's the old story. One day it goes fairly well; the next day
it won't go at all. What doggedness it takes to carry on."[151] To get her
hand in, she began by retouching one of her old stories, "La vallée
Houdou." Then she began something else, probably the long, poetic
story titled "L'arbre," which is set in Florida and describes one of those
great, age-old oak trees festooned with moss that she had seen on her
walks with Marie and the dog, Moka. Perhaps she also began *La Rivière*

sans repos, the novel she would be working on all the following summer. She spent a great deal of time reading as well, supplied once again by the kind-hearted Marie.

> I've read quite a lot since I've been at Smyrne [...] Thus I've been through the *Antimémoires* [André Malraux]. Contrary to the impression I'd had from the excerpts published here and there, it's a fascinating, superb, and majestic book. Full of heart and soul as well. I've also read the last big book by Kazantzakis; a marvellous writer, a bit Zorba himself. Now I'm beginning *Understanding Media* by Marshall McLuhan. It's rather hard to read at the start. I think it's going to interest me.

And indeed, the report she made to Marcel three weeks later could hardly have been more enthusiastic:

> Sometimes I have the feeling the man is a genius – or else an unbelievable hoax, a magician without equal. But no, I think he's a visionary, like Teilhard de Chardin, and *sees* the truth that no one else can see. Anyway, it's a fascinating theory of our world.[152]

When mid-March came and it was time to leave New Smyrna, Gabrielle had only one thought in her head, and that was to return at all costs, with Marcel if possible, and even perhaps to buy a house here – why not?

This last plan did not materialize, but as for returning to New Smyrna, this she did the very next season, without even waiting for Christmas and the really cold weather. If she left so soon, however, it was because she could not do otherwise: everything had been arranged and reserved months in advance. When it came to enthusiasm, she had not a drop left, for by the end of 1968 she was suffering a depression the like of which she had not known for a very long time. "I have a feeling," she wrote to a friend, "that I'm never again going to be able to write, that a spring has broken, this time for good . . ."

> I don't know who or what is at fault, perhaps I myself. That's to say an incurable fatigue, perhaps a whole combination of circumstances, perhaps the spirit of present times that I don't feel at home in any more, perhaps the dreariness, the nameless solitude that Marguerite Yourcenar calls "the bleakness of incommunicable thoughts." [...] If I could find at

least some other interest, some other passion to latch on to, but it's hard when for thirty years you've had no aim in life but writing, as if it's your very reason for living.[153]

The Grande Dame of Literature, or The Ambiguities of Fame

What was the cause of such deep discouragement? It is difficult to give a *complete* answer to this question, so many and diverse could be the reasons. Age may have had something to do with it, for Gabrielle was then seeing the approach of her sixtieth birthday; but since she had never attached all that much importance to youth and beauty, it seems unlikely that just growing old would have upset her so.

What seems to have triggered this depression in a more immediate way was the recent evolution of her career and standing as a writer. Since the early 1960s her situation in this regard had been growing increasingly paradoxical. To put it bluntly, she was an author who was both famous and forgotten.

Few Quebec or Canadian writers were as famous as she. To be sure, there were not many people still taking an interest in her books in France, the United States, or elsewhere in the world – outside a few marginal columnists and tiny groups of specialists and friends of Canadian culture. In Canada, however, especially on the French side, her name was known and respected everywhere. Journalists referred to her as the *grande dame* of literature and crowded about her door to obtain interviews.

She granted very few. If she behaved this way, it was less from modesty or distrust of the media than fear of the stress she experienced as soon as performance was required of her; since her experience in New York with the launching of *The Tin Flute*, she knew what disruption these episodes could bring and how much loss of time and energy they could mean, to the detriment of her work. Still, occasionally she would agree, particularly if a journalist was involved in whom she had confidence and the diffusion of the interview might carry a certain prestige. This was the case in August 1960 when she received her friend Judith Jasmin and the team from the television program *Premier Plan*, which had already featured such renowned writers as Montherlant, Mauriac, Giono, Maurois, Cocteau, and Pagnol. The interview took place at the Château Saint-Louis, in the most favourable conditions possible; and yet throughout the interview, despite her background as an actress, Gabrielle on camera cannot rid herself of a stiffness in attitude and diction that at times makes her seem like a hunted animal. This was the first and last time she appeared on television.[154] In the following years, other fairly substantial interviews would be published in the press; for example, in *Terre et Foyer*, the magazine where Adrienne Choquette worked, and in the magazine *Châtelaine* (French version), where Alice Parizeau gave her article the heading "Gabrielle Roy, grande romancière canadienne."[155] While the attention of journalists and the image of her that they conveyed to the public were important to her, however, she remained rather guarded about public disclosure of personal matters and the vanities of the small world of literature. "I admire Réjean Ducharme," she said soon after the publication of *Le Nez qui voque*. "I like his books and I like the way he goes about things. A writer's duty is to write. His books are what speak for him. He has no need to lay his whole life on the line, to appear on television and give out details of his private life."[156]

Far from damaging her reputation, this reticence only served to increase the aura of distinction and solemnity surrounding Gabrielle Roy, which in turn did nothing to stop the honours from raining upon her. Civil honours, like the title of Companion of the Order of Canada, which the government of Lester B. Pearson conferred on her in 1967, the centenary of Confederation and the year of creation of the Order; academic honours, like the honorary doctorates she was offered all over Canada and which she systematically declined, except one from the Université Laval, which she considered an homage from her city of adoption and consented to receive in 1968;[157] artistic honours, like the medal that the Canada Council for the Arts awarded her in 1968 for the body of her work, and especially the Prix Athanase-David of the Province of Quebec, which was awarded her in 1971 by a jury composed of Jean Simard, Jacques Blais, Joseph Bonenfant, and Jean Éthier-Blais. The ceremony took place on Thursday, March 11, in the Salon rouge of the Assemblée nationale. After receiving a cheque for $5,000 from the hands of François Cloutier, the minister of Cultural Affairs, the prize-winner, wearing a beige dress with an elegant Bianchini scarf lent by Madeleine Bergeron, gave a speech in which she paid tribute to Alain Grandbois and Félix-Antoine Savard, who had received the prize before her, and recalled how "all life, and with greater reason a writer's life, is tragic in the sense that the further one goes, the further one sees and the more one has to say, and the less time in which to say it."[158]

The Prix David was then the ultimate recognition for a Quebec writer.

Several months later there were rumours going around to the effect that the Nobel Prize jury was considering Gabrielle Roy, whose candidature had received the support of the great Latin American poet Miguel Angel Asturias. . . . The news made the front page of *La Presse*.[159] In fact, the rumours originated with a literary agent by the name of C. Berloty, who was then handling certain business matters for Gabrielle and was trying to interest Canadian diplomats in his client's case. Nothing came of this, except that the local journalists' curiosity was aroused and Gabrielle Roy's prestige in Quebec and Canada was further enhanced.[160]

Gabrielle viewed these developments with much agitation, as her correspondence shows. Divided between excitement and dread, she was unsure whether to rejoice or lament over this public attention and recognition. "I'm stunned almost senseless," she confided to Marcel when she learned that she was being awarded the David. Her state of nerves only worsened as the fateful day approached. "I assure you I'm in a hurry to have this Prix David business over with. I'm sleeping badly and it leaves me shaky. I had all that trouble beginning to get by a bit without mandrax and other products, and here I am at their mercy as never before."[161] And yet she had wanted this prize and prepared for it meticulously, polishing her speech and long in advance settling the smallest details of what she would wear.

Her growing renown had another effect: it brought a profusion of requests for texts. Here again, she declined most but did comply when it was impossible to do otherwise, or when there was something particularly interesting about the request. Thus in 1961 the students of the Université de Montréal invited the author of *Bonheur d'occasion* to write "Quelques réflexions sur la littérature canadienne d'expression française" for a special issue of the campus paper *Le Quartier latin*, which she accepted willingly. The following year some University of Ottawa academics obtained a text from her in response to a questionnaire on fiction for a volume of *Les Archives des lettres canadiennes*. In about this same period she agreed to write tributes to several of her artist friends, Jean-Paul Lemieux, René Richard, and, as we have already seen, Germaine Guèvremont. In 1969 the Winnipeg magazine *Mosaic*, preparing to celebrate the centenary of Manitoba's joining the Canadian Confederation, called on the great writer and native of St-Boniface for a contribution. This was to be "My Manitoba Heritage," the French text of which Gabrielle wrote in July of that year; it was her first autobiographical piece since "Souvenirs du Manitoba," published in 1954.

The most important commission of these years came from the Canadian Corporation for the 1967 World Exhibition. In 1963 Gabrielle was asked to be one of a panoply of artists and thinkers who were assembled at great expense for four days at the Château Montebello to "develop" together the theme chosen for the exhibition: "*Terre des Hommes* / Man and His World." There were people as recognized and respectable as Claude Robillard, Frank R. Scott, Dr. Wilder Penfield, and the actor Jean-Louis Roux, as well as Davidson Dunton and André Laurendeau, the co-chairmen of the newly created "B&B" Commission. Three years later when the opening of Expo 67 was drawing near, Guy Robert of Klein-Languirand Productions of Montreal, which had been commissioned to prepare the official commemorative book, signed an agreement with Gabrielle Roy that she would write the text. Like other suppliers to the exhibition, she received a phenomenal fee: $4,000. She set to work at once. After three or four months she turned over a "philosophical" essay of some thirty pages in which, drawing inspiration from Saint-Exupéry, Camus, Bernanos, Teilhard de Chardin, even Sri Aurobindo, she puts forward her vision of a classless, brotherly humanity, free of linguistic or cultural disagreements, and of one accord progressing toward universal communion and order.

> Have we not been following our path for centuries, without observing much change, it's true, along the tedious way, and yet from time to time encouraged by one pilgrim among us who has caught a flash of hope to lighten our despair, passing the word to others who take courage? And does this path not lead us, despite prejudice and obstacles, at last toward the true *Terre des hommes*?[162]

This is perhaps not the best of Gabrielle Roy's texts – her style is inflated and her optimism rather conventional – but it expresses in the clearest fashion that ideal, that Utopic "circle of mankind, full and united at last"[163] that had been nourishing her thought since the days when she had travelled Canada as a reporter, and that underlies all of her work with a vision either happy and a source of idyllic images (as in *Peoples of Canada* and *Where Nests the Water Hen*) or else critical or satirically questioning, making it appear painful and problematical (as in *The Tin Flute* or *The Cashier*). "This essay," Gabrielle would say later, "sums up, badly but as well as I am able, all of what I have thought and written."[164]

But the publication of "Terre des hommes: le thème raconté" and its translation by Joyce Marshall, "Man and His World: The Theme Unfolded" turned into a nightmare. As soon as the contractor had possession of the manuscripts, he took it upon himself to cut and shape the text as he pleased, despite letters and telegrams from Gabrielle who, "so disgusted with it all I don't know what to say about it,"[165] finally resigned herself to seeing the publication of an essay truncated and disfigured by the unwarranted intervention of rewriting experts.[166]

If the renown Gabrielle Roy had acquired was illustrated by distinctions and requests for texts, there were other more eloquent signs, particularly the position of her work on the book market and in the estimation of academics. First the book market. Gabrielle Roy's early books may have been around since the 1940s and 1950s, but they were still more present than ever on bookstore shelves and in publishers catalogues throughout Canada. In Montreal, Beauchemin republished new editions of *Bonheur d'occasion* (1965), *Rue Deschambault* (1967), *La Petite Poule d'Eau* (1970), and soon *Alexandre Chenevert* (1973), all of them reprinted regularly. In Toronto, the translations of the same four titles one after the other entered the prestigious New Canadian Library paperback series, which reprints works considered the most significant in Canadian literature.[167] Deluxe editions of *Bonheur d'occasion* and *La Petite Poule d'Eau*[168] appeared elsewhere, the latter in an art edition of two hundred copies with twenty original prints by Jean-Paul Lemieux; four years later *La Montagne secrète* would be similarly honoured with the publication by Hugues de Jouvancourt of a deluxe edition illustrated by René Richard.[169]

Vitality in publishing returned relatively high sales. Between roughly 1960 and 1975, it may be estimated (with the margin of error involved in figures often partial and approximate) that year in and year out Beauchemin sold 15,000 copies of various titles by Gabrielle Roy, while sales by McClelland & Stewart were over 8,000 copies. There were not many local authors in those days who enjoyed commercial success as real and consistent. While it was not a fortune, the money Gabrielle earned from the sale of her books, together with her other author's fees plus returns generated by her investments, now assured her a very comfortable income, far more than her earnings in the mid-1950s after the payments from New York had ceased. While her annual income had been in the neighbourhood of $3,000 or $4,000 around 1955, in 1970 it was some $20,000, ranging to $30,000 in the five years following.[170] Considering that in 1975 the average income was about $10,000, it could be said that Gabrielle Roy was not only living by her pen but living very well by it.

Such prosperity of course owed a great deal to the context of the 1960s. The rise of youth, the democratization and modernization of teaching, the feverish consumerism, and the cultural and ideological ferment characteristic of this period all were factors contributing to an enlarged reading public and hence to more prestige and influence for writers. To another phenomenon as well, the rise of a body of special-ized critics. In Quebec, as elsewhere in Canada, burgeoning universities opened their doors to professors of literature who were more numerous, more dynamic, and far better paid than their predecessors, and were making the study of national literature their priority. Armed with *la nouvelle critique*'s most formidable "schemas" and "approaches," these academics gave courses, founded magazines, wrote books, and directed theses, all focusing on home-grown authors and their works, which they addressed and interpreted from new perspectives, freed of the old infe-riority complexes vis-à-vis Europe, and centred on an updated, unapologetically Canadian or *québécois* specialization.

Gabrielle Roy and her works could only benefit from this momentum, since they were taken immediately to be proven local treasures, an illus-tration of the better quality the national literature could produce. Thus, they were the subject of a surge of dissertations, theses, and specialized studies by the most prominent academic critics of the day. Almost all "methods" were brought to bear: sociocriticism (Georges-André Vachon, Ben-Z. Shek); formal study (Réjean Robidoux and André Renaud, Jacques Blais); thematic criticism (André Brochu, Albert LeGrand, Jacques Allard); mythocriticism (Antoine Sirois, Jack Warwick); biographical interpretation (David Hayne); and psycho-analysis (Gérard Bessette).[171]

Teachers and students alike wrote to the famous novelist and sent her their articles or theses. To all she replied with grace and courtesy. Some insisted on seeing her in person. When she could, she received them politely, some in Quebec City, others at Petite-Rivière-Saint-François, and consented to the conversations – or "audiences" – they sought, transcriptions of which sometimes appeared in their books or articles, but not without first being revised by her.[172] One of these researchers received special treatment; this was Marc Gagné, a doctoral student at the Université Laval who was writing his thesis on the work and thought of Gabrielle Roy. Between 1969 and 1973, Gabrielle spent many afternoons answering his questions; she corresponded with him, opened her archives to him, allowed him to see certain of her still unpublished texts, in short, did everything possible to facilitate his work. In return he did some small services for her, being attentive and taking some work off her hands, such as correcting the proofs of the books reprinted by Beauchemin.

So Gabrielle Roy's distinction kept growing, and her body of work continued to stand as one of the most important of the national "corpus." In 1967, the publishing house Fides, to whom the novelist had refused permission to publish one of its "Classiques canadiens" studies on her ("I would rather not be too hallowed in my lifetime," she declared[173]), put out a "Dossier de documentation" on her for student use.[174] Two years later, there appeared the first book devoted entirely to Gabrielle Roy, written in English by Phyllis Grosskurth of the University of Toronto.[175] Finally, Marc Gagné's thesis, containing long passages of his conversations with the novelist, was published in 1973 by Les Éditions Beauchemin, titled *Visages de Gabrielle Roy, l'oeuvre et l'écrivain*.

More widespread recognition or more obvious celebrity than was enjoyed by the author of *Bonheur d'occasion* and *La Petite Poule d'Eau* at this time could hardly be imagined. And yet there was ambiguity in that this fame attached more to what Gabrielle Roy *had been* than what she was and was doing currently. Proof of this can be seen in the almost exclusive attention the critics gave to her very first book, which they never tired of commenting on, rereading, and interpreting, as if they had forgotten that she had written others since and was still writing books. Similarly, the treatment given her work (if not her person) in the press and learned studies often tended to portray it as belonging to the past; while it was regarded above all as "precursory," marking a turning point in local "tradition" and opening the way for current literature, its author was nevertheless categorized as belonging to a time gone by. In short, Gabrielle Roy, the *grande dame* of Quebec and Canadian literature, was increasingly a *classic* author – important, worthy of respect and of being reread, studied, and taught, but one who had already said what she had to say and was now outstripped by the much more modern form and content of present-day literature.

Hence, there is a striking contrast between the admiring interest shown Gabrielle Roy's first novels by the critics of this period and their varyingly veiled reservations over her new books. So it was, for example, when *La Montagne secrète* appeared in 1961. Without necessarily demonstrating the fury of the young Jean Paré, who compared the novel to "a picture for the Canadian National calendar," most reviewers, polite and respectful though they may have been, could not hide their disappointment. While admiring the nobility of the narration, Jean Éthier-Blais deplored the weakness of style that, he said, reminded him of "Bédier putting the legend of Tristan and Yseult into modern French," an opinion shared by Gilles Marcotte, Roger Duhamel, and Rita Leclerc. The descriptions ("appallingly outmoded, ridiculous even," wrote Gérard Tougas), the improbability of the character Pierre Cadorai, and in a general way the solemnity and heavy symbolism of the novel were also criticized. "Every admirer of Gabrielle Roy will finish this reading mortified," concluded Gérard Tougas.[176] This criticism, this disappointment, was echoed on almost all points in the English-Canadian press, where this new book of Miss Roy's was judged to be a failure.[177]

Five years later the reception given *La Route d'Altamont* and its translation, *The Road Past Altamont*, was more favourable. "Perhaps the author's finest book," Gilles Marcotte wrote; "an almost magical restraint," noted André Major; "a masterpiece, fragile as a flower, hard as a gem," concluded Phyllis Grosskurth.[178] But once again discordant voices were raised, particularly on the English side, reproaching the author for her unconvincing leading character and the sentimentality of her narration.[179] The reaction was lukewarm, neither too enthusiastic nor too hostile, respectful, not far from polite indifference. Gabrielle Roy was clearly no longer an author considered to have an integral place in the literature of the day. One was happy to read her, to know that she was still writing, but expected no further great revelations from her.

There is no question that between Gabrielle Roy's work and the period's expectations, the gap was increasingly pronounced. To begin with, she was no longer young, and in Quebec as in English Canada, the 1960s were years of triumphant youth, precocious writers, and soon the "psychedelic" culture and contestations of every description. In an environment like that, a novelist of Gabrielle's age could not help seeming out of step. This was especially so in Quebec, where almost everything made her different to the new generation of writers boisterously entering the scene on the coattails of the Quiet Revolution. To be sure, these writers recognized themselves in *Bonheur d'occasion* on account of its Montreal setting, social critique, and use of working-class language, but Gabrielle's other books and her ideas about literature, morality, or politics could not have been further removed from the winds blowing over

Quebec's "literature in ferment" at this time. Aesthetically for example, while Gabrielle by no means defended any doctrine or antiquated rule whose effects might lead her to condemn the cultural output of her day, she was by no means a revolutionary either, in the sense given the word at this time. Wanting to "subvert" traditional codes, to cultivate "rupture" and "audacity" through the use of *joual*, eroticism, derision, or New Novel and "paraliterary" techniques, this never even occurred to her and furthermore seemed to her in contradiction of what art and works of the mind should be. Similarly with the politicizing of literature and the militancy of writers; to her these ideas were contradictions. In 1961 she wrote:

> [Political] commitment is therefore a choice, but this choice could consist precisely in not committing oneself to passing ideologies that divide men more than they unite. At the risk of seeming paradoxical, I would say that a writer's commitment is above all a matter of freedom of mind. [. . .] Being a writer means above all being free. But let us not confuse freedom with language that is shocking, outrageous, with excesses and lack of restraint. Those who, on pretext of being free, write little books that are deliberately brazen seem to me the least free of writers. [. . .] Authentic independence has another aspect, another tone, and does not decline its responsibilities. The writer's true independence is his guarantee of integrity.[180]

Opinions like these obviously placed her outside the most powerful currents – and most vocal – in the literature of Quebec in those days. The same could be said of her ideological and political positions, which were hardly in tune with the thinking generally prevalent among the most "advanced" literary figures of the period – the youngest and most militant. Like many French-Canadian intellectuals of her generation and education, Gabrielle was in wholehearted agreement with the great reforms of the Quiet Revolution, which realized the platform the Liberals had been upholding since the Second World War – what they had been preaching in the desert for so many years. The former journalist for *Le Bulletin des agriculteurs* and *Le Canada*, the friend of Henri Girard and Jean-Marie Nadeau, who had admired the work of Thérèse Casgrain and Michel Chartrand, could only applaud the liquidation of the Duplessis regime and the modernization of the society and the State. By the same token, she sympathized with the feminism of the day that sought legal emancipation for married women and the right to control their own sexual lives.

This said, there was an aspect of the Quiet Revolution she could not identify with and opposed instinctively: nationalism. In the *Québec français* militancy of the day, the denunciation of Canadian "colonialism," and above all the rising tide of independentism, she saw only a retrograde and dangerous tendency toward self-absorption, rejection of others, intolerance, and hatred. To her, it was like returning to the stifling atmosphere of her birth milieu, backward-looking, vengeful, immobilized by distrust and resentment. The better organized the nationalist movement became and the more it asserted its claims, the more threatened and afraid she felt, and in a way rejected by her province of adoption. Which explains her reaction to those words of General de Gaulle's from the balcony of the Montreal City Hall in the summer of 1967. Heeding only her indignation, and despite her thinking about writers and political involvement, she immediately took up her pen and sent the Canadian Press a ringing communiqué in which she expressed both her anger and her love of Canada:

> I protest the lesson that General de Gaulle presumes to teach our country. I can see in it only disdain for the noble efforts undertaken in Canada with a view to real progress which resides nowhere if not first in a desire for understanding and mutual respect. [. . .]
>
> As a French-Canadian writer I have never suffered from a lack of freedom when I have wished to have it, either in Quebec or elsewhere in Canada. The fact that I was born in Manitoba and having spent my early years there I learned French well enough to be recognized later as a writer of the French language even in France proves it sufficiently, it seems to me.
>
> [. . .] With all my faith in the future of humankind, with all my strength, I enjoin my compatriots who consider themselves not as French in Canada but as French Canadians to demonstrate in favour of true freedom in Quebec.
>
> For it is in grave risk of being taken from us if by inertia we let it slip little by little into the hands of extremists or visionaries held back by dreams of the past rather than with eyes open to the realities of our human condition on this continent.
>
> Grandeur for us will consist not in undoing our ties but in perfecting them.[181]

This press release, which appeared in *Le Soleil* and *Le Devoir*,[182] was the only overtly political, even partisan, text that Gabrielle Roy ever wrote and made public. But the growing fear and insecurity provoked in her by the prevailing political climate in Quebec often found expression in her private correspondence. A little later in 1967, when the États généraux du Canada français were being held, she wrote to Bernadette, "What difficult times we're living through now in Quebec! On all sides tempers are frayed, and emotions are intense. Soon, I suppose, we're going to have to take sides against each other."[183] Her tone hardened subsequently. "This *fête* is going to end up having a murderous flavour," she observed in 1969 about the Saint-Jean-Baptiste celebrations.[184] In the autumn of this same year during demonstrations against the proposed Bill 63, she wrote again to Bernadette, "In Quebec these days we are awash in the most disquieting atmosphere of revolution and racism [. . .]. The climate in Quebec is becoming dangerous. It's enough to make you wonder if we'll be able to live here in freedom much longer. There's a fanatic and racist demon slumbering in all peoples, and once it's unleashed it's almost impossible to catch before it's brought violence, horror, and mortal fear."[185] Although she was "stunned" at the time, she was only half-surprised by the events of October 1970. The fears inspired in her by nationalism were joined now by frustrations for Marcel, who had just become actively involved in the strike of specialist physicians protesting the Bourassa government's introduction of health insurance. In short, everything in Quebec was going badly, it seemed to Gabrielle, who was alarmed not only by terrorism and separatism but also "the reign of theoreticians and technocrats" that she saw ahead on the horizon.[186]

After the de Gaulle affair, however, she was very careful not to make known her opinions publicly. With the October Crisis past, her political worries calmed; they would resurface episodically with other crises but without concrete actions ever resulting. For really she was not interested in politics; argument, conflict, and struggle mortified her; the only things she was in favour of were peace and understanding. The only thing that she personally was interested in was writing.

In January 1969 while she was suffering depression at New Smyrna Beach, she confided to Bernadette, "It's a cruel age in every way for anyone who's getting on in years . . . Before you can turn around, you're on the shelf. I know something about this, you know, for all the honours, which are like a kind of burial rite, in fact – rather depressing when they coincide with fewer readers and fewer sales . . . a decline of a sort . . ."[187] And yet despite the surrounding turmoil, despite the coolness of the critics, despite this feeling of "decline" and the fact that she often felt like an outsider in the literature of her time, she continued to work.

Secrets

Since finishing *La Route d'Altamont*, Gabrielle had been working on two novels. The first was titled "Baldur," after the name of a little place west of Somerset in the Pembina Mountain district, which in the manuscript becomes an immense domain where Prosper and Édouardina live. These characters were probably inspired partly by Uncle Excide and his wife, Luzina, who had died at the age of forty-seven, leaving eight children. The central theme of the novel is sex or, better, the servitude and "most frightful hidden woes" inflicted on Édouardina by her carnal relations with her husband. Prosper adores his wife, but Édouardina cannot yield to his desires without endangering her life, for she is in delicate health and unable to withstand the repeated pregnancies to which she is doomed by her married woman's duty. She dies before long in an aura of sainthood, while Prosper mopes in remorse and unassuaged lust.

Gabrielle wrote three, perhaps four versions of this tale,[188] which in the end she set aside because she saw that it was not a good book; the characters were not very believable, the action was almost non-existent, the writing forced, and the message rather too heavy-handed. The manuscript is nonetheless worthy of interest. Like certain pages of "La Saga d'Éveline," "Baldur" displays one of Gabrielle's biggest preoccupations of this period: the misery caused by sex. Far from uniting a man and a woman, the obligatory nature of physical love turns them into strangers to one another, if not enemies. The woman is always just a more or less consenting victim. To survive she must struggle against the instincts and desires of her husband. Édouardina is too good, too devoted to Prosper, to turn him away; thus she can only die, literally, from having made love. From this there emerges an extremely pessimistic view of woman's destiny – to be shackled to a man and to maternity by her biological and social condition, and thereby condemned to withering away and self-destruction, unless she renounces the flesh.

An echo of this theme is found in another novel that Gabrielle began at about this time, drawing on her memories of Ungava and particularly the picture of the young Inuk and her baby with the curly hair. To this story, one of a rape and tormented motherhood, Gabrielle first gave the title "Elsa." She worked on it during the summer of 1968 at Petite-Rivière-Saint-François. But the "feminine" theme of the novel was soon joined by another, which came directly from the "Man and His World" text of 1967, on the relationships between peoples. Whereas "Man and His World" puts forth a harmonious and idealized vision of these relationships, however, *La Rivière sans repos* presents a picture of these same relationships that is strained, not to say tragic, throughout Elsa's life, a long, wrenching experience with Elsa unable to reconcile in herself the world of whites and that of her own community of origin. Far from being made greater by her two-fold belonging, far from becoming "a citizen of the world" and a heroine of universal understanding among cultures, Elsa is a victim, someone of insecure identity – like Alexandre Chenevert in earlier days – and a defeated woman, crushed by her participation in this *Terre des hommes*.

This, the stark contrast between the ideas developed in the essay of 1967 and their "application" in *La Rivière sans repos*, provides a fine illustration of what can be called Gabrielle Roy's fictional instinct. For her as for the greatest novelists, fiction is never merely a means of promoting some theory or message, but the site where all theories and broad-based ideas are put to the test of reality and its complexities, at once turning them uncertain and problematical. In other words, while Gabrielle could proclaim her faith in humanity's "intercultural" progress in an essay like "Man and His World," in fiction this same faith – this fine, reasoned discourse – encounters the ultimate irony: the concrete existence of a character.

In September 1968 Gabrielle had the manuscript of her new novel (whose title was now "La Fleur boréale") typed by her current secretary, Marie-Blanche Devlin, and sent it to Joyce Marshall, whom she had already asked to be its translator. A month later, with the corrections finished and the title finally decided upon (*La Rivière sans repos*), she sent it to Harcourt Brace, her New York publisher, because this time she wanted both versions of her novel, English and French, to be published simultaneously.

Three weeks later, on 9 December 1968, Dan Wickenden, Gabrielle's new editor, wrote to say that *La Rivière sans repos* had been judged very severely by the reading committee and Harcourt Brace had decided not to publish it. Was this rejection based on purely literary considerations, as Wickenden declared? There is reason to doubt it. Gabrielle Roy's books had been selling poorly in the United States for years (*The Road Past Altamont* had sold barely more than 3,500 copies) and Harcourt Brace could not see this new work reversing the trend. If only the New York firm could sell directly on the Canadian market . . . but Gabrielle was opposed to it out of loyalty to McClelland & Stewart as much as literary patriotism. For Harcourt Brace, the profitability of the author of *The Tin Flute* was a thing of the past.

Gabrielle received Wickenden's letter like a bludgeon stroke. This was not only her *Rivière sans repos* being cast in the dust but also her twenty-year association with Harcourt Brace, and beyond that the diffusion of all her works in the United States. The wound to her self-respect was cruel, for in her whole career she had never before suffered a single rejection from a publisher and had always considered herself an author of international stature. "I feel like giving up, dear," she wrote to Joyce Marshall. "It is a heart wrench. But, I suppose, like so many of us these days, I have to face the reality that I am not a writer attuned to our time. [. . .] I wish I was a nurse, or a doctor, almost anything but what I am."[189]

She arrived at New Smyrna Beach in this frame of mind. The sea was as beautiful as the previous year, the sand on the beach as soft, and the welcome from Marie Dubuc as warm, yet Gabrielle's "head [was] empty, empty, empty"; she was stricken by "[a] kind of strange numbness"[190] that robbed her of interest in anything and left her in a state of moral and physical prostration from which it seemed to her she would never recover.

But the rejection of *La Rivière sans repos* by Harcourt Brace, painful though it may have been, was probably not the only factor behind this depression of the winter of 1968–1969. There were other things going on, other more private complications in Gabrielle's life that were hard on her nerves and deeply shook her confidence in herself and her inner composure.

First there was Adèle. While the *Rivière sans repos* manuscript was before the Harcourt Brace reading committee, Gabrielle wrote to Bernadette:

> I've just heard that two or three years ago Adèle was submitting a manuscript to almost all the publishers in Montreal, and elsewhere too [. . .], in which she told the story, her own spiteful version, of my childhood, my life. Were you aware of anything so abominable? Some of my friends were,

but hid it from me out of kindness. The other evening I was at some friends' house when the cat was finally let out of the bag and I learned the whole mortifying story. Someone there had seen the manuscript but didn't want to say much about it, except, of course, that it was intended to hurt me, and was as unkind as could be.[191]

Adèle had been meditating this manuscript for many years. She had never forgiven Gabrielle for that incident at Tangent, never lost an opportunity to rail against her sister, accusing her of being an opportunist, an ingrate, and of course a vile plagiarist. She even claimed that *La Route d'Altamont*, published in 1966, was "following in the footsteps" of her *La Montagne Pembina*, which however did not appear until 1970.[192] Gabrielle knew vaguely about the horrors Adèle was spreading around about her, if only because of the letters Adèle wrote her, which were full of bile and "cruelty as I've seen only with her in my life."[193] Still, certain that Anna and Bernadette would be able to prevent the worst, she paid little attention and was a good sport, even inquiring about Adèle's well-being and declaring her willingness to make up with her.

But the bitterness was so deeply rooted in Adèle's heart that nothing was going to turn her from her lust for vengeance. It seems that it was around 1962 or 1963, while she was living in Quebec, that she wrote the dreadful manuscript to which she would give a title destined to underline the difference between Gabrielle and herself: "Les Deux Sources de l'inspiration: l'imagination et le coeur," but whose subtitle revealed the true intention: "Première partie d'une étude psychologique sur un auteur bien connu."[194] This text of some fifty pages, bearing the pseudonym Irma Deloy (a partial anagram of M.-Adèle Roy), is an out-and-out rant against Gabrielle, aiming to "unmask" her true character by recounting the story of her life and relationships with her family members "without pulling punches." Everything is there: the adolescent's caprices, the tightfistedness of the young woman thirsting for glory, the abandonment of the poverty-stricken old mother, the fishy relationship with Henri Girard, and of course the shameless plundering of the works of her own sister, the narrator, whose own behaviour was never motivated by anything but the strictest virtue and the purest impartiality.

As was her custom, Adèle had typed several copies of her manuscript. She had very likely tried to place it with a publisher, as Gabrielle thought, given her long-standing frenzy to publish. Faced with repeated failure she turned to another strategy, depositing copies of her text in archives and libraries for the benefit and edification of "researchers of the future."[195] Thus it was that in the autumn of 1968 a typed manuscript of "Les Deux Sources" found its way to the Université de Montréal, into the archives of the Centre de documentation des lettres canadiennes-françaises, which was housed in the central tower of the university and run by Réginald Hamel, to whom Adèle declared as she turned over her text, "I'm going to show you that my sister is a bitch." At a conference not long after, Hamel repeated this to Ben-Z. Shek of the University of Toronto. Shek, who was writing a thesis on French-Canadian fiction, had been in contact with Gabrielle for nearly two years.

When she left for New Smyrna Beach in December 1968, Gabrielle did not know about the manuscript having been deposited at the Université de Montréal, and Marcel, who had been tipped off by Bernadette, who had been informed of it by Shek, was careful not to tell her. She did not hear about it until her return and was all the more upset by it. "I'm dreadfully shaken. [. . .] I'm afraid of Adèle, afraid of such a long-nurtured malice towards me"; "[. . .] it hurts so much it makes me feel nauseated."[196] In self-defence and in an effort to understand, she attributed Adèle's behaviour to a psychological disorder. "Something like this is the work of a sick person. In fact, I've thought for quite some time that Adèle might be a lot sicker than Clémence. [. . .] I realize now that her hatred of me is implacable, close to lunatic."[197]

This theory of mental illness, which Marcel concurred with fully and Bernadette did not contest, was also a way for Gabrielle to protect herself against all the threat that Adèle's "revelations" might conceivably offer. For the mirror that her sister was holding up to her showed a face that a part of herself could not fail to recognize, the face of ambition, the pampered child who had flown her family, the daughter who had abandoned her mother and chosen orphanhood in order to reach her goals. Gabrielle would have liked to wipe away this face of her misconduct and guilt, forget it, redeem it once and for all, but it haunted her, clung to her conscience and never really left her in peace. In a sense, all of her life and all of her work amounted to a quest for this cleansing, this redemption, or rather for this reconciliation between her face of yesteryear and that of the woman she wished with all her powers to be today, at last a woman at peace and innocent. But now here was this manuscript of Adèle's, churlishly bringing everything back to the surface. It had not only reawakened her inner uncertainties, it was endangering the public image of herself that she had been trying to build through her writings,

With Adrienne Choquette and Medjé Vézina, around 1965. (NLC NL-19165)

Medjé Vézina, Gabrielle Roy, Alice Lemieux-Lévesque, Simone Bussières.
(NLC NL-19179)

A gathering of friends on the Île d'Orléans. *From left to right*: Marcel, Madeleine Bergeron, Jean-Paul Lemieux, Madeleine Chassé, Gabrielle. *Hidden behind Gabrielle*: Jori Smith. (Madeleine Bergeron coll.)

Snowshoeing in "the tundra" at Notre-Dame-des-Laurentides. (NLC NL-19176)

Gabrielle and Marcel in their garden at Petite-Rivière-Saint-François. (NLC NL-19138)

Sister Léon (Bernadette) and Clémence at Petite-Rivière-Saint-François, summer 1965. (F. Ricard coll.)

Clémence in her room at Otterburne, around 1970. (NLC NL-19142)

Sister Berthe Valcourt
and Gabrielle with
Bernadette, March 1970.
(NLC NL-19177)

In the cottage at Petite-Rivière-Saint-François, around 1970. (Berthe Simard photo; NLC NL-19163)

In the garden at Petite-Rivière-Saint-François, around 1970. (Berthe Simard photo; NLC NL-17531)

The author of *Cet été qui chantait* (*Enchanted Summer*), by Krieber, 1972.
(NLC NL-19145)

Gabrielle Roy receiving the insignia of a Companion of the Order of Canada from the hands of Governor-General Roland Michener, 1967. (F. Ricard coll.)

Gabrielle Roy's work area the Château Saint-Louis apartment; on the wall, a portrait of her painted by Pauline Boutal. (NLC NL-19154)

Gabrielle Roy by John Reeves, 1975.

interviews, and even her correspondence with her friends. In short, Adèle's manuscript was threatening to destroy all that she had so patiently forged over so many years.

It was in this state of desolation mingled with panic that she flew off to Florida, her heart heavy with the humiliation so freshly inflicted on her by the letter of rejection from Harcourt Brace. But even this was not all. Late in 1968, her relationship with her husband had never been worse. It had been deteriorating for years in fact, and by now Marcel and Gabrielle were truly strangers to one another. Their life together was a kind of hell.

Outside, in the few interviews in which she spoke about Marcel, Gabrielle let it be understood that they formed a perfectly harmonious couple whose "incredible success" could serve as a model for all.[198] But their close friends knew that the truth was very different, and in reality the model couple fought constantly like cat and dog. Marcel, who loved parties, going out, good food and drink, accused Gabrielle of making them live like monks. She resented his lack of discipline, his apathy, his inability to be interested in anything serious. Each laid the frustrations and regrets that come with age at the other's door, and each flung them in the other's teeth at the slightest quarrel. And there were many quarrels, some of them ugly, particularly when Marcel had been drinking (which happened with increasing frequency) or when Gabrielle was more on edge than usual; then the invectives flew, and the lamentations, and there were tears. Afterwards they would be at daggers drawn for days. At Petite-Rivière or Quebec City their rows even happened occasionally in front of friends, who, though tempted, dared not intervene. While some of them sympathized with Marcel and considered him a victim of Gabrielle's selfishness and vanity, accusing her of stifling him, treating him like a slave, and preventing him from living as he might like, others commiserated with poor Gabrielle, who had to do everything herself without ever being able to count on help from Marcel, a weakling, a mollycoddle, an overgrown child.

Whatever their respective faults, the climate between the spouses after twenty years of marriage was becoming more and more strained. They had nothing in common to tell the truth, in any case none of the things that couples normally have in common, like children, property, a shared passion, or carnal complicity. Only two things really held them together. The first was Gabrielle's work, which came before all, justified all, and whose success was important to both of them. The second was money, which they did not necessarily want in vast quantities but which both of them worried about; they were afraid of being short of it, suspected others of wanting to pry it out of them, and (to put it mildly) took care not to throw it out the window. Otherwise there was almost nothing they agreed on, and both felt imprisoned in a life that weighed on them. Gabrielle would confide later that if divorce had been as easy and acceptable then as it became in the following decade, she would certainly have resorted to that solution. Short of that, she left as often as possible for other parts or withdrew to Petite-Rivière-Saint-François, while Marcel stayed alone in Quebec City, leading his own life.

And so they lived in their own worlds, from which in each case the other was virtually excluded. For the world of women that Gabrielle moved in, there was a corresponding world of men that was her husband's. A world that was equally closed and homogenous, the meeting place of a few physicians and especially artists with whom Marcel spent most of his time. It could not have escaped Gabrielle that this milieu in which he felt both happy and understood was composed largely of homosexuals. At what moment exactly she discovered that Marcel himself was a homosexual remains a mystery to which neither her correspondence nor remarks of those close to her have provided clues.

Had she realized his tendencies when they were living in France and Marcel would occasionally go to homosexual theatres with friends, or did she have to wait until they had moved to Quebec City and Marcel had a lover? The two men had met in the very early 1960s when M. C. was studying at the École des Beaux-arts in Quebec City under Jean-Paul Lemieux. Since the young man ardently wished to meet Gabrielle Roy, Jean-Paul Lemieux's wife, Madeleine, offered to bring him to the launching of a book by Alice Lemieux-Lévesque, which she knew the Carbottes would be attending. But Gabrielle was out of town, so that M. C. found himself conversing with Marcel, who after the launching took him to dinner at the Hôtel Clarendon and then invited him home for a *pousse-café*. There in the Château Saint-Louis apartment began an affair between M. C., aged twenty, and Marcel, aged forty-five, which was to last over twenty years. At times a euphoric affair, for Marcel was an experienced and sensuous initiator; at times tempestuous, for he was also a demanding and jealous lover, which did not stop him from having flings with other men of their milieu.

Because of his social standing and the period's attitudes, Marcel was obliged to keep his love life secret and not give rise to rumours, which could have spread so quickly in a tight-knit environment like upper-crust Quebec City society. But he escaped often with his friends for weekends in Montreal or elsewhere, and spent almost all his free time in their company. One summer while Gabrielle was at Petite-Rivière-Saint-François he invited one of them to move into the Château Saint-Louis apartment with him, and the two of them lived it up royally. How could Gabrielle not have known or, at least, how could she not have had strong suspicions? Without any doubt at all, Marcel's behaviour could only have deepened the gulf between them, a sexual gulf certainly, but a moral and psychological one as well. Hardly any wonder that in her husband's behaviour Gabrielle should find one more reason to feel, if not betrayed, at least overwhelmed by disappointment and perhaps a burden of guilt, both increasingly hard to bear, not to mention the threat to her public image of a possible revelation of her husband's "abnormal" tendencies.

She never mentioned Marcel's homosexuality in her letters, nor did he in his. Often during this period, however, she expressed worry over his ways, his attitudes, and the sudden changes of mood he was subject to. In June 1968 she wrote to her sister-in-law Antonia, "Marcel is suffering again this summer from a kind of neurasthenia which makes him morose and hard to bear. [. . .] I'm the one on whom his ill humour falls."[199] Shortly after her arrival at New Smyrna Beach several months later, she confided to Adrienne her worries about Marcel's "nervous system, [which is] so unsettled it frightens me sometimes,"[200] worries that were still with her in September 1969 when she wrote to Bernadette, the only one of her sisters to feel affection for Marcel:

> I confess that at times I'm worried about him and deeply discouraged, because it's his very nature that's at the root of his troubles and he doesn't seem able to change the way he lives. You've no idea what a complex person he is. [. . .] With people who have nervous illnesses like Marcel's, the trouble is that while they can't cure themselves they won't accept advice from people close to them.[201]

Had Gabrielle told Bernadette the truth about her sexual relations with Marcel? Was this the "particular sorrow in [her] life, the one [Dédette] knew about and was so upset by," as an enigmatic passage says in *Enchantment and Sorrow*?[202] Perhaps.

After the Storm

So it was a broken, downhearted woman racked by worry and disappointment who landed at New Smyrna Beach in December 1968. At first Gabrielle stayed with Marie Dubuc and her new friend Geneva, with whom she took the same excursion through the Everglades as the year before; "the weather was beautiful," she reported, "but my heart wasn't in it."[203] On New Year's Day she moved into a small apartment with windows for walls, where she tried as best she could to rebuild her health and morale. As she told her "good Drienne" the day after moving, "I'm going to make a heroic effort to do as you advise me, to take the sun, go for long walks by the sea, I'm going to try everything possible but something tells me that this year it won't work, that I'll have to find another means of salvation . . . and I'm waiting."[204] Too depressed to work, she fell back on reading, especially *L'Oeuvre au noir* by Marguerite Yourcenar, which had just won the Prix Fémina ("I wonder if I've ever read a more generous, more majestic, and at the same time more human and poignant work"[205]); but most of all, she tried "to do nothing other than let myself live, like a plant."[206]

After a few weeks the cure began to bear fruit. Gradually the moral and physical dilapidation Gabrielle was in when she arrived yielded to the sunshine, the open air, the sound of the ocean, the complete rest, and Marie's presence. On February 1 she announced a resurrection to her friend Alice:

> Just listen to this or rather just read this: you wake one fine morning with the feeling at the back of your mind that it's February, it's winter, the climate and the human condition are cruel, but on your lips and on your tongue you taste the sweetness of a summer's day in the country, listening to the birds in every corner, raising the blind and seeing a radiant sky and everywhere, on the roof, the telephone wires, the smallest twig, robins come from Canada, not by the hundreds or the thousands but incalculable numbers to gorge on the sweet little berries of the palmetto, and it's their noisy, happy gathering, and it's the magnificence of the air and the eternal song of the waves gathering you as you wake, still bruised from your thoughts while you were sleeping, and suddenly you feel yourself come alive again as if you've just set foot in a land that is truly yours. That is what happened to me this morning . . .

"I won't go as far as to say I've become as gay as a lark," she adds, "but I think I'm going to begin again to love creation." The slope was a long one to climb, however, and the progress she made from day to day was still fragile. "The fact is, M'Alice, I'm coming up from far down, from a great depth, and I probably mustn't expect to stay afloat entirely as yet."[207] But by mid-March, when it came time to return to Quebec City, the cure seemed finally to be complete. "By and large my stay in Florida has been good for me, although I didn't succeed in doing any work. I just couldn't. [...] Yet I do think my health has improved."[208] Her health, and also her composure and desire to pick up the thread of her life again. For the wounds of the autumn, while not yet completely healed, now seemed less cruel; or in any event were less important than what she had left to accomplish.

As far as Marcel's homosexuality was concerned, she really had no choice but to accept it. With her long-standing fear and abhorrence of sexual relations, did she not herself have to bear a certain share of responsibility for the state of affairs? In fact, by satisfying Marcel, M. C. freed Gabrielle of her wifely "duties," which relieved her of suffering from Marcel's frustrations or feeling guilt for her frigidity. In its fashion, her husband's affair thus contributed to what harmony there was in their life together. Consequently, she wrote him shortly before leaving New Smyrna Beach, "what is important is to preserve the friendship and esteem that are still, thank God, very healthy between us, and for which we should express gratitude, [for] it doesn't happen so frequently."[209]

In reality there was less esteem and friendship in their relationship henceforth than a kind of half-gentle, half-bitter caution, which made it hard for them to be close but at least prevented them from clashing too hurtfully. While forbidding either to invade the other's privacy, this relationship allowed them still to take an interest in one another, each wishing the other peace of mind and safety, if not happiness. Living at a respectful distance, at once caring and indifferent, it could hardy be said that there was love between them still, but neither could it be said that there was hate. They lived quite simply side by side as do many aging couples, joined by a bond both close and ambiguous, which paradoxically keeps strengthening despite misunderstandings and causes for dissatisfaction or resentment; for the most powerful bond of all is the one created between two people by the fear of finding themselves alone in the world, with no home port and no one to talk to, complain to, and come back to when one has had enough of oneself and one's freedom. Having arrived at this *modus vivendi*, neither Marcel nor Gabrielle would breach it thereafter.

More urgent was the situation created by Adèle's appalling manuscript, which had been hanging over Gabrielle's reputation since autumn. Anxious to make it impossible for her sister to do harm before it was too late, Gabrielle took action as soon as she returned from Florida. To this end, she called on her most stalwart allies, starting with Bernadette, who had inherited the authority in the family that had been Anna's. Sister Léon wrote to Adèle in response to Gabrielle's request that she try to bring her to reason.[210] Adèle's reply arrived promptly, as acerbic as usual: she had no lessons to learn from anyone, especially from the sister who had "taken off at twenty in the hour of our parents' greatest poverty" and could therefore keep her "sanctimonious preachings" to herself.[211] Germain's widow, Antonia, came to the rescue, with no more success than Bernadette. Then Gabrielle decided to stir up her friends. First Ben Shek tried intervening with Réginald Hamel, who had received the manuscript at the Université de Montréal, but Adèle on learning of it flew into a rage: "I will not allow the Anglo-Saxons to stick their noses into this," she wrote to Hamel. [. . .] "Today when contestation is everywhere, when limits are crumbling, when priests are overturning the altars of their God, the Truth can and ought to be declared!"[212]

Next Adrienne Choquette interceded with her friend Victor Barbeau, the venerable president of the Académie canadienne-française, who spoke to René de Chantal, dean of the Faculté des Lettres de l'Université de Montréal, who forced Réginald Hamel to withdraw Adèle's manuscript from his Centre de documentation. The case was thus put to rest and Gabrielle could breathe easy. To show her appreciation to Victor Barbeau, she gave him her unpublished story "L'arbre" for publication in *Les Cahiers de l'Académie canadienne-française*.

As for Adèle, "there's no longer any question of my giving [her] a cent," Gabrielle declared to Bernadette in June 1969. "I've come to the end of my patience with her and I'd rather hear no more of her."[213] She would fairly soon come around to feeling better toward her sister, however; she may not have forgiven her but at least bore her no malice. Although she no longer wished to see her or correspond with her, she would enquire after her health and well-being and send small sums of money for her. Adèle did not know that this money came from Gabrielle;

if she did she would have refused it, as she had done already in the past. The two, both advancing in age, were more estranged than ever. In 1971 Adèle, at seventy-eight, came to live in Ste-Foy, not far from Gabrielle's. The sisters never telephoned or spent two seconds together. If they met in the street it was by chance and without being certain of recognizing one another. Gabrielle wrote:

> The other day I saw pass by me an old woman, sick-looking, haggard, wretchedly dressed, apparently half blind. It was only after that I thought I'd more or less recognized my sister Adèle, and I had a shock I can't get over. (I haven't seen her for something like fifteen years, after all.) This picture of desolation and poverty haunts me . . .[214]

Old, poor as a church mouse, quavering of voice she may have been, but Adèle had not said her last word.

Of the various concerns that had triggered Gabrielle's depression of the winter of 1968–1969, the one most quickly resolved was that involving *La Rivière sans repos*. Barely a month after the rejection from Harcourt Brace, Joyce Marshall obtained Gabrielle's permission to send the manuscript to Jack McClelland, who agreed immediately to publish it. This was the original manuscript in French, which Gabrielle had not yet submitted to a Montreal publisher because she wanted to make sure that it would appear also in English, considering that her reading public was just as much English as French, if not more. As early as the end of January 1969 therefore, it was agreed that the book would come out in a translation by Joyce Marshall, who set to work at once. As soon as she was back from New Smyrna, Gabrielle too set to work, corresponding regularly with Joyce and taking advantage of the fact that her book was not yet published in French to make numerous corrections, some of which the translator found felicitous and others arguable.

At this time *La Rivière sans repos* was only the manuscript of the novel with the two characters Elsa and her son, Jimmy. The three "Eskimo stories" that precede it in the French edition did not yet exist. Gabrielle wrote these stories at Petite-Rivière-Saint-François during the summer of 1969, beginning with "Le téléphone," followed by "Le fauteuil roulant," and finally "Les satellites."[215] This addition only began all over again the endless process of correction and rewriting, which was longer for this book than any other, with the exception of *Alexandre Chenevert*. Even at night Gabrielle was "disturbed by this nightmare of seeing my manu-script covered with errors, crossings out, to be redone almost entirely."[216] In October 1969, after the final French text of *La Rivière sans repos* had been revised by Victor Barbeau, she decided to go to Toronto herself for intensive work sessions on the English version with Joyce Marshall. She was enchanted with her two weeks there. She stayed at the Westbury Hotel but spent her days and took her meals at Joyce's, with Joyce waiting on her hand and foot. Jack McClelland, whom she had not seen for many a year, dined her lavishly.

Back in Quebec City, she briefly considered leaving for the South to escape the winter but had to give up the idea because of a problem with a foot. In January she underwent an operation that left her on crutches for a time. This episode gave her even more time to polish her manu-script and find last-minute changes.

At last the final corrections and the translation of the complete book – novel and "Eskimo stories" – were finished in February 1970. Only the English title remained to be found; "River Beyond Time" was considered but set aside in favour of *Windflower*, which Gabrielle and Jack were lukewarm about but to which they resigned themselves in the end for lack of anything better. This was when Jack, on the strength of his pub-lisher's nose, decided to drop the three stories and publish only the novel. Gabrielle bowed to his decision, although, as she confided to Joyce, "I'm a little sad about the three stories, [. . .] for, after all, they are part of the story, of the theme, of the whole adventure."[217]

Once everything was settled for the English edition, the only thing left to decide was who in Quebec would publish the original French version. For *La Route d'Altamont*, Gabrielle had spurned Les Éditions Beauchemin, but the firm now had a new literary director, Paul-Marie Paquin, with whom she had much more cordial relations. The contract for *La Rivière sans repos* was signed in March 1970, the author deciding that the Beauchemin edition would contain the three "Eskimo stories" that McClelland & Stewart had chosen not to publish.[218]

Although all was ready by the end of the winter, the books were not out – in the English and French editions – until the following September and October. Meanwhile, Gabrielle was totally occupied by another event, another *oeuvre*: managing Bernadette's death.

Elegy to Bernadette

At seventy-two, Sister Léon-de-la-Croix was a very active woman. Although she had officially retired from teaching in 1966, she still gave diction lessons in the schools of St-Boniface and took on all kinds of small tasks for her sister nuns at the Académie Saint-Joseph. A good deal of her time was devoted to family matters, for which she felt responsible since Anna's death. Clémence kept her very busy, but she concerned herself also with Adèle and, across the miles, with Gabrielle, for whom she felt unbounded devotion and affection. Even the prodigal son Rodolphe received her attentions; shortly before New Year's Day 1970, Sister Léon travelled to British Columbia to take care of him, for he was increasingly unwell. Drunk as always, Rodolphe received her with foul language and ridiculed her concern for him. This was Bernadette's last journey. A few weeks later the doctor found that she had kidney cancer and prescribed an operation. On March 30, without telling her that she was dying, the nuns had her taken to the infirmary of the Académie, where they would watch over her night and day until her last breath.

As soon as she heard the bad news Gabrielle decided to go to her sister's bedside. She arrived in St-Boniface on March 21 and telephoned Adèle to ask if she could stay in her apartment. After saying some spiteful things, Adèle hung up on her. It was Antonia, Gabrielle's sister-in-law, who took her in, and then her cousin Léa, daughter of Uncle Excide Landry. Until she left on April 7 she spent nearly all her time at the dying woman's bedside, divided between the pain of watching her sister go – "almost unbearable heartache"[219] – and the pleasure of being reunited with her, for she and Bernadette had not seen one another since the summer of 1965 at Petite-Rivière-Saint-François. It was this memory that brought them closest, with Bernadette tirelessly evoking the river, the birds, the islands, the mountains, the friendship of Berthe and Marcel, and Gabrielle for her part joining gladly "in the game of dreaming of Petite-Rivière."[220]

Although there is virtually no mention of it in Gabrielle's letters to friends in Quebec at this time, she was to say in *Enchantment and Sorrow* that in the course of these days she discovered what a tortured soul was hidden beneath Bernadette's apparent candour and joviality.[221] Knowing that death was near, instead of seeking refuge in her faith, she was clinging to life and refusing to leave the world of which, as a nun, she "[hadn't] seen or known anything," although she had been so curious and enchanted with everything. And so now "she felt she'd been deprived of her share of earthly happiness" and was almost "rebelling against God." To console her, Gabrielle tried to convince her that it was perhaps she, with the freedom she had enjoyed all her life, who had best seen the marvels of creation.

"As a result," Gabrielle would say later, "Dédette and I, who'd never had much chance to get to know each other, became so close we began to feel inseparable."[222] Before leaving she made a "covenant of prayer" with her dying sister: Bernadette would offer her sufferings for Gabrielle's peace, and Gabrielle, once back in Quebec City, would go to mass every day for Bernadette's repose. She would respect it scrupulously, attending the morning or evening mass at Saint-Dominique Church next door to the Château Saint-Louis.

But this single mystic bond was not enough for Gabrielle. As soon as she was home, she added another, with letters: as long as Bernadette lived she wrote her a letter every day, the more surely to be and remain at her side across the miles. Between April 8 and May 24 she wrote forty-three letters to her, faithfully, without missing a single day except when obliged to by an intermittent postal strike.[223] At the Académie Saint-Joseph, each letter was opened by the nuns and read to Bernadette, save the last five which arrived too late.

Of the two thousand letters of Gabrielle Roy's that have been found so far, these are certainly among the finest. Perhaps because they are the "purest," the freest of any kind of message or information, of any utilitarian function. Nothing more is expressed in them than the simple desire to speak to the other, to be close to her, and not to allow the thread of "inner conversation"[224] and deep friendship uniting the two of them to be broken. "I'd like [my letters] to fly straight to you like the birds of spring, bearers of my love for you, the tenderness I feel for you . . ."[225] Like those one addresses to a person who has just lost someone dear, these letters of consolation strive to deliver Bernadette from the grief caused by her own death by reminding her what bliss awaits her and how much she is loved.

> My thought is that you are as dear to God's heart as any thing of beauty he has created in this world – flowers, the sunset, dawn, the song of a bird, the wind, or waving grasses.[226]

Gabrielle was in a way addressing this one-way correspondence also to herself. While consoling Bernadette, she was consoling herself for losing Bernadette. And in particular, by writing her every day she was putting herself in the dying woman's place, steeping herself in Bernadette's spirit, capturing Bernadette's view of the world and of those around her – and hence of herself, Gabrielle. For it was not only Bernadette for whom these letters were intended to provide "a shield that protects,"[227] it was also Gabrielle as Bernadette saw and cherished her and as Gabrielle with all her soul yearned to see herself. Coming so close to Bernadette, seeking through this writing to become one with her and share the sanctity conferred by her approaching death, Gabrielle was clinging to what she knew to be the most precious and authentic side of herself, which neither Adèle nor any one else close to her had seen: her own goodness of heart, her own capacity for saintliness. It was in this above all that Bernadette's death achieved what Anna's had begun six years earlier; it confirmed and deepened the inner conversion that was taking Gabrielle further and further away from what she had been and closer to an ideal of herself whose realization or construction was to be the major preoccupation of her last years.

Bernadette breathed her last on Monday, 25 May 1970. The next day Gabrielle wrote to Antonia, "I think we can now pray to her as a saint."[228] And a few days later, to the Mother Superior of the Académie Saint-Joseph:

> I miss her from morning to night and keep looking for her everywhere, in the passing clouds, the wind in the treetops, in her snapshots, in my own heart, and I feel sometimes that even removed from the visible world for us she is still near by, still all attentive to my well-being.[229]

Then life resumed its course. In the first week of June Gabrielle moved with her grief to Petite-Rivière. Little by little, the emptiness of these early weeks following Dédette's death began to yield to the soothing effect of the place and to Berthe's presence, and made way for other cares. Cares over Clémence certainly, to whom we shall return, but also the usual concerns of a writer with a new book about to be published.

At the beginning of autumn 1970 *La Rivière sans repos* and *Windflower* came out as planned. On both sides of the Ottawa River the critics and journalists were somewhat inattentive, preoccupied as they were with the far more spectacular fare being offered by a counter-culture in full swing. Compared to what "the new writing" was producing, Gabrielle Roy's book seemed decidedly old-hat and there were few journalists who really paid it any attention at all. Most who did were lukewarm in their judgments, like Roger Duhamel, who did not think highly of the "Eskimo Stories," and Jean Éthier-Blais, who, while praising the novel, invited his readers to see in the story of Elsa and the Eskimo genocide a presage of things to come for the Québécois within Canada.[230] This, it must be remembered, was a period of heady nationalism in Quebec; the provincial election of 1970 had created a climate of extreme tension and the demands had become particularly clamorous. That Gabrielle Roy had chosen this moment to publish her book in English and French simultaneously (the English edition even slightly ahead of the French) had done nothing to advance her cause in certain circles; denunciations were hurled.[231]

Meanwhile, things were not going much better for *Windflower* in English Canada, where Gabrielle Roy's star was continuing to fade despite her determination to be considered a truly "Canadian" author. The *Globe and Mail*, where Bill Deacon had once reigned, published a devastating review;[232] sales did not take off, reaching barely 2,500 copies in the four months following publication. In Quebec, however, where Gabrielle Roy remained a popular author despite what the critics had to say, Beauchemin succeeded in selling out two printings of 4,000 copies each in less than a year, aided perhaps by the Prix Athanase-David that the author won during this time, in spring 1971.

All in all, it cannot be said that this last book was a success. But Gabrielle was not really affected by the scant attention paid her by the critics; she was beginning to be used to it. It is true as well that current events were not playing in her favour. Throughout the autumn of 1970, people and the media were obsessed with the October Crisis and the doctors' strike, and Gabrielle was as much preoccupied by these events as by the fortunes of her book. It was partially to escape this agitated atmosphere (which affected Marcel's mood in particular) that she decided to leave once more for the South. Instead of Florida, where her last stay had not been the happiest, this time she chose Arizona, which she had discovered seven years earlier and where she had always hoped to return.

She was attracted not only by the scenery and the climate. First of all, Phoenix was the city where Anna had died, a place eminently propitious for reflection on mourning and the inner conversion under way in Gabrielle since the death of Bernadette. But Phoenix also held the attraction of Anna's eldest son, Fernand Painchaud and his wife, Léontine, whom Gabrielle had come to know during her previous trip, and whom she could count on to look after her appropriately. There, it seemed to her, she could lead the gentle, meditative, slower life she was yearning for.

She would not be disappointed. Alerted that she would arrive on December 15, Fernand and Léontine had found her a comfortable motel on the outskirts of the city not far from the Blue Skies Trailer Park where they lived near their two adopted sons, Reynald and Roger, who were now married. Moreover, since Fernand's work at the race track (where he was a ticket vendor) allowed him a great deal of free time during the day, he and his wife took the visitor under their wing; "[they] shower me with the most delicate attentions," she wrote.[233] They invited her to take all her meals with them, respected her diet, and threw a little Christmas party in her honour; they were always available to go with her on her walks or take her on drives into the mountains round about. For Gabrielle never ceased to admire the harsh, wild vegetation of the region. She wrote to Adrienne:

> This country is different from Florida. First, for me in Florida it was above all the great sound of the waves retreating, the beautiful beach of white sand. Here – from the moment you leave the city – it's the harshness of the desert, but I've always loved – almost as much as the sea – lands scorched by the sun, that are dry and impoverished of everything, except light. At times when I walk along little streets partly developed where there are patches of country, patches of desert all over, from the sounds, the smells, a certain quality to the air, I would swear I was back in my beloved Provence, probably because I knew it when I was young, and this makes me feel all young again.[234]

As usual she read a great deal (in particular *Kamouraska* by Anne Hébert, which was just out) and stayed in contact with those close to her through correspondence. Her niece Yvonne, Jos's elder daughter, came to visit at the end of January. Yvonne, who was now in her fifties, had married an officer in the American army and was living in Texas. The two women had not seen each other for nearly forty years. It does not seem that Gabrielle did any writing while she was in Phoenix. At the beginning she was too tired and was trying only to relax and benefit from the climate. Then when the time came that she might have got back to work, the news arrived of her Prix David, which so excited her she could no longer concentrate at all. When she returned to Quebec City on February 22, tanned but agitated, she had no new manuscript in her luggage.

She began nothing that spring, the excitement of the Prix David leaving her in worse state than before her departure for Arizona. On March 14 she wrote to Antonia, "Here I am tired to death now that the flame of overexcitement has burned down – and it's always this way with me. All fire and frenzy . . . then nothing left but cold ashes. Thus have I lived."[235] During this time Marcel was having difficulty accepting his new working conditions. He and Gabrielle were both feeling increasingly outstripped by the events of the day. They were bewildered by it all and began to think of retirement, which they could take elsewhere, they said, if things turned really bad in Quebec. This plan of expatriation was just talk and they did nothing to realize it, but the ill-ease it betrayed was nonetheless real, the sign of old age gradually catching up with them. In any event catching up with Gabrielle, who was more than ever obsessed by the need for tranquillity and withdrawal into herself. She confided to Antonia:

> The world here is topsy turvy. [. . .] You feel yourself get out of kilter just by thinking about it. I know now that there's no solution, nothing else to do but find a refuge and try to live there peacefully, busy with humble eternal chores, one's flowers, one's garden. I'd like to get myself back to work. There alone is salvation . . .[236]

Feeling the need to put herself back to work, flee the century's disruptions, draw closer to "eternal" realities – this was her state of mind when she moved back to Petite-Rivière-Saint-François at the beginning of summer 1971.

This was when news arrived of another death, Rodolphe's. The last of her brothers had succumbed to a heart attack at the age of seventy-one. Gabrielle, who had not seen Rodolphe since leaving Manitoba thirty-five years before, had quite simply fallen out with him since he had several times attempted to extort money from her friends by using her name. Bernadette had tried to reconcile them but in vain. In the past year or two, thanks to Jos's son Bob Roy and his wife, Brenda, who had become fond of him, Rodolphe had mended his ways a bit and had attempted to make up with Gabrielle; he had written to her (in English), had taken her side against Adèle's pernicious writings and, sensing the approach of death, had generally made efforts to return to her good graces through demonstrations of fidelity and devotion. "Poor wretch!" Gabrielle wrote. "After not giving a damn for the family for three-quarters of his life, now all he wants are whatever letters, visits, and reconciliations he can raise."[237] But she did not go to Vancouver for his funeral; the only family member attending was Adèle, who succeeded in preventing the cremation of the body, contrary to the wishes of the deceased. Rodolphe's death inspired neither grief nor any particular feeling in Gabrielle, unless it pacified her resentment toward him, now that he could do nothing more to hurt her nor she to benefit him. In the months following, she would offer to settle his debts, but Bob Roy, citing "Rod's" honour, would turn the offer down.

When she learned of Rodolphe's death, Gabrielle had not long since begun writing a new book. "When I begin writing a book" she told Berthe, "I get the terrifying feeling that I'm going to shut myself up for ages in a kind of dungeon . . . [reaping] both my greatest misery and unspeakable joy."[238] Misery and joy intermingled, enchantment and sorrow, this was the background from which *Cet été qui chantait* would emerge.

Gabrielle drew her immediate inspiration for these texts from her familiar surroundings and company at Petite-Rivière, where she had been spending all her summers for nearly fifteen years. Over this time she had already begun a number of stories set there, mostly using stories that Berthe would tell her, but she had never succeeded in finding the form or tone she wanted.[239] Only one of these abandoned manuscripts, titled "L'été qui ne vint pas," featuring an octogenarian by the name of Mathilda, in a way heralds *Cet été qui chantait*, but apart from this there is practically nothing in all Gabrielle Roy's work that leads one to expect a book like this one, where the essential has less to do with the material evoked – the people and things of La Grande-Pointe – than the spirit moving it, a profoundly religious, even mystic spirit that is completely detached from everything preoccupying the contemporary era. This "Franciscan" spirit, this enchanted view of the marvels of creation, Gabrielle owed above all to Bernadette, to the presence in herself of Bernadette's saintliness. Writing *Cet été qui chantait* meant rejoining Bernadette's orbit, following in her wake, reliving in memory that wonderful summer of 1965, and so much more intensely than she had at the time, seeing through Bernadette's enchanted eyes the world that

Bernadette had loved so much, and now had lost; for Gabrielle it meant forgetting who she was and had been and, through her writing, herself becoming her departed sister.

In this sense, it could be said that this book begun in the spring or summer of 1971 had been in preparation for over a year. "I think your memory will always sing in the gentle breeze of summer," Gabrielle wrote in one of her daily letters to the dying woman, "you'll be forever present on the broad horizon of the river, and I shall always hear your dear voice mingled with the rustle of birch leaves and the murmur of the rising tide."

> If I ever write another book, believe me, my Bernadette, it will largely be owing to what you have wrought in me. It will be the work of a soul cleansed by your example. And you will whisper to me what must be said to humankind about suffering, about separation, and about our reunion and homecoming in love triumphant.[240]

This is a book filled with light and innocence, in which frogs talk, trees sing, animals and humans fraternize, and nothing dismal or bad is allowed. And yet *Cet été qui chantait* is also a book about bereavement, in which death and absence are present throughout. This is the focus particularly in "L'enfant morte" ("The Dead Child"), which may seem a puzzling insertion but in a way provides a summation or emblem for the whole book: a dead body covered in flowers. A pastoral that happens to be a tomb.

A preliminary version of the "tales" of *Cet été qui chantait*, as Gabrielle called them, was finished by November 1971. The work of revision and tidying – in the course of which several texts judged marginal were set aside[241] – went on until spring 1972. A contract was then signed with Les Éditions françaises of Quebec City, a firm affiliated with Larousse of France. It was Simone Bussières who was Gabrielle's intermediary with the publisher and who took care of most of the chores involved in publication. The firm was delighted to be able to publish an author as important as Gabrielle Roy and left no stone unturned in an effort to please her. Guy Lemieux, a nephew of Alice Lemieux-Lévesque, received an order for six full-page illustrations in colour; a new portrait of Gabrielle was taken by the photographer Krieber; Adrienne Choquette wrote a preface; the regular edition was given a jacket in full colour, and a special edition of a hundred copies was printed on deluxe vellum.

Finally, although the author did not approve and was not present, a big launch was held on 13 October 1972 at the Éditions françaises bookstore on Côte de la Fabrique, attended by Claire Kirkland-Casgrain, the Quebec minister of Cultural Affairs.

"I do wonder what impression this book will create," Gabrielle wrote when she received her first copy. "I really have no idea."[242] There was little in common between *Cet été qui chantait* and the books the reading public and critics were used to receiving from her. The dedication she placed at the beginning may have stated that the book was intended for young people, but she knew very well that the realistic, politically minded novelist who had written *Bonheur d'occasion* could hardly offer this naïve, childlike style of writing so oblivious to modern literature and contemporary concerns without raising eyebrows, without disconcerting and perhaps even disappointing her readers.

These apprehensions were only partly confirmed. From the moment of publication, *Cet été qui chantait* sold very well, as well and perhaps better than *La Route d'Altamont* and *La Rivière sans repos*, her two previous books. After four months the publisher had to go to a second printing, bringing the number of copies sold in the first year to 8,000. All of which showed that Gabrielle Roy had a faithful reading public and this reading public was ready to follow her into the new ground she was proposing, diametrically opposed though it may have been to the stamping ground of the advanced wing of Québécois literature.

As far as the critics were concerned, however, the book was a disaster. There were a good number of columnists talking about the "innocence rediscovered" and "country joys" evoked by this book, which in their eyes was about "serenity"; there were even a few who grasped the gravity hidden beneath the apparent artlessness of the stories,[243] but these were marginal for the most part. Where the opinions counted, in the major dailies, the reviews were very negative. Réginald Martel, the critic for *La Presse*, could not get over the "mawkishness" and "childish nonsense" that Gabrielle Roy had lapsed into; even Jean Éthier-Blais, who was touched by "the total simplicity of the great artist," considered the book to be an interlude pending "a work of greater importance, with numerous ramifications" finally from the pen of this major writer. But the harshest criticism came from Quebec City, where Gilles Constantineau, the literary columnist for *Le Soleil*, delivered a stinging charge against the "veterinary bucolics" and "affected preciosity" that, he said, made *Cet été qui chantait* "a pointless work," one for "lovers of

insipidities."[244] Constantineau's article drew public condemnations –
"Ignominious, disgusting, bestial," fumed the writer Jean-Jules
Richard[245] – but Gabrielle was still profoundly shocked by it. In January
1973 she wrote to Joyce Marshall, "Our book reviews in French in
Quebec are getting poorer, madder, sillier every day, and so full of hatred
and racism that it's unbelievable. [. . .] Pretty soon, we will look upon
the reviews given in English of French publications to know what they
are about."[246]

But when the book, translated by Joyce Marshall, was published in
English by McClelland & Stewart in 1976 under the title *Enchanted
Summer*, there was not much enthusiasm shown by the English-
Canadian critics either. For each one who as usual praised the book's
"Canadianness" and saw it to be "the work of a writer in full possession
of her talent," there was another for whom it contained only "saccharin
sentiment and schmaltz," as Adele Freedman wrote in *Maclean's* of
Toronto. In other words, these circles too found it disconcerting. As one
columnist put it, "If it had been written by someone unknown [. . .], who
would read it?"[247]

The period not long past when Gabrielle Roy had been the darling
of the critics was over and done with. In fact, with the publication of
Cet été qui chantait and *Enchanted Summer*, one might say that the gulf
between Gabrielle Roy and the segment of the literary world represented
by the most influential or highly regarded critics reached its widest.
Papers, magazines, and literary periodicals felt obliged to cover what she
wrote, but they were no longer receptive to what she had to say, perhaps
not even interested.

CHAPTER 9

A Time for Remembrance

"*I*cannot look at the sky or at the river or at treetops swaying in the wind without trying to describe, for myself, just what is happening, just trying to capture the movement, or the sound, in an image that would be so perfect."[1]

These words spoken in 1972 put in a nutshell the one and only rule, the one and only quest that governed all of Gabrielle Roy's acts, desires, and thoughts in her final years. As old age approached, as her health declined, her friends disappeared, and her professional cares faded, as her life and existence simplified, the supremacy of her writing kept increasing. The woman in old age literally counted on nothing else, identified with nothing else – the words, sentences, stories that flowed from her pen and justified her for living and having lived. Writing, she declared to her friend Joyce Marshall, "is our only possible salvation, our only way out of the confines of ourselves . . . and thus perhaps freeing ourselves to some extent, help[ing] others to free themselves."[2]

To free herself, give an honourable account of herself in her own eyes and the eyes of the world, this was the obsession at the source of both the sufferings and the tranquillity of these last years. With her physical as well as moral stamina ebbing, she lived increasingly with her end in view and prepared consciously for it. She felt or at least expressed no fear or regret over this approaching end, just detachment, consolation, but at the same time an urgent need to leave her house in order, settle her accounts, and complete her work.

In 1975 Gabrielle allowed a Toronto magazine to publish a new picture of her that surprised, even sowed consternation among, many of her readers.[3] This photograph by John Reeves for the first time shows a woman shorn of all signs of youth: blotched hands, grey wisps of hair carelessly dangling over an ear, unsmiling mouth, face tanned and deeply lined. The chin cupped in a palm and the bent upper body express infinite weariness, relieved only by the gaze of the right eye, which is clear and steady, the other side of the face remaining hidden in shadow. Gabrielle loved this picture despite its brutality, or perhaps because of it: "It is slightly poignant, it seems to me, it shows the scars and pain of life, but I have learned now to love such images of truth."[4] Which are also images of beauty, as shown by this picture of an old woman full of wrinkles, weariness, and shadow.

Although recapitulation and death were the keynotes of this entire period of Gabrielle Roy's life, it was not at all a period of decline. On the contrary, and paradoxical as it may seem, it was perhaps the richest and most productive of her career. Despite increasing ill-health, in less than ten years she not only published regularly but produced some of her finest work: *Un jardin au bout du monde* (1975; *Garden in the Wind*, 1977), *Ces enfants de ma vie* (1977; *Children of My Heart*, 1979), and eventually *La détresse et l'enchantement* (*Enchantment and Sorrow*), books which are by no means mere repetitions or reworkings of predecessors, but in the best sense of the term works of creation, of search and discovery, thus marking a new, final, and magnificent phase of her work. The writing here is not only more assured, efficient, and uncluttered than ever, it achieves a luminous quality, a purity of tone and purpose attained no doubt only by those artists who have spent their lives in pursuit of these things and sacrificed all to them.

Her Sister's Keeper

When she died, Bernadette gifted Gabrielle with a saintly model and vision of the world that yielded *Cet été qui chantait* (*Enchanted Summer*), but she also left her another legacy that would occupy Gabrielle's life and thoughts until her last breath: Clémence.

Among Mélina's daughters, Clémence held a special place. Ailing since an early age, incapable of providing for herself, to her four sisters she was the picture and relic of their past, and the bond – the only bond perhaps – that held them together after the death of their mother, from whom they had inherited her. "Our Clémence," we read in *Enchantment and Sorrow*, "has been an enduring sorrow bequeathed by one sister to another, each one as she dies passing on the legacy to a younger sister; strange, priceless legacy."[5]

For Anna, then Bernadette, for Adèle too (who did try inadeptly), taking care of Clémence was keeping alive the memory of their *moudra*, and keeping faith with the family. Gabrielle had never ducked this responsibility (or shackle), whatever Adèle said. Immediately after her mother's funeral in the summer of 1943, as she was throwing herself into the frenzy of writing *Bonheur d'occasion*, she pledged never to abandon Clémence, as she would tell her in a letter in 1981:

> It's a solemn promise I made to myself one day when I was in the Gaspé looking out at the Ocean. There, I resolved to watch over you as long as I live and do my best always to be sure you're never in need of anything.[6]

While she had made this promise at a time of bereavement and to assuage her guilt over having abandoned her mother, she had never forgotten it. As long as Anna and Bernadette were alive, of course, the worry over Clémence was rather slight, for they could be depended upon. But Adèle being too old, too poor, and too volatile in nature to take responsibility for Clémence, the duty of family solidarity would fall henceforth to Gabrielle alone, like a debt repayment long postponed and now due.

Called upon now by the circumstances, Gabrielle would keep her promise. From the time of Bernadette's death in 1970, Clémence became her major worry, constantly in her thoughts and certainly one of her most powerful reasons for living. In the remaining ten or twelve years of her life, not a week, hardly a day, went by when she did not send Clémence a message or do something for her benefit. Clémence's comfort and pleasure were a real obsession for her, as though in devoting herself to her sister in this way she were obeying some mysterious, forceful command from herself or someone inside her whose authority she could not and did not wish to escape.

Early in May 1970, realizing that Bernadette did not have long to live and fearing that Clémence would react badly to losing her, Gabrielle invited Clémence and Antonia, Germain's widow, to come and spend the summer at Petite-Rivière-Saint-François, but Antonia had to undergo an operation and the trip was postponed. Other attempts would also fall through in the years that followed, so that Clémence never again set foot in Quebec and the two sisters never managed to have another "enchanted summer" like the one of 1965,[7] as Gabrielle had so hoped they would. Clémence was not really keen on the idea anyway; she worried about the tiring effects of the journey and much preferred excursions to the village of Somerset in the Pembina Mountain district where she had been born and had spent the best times of her youth. There she could visit old Aunt Anna Landry, Zénon's widow, who still lived there and with whom she would have endless chats, "which is always a treat for her," wrote Gabrielle, "for Somerset brings back all her childhood memories and for a little while restores her spirit of those days, its wonder and artlessness."[8]

Since Clémence hated travelling, Gabrielle had to go to Manitoba to see her sister and attend to her needs. She took the first of these trips in early autumn 1970. Marcel stayed in Quebec, taking part in doctors' demonstrations against medicare; *La Rivière sans repos* was beginning to appear on bookstore shelves. Arriving in Winnipeg on September 24, she took a room at the Westminster Hotel and immediately contacted Sister Berthe Valcourt, the Mother Superior of the Académie Saint-Joseph, who drove her to the village of Otterburne, some thirty miles south of the capital. It was here, to remove her from Adèle's influence, that Bernadette had succeeded in placing Clémence two years earlier as a boarder in the Résidence Sainte-Thérèse, a retirement home for ladies run by the Sisters of Providence.

In *Enchantment and Sorrow*, Gabrielle would recount this first visit to Clémence, the desolation of the little village surrounded by prairie, the twilight, the dreariness of the home full of abandoned elderly women, and especially the state of physical and mental deterioration in which she found her sister: "frighteningly thin, her face terribly small, her body all huddled up as if trying to take as little room as possible in this world, perhaps even to disappear completely," because she "felt we'd abandoned her."[9] Until now on her visits to Manitoba, Gabrielle had only seen Clémence surrounded and protected by her sisters; this was the first time she was discovering her in her natural surroundings so to speak, cut off from everything, enclosed in the silence and dismal monotony of her usual existence. The experience affected her deeply. Seized with remorse, she decided that her duty henceforth was to do everything possible to draw Clémence out of her torpor and infuse her with a taste for life. In the weeks following this first visit she returned regularly to Otterburne, either from Winnipeg or from the village of St-Jean-Baptiste, where Sister Berthe had invited her to rest for a few days at the convent of the Soeurs des Saints Noms de Jésus et de Marie. Gabrielle and Clémence went for long walks in the deserted village; they talked about the past. Sometimes when she could get away, Sister Berthe would take them for drives along the section roads, even as far as Somerset where Gabrielle saw the house of her grandmother Landry, "the one who made me a doll one day. [. . .] The house is all ramshackle," she wrote to Berthe Simard, "but the land is really beautiful. If it weren't so far away I might be tempted to buy it."[10] After the party organized on October 16 for Clémence's seventy-fifth birthday, she took Clémence shopping to buy her a decent wardrobe. When it came time to return to Quebec, where the murdered body of the cabinet minister Pierre Laporte had just been discovered, she knew that she was now her sister's keeper and her work with Clémence had only just begun.

Four times in the next four years, toward the end of each summer, she would make the same trip to Otterburne to attend to Clémence's needs and bring her a little comfort. In 1971 she spent the last two weeks of August there, interrupting the writing of Cet été qui chantait to do so. With Antonia, who drove the rental car, she stayed in the village of St-Pierre-Jolys, a few minutes away from the Résidence Sainte-Thérèse. The two women went to the home every day, happy to see Clémence's improving condition. Sister Berthe came to help as well. One day on the way back from a drive to Tolstoy, Gabrielle and Sister Berthe stopped at Marchand and went to see the old school where Gabrielle had had her first teaching job and had covered the body of a dead child with flowers.

But the attention she was giving Clémence was not limited to these annual trips to Manitoba. Once home, and throughout the year, Gabrielle kept in touch, alert to the slightest change in Clémence's mood and from a distance overseeing all aspects of her health and comfort: food, medication, clothing, hygiene, budget. Every week, if not twice or three times a week, she wrote her letters full of affection and gaiety, "to entertain you a bit and try to encourage you."[11] Berthe Simard or Bibiane Patry, Gabrielle's neighbour in Quebec City, would take charge of dispatching the books, magazines, flowers, and little treats that Gabrielle wanted to send her sister, as if to a delicate child she was afraid of losing again. With equal regularity Gabrielle communicated with the nuns and doctors at the Résidence Sainte-Thérèse, making sure that all was well with her. Most important, however, she kept in touch with the two women who had become her chosen stand-ins with Clémence, Antonia and Sister Berthe Valcourt.

In all the years she had known her, Gabrielle had always been very fond of Germain's wife. Antonia was about her own age and she too had been a teacher. Her calm, gentle nature was very different to that of

Gabrielle and her sisters, who were constantly flying off the handle or having crises of one kind or another. Their contacts had been somewhat episodic until Bernadette was dying, but at that time Antonia had been accommodating and considerate to an exemplary degree. Gabrielle had been deeply attached to her sister-in-law ever since; she worried about her health, took an interest in her children, invited her to come and visit, and wrote her numerous letters expressing deep friendship, seeking in her, as in all her friends, both a sister and a mother, someone who loved her without motive and brought her the help and affection she was so sadly lacking. In May 1970 she wrote to Antonia:

> I so need a shoulder to lean on, I think only of that. I've tried to reason with myself but in vain; with our Dédette, all that is fine, good, and marvellous left in our family is disappearing; after her there'll be nothing but sick people and crazy people.[12]

Antonia was Gabrielle's only remaining direct relation still living in Winnipeg, apart from Adèle, since her two daughters, Lucille and Yolande, were now married and settled in the East. Gabrielle therefore came to count on her to attend to Clémence, either by going to visit her at Otterburne or having her for short stays at home in town to break the monotony of her life at the Résidence Sainte-Thérèse. Bombarded by Gabrielle with supplicating letters, with her great kindness, and despite her health problems, Antonia fulfilled her role impeccably, becoming one of Clémence's on-the-spot guardians.

The other charitable soul was Sister Berthe. Bernadette, before she died, knowing what a heavy responsibility Clémence was going to be for Gabrielle and how it could endanger the freedom necessary for her work, seeing too that Clémence would never agree to go and live in Quebec or Gabrielle to come back and live in Manitoba, had made arrangements for Clémence's care not to fall entirely on Gabrielle's shoulders. For some years already, Sister Léon had had help from other nuns of her community, so that Clémence had become in a way everyone's child, especially for Sister Berthe Valcourt, the Mother Superior. Then, a few days before she died, "she had been perfectly lucid and had clearly and unmistakably given Clémence into Soeur Berthe's care"; and "Sister Berthe had accepted responsibility for Clémence as though she hadn't needed to be asked."[13]

This tiny woman with the laughing eyes, talkative and vivacious, a bundle of energy and tenderness, who was about forty at this time, took upon herself Clémence's maintenance and well-being from 1970 on. Only too happy to find someone local to perform the duties that were hers, and captivated from the moment of their first meeting by Sister Berthe's kindness and insightfulness, Gabrielle had total confidence in her. And with reason; from the moment of Bernadette's death and through all the years to follow, Sister Berthe showed that she could be relied upon. With unfailing diligence and efficiency she saw to Clémence's every need, visited her whenever the opportunity arose, clothed her, took her on drives, entertained her, had her see a doctor when necessary – looked after her as if she were her own sister.

But it was not only for Clémence that Sister Berthe was doing all this. She was doing it as much, perhaps more, for Gabrielle, to relieve Gabrielle of anxiety and make her happy. Despite the difference in their ages, the friendship that bound Berthe to Gabrielle continued to deepen over the years through letters exchanged and meetings, sometimes in Manitoba, sometimes at Petite-Rivière-Saint-François or the Château Saint-Louis when the service of Sister Valcourt's community brought her to Quebec. And Gabrielle too became deeply attached to the woman she called "dear sister, dear friend," and who soon became one of her most intimate confidantes. A relationship developed between them similar to those she had had with Esther Perfect, Henri Girard, and Adrienne Choquette, and which she still had with the other Berthe, her friend at Petite-Rivière-Saint-François. A relationship that was both maternal and adoring, at least on Berthe's part, in which she, Gabrielle, was the object of unbounded affection, admiration, and devotion, feelings to which she responded and nourished with repeated expressions of her own attachment and especially her total dependence on the other for the maintenance of her peace of mind and happiness.

> I've had no one in the world, aside from my mother perhaps, who has given me as much as you, who has helped me with as much generosity and love.[14]

Gabrielle in Quebec City or Petite-Rivière-Saint-François, Antonia and Sister Berthe in Winnipeg, Clémence at Otterburne: among them was woven a web of thought and action sustained by a vigorous exchange of letters, telephone calls, cheques, and objects of all descriptions on their way to Clémence. Although Clémence was at the centre of this web, everything depended on Gabrielle, who from a distance was its brain and soul. All communications came from her, to her, and through her. Between Sister Berthe and Antonia, as between each of them and Clémence, there were few spontaneous contacts; their contacts were always instigated and piloted by Gabrielle, who wrote all the letters, took all the initiatives, and paid all the expenses, rather liberally besides. "Money is not a problem," she wrote to Sister Berthe. "Think of the budget as generous."[15] She was the director of operations, the master strategist of Clémence's well-being, and Clémence had only to let her know her moods and needs, even in veiled terms, for the web to activate and get her what she wanted. The process was almost always the same; among the news and amiable chitchat of Clémence's letters to Gabrielle, a sentence would suddenly bring to mind, in a by-the-way fashion, how bereft she felt and what a dreary life she led: "It's so country and fields at Otterburne"; "we're not at Niagara Falls"; "it's hard when boredom eats you up."[16] Then Gabrielle would try to lift her spirits, telling her that she mustn't let herself go and something good might be going to happen, and without saying so to Clémence would write or telephone the same day or the next to Sister Berthe or Antonia to tell her about "the anguish Clémence is communicating to me" and what consolation it would be to know that she was doing better: "our poor little Clémence whose lot makes my heart ache. So alone in that boring little village, I could cry just to think of it."[17] Then Sister Berthe or Antonia would go to Otterburne and take Clémence to Winnipeg or Somerset for a day or two. When she got back, Clémence would write to Gabrielle again and tell her all about it, and Gabrielle would hasten to write one of her "letters from the heart" to Sister Berthe or Antonia praising her act of pure kindness to Clémence.

> With you, with your help, I shall have accomplished some of the finest acts of my life, perhaps the only ones of value.[18]

Never since her mother's death had Clémence had so much company. Never had anyone written her so many letters, paid so many visits, shown her so much kindness and attention. Never had she received so many gifts, new dresses, hats, boxes of chocolates, so much pocket money. To the point sometimes of finding it a bit much. And yet for all that, Clémence was not happy. Nothing seemed to fill the vast melancholy gnawing at her. As clean and well run as the Résidence Sainte-Thérèse may have been, it was still a place filled with powerless old women their families had left there to die, all as mournful and silent as she, as downcast, wanting only one thing as they sat for hours in the same chair before the same window looking out at the same scene with its naked horizon: someone to come and take them out of there, when time would stop at last. "Several very old women have died here in the last while," Clémence announced in one of her letters to Gabrielle. "But that doesn't change things much here in the home."[19]

Clémence being cyclical like Gabrielle, she did have less gloomy periods, thanks to some new medication or some minor event that briefly brought joy to her heart – a visit, an outing, a book she enjoyed more than most. But these phases of remission never lasted long and made the inevitable crises of gloom that followed even more painful. Then everything about her would seem devoid of life. She would not eat, would do a minimum of washing and dressing, refuse to leave her room or speak to anyone, as if her whole being were near extinction and she had withdrawn into some parallel, unreachable, devastated world.

The only way to put an end to these phases of depression would have been to deliver her from her Otterburne prison. Gabrielle had tried everything to find her a place in a home in St-Boniface and had to keep urging Clémence to have patience. On her third trip in 1972, however, she arranged for Clémence to come and spend a week in Winnipeg, staying with Antonia in her little apartment while Gabrielle stayed at the Westminster Hotel. She and Clémence went shopping together, to the cemetery to pray beside the graves of their parents and siblings, and on an excursion to Lake Manitoba. Clémence was enchanted. "All went well," Gabrielle wrote to Berthe Simard, "until we took her back to the home at Otterburne. Then I saw her become tense, rather like a child you're sending back to school against her will, or even like a prisoner you're taking back to her cell."[20]

That year Gabrielle had decided to take the train from Winnipeg to the West Coast, where her nephew Bob, Jos's son, had invited her when he had come to visit the previous year. This also offered a convenient way of not being in Quebec for the launching of *Cet été qui chantait*, hence escaping the media hoopla involved in it. Before leaving she asked Sister Berthe to buy Clémence a television set, but Clémence turned the gift down because, she said, "I don't like those things."[21] Then, having persuaded Antonia to go with her, Gabrielle left for Coquitlam, an east suburb of Vancouver, where Bob and his wife, Brenda, gave them a warm welcome. From there they went to spend a few days of rest by the sea at White Rock, in a little cottage found for them by a friend of Antonia's. Gabrielle took the opportunity to continue on as far as Victoria in hope of finding a spot where she and Marcel might retire, as they had been talking of doing for some time, but she did not like the climate and promptly dropped the idea. She returned directly to Quebec on 14 October 1972 without stopping in Manitoba.

In Which the Biographer Meets His Subject

Although her three weeks by the Pacific Ocean had done her a world of good, as soon as she was home Gabrielle slumped into one of those periods of extreme fatigue she was always prey to with the approach of winter. "I have no taste for anything but staying still doing nothing, I feel so tired," she wrote to Antonia on November 23.[22] As in previous years, she decided to escape to a kinder climate where she might perhaps begin to write again. But where?

One of her Belgian readers, Suzanne Boland, a painter who had been writing her long, admiring letters for the last two or three years, was spending the winter with her family in the Maritime Alps; she owned a house at Tourrettes-sur-Loup, a few miles from Vence. Suzanne had kept vaunting the beauty of the countryside to Gabrielle and telling her she should come there for a rest. Still attached to her "beloved Provence," despite her unhappy experience at Draguignan seven years earlier, and at a loss to know where to turn to satisfy her need for solitude and genial idleness, Gabrielle decided to take up Suzanne's invitation. She took flight for the South of France on 9 December 1972, without Marcel.

Once again the sojourn quickly turned out to be a disappointment. Yes, the village, the mountains, the vegetation were magnificent; yes, she could breathe better in this temperate climate than in her overheated apartment at the Château Saint-Louis, but the conditions were far from ideal and she complained about it in every one of her letters. The comfort in the little house in which she had rented an apartment was rudimentary; the population, consisting of untalkative peasants and the fauna of daubster artists and long-haired hippies that descended on all the rivieras of the world, was not very reassuring. But hardest of all to endure was that Suzanne, contrary to what Gabrielle had hoped and expected, was not really prepared to do anything for her at all and left her to fend for herself. Gabrielle was simply not used to doing her own shopping, cooking, dishwashing, and all those other chores ordinarily taken care of by someone else. Here she had to do everything herself, losing absurd amounts of time "running to get one's bread, meat, heating, washing, etc.,"[23] which was tiring and prevented her from arranging her days as she would like. What she was missing of course was a kindly soul like Berthe Simard, Antonia, or even her New Smyrna Beach friend Marie Dubuc, a presence common to all her successful retreats. Suzanne, whom Gabrielle had known only through correspondence, was a distant and complicated person, "as stiff as a broom handle and about as warm as washing hung out to dry in winter."[24] Soon the two women were seeing each other only on rare occasions, and the vacationer ended her sojourn alone, going for walks in the sunshine, reading, being lonely sometimes, writing to friends and relatives, and every morning holding herself in readiness for the muse.

But the muse did not come, it seems. Since she had finished *Cet été qui chantait*, Gabrielle had not started any new book, nor would she really before 1974 or 1975. Brief though it was, this period of drought raised the fear in her that she had come to the end. It haunted her constantly, this fear of no longer finding the stuff in her that she needed in order to write, of being short of strength, or time, or inspiration, and finding herself in the midst of a desert, abandoned. A few years later, after the death by suicide of Hubert Aquin, she would write:

> Perhaps he had also perceived – or thought he had perceived – that he could no longer write. This torment for someone who has enchanted, guided, consoled is unimaginable. Nevertheless the threat of it hangs over every writer, and this perhaps is the reason for the attraction [. . .] of suicide for so many writers. For talent is never given. They say "the gift," but that is wrong, it is never more than a loan, and it can be withdrawn. Or at least one can feel that it is withdrawn, and then life becomes a torture. [25]

For herself, in the time she had been giving her whole life to writing, she had learned not to despair over these arid phases and to live through them as slow periods, waiting periods. To hold herself ready, however, she would keep herself busy revising texts she had written and set aside for the time being. Among these was a novella whose theme had been haunting her for nearly thirty years, but which she had never succeeded in getting to gel in satisfactory shape. This theme, the consolation brought to a love-starved woman by embellishing the world around her, had produced two or three isolated or partial texts like "La lune des moissons," which was published in 1947, the screenplay "Le plus beau blé du monde," and the unfinished and unpublished novel about "Madame Lund," the last two written in the 1950s. Still, in none of these efforts had she felt she had given her principal character all the depth, complexity, or poetry she believed was potential in this woman, nor ever found adequate words to re-create the full power of her initial vision, which had come to her at the time of her first stay at Tangent. So she set back to work, concentrating this time on the most powerful image involved in the theme, that of a flower garden in the midst of a vast, hostile, deserted countryside. The title of the story, "Le printemps revint à Volhyn," was soon replaced by the one that became permanent, "Un jardin au bout du monde." Whether Gabrielle finished this story during her sojourn at Tourettes-sur-Loup is impossible to say, but it is certain that a relatively final version was ready at about this time.

She returned to Quebec City on 2 February 1973. This was the last time that she crossed the Atlantic. It was also the last time she allowed herself to be lured by that old, long-nurtured dream of a haven somewhere, a house, a secluded spot, a deserted island, where she would be happy and at peace forever, as she had been at her Upshire, Port-Daniel, and Rawdon Shangri-Las. After this new disappointment at Tourettes, Gabrielle would rely on only two havens already proven to satisfy her need for escape: Petite-Rivière-Saint-François, with Berthe and her kindness to care for her, and the inexhaustible world of her memories.

That spring she left Quebec City and settled in at Petite-Rivière in mid-May, much earlier than ever before. Berthe of course had made everything ready and the cottage was comfortable despite the lingering cold. Then the familiar pattern resumed, the walks along *la track*, the evenings by the stove in the old Simard house, the maintenance of the web of friends protecting Clémence. Gabrielle had brought a manuscript she had been working on for some years, "Où iras-tu, Sam Lee Wong?," a story inspired by a picture in her mind from her reporting days in the West, enriched by others brought back from her stay in Dollard shortly before the death of her brother Joseph. Having finished the character's story and the evocation of the village of Horizon, she was hesitating between two possible endings: either Sam would commit suicide or he would move to the next village and begin the same life all over again . . .

At this point I had my first meeting with Gabrielle Roy, in midsummer 1973. I was twenty-six. I had been a teacher of French literature at McGill University for two years and was small potatoes in the parade of academics and admirers filing through Petite-Rivière-Saint-François in those years. Joan Hind-Smith of Toronto, who was writing biographical essays on the three great "voices" of Canadian literature, Margaret Laurence, Frederick Philip Grove, and Gabrielle Roy, had been visiting a week or two before me; Jeannette Urbas and Paul Socken, of the Universities of Toronto and Waterloo respectively, were to come the following year. Marc Gagné, whose thesis on her had just been published, had been coming from time to time. The result was that Gabrielle was beginning to feel besieged. As she wrote to Antonia:

> I have goodness knows how many professors on my heels who have books under way about me and who write from all corners of the country asking to see me. For several years I have given a lot of my time to a professor from [l'Université] Laval whose book, *Visages de Gabrielle Roy* (very learned) has just come out. I thought, having spared no effort this time, that afterwards others would leave me alone, taking what information they needed from this book. But no! They're in hotter pursuit than ever for their own books. My Petite-Rivière hideaway has long since been uncovered.[26]

Yet she was pleased with the interest being shown in her and did not refuse the interviews being requested. "Of course," she confessed to Joyce Marshall, "this is better than the total indifference of several years back."[27] I myself was writing a little book on her work and had written her asking for photographs and permission to use some excerpts from a few of her diverse texts. She had at once telephoned and invited me to Petite-Rivière for an afternoon in July. The weather was magnificent. When I arrived she introduced me to Marcel, who then got in his car and made himself scarce for the day. First we went for a walk in the neighbourhood; she took me to Berthe's and we talked a bit. Then we came back and sat in the lawn swing. We must have stayed there for an hour, perhaps two, talking about her, about her books, about my book in progress. She swung the swing so energetically, so fast and furiously that suddenly I could barely keep from throwing up; I managed not to show my distress and made do with stiffening my legs as best I could to slow the movement of the swing. Did she notice? Whether she did or not, the swing did not slow down.

Since the mosquitoes were arriving, we took refuge in the house. She sat in a rocking chair beside her little desk in front of the window, and had me sit on a sofa facing her. Then she brought out the "Sam Lee Wong" manuscript and read it to me from beginning to end. She read very well, in a firm if slightly hoarse voice, miming the dialogue and varying the rhythm to suit the emotional colour of the words and sentences. She read me both conclusions she had written, adding that she could not decide which was the better. I told her I preferred the second, where the leading character goes to the other village and finds himself back with his hills. Then she told me she would keep that one, and she did; but I think she had already made her decision. Shortly after, I got up to leave and we gave each other a goodbye kiss.

I came back to Petite-Rivière twice more that summer. Never, if I recall correctly, did she speak to me of her sister Clémence, who was a worry to her at the time as shown by the letters to Berthe Valcourt and Antonia that I have read since. However, she talked to me at length about her friendship for Adrienne Choquette, who for some time had been suffering from a cancer that was progressing and was no longer a mystery for anyone; the prospect of losing Adrienne was upsetting her exceedingly, she said, haunting her dreams and preventing her from working.

Since learning that Adrienne was dying she had been thinking constantly of her friend. She wrote her letters of encouragement and tenderness, enquired of her condition from Simone Bussières, went to see her at Notre-Dame-des-Laurentides, prayed for her before the little statue of "Notre-Dame-des-Bouleaux" that Berthe had put up for her in the garden above the river; in short, she was doing the same things she had done three years earlier when Bernadette was dying. On her return from an afternoon at Notre-Dame-des-Laurentides, she wrote to Adrienne:

> In spite of your illness which pains all of us so, this hour spent in your sweet, slightly tousled little garden, like Esther's – hers was the only other precious feminine friendship of my life, with yours, and two sibling gardens, isn't that strange? – this hour remains filled with memories that I know are ready to live in my mind forever. [. . .] Above all there is the colour, the expression both tender and a little sad – which I think by now I can read – of your eyes . . .[28]

Although Gabrielle worried a great deal about her friend, her first responsibility was to her sister, her sister Clémence who was pining for her out there in Manitoba and impatiently awaiting her arrival. At the end of August she left Petite-Rivière-Saint-François, stopped for a few days in Quebec City to see Adrienne, who was now in hospital, then for the fourth time flew off to Otterburne.

She stayed three weeks. Happy to receive such a distinguished visitor, the nuns made available a little house across the road from the Résidence Sainte-Thérèse. Living there for the duration with Antonia, who took care of the cooking and housekeeping, Gabrielle saw Clémence every day and tried to bring her comfort. But it was not easy. Clémence was in terrible condition; dejected, thin, completely sunken into herself and indifferent to everything around her, she looked like "a little ghost [. . .] out of the concentration camps."[29] Still, by dint of walks, conversation, coaxing, and antidepressants, Gabrielle and Antonia succeeded in bringing her back to a degree of vitality and good humour. But how long would it last, Gabrielle wondered. "What is unfortunate – or fortunate – is that Clémence becomes accustomed to having us here, acquires a taste for it, poor child. So after we've gone she'll feel her isolation more than ever. It's so difficult sometimes to know what to do in life."[30]

"Adrienne dying and refusing to die, Clémence living and refusing to live";[31] when Gabrielle returned to Quebec City at the end of September, her distress was at a peak. Adrienne died three weeks later, with Simone and Medjé beside her. Then Gabrielle received news of another death, that of her old friend of St-Boniface days, Paula Sumner. During her vacation at Tourrettes-sur-Loup the previous winter, she had briefly seen Paula, who had been going from one clinic to another for the past five or six years, unsuccessfully seeking to regain her mental balance. This death was a shock for Gabrielle; with it, a last vestige of her youth had disappeared, and the solitude around her was looming larger than ever.

In the course of the autumn and winter following our first meeting, she invited me several times to the Château Saint-Louis. Thus our friendship was beginning to be sealed, a friendship which I think lasted until the end. In any case we never ceased to be in contact by letter and telephone and to see each other frequently. Each year I would go once or twice during the winter to Quebec City and once or twice during the summer to Charlevoix County. I would stay for several days in Baie-Saint-Paul, from where I would drive to Petite-Rivière for lunch and the afternoon, which as always we would spend talking (despite the torture

of the lawn swing) and going for walks. From time to time I would
suggest a little drive to St-Joseph-de-la-Rive or La Malbaie, which would
delight Gabrielle.

There was nothing complicated about out conversations. I would ask
her about episodes of her life, which she would happily reminisce about,
especially her first stay in Europe and her Montreal years. She would ask
me for news of the Montreal literary community and talk about what
she had been reading, her travels, her worries over the political climate.
But the most important part of our conversations concerned her work.
I quickly became a kind of secretary for her, in this role replacing Marc
Gagné, who was busy with other things and had drifted away from her.
In the first years she asked me to help her mostly with the correction of
proofs and things of that kind; my first "assignment" was to prepare the
revised edition of *Alexandre Chenevert*, which was published by
Beauchemin in the autumn of 1973. Subsequently I corrected almost all
her books, the new ones before their first publication, the old ones as
they came up for republication. In other words, I was doing for her in
French what Joyce Marshall was doing at the same time in English. It was
a fascinating process. Gabrielle would give me the manuscript or book,
which I would read and reread at home and annotate meticulously. Then
we would meet to examine and discuss my corrections, consulting
grammars and dictionaries, looking for the word, turn of phrase, punc-
tuation that would work best; we would try it out, then try another, then
still another, until we felt that nothing more should be changed. Then
we would rejoice together in the result. I learned a great deal from this
game (for it was very nearly a game) about the way she wrote, her language, and a good many other things as well.

During the winter of 1974 we began work on what was to become
Fragile Lumières de la terre (The Fragile Lights of Earth). For some time
Gabrielle had been toying with the idea of putting together a number of
texts she had published here and there in the course of her career and
which were languishing in periodicals that no one read any more.
Dreading the day when misguided "researchers" would unearth this
material, she had decided it would be better that she judge for herself
which of these texts deserved to be saved from oblivion. In the summer
of 1969, when Marc Gagné had been digging in this early production
for material for his thesis, she had discussed the matter with Victor
Barbeau, who wanted to publish such a "retrospective" in one of his
Cahiers de l'Académie canadienne-française. Two years later, Gilles

Marcotte invited her to give him a collection of her diverse writings for publication by Les Éditions HMH in the Reconnaissances series under his direction. But she always backed out in the end, having neither the desire nor the courage to stir up all those old ashes. "The only thing that keeps me going is doing more that's new,"[32] she used to say.

And yet when I met her she had already turned over a preliminary manuscript for typing. It consisted of some twenty texts, only one of which was unpublished, a brief account of her "Rencontre avec Teilhard de Chardin." The others had all appeared in magazines or works that were more or less impossible to find. Of the prolific production of her early years, she had chosen only the series of articles from *Le Bulletin des agriculteurs* titled "Peoples of Canada," whose inspiration and tone she felt were still relevant; however, since the last article of the series (on the French Canadians of Alberta) contained opinions that could be misinterpreted, she had replaced it with another on the fishermen of the Gaspé, taken from the series *Horizons du Québec*. Apart from these, all the other texts of the manuscript postdated *Bonheur d'occasion*. They had been slightly revised and arranged in chronological order of their first appearance.

My discussions with her bore mostly on the title of the book and its organization. We agreed that to give a certain unity to the collection it would be better to eliminate the fictional texts. The stories "Ma cousine économe" and "L'arbre" were therefore removed from the manuscript, as well as "Ma vache," which I then busied myself getting published separately as a children's book at Les Éditions Leméac, where I was editor of a series with André Major. The children's book appeared in 1976 under the title *Ma vache Bossie*, with beautiful illustrations by Louise Pomminville (*My Cow Bossie*, 1988); this was Gabrielle Roy's first incursion into the realm of children's literature.

With this housecleaning done, the next step was to compose the frame of the book, which we divided into three parts, first the documentary articles, then the personal recollections, and finally, in a section by itself, the "Terre des hommes" text, which Gabrielle was very anxious to publish in its original version. Then all that remained was the title, over which she hesitated at length before coming around to my suggestion of taking five words from "Terre des hommes," *Fragiles Lumières de la terre*.

All this work was spread over several years, moving ahead only when we met and without Gabrielle ever feeling any urgency to publish, as if this book were more a pretext for exchange and discussion than a real project. Which is why, although begun in 1974, it finally appeared only in 1978.

Meanwhile our contacts became more frequent and I became the equivalent of a literary agent or proxy. Besides involving me in her work, Gabrielle was entrusting a variety of chores to me, like part of her correspondence, negotiations, certain dealings with publishers and journalists, replies to requests for permissions which were arriving in great number. All of this, which she knew was unavoidable, was tiring her increasingly and she wanted desperately to be relieved of it. "The further I go," she wrote to me, "the bigger and heavier is the burden of business attached to the trade. So much that some days I wonder if I'm not going to give up all publication so as to get back my freedom if necessary."[33] Sometimes, I can say it now, there were days when I found the role she made me play pretty hard to take and I felt sorry for myself. But not for an instant did I dream of refusing her my help, or stop serving her to the best of my ability. Like the two Berthes, like Joyce, like Adrienne, and like so many others, I was captured by that mysterious magnetism that made all of us long to see her happy at any price, and incapable of offering her the least resistance.

Our devotion was amply repaid, I hasten to add. Not in money, but in affection, gratitude, and confidence, expressed with generosity worth more than all else and which I, for one, shall never forget.

"Memory Is a Poet"

May 1974. As she had done the year before, Gabrielle hurried to move to Petite-Rivière-Saint-François the moment the first fine days appeared. The winter had been even more difficult than usual; besides Adrienne's and Paula's deaths, besides the worry over Clémence sunk in her "bottomless pits of depression,"[34] besides the low spirits and listlessness always brought to her by winter, there had been illnesses even more taxing than in previous years, particularly recurrent attacks of asthma and fits of coughing like those her brothers Joseph and Rodolphe had experienced before her. It was in hope of escaping these by breathing more freely that she had sought the clean air of Petite-Rivière so early. Little good it did her, for the cold and dampness soon brought on a relapse and forced her to spend some time in hospital at Baie-Saint-Paul. Fortunately the sunshine, resumption of warm weather, and Berthe's ministrations quickly overcame the trouble, and then summer, the real summer, could finally begin.

Gabrielle spent it mostly finishing *Un jardin au bout du monde*. Her idea for this book was to add to the two unpublished novellas she had just finished, "Où iras-tu, Sam Lee Wong?" and "Un jardin au bout du monde," two texts that had been published in magazines a quarter of a century earlier and that she had polished up since, "Un vagabond frappe à notre porte" and "La vallée Houdou." This was her first real collection of short stories. Several of her previous books, like *La Petite Poule d'Eau*, *Rue Deschambault*, and *La Route d'Altamont* (*Where Nests the Water Hen*, *Street of Riches*, and *The Road Past Altamont*), were assemblages of stories but their unity of action and characterization was too strong and their writing too continuous for her to consider them "collections"; in her mind they were novels, loose and open in form, but novels all the same. With *Un jardin au bout du monde* it was different; as she wrote to Joyce Marshall, these were "real short stories this time, I mean with no link between them, except perhaps a sort of climate."[35] When she brought these four stories together between the same covers, she was realizing an old project she had called "Contes de la plaine," which she had conceived and abandoned many years before in the days of *Bonheur d'occasion*, a book inspired by her knowledge of the West and devoted to tales of the prairies. She added a brief two-page preface to the four short stories and the manuscript was finished by the end of August.

It was also during this summer of 1974, it seems, that she wrote a text of recollections that the Cercle Molière had asked of her for a book intended to celebrate the fiftieth anniversary of its founding. A few months before, she had given *Le Devoir* of Montreal a short article titled "Le pays de *Bonheur d'occasion*" in which she nostalgically recalls her days of journalism in Montreal, her discovery of the Saint-Henri district, and the beginnings of her first book. "Le Cercle Molière . . . porte ouverte" is in somewhat the same vein, an autobiographical narrative in which she recalls Arthur and Pauline Boutal, the atmosphere of fervour reigning at rehearsals, and the troupe's successes in which she participated in the days of her Manitoban youth. It was in April 1975 that this text was sent to Lionel Dorge, who was head of both the Société historique de Saint-Boniface and Les Éditions du Blé, but since the book in which it was to figure could not appear in time, the article was published only six years later, in a collection on the musical and literary history of French Manitoba.

Then in August 1974 came the annual trip to Manitoba, to the "forsaken little village where my poor, half-confined sister awaits me. [...] I hate to leave my work," she wrote me, "[...] but if we did not sacrifice it once in a while to the responsibilities of solidarity and the heart, it would soon be sterile."[36] She and Antonia moved into the same little house as the previous year and for three weeks tried to cheer up Clémence, who was still frighteningly thin but whose morale seemed better this year. Sister Berthe joined them and they drove to Somerset to chat with the aged Aunt Anna and revisit the scenes of their childhood. They went all the way to great Lake Winnipeg for a day of lazing on the beach at Camp Morton, where Bernadette used to come on vacation with her community and where she had written those "summer letters" of hers to Gabrielle. Finally, before leaving, Gabrielle took Clémence to Winnipeg and bought her new clothes from head to foot. With her peace of mind restored and new confidence, she took the plane home on September 18, having asked me to join her at Dorval where she was to change planes. I found her very pleased with the way her trip had gone.

But what we talked about mostly was *Un jardin au bout du monde*. All the manuscript needed at that point was to be delivered to the publisher. Dreading the work involved in publication, Gabrielle was hanging back. "The drive in me to publish is broken so to speak," she wrote to me several days later, "not the necessity or duty of writing, though."[37] Six months would go by before she decided to "let [her book] go," once again entrusting it to Les Éditions Beauchemin. The contract was signed on 11 March 1975. But with the approach of publication, scheduled for the end of May, she was gripped by anxiety. "Here I am [...] as scared stiff as the first time, even worse than ever. I suppose it will always be this way with me. But what judgment is to be feared so, when you think of it? Or what mysterious approval does one need so urgently?"[38]

The reception given *Cet été qui chantait* three years earlier had given her cause to be nervous, true enough. This time, however, things went relatively well. The *péquiste* daily *Le Jour* may have deplored the fact that the novelist had not chosen "to counter the erosion of our culture, [being content] to witness it without understanding the historic process to the point of actively committing herself," but most critics were quick to agree with the one who welcomed "the moving and beautiful return of Gabrielle Roy."[39] At *Le Devoir* in particular, she was positively celebrated. The previous year the editor of the paper's literary section, Robert Guy Scully, had published a major interview with her, while the opinionated Victor-Lévy Beaulieu, who had poured scorn on *La Rivière sans repos* and *Cet été qui chantait*, announced his sudden conversion to Gabrielle Roy's work, to which Jacques Ferron had just finished opening his eyes.[40] When *Un jardin au bout du monde* appeared, Scully delivered a long panegyric celebrating the "North-American quality" of the book, and reproduced "La vallée Houdou" in its entirety.[41] But the praise was even warmer when, two years later, the book appeared in English translation, titled *Garden in the Wind*; here again, after being supercilious over her recent books, the columnists expressed the opinion that with this one the author had attained the summit of her art.[42] The political context in late 1977 was of special significance in this, it should be noted, for the Parti Québécois had come to power for the first time and its language law, Bill 101, had been adopted, contributing to the English-Canadian critics' appreciation of a work that represented "Canadian literature par excellence," since it extolled the immigrants and landscapes of the West and broke with the usual narcissistic and demanding clamour of modern Québécois culture; here, they said, is a book in which language does not divide and in which men get along together. Gabrielle Roy, wrote George Woodcock, is really and truly "one of us."[43]

But sales did not follow suit, at least in Quebec. Les Éditions Beauchemin had printed 5,000 copies but for all the critics' enthusiasm sold less than 1,500 in a year. The book had not come out at an opportune moment, it is true, and in this period Beauchemin occupied a very marginal position in the literary market. McClelland & Stewart, however, sold about 4,000 copies of *Garden in the Wind* in the first year (1977–1978), confirming Gabrielle Roy's return at least temporarily to the English-Canadian literary scene.

While she did not lose interest completely in the fortunes of her book, Gabrielle had plenty of other worries in the course of that spring and summer of 1975. Her health, to start with. The winter just past had been even harder than the one before; she would gladly have escaped to the South, but finding no one to go with her had had to resign herself to staying at the Château Saint-Louis, where she had soon fallen prey to fits of coughing and attacks of asthma, along with insomnia for weeks on end. She had had one injection after another and undergone sessions of inhalation therapy, leading a snail-paced, almost vegetative life, so weak and incapable of the least effort had she been. A new affliction had been sharp pains in her fingers, preliminary signs of the arthritis she would soon be suffering. Trouble with her sinuses and her right eye required surgery in May, from which, thanks to the good, clean air of Petite-Rivière, she was just beginning to recover as summer began.

From now on the same pattern would be repeated year after year – the same contrast between increasingly wretched winters and summers awaited with growing, almost pathetic impatience. From November to March, Gabrielle in her sixties lived as though half-dead, shut up in her Château Saint-Louis "dungeon," subject to coughs, insomnia, attacks of arthritis and allergies of all kinds, constantly tired and totally lacking in energy. What strength remained she spent writing a few letters, mostly to Clémence, whom she never neglected. Then with the first breath of spring the life instinct would take over and she would come alive again, and there would be one thought in her head, to "reach Petite-Rivière, fresh pure air, and if God will, sunshine at last."[44] The air, the sunshine, Berthe's kindly friendship, relief at least temporarily from her woes – finding herself able and wanting to re-enter the only real world, the world of her writing, this was what this paradise, this Petite-Rivière-Saint-François, meant to Gabrielle, and would remain for her until the very end.

A paradise that seemed in peril, however, if one listened to rumours going round in the village since the early 1960s. Promoters backed by local and provincial authorities were eyeing the topography of Petite-Rivière for the development of a major ski centre that, they said, would attract floods of tourists and rouse the village from its economic torpor. For the purpose, the powers that be would expropriate all the land of La Grande-Pointe, hence the entire Simard domain and Gabrielle Roy's little house. Berthe was all upset, torn between her attachment to the old family property and her loyalty in spite of all (or in spite of herself) to the villagers, who were almost unanimously in favour of the plan. Gabrielle had no such scruples and did everything in her power to prevent what she considered not only a violation of her property owner's rights but an ecological disaster. She stirred up her summer-resident neighbours, protested to the mayor, and did not hesitate to put her prestige as a writer on the line. The ski centre project went ahead in spite of her efforts, although she did succeed in limiting the damage. The expropriation of 1980 affected only the north side of the road, so that her house was left untouched. Berthe had to give up hers, however, and move to the other side of the road into a new house that she and Aimé had built for them, opposite the old one.

During the summer of 1975 these preoccupations, added to those that Clémence was causing her, prevented Gabrielle from getting seriously down to work. Still, she had had a new manuscript under way for a year whose tentative title was "Mes enfants des autres." She was determined to finish it whatever the cost, and confided to me:

> But when this one is finished, I suppose I'll be asking heaven for time to do another. Always another to blot out the weaknesses of the one before, to do a little better, to dig deeper in the scrap of truth you're exploring [...]. But when all is said and done, you know – in any case I have long known – that the best, the finest book will be the one there won't be time to write. And in a sense it's better that way. You die wanting more, which is the best way to die.[45]

Gabrielle would spend the whole of the following summer, 1976, writing *Ces enfants de ma vie* – this was the title she would settle on shortly with the help of Sister Berthe. She moved to Petite-Rivière in the middle of May and brimming with energy threw herself into the work; not content just to spend her mornings on it as was her custom, she returned to it in the afternoon and often continued until late in the evening. As if there were an urgency, or as if the words were coming to her with unaccustomed ease and she was anxious to lose nothing for fear the flow might stop. By the end of that summer the manuscript was finished; one typewritten copy was ready by the beginning of November.

Judging from the manuscripts, it would seem that the six stories of *Ces enfants de ma vie* (*Children of My Heart*) were written in the order of their appearance in the book, the first being "Vincento," the last "De la truite dans l'eau glacée." There is no question that they were written one after the other without interruption, as different parts of a single work, "together clarifying, complementing, overlapping each other, and contributing to a common end," as a single "novel" in short, even though, Gabrielle conceded, "it's not the traditional form of a novel."[46] Although it consists of six stories, the book is divided into two parts corresponding to the two places where Gabrielle had been a teacher, but their succession in time is reversed. The first four stories are fairly short ("Vincento," "L'enfant de Noël," "L'alouette," and "Demetrioff") and take place in a city school modelled on the Institut Provencher, while the last two ("La maison gardée" and "De la truite dans l'eau glacée"), which are longer and more probing, are set in a rural school evoking the world of Gabrielle's first year of teaching at Cardinal. And so *Ces enfants de ma vie*, to the extent that its subject matter is autobiographical, can be read as moving in reverse order, toward older and more fundamental memories.[47]

This perhaps explains the rapidity and verve with which Gabrielle wrote the book, recalling her state of mind when writing *La Petite Poule d'Eau* and *Rue Deschambault*. The fact is that *Ces enfants de ma vie*, like these two earlier books, is a work whose inspiration sprang from what for Gabrielle was the most vigorous, most generously available source: her own life, the inexhaustible material of her past. This said, the thrust of the book is not primarily autobiographical, any more than it is with *La Petite Poule d'Eau* or *Rue Deschambault*. It is not a question of the author faithfully relating her past, but of allowing her imagination to use it as a base in a way, and to feed on it in order to compose a world in which one can no longer distinguish memory from invention, real people from fictional characters, familiar places of yesteryear from scenes of pure poetic creativity. As if embodying this ambiguity, there is a narrator central to *Ces enfants de ma vie* who, like Christine of *Rue Deschambault* and *La Route d'Altamont*, at one and the same time is and is not the young woman Gabrielle used to be. Except that this narrator has no name, no identity other than the simple "I" by which she designates herself.

Early in this chapter we saw that Gabrielle Roy in her old age, unlike so many other writers who fade or decline in their last years, experienced a burst of extraordinary creative power as great as in her youth and middle age, if not greater. This was perhaps owing to the fact that this entire last period of her career drew inspiration from remembrance and autobiographical imagination. A period that could therefore be qualified as "Proustian." *Un jardin au bout du monde* was already largely based on her past. More openly so were "Le pays de *Bonheur d'occasion*" and "Le Cercle Molière . . . porte ouverte," which she wrote around 1975. Then came *Fragiles Lumières de la terre*, the collection of old texts from earlier years that she had assembled and was preparing to publish. Things were happening as though she was taking less and less interest in the contemporary world and, feeling the approach of her own end, was detaching herself from the present and in the process discovering or rediscovering under a new light the vast space within herself that, although now lost, was begging to be recounted, explored, inhabited anew.

"Time does its work," she declared to Marc Gagné. "It decants what we remember, leaving aside what should not last. Memory is a poet."[48] And to Jacques Godbout a few years later, "There is no imagination, there is only a collage of memories."[49]

Fame Again

The manuscript of *Ces enfants de ma vie* was finished by the end of summer 1976 and was typed and corrected during the autumn and winter. By the following summer all was ready for publication by Les Éditions Stanké, and the book came out in September. It was an immediate and spectacular success. In the press and on radio and television, the critics gushed their enthusiasm. "Gabrielle Roy has never written anything as passionate, as troubling," Gilles Marcotte declared in *Le Devoir*; "[. . .] from *Bonheur d'occasion* to *Ces enfants de ma vie*, how far she has come, to the heart's most hidden recesses." "Luminous prose," "keenness of observation" trumpeted *La Presse* and *Le Droit*. Gabrielle Poulin ("one of the finest gifts that [Gabrielle Roy] has made to life and literature"), François Hébert ("unforgettable experience"), Jacques Godbout ("a great moment of emotion"), all those who made it their business to pass judgment on new books sang praises unreservedly and unequivocally.[50] Among all the expressions of admiration, one of the most moving came from the writer Yves Thériault, who had begun his career at the same time as Gabrielle Roy and whose work had often been compared to hers:

> I have written a lot in my life, in every genre, in every geographical setting, about all kinds of people, great and weak, powerful and abject, and through all these years, in all this writing, and today more than ever, I would have liked, would like still, and always will want to be able to write the way Gabrielle Roy does, to be able to love my characters as she loves hers, and [understand them] as she understands them.[51]

The primary reason for this critical success was of course the quality of the book, its power of evocation, the beauty of its writing, its capacity to please, as André Brochu observed, "both *connaisseur* readers and readers at large."[52] But there was also the literary context of the late 1970s, when the avant-garde aesthetics that had held sway for a decade were beginning to look shopworn and a desire was felt in many quarters for a return to a more human and readable literature. *Ces enfants de ma vie* sold like hotcakes in the bookstores as a result, over 25,000 copies in a year, more than any previous book of Gabrielle Roy's in so little time.

"I don't understand what's happening to me," she wrote to Berthe Valcourt. "Since my last book, *Ces enfants de ma vie*, came out there's been nothing but praise, praise, praise to the heavens! Even my old enemies are sending praise my way. In any case I'm climbing the last rungs of my life in glory. [. . .] It's true," she added, "that I still have time to come down again . . ."[53] However, the publication of *Fragiles Lumières de la terre* a few months later in the spring of 1978, far from bringing her down again gave a new boost to the celebration. Although this book, given its special nature, did not attract as many readers (about 2,000 copies sold in the first year), it brought its author a renewed flood of adulatory praise from the critics. "Honour to Gabrielle Roy," Réginald Martel exclaimed, while Jean Éthier-Blais declared himself "proud to be the contemporary of such a woman," and Yves Thériault once again expressed the "envy" he had always felt toward "this lacemaker of literature."[54]

Remembering that, while *Ces enfants de ma vie* and *Fragiles lumières de la terre* were having such success in Quebec, in the same year *Garden in the Wind* was being received enthusiastically in English Canada, one can only be struck how similar this year of 1977–1978 was to the time thirty years earlier when *Bonheur d'occasion* and *The Tin Flute* were rocketing Gabrielle Roy to the forefront of the literary scenes in Quebec and Canada. The context was not the same, of course; there were more books being published now, book distribution was better organized, and there were more readers. Still, all things considered, and leaving aside the international dimension that was not a factor this time, broadly speaking it was the same triumph, the same sudden fame all over again. The phenomenon was even more striking in its contrast with the relative eclipse that Gabrielle Roy's work had suffered since the 1960s and particularly since the early 1970s, when many readers and critics, while respecting her, considered her more or less old hat, even obsolete. André Brochu wrote, "It was even thought that [her] last works, particularly *Cet été qui chantait*, displayed a progressive waning of inspiration. But it was not so," he continued, "in *Ces enfants de ma vie*, Gabrielle Roy's voice rises with the mastery and inimitable purity of her most beautiful narrations."

The publication of *Ces enfants de ma vie* and *Fragiles Lumières de la terre*, which strictly speaking were the last books of her lifetime, brought

Gabrielle the pleasure of being rediscovered, winning back a wide readership and being in the limelight again. All the spotlights were turned on her, and the long succession of honours throughout her life and career entered a new, accelerated phase. Four major distinctions came one after the other. In May 1978 she received the Governor General's Award for *Ces enfants de ma vie*; this was the third time she had received this award, a record in Canadian history. A month later the Canada Council presented her with the Molson Prize of $20,000; the painter Jack Shadbolt and the lexicographer George Story were also recipients on the same occasion. In 1980, the same Canada Council awarded her its Prize for Children's Literature for *Courte-Queue* (*Cliptail*), a story for children published in the autumn of 1979. A few days later, the Canadian Conference of the Arts awarded her one of its prestigious Diplômes d'honneur. Hardly surprising in the course of these fertile years that there should be recurrent Nobel Prize rumours, always nerve-racking for Gabrielle and always coming to nothing.

Ever since the days of the Académie Saint-Joseph and the Association d'éducation medals, Gabrielle had never ceased to be excited over winning prizes. She wrote to Clémence, "I don't think there are many [prizes] I haven't had. Hey, who could have said, back in the days of Deschambault Street, that so many extraordinary things would happen to me that even to me they seem more dreamlike than real."[55]

However, moved though she was by all these manifestations of admiration, she was also flustered, even overwhelmed by it all, as she had been years before by the success of *Bonheur d'occasion* and *The Tin Flute*. For honours never came without their retinue of obligations and requirements, which tired her and prevented her from working. If she allowed herself to be snared by an invitation she was immediately sorry for it. Thus in February 1978 she agreed to go to Calgary for a conference on Canadian fiction organized by Jack McClelland on the occasion of the twentieth anniversary of the New Canadian Library series; it was her last trip to the West. Tributes were paid from every quarter; she was fêted, surrounded, but could take only four days of it and returned home exhausted. Fortunately she had been able to spend a great deal of time with the novelist Margaret Laurence, whom she was meeting for the first time but with whom she had begun exchanging letters not long before and would continue until the end of her life. A little later that spring I persuaded her to go with me to a cocktail party in conjunction with the Salon du livre de Québec; when I brought her home to her apartment I bitterly regretted my insistence when I saw how tense and overexcited the experience had made her, for she was barely able to catch her breath. The next day I learned that she had not slept a wink all night. This was the reason she shrank from all public gatherings, even those organized especially for her; when she was to receive a prize, instead of going herself to the ceremony she would ask someone close to represent her.[56] Social events were decidedly not for her.

She much preferred relationships by letter, although sometimes she despaired of the number she found she had to write. She considered it a duty to reply to all the letters she received. If they were from readers or fellow writers, she replied herself, but for the rest of her mail – more or less official inquiries, invitations, and requests for information or permissions – usually she had me reply for her. The most diligent letter-writers were journalists looking for interviews. To most of these she continued to give a categorical "no," refusing as always to play the game of promotion via the media. But when she felt she was dealing with someone sensitive, with whom she could feel confident, she did occasionally accept, provided the visitor had no tape recorder or camera of any kind. In fact, as she confided to Joyce Marshall, there was not as much stress in this exercise as there used to be:

> I am still a little afraid of interviews [...] but not frightened to death as I used to [be]. Perhaps, now, the fear is attenuated by the feeling that however they dig and I with them, there remains a hidden core to their eyes and my eyes, which is to the best, for therein lies the never rooted secret which alone enables us to continue living. Just imagine the despair if suddenly we knew everything about [ourselves] and saw clearly to the very bottom of the riddle.[57]

Among the rare interviews she granted during these years, the finest and warmest were one she granted in 1976 to the journalist David Cobb and another two years later to Jacques Godbout, who came to see her at Petite-Rivière-Saint-François for the magazine *L'Actualité.*[58] She also continued to receive academics from time to time, some of whom would publish accounts of their private conversations with her, after her death.

As a public personage, an admired and celebrated novelist, Gabrielle Roy was therefore once again in a position of prominence in the late 1970s. The political and ideological context being what it was at the time, it is understandable that she be invited to take a position in the great debates of the hour. She was wary of such solicitations, however, and kept as far as possible from controversy. She had her own ideas, to be sure, and did not hesitate to express them in private, but taking public positions seemed to her dangerous and contrary to her role as a writer. She felt this way for example about feminism, whose recent evolution toward ever more radical theory and action repelled her, as it repelled many women of her generation who, after sympathizing in the past with women's causes, could no longer identify with the positions of the neo-feminists, whom they saw as extreme. Gabrielle would talk about her hesitations in private conversation with those close to her and even a few admirers, but never publicly and never committing herself on these questions.

The same wariness applied to her attitude with regard to Québécois nationalism, which in these pre-referendum years was certainly the principal subject of discussion and discord in Québécois and Canadian political and intellectual circles. Here again, the election of the Parti Québécois, the rise of independentism, the promulgation of Bill 101, the "language law," all clashed with her federalist convictions and her attachment to Canada, or at least the ideal vision she had always had of a multi-ethnic and fraternal Canada. The situation in Quebec worried her; she was afraid of the intolerance "which often goes with a certain form of incorruptibility," she said in private. "I was brought up in much the same atmosphere. I dread it like the worst evil."[59] When we met we often had discussions on this subject; she knew my opinions, which were not hers, and respected them, but did not hide the hostility, even anxiety, inspired in her by the Parti Québécois and the nationalist intellectuals.

This said, she did not for an instant dream of becoming involved in the debate, aware that in the state the province was in, with almost all the writers backing the Parti Québécois, her voice might not be heard, or worse, might be heard in a negative way, attracting a tempest of fury similar to that being suffered currently by Félix-Antoine Savard after his public stand in favour of Canada.[60] How, in the midst of this extreme polarization of ideas and feelings, could she possibly put across her own personal vision of things, affirming "my loyalty to Quebec," but without being able or wanting to exclude from her affections "the rest of Canada, where we as a people have wandered and suffered, yes, but throughout which we have also left our mark"?[61] She tried therefore not to get involved. "It is a time indeed for silence, meditation, or, if words it must be, let them be of friendship and understanding."[62]

Not that there was any shortage of opportunity for involvement. In English Canada her ideas were known and invitations kept arriving for her to take a public stand. She declined them all, or at least refused to associate herself with any side, preferring in an unobtrusive way to advocate tolerance and mutual understanding.[63] In Quebec, as the May 1980 referendum approached, the No side pressed her increasingly to declare herself publicly in its favour. Despite her convictions she remained firm. And so to Solange Chaput-Rolland, whom the "No Committee" had delegated to recruit her, she replied in April 1980:

> The use of their names for political purposes to which so many stars, singers, poets, writers have lent themselves *chez nous*, inspires such sadness in me, I see in it so little respect for moral and intellectual integrity, and a conformity so contrary to the creative spirit that I could not bring myself to imitate them, even for the benefit of the cause that I consider to be good and just. In our desire to succeed, I think we should take care not to use methods of which we disapprove.[64]

Her one and only intervention was the publication in the Montreal literary magazine *Liberté* in 1979 of her short story titled "Ély! Ély! Ély!," which she had written some time before and in which she remembered her major reporting tour of 1942 through the prairies of the West, to her the image of the poetry and grandeur of Canada.[65] This text, in which once again fiction and autobiography are mingled, was to her in no way a political statement. She was offering it essentially as the statement of a writer, bearing, in her mind, the same message of harmony and fraternity expressed by her entire life's work.

Leaving Her House in Order

Her life's work. Although she felt intensely the political turmoil that rocked these years, one of Gabrielle's major concerns through the 1970s was tending the fortunes and future of the books she realized she would soon be leaving behind. She therefore devoted a great deal of her failing energy to putting her professional and family affairs in order, as though all this must be settled before she could depart in peace.

In practical terms, this meant masses of agreements to be negotiated and signed, endless correspondence, telephone calls, files to be opened and kept – all the thankless, harrowing administrative work she complained about constantly. "I have a feeling," she wrote to Margaret Laurence, "that you and I have been worn out far more by the business letters and all the demands on us [than] by our own work. It seems to me there must have been a time when writers wrote their books and were otherwise left alone. [. . .] And where are we to find the time to dream our dreams out of which come our books?"[66]

Still, these chores simply had to be done in her estimation, and she did them with great care and competence. People close to her – friends, publishers – offered what help they could, and she made abundant use of their services or counsel while keeping a watchful eye on everything and meticulously following developments under each heading. For final decisions she looked to no one but herself, confident in her thirty-five years of experience in the trade and anxious to keep a controlling hand on the literary and commercial destiny of her work.

Publishing was the first thing she tackled. Over the years, ownership of her rights had become rather scattered. Her aim now was to regain ownership of as much as possible of those scattered rights so as to exercise direct control herself over all publication and distribution of her works. First she must repatriate the rights she had granted her publishers in New York and Paris years before.

She approached Harcourt Brace (subsequently Harcourt Brace & World), which still held world English-language rights (excluding Canada) for all her books up to and including *The Road Past Altamont*, but to whom she felt she owed nothing since the firm had declined to publish *Windflower*. The head of the firm complied willingly with her request. The same request to Les Éditions Flammarion met with a very different reaction. The house had published seven of Gabrielle's books, the last being *La Rivière sans repos*, which appeared in 1972, two years after the Montreal edition; despite a few sympathetic reviews,[67] once again the book had sold poorly. No other title of hers appeared in Paris subsequently in her lifetime, either with Flammarion or any other publisher.[68] And yet by the terms of the contracts signed with Jean-Marie Nadeau and more recently with Gabrielle herself, Flammarion retained not only the right to sell her early books on the French-language market (excluding Canada), and to continue to do so for fifty years after her death, but had exclusive translation rights for all languages of the world except English. Flammarion was doing nothing to lift Gabrielle Roy's name from the oblivion into which it had sunk in France, having more lucrative fish to fry, and was making no effort to sell her rights abroad, merely replying routinely to the occasional inquiries that happened to come along from European and Asiatic translators or publishers. Wishing to regain her freedom in this quarter as well, Gabrielle wrote asking for the return of her rights. No reply. She wrote again. Still no reply. After the third letter, Henri Flammarion, the head of the firm, deigned at last to write her a letter containing, behind its complimentary phrases, an unmistakable message: there was no question of returning her rights; Flammarion valued its authors and gave them all the attention required, the proof being that the minimum number of copies stipulated in the contract was always kept on hand. Gabrielle kept badgering, called on support from friends and acquaintances, considered bringing the newly founded Union des écrivains québécois into the picture, all to no avail: "Flammarion's talons"[69] remained firmly closed. Gabrielle would remain a Flammarion author, a prisoner, until the very end.

Flammarion's refusal to let her go was far more a matter of principle than profit, for her career in France had been over for many a year, as in the United States. Except in academic circles specializing in Canadian or Quebec studies, hardly anyone on the international scene spoke of her or read what she wrote, unless it was the story titled "De la truite dans l'eau glacée," which had been adapted and published in several editions of The Reader's Digest.[70] Although she considered herself to have a "universal" vocation and to be writing "for all men," she found her real readership above all, if not solely, in Canada. In the Canadian context, her work was and still is unquestionably universal, for it has been read, admired, and studied as much in English-speaking circles as French-speaking, as much in Toronto and Winnipeg as Montreal, which at the time could be said of very few authors either French Québécois or English Canadian. To this day, Gabrielle Roy is probably the only truly "Canadian" writer in the federal sense of the word, meaning the only one whose work genuinely transcends the language barrier and is embraced unreservedly by the two communities as their own – and by the two literary establishments.

This was why Gabrielle paid such close attention to the English translation of her works and their publication on the English-Canadian market. She considered the English versions of her books to be practically the equals of the French, in fact, more or less a second original addressed to a readership as important in her eyes as her French readers. Beginning with the advent of Joyce Marshall, she took up the habit of very closely following and even intervening in the translations, which did not always sit well with Joyce, who felt sometimes that Gabrielle had an inflated idea of her own grasp of literary English. Nevertheless the two continued to work together closely and amicably, and their abundant correspondence stands as a fine example of the counterpoint in writing that translation can stimulate when conditions are right.

However, around 1973 after she had finished the translation *Enchanted Summer*, for which she won the Canada Council Translation Prize, Joyce decided to stop translating in order to give more time to her own writing.[71] For Gabrielle it was a great loss. "I so dislike the thought of working with someone else than you," she wrote, "specially now that we had acquired a sort of ease and harmony which only come from the experience of working together."[72] Several years would have to go by before she would accept a new translator, one chosen by Jack McClelland for *Garden in the Wind* in 1976. This was Alan Brown of Montreal, who had a distinguished career behind him begun in France with translations of Cendrars and Giono and continued in Canada with poems by Anne Hébert. Gabrielle very quickly came to appreciate his competence and dedication and expressed her delight with the quality and diligence of his work. She never had as friendly an association with him as she had had with Joyce, but their professional relationship was always harmonious. Thus Brown became Gabrielle Roy's regular translator. After *Un Jardin au bout du monde* (*Garden in the Wind*, 1977), he translated *Ces enfants de ma vie* (*Children of My Heart*, 1979), *Fragiles Lumières de la terre* (*The Fragile Lights of Earth*, 1982), and *Courte-Queue* (*Cliptail*, 1980).[73] All these translations were published by the same publisher, McClelland & Stewart, to whom Gabrielle had remained faithful since the first contacts in the late 1940s. The head of the firm, Jack McClelland, had become a friend. However, at the end of 1973 this relationship was clouded briefly when *The Hidden Mountain* came out in the New Canadian Library series; Gabrielle was revolted by the introduction written by Mary Jane Edwards, which essentially repeated a psychoanalytical interpretation put forward several years earlier by Gérard Bessette that turns the cariboo hunt into a metaphorical "mother-killing." Knowing that her words would reach Jack's ears, she wrote to Joyce Marshall, "I don't think I'll ever have another book published at McClelland & Stewart. [...] I consider [this foreword] not only a gross lack of intelligence, taste and judgment, but a sort of villainy. [...] There was a time when [Jack] would not have tolerated such mediocrity, but now!"[74] As soon as he got wind of it, Jack fell over himself with apologies and had the offending introduction removed from subsequent printings and replaced with a far more amenable text by Malcolm Ross, the series editor. Gabrielle's attitude changed forthwith. "You," she was soon telling Jack, "are one of the few left of the breed of friendly publishers who genuinely love their writers."[75] The fact was that there was not a single English-Canadian publisher in a position to look after her interests as well as McClelland & Stewart, and she knew it. Jack was always unfailingly honest and kind with her, her new books were promptly translated and published, her royalties were paid on schedule, and the body of her works enjoyed a sort of permanence in the schools and bookstores of English Canada through the paperback New Canadian Library series. Joining her first four novels in the series, after *The Hidden Mountain* there appeared *Windflower* (1975), *The Road Past Altamont* (1976), and *Garden in the Wind* (1981).[76]

The situation was far less rosy in Quebec, where Gabrielle had been having rather serious publication problems for some time. Beauchemin, which had been publishing her since 1947, was in steep decline as a literary publisher, its managers having decided to concentrate on the far more lucrative textbook field. For some ten years or so Gabrielle had been distancing herself from the firm, obtaining cancellation of her original contracts and replacing them with licences of limited scope. She even gave three of her books to competitors. However, her flirtations with HMH (*La Route d'Altamont*), les Éditions françaises (*Cet été qui chantait*), and Leméac (*Ma vache Bossie*) did not lead to anything more permanent, so that around 1976 she found she was at a loose end as an author, without a steady publisher on the Quebec scene. Enter Alain Stanké, who had founded a firm named les Éditions internationales Alain Stanké two years earlier and was on the hunt for blue-chip authors. He made contact with Gabrielle Roy in the spring of 1977 and urged her to let him publish her new book. She agreed, and *Ces enfants de ma vie* appeared that fall with resounding success. That same year Stanké was starting a Quebec literature paperback series, Québec 10/10, in which he suggested a reprint of *Bonheur d'occasion*, the only available French-language version at the time being the original Beauchemin edition, which was too expensive for large-scale school purchases. The book appeared in the series with Stanké at the end of 1977. Since this first experience was positive, Gabrielle authorized a reprint edition of *La Montagne secrète* in 1978, and then the same with her other books. These were not strictly speaking new editions but photographic reproductions of the regular editions, after a number of corrections. So that this work, which she found tiring, would be attended to, she asked Stanké to appoint me editor of the series. And so from 1979 until my departure from the firm in 1982, there appeared six more of her books in the Québec 10/10 series.[77]

In 1979, to mark the International Year of the Child, Gabrielle also published the children's story *Courte-Queue* with Stanké; the royalties from the first printing of 3,000 copies went to UNICEF. But while her ties with Les Éditions Stanké were close, they were not of the same order as those she had with McClelland & Stewart. In the first place they did not prevent her from publishing elsewhere; *Fragiles Lumières de la terre* appeared with Les Éditions Quinze in the Prose entière series I was editing with François Hébert at the time. And then, Gabrielle was determined to remain entirely free in her relationship with her new publisher so as never again to be caught in the powerless position her relations with Flammarion had placed her. She was therefore extremely cautious in all her agreements with Stanké, as with her other publishers in this period, never giving up her copyright or any subsidiary rights and signing short, straightforward contracts that she drew up herself, had limited application, and were revocable at any time. In this way she could extricate herself without difficulty, if and when she wished.

And so Gabrielle had a full plate as a businesswoman. Her long winter days were amply occupied with these matters. Something that concerned her greatly, aside from publication, was film adaptation of her novels. She had not had much luck with this, but then she had not made much effort to induce movie and television producers to bring her books to the screen; any overtures on their part had met with indifference on hers, even hostility. In the 1970s, with the movie industry becoming more prosperous and open-handed, her attitude changed. For a time she thought fortune was smiling on her when Paul Blouin, a Radio-Canada producer, began an adaptation of "De la truite dans l'eau glacée," and a young Hollywood screenwriter, Paula Mason, was interested in a number of her books and even took out an option on *Windflower*. Both projects fell through, however, as happens more often than not in such cases. It was a different story with *The Tin Flute*. In view of its widespread popularity, various groups had been expressing interest in producing a film based on the novel for some dozen years. But the rights were still locked up in Hollywood with Universal Studios, which had declared in 1969 that they would not be released for less than $150,000. Other approaches had been made since, but none had led anywhere. Gabrielle had come to the point of resigning herself to the permanence of the situation when in 1976 she learned that the Montreal filmmaker Claude Fournier was considering buying the rights from Universal. With this news "I experienced the fear of my life," she wrote to Jack McClelland, for in her opinion Fournier was a filmmaker "who [did] inferior work on the porno side."[78] She also notified Gratien Gelinas, president of the Canadian Film Development Corporation, hoping that he would intervene and enable her to recover control of her film rights for *The Tin Flute*. Gelinas promised to do his best, but had no success. Rose Films, Fournier's company, acquired the rights and began production of the feature film, *Bonheur d'occasion*. Its première took place in Moscow on 12 July 1983, the day before Gabrielle's death. Gabrielle therefore had neither seen it nor had a hand in shaping it.[79] None of her books were brought to the screen in her lifetime, in fact. That, she confided to me, was one of her great regrets.

The business matters she dealt with in her final years also included the preparation of her literary estate, beginning with her personal papers. For a long time she had kept practically none of her manuscripts, letters, or other documents relating to her life and career, not being a "packrat" by nature and wanting to be burdened with as little as possible so as to be free to pull up stakes and move on at any moment. It was Marcel, after their marriage, who put a stop to this practice. Careful collector that he was, he went about saving at least the essential, the manuscripts, which he sometimes even had to go and fish out of the garbage can. Then, after Jean-Marie Nadeau's death in 1960, Gabrielle received boxes full of files that she did not take the trouble to put in order but that she did keep, despite her lack of interest in her own archives. For her, all that counted was whatever she was working on currently, not the relics of the past.

And then as her reputation grew, official institutions began to show an interest. In 1969 she was approached by the National Library of Canada. The initiative did not lead anywhere, but it made Gabrielle aware of the potential value of her papers. In her spare time she started putting them in order with the help of Berthe Simard. Berthe, who was good at carpentry, made some wooden boxes and began a preliminary sorting of the documents stored in the Simard house at Petite-Rivière-Saint-François. This went on through the winter of 1975. Less than a year later, Gabrielle received a firm offer from Kenneth M. Glazier, the head librarian at the University of Calgary, for the purchase of her archives.

Backed by the petrodollars then pouring into Alberta, Glazier was combing Canada from ocean to ocean for the manuscripts of famous writers. He had already acquired some prestigious papers: Hugh MacLennan, Brian Moore, Mordecai Richler; and discussions were well under way with André Langevin, Roger Lemelin, and Claude Péloquin. Glazier was proposing to pay her $60,000 for the entirety of her papers – a fairly tidy sum on the Canadian archivistic market at the time.

Jack McClelland, who was the intermediary between Glazier and Gabrielle, urged her to accept; Mordecai Richler came to Quebec City to see her and try to convince her. She was not too categorical but her mind was made up, had been made up since the beginning – since her work belonged "to the country as a whole,"[80] and was written in French, there was no question of giving over her manuscripts to an Albertan university. As to the money she was being offered, she wrote to Jack:

> I discovered what has been true most of my life but has become more and more evident to me lately, the fact that I care very little for money. Professionally, I care for almost nothing, except, I think, to write according to the inner commands and thus reap friendship perhaps through my efforts. All the rest now seems quite insignificant to me. And so I have attained extraordinary freedom, just by not caring for wealth and even, I suppose, fame. Have you ever weighed the bizarre strength that comes from such a liberation in our present day society? It is almost incredible.[81]

There is no reason to doubt the sincerity of this declaration. However, this detachment from material things at which Gabrielle says she has arrived did not prevent her, at the time of this letter as always, from keeping a sharp eye on the management of her finances, insisting on prompt payment of her royalties at each due date, and never spending more than necessary, as if she were short of money. In fact, her income in these years was not only more than respectable but kept increasing. From some $14,000 in 1976, her royalties rose to over $33,000 in 1979 (after publication of *Ces enfants de ma vie*), and thereafter stabilized at around $25,000 a year. Added to this there were soon government pension payments and especially her investment income, which was growing each year. In total, her annual income climbed from $32,000 in 1976 to over $86,000 in 1982.[82]

Jack McClelland and the librarian-collector Glazier tried again in the months following Gabrielle's first refusal, then again a year later. In vain.

The precious papers were going to remain in the East. Offers came from the Bibliothèque nationale du Québec and the National Archives of Canada, neither of which suited her but which inspired her to pay even more attention to assembling her archives. She asked Sister Berthe to return the many letters she had written Clémence and took good care of Bernadette's personal papers, which Bernadette's community had turned over to her. She knew now that all these papers were worth a lot of money and could arouse greed.

Finally, in the closing months of 1980, Guy Sylvestre, the national librarian at the National Library of Canada, made her a new offer that she decided to accept, stipulating that the news could not be made public until after her death. The papers were stored in the meantime in two huge wooden boxes in Montreal, in my office at McGill University, where I had taken them several months earlier at Gabrielle's request. There they would stay until the winter of 1983 after an expert consulted by the library had estimated their value at $165,000. But Gabrielle did not want to touch this money for fear of incurring income tax, and because she intended it for the foundation she was setting up to receive her literary estate.

Thinking of the posthumous destiny of her oeuvre, she had for some time been considering creating a small non-profit company to which she could bequeath her royalties, and which would administer her works when she was no longer there. Beginning in 1978 or 1979, a large part of the conversations I had with her were on this subject, which was a major preoccupation for her. But I was not the only one helping her; she also discussed the project with Pierre Morency, who was living in Quebec City and was in regular contact with her. She and Morency had known each other since 1976 when he had sent her a copy of the first issue of the magazine *Estuaire*, which he had just founded. They had taken to phoning and seeing each other often after that. When he had time, Pierre would drive her to the Île d'Orléans where he had a little house by the river. They became friends this way, united not only by being writers but also their shared passion for nature.[83] Renée Dupuis, Pierre Morency's wife, is a lawyer; she undertook the incorporation of the non-profit company, which received its letters patent in November 1981 under the name "Fonds Gabrielle Roy." Its first directors were Pierre and Renée Morency, Marcel, and I. Gabrielle asked André Major and Gilles Marcotte to join us, which they accepted at once.

It was therefore the Fonds Gabrielle Roy that finally fell heir to Gabrielle's archives and in 1984, after her death, received the National Library's $165,000.[84]

Looking Back

Over these final years of her life, settling her professional affairs mattered a great deal to Gabrielle, with the thought of death more present in her mind each day. But far from trying to forget it, far from thrusting it away or rebelling against it, she accepted the thought without distress and let it be the guide for most of what she was doing. She wanted to leave everything in order and provide in minutest detail how things would be handled after her demise.

One of these things was how Clémence would be cared for. In the spring of 1975, about eight months after her last visit to Otterburne, Gabrielle learned that the Sisters of Providence were going to close the Résidence Sainte-Thérèse. Some other place would have to be found for Clémence, who was more cheered than distressed at having to leave this village she had found such a crushing bore. "Let's let Saint Providence do as she will," she wrote to Gabrielle, who was sick with worry, adding wickedly, "if there is one."[85] With or without the help of divine Providence, Gabrielle and Sister Berthe moved heaven and earth to find Clémence a place in St-Boniface, as she wished. In the autumn they succeeded, when the managers of the newly built nursing home on Archibald Street agreed to take Clémence, beginning the following March. In order to see to the final details of the move, Gabrielle came with Marcel to spend Christmas in St-Boniface. As soon as she had bought what was needed for Clémence's move and seen to the formalities, however, she left Marcel with his family in St-Boniface and took refuge for a week at the St-Jean-Baptiste convent with Sister Berthe.

More than ever, Sister Berthe was the one that Gabrielle relied on to ensure Clémence's care and future – "my Berthe, my hummingbird, my message runner, my lantern bearer, my silent partner too sometimes, my big sister or my little sister, I hardly know what any more."[86] Her role with Clémence had hitherto been mostly one of moral and psychological support, but Gabrielle now felt she no longer had the strength to look after her aged, ailing sister as she had been doing and so placed full

responsibility for her care in Sister Berthe's hands, with the new relationship taking a more official turn and becoming a true legal tutorship.
But complications arose over the transfer.

Gabrielle had had legal responsibility for Clémence since 1973,
Clémence having signed a power of attorney making her younger sister
her guardian and administrator of her assets, meaning the sums banked
in her name to cover her living and burial expenses. These sums all came
from Gabrielle, who continued besides to add between $500 and $1,000
a year to Clémence's capital so as to give her as much protection as possible in case of need. In practice, it had been Sister Berthe who had been
seeing to Clémence's interests and managing her money. To simplify
things, to better protect Clémence, and, to be frank, free herself of a
burden that was weighing on her, Gabrielle now wanted a new power of
attorney making Berthe her replacement as manager of Clémence's
assets. However, in the summer of 1977, a psychiatrist sent by the provincial social services to examine the occupants of the Résidence Sainte-
Thérèse declared Clémence "mentally disordered and incompetent to
manage her own personal affairs," which meant she was declared unfit
to sign anything whatever and made a ward of the State. Gabrielle was
outraged and protested immediately with the utmost vigour, in support
of her case quoting Clémence's letters "which show sensitivity, delicacy,
and intelligence." She threatened to use her personal prestige to appeal
directly to the Manitoban government. Her protest had the desired
effect. Less than a month after having judged Clémence to be suffering
from "senile dementia," the psychiatrist admitted to mistaking patients
and ordered his diagnosis destroyed; one of his colleagues then examined Clémence and declared, "I find no element in her suggesting mental
debility or senility."[87] Clémence was therefore free to entrust anyone she
wished with the management of her money. With much careful explanation, for Clémence was mistrustful, Gabrielle persuaded her to sign
a power of attorney in favour of Sister Berthe. And so the heritage
bequeathed by Mélina to her daughters and handed from one to
another over thirty-five years was finally received by Sister Berthe
Valcourt. From that moment Berthe became much more than a friend
or even a sister to Gabrielle – she became the surrogate, even the rein-
carnation of Gabrielle's mother, with whom Gabrielle found herself
once more in the position she had never really wanted to lose, had
never really accepted having lost: that of the favourite child with a
loving soul to watch over and protect her, the daughter so much freer,

more self-assured, more able to confront the world for having someone back there looking after everything, keeping the home fires burning, and waiting for her.

After her brief visit to St-Boniface and St-Jean-Baptiste in the final days of 1975, Gabrielle would never again return to Manitoba. She would never again see Clémence either. The sisters continued to correspond, however, and sometimes talked on the telephone, for poor Clémence's morale still had to be boosted on a regular basis. She soon became almost as bored in St-Boniface as at Otterburne; "it's not the most ideal place in the world," she announced barely six months after moving.[88] Gabrielle did her best to cheer her up, but Clémence always found cause to complain about her loneliness, or the monotony of the neighbour-hood, or the all-round dreariness of life. "You know," she told Gabrielle one day, "I was born old."[89] The fact was that being sad was her way of life and her only way of getting to feel loved a little. Gabrielle kept sending her small gifts – clothes, books, sugary treats – and continued supplying money, but in all other respects it was Berthe who took care of everything, and on that score Gabrielle's heart and mind were now at peace.

Little by little, a kind of peace had also settled in between Gabrielle and Marcel. To be sure, they still quarrelled, and the tone between them was often impatient or surly; they no longer really liked being in each other's company and spent long periods without even seeing one another, or very nearly. In summer, Gabrielle would escape to Petite-Rivière-Saint-François, where Marcel made increasingly rare appear-ances. In winter, Marcel often went to Manitoba alone to spend Christmas with his mother and sisters, and the rest of the year regularly made other short trips with his friends. When they were together they talked little, preoccupied as they were with their own worries and each more or less indifferent to those of the other. Yet they did not consider breaking up. "You don't separate two old horses," Gabrielle sometimes used to say to her friends with a note of tenderness in her voice. Too old for resentment, the two of them had learned to accept each other's faults and frustrations, or at least not to harbour grudges over them, and to live side by side as strangers who needed one another so as not to feel totally abandoned and bereft.

They continued to move in parallel worlds for all that, and the apart-ment in the Château Saint-Louis, which had not seen a new coat of paint in many a year, was now no more than a neutral meeting ground where each was shut away in a separate room and spoke no more than was strictly necessary to the other. Beyond this, she had her life and he had his. Gabrielle was more and more solitary. She did maintain a few occasional contacts with Simone Bussières, Jacqueline Deniset, and Cécile Chabot and still saw the Madeleines, but no longer had a friend she felt as close to as she had been to Adrienne. Her only really regular contacts were with Berthe Simard, who was ever more devoted to her, and Bibiane Patry, the Quebec City neighbour and part friend, part servant who came running at the crook of a finger and did a great many things for her, from buying her clothes at Holt Renfrew's to sending off parcels to Clémence, to running errands in the neighbourhood. Marcel's affair with M. C. continued despite frequent tempests. Perhaps on account of his increasing age, he had taken to haunting gay bars and roaming the Plains of Abraham at night in search of new companions. Gabrielle was always afraid of scandal and this behaviour worried her, and so she urged M. C. to keep an eye on "the llama," as they had nicknamed Marcel, to make sure he did nothing asinine.

Gabrielle's fondest wish these days was not to have to worry any more over either Clémence or Marcel as she had been doing, not to feel responsible for their happiness. First because she no longer felt capable of it either physically or psychologically, but also because she was absorbed by something else, held to another obligation that she wanted at all costs to fulfil before departing. This other obligation was still the same as ever, perhaps the only one she had never been free of, once committed – her compulsion to write.

By 1977, even before putting the finishing touches to *Ces enfants de ma vie*, she had embarked on a new project that was engrossing her totally. We find this project announced in a letter to Jack McClelland dated 30 December 1976:

> It has [come] down on me lately that my own life, could I relate it simply as it unfolded and went on its bizarre way, would be my best novel.[90]

She had been cultivating memories of her own life for many years, in fact. She had barely turned fifty before she entered "the age when we never stop digging things about the past out of the backs of our minds"; "and it's good that it should be so," she added; "that's what makes up for the sadness of growing old."[91] Then came the death of Bernadette, the trips to Otterburne, the exchanges of letters with Clémence, all circumstances which "[reawakened] the memories of my youth and my childhood in Manitoba by the thousands, some of them sweet, others stifling,"[92] and which in her life and imagination gradually created another world that was almost more real to her than the present and certainly closer, richer in emotions and imagery, and come to her directly from the past. Her writing had been delving more and more into this world, as we have seen, beginning with *Un jardin au bout du monde*, (*Garden in the Wind*), and especially when she came to *Ces enfants de ma vie* (*Children of My Heart*).

Until that point, however, she had always kept autobiography and fiction separate in her work. The "true" story of her past she had carefully limited to short texts that in her mind had less literary than historical or documentary interest, like "Souvenirs du Manitoba," "My Manitoba Heritage," "Le pays de *Bonheur d'occasion*," and "Le Cercle Molière . . . porte ouverte," texts whose purpose was not so much to tell about her life as to reminisce about periods and people she had known. The subject or focus of these writings had not been herself but the people she had associated with and the events and circumstances she had been part of. Her really personal memories, those about her most private and unforgettable past, her deepest awareness of what she had been and become, had found ample place in her writings, but always in fictional mode, through characters who, as like as they might appear to their author, were still invented. This is the case with first-person narrations like *Street of Riches*, *The Road Past Altamont*, and *Children of My Heart*, but also novels as "objective" as *Where Nests the Water Hen*, *The Cashier*, *The Hidden Mountain*, and even *The Tin Flute* and *Windflower*. From one end to the other, Gabrielle Roy's oeuvre, like that of many other writers, is suffused with memory, nourished with experiences and imagery reaped throughout a lifetime and which, captured by her writing, are both revealed and transformed.

In fictional creation, the aim of this process is the make-up of a story and universe that are not those of the novelist but of the characters, and only theirs. In autobiography it is different, for the author's past is not just a storehouse of impressions and images but the subject of the text, and the primary purpose is not invention but avowal, a search for the self and the expression of what ought to be given and received as the truth about the person writing. This is probably why aging writers so often show an urge to write autobiographies, at a point where their fictional oeuvre seems to be complete and all they have left to put into writing is their own lives, whole and shorn of secrets, so that they too may emerge and be properly completed.

When she began the story of her life, Gabrielle knew she did not have any other book to write than this one. What triggered it was perhaps a short text commissioned by the *Globe and Mail* of Toronto in the autumn of 1976 for its "Mermaid Inn Column." Since she was left free to choose any subject she wanted, she chose to write about her years at the Académie Saint-Joseph, under the title "My Schooldays in St. Boniface," about the atmosphere of clandestinity in which the nuns taught French, her discovery of Shakespeare and English literature, and especially the episode of "saving the class" before the astonished inspector, which would reappear almost word for word in the fifth chapter of *Enchantment and Sorrow*.[93] The *Globe and Mail* article appeared on 18 December 1976 in an English translation by Alan Brown, but was never published in French.

In the Gabrielle Roy archives at the National Library of Canada there is another unpublished manuscript of the same kind, probably written in 1977, likely predating only briefly the beginning of *La détresse et l'enchantement*, the original French version of *Enchantment and Sorrow*. Titled "Ma petite rue qui m'a menée autour du monde," this is a long remembrance of Gabrielle's birth milieu that would be rather clumsy and uninteresting if it were not for two features directly prefiguring the autobiography. First, there is a striking scene in which the sixteen-year-old girl discovers her mother's face and suffering for the first time, an important scene because it shows the mother as the key character in the narrator's personal development; then there is the evocation of the "little street," which is entirely built on the juxtaposition of two extremes, on one side looking toward Nature and peaceful solitude, on the other toward city life, all disorder and fraternity. Thus was announced one of the fundamental motifs of the autobiography, the thematic polarization between euphoria and suffering, bursts of optimism and slumps of discouragement, confidence and regret – in other words, Gabrielle's realization that she was a divided, torn creature who could never come to rest anywhere and would find her true nature only in this very oscillation.

This both metaphysical and psychological form of cyclothymia had always defined Gabrielle's temperament, a fact she recognized herself. Even at the early age of twenty when she was a young teacher at Cardinal, she described herself as being "light and shadow, gaiety and melancholy, smiles and tears."[94] The recognition recurs repeatedly in her writings and correspondence. In 1972 she declared in an interview, "I'm constantly torn between two forces pulling me in opposite directions, hope and sorrow,"[95] a split that was not only a trait of character in her, although it was that too (and hence one of the sources of her chronic swings of mood), but with advancing age became a basic characteristic of her writing and more broadly her view of the world. Shortly after I met her for the first time, she wrote me a letter in which she spoke of "the complicity of pain and joy, sorrow and hope, grief and wonderment":

> Perhaps this is not only a complicity but an indispensable union. Is it not their cohabitation in a single soul that renders that soul capable of grasping the ultimate reality as at no other moment in life . . .[96]

With this mingling of darkness and light, suffering and wonder, remorse and contentment, her recognition, her acceptance of this impossible resolution of her own opposing tendencies of mind and sensitivity was one of the most powerful factors impelling the autobiographical undertaking she then launched. Having toyed with insipid phrases like "Des heures de ma vie," she soon knew what the title of her book was going to be, a title that was also going to be the central "hypothesis" through which she would tell her story and try to justify it: *La détresse et l'enchantement – Enchantment and Sorrow*.

She began work on it at Petite-Rivière-Saint-François, where she settled in at the end of May 1977. When she left the cottage in mid-September she already had a manuscript of several chapters; the memories had been coming forth and the words flowing. Once the excitement over the launching of *Ces enfants de ma vie* had passed, she went back to work and contrary to her usual custom continued to write during the winter of 1978 until the Governor General's Award and the Molson Prize she won that spring disrupted her tranquillity again and for the moment obliged her to stop. Having escaped to Petite-Rivière on May 26, she immediately set to work again. In June 1978 when I went to see her she read me a few pages of "Le bal chez le gouverneur" for the first time; this was the title she had chosen for the first part of her autobiography. She had seen the magnitude of her project and knew already that the book would be divided into four parts: to the first, which would be about her early years in Manitoba, and the second, which would recount her first sojourn in Europe, she intended to add a third part on her years in Montreal and on *Bonheur d'occasion* and *The Tin Flute*, then a fourth about the last three decades of her life.

It was a monumental plan and time was short. "All I want is silence, peace and quiet, and rest, so I can work on my last book,"[97] she wrote to Sister Berthe. But hard as she tried to isolate herself and concentrate, she was constantly interrupted by visitors or, increasingly, physical weaknesses – allergies, shortness of breath, arthritic pains in her wrists and fingers, not to mention those sudden waves of fatigue and depression that kept sweeping over her periodically, immobilizing her for days at a time.

On advice from her doctor, "in order to rebuild [her] strength and find the courage to finish [her] last book,"[98] she decided to spend the worst of the winter in Florida. She chose Hollywood, north of Miami, hoping that the peacefulness of the place and its balmy air would be conducive to her work. She arrived on 2 December 1978, moved into a small apartment on Johnson Street, and immediately began the seaside vacation routine of earlier years: walks on the beach at sunset, letters to Marcel and friends, periods of rest by the swimming pool, daily reading (I lent her *Djann* by Platanov and *Le Communiste* by Guido Morselli). But she had come here first and above all to write. "I would like to get down to work," she confided to Antonia. "That is still the best way – for me the only way – to endure life."[99]

But the days passed and the book waited. "I'm resting as much as I can," she wrote to Marcel shortly before Christmas. "I don't think I'll ever manage to work here. I feel too out of place. The climate doesn't lend itself to work either."[100] While the heat and humidity did her some good at first, they were soon crippling her. The infernal round of allergies and bronchial infections began again, treated with medications that robbed her of all capacity to concentrate. These malaises were soon joined by loneliness and boredom, as well as anxiety at wasting precious time that would be lost forever. She left again for Quebec City on 22 February 1979, having expected to stay in Florida at least four months. When her friend Pierre Boutin picked her up at Dorval, the manuscript of her autobiography weighed no more in her baggage than it did when she left.

Her health problems persisted through the spring, after her seventieth birthday. Nevertheless, from the first days of June, as soon as she arrived at Petite-Rivière-Saint-François and found herself enveloped in Berthe's kindly protection, the desire and courage to write returned. By mid-July when I came to see her she had finished a first draft of "Le bal chez le gouverneur," which she would correct and hand over for typing in the following months. But the task she had set herself was not over, she knew well; in a letter she wrote to me she said, "What I see before me is so long, so long that I'm afraid of it."[101]

Still, stronger than fear was her will to complete her project. A will so dogged that no obstacle short of death could turn her from it. For there was much more to this book than just the story of her life; *La détresse et l'enchantement* was both a monument and a testament, and in its writing she was setting forth the meaning, even the value of her life, and therefore all of what she was and had been. At this time when her strength was failing and there would soon be nothing to add to what had already been said, this autobiography was the old woman's last chance to write a book in which she could build an expanded image of herself, of that ideal person she had never, all her life since adolescence, ceased trying to build through her acts and thoughts. With this book she would leave all in order behind her, once and for all redeem herself, justify herself. There was no way to achieve this salvation other than by turning on her own life the same compassionate eye she had given to Alexandre Chenevert, Christine, Pierre Cadorai, Elsa, and the other characters born of her imagination; becoming herself the narrator and principal character of her own novel; transforming her life totally, irrevocably into literature. Hence the determination and feeling of urgency with which she wrote her book, feverishly, passionately, without a second thought or allowing herself to be deterred by the health risks posed by so much work. As she wrote to Margaret Laurence:

> Only one thing now is important to me: to finish the book I'm fighting my way through with poor hands, poor breath, poor heart. Yet the miracle may happen and I may give it my last efforts, which is a fine way, I feel, to come to a conclusion. Is the work worth all that much, I don't know, possibly not, probably not, but I don't care.[102]

But in the summer of 1979 a major obstacle raised its head. As she was putting the finishing touches to "Le bal chez le gouverneur," Gabrielle learned that Adèle, at the age of eighty-six, had finally found a taker for the dreadful indictment she had written against her youngest sister. Since 1969, the matter seemed to have been over and done with. In spite of a new alarm in 1971 – which had faded as quickly as the first – there had seemed to be every indication that Adèle had given up thought of trying to make known publicly the "true face" of her sister and the resentments she harboured against her. Although she and Gabrielle never saw one another, there had even been a certain renewal of friendship between them, and they had begun to correspond again and tell each other of their work in progress. Adèle's was pious and insipid; poor and almost blind, confined to some cramped, dilapidated lodgings, she would be typing her memories of her family and the Manitoba of her youth for the umpteenth time on her little typewriter. To encourage her, Gabrielle would send her a few hundred dollars two or three times a year, which Adèle accepted gratefully. In 1977 she self-published a little book titled *Les Capucins de Toutes-Aides*, which was intended to be a contribution to the religious history of the Canadian West. The book contained a rather harsh criticism of *La Petite Poule d'Eau*, judging its documentary value to be virtually nil by reason of its author's "unbridled imagination."[103] Gabrielle was a good sport about it and wrote to Clémence:

> Of course I won't take offence at Adèle's book. I can't do anything about it, you know, and then after all it can't do me any harm if she writes in her own way about what I write with the talent I have and in the way it comes to me. I only wish her well.[104]

Gabrielle knew very well that her "talent" outweighed her sister's by far. Besides, this new book of Adèle's, like all its predecessors, struck no chord with the public. But this was exactly what enraged Adèle, whose jealousy and spite were fanned, not mollified, by Gabrielle's good will and generosity. Adèle truly believed in her writerly talent, "even though [her] works," as she said, "were not in the fashion of the day [and] not to the liking of young people hungry for erotic sensations."[105] Gabrielle's fame seemed to her the more revoltingly unfair in that Gabrielle, who was such a power in the literary world, did nothing to get her sister's "humble works" known and published. What could Adèle do about such a situation except harbour her ill temper and wait for the moment of revenge?

That moment came at last in September 1978 when the novelist Gérard Bessette, who also made a specialty of psychoanalytical criticism and had been interested in Gabrielle Roy's oeuvre for some time, appeared at Adèle's Tupper Street rooming house in Montreal asking if Adèle had anything "unpublished" on Gabrielle.[106] Only too happy to be approached by someone that important – "a first-class writer" – Adèle handed over a fat manuscript titled "Journal intime d'une âme solitaire: Reflet des âmes dans le miroir du passé." It was essentially the same text as that of 1968, meaning the same denunciation of Gabrielle's selfishness and unscrupulous ambition, augmented this time with several chapters on other family members, particularly Anna, Bernadette, and Rodolphe, who all received unflattering portraits. Bessette was delighted; Adèle's story meshed perfectly with his own theories about Gabrielle Roy. Adèle did feel a compunction as she turned over the manuscript, for, she said, "I thought about the *Petite Misère* of long ago and did not want to give grief to the grownup Gabrielle of today, even though she had not wanted to encourage my efforts to write." Several days later when Gabrielle sent her another cheque for $500, she returned it, saying nothing about Bessette's visit and declaring simply, "I do not want to see any face again! Or hear any voice!"[107] But what price last-minute remorse beside the sheer joy of being published at long last?

At this time, Bessette was associated with Les Éditions Québec/Amérique, founded several years earlier by Jacques Fortin, and more particularly with its literary editor, the novelist Gilbert La Rocque. La Rocque found the literary quality of the manuscript to be pitiful but yielded to pressure from Bessette and agreed to publish it; after all, a book on Gabrielle Roy, even an unkind one – and especially one written by her own sister – could not fail to be a success, at least among scandal-seekers.

The minute she had wind of what was being planned, Gabrielle was crushed. These hateful accusations were not only threatening to damage her reputation, but more seriously and distressingly, they were a negation of the undertaking to which she had given herself totally in this period, the building of an autobiographical image of herself and her relationships with her family. Adèle's story was threatening to knock all this down like a house of cards. For between Adèle's Gabrielle and the Gabrielle on stage in *La détresse et l'enchantement*, the contrast could not be more harsh. Literally panic-stricken, Gabrielle tried everything to stop the publication of the fratricidal book. She implored Alain Stanké to intervene with Jacques Fortin; she asked me to contact the Franciscan fathers to have them use their influence with Adèle. From August to October she telephoned me two or three times a week, in tears, each time fluctuating between despair and rage, a towering rage whose target was less Adèle herself – "a poor thing who's very sick really"[108] – than Adèle's publisher, "one of those vultures who deliberately exploit sensational themes."[109] But nothing worked. *Le Miroir du passé* by Marie-Anna A. Roy appeared in November 1979 in the Littérature d'Amérique series, which was edited by Gilbert La Rocque; the cover bore a photograph of Adèle, but the back-cover blurb talked mostly about Gabrielle; nowhere was there any mention of Gérard Bessette.

Three weeks before Adèle's book came out, Gabrielle suffered a heart attack. Rushed to the Hôtel-Dieu Hospital in Quebec City, she spent eleven days in the coronary unit. Then she was moved to a private room for a complete rest and tests. She went home only around November 15, after more than a month in hospital. On December 2 she wrote to Sister Berthe:

> For several months, with the Adèle business and my illness, it's been as if a great shadow has been spreading over my life. At times, I feel almost suffocated.[110]

The End, Incompletion

In Adèle's opinion Gabrielle's heart attack had nothing to do with the publication of *Le Miroir du passé*; it was owing, she said, "to the devouring and inexorable passion to write that was consuming her."[111] While this interpretation is hard to reconcile with the facts, it would also be excessive to attribute the heart attack solely to what Adèle was up to, as did some of Gabrielle's friends at the time. Gabrielle had been having chronic respiratory and coronary problems for some years; Adèle's book, through the extreme and prolonged agitation it provoked, hastened rather than caused the heart attack of the fall of 1979.

With all the medication being poured into her, the patient soon recovered enough energy to get back to work. Despite her anxiety over the approaching sovereignty-association referendum of May 1980, she began work on Part Two of *La détresse et l'enchantement*, titled "Un oiseau tombé sur le seuil," and succeeded in writing a good piece of it. More linear in construction than "Le bal chez le gouverneur," the story of her two years of adventure in Europe practically wrote itself, with an ease that almost made her forget the troubles she had just been through, all the more since Adèle's book did not do nearly as well as had been expected and feared. Starting in the middle of June Gabrielle was once again at Petite-Rivière, where as before she put in a good spell of writing every morning; since the arthritis in her hands prevented her from writing for more than an hour at a time, she would get up after an hour, walk around the house a bit, then come back to her notebook for another hour before breaking off for another walk, followed by another hour of writing, and so on until early afternoon. "My health has improved quite a bit," she wrote to Jack McClelland, "and I have been able to do a fairly good bit of work this summer. Not as much as before and not as much as I would like, still I am not entirely displeased with what I have done."[112]

Things went so well that when she returned to Quebec City in mid-September the manuscript of "Un oiseau tombé sur le seuil" was finished and ready for typing. A month later, on October 22 precisely, she had Pierre Morency bring me two thick binders containing the clean copy of the text; together with the two binders of "Le bal chez le gouverneur" already in my possession, they made up the complete manuscript of what would finally be *La détresse et l'enchantement*.

It had been agreed between us since the beginning that the four volumes of the autobiography would be published only after Gabrielle's death. This was why she had given me one of the two copies of the typed manuscript, keeping the other for herself.[113] This way, each of us working with a copy, we were able to make a certain number of improvements and corrections, which we examined together at our meetings in Quebec City that autumn. By December 1980 the final text was ready.

But once again the winter soon had Gabrielle coping with the horrors of coughs, insomnia, and chronic fatigue, with the addition of digestive problems that required hospitalization again at the Hôtel-Dieu in February, while Marcel was in hospital at Saint-Sacrement for a virulent case of the flu. And so she did nothing until the spring of 1981 except wait patiently for her troubles to end, while doing her best to bolster Clémence's morale as well as her own. She wrote to her on February 19:

> Spring is not far off. You'll be able to see the little Seine I used to love so as a child, and where we used to go for walks hand in hand, you and I. As in those days, I love you and long to help you.[114]

June had hardly begun before she hurried back to her refuge at Petite-Rivière-Saint-François. Not having the strength to go for walks any more, she spent most of her time in her lawn swing or visiting Berthe Simard, who watched over her as if she were her own sick child. She cooked for her, cared for her, dressed her, looked after everything in the house, always worrying, always attentive to the moods and desires of her old friend and ready to come running at the slightest alarm. Coddled this way, Gabrielle managed to take up her pen again and with monumental effort began Part Three of *La détresse et l'enchantement*:

> For years and years I thought the rails would never sing to me of anything but happiness . . .[115]

In a shaky, almost illegible hand, she wrote three successive drafts of sixty or so pages that were to begin the sequel to her autobiography. These pages, set during her years of journalism in Montreal, tell of going to St-Boniface by train in the spring of 1943 to attend her mother's funeral. Imbued with sorrow and remorse, they end in the Gaspé, where the orphan tries to fill the void of her loss writing *Bonheur d'occasion*.

These were the last pages written by Gabrielle Roy. They are unfinished, to be sure, as remains the great autobiographical project she had planned. But this incompletion was in a sense the only possible end, not only for the autobiography, which thus closes with the writing of her first novel, the beginning of her whole oeuvre, which the autobiography finishes and culminates, but also and even more for Gabrielle herself, who put her last remaining efforts into bringing back, reliving through writing and imagination the deed that had underlain her whole existence: her fatal abandonment of her mother. In this way she finally took charge of the shameful deed and redeemed it for ever.

And so the circle was closed. As if she sensed in a vague kind of way that almost all of what she had to write was now written, beginning in the autumn of 1981 Gabrielle slipped into a state of physical weakness and inner disarray more terrible than anything she had been through before. Everything in her seemed broken, overwhelmed, devastated by the health problems falling upon her and leaving her limp and lifeless – like a corpse with a reprieve. The following winter, that of 1982, was worse still than usual, perhaps because her customary ills were now joined by a resignation, a refusal to fight that made her the more vulnerable, as if beyond willing herself better. Total collapse. "She was not writing," Marcel would recall, "and not reading any more, she who could read a book a day. She wanted to die. I was worried; for months I would get up at night and go to the door of her room to see if she was still breathing."

The return of summer brought her no relief. For the first time in twenty-five years she dropped the idea of going to Petite-Rivière and spent the whole summer of 1982 in Quebec City, exhausted, lifeless, incapable of the least sustained physical or mental effort. She did, however, manage to reread "De quoi t'ennuies-tu, Éveline?," a story I had requested for Les Éditions du Sentier, which I was then running with Jacques Brault, Gilles Archambault, and Martin Dufour. Our little team was very anxious to publish something of hers, and in May 1981 she had given me a bundle of unpublished manuscripts, telling me to choose the best; in it there had been some fragments of her old abandoned saga, a draft of "La route d'Altamont," and this story with the enigmatic title, "De quoi t'ennuies-tu, Éveline?" All were first drafts, typed long ago by Gabrielle herself, with some corrections entered by hand. They were therefore not in publishable condition as they stood. Having chosen "De quoi t'ennuies-tu Éveline?" because of the beauty of the story and the principal character, and because its length was more appropriate to the kind of book my friends and I wanted to publish, I undertook to rewrite it all myself to turn the draft into a finished text whose tone and style would be as faithful as possible to Gabrielle's own. When I showed her this work in July 1982 she declared herself delighted with the result; the idea of publishing under her name a text that was rewritten by me, therefore confounding the critics, appealed to her sense of humour. But she insisted that my name appear at least in the dedication of the book. *De quoi t'ennuies-tu, Éveline?* came off the presses in November 1982; it was not put on sale in bookstores because Les Éditions du Sentier published in very small print runs (two hundred copies in this case) and sold only by correspondence.

I like to believe that this last publication gladdened her heart. But that gladness was not enough to relieve her ailments, which on the contrary worsened through all of that autumn and the following winter. Ailments both physical, tormenting her for weeks on end and necessitating constant visits to the hospital, and psychological, as if everything in her were collapsing, leaving a vast wasteland, a bleakness without possibility of remission.

On the two or three occasions that I went to see her in Quebec City, I found her in a dressing gown, her face either puffy from cortisone, or grey and thin. I would stay with her for half an hour or an hour at most. We would talk about the Fonds Gabrielle Roy, small current business matters, the manuscript of *La détresse et l'enchantement*. Since she became exhausted very quickly, I would be sure to leave before long.

Close friends did their best to help, for Marcel was himself too weak and too depressed to be up to it. The most faithful was Julie Simard, who was a nurse as well as a friend, and who came almost every day to cook, run errands, and give Gabrielle the treatments her condition required. In February Berthe Simard herself, only just recovered from the loss of her brother Aimé, came from Petite-Rivière and spent a week at her old friend's bedside, doing "a thousand little things" for her and trying to console her.[116] Yolande Cyr, Antonia's daughter, called often from Ottawa to hear how she was. Yolande, a psychologist, was anxious for Gabrielle to consult a therapist and found her one in Quebec City, but Gabrielle refused to see him. As for the Madeleines, they did what they could, but they knew that their friend did not have long now to live.

Gabrielle knew it too. At the beginning of April 1983 she wrote what would be her last letter to Sister Berthe Valcourt:

> I don't feel any better, not at all well, dear Berthe. Not well enough to write you in the singing tone I'd like to find for you at least. Be sure nevertheless that I love you with all my heart and put my trust in yours.[117]

Again that year, spring brought her neither relief for her ailments nor the surge in morale it would have taken to lift her from the depths she had been sinking into for a year and a half. Being shut up in the Château Saint-Louis was living in hell for her. Marcel was not much better either; in May he had to be hospitalized again, for an embolism. Léona, his sister in St-Boniface, on learning of this announced that she was arriving in mid-June. Gabrielle, unable to bear the thought of living with Léona for even a few days, decided against all reason to escape to Petite-Rivière-Saint-François, her only refuge, the only place in the world where she was not afraid to die, she told Berthe, as long as Berthe would be there holding her hand.

Marcel could do nothing to dissuade Gabrielle, who arrived at Petite-Rivière on Sunday, June 12. Victorine Simard, Berthe's grand-niece who was working in Quebec City, had a car and drove her there. Despite her extreme weakness, Gabrielle would live alone for three weeks in her little house, looking out the window at the river and the trees, taking a few steps in the garden, rereading the poetry by Francis Jammes that Henri Girard had given her years ago, jotting down thoughts, quotations, fragments of poems that sprang to her memory. Calmly, imperturbably, she waited for death.

Since she did not have the strength left to walk as far as Berthe's house, Berthe came to her house every day as soon as Gabrielle raised the blind in her room, as they had agreed. If she saw that the blind had not been raised by nine o'clock, Berthe was to come post-haste, because that would be the sign that something serious had happened. From morning till night, Berthe saw to everything, meals, housework, personal and every other kind of care for Gabrielle, whose condition she found more and more worrying.

On the afternoon of July 7 Madeleine Bergeron, who was briefly in Baie-Saint-Paul with Madeleine Chassé, telephoned the cottage and learned that Gabrielle was in a very bad way. She immediately phoned the Château Saint-Louis but Marcel was at a loss to know what to do. Without losing a second she decided to alert Doctor Yvon Ouellet, a lung specialist and Gabrielle's personal physician for the past twelve years or so. Ouellet ordered Gabrielle to be returned to Quebec City. An ambulance arrived at Petite-Rivière the next day. Berthe proposed to go with her friend but Gabrielle declined her offer; so Berthe kissed her and said, "Bon voyage." The ambulance left. They never saw each other again.

It was a summer weekend and there was no available room at the Hôtel-Dieu, so Gabrielle had to stay at the Château Saint-Louis at first, where Julie Simard took care of her until Sunday, July 10. On Monday and Tuesday, Doctor Ouellet had a battery of tests run. In extreme discomfort and deeply depressed, Gabrielle was asking only for "deliverance." Cardinal Maurice Roy, archbishop of Quebec City, himself in hospital at the Hôtel-Dieu, administered the last rites to her. On Wednesday, July 13 she had a heart attack early in the afternoon and was taken to the coronary unit where she was resuscitated. A nurse phoned Marcel to ask him to come. Julie Simard was already there. Although weak, Gabrielle was fully conscious and able to express her worries about Marcel.

Shortly after suppertime a strong fibrillation took hold, announcing another attack. While doctors and nurses worked, Julie Simard would recall, Marcel began to cry and whimper "like a little animal." The attack was massive. At 9:45 it was all over.

Epilogue

*T*he body was not exposed. The funeral took place on Saturday, 16 July 1983, in Saint-Dominique Church. It was a sunny, beautiful morning. At the door of the church, Marcel and Léona received condolences. Berthe Simard recorded the whole ceremony on her little tape recorder; at the end, when the procession passed her pew, she put out her hand and touched the coffin. Friends and relatives gathered afterward at the Salon Lépine on chemin Ste-Foy, while the remains were being cremated as Gabrielle had wished. The ashes were placed in the Jardin du Repos (today the Parc de la Souvenance).

In the following months the Quebec City office of the Trust Général, which Gabrielle had appointed as her executor, proceeded with the settlement of her estate.[1] Ownership of all her papers and copyrights was transferred to the Fonds Gabrielle Roy. The house at Petite-Rivière-Saint-François went to Marcel, while Berthe Simard inherited all Gabrielle's clothes and personal effects. The money left by Gabrielle Roy amounted to some $565,000, about a tenth of which was distributed in individual bequests: $10,000 to Sister Berthe Valcourt for Clémence's upkeep; $10,000 to Brenda, Bob's wife; $2,000 to Antonia; $1,000 to Léontine, Fernand's wife, who was still living in Phoenix; $5,000 each to Yolande and Lucille, Germain's daughters, and to Blanche, Jos's daughter; $8,000 finally to various local charities. The balance was left with the company in trust; Marcel would receive the income from this capital of about $500,000 as long as he lived; on his death, the capital was to be divided among three international charitable organizations, UNICEF, Oxfam, and Fame Pereo.

When he returned to the Château Saint-Louis, Marcel was taken in hand by M. C. and his friends, who redecorated the apartment and looked after him. His health declined rapidly, however. He died in Quebec City on 8 July 1989, leaving the house at Petite-Rivière-Saint-François to the Fonds Gabrielle Roy and his collection of antique furniture and art works to the Musée du Québec. Four years later, on 28 October 1993, Clémence died in St-Boniface at the age of ninety-eight. As for Adèle, far from prompting a mood of forgiveness in her, Gabrielle's death left her free to slake her thirst for vengeance unimpeded; at the rest home in St-Boniface where she had retired, she devoted herself to rehashing her memories and losing no opportunity to settle her old scores with her youngest sister, whom she accused of having bathed all her life "in the troubled waters of lies and hallucination."[2] Adèle died in St-Boniface on 3 April 1998 at the age of a hundred and five.

For my part, in 1984 I attended to the publication of *La détresse et l'enchantement*, which met with enormous success with the critics and public alike in Quebec. Then I began this biography. Almost against my better judgment, I have to admit. As a reader of Valéry and Kundera, I have always had the most serious reservations about the biographical genre which, in subordinating knowledge of an author's works to the very circumstantial, very uncertain knowledge of the individual who created those works, most often obscures rather than provides access to that intangible "other *me*" who in Proust's opinion is the only true author of works and is met undisguised only *through* his or her works and their re-creation in each of us. I still have these reservations, even after the years of research and writing that this book have taken me, reflecting that although I have tried to leave no stone unturned in my efforts to know everything about Gabrielle Roy, I still know so little about her really, about the woman, the writer that she was. You can comb through all the archives, read everything ever written about a person, put questions to all the people who knew that person, but something is always missing, and that something, especially when your subject is an artist, is bound to be the most important thing of all.

Knowing this, how could I ever have become involved in such a perilous adventure as writing this enormous book? Two things led me, or drove me, to it. The first has to do with my feeling ever since I began reading Gabrielle Roy that her oeuvre calls for a biography, and my urge as a critic to respond to that call. Unlike others, hers is an oeuvre so imbued with autobiography, so richly nourished from its author's life and especially so focused on the revelation of that life and its transformation into a work of art that it begs to be extended, echoed in a biographical enterprise that, for all my reservations about biographies in general, still seems to me about the fairest and most compassionate way one could choose to respond. My second reason is to the same effect, but it concerns Gabrielle Roy personally, not her works. Between us, and once again despite whatever reservations I might have about the validity of biographies, there was always the agreement that one day I would tell the story of her life. She took it for granted. She even wanted me not to publish *La détresse et l'enchantement* until after I had used it as a privileged source for my biography. I do not remember ever actually having told her in so many words that I would write this biography – but then I never told her either that I would not. So she departed believing that I would, and since the agreement between us was no longer renegotiable, it became a promise.

Now I have kept my promise, if that kind of promise can ever really be kept.

Notes

ABBREVIATIONS USED IN THE NOTES

ANQ: Archives nationales du Québec, Quebec City and Montreal.

BNQ: Bibliothèque nationale du Québec, Montreal.

BUA: Bishop's University Archives, Lennoxville, Quebec.

FGR: Fonds Gabrielle Roy, Montreal.

MMU: McMaster University, William Ready Division of Archives and Research Collections, Hamilton, Ontario.

MPA: Manitoba Provincial Archives, Winnipeg.

NAC: National Archives of Canada, Ottawa.

NLC: National Library of Canada, Ottawa.

SDSB: School Division of St-Boniface, Winnipeg.

SHSB: Société historique de Saint-Boniface, Winnipeg.

SSNJM: Archives des Soeurs des Saints Noms de Jésus et de Marie, Académie Saint-Joseph, St-Boniface, Manitoba.

UOT: University of Toronto, Thomas Fischer Rare Books Library, Toronto.

UQTR: Université du Québec à Trois-Rivières, Trois-Rivières.

YUT: York University Archives and Special Collections, Toronto.

NOTES TO CHAPTER 1

Daughter of Immigrants

1. The name that appears in the Registre des baptêmes de la paroisse-cathédrale de Saint-Boniface (23 March 1909); the child's godfather was her brother Rodolphe and her godmother was her sister Adèle.
2. According to Marie-Anna A. [Adèle] Roy (1989–1990, episodes 5 and 8), Léon journeyed briefly to Quebec to see his family during the year 1906.
3. This is the date on Léon Roy's baptismal certificate reproduced in Marie-Anna A. [Adèle] Roy, "Généalogie des Roy-Landry," unpublished manuscript (MPA, NAC, BNQ); in the Registre des mariages de Saint-Léon, Manitoba, the date of birth indicated is 4 June 1855; later, in the declaration of 14 May 1897 accompanying his engagement by the Department of the Interior, Léon gave 4 March 1850 as his date of birth (Department of the Interior, Immigration Branch, RG 76, vol. 688, file 34686); finally, the year of birth engraved on his tombstone in St-Boniface is 1851.
4. Marie-Anna A. [Adèle] Roy, 1954, p. 105.
5. Most of this information is obtained from the writings of Marie-Anna A. [Adèle] Roy; Gabrielle Roy, in *Enchantment and Sorrow* ("The Governor's Ball," VII, pp. 76–77), presents the facts in a slightly different order.
6. See Marie-Anna A. [Adèle] Roy, 1954, p. 105.
7. See Yvette Brandt, 1980, p. 161.
8. For a topographical description and history of the region and its parishes, see Marie-Anna A. [Adèle] Roy, 1969.
9. The source of this information and several others following is the declaration by Léon Roy in his Application for Homestead Patent, dated 2 October 1887, and accompanied by statements from two neighbours, Félix-Raoul Lussier and Olivier Gendron; the official patent was granted on 19 March 1888. Majorique Roy, Léon's brother, occupied the southwest quarter of the same section.

10. Land division in the Canadian West is done by the grid method. The base unit is the "section," which has an area of one square mile; for the sale or attribution of lots, however, the section is divided into four "quarter sections," identified according to their position (northeast, southeast, southwest, northwest). A square of thirty-six sections (six miles by six miles) forms a larger unit identified by two numbers, a "township" or latitude number indicating its relative position north of the U.S. border, and a "range" number relating to its position east or west of the meridian of the province running through Winnipeg. Within the "township/range" thus constituted, the sections are numbered consistently; section 4 in which Léon Roy's homestead was located is the fourth section west of the eastern edge of the range and the first above the meridian line of the township.

11. Léon Roy would remain a municipal councillor almost without interruption until he left the region in 1896 (see Y. Brandt, 1980, p. 27, 49).

12. The *Manitoba Gazette* announced the appointment of Léon Roy in 1888 (vol. XVII, no. 28), 1889 (vol. XVIII, no. 5), and 1893 (vol. XXII, no. 17), but he was already signing as justice of the peace as early as 1886.

13. Léon Roy's children knew directly only two paternal uncles, Majorique and Édouard, who, like their brother Léon, had come to settle in Manitoba.

14. *Enchantment and Sorrow*, "The Governor's Ball," VII, p. 76 (trans. P. Claxton); this simile rests also on a certain facial resemblance between Charles Roy as shown in an old photograph kept by Léon and portraits of the Florentine reformer.

15. Ibid., p. 75; this vision of the Roy grandparents was to be vigorously contested some years after Gabrielle Roy's death by her sister Adèle (Marie-Anna A. Roy, 1989–1990, episodes 7 and 8).

16. Ibid., II, pp. 12–20.

17. A long unpublished novel, "La Saga d'Éveline," which will be discussed later in this work, in Chapters 7 and 8.

18. "My Manitoba Heritage" (1970), *The Fragile Lights of Earth*, p. 144 (trans. A. Brown).

19. T.-Alfred Bernier, 1887, p. 16.

20. Baptised on February 10, 1867, Émélie Landry, Gabrielle Roy's mother, was born the previous day (Registre des baptêmes de la paroisse de Saint-Alphonse, County of Joliette); her godfather and godmother were David Jeansonne and Adélaïde Pellerin.

21. T.-A. Bernier, 1887, p. 143.

22. "My Manitoba Heritage" (1970), *The Fragile Lights of Earth*, p. 144 (trans. A. Brown).

23. See the Application for Homestead Patent signed by Élie Landry on 4 July 1884 (MPA, Dominion Lands Office). The "patent" was granted the following 26 October, but documents show that the acquisition was attended by somewhat muddied circumstances: in July 1884, Élie had apparently assigned his property rights to a financial institution, which attempted to

take possession of the land two years later, in November 1886. However, Élie, in an affidavit sworn by Justice of the Peace Léon Roy, denied the pretensions of his "creditors."

24. "We call ploughing the prairie for the first time 'breaking' it. [. . .] This is an operation done only once for a single piece of land; one clears wooded land; one breaks the prairie" (T.-A. Bernier, 1887, p. 114).

25. *Enchantment and Sorrow*, "The Governor's Ball," IV, p. 33–34 (trans. P. Claxton).

26. Calixte established himself as early as the month of July 1881 on the south half of Section 10, 6th Township, 9th Range, not far from his father's homestead. From July 1887, Moïse would occupy the northeast quarter of Section 2, 5th Township, 12th Range, near Léon Roy's farm (MPA, Dominion Lands Office, Applications for Homestead Patent, dated 20 July 1887 and 19 April 1892 respectively).

27. Marie-Anna A. [Adèle] Roy, 1979, p. 12.

28. On Mélina's youth, see Marie-Anna A. [Adèle] Roy, 1954 (p. 232) and 1988.

29. In one version of "La Saga d'Éveline," "Conversations sur la galerie" was the title that Gabrielle Roy intended to give to those chapters treating of the period when Éveline and Édouard were courting.

30. Registre des baptêmes, mariages et sépultures de la paroisse de Saint-Léon, 23 November 1886; the marriage took place before Théobald Bitsche; Élie Landry, Moïse Landry, Délima Desrochers, and Romuald Fournier signed as witnesses.

31. "My Manitoba Heritage" (1970), *The Fragile Lights of Earth*, p. 144 (trans. A. Brown).

32. *Enchantment and Sorrow*, "The Governor's Ball," ch. 2, p. 16 (trans. P. Claxton).

33. "My Manitoba Heritage" (1970), *The Fragile Lights of Earth*, p. 144 (trans. A. Brown).

34. The child's name was Joseph Armand; his godfather was Élie Landry, his godmother Adélina Campeau (Registre des baptêmes de la paroisse de Saint-Alphonse, Manitoba, 29 August 1887).

35. The child's name was Marie Anna Antoinette Léona; her godfather was Zénon Landry, her godmother Thérèse Généreux (Registre des baptêmes de la paroisse de Saint-Léon, Manitoba, 27 September 1888).

36. *Canada Gazette*, vol. 25, no. 26, 26 December 1891.

37. On Léon's postal activities, see the *Report of the Postmaster General* (Ottawa: Queen's Printer, editions 1892, 1893, and 1894); also see the Canada Official Postal Guide (Ottawa: Queen's Printer, January 1892, January 1983 and January 1894 editions).

38. The Lands Office archives of the municipality of Lorne (Morden, Manitoba) show that Léon Roy mortgaged his quarter-section at St-Alphonse (NE-4-5-12) for $350 on 16 August 1888 before selling it in November 1890 for $497, but did not pay off the mortgage until 1899.

39. See Y. Brandt, 1980, p. 153; in the *Public Accounts of the Province of Manitoba for the Year 1896* (Winnipeg: Queen's Printer, 1897, p. 18), Léon Roy appears as a liquor permit holder for a hotel located in Somerset.

40. Born on 29 September 1890 at his maternal grandparents' house and baptised two days later, this child was named Joseph Léon Alcide; Excide and Rosalie, Mélina's brother and sister, were his godfather and godmother (Registre des baptêmes de la paroisse de Saint-Léon, 1 October 1890); on the child's death, see M.-A. A. Roy, 1954, p. 105.

41. The name of the child was Marie Agnès Joséphine; her godfather was Joseph Landry, represented by his brother Moïse, and her godmother was Catherine Callahan, represented by Thérèse Généreux (Registre des baptêmes de la paroisse de Saint-Alphonse, Manitoba, 24 November 1891); on Agnès's tombstone, the year of birth inscribed is 1892.

42. The name of the child was Marie Anna Adèle; her godfather was Herménégilde Bessette, her godmother Florence Weller (Registre des baptêmes de la paroisse de Saint-Léon, Manitoba, 12 February 1893).

43. The name of the child was Marie Clémence Ernestine; her godfather and godmother were Moïse and Rosalie Landry (Registre des baptêmes de la paroisse de Saint-Léon, Manitoba, 20 October 1895).

44. On these developments, see Jacqueline Blay, 1987, p. 15–31; Lionel Groulx, 1933, p. 71–129; and L. Dorge, 1976, p. 111–119.

45. Archives of the Archbishopric of St-Boniface, Langevin Collection, L3789; a copy of this letter was found in Gabrielle Roy's personal archives (NLC). Joseph-Anthime Decosse was the Conservative organizer and "one of Somerset's most influential men." (M.-A. A. Roy, 1969, pp. 210–211).

46. See Abbé Noël Perquis to Mgr Langevin, St-Alphonse, 26 May and 8 June 1896 (Archives of the Archbishopric of St-Boniface, Langevin Collection, L5175 and L5295).

47. Léon Roy to W. Laurier, Somerset, 30 June 1896 (NAC, Laurier Collection, reel C741, folio 5037–5040).

48. Léon Roy to C. Sifton, Somerset, 7 December 1896 (NAC, Laurier Collection, reel C453, folio 4879–4880; Léon Roy's second letter to Laurier, also dated December 7, 1896, is on the same reel, folio 4882–4884).

49. See correspondence during the winter of 1896–97 among Sifton, John A. Macdonell, R. L. Richardson, and Léon Roy: NAC, Sifton Collection, reels C402 (passim), C446 (folio 549), C452 (folio 3485, 3487), C453 (folio 4971), C462 (folio 15695), and C466 (folio 20423–20424, 20433, 20436).

50. NAC, Department of the Interior, Immigration Branch, RG 76, vol. 688, file 34686.

51. The population of St-Boniface in 1891 was 1553, rising in 1901 to 2019, and by 1911 to 7483. In the same period, the population of Winnipeg rose from 25,639 to 42,340 and then to 136,035 (*Canada Census, 1921*, vol. 1, table 12). At the time of Léon Roy's arrival, St-Boniface was a town; it became a city in 1908.

52. According to *Canada Census, 1921* (vol. 1, tables 23 and 28), after addition of the populations of French and Belgian origin, the French-speaking proportion

for all of Manitoba was around 7% in 1901, 1911, and 1921. For St-Boniface, in 1921, the only year for which statistics are available, the French-speaking proportion was 47%, while for Winnipeg it was only 2.4%; we may suppose that the proportion for St-Boniface was at least as high or perhaps higher in 1901 and 1911.

53. On this neighbourhood and this house, see Marie-Anna A. [Adèle] Roy, 1970, pp. 7–16; and 1954, pp. 17–45.

54. The child's name was Marie Louise Marguerite Bernadette; her godfather and godmother were Napoléon Houde and his wife (Registre des baptêmes de la paroisse-cathédrale de Saint-Boniface, 19 July 1897).

55. The child's name was Joseph Rodolphe Léon; his godfather was Adolphe Blais, his godmother Mary Bell Roy (Registre des baptêmes de la paroisse-cathédrale de Saint-Boniface, 16 July 1899).

56. The child's name was Grégoire Valmor Germain; his godfather and god-mother were Excide Landry and his wife, Luzina Major (Registre des baptêmes de la paroisse de Saint-Léon, Manitoba, 11 May 1902).

57. On Léon Roy's activities as an Immigration Bureau employee, see the *Annual Reports of the Department of the Interior* (Ottawa, Queen's or King's Printer); texts signed by Léon Roy appear in the *Reports* covering the years 1897 (pp. 197–199), 1898 (p. 230), 1899 (p. 136), and 1900 (pp. 120–121), while his name and summaries of his activities appear in those of 1900–1901 (p. 116), 1901–1902 (p. 108), and 1902–1903 (p. 93); until 1899 his title was "Interpreter," but that year he was appointed "Inspector of Colonies" (*Winnipeg Free Press*, 22 June 1899, p. 6).

58. *Annual Report of the Department of the Interior for the Period July 1, 1906 to March 31, 1907*, Ottawa: King's Printer, 1908, p. 87.

59. See Vladimir J. Kaye, *Early Ukrainian Settlements in Canada, 1895–1900*, (Toronto: University of Toronto Press, 1964) pp. 171–172, 239–241, 309–310.

60. See G. W. Spiers to J. Bruce Walker, 26 February 1912, published in English in *La Liberté*, St-Boniface, 28 December 1915, p. 6. On the Doukhobor immigrants, see Craig Brown, 1987, pp. 388–390; George Woodcock and Ivan Avakumovic, *The Doukhobors*, Toronto, Oxford University Press, 1968.

61. See NAC, Department of the Interior, Immigration Branch, RG 76, vol. 688, file 34686.

62. See Ramsay Cook, "Peopling the New Canada," in Craig Brown, 1987, pp. 383–393.

63. Ed. K. Leep to J. Bruce Walker, Chicago, 12 May 1910 (NAC, Department of the Interior, Immigration Branch, RG 76, vol. 688, file 815251).

64. Martin Jérôme to C. Sifton, Winnipeg, 4 March 1902 (NAC, Sifton Papers, reel C420).

65. *Street of Riches*, "The Well of Dunrea," p. 75 (trans. H. L. Binsse).

66. *Le Manitoba*, St-Boniface, 8 October 1902.

67. See Marie-Anna A. [Adèle] Roy, 1989–90, episodes 4 and 5. Gabrielle Roy would later use the story of this journey, which took place before her birth, as inspiration when writing "The Gadabouts" (*Street of Riches*).

68. Part One of *Enchantment and Sorrow* is, in fact, entitled "The Governor's Ball"; the event is recounted in Chapter VII (pp. 74–80), and Gabrielle Roy places it less than a year before the birth of Marie-Agnès (p. 80), which would be the spring of 1905; this episode also appears in fictional transposition in the unpublished manuscript "La Saga d'Éveline" (NLC).

69. According to the documents preserved at the MPA (Manitoba Lands Office, Lots 1 to 5 on Plan 947, formerly Lot 79 of the parish of St-Boniface, certificate numbers 27260, 51048, 62785, 112348, 124099, 199581, 207530), a first plot was purchased in April 1904; a year later the land was subdivided and Léon Roy found himself the owner of five contiguous plots, "three plots on des Meurons Street and two on Deschambault Street" (M.-A. A. Roy, 1970, p. 40).

70. See *Le Manitoba*, 25 May 1904, p. 3; 6 July 1904, p. 3; 13 July 1904, p. 1; 31 January 1906, p. 3; 28 February 1906, p. 2.

71. See *Le Manitoba*, 5 December 1906, p. 3; the official in question was Théo. Bertrand, Secretary-Treasurer of the municipality.

72. The street number of the house became 375 in 1925 (see the annual issues of *Henderson's Winnipeg Directory* for these years).

73. M.-A. A. Roy, 1979, p. 20. For descriptions of the house, see Marie-Anna A. [Adèle] Roy, 1954, pp. 84–96; 1970, pp. 40–42; 1979, pp. 20–21; and Anna Roy-Painchaud, "Christmas at Deschambault Street," unpublished manuscript (NLC).

74. Marie-Anna A. [Adèle] Roy, 1954, p. 132.

75. *Street of Riches*, "The Well of Dunrea," p. 73; see also Clémence to Gabrielle, St-Boniface, 18 November 1976 (NLC).

76. Although Adèle calls the illness meningitis (M.-A. A. Roy, 1979, p. 22), it was more likely typhoid fever, according to what Gabrielle Roy told Joan Hind-Smith (1975, p. 66).

77. The name of the child, born March 2, was Marie Agnès Émérancienne (Registre des baptêmes de la paroisse-cathédrale de Saint-Boniface, 4 March 1906).

78. On the founding of Villeroy-Dollard, see an account by A. Roger, a priest, dated 11 September 1920 (NLC).

79. Pierre Lardon to Léon Roy, 30 June 1898 (MPA, Dominion Lands Office; underlinings by the letter-writer); on Pierre Lardon (1854–1941), see J. R. Léveillé, *Anthologie de la poésie franco-manitobaine* (St-Boniface: Éditions du Blé, 1990) pp. 189–205.

80. See *Les Cloches de Saint-Boniface*, St-Boniface, 1 September 1906, p. 233.

81. See ibid., 15 November 1907, p. 279.

NOTES TO CHAPTER 2

A Singular Childhood

1. "Souvenirs du Manitoba" (1954), p. 6.

2. See in particular "Mes études à Saint-Boniface" (unpublished in French;

published in English as "The Disparate Treasures of a Young Girl Who Came from Deschambault Street," translation by Alan Brown, *Globe and Mail*, Toronto, 18 December 1976) and "Ma petite rue qui m'a menée autour du monde," manuscripts in French conserved at the NLC; the second of these stories was published posthumously in the magazine *Littératures*, 1996 (page numbers in notes following refer to this publication).

3. "Mon héritage du Manitoba" (1970), in *Fragile Lumières de la terre*, p. 160.

4. Gabrielle Roy to Joan Hind-Smith, in English, 4 June 1973 (reproduced in J. Hind-Smith, 1975, p. 67); the death of Marie-Agnès is recounted in detail by Marie-Anna A. [Adèle] Roy, 1954, pp. 117–119.

5. Gabrielle Roy to J. Hind-Smith, ibid.

6. Interview of 19 April 1973, reported in J. Hind-Smith, 1975, p. 67.

7. Marie-Anna A. [Adèle] Roy, 1954, p. 25.

8. Clémence to Gabrielle, St-Boniface, 13 March 1978 (NLC).

9. Marie-Anna A. [Adèle] Roy, 1979, p. 25.

10. *Street of Riches*, "Petite Misère," p. 15 (trans. H. L. Binsse).

11. G. V. R. [Germain Roy], "Gabrielle Roy: La Petite Misère Comes Into Her Own." *St. Paul's Library Bulletin*, March 1954, p. 25.

12. See Anna Roy-Painchaud, "Christmas on Deschambault Street," unpublished manuscript (NLC); Marie-Anna A. [Adèle] Roy, 1979, p. 12.

13. "My Manitoba Heritage" (1970), *The Fragile Lights of Earth*, p. 148 (trans. A. Brown).

14. Clémence to Gabrielle, St-Boniface, 23 February 1981 (NLC).

15. Marie-Anna A. [Adèle] Roy, 1979, p. 55; see also M.-A. A. Roy, 1954, p. 90.

16. Gabrielle to Clémence, Quebec, 28 February 1981 (BNQ, fonds Marie-Anna A. Roy).

17. *Street of Riches*, "The Gadabouts," I, p. 55 (trans. H. L. Binsse).

18. Irma Deloy [Adèle Roy], "Les Deux Sources de l'inspiration: l'imagination et le coeur," unpublished manuscript (MPA, BNQ).

19. The story of Rosalie (called "Rosalinde") is told by Marie-Anna A. [Adèle] Roy, 1954, pp. 60–64, 145–150; the story is also told by Gabrielle Roy in her unpublished novel "La Saga d'Éveline" (NLC), in which some of Rosalie's adventures are attributed to the principal heroine, Éveline.

20. Clémence to Gabrielle, St-Boniface, 10 March 1981 (BNQ, fonds Marie-Anna A. Roy).

21. Gabrielle Roy in conversation with Rex Desmarchais, 1947, p. 9.

22. *Street of Riches*, "The Voice of the Pools," p. 132 (trans. H. L. Binsse).

23. On Adèle's works and literary thinking, see Paul Genuist, 1992.

24. "Ma rue qui m'était l'univers." This phrase is from "Ma petite rue qui m'a menée autour du monde" (1996), p. 142.

25. Ibid., p. 149.

26. Irma Deloy [Adèle Roy], "Les deux sources de l'inspiration: l'imagination et le coeur," unpublished manuscript (MPA, BNQ).

27. "Ma petite rue qui m'a menée autour du monde" (1996), p. 144.

28. Ibid., p. 142.

29. "My Manitoba Heritage" (1970), *The Fragile Lights of Earth*, p. 154 (trans. A. Brown).

30. Marie-Anna A. [Adèle] Roy, 1954, pp. 142–143; this passage refers to the character Gaétane, nicknamed *Misère*, but is repeated in reference to Gabrielle herself in "Les deux sources de l'inspiration: l'imagination et le coeur" (MPA, BNQ).

31. "Le Cercle Molière, porte ouverte," in Lionel Dorge, *Chapeau bas*, 1, (1980), p. 118.

32. "Ma petite rue qui m'a menée autour du monde" (1996), pp. 140–141.

33. For instance, see "Petite Misère" (p. 17) and "Alicia," (I, p. 89) in *Street of Riches* (trans. H. L. Binsse) or "The Old Man and the Child" (I, pp. 36–37) in *The Road Past Altamont* (trans. J. Marshall).

34. "Gérard le pirate" (*RM*, May 1940).

35. Gabrielle to Clémence, Quebec City, 19 February 1981 (FGR, dossier Clémence Roy).

36. This lady's name was Blanche Borghesi (*Henderson's Winnipeg Directory*, 1920, p. 305); Gabrielle Roy was remembering her when she wrote "L'Italienne" in *Street of Riches*.

37. See the subscribers' lists of the Association d'éducation des Canadiens français du Manitoba published annually in the newspaper *La Liberté* (e.g., 25 October 1921, 19 September 1922, 11 December 1923).

38. "Souvenirs du Manitoba" (1954), p. 1.

39. Ibid., pp. 1–3.

40. "Ma petite rue qui m'a menée autour du monde" (1966), p. 144.

NOTES TO CHAPTER 3

The Last Family Picture

1. Marie-Anna A. [Adèle] Roy, 1954, pp. 170–171, 193.

2. Marie-Anna A. [Adèle] Roy, 1979, p. 253.

3. Ibid., 255.

4. Registre des mariages de la paroisse-cathédrale de Saint-Boniface; there was not a single member of Anna's own family among the three witnesses to the marriage.

5. Marie-Anna A. [Adèle] Roy, 1988, p. 3.

6. Marie-Anna A. [Adèle] Roy, 1954, p. 134.

7. *Enchantment and Sorrow*, "The Governor's Ball," XI, p. 106 (trans. P. Claxton).

8. On the life of Adèle, see her autobiographical writings, published under the name Marie – Anna A. Roy (1954, 1979, 1988, 1989–90), as well as her unpublished manuscript titled "À vol d'oiseau à travers le temps et l'espace" (NAC, MPA).

9. Marie-Anna A. [Adèle] Roy, 1988, p. 3.

10. Marie-Anna A. [Adèle] Roy, 1954, pp. 138–139.

11. Marie-Anna A. [Adèle] Roy, "À vol d'oiseau," unpub. ms (NAC, MPA).

12. Marie-Anna A. [Adèle] Roy, 1970, p. 69.

13. Marie-Anna A. [Adèle] Roy, "À vol d'oiseau," unpub. ms (NAC, MPA).

14. Ibid.

15. See *La Liberté*, 12 January 1915, p. 8; the wedding is reported to have taken place on 7 January, with Joseph, the older brother, giving the bride away in place of the father.

16. Gabrielle Roy recalls this journey of many years before in a letter to her husband, Marcel Carbotte, Dollard, 25 August 1955 (NLC); it also inspired her to write "To Prevent a Marriage" (*Street of Riches*, pp. 25–30).

17. Was Adèle divorced? No document confirming this has been located. In 1937, in her application for the old-age pension, Mélina Roy declared that her daughter was still married and bore the name "Morin," but the mother might not have been fully cognizant of Adèle's status.

18. *Enchantment and Sorrow*, "The Governor's Ball," XI, p. 106. (trans. P. Claxton).

19. Marie-Anna A. [Adèle] Roy, "À vol d'oiseau," unpub. ms (NAC, MPA).

20. Adèle's words as reported by Sylviane Lanthier ("Les 100 ans de Marie-Anna Roy," *La Liberté*, week of 5–11 February 1993) and Jean-Pierre Dubé ("L'auteur franco-manitobaine Marie-Anna Roy à 99 ans," ibid., week of 20–26 March 1992).

21. *Enchantment and Sorrow*, "The Governor's Ball," X, p. 101 (trans. P. Claxton).

22. Ibid., XI, p. 106.

23. In *Street of Riches*, Gabrielle Roy evokes Clémence's youth through the character Alicia.

24. This fever was typhoid, according to Adèle (Marie-Anna A. Roy, 1979, p. 61), but it was more likely meningitis in the opinion of Marcel Carbotte, Gabrielle Roy's husband, who was a physician; in *Street of Riches*, the young Alicia's condition is also attributed to "a fever which had, as it were, consumed her" (*Street of Riches*, "Alicia," II, p. 90; trans. H. L. Binsse).

25. This explanation is advanced by Antonia Houde-Roy, Germain's wife, who recalls that Clémence never used to go to confession; see also a passage in *Enchantment and Sorrow*, "The Governor's Ball," XIX, pp. 185–187 (trans. P. Claxton).

26. Clémence to Gabrielle, St-Boniface, 12 February 1981 (NLC).

27. Mélina Roy to Éliane Landry, St-Boniface, 23 October 1922 (R. Jubinville Collection).

28. Clémence to Gabrielle, St-Boniface, 16 September 1982 (NLC).

29. *Street of Riches*, "A Bit of Yellow Ribbon," p. 31 (trans. H. L. Binsse). The phrase applies to Odette, a character inspired by Bernadette.

30. *Street of Riches*, "The Two Negroes," IV, p. 11 (trans. H. L. Binsse).

31. Bernadette's temporary profession took place on 21 August 1921, and her perpetual profession on 21 August 1924. On Bernadette's religious career, see "Dossier personnel 2044" (SSNJM).

32. *The Tin Flute*, XV. p. 188 (trans. A. Brown).

33. "Noëls canadiens-français" (December 1938).

34. *Enchantment and Sorrow*, "The Governor's Ball," IV, p. 46 (trans. P. Claxton).

35. *The Road Past Altamont*, "The Road Past Altamont," IV, p. 128 (trans. J. Marshall).

36. "My Manitoba Heritage" (1970), *The Fragile Lights of Earth*, p. 146 (trans. A. Brown).

37. See *The Tin Flute*, XV, pp. 188–198.

38. "My Manitoba Heritage" (1970), *The Fragile Lights of Earth*, pp. 145–146 (trans. A. Brown).

39. *The Road Past Altamont*, "My Almighty Grandmother," I, p. 14 (trans. J. Marshall).

40. "My Manitoba Heritage" (1970), *The Fragile Lights of Earth*, p. 145 (trans. A. Brown).

41. See Marie-Anna A. [Adèle] Roy, 1954, pp. 237–238; Émilie's last months also inspired the third chapter of "My Almighty Grandmother" (*The Road Past Altamont*, pp. 20–30).

42. J. Bruce Walker to W. D. Scott, Winnipeg, 14 February 1912 (NAC, Department of the Interior, Immigration Branch, RG 76, vol. 688, file 34686); a copy of this letter was found among Gabrielle Roy's personal papers (NLC).

43. W. D. Scott to J. Bruce Walker, Ottawa, 14 April 1912 (ibid.).

44. Ibid.; see also W. D. Scott to J. Bruce Walker, Ottawa, 12 October 1915, and Walker's reply dated 15 October.

45. Léon Roy to J. Bruce Walker, St-Boniface, 19 October 1915, transmitted by Walker to W. D. Scott, 23 October, then by Scott to M. Cory, 29 October (ibid.).

46. "Tribune libre," *La Liberté*, 28 December 1915, p. 6; Léon added to this letter (dated 12 December) two expressions of praise for his work, dating from 1910 and 1912 respectively; a previous letter on colonization from Léon Roy had appeared in *La Liberté*, 9 November 1915, p. 1.

47. On this subject, see documents of January and February 1916 and 15 May 1917 (NAC, Department of the Interior, Immigration Branch, RG 76, vol. 688, file 34686).

48. It has not been possible to corroborate this. According to information obtained from the federal Department of Supplies and Services (*Record of Pension Legislation*, "Administration of Pension Plans," 1.2, p. 1.), it was not until 1924 that federal employees began to have the benefit of a legally constituted pension plan.

49. See letters from Mgr Langevin to Léon Roy between 1902 and 1914 (Archives of the Archbishopric of St-Boniface, Langevin Papers, "Letterbook," vol. IV, pp. 222–223; V, p. 641; IX, p. 279; X, pp. 1, 5; XI, p. 211; XVIII, pp. 404–405. During these same years, Léon Roy's activities were quite often mentioned in *Les Cloches de Saint-Boniface*, "the organ of the Archbishopric and the entire ecclesiastical province of St-Boniface."

50. *Enchantment and Sorrow*, "The Governor's Ball," III, pp. 30, 28 (trans. P. Claxton).

51. Ibid, p. 28.

52. *Street of Riches*, "By Day and By Night," p. 142 (trans. H. L. Binsse).

NOTES TO CHAPTER 4

"That Person All Unknown to Me"

1. MPA, Department of Education (GR 1628): "Half-yearly Returns of Attendance," 1915–1928, District 1188. Gabrielle Roy's teachers in subsequent years were: Sister Marie de Sion (Héléna Perrault) in Grade 2; Sister Marie Auxiliatrice (Anastasie Bertrand) in Grade 3; Sister Marie de la Foi (Albertine Bertrand) in Grade 4; Sister Gilles de Saint-Joseph (Marie-Louise Laporte) in Grade 5; and Sister Marie-Dominique (Éva Daigneault) in Grade 6. At the secondary level, her home-class teachers were Sister Agathe de Sicile (Adéla Gauthier) in Grades 7 and 10, Sister Joseph de Bethléem (Élisa Marion) in Grades 8 and 11, Sister Jeanne de Chantal (Marie-Antoinette Lépine) in Grade 9, and Sister Marie Maxima (M.-A. Bellemare) in Grade 12.

2. Lionel Groulx, 1933, p. 123.

3. On this question, see the "Chroniques" of the Académie Saint-Joseph (SSNJM).

4. Marie-Anna A. [Adèle] Roy, 1979, p. 27.

5. Ibid., p. 28.

6. *Street of Riches*, "My Whooping Cough," p. 41 (trans. H. L. Binsse).

7. Marie-Anna A. [Adèle] Roy, 1979, pp. 27–28.

8. Marie-Anna A. [Adèle] Roy, "À vol d'oiseau à travers le temps et l'espace," unpublished manuscript (NAC, MPA).

9. Marie-Anna A. [Adèle] Roy, 1954, p. 177.

10. Interview, 19 April 1973, by Joan Hind-Smith, 1975, p. 71.

11. Clémence to Gabrielle, St-Boniface, 2 March 1981 (NLC).

12. In one of Gabrielle Roy's early short stories titled "La grande Berthe" (June 1943), the nickname *petit misère* is given contemptuously to "a puny, sickly-looking little child."

13. *Street of Riches*, "Petite Misère," p. 16 (trans. H. L. Binsse).

14. Gabrielle to Adèle, quoted by Adèle in "L'arbre grandit," unpublished manuscript (MPA, BNQ); the letter is not dated but was written about 1970.

15. Marie-Anna A. [Adèle] Roy, 1954, p. 177.

16. Marie-Anna A. [Adèle] Roy, 1979, p. 30.

17. Marie-Anna A. [Adèle] Roy, 1974, p. 177.

18. Gabrielle to Bernadette, Quebec City, 23 June 1960 (NLC; *Letters to Bernadette*, p. 32, trans. P. Claxton).

19. Marie-Anna A. [Adèle] Roy, 1979, p. 143.

20. Marie-Anna A. [Adèle] Roy, 1954, p. 177.

21. Ibid.

22. These events are mentioned in *Enchantment and Sorrow* ("The Governor's Ball," II and III, pp. 19–30, trans. P. Claxton).

23. MPA, Department of Education (GR 1628), "Half-yearly Returns of Attendance," 1920–21, district 1188.

24. "Chroniques" of the Académie Saint-Joseph (SSNJM).

25. *Enchantment and Sorrow*, "The Governor's Ball," IV, p. 47 (trans. P. Claxton).

26. "La caravane en détresse," unpublished manuscript (F. Ricard Collection).

27. *La Saga d'Éveline* (NLC, box 74, file 2, folio 54).

28. *Enchantment and Sorrow*, "The Governor's Ball," XIX, p. 190 (trans. P. Claxton).

29. Ibid., II, p. 24.

30. Ibid., V, p. 50.

31. MPA, Department of Education (data conveyed by Denise Lecuyer).

32. See *La Liberté*, 12 August 1925, p. 4; the others in her class were promoted "with satisfaction."

33. *La Liberté*, 13 July 1927, p. 9; this paper also announced that Gabrielle had come first in the semi-annual examinations for Grade 10 (20 January 1926, p. 8) and Grade 11 (12 January 1927, p. 8) with marks of 96 per cent in the first case and 94 per cent in the second.

34. MPA, Department of Education, RG 19-B1 (box 10).

35. See *La Liberté*, 30 March 1920, p. 1; 29 June 1920, p. 1; 25 October 1921, p. 1; 27 June 1922, p. 1; 19 September 1922, p. 1; 11 December 1923, p. 8; 9 December 1925, p. 4; 16 November 1927, p. 4; 16 January 1929, p. 8. After Léon's death, in the lists of subscribers published annually in *La Liberté* we find Melina (3 February 1932, p. 5; 8 February 1933, p. 2; 23 January 1934, p. 2), Anna, her husband Albert, and their son Fernand (15 January 1930, p. 4; 3 February 1932, p. 5), and once, "Mlle Gabrielle Roy" for a sum of one dollar (11 March 1931, p. 11).

36. "Chroniques" of the Académie Saint-Joseph (SSNJM).

37. "Souvenirs du Manitoba" (1954), p. 5.

38. *La Liberté*, 17 July 1923, p. 7.

39. On the organization of the contest, see the AECFM Papers (SHSB).

40. See *La Liberté*, 17 June 1924, p. 1; 26 August 1924, p. 5; 12 August 1925, p. 7.

41. See ibid., 23 June 1926, p. 9.

42. See ibid., 22 June 1927, p. 1, 11; 13 June 1928, p. 1; 27 June 1928, p. 11.

43. Ibid., 6 April 1927, p. 2; although the winner for the Académie Saint-Joseph, Gabrielle was eliminated in the subsequent round of the provincial contest (ibid., 27 April 1927, p. 1). She may also have participated (but without notable success) in the contest for 1928, whose theme was "The Future of Canada."

44. She was a "maid of honour" in Grade 9 (ibid., 10 May 1925, p. 8), Grade 10 (ibid., 16 June 1926, p. 8) and Grade 11 (ibid, 13 July 1927, p. 8).

45. "Chroniques" of the Académie Saint-Joseph (SSNJM); see also *La Liberté*, 10 June 1925, p. 8; 16 June 1926, p. 8; 4 July 1928, p. 8.

46. *Enchantment and Sorrow*, "The Governor's Ball," V, p. 51 (trans. P. Claxton).

47. See ibid.

48. Ibid., V, p. 58; II, p. 21.

49. Ibid., V, p. 51.

50. "Chroniques" of the Académie Saint-Joseph (SSNJM).

51. *La Liberté*, 3 July 1923, p. 5.

52. Ibid., 23 December 1925, p. 8.

53. Ibid., 14 December 1927, p. 7.

54. *Enchantment and Sorrow*, "The Governor's Ball," V, p. 51 (trans. P. Claxton).

55. Ibid., p. 53.

56. Ibid., p. 54.

57. "The Disparate Treasures of a Young Girl Who Came from Deschambault Street," 1976 (trans. A. Brown).

58. Gabrielle to Bernadette, Rawdon, 4 January 1946 (NLC; *Letters to Bernadette*, p. 5, trans. P. Claxton); see also a letter from Gabrielle Roy to Sister Anna-Josèphe [Quebec City], 28 February 1958 (SSNJM). On Sister Marie-Diomède, see also C. Bahuaud and F. Lemay, 1985, pp. 66–68.

59. Gabrielle to Bernadette, Saint-Germain-en-Laye, 24 October 1949 (NLC; *Letters to Bernadette*, p. 18, (trans. P. Claxton).

60. *Enchantment and Sorrow*, "The Governor's Ball," V, pp. 54–55 (trans. P. Claxton).

61. See the advertisement in the *Winnipeg Tribune*, 13 October 1928, p. 26. The troupe was visiting Winnipeg for the first time and spent five days there, performing, besides *The Merchant of Venice*, *The Taming of the Shrew*, *The Merry Wives of Windsor*, *Richard III*, *Henry IV*, Part I, *Julius Caesar*, and *Hamlet*. For reviews of the performance of *The Merchant of Venice*, see the *Manitoba Free Press* (p. 8) and the *Winnipeg Tribune* (p. 19) of 25 October 1928.

62. *Enchantment and Sorrow*, "The Governor's Ball," V, p. 54 (trans. P. Claxton).

63. *The Hidden Mountain*, XVII, p. 122 (trans. H. L. Binsse).

64. *Enchantment and Sorrow*, "The Governor's Ball," V, p. 55 (trans. P. Claxton).

65. Marie-Anna A. [Adèle] Roy, 1954, pp. 201–203.

66. *Street of Riches*, "The Jewels," p. 127; "To Earn My Living," p. 151; "The Voice of the Pools," p. 130 (trans. H. L. Binsse).

67. *Enchantment and Sorrow*, "The Governor's Ball," II, p. 22 (trans. P. Claxton).

68. Ibid., IV, p. 39.

69. Gabrielle to Éliane Landry, St-Boniface, 19 April 1925 (R. Jubinville collection). In the same collection, there is another letter to Éliane, written in late December 1924; this is the earliest of Gabrielle Roy's letters to have been found so far.

70. Éliane was born in 1903, Philippe in 1905, Léa in 1908, and Cléophas in 1910; their father, Excide Landry, was born in 1875; Excide and Luzina's other children were Ovide (1906, died in early childhood), Wilfrid (1914, died shortly after birth), Alberta (1916), and Germain (1917).

71. *Enchantment and Sorrow*, "The Governor's Ball," IV, p. 39 (trans. P. Claxton).

72. Ibid., XIV, p. 139; IV, p. 45.

73. *Children of My Heart*, III, p. 131. (trans. A. Brown).

74. *La Détresse et l'Enchantement*, "Le bal chez le gouverneur," XIX, p. 231.

75. *Street of Riches*, "The Voice of the Pools," p. 130 (trans. H. L. Binsse).

76. *Enchantment and Sorrow*, "The Governor's Ball," I, p. 3 (trans. P. Claxton).

77. Ibid., p. 6.

78. "Ma petite rue qui m'a menée autour du monde," pp. 149–152; in *Enchantment and Sorrow*, ("The Governor's Ball," XV, p. 153) Gabrielle Roy briefly recalls a similar scene, which she places in the autumn of 1936.

79. *Enchantment and Sorrow*, "The Governor's Ball," II, pp. 19–20 (trans. P. Claxton).

80. "Notre histoire," *La Liberté*, 14 November 1922, p. 5.

81. See ibid., 8 December 1926, p. 11.

82. *Enchantment and Sorrow*, "The Governor's Ball," XIX, pp. 192–193 (trans. P. Claxton).

83. Ibid., p. 193.

84. *The Tin Flute*, IX, pp. 115–116 (trans. A. Brown).

85. Ibid., p. 116.

86. "Ma petite rue qui m'a menée autour du monde," p. 148.

87. In St-Boniface itself, the proportion of francophones (Canadians of French and Belgian origin) was 46.7 per cent in 1921 (*Canada Census, 1921*, vol. 1, tables 23 and 28); twenty years or so later, it had dropped to 31.6 per cent, according to Gabrielle Roy in an article she published in 1940 ("Où en est Saint-Boniface?").

88. Gabrielle to Bernadette, Quebec, 4 May 1970 (NLC; *Letters to Bernadette*, p. 180, trans. P. Claxton).

89. Gabrielle to Clémence, Quebec, 23 February 1972 (NLC); she adds, "No one could make people laugh as he could when he felt like making the effort and when he was 'in the pink' as Maman would have said."

90. In the children's story *My Cow Bossie*, Gabrielle Roy draws on this episode and another that took place before she was born, when her parents lived on La Vérendrye Street and Uncle Édouard, Léon's brother, had made them a present of a cow named Bossée, which they had kept for a number of months (see Marie-Anna A. [Adèle] Roy, 1954, pp. 37–38).

91. Of the five lots at the corner of Desmeurons and Deschambault Streets that he had acquired in 1904–1905, Léon sold four between 1908 and 1913 (MPA, Manitoba Lands Office, lots 1 to 5 on Plan 947, formerly lot 79 of the Parish of St-Boniface, certificates no. 27260, 51048, 62785, 112348, 124099, 199581, 207530). According to *Henderson's Directory*, Winnipeg (1904, p. 723; 1905, pp. 109, 985), he may also have owned land on Aubert St., but it has not been possible to confirm this.

92. See *La Liberté*, 29 November 1916, p. 8.

93. See ibid., 13 March 1923, p. 1.

94. Remarks of April 1973 [in English], reported by Joan Hind-Smith, 1975, p. 68.

95. In 1973, Gabrielle Roy told Joan Hind-Smith (1975, p. 69) that, thanks to her mother, "[she] acquired a taste for the exquisite in the midst of poverty."

96. Marie-Anna A. [Adèle] Roy, "Indulgence et Pardon," unpublished manuscript (MPA, BNQ).

97. Gabrielle Roy's remarks reported in English by Myrna Delson-Karan, 1986, pp. 195–196.

98. See *La Liberté*, 8 January 1924, p. 8; 14 January 1925, p. 9. In 1924, one of the first prizes went to a cousin of Gabrielle's, Blanche McEachran, daughter of Rosalie.

99. *Enchantment and Sorrow*, "The Governor's Ball," V, p. 60 (trans. P. Claxton).

100. *Street of Riches*, "The Voice of the Pools," p. 131 (trans. H. L. Binsse).

101. Ibid.

NOTES TO CHAPTER 5

Real Life Is Elsewhere

- The chapter title alludes to a line from the poem *Une Saison en enfer* by Arthur Rimbaud, "La vraie vie est absente," modified in the original title as "La vraie vie est ailleurs."
- The title of the final section of this chapter, "Fly! Oh, to Fly Away!," is a quotation from the poem "Brise marine" by Stéphane Mallarmé, "Fuir! la-bas fuir!" in the original French.

1. *Enchantment and Sorrow*, "The Governor's Ball," V, p. 51 (trans. P. Claxton).

2. *Manitoba Free Press*, Winnipeg, 22 February 1929, p. 2 (with a picture of Léon Roy).

3. *Enchantment and Sorrow*, "The Governor's Ball," VII, pp. 72–73 (trans. P. Claxton).

4. Irma Deloy [Adèle Roy], "Les deux sources de l'inspiration: l'imagination et le coeur," unpublished manuscript (MPA, BNQ).

5. Gabrielle to Bernadette, Quebec City, 3 December 1961 and 25 June 1963 (NLC; *Letters to Bernadette*, pp. 43, 51, trans. P. Claxton).

6. Gabrielle to W. A. Deacon, Encinitas, 11 March 1946 (UOT; in J. Lennox and M. Lacombe, 1988, p. 208).

7. SHSB, fonds AECFM.

8. In *Enchantment and Sorrow* ("The Governor's Ball," VI, p. 62), Gabrielle Roy writes that the Winnipeg Normal Institute [the original name inscribed on the building] was "on Logan Street as I recall"; in fact, the building, built in 1906 and today a classified historic monument, is located at 442 William Avenue, which is parallel to and south of Logan (see Treena Khan, "City Heritage Site Celebrates History," *Winnipeg Free Press*, 15 May 1994, p. A10).

9. This information has been provided by Maria Pronovost and Léonie Guyot, who attended the Provincial Normal School at about the same time as Gabrielle Roy.

10. MPA, Provincial Normal School (GR 1231), registers E-16-3-3, E-16-3-13, and E-16-3-16. In 1928–1929, the school took in approximately 400 students, who

were divided into five classes: two (A and B) designated "Second Class," for students who had only a Grade 11 previous education, two (C and D) at the "First Class" level for those who had completed Grade 12, and one (E) called "Graduate" for those who had already obtained teaching certificates and wished to qualify to teach at the secondary school level. Gabrielle was in Class D, in which there were 78 students.

11. See *Enchantment and Sorrow*, "The Governor's Ball," VI, pp. 63–66. Further to this, Léonie Guyot wrote on 1 February 1994 (F. Ricard Collection), "I never felt that Dr. McIntyre had a remarkably 'open mind' about things to do with French. [...] It may be that Gabrielle had reason to feel warmly toward Dr. W. A. McIntyre. I have trouble understanding how he seemed so kind and so interested in the preservation of the French language."

12. Excerpt from the Provincial Normal School *Year-Book* for the year 1928–1929, cited in Clayton Bricker to Gabrielle Roy, 23 February 1976 (NLC).

13. *Enchantment and Sorrow*, "The Governor's Ball," VI, p. 66 (trans. P. Claxton).

14. See ibid., p. 62.

15. Ibid., p. 66.

16. This first certificate was temporary; it was renewed on 22 November 1930 and became permanent on 31 July 1931 (NLC).

17. "Ma petite rue qui m'a menée autour du monde," p. 152.

18. See "The Dead Child," in *Enchanted Summer*.

19. *Enchantment and Sorrow*, "The Governor's Ball," VIII, pp. 84–85 (trans. P. Claxton).

20. Ibid., IX, p. 88.

21. Message on the occasion of the inauguration of the École Gabrielle Roy in Toronto, unpublished manuscript, June 1976 (NLC).

22. See *Street of Riches*, "To Earn My Living," pp. 153–154. Toward the end of her life, Gabrielle Roy wrote, "In the last chapter of *Street of Riches* I think I recreated the atmosphere of that village fairly accurately. It also figures briefly in *Children of My Heart*, the book I'm putting the final touches to at present." (*Enchantment and Sorrow*, "The Governor's Ball," IX, p. 87; trans. P. Claxton).

23. *Children of My Heart*, Part II, pp. 79–80 (trans. A. Brown).

24. See Gabrielle to Léa Landry, Cardinal, 22 January and 27 February 1930 (R. Jubinville Collection).

25. This evocation of Cardinal and the year that Gabrielle Roy spent there draws almost entirely on the recollections of Victorine Vigier, Aimé Badiou, and Marcel Lancelot, who all three attended the Cardinal school in 1929–1930.

26. *Street of Riches*, "To Earn My Living," p. 153 (trans. H. L. Binsse).

27. MPA, Department of Education, (GR 1628): Half-Yearly Returns of Attendance, 1929–1930, District 964 (M 444, 445); in *Children of My Heart* (Part II, p. 81), the name given is "Cellini" rather than "Cenerini."

28. With respect to this story, Gabrielle Roy told a correspondent that it was inspired by two memories of her time at Cardinal; one of a teenaged pupil

whose confidence she had gained, "perhaps even more than confidence," and the other of a bouquet of wildflowers that someone (the same pupil? one of her cousins? her friend Jean Coulpier?) had thrown to her through a train window (Gabrielle Roy to Antoine Gaboriau, 15 February 1980, reproduced in *Cahiers franco-canadiens de l'Ouest*, St-Boniface, Spring 1991, p. 141). As for the sleighride through the snowstorm, it may have been inspired by a similar event which Gabrielle Roy, according to her account in *Enchantment and Sorrow* ("The Governor's Ball, IX, pp. 90–91), had experienced that year in the company of one of her cousins, and which she most likely used as well for the story entitled "The Storm" in *Street of Riches*. There are various theories about the pond where the trout allow themselves to be touched, some linking this image to the Cardinal region in Manitoba and others to the environs of Petite-Rivière-Saint-François in Quebec.

29. *Children of My Heart*, Part III, p. 167 (trans. A. Brown).

30. Remarks by Gabrielle Roy reported by Pauline Beaudry, 1968–1969, p. 6.

31. *Street of Riches*, "To Earn My Living," p. 158 (trans. H. L. Binsse).

32. SHSB, fonds AECFM, chemise 195, document dated 29 September 1929.

33. See Marie-Anna A. [Adèle] Roy, 1969, pp. 103–145. On French immigration to the Canadian West in the late nineteenth and early twentieth centuries, see Donatien Frémont, 1980 (in particular chapters 10 and 11 for the Pembina Mountain region); also the fine work by Jacques Bertin, *Du vent, Gatine! Un rêve américain* (Paris: Arléa, 1989).

34. "Manitoba" (1962), *The Fragile Lights of Earth*, p. 106 (trans. A. Brown).

35. "Cent pour cent d'amour," October 1936.

36. *Enchantment and Sorrow*, "The Governor's Ball," VIII, p. 86 (trans. P. Claxton).

37. Gabrielle Roy to Léa Landry, Cardinal, 27 February 1930 (R. Jubinville Collection).

38. *Children of My Heart*, Part III, p. 151 (trans. A. Brown).

39. Gabrielle Roy to the School Commission of St-Boniface, Marchand, 12 June 1929, Cardinal, 29 December 1929, and 14 May 1930 (SDSB).

40. Louis Bétournay to Gabrielle Roy, St-Boniface, 20 June 1930 (ibid.).

41. This and much of the subsequent information comes from Léonie Guyot, Marcel Lancelot, and Thérèse Gauthier.

42. In Quebec, the average annual salary for Catholic teachers fell from $402 in 1931–1932 to $337 in 1936–1937; among rural schoolteachers it did not exceed $300 (see P.-A. Linteau, R. Durocher, J.-C. Robert, and F. Ricard, 1989, pp. 103–104).

43. MPA, Department of Education (GR 1628): Half-Yearly Returns of Attendance, 1930–1937, District 1188, (447–463).

44. *Children of My Heart*, Part I, p. 58 (trans. A. Brown).

45. On Léonie Guyot, see C. Bahuaud and F. Lemay, 1985, pp. 54–56; and Bernard Boquel, "En éducation, il n'y a jamais rien de définitif," *La Liberté*, 21 September 1984.

46. This sixteen-page unpublished manuscript, conserved by Léonie Guyot, is the earliest known manuscript of Gabrielle Roy.

47. *La Liberté*, 10 May 1933, p. 4.

48. See ibid.; also the South Eastern Teachers' Association of Manitoba convention program, 9 November 1934 (L. Guyot Collection).

49. Gabrielle Roy to Léonie Guyot, St-Boniface, 26 April 1937 (L. Guyot Coll.).

50. See "The Governor's Ball," X, pp. 97–98 (in which Gabrielle Roy erroneously calls him "Hinks"); see also *Children of My Heart*, Part I, pp. 38–39.

51. See MPA, Department of Education (GR 129A): Correspondence with School Districts, District 1188.

52. *Enchantment and Sorrow*, "The Governor's Ball," X, p. 98 (trans. P. Claxton).

53. MPA, Department of Education, (GR 1628): Half-Yearly Returns of Attendance, 1930–1937, District 1188 (M 447–463). There is no student with the given name Nil or the surname Galaïda in these lists. Vincenzto Rinella (called Vincent) was five when he entered Gabrielle Roy's class in the second semester of the year 1931–1932, and he stayed until June 1933. William Demetrioff was there in 1930–1931 and 1931–1932; Walter Demetrioff in 1932–1933 and 1933–1934, as was Tony Tascona; Clare Atkins was in Gabrielle's class in 1934–1935 and 1935–1936, as was Nikolaï Susick (called Nick). The latter name heralds not only that of the postman (Nick Sluzick) in *Where Nests the Water Hen*, ("Luzina Takes a Holiday"), but also the title of one of Gabrielle Roy's first stories ("Nikolaï Suliz," February 1940), which evokes the hardship experienced by an immigrant family living in a working-class milieu.

54. Except for her last year (1936–1937), when about half her pupils were in Grade 2.

55. From a 1990 interview conducted and reported by C. J. Harvey, 1993, p. 223; Tony Tascona is named in *Children of My Heart* (Part I, pp. 29–30); see also Gabrielle Roy to Tony Tascona, Quebec City, 20 April 1963 (reproduced in *Cahiers franco-canadiens de l'Ouest*, St-Boniface: spring 1991, p. 41).

56. These photographs have been kindly provided to me by Brother Joseph G. André, Marianist, of St-Boniface.

57. *Enchantment and Sorrow*, "The Governor's Ball," X, p. 152. (trans. P. Claxton).

58. T. Goulet Courchesne, "Mlle Gabrielle Roy," *La Liberté et le Patriote*, 9 May 1947, p. 10. Thérèse Goulet published a number of texts under the pseudonym Manie Tobie (see René Juéry, *Mani Tobie, femme du Manitoba*, St-Boniface: Éditions des Plaines, 1979).

59. See André Belleau, *Le Romancier fictif* (Sillery: Presses de l'Université du Québec, 1980), II and III.

60. See *Catalogue de la Bibliothèque paroissiale de St-Boniface*, no place or date, self-published, 23 pp. (SHSB); the publication of this catalogue likely dates from the 1930s.

61. An observer visiting Winnipeg in 1936 found only one French bookstore, about which he wrote, "Its stock is poor. Buyers have practically no choice. French books arrive with difficulty" (quoted by Philippe Prévost, *La France et le Canada d'un après-guerre à l'autre, 1918–1944*, St-Boniface: Éditions du Blé, 1944, p. 81).

62. See Gabrielle Roy's "[Témoignage sur le roman]" (1963), her remarks of 1970 reported by Marc Gagné (1973, p. 164), and *Enchantment and Sorrow*, "A Bird Knows Its Song, III, p. 222.

63. "The Governor's Ball," XI, pp. 107–108 (trans. P. Claxton).

64. See Blanche Ellinthorpe, "From Teaching to Writing," *The Country Guide*, Winnipeg, February 1953, pp. 68, 76, and a brochure entitled *Lillian Benyon Thomas (1874–1961)*, Winnipeg: Manitoba Culture, Heritage and Recreation, 1986; noted in particular is the role played by Mrs. Thomas in the campaigns for women's suffrage, which Manitoba was the first province to recognize in 1916, before the federal government (1917–1918), and well before Quebec (1940).

65. Léon Dartis [Henri Girard], 1947, p. 26.

66. See Tony Dickason, 1947, p. 9.

67. And not twenty, as she said in 1973 to Joan Hind-Smith (1975, p. 76), speaking of the *Free Press* episode; in the same interview she added that another of her detective stories, this time in French, had appeared at this time in *Le Samedi* of Montreal, but, in fact, the first text by Gabrielle Roy in this magazine did not appear until 1936, and it was not a detective story.

68. "Souvenirs du Manitoba" (1954), p. 6.

69. Gabrielle Roy, "Les gens de chez nous" (May 1943).

70. *La Liberté*, 29 November 1933, p. 1; see ibid., 15 November 1933, p. 1; see also the program of the evening (L. Guyot Coll.).

71. Ibid., 9 April 1930, p. 6.

72. The program for the evening is reproduced in L. Dorge, 1980, p. 119; see also *La Liberté*, 21 January 1931, p. 8.

73. See *La Liberté*, 25 March 1931, p. 8; 10 May 1933, p. 8; 23 November 1932, p. 8; 16 March 1932, p. 10; 14 December 1932, p. 6; 8 November 1932, p. 8; 23 December 1931, p. 4; 6 April 1932, p. 4; 26 October 1932, p. 4.

74. See "The Governor's Ball," XII–XII, pp. 115–126. For the names of her companions, see Gabrielle to Clémence, Quebec City, 15 November 1968, and Petite-Rivière-Saint-François, 8 July 1969 (NLC). According to a poster saved by Léonie Guyot, other probable members of the group were Yvonne Thorimbert, Paul Dugal, and Fernando Champagne.

75. On the history of Le Cercle Molière and on the Boutals, see especially: Pauline Boutal, 1985; Collaborative authorship, *Le Cercle Molière: 50ᵉ anniversaire*, St-Boniface: Éditions du Blé, 1975; and two pages in *La Liberté* (8–14 May 1992) on Pauline Boutal on the occasion of her death.

76. A. LaFlèche, "Souvenirs d'un comédien amateur," in L. Dorge, 1980, p. 146.

77. "Le Cercle Molière, porte ouverte" (1980), p. 117.

78. See *La Liberté*, 4 February 1931, p. 8.

79. SHSB, fonds Cercle Molière; see in particular the minutes of meetings of 16 May and 22 October 1932, and in 1933, of 27 January, 18 February, 18 March, 15 April, and 19 May; see also *La Liberté*, 23 November 1932, p. 8; 22 February 1933, p. 3; 24 October 1934, p. 10.

80. *La Liberté*, 6 December 1933, p. 3; the other actors were Victor Masson, Jean de la Vignette, Henri Pinvidic, Georgeline Bélanger, Joseph Plante, Antoine LeGoff, Bernard Goulet, and Albert Prendergast (see ibid., 22 November 1933, p. 8).

81. See ibid., 28 March 1934, p. 3.

82. See ibid., 4 April 1934, p. 4; 18 April 1934, p. 8.

83. See Gabrielle Roy to L. Bétournay, St-Boniface, 19 April 1934 (SDSB).

84. *La Liberté*, 2 May 1934, pp. 1, 3; see ibid., 16 May 1934, p. 8; *Winnipeg Tribune*, 14 May 1934; SHSB, fonds Cercle Molière, chemise 664.

85. *La Liberté*, 6 February 1935, p. 3. Besides Gabrielle Roy, the cast consisted of Marc Meunier, Jean Trudel, Denys Goulet, Armand Schwartz, and Jean Boily (see *Winnipeg Tribune*, 4 February 1935).

86. *La Liberté*, 19 February 1836, p. 1.

87. The cast also included Pauline and Arthur Boutal, Joseph Plante, and three young boys, J.-M. Deniset and Georges and Gabriel Sourisseau.

88. *La Liberté*, 26 February 1936.

89. See ibid., 18 March 1936, p. 4; 1 April 1936, p. 4; 15 April 1936, p. 3; 22 April 1936, p. 8; 29 April 1936, p. 1. See also Gabrielle Roy to the St-Boniface School Commission, 29 March 1936 (SDSB).

90. See an article from *Le Canada*, Montreal, 30 April 1936 (reproduced in *Le Cercle Molière: 50ᵉ anniversaire*, St-Boniface: Éditions du Blé, 1975).

91. Paul Guth, 1947, p. 1.

92. See that evening's program (L. Guyot Coll.).

93. *La Liberté*, 14 December 1932, p. 6 (the second declamation was "Le Retour" by Lucienne Boyer, in French).

94. This and the following information comes from the archives of the Winnipeg Little Theatre (MPA). On the history of the troupe, whose activities ceased in 1937, see Eugene Benson and L. W. Conolly, eds., *The Oxford Companion to Canadian Theatre* (Toronto: Oxford University Press, 1989), p. 324.

95. SHSB, fonds Cercle Molière, chemise 5. The play was presented on 26, 27, 29, and 30 April 1935; the other parts were played by Florence Zachary, Harry Harrod, Norman West, Kenneth Gosling, Edith Myers, Alan Jenkins, Wootton Goodman, and Phyllis Roberts; John Craig was director (see *Winnipeg Free Press*, 20 April 1935, p. 26).

96. In "Le Cercle Molière, porte ouverte" (1980, p. 118) and in *Enchantment and Sorrow* ("The Governor's Ball," XV, p. 146), Gabrielle Roy writes that she played also in *Le chant du Berceau*; Le Cercle Molière won two prizes for its performance of this play at the finals of the Dominion Drama Festival, but not until the spring of 1938, six months after Gabrielle's departure for Europe; she may have taken part in the very early rehearsals, but her name does not appear in the cast listing for the performances of the play on 5 February and 18 May 1938 (see *La Liberté*, 26 January 1938, p. 1; 9 February 1938, p. 1; 25 May 1938, p. 1). The confusion arises perhaps from the fact that when Gabrielle was studying dramatic arts in London early in 1938, she played a part in this same play, mounted by the students of the Guildhall

School (see Gabrielle Roy to Brother J. Bruns, 26 February 1938 (archives des frères Marianistes, St-Boniface) and to Renée Deniset, undated (FGR, dossier J. Helliwell).

97. She played the part of a lady's maid. Her mistress was played by Margot Syme, who had scored a resounding success the preceding month in a *Romeo and Juliet* attended by the Governor General himself (see *Winnipeg Tribune*, 4 December 1936, p. 12); the other actors were Ethel Watson, Graeme Norman, Thomas McEwen, and Herbert Marsden; John Craig was director (see *Winnipeg Free Press*, 23 January 1937, p. 12, which includes a picture of Gabrielle Roy).

98. See *Winnipeg Free Press*, 27 April 1935, p. 11; 1 February 1937, p. 20; and *Winnipeg Tribune*, 27 April 1935, p. 5; 30 January 1937, p. 4.

99. Gabrielle Roy to W. A. Deacon (in English), Encinitas, 11 March 1946 (UOT; in J. Lennox and M. Lacombe, 1988, p. 208). To Rex Desmarchais (1947, p. 36) Gabrielle Roy declared, referring to these years, "I used to tell myself that if I left teaching I could have a fine career on the stage."

100. "Le Cercle Molière, porte ouverte" (1980), pp. 117–118.

101. Ibid., p. 118.

102. *Enchantment and Sorrow*, "The Governor's Ball," I, pp. 6, 3 (trans. P. Claxton).

103. On this subject, see D. Frémont, 1980, chapters XIII and XIV.

104. On Élisa Houde, née Charlet (1887–1978), to whom Gabrielle Roy pays tribute in "Le Cercle Molière, porte ouverte" (1980, pp. 119–121), see C. Bahuaud and F. Lemay, 1985, pp. 57–58; and P. Boutal, 1985, pp. 210–211.

105. See *La Liberté*, 10 April 1935, p. 3; see also the poster reproduced in L. Dorge, 1980, p. 119.

106. These and many of the following details have been provided by Jacqueline Deniset-Benoist, Léonie Guyot, Louis-Philippe Gauthier, Antonia Roy-Houde, and Guy Chauvière.

107. *La Liberté*, 24 July 1935, p. 4.

108. See ibid., 31 December 1935, p. 4.

109. Ibid., 19 December 1934, p. 4; see also 21 August 1935, p. 4.

110. Gabrielle Roy to Marcel Carbotte, Paris, 8 July 1955 (NLC).

111. See *La Liberté*, 21 July 1937, p. 1.

112. *Enchantment and Sorrow*, "The Governor's Ball," XI, p. 108 (trans. P. Claxton).

113. "Les petits pas de Caroline" (October 1940), p. 11.

114. Léonie Guyot to F. Ricard, Winnipeg, 23 May 1991 (F. Ricard Collection).

115. Ibid. Léonie thinks she remembers the young man's first name as Richard, but is not certain.

116. Guy Chauvière in conversation with Lucien Chaput, Winnipeg, February 1991. Born in Winnipeg in 1908, Guy Chauvière died there on 27 May 1992.

117. Irma Deloy [Adèle Roy], "Les Deux Sources de l'Inspiration: l'imagination et le coeur," unpublished manuscript (MPA, BNQ).

118. *Enchantment and Sorrow*, "The Governor's Ball," XI, p. 107 (trans. P. Claxton).

119. Marie-Anna A. [Adèle] Roy, "L'arbre grandit," unpublished manuscript (MPA, BNQ).

120. L. Groulx, 1933, p. 135.

121. Gabrielle Roy to W. A. Deacon (in English), Encinitas, 11 March 1946 (UOT; in J. Lennox and M. Lacombe, 1988, p. 208).

122. *Enchantment and Sorrow*, "The Governor's Ball," XI, p. 109 (trans. P. Claxton).

123. Léonie Guyot to F. Ricard, Winnipeg, 15 June 1991 (F. Ricard Coll.).

124. Gabrielle to Adèle, [Montreal], 14 March 1944 (NAC, Marie-Anna A. Roy Papers).

125. *Enchantment and Sorrow*, "The Governor's Ball," XIX, p. 189 (trans. P. Claxton).

126. See Fulgence Charpentier, 1983; see also Ben-Z. Shek, 1989, p. 451.

127. It was in March 1926 that Léon Roy made a gift of his house to Mélina (MPA, Manitoba Lands Office, lot 5 on plan 947, formerly lot 79 of the Catholic Parish of St-Boniface, certificate no. 387113).

128. *La Liberté*, 13 December 1933, p. 4.

129. See ibid., 13 July 1932, p. 4.

130. See "The Governor's Ball," XI, pp. 110–111.

131. *La Liberté*, 7 September 1932, p. 4.

132. Ibid., 2 May 1934, p. 4.

133. Marie-Anna A. [Adèle] Roy, 1954, p. 218.

134. "The Governor's Ball," XI, p. 113 (trans. P. Claxton).

135. Ibid., p. 112.

136. Ibid., XV, p. 148.

137. Gabrielle Roy in interview with Dorothy Duncan (in English), 1947.

138. *Enchantment and Sorrow*, "The Governor's Ball," XIX, p. 193. (trans. P. Claxton).

139. *La détresse et l'enchantement*, "Le bal chez le gouverneur," XVI, p. 198.

140. Gabrielle Roy in interview with Rex Desmarchais, 1947, pp. 36–37.

141. *Enchantment and Sorrow*, "The Governor's Ball," ch. 15, p. 145 (trans. P. Claxton).

142. Ibid., XVI, p. 155.

143. *The Road Past Altamont*, "The Road Past Altamont," I, p. 111; II, p. 114 (trans. J. Marshall).

144. *Children of My Heart*, Part I, p. 44 (trans. A. Brown).

145. Ibid., p. 41.

146. *Enchantment and Sorrow*, "The Governor's Ball," XV, p. 146 (trans. P. Claxton).

147. *The Road Past Altamont*, "The Road Past Altamont," V, pp. 132–134 (trans. J. Marshall).

148. "The Governor's Ball," X, p. 100 (trans. P. Claxton).

149. See the correspondence between Mélina Roy and the municipality of St-Boniface (SHSB, fonds 123, boîte 6, chemise 19). The official transfer of the title deeds to F. Saint-Germain is dated September 1937 (MPA, Manitoba Lands Office, lot 5 of plan 947, formerly lot 79 of the parish of St-Boniface, certificate no. 508956).

150. The manuscript is at the NLC; a posthumous edition of the text was published in 1991.

151. "The Governor's Ball," XV, p. 150 (trans. P. Claxton); see Gabrielle Roy to Helen Sisson, Petite-Rivière-Saint-François, 18 August 1976 (NLC).

152. See the presentation of the article by Gabrielle Roy, "Winnipeg Girl Visits Bruges" (December 1938).

153. See Anna Roy-Painchaud to Mélina Roy, St-Vital, 1 September, 1941, and Dr. A. P. Mackinnon to Mélina Roy, Winnipeg, 24 April 1942 (NLC).

154. See *La Liberté*, 18 November 1936, p. 4.

155. Fragment of a letter from Mélina to Adèle, St-Boniface, 3 January 1937 (NLC; photocopy).

156. MPA, GR 267 Health and Public Welfare, Old Age Pension, file 20015. The document is countersigned by Marie-Agnès Bernier, Mélina's neighbour since 1905, as sworn witness.

157. This pension was raised to $20 in December 1939.

158. Gabrielle Roy to the St-Boniface School Commission, 19 April 1937 (SDSB).

159. Louis Bétournay, Secretary of the St-Boniface School Commission, to Gabrielle Roy, 28 April 1937 (SDSB).

160. *Enchantment and Sorrow*, "The Governor's Ball," XVII, p. 166 (trans. P. Claxton).

161. These details are given by Marie-Anna A. [Adèle] Roy, 1977, ch. 6.

162. *Enchantment and Sorrow*, "The Governor's Ball," XVIII, p. 180 (trans. P. Claxton).

163. "Memory and Creation, Preface to *Where Nests the Water Hen*" (1957), *The Fragile Lights of Earth*, p. 187 (trans. A. Brown).

164. In the passport that Gabrielle Roy obtained in 1943 is inscribed this note: "Bearer previously travelled on passport No. 47309 issued on August 31, 1937" (NLC).

165. See "The Governor's Ball," XVII, pp. 166–171 (trans. P. Claxton).

166. Marie-Anna A. [Adèle] Roy, 1979, p. 123.

167. Gabrielle to Bernadette, 15 September 1943 (NLC; *Letters to Bernadette*, p. 3 (trans. P. Claxton).

168. *Enchantment and Sorrow*, "The Governor's Ball," XV, p. 146 (trans. P. Claxton).

169. See ibid., XIX, pp. 183–190.

170. See a postcard from Gabrielle Roy to Renée Deniset, [North Bay,] 30 August 1937 (FGR, dossier J. Helliwell).

171. *La Liberté*, 8 September 1937, p. 4.

NOTES TO CHAPTER 6

Adventure

1. *Enchantment and Sorrow*, "A Bird Knows Its Song," V, p. 233 (trans. P. Claxton).

2. Her passage through the city was noted in *Le Canada*, Montreal, 9 September 1937, p. 4.

3. Gabrielle Roy in interview with Rex Desmarchais, 1947, p. 37.

4. And not "Madame Jean-Pierre Jouve" as in *Enchantment and Sorrow*, "A Bird Knows Its Song," I, p. 202; or "Madame Pierre-Jean Jouve" as in the French original (*La détresse et l'enchantement*, "Un oiseau tombé sur le seuil," I, p. 254).

5. See ibid., II, p. 210.

6. Archives de la Police, Paris; handwritten register of the 52e *quartier*, entry no. 1027, Wednesday, 20 October 1937.

7. The play, first presented in 1928, was mounted at the Théâtre de l'Atelier (in the XVIIIe arrondissement) from 17 September 1937 to 26 January 1938. This and subsequent information is found in the Bibliothèque de l'Arsenal, Paris, and the daily newspaper *Le Figaro* (Bibliothèque nationale, Paris, microfilm D-13).

8. *La sauvage* was presented from 11 January until 3 April 1938, with Ludmila Pitoëff in the title role; *La Mouette*, which was first performed in 1922, was presented from 17 January to 13 May 1939.

9. Herbert R. Lottman, *The Left Bank: Writers, Artists, and Politics from the Popular Front to the Cold War* (Boston: Houghton Mifflin, 1982).

10. Gabrielle to Marcel Carbotte, Paris, 9 May 1955 (NLC).

11. This registration was found by Pierre Castonguay and Mireille Attas of Radio-Canada in the course of their research for a film on Gabrielle Roy's London period.

12. See Gabrielle Roy to Brother Joseph Bruns, London, 26 February 1938 (Archives des frères Marianistes, St-Boniface).

13. Gabrielle to Léonie Guyot, London, 25 February 1938 (L. Guyot Collection).

14. Gabrielle Roy in interview with Rex Desmarchais, 1947, p. 37; see also "Mlle Gabrielle Roy," *La Revue populaire*, Montreal, October 1939, p. 67; R.-G. Scully, 1974, p. 15; and *Enchantment and Sorrow*, "A Bird Knows Its Song," VII, pp. 260–261.

15. See Gabrielle Roy to Messieurs de la Commission scolaire de Saint-Boniface, London, 28 February 1938, and the reply from Louis Bétournay, Secretary, St-Boniface, 24 March 1938 (SDSB).

16. And not "Wickendon," as Gabrielle wrote in *Enchantment and Sorrow* ("A Bird Knows Its Song," VI, p. 241) where she says also that her address was "Number 72" (p. 247). The address given here is that appearing on Gabrielle's registration card at the Guildhall School and in letters that she wrote in this period.

17. And not "Lily" as in the French original of *Enchantment and Sorrow* (*La Détresse et l'Enchantement*, "Un oiseau tombé sur le seuil," VI, p. 314).

18. Gabrielle to Renée Deniset, London, November 1937 (FGR, dossier J. Helliwell).

19. See Gabrielle Roy, "Lettre de Londres: Les jolis coins de Londres" (December 1938).

20. See Gabrielle Roy, "La Maison du Canada" (August 1939).

21. "Lettre de Londres: Si près de Londres . . . si loin . . ." (October 1938).

22. Gabrielle to Léonie Guyot, London, 25 February 1938 (L. Guyot Coll.).

23. And not "Bridgeport" (*Enchantment and Sorrow*, "A Bird Knows Its Song," XV, p. 357).

24. See "Lettre de Londres: Choses vues en passant" (July 1938); "Lettre de Londres: Si près de Londres . . . si loin . . ." (October 1938); see also Gabrielle to Léonie Guyot, London, 25 February 1938 (L. Guyot Coll.); and a postcard to Renée Deniset ([London,] 26 May 1938; FGR, dossier J. Helliwell) written on her return from Monmouthshire.

25. That spring it seems that she had even got as far as Belgium, judging by the articles on Bruges that she published in July ("Lettre de Londres: Choses vues en passant") and December 1938 ("Winnipeg Girl Visits Bruges").

26. On this trip, see an article by Gabrielle Roy, "Lettre de Londres: Londres à Land's End" (October 1938).

27. *Enchantment and Sorrow*, "A Bird Knows Its Song," XVIII, p. 388 (trans. P. Claxton).

28. Ibid., VII, p. 282.

29. According to *Enchantment and Sorrow* (ibid., p. 279), their first date took them to a performance of *Boris Godunov* at the Sadler's Wells; P. Castonguay and M. Attas have verified that this opera was being performed in April 1938, but in English, not Russian.

30. *Enchantment and Sorrow*, "A Bird Knows Its Song," IX, p. 290 (trans. P. Claxton).

31. Ibid., p. 293.

32. See Marie-Anna A. Roy, 1979, p. 142; this scene reported by Adèle took place in 1942.

33. *Enchantment and Sorrow*, "A Bird Knows Its Song," VIII, p. 281 (trans. P. Claxton).

34. Ibid., IX, p. 293.

35. Ibid., VIII, p. 281.

36. See what Gabrielle Roy has to say about this in "Lettre de Londres: Si près de Londres . . . si loin . . ." (October 1938).

37. *Enchantment and Sorrow*, "A Bird Knows Its Song," XI, p. 309 (trans. P. Claxton).

38. The data following is drawn from research by Pierre-Marie Dioudonnat, 1973 and 1993.

39. *Enchantment and Sorrow*, "A Bird Knows Its Song," XII, p. 326 (trans. P. Claxton).

40. Ibid., p. 317.

41. Gabrielle Roy in interview with Donald Cameron (in English), 1973, p. 130.

42. Gabrielle Roy in interview with Myrna Delson-Karan (in English), 1986, p. 199.

43. This was a play entitled "The Devil's Trump," unpublished manuscript (NLC). The typewritten manuscript bears no indication of date. Judging from a remark in an interview that Gabrielle Roy granted to John J. Murphy (1963, p. 454: "Travelling to London to study dramatics, she began to write sketches in English"), it could have been written in England, but its theme (conjugal strife in the Canadian West) suggests a closer link with her *Peoples*

of Canada articles, which she published in the original French as *Peuples du Canada* in 1942–1943.

44. See Gabrielle Roy to Messieurs de la Commission scolaire, 23 July 1938, and the replies from J.-A. Marion, President, and Louis Bétournay, Secretary, dated respectively 29 July and 29 September [1938] (SDSB).

45. Although it is impossible to state with certainty since the manuscripts have disappeared, from their content one can imagine that some stories published later in fact date from this period, like "La conversion des O'Connor" (September 1939), "Une histoire d'amour" (March 1940), or "La fuite de Sally" (January 1941), in which are mentioned Epping Forest and the tiny house of Felicity, the little hunchbacked innkeeper who suggested that Gabrielle should go and knock at Esther Perfect's door (see *Enchantment and Sorrow*, "A Bird Knows Its Song," X, pp. 301–304).

46. Gabrielle Roy to Léonie Guyot, London, 24 November 1938 (L. Guyot Coll.).

47. See *Enchantment and Sorrow*, "A Bird Knows Its Song," XVI, pp. 367–370.

48. *La Liberté*, 21 December 1938, p. 4; the information was repeated several days later in the *Northwest Review*, Winnipeg, 29 December 1938, p. 5.

49. Gabrielle Roy in interview with Pauline Beaudry, 1968–1969, p. 6.

50. *Enchantment and Sorrow*, "A Bird Knows Its Song," XVII, p. 374 (trans. P. Claxton). The use of the name "Provence" as a synonym for the Midi or South of France in general is not strictly accurate but is a common practice among the French themselves.

51. "Ma petite rue qui m'a menée autour du monde," p. 155.

52. On one of these episodes, see two published articles by Gabrielle Roy, "En vagabondant dans le midi de la France: Ramatuelle à Hyères" (December 1939) and "Une messe en Provence" (January 1940).

53. Gabrielle Roy evokes this stay in an article titled "Chez les paysans du Languedoc" (August 1939).

54. See Gabrielle Roy in interview with Rex Desmarchais, 1947, p. 38; and with Marie Bourbonnais, 1947, p. 13.

55. See *Enchantment and Sorrow*, "A Bird Knows Its Song," XIX, p. 398; the manuscript of this article seems to have disappeared.

56. Ibid., XX, p. 403 (trans. P. Claxton).

57. See ibid., p. 409; see also Gabrielle Roy in interview with Judith Jasmin, 1961.

58. "Ma petite rue qui m'a menée autour du monde," p. 155.

59. Marthe Robert, *Origins of the Novel*, trans. Sacha Rabinovitch (Brighton: Harvester Press, 1980), p. 83.

60. "Ma petite rue qui m'a menée autour du monde," p. 155.

61. Gabrielle Roy to W. A. Deacon, Encinitas, 11 March 1946 (UOT; in J. Lennox and M. Lacombe, 1988, p. 208); Gabrielle Roy's translator Joyce Marshall (1983, p. 37) remembers Gabrielle speaking of this period as her "glorious years."

62. The ship from Liverpool must have docked at St. John, New Brunswick, on account of ice; the passengers were brought from there to Montreal by rail (see *Enchantment and Sorrow*, "A Bird Knows Its Song," XX, p. 404).

63. Ibid., p. 406 (trans. P. Claxton).

64. "Quelques jolis coins de Montréal" (July 1939).

65. *Le temps qui m'a manqué*, I, p. 26.

66. On this subject, see Ben-Z. Shek, 1989.

67. She used his name in "Ély! Ély! Ély!" (1979), a story based on a memory dating from 1942 (*De quoi t'ennuies-tu, Éveline?*, pp. 112–113).

68. "Quelques jolis coins de Montréal" (July 1939).

69. In his memoirs (*Sacré menteur: mémoires d'un journaliste*, Montreal: Louise Courteau, 1990, pp. 73, 187), Ernest Pallascio-Morin recounts that Gabrielle Roy, soon after her return from Europe, offered him some articles for *Photo-Journal*, of which he was editor-in-chief; however, Gabrielle Roy's name does not appear over any contribution in the pages of this paper between 1939 and 1943.

70. Except that of 15 July; but the 8 July issue carried two articles by her.

71. Thirty texts appeared; among Émile-Charles Hamel's papers were also found two typewritten manuscripts that Gabrielle Roy no doubt intended for *Le Jour* but which were not published. These were two short stories titled "La photographie d'il y a cinquante ans" and "Nowhere Tour" (NLC, François Côté Papers).

72. See Victor Teboul, 1984.

73. This was the case with Gabrielle Roy's two last texts in *Le Jour*: "Nikolaï Suliz" and "De la triste Loulou à son amie Mimi" (February 1940).

74. *Enchantment and Sorrow*, "A Bird Knows Its Song," XX, p. 410 (trans. P. Claxton).

75. On this periodical, see André Beaulieu and Jean Hamelin, 1982, pp. 294–295; and F. Ricard, 1991.

76. H. Girard, "La vie artistique. *Regards et Jeux dans l'espace*," *Le Canada*, Montreal, 30 March 1937, p. 2.

77. See P.-É. Borduas, "Projections libérantes," in *Écrits I*, A.-G. Bourassa, J. Fisette, and G. Lapointe, eds., (Montreal: Presses de L'Université de Montréal, 1987, "Bibliothèque du Nouveau Monde"), pp. 421–422; H. Girard, "Aspects de la peinture surréaliste," *La Nouvelle Relève*, Montreal, September 1948.

78. On Henri Girard's writings and thinking on art criticism, see Esther Trépanier, "L'émergence d'un discours de la modernité dans la critique d'art (Montréal, 1918–1938)," in Y. Lamonde and E. Trépanier, eds., *L'Avènement de la modernité culturelle au Québec* (Quebec: Institut québécois de recherche sur la culture, 1986), pp. 69–112.

79. H. Girard, "Concours de littérature," *La Revue moderne*, Montreal, May 1939, p. 39.

80. Roger Duhamel, "Ce qu'on lit. Canadiens et français," ibid., March 1944, p. 30.

81. H. Girard, "Entre nous," ibid., May 1940, p. 4.

82. Léon Dartis [H. Girard], 1947, p. 9.

83. Although the English version of this text was published before the French, since the manuscripts are inaccessible it is impossible to determine which of the two was written first. We do not know which version is the translation or adaptation of the other.

84. Subsequent information comes from *Radiomonde*, Montreal, 9 December 1939, 24 February, 13 April, and 25 May 1940; see also P. Pagé, R. Legris, and L. Blouin, 1975, p. 239. It seems also that Gabrielle Roy had a role on English radio on the program *Miss Trent's Children*, at least during the autumn of 1939 (see *La Revue populaire*, Montreal, October 1939, p. 67).

85. On this troupe, see Philip Booth, 1989; and Jean Béraud, *350 ans de théâtre au Canada français* (Montreal: Cercle du Livre de France, 1958), chapters VIII and IX.

86. See "Le MRTF à Saint-Sulpice," *Le Jour*, Montreal, 2 September 1939, p. 4; and Jacques Gadbois, "Le Théâtre à Montréal," ibid., 28 October 1939, p. 3.

87. "La Femme de Patrick," unpublished manuscript (NLC); the text is accompanied by documents relating to its staging and bears annotations anticipating its reading on radio.

88. J. Desprez, "Lettre à Suzy," *Radiomonde*, Montreal, 15 June 1940, p. 7.

89. P. Guèvremont played the part of Pat (the father) and P. Dagenais that of Don (the son); the other actors were Phil Lauzon (Mike), Thérèse Rochon (Kathleen), Alda Micheli (Lizzie, the mother), and the child Arlette Desforges (Dodie).

90. M. Boulianne, "Le deuxième gala de pièces canadiennes," *Le Jour*, Montreal, 8 June 1940, p. 3; J.-J. L., "Talents canadiens qui s'affichent," *Le Canada*, Montreal, 4 June 1940, p. 6; J. Desprez, "Lettre à Suzy," *Radiomonde*, Montreal, 15 June 1940, p. 7.

91. See *La Presse*, Montreal, 4 June 1940, p. 10; *Radiomonde*, Montreal, 22 June 1940, p. 10.

92. "Oui, mademoiselle Line," unpublished manuscript (NLC); the text is not dated, but an allusion to the war in Spain and thematic similarity to short stories like "Le roi de coeur" (April 1940) and "Les petits pas de Caroline" (October 1940) suggest that it too is from 1940.

93. "Pêcheurs de Gaspésie," unpublished manuscript (NLC); it was broadcast over CBF on 27 February 1941, produced by Paul Leduc (see P. Pagé, R. Legris, and L. Blouin, 1975, p. 515); this was an adaptation for radio of "La dernière pêche," a story published in *La Revue moderne* of November 1940.

94. This is "The Devil's Trump," the English play referred to in note 43.

95. Little is known of these radio readings. In a note that she herself wrote to publicize *Bonheur d'occasion* (NLC, Éditions Pascal Papers), Gabrielle Roy mentions two "tales" from this period that had been read on radio by Albert Duquesne: "La pension de vieillesse" (published in November 1943) and "La vallée Houdou" (published in February 1945); documents relating to the radiobroadcast of the second – but not the first – are at the NLC. In *L'Explication des textes littéraires* (Quebec: Presses de l'Université Laval, p. 289), Maurice Lebel, who claims to have the information from Gabrielle Roy herself, gives, in addition to "La vallée Houdou" and "La pension de vieillesse," the following list of stories that were radiobroadcast (all of them already published at the time): "Cendrillon ['40]," "Une histoire d'amour,"

"Girard le pirate," "[À] O.K.K.O.," "Embobeliné," "La grande voyageuse," and "La source au désert."

96. Gabrielle Roy in interview with Rex Desmarchais, 1947, p. 38.

97. See, for example, her remarks to Rex Desmarchais, 1947, p. 38. Later she would tell Jacques Godbout (1979, p. 32) that it was Jean Desprez (who had herself published a number of articles in *Le Bulletin* in that period) who recommended her.

98. See, for example, the version given by Marc Gagné (1973, p. 23) and by Joan Hind-Smith (1975, pp. 80–81).

99. On this subject, see especially Richard Giguère and Jacques Michon, 1985 and 1991.

100. On this periodical, see A. Beaulieu and J. Hamelin, 1982, pp. 171–174.

101. *Le temps qui m'a manqué*, IV, p. 79.

102. Ibid.

103. Gabrielle Roy, "Une voile dans la nuit" (May 1944), p. 9.

104. These are the manuscripts entitled "Excusez-moi . . .," "Blandine," "Les trois Mac," "La maison au bord de la mer," and "Le vieux Prince" (NLC).

105. Gabrielle Roy to François Ricard, Quebec City, 3 October 1973 (F. Ricard Collection); this remark was specifically about "Un Noël en route" (December 1940).

106. On this subject see Guy Laflèche, "Les bonheurs d'occasion du roman québécois," *Voix et Images*, Montreal, September 1977, pp. 96–115.

107. *Enchantment and Sorrow*, "A Bird Knows Its Song," XX, p. 406 (trans. P. Claxton).

108. This is the address that appears in an item in *La Liberté et le Patriote*, 26 May 1943, p. 4; as for the date on which Gabrielle Roy moved there, it is difficult to establish exactly, but, according to Guy Savoie, who has his information from Gabrielle Roy herself, it was the end of 1940.

109. Gabrielle Roy in interview with Rex Desmarchais, 1947, p. 38.

110. See the articles entitled "Mort d'extrème vieillesse" (February 1941), "La ferme, grande industrie" (March 1941), "Nos agriculteurs céramistes" (April 1941), "Un homme et sa volonté" (August 1941), and "Vive l'Expo" (October 1941).

111. On this subject, see Ginette Michaud, "De la 'Primitive Ville' à la Place Ville Marie," in Pierre Neveu and Gilles Marcotte, eds., *Montréal imaginaire: ville et littérature* (Montreal: Fides, 1992), pp. 13–95.

112. "Les deux Saint-Laurent" (June 1941), p. 40; see *The Tin Flute*, XXVII, pp. 307–309.

113. "Du port aux banques" (August 1941), p. 11.

114. *Le temps qui m'a manqué*, I, p. 27.

115. Gabrielle Roy in interview with D. Cameron, 1973, p. 135.

116. "Le pays de *Bonheur d'occasion*" (1974), p. 115.

117. Gabrielle Roy in interview with Rex Desmarchais, 1947, p. 39.

118. Gabrielle Roy in interview with D. Cameron, 1973, p. 135.

119. Gabrielle Roy in interview with Judith Jasmin, 1961.

120. *Enchantment and Sorrow*, "A Bird Knows Its Song," XX, p. 410 (trans. P. Claxton).

121. "La côte de tous les vents" (October 1941), p. 44.

122. See among others *Le Canada*, Montreal, 4 September, 1941, p. 1; by error, Robert Rumilly situates this event in 1940 in his *Histoire de la Province de Québec*, vol. XXXVIII: *La Guerre de 1939–1945. Ernest Lapointe* (Montreal: Fides, 1968), pp. 213–214.

123. "Le chef de district" (January 1942), p. 7.

124. Ibid., p. 29.

125. These characters appear respectively in "Plus que le pain" (February 1942), in "La terre secourable" (November 1941), and in "Le pain et le feu" (December 1941).

126. "Pitié pour les institutrices!" (March 1942), p. 7.

127. See "Le plus étonnant: les Huttérites" (November 1942), p. 8; "De Prague à Good Soil" (March 1943), p. 46. According to Jacqueline Deniset-Benoist, it was thanks to Émile Couture that Gabrielle joined *Le Bulletin des agriculteurs*; however, René Soulard, who hired Gabrielle, remembers neither this intervention nor even Émile Couture's name. It may (hypothetically) be concluded that Émile Couture's role in Gabrielle's career at *Le Bulletin* consisted of obtaining her the CNR sponsorship for her trip to the West in the summer of 1942, and perhaps also for her Abitibi tour of the previous summer, which one suspects on finding praise for the CNR contained in "Bourgs d'Amérique I" (April 1942, p. 9).

128. "Femmes de dur labeur" (January 1943), p. 10.

129. "Le plus étonnant: les Huttérites" (November 1942), p. 32.

130. "Les gens de chez nous" (May 1943), pp. 33, 37–39.

131. See Edmond de Nevers, *L'Avenir du peuple canadien-français* (Paris: Jouve, 1896; new edition, Montreal: Fides, 1964, Collection du Nénuphar).

132. "Les gens de chez nous" (May 1943), p. 38.

133. See "Ukraine" (April 1943), pp. 43–44 (this article would appear later in *The Fragile Lights of Earth*, trans. A. Brown).

134. "Vers l'Alaska. Laissez passer les jeeps" (November 1942); see *The Hidden Mountain*, III, pp. 22–28.

135. M. Kundera, *Immortality*, trans. Peter Kussi, New York, Weidenfeld, 1991, p. 109.

136. *Le temps qui m'a manqué*, I, p. 18.

137. See Marie-Anna A. [Adèle] Roy, 1988, pp. 4–5; and 1979, pp. 129–130. Later, Gabrielle Roy would recall this episode with the writing of "De quoi t'ennuies-tu, Éveline?"

138. Marie-Anna A. [Adèle] Roy, 1989–1990, épisode 16.

139. On Adèle's house at Tangent and her mother's and sisters' visits there, see Marie-Anna A. [Adèle] Roy, 1979 (pp. 131–140) and 1958 (passim.).

140. See Anna to Gabrielle, [Tangent,] 1, 2, and 3 September 1941 (NLC).

141. Marie-Anna A. [Adèle] Roy, 1979, p. 140.

142. Gabrielle Roy, "Les gens de chez nous" (May 1943), p. 36.

143. See Gabrielle to Adèle, [Montreal], 8 February 1943 and [Rawdon], 14 March 1944 (NAC, Marie-Anna A. Roy Papers, manuscripts mutilated and annotated by the addressee).

144. See *Le temps qui m'a manqué*, I, pp. 14–15.

145. Germain Roy and his wife were staying in St-Boniface at the time of Gabrielle's visit (see *La Liberté et le Patriote*, 28 October 1942, p. 4; 4 November 1942, p. 4).

146. On Gabrielle Roy's life at Rawdon, see *Le temps qui m'a manqué*; see also Gabrielle to Adèle, Rawdon, 13 February 1944 (NAC, Marie-Anna A. Roy Papers).

147. *Le temps qui m'a manqué*, I, p. 21.

148. Gabrielle to Mélina, Montreal, 2 May 1943 (NLC).

149. Mélina to Gabrielle, St-Boniface, 5 April 1943 (NLC).

150. Mélina to Gabrielle, St-Boniface, 22 March 1943 (NLC).

151. See *Le temps qui m'a manqué*, I, p. 28; the contract was announced in St-Boniface in an item in *La Liberté et le Patriote*, 26 May 1943, p. 4.

152. Mélina to Gabrielle, St-Boniface, 19 June 1943 (NLC); Gabrielle's story entitled "La grande Berthe" appeared in *Le Bulletin des agriculteurs* of June 1943.

153. This is the text that Gabrielle Roy cites in *Le temps qui m'a manqué*, I, p. 15.

154. Ibid, p. 14.

155. Ibid., pp. 25–26; the date in the manuscript, erroneously, is "June 1944."

156. Anna to Adèle, St-Vital, 7 May 1943 (carbon copy, NLC).

157. See *La Liberté et le Patriote*, 7 April 1943, p. 7; 25 August 1943, p. 4.

158. See ibid., 7 July 1943, p. 4; for an account of these days, see *Le temps qui m'a manqué*, III.

159. Gabrielle to Bernadette, Montreal, 15 September 1943 (NLC; *Letters to Bernadette*, p. 4, trans. P. Claxton).

160. Gabrielle to Bernadette, Montreal, 15 September 1943 (NLC; *Letters to Bernadette*, p. 3, trans. P. Claxton).

161. Gabrielle to Adèle, 16 September 1943 (NAC, Marie-Anna A. Roy Papers).

162. Gabrielle to Adèle, [Rawdon], 14 March 1944 (ibid.).

163. Gabrielle to Adèle, [undated], (ibid.); although the mutilated manuscript bears no date, the contents of the letter indicate that it dates from December 1944 or January 1945.

164. *Le temps qui m'a manqué*, IV, p. 90.

165. Ibid., p. 92; these are the closing words of the book.

166. Gabrielle to Bernadette, Montreal, 15 September 1943 (NLC; *Letters to Bernadette*, p. 3, trans. P. Claxton).

167. Gabrielle to Adèle, [Rawdon], 13 February 1944 (NAC, Marie-Anna A. Roy Papers).

168. Gabrielle to Adèle, Montreal, 16 September 1943 (ibid.).

169. Ibid.

170. Gabrielle Roy to Henri Girard, [Rawdon], 21 May [1944] (NLC, Éditions Pascal Papers).

171. Henri Girard to Gabrielle Roy, Montreal, 23 May 1944 (ibid.).

172. Gabrielle to Adèle, [Rawdon, December 1944 or January 1945] (NAC, Marie-Anna A. Roy Papers).

173. Henri Girard to Gabrielle Roy, Montreal, 23 May 1944 (NLC, Éditions Pascal Papers).

174. Gabrielle to Adèle, Montreal, 1 December 1944 (NAC, Marie-Anna A. Roy Papers).

175. Gabrielle to Adèle, [Rawdon, December 1944 or January 1945] (ibid.).

176. Gabrielle to Adèle, Montreal, 1 December 1944 (ibid.).

177. This portrait is based on the memories of Jori Smith, Françoise Dagenais, Paul Dumas, and Marcel Carbotte.

178. Gabrielle to Adèle, [Rawdon, December 1944 or January 1945] (NAC, Marie-Anna A. Roy Papers).

179. See Henri Girard to Adèle Roy, Montreal, 8 January 1947; a transcription of this letter figures in Adèle's unpublished manuscript, "Les deux sources d'inspiration: l'imagination et le coeur" (MPA, BNQ).

180. "Qui est Claudia?" (May 1945), p. 49.

181. See Gabrielle Roy in interview with Paul Goth (1947), Marguerite Audemar (1948), and Paul G. Socken (1987, p. 92); see also Gabrielle Roy to Marcel Carbotte, Rawdon, 24 April 1952 (NLC).

182. Marie-Anna A. [Adèle] Roy, 1979, pp. 141 and 174–175.

183. Jori Smith painted a portrait of Gabrielle Roy at about this time; today the picture seems to have been lost.

184. This work never materialized; its publication was announced in the first volume of the series (Maurice Gagnon, *Pellan*, Montreal: Éditions de l'Arbre, 1943, p. [2], then in *Borduas* by R. Élie (1943), in *Roberts* by J.-G. de Tonnancour (1944), and in *Lyman* by Paul Dumas (1944), but not in *Morrice* by John Lyman (1945).

185. *Le Bulletin des agriculteurs*, Montreal, January 1944, p. 6; see also Gabrielle to Adèle, 16 September 1943 (NAC, Marie-Anna A. Roy Papers).

186. Jean Palardy also published an article on this subject in *La Revue moderne* ("Au pays des goélettes," April 1942).

187. Gabrielle to Adèle, Rawdon, 19 January 1944 (NAC, Marie-Anna A. Roy Papers).

188. "Allons, gai, au marché" (October 1944).

189. Gabrielle to Adèle, Rawdon, 13 February 1944 (NAC, Marie-Anna A. Roy Papers).

190. See Gabrielle to Adèle, [Rawdon, December 1944 or January 1945] (ibid.).

191. Gabrielle Roy's second passport, issued in January 1943 (NLC).

192. This was the case with "La vieille fille" (February 1943), "La grande Berthe" (June 1943), and "Qui est Claudia?" (May 1945).

193. In "La grande Berthe" (June 1943), the characters are inspired by the family of Gabrielle's Uncle Zénon Landry, brother of Mélina (see on this subject Mélina to Gabrielle, [St-Boniface,] 19 June 1943; NLC); in "La pension de vieillesse" (November 1943), the character Hermine, the septuagenarian who

works herself to death while waiting to qualify for a government pension, has many of Mélina's traits.

194. "François et Odine" (June 1944), p. 53.

195. "Qui est Claudia?" (May 1945), pp. 6–7, 49.

196. In "How I Found the People of Saint-Henri" (1947, p. 3), she says that the novel took "three years" to write; in *Le temps qui m'a manqué* (IV, p. 88) that, in the summer of 1943, she had been working on it for "two years."

197. Thus, she told D. Duncan (1947) that she had begun *Bonheur d'occasion* "nearly four and a half years" before its publication in June 1945; 1941 is also the date cited by Gabrielle Roy's translator Harry Binsse in a text he wrote in 1958 ("Gabrielle Roy," manuscript, NLC), and by Marc Gagné (1973, p. 39).

198. This was the year that Gabrielle Roy mentioned in her interview with R. G. Scully (1974) and in conversations that I myself had with her before publication of my first book on her (Ricard, 1975).

199. See T. Dickason, 1947: the novel was likely begun "two years before publication in Canada"; however, this statement is from Anna, Gabrielle's elder sister.

200. Gabrielle Roy to Joan Hind-Smith (in English), 4 June 1973 (reported in J. Hind-Smith, 1975, p. 83); see also the interview with Maryse Elot (1947): "Suddenly, in a rush of inspiration, I knew the theme, the characters, the plot, and the ending."

201. See P. Beaudry, 1968–1969, p. 7; J. Godbout, 1979, p. 32; this was also the story she told me in 1973.

202. "How I Found the People of Saint-Henri" (1947).

203. "Le pays de *Bonheur d'occasion*" (1974), p. 117.

204. Gabrielle Roy in interview with Rex Desmarchais, 1947, p. 39.

205. "Le pays de *Bonheur d'occasion*" (1974), p. 120.

206. Henri Girard to Adèle Roy, Montreal, 11 November 1945 (reproduced in Irma Deloy [Adèle Roy], "Les deux sources de l'inspiration: l'imagination et le coeur," unpublished manuscript, MPA, BNQ).

207. Léon Dartis [Henri Girard], 1947, p. 26.

208. *The Tin Flute*, I, p. 18 (trans. A. Brown).

209. André Brochu, in one of his excellent studies on the works of Gabrielle Roy, has noted this aspect of *Bonheur d'occasion* (see *La Visée critique*, Montreal: Boréal, 1988, pp. 214–230).

210. To Rex Desmarchais (1947, p. 43), she said there were two versions; to Pauline Beaudry (1968–69, p. 6) and Alice Parizeau (1966, p. 121), three versions; to Jeannette Urbas (23 March 1979, notes provided by J. Urbas), five or six versions; what Henri Girard, alias Léon Dartis (1947, p. 26), has to say, however, leads us to conclude that there were only two versions.

211. See *Le temps qui m'a manqué*, IV, p. 88; eight hundred is also the number of pages mentioned by Gabrielle Roy to Pauline Beaudry (1968–69, p. 7) and R. G. Scully (1974, p. 15).

212. *Le temps qui m'a manqué*, IV, pp. 88–89.

213. Léon Dartis [Henri Girard], 1947, p. 26.

214. Only the second of these binders (comprising pages 281 to 499, whose text corresponds to the second volume of the first edition of *Bonheur d'occasion*, Montréal: Éditions Pascal, 1945) has been found (NLC, Éditions Pascal Papers); the first binder and all other manuscripts of the novel seem to have disappeared.

215. See Richard Giguère, 1983, pp. 53–63.

216. Gérard Dagenais, *Nos écrivains et le français*, Montreal, Éditions du Jour, 1967, pp. 51–52.

217. A copy of this contract is preserved at the NLC.

218. Gabrielle Roy to Gérard Dagenais, Rawdon, 15 January 1945 (NLC, Éditions Pascal Papers).

219. *Amérique française*, Montreal, February 1945, p. 4.

220. See Gabrielle Roy to Gérard Dagenais, 26 December 1944 (NLC, Éditions Pascal Papers).

NOTES TO CHAPTER 7

The Burden of Fame

1. On the career of Jean-Marie Nadeau (1906–1960), see Jean-Jacques Lefebvre, "Jean-Marie Nadeau," *Revue du Barreau de la Province de Québec*, Montreal, February 1961. In 1944, Nadeau published two books, *Horizons d'après-guerre* and *Entreprise privée et Socialisme*; his *Carnets politiques* were published after his death (preface by René Levesque, Montreal: Éditions Parti pris, 1966).

2. On J.-M. Nadeau's death, the files he had kept for his client were turned over to Gabrielle Roy; today they form part of the Gabrielle Roy Papers at the NLC. Most of the information given here regarding the success of *Bonheur d'occasion* and its translation, *The Tin Flute*, as well as Gabrielle Roy's business matters between 1945 and 1950, are drawn from these files.

3. É.-Ch. Hamel, *Le Jour*, Montreal, 4 August 1945, p. 5. See also J. Béraud, *La Presse, Montreal*, 21 July 1945, p. 30; R. Garneau, *Le Canada*, Montreal, 11 August 1945, p. 4; B. Brunet, *La Nouvelle Relève*, Montreal, September 1945, pp. 352–354.

4. Roger Duhamel, "*Bonheur d'occasion*," *L'Action nationale*, Montreal, October 1945, p. 137 (article reproduced in Gilles Marcotte, ed., *Présence de la critique*, Montreal: HMH, 1966, pp. 43–46); Albert Alain, *Le Devoir*, Montreal. 15 September 1945, p. 8.

5. Roger Lemelin to Gabrielle Roy, Quebec, 5 August 1945; Marcel Dugas to Gabrielle Roy, undated [1945]; Michelle LeNormand to Gabrielle Roy, undated [1945] (NLC). Michelle LeNormand was the wife of Léo-Paul Desrosiers, author of *Les Opiniâtres* (1941).

6. The annotated copy of the first edition of *Bonheur d'occasion* that served for making these corrections is at the NLC, Éditions Pascal Papers.

7. See Gabrielle Roy's remarks reported by Rex Desmarchais (1947, p. 43), by D. Duncan (1947), and by a journalist for the *New York Times* (17 March 1947).

8. "La vallée Houdou" was read by Albert Duquesne on the Radio-Canada radio program *Histoires de chez nous* on 8 August 1944; the text was announced as being "from a book in preparation, Les Contes de la Plaine."

9. Gabrielle to Bernadette, Rawdon, 4 January [1946] (NLC; *Letters to Bernadette*, p. 6, trans. P. Claxton).

10. See R. Barthes, "L'acteur d'Harcourt," in *Mythologies*, Paris: Seuil, 1970, Points Series, pp. 24–27 (the relevant passage does not figure in the published English translation, *Mythologies).*

11. See Colette Beauchamp, 1992, p. 152; and Beth Paterson, "Gabrielle Roy's Novel of St. Henri Realizes Fragile Five-Year Hope," *The Gazette*, Montreal, 29 August 1945.

12. See *La Liberté et le Patriote*, 9 November 1945, p. 4.

13. Gabrielle to Bernadette, Rawdon, 4 January [1946] (NLC; *Letters to Bernadette*, p. 6, trans. P. Claxton); Gabrielle Roy to Léonie Guyot, Rawdon, 1 November 1945 (L. Guyot Collection).

14. Gabrielle Roy to J.-M. Nadeau, Encinitas, 27 February 1946 (NLC).

15. See Gabrielle Roy's second passport (NLC).

16. Gabrielle Roy to W. A. Deacon, Encinitas, 11 March 1946 (UOT; in J. Lennox and M. Lacombe, 1988, p. 208).

17. Gabrielle to Adèle, undated (NAC, Marie-Anna A. Roy Papers); only page 2 of the original is preserved, at the top of which Adèle has written "1944," but the contents of the letter date it in the autumn of 1945.

18. Gabrielle to Adèle, Montreal, 1 December 1944 (NAC, Marie-Anna A. Roy Papers).

19. Henri Girard to Adèle Roy, Montreal, 11 November 1945; a transcription of this letter figures in Irma Deloy [Adèle Roy], "Les deux sources de l'inspiration: l'imagination et le coeur," unpub. ms. (MPA, BNQ).

20. Gabrielle to Adèle, Montreal, 1 December 1944 (NAC, Marie-Anna A. Roy Papers).

21. Marie-Anna A. Roy, "Indulgence et pardon," unpub. ms. (MPA, BNQ).

22. Ibid.

23. Léon Dartis [H. Girard], 1947, p. 9.

24. Gabrielle Roy to J.-M. Nadeau, Montreal, 28 April 1946, and Rawdon, 22 May 1946 (NLC). Gabrielle Roy subsequently received other offers for radio or stage adaptations of *Bonheur d'occasion* or its English translation, *The Tin Flute*: in October 1947 from CKAC; in September 1948 from Radio-Canada, Montreal; in October 1949 from Jean Laforêt; in August 1952 from the CBC, Toronto; in June 1953 from CKVL, Montreal; in December 1955 from a Montreal theatre company. She turned them all down. "I'm sorry to discourage the kind intentions of so many people who are interested in continuing the memory of *Bonheur d'occasion* on radio or on the stage, but I always have the same reason to be negative: I do not have the time to oversee an adaptation

myself and I cannot agree not to oversee it if it is to be undertaken."
(Gabrielle Roy to J.-M. Nadeau, Saint-Germain-en-Laye, 24 October 1949,
NLC).

25. On W. A. Deacon (1890–1977), see Clara Thomas and John Lennox, 1982; and
Jessie L. Beattie, *William Arthur Deacon: Memoirs of a Literary Friendship*
(Hamilton: Fleming Press, 1978).

26. H. MacLennan to W. A. Deacon, Montreal, 7 March 1946 (J. Lennox and M.
Lacombe, 1988, p. 207).

27. See Gabrielle Roy to W. A. Deacon, Encinitas, 11 March 1946 (UOT; J. Lennox
and M. Lacombe, 1988, p. 208).

28. On the relationship between Deacon and Gabrielle Roy, see Mariel O'Neill-
Karch, 1992; most of the information contained here is drawn from this study.

29. See Edith Ardagh, "Magnificent Canadian Novel from Pitiful Montreal
Slum," *Globe and Mail*, Toronto, 27 April 1946, p. 10 (the review is accompa-
nied by a photograph of Gabrielle Roy and an article on her by Deacon);
Stewart C. Easton, "French-Canadian Tale Has Social Import," *Saturday
Night*, Toronto, 2 March 1946, p. 17.

30. J.-M. Nadeau to Oxford University Press, Montreal, 6 December 1945 (NLC).

31. See in particular W. A. Deacon, *My Vision of Canada* (Toronto: Ontario
Publishing Co., 1933) and *A Literary Map of Canada* (Toronto: Macmillan,
1936).

32. Gabrielle Roy to W. A. Deacon, Encinitas, 11 March and 27 February 1946
(UOT; J. Lennox and L. Lacombe, 1988, pp. 208, 203).

33. See W. E. Collin, "Letters in Canada," *The University of Toronto Quarterly*,
July 1946, pp. 412–413.

34. G. Constantineau, "Requiems pour Gabrielle Roy," *Le Nouveau Journal*,
Montreal, 4 November 1961, supplement, p. 7.

35. H. MacLennan to W. A. Deacon, 29 May 1947 (J. Lennox and M. Lacombe,
1988, p. 251).

36. The phrase occurs early in Chapter XII (*Bonheur d'occasion* [Montreal:
Pascal, 1945], p. 197; *The Tin Flute* [New York: Reynal & Hitchcock, 1947],
p. 117). The current translation reads, ". . . the powdery snow was loosed on
the city" (*The Tin Flute*, p. 144, trans. A. Brown).

37. For Canadian Literary Guild subscribers, *The Tin Flute* was the Book of the
Month for June 1947.

38. The source of this information is a file kindly provided by Arlene Friedman
of Doubleday New York (which today administers the Literary Guild of
America). The only Canadian author to have been chosen before Gabrielle
Roy was Mazo de la Roche; others since have been Brian Moore (July 1968),
Robertson Davies (April 1971), and Mordecai Richler (August 1971).

39. With the book was mailed the May 1947 issue of *Wings, the Literary Guild
Review*, which contains an article on Gabrielle Roy and her novel as well as
her own text entitled "How I Found the People of St. Henri."

40. Gabrielle Roy's remarks to David Cobb, 1976, p. 14.

41. Remarks by Jacqueline Deniset-Benoist, Montreal, 10 January, 1990.

42. For examples of critics' responses, see reviews by James Hilton (*New York Herald Tribune Weekly Book Review*, 20 April 1947), Mary McGory (*New York Times Book Review*, 20 April 1947), and Orville Prescott (*New York Times*, 22 April 1947); as for Reynal & Hitchcock's sales, for the first year they totalled 16,458 copies (accounts preserved at the NLC).

43. Gabrielle Roy to Francine Lacroix (secretary to J.-M. Nadeau), Kenora, 15 July 1947 (NLC).

44. See W. A. Deacon, 1947; W. A. Deacon, "Superb French Canadian Novel Is All About Montreal's Poor Folk," *Globe and Mail*, Toronto, 26 April 1947.

45. See, for example, A. V. Thomas, 1947. On the reception given *The Tin Flute* by English Canadian critics, see Antoine Sirois, "Gabrielle Roy et le Canada anglais," *Études littéraires*, Quebec City, Winter 1984.

46. R. Lemelin, "A Tribute to Gabrielle Roy," *Canadian Review of Music and Art*, Toronto, vol. 6, 1947; Rex Desmarchais (1947, p. 8) writes the same thing: *Bonheur d'occasion* "proves irrefutably that our writers are not inferior to those of other countries, and that we too are capable of an international role, we French Canadians."

47. R. Charbonneau, *La France et nous. Journal d'une querelle* (Montreal: Éditions de l'Arbre, 1947). On this polemic, see Robert Dion, "*La France et nous* après la Seconde Guerre mondiale: analyse d'une crise," *Voix et Images*, Montreal, No. 38, Winter 1988; and Gilles Marcotte, "Robert Charbonneau, la France, René Garneau et nous," *Écrits du Canada français* 57, Montreal, 1986.

48. Gabrielle Roy to Robert Charbonneau, St-Vital, 26 June 1947 (copy provided by Madeleine Ducrocq-Poirier).

49. See, for example, letters from J.-Claude Gagnon (Los Angeles, 25 May 1947), R. J. Chandonnet (San Francisco, 7 June 1947), and Paul J. Gelinas (Long Island, 10 July 1947), all preserved at the NLC.

50. Letter from Fred J. Poirier, Collette, 10 June 1947 (NLC).

51. See the letter from James D. Phinney, Moncton, 2 July 1947 (NLC) and Gabrielle Roy's remarks to G. V. R. [Germain Roy], 1954.

52. The short story "The Vagabond" (translation of "Un Vagabond frappe à notre porte") appears in the May 1948 issue of *Mademoiselle*, which is almost entirely devoted to Canada; no translator's name is given for this story by Gabrielle Roy. A new translation of this story appeared later in *Garden in the Wind*, translated by Alan Brown. The sales of foreign rights took place between May 1947 and summer 1948; in July 1947, *The Tin Flute* was sold to the publisher Heinemann's for a British edition.

53. The document is at the NLC.

54. Gabrielle Roy to J.-M. Nadeau, St-Germain-en-Laye, 10 January 1949 (NLC); around 1950, Universal offered to sell the screenplay back to Gabrielle Roy for $16,000, but Nadeau declined.

55. Gabrielle Roy to F. Lacroix, Kenora, 15 July 1947 (NLC).

56. The novel by Lockridge (1914–1948) is entitled *Raintree County*; see Larry Lockridge, *Shade of the Raintree*, New York, Viking, 1994; see also on this and another similar case in the same period, that of the successful novelist

Thomas Heggen (1919–1949), a book by John Leggett, *Ross and Tom, Two American Tragedies*, New York, Simon & Shuster, 1974.

57. Gabrielle Roy to J.-M. Nadeau, St-Vital, 5 May 1947 (NLC).

58. See *Winnipeg Tribune*, 1 March, 26 April, and 1 May 1947; *Winnipeg Free Press*, 3 May 1947.

59. See A. Le Grand, "*Bonheur d'occasion*," *La Liberté et le Patriote*, 7 September 1945; Alice Raymond, "Gabrielle Roy et son *Bonheur d'occasion*," ibid., 2 November 1945, p. 9; anonymous, "*Bonheur d'occasion*," *Le Bonifacien*, St-Boniface, December 1945, pp. 6–7.

60. This article was published in *La Libeté et le Patriote* of 3 October 1947, p. 3; "Marie-Reine" wrote again in the same vein six months later (ibid., 16 April 1948, p. 3), this time drawing a retort from Alfred Rivest of Montreal (ibid., 14 May 1948, p. 13).

61. See, for example, an article by Donatien Frémont, 1947.

62. Gabrielle Roy to J.-M. Nadeau, St-Vital, 5 May 1947 (NLC).

63. Clémence to Gabrielle, St-Boniface, 20 December 1945 (NLC).

64. According to the interview she granted to A. Vernon Thomas (1947), Gabrielle Roy was thinking at this time of writing a novel about the world of journalism.

65. All these manuscripts are preserved at the NLC; none of them bear any indication of the precise date of writing.

66. Gabrielle Roy to Séraphin Marion, Montreal, 28 April 1947 (NLC).

67. "Return to Saint-Henri" (1947), *The Fragile Lights of Earth*, p. 170 (trans. A. Brown).

68. Marie-Anna A. Roy, "À vol d'oiseau à travers le temps et l'espace," unpub. ms. (NAC, MPA).

69. Gabrielle Roy to J.-M. Nadeau, St-Vital, 5 May 1947 (NLC).

70. *La Liberté et le Patriote*, 9 May 1947, p. 4.

71. Marcel Carbotte to Gabrielle Roy, Winnipeg, 7 November 1945 (NLC); see also SHSB, fonds Cercle Molière, chemise 6.

72. This copy is preserved by Pierre Morency, Quebec City; the dedication is dated 10 May 1947.

73. Gabrielle Roy to Judith Jasmin, St-Vital, 27 May 1947 (ANQ-Montreal, fonds Judith Jasmin).

74. See the notice of Joseph Carbotte's death, *La Liberté et le Patriote*, 12 December 1947, p. 4. The information that follows regarding the life of Marcel Carbotte is based on my conversations with him and with his sister, Léona Carbotte-Corriveau.

75. Texts by Marcel Carbotte appearing in *La Liberté*: 21 May 1930, p. 4; 15 October 1930, p. 4; 12 November 1930, p. 4; 11 November 1931, p. 2; 27 April 1932, p. 2; 28 September 1932, p. 3; 26 October 1932, p. 2; 17 May 1933, p. 2; 7 March 1934, p. 2.

76. In an interview published by *Le Devoir* (Montreal, 6 October 1984), Marcel Carbotte recounts that he knew Gabrielle in the early 1930s and found her "extremely pretentious."

77. Marcel performed in at least three plays: *Prenez garde àla peinture* (1941–1942), *Le Quatrième* (1942–1943), and *Gai, marions-nous* (1944–1945); see the reviews of his performances in *La Liberté et le Patriote* (6 May 1942, p. 3; 16 December 1942, p. 4; 18 May 1945, p. 12). He was president of Le Cercle Molière for the seasons 1944–1945, 1945–1946, and 1946–1947 (SHSB, fonds Cercle Molière).

78. Gabrielle Roy to Joan Hind-Smith, 4 June 1973 (quoted in J. Hind-Smith, 1975, p. 89).

79. Marie-Anna A. Roy, 1979, p. 175.

80. See J.-M. Nadeau to H. Girard, Montreal, 1 April 1947 (NLC).

81. Marie-Anna A. [Adèle] Roy, 1979, pp. 172, 175.

82. Gabrielle to Marcel, Kenora, 16 July, 20 July, and 14 July 1947 (NLC).

83. Marcel to Gabrielle, St-Boniface, 22 July and 19 July 1947 (NLC).

84. Gabrielle to Marcel, Kenora, 20 July 1947 (NLC).

85. Gabrielle to Marcel, Kenora, 22 July, 23 July, and 6 August 1947 (NLC).

86. Gabrielle to Marcel, Kenora, 18 July 1947 (NLC).

87. See the remarks by Madame de Pange quoted by Bertrand Lombard, "Le Prix Fémina à *Bonheur d'occasion*," *Revue de l'Université Laval*, Quebec City, January 1948, p. 443.

88. FGR; the book was found in Gabrielle Roy's house at Petite-Rivière-Saint-François at the time of her death. The phrase *tous mes voeux de bonheur*, a graceful if standard formulation, is the equivalent of "my best wishes for every happiness."

89. Henri Girard to Adèle Roy, Montreal, 8 January 1948 (a transcription of this letter figures in Irma Deloy [Adèle Roy], "Les deux sources de l'inspiration: l'imagination et le coeur," unpub. ms., MPA, BNQ).

90. See Gabrielle Roy to J.-M. Nadeau, Paris, 9 December 1947; Saint-Germain-en-Laye, 13 June 1949; Marcel to Gabrielle, Paris, 16 January 1948; and J.-M. Nadeau to Gabrielle Roy, Montreal, 2 and 4 August 1949 (NLC).

91. Marcel to Gabrielle, Quebec City, 4 March 1954 (NLC).

92. As for Gabrielle's letters to Henri, only two or three are accessible (NLC, Éditions Pascal Papers); it is impossible to know whether the rest of these letters, which must have been very numerous, still exist.

93. See the reports of this event in *Le Canada* (Montreal, 29 September 1947, p. 3), *Le Devoir* (Montreal, 4 October 1947, p. 8), *Combat* (Montreal, 4 October 1947, p. 2), *Le Droit* (Ottawa, 18 October 1947, p. 4), and *Pour vous Madame* (Montreal, November–December 1947, pp. 5–20).

94. See G. Lanctôt, 1947.

95. Jacques Ferron, "Des sables, un manuscrit," in *Du fond de mon arrière-cuisine* (Montreal: Éditions du Jour, 1973), p. 109.

96. Gabrielle Roy to J.-M. Nadeau, Paris, 26 October 1947 (NLC).

97. Press release prepared by Les Éditions Flammarion for the publication of *Bonheur d'occasion* (reproduced in Mireille Trudeau, 1976).

98. "How I received the Fémina" (1956), *The Fragile Lights of Earth*, p. 178 (trans. A. Brown).

99. Ibid., p. 174.

100. See "Le Fémina," *Nouvelles littéraires*," 4 December 1947, p. 4; and B. Lombard, "Le Prix Fémina à *Bonheur d'occasion*," *Revue de l'Université Laval*, Quebec City, January 1948, p. 443.

101. Gabrielle Roy to J.-M. Nadeau, St-Vital, 6 July 1947 (NLC).

102. Maryse Elot, 1947; Paul Guth, 1947; see also Marguerite Audemar, 1948; Francis Ambrière, 1947.

103. "Rencontre avec Teilhard de Chardin," unpub. ms. (NLC; this typewritten manuscript dates from the mid-1970s, but the text itself was probably written earlier); on this meeting, see also M. Gagné (1973, pp. 226–228) and J. Hind-Smith (1975, pp. 91–92).

104. See A. Rousseaux, "Un roman canadien," *Figaro littéraire*, Paris, 8 November 1947, p. 2.

105. Thierry Maulnier, "*Bonheur d'occasion*," *Hommes et Mondes*, Paris, January 1948, p. 137.

106. M. Audemar, 1948, pp. 27–28.

107. R. Kemp, "La vie des livres," *Nouvelles littéraires*, Paris, 11 December 1947, p. 3.

108. L. Barjon, "Chronique des lettres," *Études*, Paris, January 1948, p. 104; Magot solitaire, "J'ai rêvé du prix Fémina," *Carrefour*, Paris, 16 December 1947 (reproduced in *Notre temps*, Montreal, 21 February 1948, p. 4).

109. On the critical reception given *Bonheur d'occasion* in France, see Mireille Trudeau, 1976; Jacqueline Gerols, *Le Roman québécois en France* (Montreal: HMH, 1984); and Antoine Sirois, "Prix littéraires pour les écrivains québécois," in M. Shaddy, ed., *International Perspectives in Comparative Literature* (Lewiston: Edwin Mellen Press, 1991), pp. 147–159.

110. See especially, in *Le Devoir*, articles by Pierre Descaves ("Un grand prix littéraire français à une romancière canadienne," 20 December 1947, pp. 9–10); Pierre de Grandpré ("Courrier de France," 3 January 1948, pp. 1–2); and Germaine Bernier ("Hommages et critiques autour de *Bonheur d'occasion*," 24 January 1948, p. 6).

111. R. Charbonneau, *Romanciers canadiens*, Quebec City, Presses de l'Université Laval, 1972, pp. 109–110 (text of a radio talk, one of a series given in 1952–53).

112. "Une controverse sur *Bonheur d'occasion*: Saint-Henri présenté sous un mauvais jour," *La Voix populaire*, Montreal, 25 June 1947, p. 1; see also "Critique de *Bonheur d'occasion*," *La Liberté et le Patriote*, 31 October 1947, p. 1.

113. The ceremony took place on 12 June 1948, in Gabrielle Roy's absence; she was represented by the French ambassador, Francisque Gay; Deacon had been chairman of the jury (see *Lectures*, Montreal, February 1949. p. 345; M. O'Neill-Karch, 1992, p. 78).

114. This first thesis was by James E. LaFollette, "Le Parler franco-canadien dans *Bonheur d'occasion*," M.A. thesis, Université Laval, October 1949. For the criticism, see Gilles Marcotte, "En relisant *Bonheur d'occasion*," *L'Action nationale*, Montreal, July 1952, pp. 53–74.

115. Gabrielle to Marcel, Geneva, 15 January [1948; first letter of this day, dated in error "1947"] and 21 January 1948 (NLC).

116. Gabrielle to Marcel, Geneva, 20 January 1948 (NLC).

117. Gabrielle to Marcel, Geneva, 15 January 1948, 9 P.M. [second letter of this day] (NLC).

118. Gabrielle to Marcel, Geneva, 21 January 1948 (NLC); see *The Cashier*, VIII, pp. 124–125.

119. Gabrielle to Marcel, Geneva, 18 January 1948 (NLC).

120. Gabrielle to Marcel, Geneva, 23 [January 1948; second letter of this day, dated in error "February."] (NLC).

121. Gabrielle to Marcel, Geneva, 25 January 1948 (NLC).

122. "The leading character in this story I'm writing is an unhappy man [...], one of the minor civil servants of which there are any number in every city – and you'll see why he could not sleep" (Gabrielle to Marcel, Geneva, 26 January 1948; NLC).

123. Gabrielle Roy to J.-M. Nadeau, Geneva, 25 January 1948 (NLC).

124. Gabrielle to Marcel, Geneva, 26 January 1948 (NLC).

125. Marcel to Gabrielle, Paris, 16 and 29 January 1948 (NLC).

126. Gabrielle to Marcel, Geneva, 12 January 1948 (NLC).

127. Gabrielle to Marcel, Geneva, 29 January 1948 [second letter of this day] (NLC).

128. Gabrielle to Marcel, Geneva, 12 January and 15 January 1948 [second letter of this day] 1948 (NLC).

129. Gabrielle to Marcel, Geneva, 31 January 1948 (NLC).

130. "How I received the Fémina" (1956), *The Fragile Lights of Earth*, p. 184, trans. A. Brown.

131. See J.-M. Nadeau to Gabrielle Roy, Montreal, 25 June 1948 (NLC).

132. On this arrangement, see the "Jean-Marie Nadeau files" for 1948, and Gabrielle Roy to J.-M. Nadeau, Quebec City, 24 November 1954, 10 November 1955, and 10 December 1956 (NLC). From her income tax declarations, Gabrielle Roy's gross income, "spread" under the agreement, was as follows: $4,592 in 1945; $9,007 in 1946; $20,299 in 1947; $26,843 in 1948; $15,200 in 1949; $16,797 in 1950; $17,013 in 1951; $15,718 in 1952; $15,408 in 1953; I have not been able to find the figure for 1954, but from the amount of income tax paid that year ($2,428.35), it must have been in the same range as the five preceding years.

133. Anna Roy-Painchaud to J.-M. Nadeau, St-Vital, 18 February 1948 (NLC).

134. Gabrielle to Anna, Paris, 28 February 1948 (NAC, Marie-Anna A. Roy Papers); reproduced in Marie-Anna A. [Adèle] Roy, 1979, pp. 181–183.

135. Anna to Gabrielle, St-Vital, 3 March 1948 (NAC, Marie-Anna A. Roy Papers); reproduced in ibid., pp. 183–186.

136. Anna to Adèle, St-Vital, 22 March 1948 (NAC, Marie-Anna Roy Papers).

137. Anna to Adèle, St-Vital, 27 March 1948 (ibid.).

138. See J.-M. Nadeau to Heward Stikeman, Montreal, 13 February 1950 (NLC).

139. Gabrielle Roy to W. A. Deacon (in English), Saint-Germain-en-Laye, 9 April 1949 (UOT).

140. For this period, the account of Gabrielle and Marcel's life is based on inter-views with Jeanne Lapointe, Cécile Chabot, Jean Soucy, Marcel Carbotte, Paul Dumas, Jori Smith, and Jacqueline Deniset-Benoist.

141. Gabrielle to Bernadette, Saint-Germain-en-Laye, 13 June 1949 (NLC; *Letters to Bernadette*, p. 16, trans. P. Claxton).

142. Gabrielle Roy to Jeanne Lapointe, Saint-Germain-en-Laye, 13 June 1949 (NLC, Jeanne Lapointe Papers).

143. See F. Charpentier, 1983.

144. Gabrielle to Bernadette, Saint-Germain-en-Laye, 16 June 1949 (NLC; *Letters to Bernadette*, p. 17, trans. P. Claxton).

145. Gabrielle Roy to Pauline Boutal, Paris, 23 March 1948 (SHSB, fonds Pauline Boutal).

146. *Enchantment and Sorrow*, "A Bird Knows Its Song," XIX, p. 394 (trans. P. Claxton).

147. Gabrielle Roy to J.-M. Nadeau, Ascain, 5 July 1949 (NLC).

148. Gabrielle to Marcel, Upshire, 8 September 1949 [dated in error "August"] (NLC).

149. Two of these texts became magazine articles, "Sainte-Anne-la-Palud" (1951) and "La Camargue" (1952); they were republished in 1978 in *Fragiles lumières de la terre* (*The Fragile Lights of Earth*, trans. A. Brown) under the heading "Paysages de France" ("Landscapes of France").

150. Gabrielle to Marcel, Concarneau, 6 August 1948 (NLC).

151. Gabrielle to Marcel, Geneva, 22 January 1948 (NLC).

152. Marcel to Gabrielle, Paris, 22 January 1948 (NLC).

153. Gabrielle to Marcel, Concarneau, 6 July 1948 (NLC).

154. Gabrielle to Marcel, Concarneau, 12 July 1948 [first letter of this day] and 6 August 1948 (NLC).

155. Gabrielle to Marcel, Concarneau, 3 July 1948 (NLC).

156. Gabrielle to Marcel, Concarneau, 16 July 1948 (NLC).

157. Gabrielle Roy to Jeanne Lapointe, Concarneau, 14 September 1948 (NLC, Jeanne Lapointe Papers).

158. Gabrielle to Marcel, 10 July 1948 (NLC).

159. The two stories, both dated "Concarneau, September 1948," are entitled "Pitié" and "Le petit liftier"; the other text is "L'île de Sein"; these unpub-lished manuscripts are at the NLC.

160. See the voluminous set of undated manuscripts at the NLC. As this set bears no title, I have proposed calling the projected work "La Saga d'Éveline" (F. Ricard, 1992a, p. 251). For a description of the manuscripts, see Christine Robinson, 1995; according to her research, the manuscripts at the NLC dating from the late 1940s are those in box 72, files 8–12, and box 73, files 1–6.

161. See Gabrielle Roy to J.-M. Nadeau, Paris, 11 April and 31 May 1948; to Ronald [Everson], Paris, 21 April 1948; also J.-M. Nadeau to Gabrielle Roy, Montreal, 17 June 1948 (NLC).

162. Gabrielle to Marcel, Concarneau, 6 July 1948 (NLC).

163. These unpublished manuscripts are at the NLC; that of "Dieu" is dated "Paris, October 1948."

164. "La première femme," unpub. ms. (NLC).

165. These were "Julia de Grandvoir" and "Rose en Maria" (NLC); although these manuscripts bear no date, it can reasonably be supposed that they were written during the winter or spring of 1949.

166. Gabrielle Roy to W. A. Deacon, Saint-Germain-en-Laye, 9 April 1949 (UOT).

167. Gabrielle to Marcel, Concarneau, 25 July 1948 (NLC).

168. See Gabrielle Roy to Jeanne Lapointe, undated [but which may be dated December 1950] (NLC, Jeanne Lapointe Papers).

169. "Memory and Creation" (1957), *The Fragile Lights of Earth*, pp. 188–189 (trans. A. Brown).

170. On Father Antoine-Marie, see Marie-Anna A. [Adèle] Roy, 1977, pp. 79–99 (with a photograph, p. 84).

171. "Memory and Creation" (1957), *The Fragile Lights of Earth*, p. 189 (trans. A. Brown)

172. Gabrielle Roy writes of this return to Upshire in *Enchantment and Sorrow*, "A Bird Knows Its Song," XIX, pp. 400–401 (trans. P. Claxton).

173. Gabrielle to Marcel, Upshire, 26 August 1949 (NLC).

174. Gabrielle to Marcel, Upshire, 19 and 21 August 1949 (NLC).

175. Gabrielle to Marcel, Upshire, 13 September 1949 (NLC).

176. Gabrielle to Marcel, Upshire, 19 August, 3 and 13 September 1949 (NLC).

177. "Memory and Creation" (1957), *The Fragile Lights of Earth*, p. 186 (trans. A. Brown).

178. In "Memory and Creation" (1957; *The Fragile Lights of Earth*, p. 189, trans. A. Brown), Gabrielle Roy recounts that it was during her stay at Upshire that she invented the Tousignant children who were "seized by a desire to learn," and who were the characters in "The School on the Little Water Hen." According to her conversation with Ringuet (1951), however, the text she wrote at Upshire was "all the second part of my book, the one in which the Capuchin missionary is the central character."

179. René d'Uckermann to Gabrielle Roy, Paris, 23 June 1950 (NLC).

180. Gabrielle to Bernadette, Saint-Germain-en-Laye, 11 May 1950 (NLC; *Letters to Bernadette*, p. 19, trans. P. Claxton).

181. Gabrielle to Marcel, Saint-Germain-en-Laye, 13 June 1949 (NLC; *Letters to Bernadette*, p. 17, trans. P. Claxton).

182. Gabrielle to Marcel, Port-Daniel, 25 June 1951 (NLC).

183. Gabrielle Roy to J.-M. Nadeau, Saint-Germain-en-Laye, 10 August 1950 (NLC).

184. Gabrielle Roy to Cécile Chabot, Ville LaSalle, 9 October 1950 (NLC).

185. Gabrielle to Marcel, Upshire, 30 August 1949; see also Gabrielle to Marcel, Upshire, 15 September 1949 (NLC).

186. Théophile Bertrand, "Quatre romans canadiens," *Lectures*, Montreal, February 1951, p. 306; Paul Gay, "*La Petite Poule d'Eau*," *Le Droit*, Ottawa, 16 December 1950, p. 2.

187. A. Maillet, "Lettre à Gabrielle Roy," *Amérique française*, Montreal, March–April 1951, pp. 60–61.

188. G. Sylvestre, "*La Petite Poule d'Eau*," *Nouvelle Revue canadienne*, Ottawa, April–May 1951, p. 69; G. Marcotte, "Gabrielle Roy retourne à ses origines," *Le Devoir*, Montreal, 25 November 1950, p. 18 (see also, by the same author, "Rose-Anna retrouvée," *L'Action nationale*, Montreal, January 1951, pp. 50–51). See J. Richer, "*La Petite Poule d'Eau* de Gabrielle Roy," *Notre temps*, Montreal, 25 November 1950, p. 3; L'Illettré [H. Bernard], "Le nouvel ouvrage de Gabrielle Roy," *Le Travailleur*, Worcester, 28 December 1950, pp. 1, 4 (reprinted in *Le Droit*, Ottawa, 5 January 1951, p. 3).

189. See Gabrielle Roy to W. A. Deacon, Ville LaSalle, 14 December 1950 (UOT); and Gabrielle to Marcel, Port-Daniel, 11 July 1951 (NLC).

190. Gabrielle Roy to Jeanne Lapointe, undated [December 1950] (NLC, Jeanne Lapointe Papers).

191. Harry L. Binsse, "Gabrielle Roy," manuscript, 1958 (NLC).

192. Ringuet, 1951.

193. Gabrielle to Marcel, Ville LaSalle, 16 February 1952 (NLC).

194. J. Jasmin, "Quelques brèves rencontres," speech given in October 1971 (ANQ, fonds Judith Jasmin; quoted by Colette Beauchamp, 1992, p. 153).

195. Gabrielle to Marcel, Port-Daniel, 24 July 1951 (NLC).

196. Gabrielle Roy to Jeanne Lapointe, Port-Daniel, 24 July 1951 (NLC, Jeanne Lapointe Papers).

197. Gabrielle to Marcel, Port-Daniel, 13 July 1951 (NLC).

198. Gabrielle to Marcel, Port-Daniel, 2 July 1951 (NLC).

199. Gabrielle to Marcel, Port-Daniel, 18 July 1951 (NLC).

200. E. Reynal to Gabrielle Roy, New York, 6 October 1950; the same to J.-M. Nadeau, New York, 17 October 1950 (NLC).

201. Ruth M. Gerbig, "Books for Lenten Reading and Contemplation," *The Catholic Woman Review*, Detroit, March 1952.

202. See S. North, "A Classic of French Canada," *New York World, Telegram & Sun*, New York, 23 October 1951 (reproduced in a number of newspapers, notably the *Vancouver Sun* of 10 November 1951, under the title "A Canadian Classic").

203. W. A. Deacon, "One Isolated Family in Northern Manitoba," *Globe and Mail*, Toronto, 3 November 1951; W. E. Collin, "Letters in Canada," *University of Toronto Quarterly*, July 1951, p. 396.

204. Gabrielle to Marcel, Port-Daniel, 8 July 1951 (NLC).

205. Gabrielle to Marcel, Port-Daniel, 13 July 1951 (NLC).

206. See Gabrielle Roy in interview with Paul G. Socken, 1987, p. 90.

207. Gabrielle to Marcel, Geneva, 26 January 1948 (NLC).

208. Gabrielle Roy in interview with John J. Murphy, 1963, p. 449.

209. Remarks reported by M. Audemar, 1948, p. 28.

210. Remarks reported by P. G. Socken, (1987, p. 90) and by J. J. Murphy (1963, p. 449).

211. Gabrielle Roy to W. A. Deacon, Ville LaSalle, 7 December 1951 (UOT; in J. Lennox and L. Lacombe, 1988, p. 276).

212. Gabrielle to Marcel, Ville LaSalle, 16 February 1952 (NLC).

213. Gabrielle to Marcel, Ville LaSalle, 1 and 11 February 1952 (NLC).

214. Marcel to Gabrielle, Quebec City, 31 January 1952 (NLC).

215. Gabrielle to Marcel, Ville LaSalle, 10 February 1952 (NLC).

216. Gabrielle to Marcel, Ville LaSalle, 28 January 1952 (NLC).

217. Gabrielle to Marcel, Rawdon, 15 and 26 April 1952 (NLC).

218. René d'Uckermann to Gabrielle Roy, Paris, 4 March 1952 (NLC).

219. Gabrielle to Marcel, Rawdon, 22 April 1952 (NLC).

220. Gabrielle to Marcel, Rawdon, 24 April 1952 (NLC).

221. Gabrielle to Marcel, Rawdon, 2 May 1952 (NLC).

222. Gabrielle Roy to Cécile Chabot, Port-Daniel, 18 August 1952 (BNQ); and to Jeanne Lapointe, 28 August 1952 (NLC, Jeanne Lapointe Papers).

223. Gabrielle Roy to Jeanne Lapointe, Rawdon, 29 August 1952 (NLC, Jeanne Lapointe Papers).

224. Gabrielle to Marcel, Port-Daniel, 15 August and 21 July 1952 (NLC).

225. Gabrielle to Marcel, Port-Daniel, 6 August 1952 (NLC) [Gabrielle wrote the French word *stage* instead of *stade*].

226. Gabrielle Roy to Jeanne Lapointe, Rawdon, 29 August 1952 (NLC, Jeanne Lapointe Papers).

227. The manuscript annotated by J. Lapointe is today at the NLC, Jeanne Lapointe Papers; marked "4e copie," it includes all Jeanne Lapointe's pencilled corrections, certain of which have been traced over in ink by Gabrielle Roy to indicate her approval.

228. Gabrielle to Marcel, Rawdon, 2 June 1953 (NLC).

229. René d'Uckermann to Gabrielle Roy, Paris, 2 July 1953 (NLC).

230. E. Reynal to Gabrielle Roy (in English), New York, 23 July 1953 (NLC).

231. Firmin Roz, "Témoignage d'un roman canadien," *Revue française de l'élite européenne*, Paris, August 1954, pp. 33–34; see also Robert Kemp, "Pensées d'Ève," *Nouvelles littéraires*, Paris, 13 May 1954, p. 2; André Thérive, "Le Canada et la littérature," *La Table ronde*, Paris, September 1954, pp. 113–116.

232. See especially Eizabeth Janeway, "The Man in Everyman," *New York Times Book Review*, New York, 16 October 1955, p. 5; Marjorie Holligan, "Why Suffering," *America*, New York, 5 November 1955, p. 160.

233. J. Béraud, "*Alexandre Chenevert* de Gabrielle Roy," *La Presse*, Montreal, 13 March 1954, p. 74; G. Marcotte, "Vie et mort de quelqu'un," *Le Devoir*, Montreal, 13 March 1954, p. 6; see also Julia Richer, "*Alexandre Chenevert* de Gabrielle Roy," *Notre Temps*, Montreal, 6 March 1954, p. 5; Roger Duhamel, "Livres de notre temps," *La Patrie*, Montreal, 21 March 1954, p. 75. On the critics' reception of *Alexandre Chenevert*, see Lise Gauvin, 1986.

234. Gabrielle Roy to W. A. Deacon, Quebec City, 16 March 1954 (UOT; in J. Lennox and M. Lacombe, 1988, p. 305).

NOTES TO CHAPTER 8

"Writing, As If It's Your Very Reason for Living"

Gabrielle Roy's letters to W. A. Deacon, Joyce Marshall, and Jack McClelland were all written in English.

1. M. Robert, *Origins of the Novel*, trans. Sacha Rabinovitch (Brighton: Harvester Press, 1980), pp. 222–223.
2. Gabrielle to Marcel, Kenora, 16 July 1947 (NLC).
3. Remarks reported by Ringuet, 1951.
4. Remarks reported by Pauline Beaudry, 1968–1969, p. 8.
5. Remarks reported by G. Bessette, 1968, p. 304.
6. According to Adèle (M.-A. A. Roy, 1979, p. 197), Radio-Canada was the sponsor, but according to a letter from Marcel to Gabrielle (Quebec City, 29 July 1953; NLC), it could have been the NFB.
7. See Gabrielle to Marcel, Edmonton, 18 September 1953 (NLC).
8. Typewritten manuscript with annotations in Gabrielle Roy's hand, undated (F. Ricard Collection).
9. Anna [Roy-] Painchaud, 1955; there is also at the NLC an unpublished manuscript by Anna entitled "Christmas on Deschambault Street," which likely dates from the same period.
10. Marie-Anna A. [Adèle] Roy to Éditions du Lévrier, Tangent, 6 October 1953; this letter, as well as much of the information that follows concerning the publication of *Le Pain de chez nous*, are found in the archives of Les Éditions du Lévrier (Université de Sherbrooke).
11. On this publisher, see Yvan Cloutier, "L'activité éditoriale des dominicains: les Éditions du Lévrier (1937–1975)," in Jacques Michon (ed.), *L'Édition littéraire en quête d'autonomie: Albert Lévesque et son temps* (Quebec City: Presses de l'Université Laval, 1994).
12. Marie-Anna A. [Adèle] Roy, 1979, p. 204.
13. Gabrielle to Adèle, [Rawdon, 30 avril 1953] (NAC, Marie-Anna A. Roy Papers; the original is incomplete and covered with annotations in the hand of Adèle, who has herself inscribed the date; the letter is reproduced in part in M.-A. A. Roy, 1979, p. 196).
14. Gabrielle to Adèle, Edmonton, [September 1953] (NAC, Marie-Anna A. Roy Papers; the date is in Adèle's hand).
15. Marie-Anna A. [Adèle] Roy, 1989–1990, épisode 27.
16. "Les deux sources de l'inspiration: l'imagination et le coeur," unpublished manuscript (MPA, BNQ).
17. Marie-Anna A. [Adèle] Roy, 1979, p. 207.
18. For example, the name Édouard, which is given to Christine's father in *Rue Deschambault*, was already figuring in saga manuscripts dating from the late 1940s, and the mother was called Évangéline, Line, or Lina.
19. Remarks reported by Gérard Bessette, 1968, p. 304.

20. René d'Uckermann to Gabrielle Roy, Paris, 30 December 1954 (NLC).

21. Among the best reviews are those of Pierre Lagarde for France ("*Rue Deschambault* par Gabrielle Roy," *Nouvelles littéraires*, Paris, 29 September 1955, p. 3) and Richard Sullivan for the United States ("Amid Sadness, Green Hope," *New York Times Book Review*, New York, 6 October 1957, p. 4).

22. German translations of *La Petite Poule d'Eau* and *Alexandre Chenevert* appeared in Munich in 1953 and 1956, and an Italian translation of *Rue Deschambault* in Milan in 1957; except for one of *La Route d'Altamont* published in Zurich in 1970 and some of *Bonheur d'occasion*, notably into Romanian (Bucharest, 1968) and Russian (Moscow, 1972), no other foreign-language translations of her books appeared in Gabrielle Roy's lifetime.

23. René Garneau, "*Rue Deschambault*," *Livres de France*, Paris, December 1955, p. 17 (reprinted in *Le Droit*, Ottawa, 11 April 1956, and reproduced in *Écrits du Canada français 49*, Montreal, 1983); R. Leclerc, "*Rue Deschambault* de Gabrielle Roy," *Lectures*, Montreal, October 1955, p. 33; Jean-Paul Robillard, "Lisez *Rue Deschambault*," *Le Petit Journal*, Montreal, 30 October 1955, p. 56; Jean-Louis Madiran, "*Rue Deschambault*," *L'Action catholique*, Quebec City, 31 March 1956, p. 4; G. Marcotte, "Comme lieu de rencontres fraternelles," *Vie étudiante*, Montreal, 15 November 1955, p. 13.

24. See W. O'H., "Gabrielle Roy's Charming Recollections of Youth," *Montreal Star*, 12 October 1957, p. 23; Harriet Hill, "Excursion into Childhood," *The Gazette*, Montreal, 12 October 1957, p. 33; Marielle Fuller, "New Tales by Gabrielle Roy Recall Her Manitoba Youth," *Globe and Mail*, Toronto, 23 June 1956, p. 17; W. E. Collin, "Letters in Canada," *University of Toronto Quarterly*, April 1956, pp. 394–395; Miriam Waddington, "New Books," *Queen's Quarterly*, Winter 1957–1958, pp. 628–629.

25. See R. Duhamel, "Livres de notre temps," *La Patrie du dimanche*, Montreal, 6 November 1955, p. 78.

26. Marcel Valois [Jean Dufresne], "Le dernier-né de Gabrielle Roy," *La Presse*, Montreal, 8 October 1955, p. 73; René Garneau, "*Rue Deschambault*," *Livres de France*, Paris, December 1955, p. 17 (reprinted in *Le Droit*, Ottawa, 11 April 1956, and reproduced in *Écrits du Canada français 49*, Montreal, 1983); Miriam Waddington, "New Books," *Queen's Quarterly*, Winter 1957–1958, pp. 628–629.

27. G. Sylvestre, "Au jour le jour dans le monde littéraire," *Le Droit*, Ottawa, 19 November 1955; P. de Grandpré, "La vie des Lettres," *Le Devoir*, Montreal, 8 October 1955, p. 32.

28. Besides R. Duhamel, the jury was composed of Guy Sylvestre, Marcel Raymond, Canon Arthur Sideleau, and Eugène Therrien, president of the SSJB (ANQ, fonds de la Société Saint-Jean-Baptiste de Montréal).

29. See Alan Brown, "Gabrielle Roy and the Temporary Provincial," *Tamarack Review*, Toronto, Autumn 1956; Hugo McPherson, "The Garden and the Cage: The Achievement of Gabrielle Roy," *Canadian Literature*, Vancouver, Summer 1959.

30. For 1955, the amount can be estimated from the amount of income tax paid ($1,246.34); for 1956 ($2,989.33) and 1957 ($2,325.21), see Gabrielle Roy to

J.-M. Nadeau, Quebec City, 24 December 1956 and 13 January 1958 (NLC); no figures for the period 1958–1969 have been found.

31. Gabrielle Roy to J.-M. Nadeau, Quebec City, 31 December 1955 (NLC).

32. J.-M. Nadeau to Gabrielle Roy, Montreal, 22 November 1957; Gabrielle Roy to J.-M. Nadeau, Quebec City, 26 November 1957 (NLC).

33. Gabrielle Roy to J.-M. Nadeau, Quebec City, 10 December 1955 (NLC).

34. Gabrielle Roy to J.-M. Nadeau, Quebec City, 31 December 1955 (NLC).

35. Gabrielle Roy to Cécile Chabot, Rawdon, 24 May 1953, and Quebec City, 16 December 1953 and 14 February 1954 (BNQ).

36. Gabrielle Roy to Cécile Chabot, Quebec City, 16 January 1954 (BNQ).

37. This speech, whose manuscript has been lost, was entitled "Jeux du romancier et des lecteurs."

38. Gabrielle Roy to Cécile Chabot, Quebec City, 16 December 1955 (BNQ).

39. Gabrielle to Adèle, [Rawdon, 30 April 1953] (NAC, Marie-Anna A. Roy Papers).

40. J. Lapointe, "Quelques apports positifs de notre littérature d'imagination," *Cité Libre*, Montreal, October 1954; reproduced in Gilles Marcotte, ed. *Présence de la critique* (Montreal: HMH, 1966).

41. Gabrielle Roy to J. Lapointe, Quebec City, 1 February 1954 (NLC, Jeanne Lapointe Papers).

42. Gabrielle Roy to Cécile Chabot, Quebec City, 25 October 1954 (BNQ).

43. Conversation with Antonia Houde-Roy, Ottawa, 23 March 1993.

44. Gabrielle Roy to Madeleine Bergeron, Port-Daniel, 6 July 1954 (FGR).

45. Gabrielle to Marcel, Port-Daniel, 13 July 1954 (NLC).

46. Gabrielle to Marcel, Petite-Rivière-Saint-François, 1 August 1956 (NLC).

47. Gabrielle Roy to Madeleine Bergeron, Paris, [13 May 1955] and 26 May 1955 (FGR).

48. See Gabrielle to Marcel, Port-Navalo, 25 June 1955 (NLC); in *La Montagne secrète* (*The Hidden Mountain*), the name Le Bonniec was to be that of the missionary father who came to the aid of the hero, Pierre Cadorai.

49. Gabrielle to Bernadette, Port-Navalo, 4 June 1955 (NLC; *Letters to Bernadette*, p. 23, trans. P. Claxton).

50. Gabrielle Roy to Madeleine Bergeron, Paris, 5 July 1955 (FGR).

51. Ibid.

52. Gabrielle to Marcel, Paris, 10 July 1955 (NLC).

53. Gabrielle to Bernadette, Quebec City, 19 November 1964 (NLC; *Letters to Bernadette*, p. 70, trans. P. Claxton).

54. Gabrielle to Marcel, Dollard, 25 August 1955 (NLC).

55. Gabrielle to Marcel, Dollard, 29 August and 4 September 1955 (NLC).

56. See Gabrielle to Marcel, Dollard, 25 and 27 [second of that day] August 1955 (NLC); Gabrielle Roy would later use these names in *The Hidden Mountain* (whose hero is called Pierre Cadorai) and in *Garden in the Wind* (one of the characters in the story "Where Will You Go, Sam Lee Wong?" is called Smouillya and is of Basque origin).

57. Gabrielle to Marcel, Dollard, 29 August 1955 (NLC).

58. Gabrielle to Marcel, near Washington, 18 February 1957 (NLC).

59. Gabrielle to Marcel, near Augusta, 20 February 1957 (NLC).

60. Gabrielle to Marcel, Panama City, 23 February 1957 (NLC).

61. Gabrielle to Marcel, Gulf Breeze, 1 March 1957 (NLC).

62. Gabrielle to Marcel, New Orleans, 10 March 1957 (NLC).

63. Ibid.

64. For an idea of the substance of these conversations, see René Richard, *Ma vie passée* (Montreal: Art Global, 1990).

65. Gabrielle Roy to Cécile Chabot, Quebec City, 24 February 1958 (BNQ).

66. Gabrielle Roy to Madeleine Bergeron, Port-Daniel, 6 July 1954 (FGR).

67. Gabrielle Roy to Cécile Chabot, Port-Daniel, 9 July 1954 (BNQ).

68. Gabrielle to Marcel, Rawdon, 26 March 1959 (NLC).

69. Gabrielle to Marcel, Laterrière, 13 July 1953 (NLC).

70. This portrait today hangs in the Bibliothèque Gabrielle-Roy in Quebec City.

71. Gabrielle to Marcel, Port-au-Persil, undated [16 or 17 July 1953] (NLC).

72. Gabrielle Roy to Berthe Simard, Quebec City, 15 October 1956 (NLC, Berthe Simard Papers).

73. Gabrielle Roy to Madeleine Bergeron and Madeleine Chassé, 2 October [1956] (FGR).

74. This passage is based on the memories of Berthe Simard.

75. Gabrielle Roy to Berthe Simard, Quebec City, 11 May 1959 (NLC, Berthe Simard Papers).

76. Gabrielle to Bernadette, Quebec City, 2 October 1957 (NLC; *Letters to Bernadette*, p. 24, trans. P. Claxton).

77. Ibid.

78. Gabrielle to Antonia Houde-Roy, [Quebec City], 12 March 1974 (Yolande Roy-Cyr Collection).

79. Gabrielle Roy to Madeleine Bergeron and Madeleine Chassé, Petite-Rivière-Saint-François, 8 June 1956 (FGR); with *cachot*, meaning a dungeon cell, Gabrielle is making a word play with *Château* Saint-Louis.

80. Gabrielle Roy to Berthe Simard, Quebec City, 2 February 1970 (NLC, Berthe Simard Papers).

81. Gabrielle Roy to Berthe Simard, Quebec City, 2 December 1969 (ibid.).

82. Gabrielle Roy to Madeleine Bergeron and Madeleine Chassé, Petite-Rivière-Saint-François, 1 July [1957] (FGR).

83. This edition (which is incomplete, consisting of fourteen of the original sixteen volumes) today belongs to André Fauchon of the Collège universitaire de Saint-Boniface.

84. Only one of these notebooks has been found (FGR).

85. Interview with Judith Jasmin, 1961.

86. These manuscripts are preserved at the NLC; there are allusions to the first two titles in Gabrielle Roy to Madeleine Bergeron, Port-Daniel, [12 or 13 July 1954] and Port-Navalo, 12 June 1955 (FGR); "La petite faïence bleue" is included in the list of Gabrielle Roy's unpublished works cited by Marc Gagné, 1973, p. 287.

87. Gabrielle Roy to Madeleine Bergeron and Madeleine Chassé, Petite-Rivière-Saint-François, 17 July 1957 (FGR).

88. Gabrielle to Bernadette, Quebec City, 2 October 1957 (NLC; *Letters to Bernadette*, p. 25, trans. P. Claxton).

89. According to C. Robinson (1995), the manuscripts of the saga dating from the 1950s preserved at the NLC are those in box 73, files 7–15, and box 74, files 5–7; certain manuscripts of the F. Ricard Collection are also of this period.

90. Gabrielle Roy to Cécile Chabot, Quebec City, 1 October 1959 (BNQ).

91. Gabrielle Roy to Joyce Marshall, Quebec City, 23 November 1960 (BUA).

92. Ibid.

93. "[René Richard] yesterday showed me a portrait of himself that he had painted in Paris. It is I think the loveliest portrait I have seen in Canada. He was ill at the time. In a few brush strokes he had succeeded in conveying a truly pathetic face." (Marcel to Gabrielle, Baie-Saint-Paul, 24 August 1955; NLC).

94. The hero of this story is called Gédéon, like the first character to appear in *La Montagne secrète* (*The Hidden Mountain*).

95. René D'Uckermann to Gabrielle Roy, Paris, 5 April 1956 (NLC).

96. The date of composition of this manuscript (F. Ricard Collection) is uncertain. When Gabrielle Roy gave it to me in May 1981, she told me she had written it some twenty years earlier (see also Gabrielle to Clémence, Quebec City, 2 June 1893; FGR, dossier Clémence Roy). However, C. Robinson (1995), subsequent to her analysis of the manuscripts of "La Saga d'Éveline," tends to place it in the late 1950s, hence before *La Montagne secrète*.

97. *De quoi t'ennuies-tu, Éveline?*, p. 11.

98. According to C. Robinson (1995), the saga manuscripts at the NLC dating from the 1960s are in box 74, files 1–4.

99. According to what Gabrielle wrote at the time to Bernadette (Quebec City, 20 January 1963; NLC, *Letters to Bernadette*, p. 50, trans. P. Claxton), this story was inspired by Sister Marie Girard; "In other respects, the story I tell is almost entirely invented. However, it's invented in a way that expresses the truth better than reality does."

100. This story (manuscripts at the NLC) was first titled "Un air de famille," then "La maison rose près du bac."

101. This screenplay, written for Radio-Canada, was never produced; it is conserved today at the NLC. After Gabrielle Roy's death, the filmmaker Claude Grenier produced his own adaptation of "Le vieillard et l'enfant" for the National Film Board of Canada.

102. Gabrielle to Bernadette, Quebec City, 26 November 1962 (NLC; *Letters to Bernadette*, p. 48, trans. P. Claxton).

103. Gabrielle Roy to Jack McClelland, Quebec City, 20 January 1965 (MMU).

104. Remarks of 8 July 1969 reported by M. Gagné, 1973, p. 179.

105. Gabrielle to Bernadette, Quebec City, 26 November 1962 (NLC; *Letters to Bernadette*, p. 48, trans. P. Claxton).

106. Gabrielle Roy to Jack McClelland, Quebec City, 11 November 1965 (MMU).

107. É. Lalou to Gabrielle Roy, Paris, 13 May 1966; see also Gabrielle Roy's reply, Quebec City, 15 June 1966 (NLC).

108. Gabrielle Roy to W. A. Deacon, Quebec City, 16 March 1954 (UOT; in J. Lennox and M. Lacombe, 1988, p. 305).

109. The expression is from Émilia-B. Allaire (1963), who writes portraits of S. Bussières (pp. 65–74) and A. Choquette (pp. 105–114).

110. See Gabrielle Roy to Simone Bussières, Quebec City [in fact, Port-au-Persil], 5 March 1954 (S. Bussières Collection).

111. Gabrielle Roy to Alice Lemieux-Lévesque, New Smyrna Beach, 21 February 1969 (ANQ-Quebec City)

112. Gabrielle Roy to Cécile Chabot, Quebec City, 2 October 1967 (BNQ).

113. *Presently Tomorrow* (1946) and *Lovers and Strangers* (1957).

114. Excerpt from the diary of Joyce Marshall, reproduced in Joyce Marshall to F. Ricard, Toronto, 25 May 1989, and quoted in part in J. Marshall, 1990.

115. Gabrielle Roy to Alice Lemieux-Lévesque, [New Smyrna Beach,] 1 February 1969 (ANQ-Quebec City).

116. She was to see Léo-Paul Desrosiers and Michelle LeNormand the following winter at St-Sauveur, where she went for another period of rest; as for Percé, Gabrielle would return there one last time in the summer of 1964.

117. Gabrielle to Marcel, Percé, 12 August 1962 (NLC).

118. Gabrielle to Marcel, Montreal, 7 May 1961 (NLC).

119. "Manitoba" (1962), *The Fragile Lights of Earth*, p. 103 (trans. A. Brown).

120. There are two versions of this unpublished text at the NLC; excerpts were published by Marc Gagné, 1976.

121. Remarks of 6 March 1969, reported by Marc Gagné, 1976.

122. See her remarks in 1969 to M. Gagné (1973, pp. 180–181), in 1972 to D. Cameron (1973: transcription at the NLC) and in 1982 to M. Delson-Karan (1986, pp. 202–203; there is some confusion here between the trip to Ungava and the one Gabrielle Roy had made to Alaska nineteen years earlier); in 1973, she also recounted her trip to Joan Hind-Smith (1975, pp. 116–117).

123. "My Manitoba Heritage" (1970), *The Fragile Lights of Earth*, p. 103 (trans. A. Brown).

124. Gabrielle to Marcel, London, 6 August 1963 (NLC).

125. Gabrielle Roy to A. Choquette, London, 21 August 1963 (UQTR).

126. Gabrielle to Marcel, London, 9 August 1963 (NLC).

127. Gabrielle Roy to Berthe Simard, London, [7 August 1963] (NLC, Berthe Simard Papers).

128. *Enchantment and Sorrow*, "A Bird Knows Its Song," VIII, p. 280 (trans. P. Claxton).

129. Gabrielle to Marcel, Upshire, 23 August 1963 (NLC).

130. Gabrielle to Marcel, Upshire, 21 August 1963 (NLC).

131. Gabrielle to Marcel, Paris, 29 August [second letter of the day] and 17 september 1963 (NLC).

132. Gabrielle to Bernadette, Quebec City, 4 February 1965 (NLC, *Letters to Bernadette*, pp. 72–73, trans. P. Claxton).

133. *Enchantment and Sorrow*, "The Governor's Ball," XIII, p. 131 (trans. P. Claxton).

134. Gabrielle to Bernadette, Quebec City, 22 May 1965 (NLC; *Letters to Bernadette*, p. 74, trans. P. Claxton).

135. Remarks of 2 April and 6 July 1971, reported by M. Gagné, 1973, p. 227.

136. Gabrielle to Marcel, St-Vital, 22 July 1958 (NLC).

137. Gabrielle to Bernadette, Quebec City, 5 January 1965 (NLC; *Letters to Bernadette*, p. 71, trans. P. Claxton).

138. Anna to Bernadette, [Montreal] 1 January 1963 (NLC).

139. Gabrielle to Bernadette, Quebec City, 20 January 1963 (NLC; *Letters to Bernadette*, p. 50, trans. P. Claxton).

140. Gabrielle to Bernadette, Quebec City, 10 January 1958 (NLC; ibid., p. 26).

141. Gabrielle to Bernadette, Petite-Rivière-Saint-François, 16 August 1965 (NLC; ibid., p. 91).

142. Gabrielle to Bernadette, Petite-Rivière-Saint-François, 16 August 1965 (NLC; ibid., p. 81).

143. Gabrielle to Bernadette, Quebec City, 22 May 1965 (NLC; ibid., p. 73).

144. Gabrielle to Bernadette, Quebec City, 3 December 1965; New Smyrna Beach, 25 February and 8 March 1969 (NLC; ibid., p. 83; *Ma chère petite soeur*, pp. 147–148.)

145. Gabrielle Roy to Simone Bussières, Draguignan, undated [February or March 1966] (S. Bussières Collection).

146. Gabrielle to Marcel, Draguignan, 22 February and 2 March, 1966 (NLC).

147. Gabrielle Roy to Cécile Chabot, Quebec City, 20 December 1965 (BNQ).

148. Gabrielle Roy to Berthe Simard, New Smyrna Beach, 6 January 1968 (NLC, Berthe Simard Papers).

149. Letters from Gabrielle Roy at New Smyrna Beach to Adrienne Choquette, 12 January 1968 (UQTR); to Bernadette, 19 February 1968 (NLC; *Ma chère petite soeur*, p. 129, trans. P. Claxton); and to Cécile Chabot, 4 March 1968 (BNQ).

150. Gabrielle to Bernadette, undated postcard [New Smyrna Beach, January or February 1968] (NLC; *Letters to Bernadette*, p. 101, trans. P. Claxton).

151. Gabrielle to Marcel, New Smyrna Beach, 10 and 20 January 1968 (NLC).

152. Gabrielle to Marcel, New Smyrna Beach, 1 and 22 February 1968 (NLC).

153. Gabrielle Roy to Alice Lemieux-Lévesque, New Smyrna Beach, 25 January 1969 (ANQ-Quebec City).

154. The program was produced by Claude Sylvestre; recorded on 1 August 1960, it was broadcast over CBFT on Monday, 30 January 1961.

155. P. Beaudry, 1968–1969; A. Parizeau, 1966.

156. Remarks reported by Alice Parizeau, 1967. The novelist Réjean Ducharme is media-shy to the point that there was speculation for a time whether he really existed.

157. The only other university degree that Gabrielle Roy would accept, because she was not required to go herself to receive it, was an honorary doctorate conferred by the University of Lethbridge, Alberta, at the instigation of Professor M. G. Hesse.

158. This speech, remaining unpublished, is conserved at the NLC.
159. See *La Presse*, 29 May 1971, p. 1.
160. See copies of letters from C. Berloty to J.-Z.-L. Patenaude (Conseil supérieur du livre) and M. A. Asturias (Guatemalan ambassador in Paris), Neuilly-sur-Seine, 27 April 1971 (FGR).
161. Gabrielle to Marcel, Phoenix, 25 January and 9 February 1971 (NLC).
162. "Man and His World: A Telling of the Theme" (1967), *The Fragile Lights of Earth*, p. 222 (trans. A. Brown).
163. "My Manitoba Heritage" (1970), *The Fragile Lights of Earth*, p. 155 (trans. A. Brown).
164. Gabrielle Roy to F. Ricard, Quebec City, 27 September 1974 (F. Ricard Collection).
165. Gabrielle Roy to Cécile Chabot, Quebec City, 25 August 1967 (BNQ).
166. A file on this dispute, consisting of the correspondence and other documents, is included in the Yolande Roy-Cyr Collection.
167. The series was created by McClelland & Stewart in 1958. *The Tin Flute* appeared in it in 1958, *Where Nests the Water Hen* in 1961, *The Cashier* in 1963, and *Street of Riches* in 1967; in each volume the text is accompanied by a critical introduction.
168. *Bonheur d'occasion* (Geneva: Le Cercle du Bibliophile, 1968); *La Petite Poule d'Eau* (Paris: Éditions du Burin et Martinsart, 1967).
169. *La Petite Poule d'Eau* (Montreal: Gilles Corbeil éditeur, 1971); *La Montagne secrète* (Montreal: Éditions de la Frégate, 1975), edition limited to 230 copies.
170. According to Gabrielle Roy's income tax declarations, her income was as follows: in 1970, she earned $20,834 ($13,494 net royalties, that is, after deduction of professional expenses + $7,340 interest and dividends); in 1971, $20,446 ($12,913 + $7,533); in 1972, $21,432 ($13,354 + $8,078); in 1973, $30,529 ($14,383 + $16,146); in 1974, $25,001 ($9,080 + $15,921); and in 1975, $27,440 ($10,926 + $16,514).
171. See G.-A. Vachon, "Chrétien ou Montréalais" (*Maintenant*, Montreal, February 1965), "L'espace politique et social dans le roman québécois" (*Recherches sociographiques*, Quebec City, September–December 1966); Ben-Z. Shek, "L'espace et la description symbolique dans les deux romans montréalais de Gabrielle Roy" (*Liberté*, Montreal, no. 73, May 1971); R. Robidoux and A. Renaud, "*Bonheur d'occasion*" (in *Le Roman canadien-français du xxe siècle*, Ottawa: Éditions de l'Université d'Ottawa, 1966); J. Blais, "L'unité organique de *Bonheur d'occasion*" (*Études françaises*, Montreal, February 1970); A. Brochu, "Un aperçu sur l'oeuvre de Gabrielle Roy" (*Le Quartier latin*, Montreal, 20, 22, and 27 February 1962); "Thèmes et structures de *Bonheur d'occasion*" (*Écrits du Canada français*, Montreal, no. 22, 1966); A. LeGrand, "Gabrielle Roy ou l'être partagé" (*Études françaises*, Montreal, June 1965); J. Allard, "Le chemin qui mène à la Petite Poule d'Eau" (*Cahiers de Sainte-Marie*, Montreal, May 1966); A. Sirois, "Le mythe du Nord" (*Revue de l'Université de Sherbrooke*, Sherbrooke, October 1963); J. Warwick, *The Long Journey: Literary Themes of French Canada* (Toronto: University of Toronto

Press, 1968, pp. 86–100, 140–144); D. Hayne, "Gabrielle Roy" (*Canadian Modern Language Review*, Toronto, October 1964); G. Bessette, "*La Route d'Altamont* clef de *La Montage secrète*" (*Livres et Auteurs canadiens 1966*, Montreal, 1967), "Gabrielle Roy" (*Une littérature en ébullition*, Montreal: Éditions du Jour, 1968), "*Alexandre Chenevert* de Gabrielle Roy" (*Études littéraires*, Quebec City, August 1969). For selections of learned criticisms of Gabrielle Roy's work during her lifetime, see P. Socken (1979), R. Chadbourne (1984), and L. Saint-Martin (1998).

172. See in particular the conversations reported by John J. Murphy (1963), Gérard Bessette (1968), Robert Morissette (1970), Don Cameron (1973) and Joan Hind-Smith (1975). Also received by Gabrielle Roy around 1970 were the academics Lise Gauvin (1986, p. 230) and Jeannette Urbas (1988).

173. Gabrielle Roy to Antoine Sirois, Quebec City, 2 March 1964 (FGR); in 1960, Gabrielle Roy also refused Fides permission to publish a pocket paperback edition of *Bonheur d'occasion* in the series "Alouette bleue."

174. R.-M. Charland and J.-N. Samson, 1967.

175. Phyllis Grosskurth, 1969.

176. J. Paré, "*La Montagne secrète,*" *Le Nouveau Journal*, Montreal, 28 October 1961, supplement, p. 27; J. Éthier-Blais, "*La Montagne secrète* de Gabrielle Roy," *Le Devoir*, Montreal, 28 October 1961, p. 11; G. Marcotte, "À chacun sa montagne secrète," *La Presse*, Montreal, 21 October 1961, supplement, p. 5; R. Duhamel, "*La Montagne secrète,*" *La Patrie du dimanche*, Montreal, 12 November 1961, p. 8; R. Leclerc, "*La Montagne secrète* de Gabrielle Roy," *Lectures*, Montreal, January 1962, pp. 135–138; G. Tougas, "*La Montagne secrète* de Gabrielle Roy," *Livres et Auteurs canadiens 1961*, Montreal, pp. 11–12.

177. See in particular the reviews by Constance Beresford-Howe ("Gabrielle Roy's New Novel," *Montreal Star*, Montreal, 3 November 1962, supplement, p. 60), Harriet Hill ("The World of Spirit," *The Gazette*, Montreal, 3 November 1962, p. 31), Hugo McPherson ("Prodigies of God and Man," *Canadian Literature*, Vancouver, Winter 1963, pp. 74–76), and Michael Hornyansky ("Countries of the Mind," *Tamarack Review*, Toronto, Spring 1963, pp. 85–86).

178. G. Marcotte, "Toutes les routes vont par Altamont," *La Presse*, Montreal, 16 April 1966, supplement, p. 4; A. Major, "*La Route d'Altamont* de Gabrielle Roy," *Le Petit Journal*, Montreal, 17 April 1966, p. 42; Phyllis Grosskurth, "Quebecker with a Flaubert Accent," *The Globe Magazine*, Toronto, 8 October 1966, p. 27.

179. See John Clute, "New Fiction," *Toronto Daily Star*, Toronto, 1 October 1966, p. 34; Arrol Toplitsky, "Gabrielle Roy's *The Road Past Altamont*," *The Vanity*, Toronto, 7 October 1966; Michael Gordon, review of the novel on CBC radio, 10 October 1966 (transcription at the NLC).

180. "Quelques réflexions sur la littérature canadienne d'expression française" (1962), p. 7.

181. "Prière de communiquer," copy of the unpublished manuscript (Yolande Roy-Cyr Coll.).

182. See *Le Soleil*, Quebec City, 29 July 1967, p. 3; *Le Devoir*, Montreal, 31 July 1967, p. 3.

183. Gabrielle to Bernadette, Quebec City, 29 November 1967 (NLC; *Letters to Bernadette*, p. 99, trans. P. Claxton).

184. Gabrielle Roy to Alice Lemieux-Lévesque, Petite-Rivière-Saint-François, 19 June 1969 (ANQ-Quebec).

185. Gabrielle to Bernadette, Quebec City, 30 October 1969 (NLC; *Letters to Bernadette*, pp. 130–131, trans. P. Claxton).

186. Gabrielle to Marcel, Phoenix, 14 January 1971 (NLC).

187. Gabrielle to Bernadette, New Smyrna Beach, 22 January 1969 (NLC; *Letters to Bernadette*, p. 113, trans. P. Claxton).

188. The "Baldur" manuscripts are at the NLC; Pierre Morency also has a copy. See Monique Roy-Sole, *En ce pays d'ombre: analyse génétique de «Baldur», un roman inédit de Gabrielle Roy*, M.A. thesis, Carleton University, Ottawa, 1993.

189. Gabrielle Roy to Joyce Marshall, Quebec City, 12 December 1968 (BUA).

190. Gabrielle Roy to Adrienne Choquette, New Smyrna Beach, 14 December 1968 (UQTR).

191. Gabrielle to Bernadette, Quebec City, 18 December 1968 (NLC; *Letters to Bernadette*, p. 106, trans. P. Claxton).

192. M.-A. A. Roy, 1989–1990, episode 27.

193. Gabrielle to Anna, Quebec City, 26 December 1962 (NLC).

194. This subtitle figures in the copy at the MPA, Marie-Anna A. Roy Papers.

195. Gabrielle to Bernadette, Quebec City, 24 May 1969 (NLC; *Letters to Bernadette*, p. 123, trans. P. Claxton).

196. Gabrielle to Bernadette, Quebec City, 7 and 17 May 1969 (NLC; ibid., pp. 120, 122).

197. Gabrielle to Bernadette, Quebec City, 18 October 1968 (NLC; ibid, p. 106).

198. A. Parizeau, 1966, p. 140.

199. Gabrielle to Antonia Houde-Roy, Quebec City, 9 June 1968 (Yolande Roy-Cyr Coll.).

200. Gabrielle Roy to A. Choquette, [New Smyrna Beach,] 2 January 1969 (UQTR).

201. Gabrielle to Bernadette, Quebec City, 3 September 1969 (NLC; *Letters to Bernadette*, p. 129, trans. P. Claxton).

202. *Enchantment and Sorrow*, "The Governor's Ball," VII, p. 81 (trans. P. Claxton).

203. Gabrielle Roy to Adrienne Choquette, [New Smyrna Beach,] 2 January 1969 (UQTR).

204. Ibid.

205. Gabrielle to Marcel, New Smyrna Beach, 26 January 1969 (NLC).

206. Gabrielle Roy to Adrienne Choquette, New Smyrna Beach, 17 January 1969 (UQTR).

207. Gabrielle Roy to Alice Lemieux-Lévesque, New Smyrna Beach, 1 and 21 February 1969 (ANQ-Québec).

208. Gabrielle to Bernadette, New Smyrna Beach, 15 March 1969 (NLC; *Letters to Bernadette*, p. 118, trans. P. Claxton).

209. Gabrielle to Marcel, New Smyrna Beach, 22 March 1969 (NLC).

210. See the copy of this letter in Bernadette to Gabrielle, St-Boniface, 12 May 1969 (NLC).

211. Adèle to Bernadette, recopied in Bernadette to Gabrielle, St-Boniface, 20 May 1969 (NLC).

212. Copy of a letter from Adèle Roy to R. Hamel, St-Boniface, 16 May 1969 (Ben-Z. Shek Collection).

213. Gabrielle to Bernadette, Petite-Rivière-Saint-François, 30 June 1969 (NLC; *Letters to Bernadette*, pp. 125–126, trans. P. Claxton).

214. Gabrielle Roy to Berthe Valcourt, Quebec City, 4 December 1971 (SSNJM).

215. Remarks of 29 July 1969 reported by Marc Gagné, 1973, p. 180.

216. Gabrielle Roy to Berthe Simard, Quebec City, 15 September 1969 (NLC, Berthe Simard Papers).

217. Gabrielle Roy to Joyce Marshall, Quebec City, 29 January 1970 (BUA).

218. Joyce Marshall had already translated the "Three Inuit Short Stories" (NLC); around 1977, there was even talk of making a book of them, but the project did not materialize; finally, "The Satellites" was published in *The Tamarack Review*, Toronto, no. 74, 1978; a different translation by Sherri Walsh of "Le fauteuil roulant" also appeared in *Arts Manitoba*, Autumn 1984.

219. Gabrielle Roy to Adrienne Choquette, St-Boniface, 3 April 1970 (UQTR).

220. Gabrielle to Marcel, [St-Boniface,] 21 March 1970 (NLC).

221. *Enchantment and Sorrow*, "The Governor's Ball," XIII, pp. 126–136, and XVIII, pp. 171–173 (trans. P. Claxton).

222. Ibid., XIII, pp. 126–127.

223. These letters, which were sent back to Gabrielle Roy after Bernadette's death, are at the NLC and are published in *Letters to Bernadette*, pp. 144–197 (trans. P. Claxton).

224. Gabrielle to Bernadette, Quebec City, 18 April 1970 (NLC; *Letters to Bernadette*, p. 159, trans. P. Claxton).

225. Gabrielle to Bernadette, Quebec City, 9 April 1970 (NLC; ibid., p. 146).

226. Gabrielle to Bernadette, Quebec City, 15 April 1970 (NLC; ibid., p. 155).

227. Gabrielle to Bernadette, Quebec City, 17 April 1970 (NLC; ibid, p. 157).

228. Gabrielle to Antonia Houde-Roy, Quebec City, 26 May 1970 (Yolande Roy-Cyr Coll.).

229. Gabrielle Roy to Berthe Valcourt, Quebec City, 4 June 1970 (SSNJM).

230. See R. Duhamel, "L'amour de chair et l'amour de coeur," *Le Droit*, Ottawa, 5 December 1970, p. 9; J. Éthier-Blais, "Une lecture émouvante et mélancolique," *Le Devoir*, Montreal, 28 November 1970, p. 12.

231. See, for example, Robert Dickson, "Un échec pour Gabrielle Roy," *Le Soleil*, Quebec City, 31 October 1970, p. 37; there was also a virulent indictment on the television program *Format 30* (see Victor Barbeau to Gabrielle Roy, Montreal, 29 October 1970; NLC).

232. Phyllis Grosskurth, "Maternity's Fond but Tedious Tune," *The Globe Magazine*, Toronto, 19 September 1970, p. 20.

233. Gabrielle Roy to Berthe Valcourt, [Phoenix,] 3 January [1971, dated in error "1970"] (SSNJM).

234. Gabrielle Roy to Adrienne Choquette, Phoenix, 29 December 1970 (UQTR).

235. Gabrielle to Antonia Houde-Roy, Quebec City, 14 March 1971 (Yolande Roy-Cyr Coll.).

236. Gabrielle to Antonia Houde-Roy, Quebec City, 25 March 1971 (Yolande Roy-Cyr Coll.).

237. Gabrielle to Antonia Houde-Roy, Quebec City, 29 April 1971 (Yolande Roy-Cyr Coll.).

238. Gabrielle Roy to Berthe Simard, 20 September 1971 (NLC, Berthe Simard Papers).

239. These are four unpublished manuscripts kept at the NLC: "Anne-Marie," "L'été qui ne vint pas," "Le merveilleux," and "Le petit garçon trop tendre"; none are dated but their manner of writing suggests that they were written in the late 1950s or early 1960s.

240. Gabrielle to Bernadette, Quebec City, 28 and 29 April 1970 (NLC; *Letters to Bernadette*, pp. 170, 172, trans. P. Claxton).

241. We know of three stories that were written for *Cet été qui chantait* but did not find their way into the final composition of the book, Gabrielle Roy having decided to keep them for separate publication as children's books; only one appeared during her lifetime, *Courte-Queue* (1979; *Cliptail*, trans. A. Brown, 1980); the two others were published posthumously: "L'empereur des bois" (1984) and *L'Espagnole et la Pékinoise* (1986) (*The Tortoiseshell and the Pekinese*, trans. P. Claxton, 1989).

242. Gabrielle to Marcel, White Rock, 27 September 1972 (NLC).

243. See Paul Gay, "*Cet été qui chantait*," *Le Droit*, Ottawa, 30 December 1972, p. 13; Paule Saint-Onge, "De la sérénité à la dignité," *Châtelaine*, Montreal, January 1973, p. 4; François Hébert, "De quelques avatars de Dieu," *Études françaises*, Montreal, November 1973, pp. 346–348.

244. R. Martel, "Bonheurs mièvres et enfantillages," *La Presse*, Montreal, 9 December 1972, p. E-3; J. Éthier-Blais, "Comme si la terre elle-même écrivait son histoire," *Le Devoir*, Montreal, 11 November 1972, p. 16; G. Constantineau, "Un bestiaire, car finalement c'en est un, mais anodin," *Le Soleil*, Quebec City, 18 November 1972, p. 16.

245. J.-J. Richard, "Cet été qui chantait," *Le Soleil*, Quebec City, 16 December 1972, p. 49.

246. Gabrielle Roy to Joyce Marshall, Tourettes-sur-Loup, 19 January 1973 (BUA).

247. Sylvia Fraser, "Two Quebec Authors Plumb Mystery of Life, Poignancy of Death," *Toronto Star*, 2 October 1976, p. F-7; Pierrette Ferth, "*Enchanted Summer*," *Prince Albert Daily Herald*, 8 October 1976; A. Freedman, "Summer Doldrums," *Maclean's*, Toronto, 20 September 1976, p. 66; James Ross, "Gabrielle Roy's *Enchanted Summer*," *Hamilton Spectator*, 23 September 1976.

NOTES TO CHAPTER 9

A Time for Remembrance

Gabrielle Roy's letters to W. A. Deacon, K. M. Glazier, Margaret Laurence, Joyce Marshall, and Jack McClelland were all written in English.

1. Remarks in interview with Don Cameron (1973, p. 141).
2. Gabrielle Roy to Joyce Marshall, Quebec City, 31 March 1974 (BUA).
3. See John Reeves, 1975.
4. Gabrielle Roy to Jack McClelland, [Quebec City] 9 January 1975 (MMU).
5. *Enchantment and Sorrow*, "The Governor's Ball," XIII, p. 129 (trans. P. Claxton).
6. Gabrielle to Clémence, [Quebec City, 28 February 1981] (BNQ, fonds Marie-Anna A. Roy; CEFCO).
7. Gabrielle to Antonia Houde-Roy, Quebec City, 17 March 1971 (Yolande Roy-Cyr Collection).
8. Gabrielle to Antonia Houde-Roy, Petite-Rivière-Saint-François, 12 August 1970 (Yolande Roy-Cyr Coll.).
9. *Enchantment and Sorrow*, "The Governor's Ball," XIV, p. 140 (trans. P. Claxton).
10. Gabrielle Roy to Berthe Simard, Winnipeg, 5 October 1970 (NLC, Berthe Simard Papers).
11. Gabrielle to Clémence, Quebec City, 29 March 1971 (NLC).
12. Gabrielle to Antonia Houde-Roy, Quebec City, 8 May 1970 (Yolande Roy-Cyr Coll.).
13. *Enchantment and Sorrow*, "The Governor's Ball," XIII, p. 137 (trans. P. Claxton).
14. Gabrielle Roy to Berthe Valcourt, Quebec City, 27 November 1977 (SSNJM).
15. Gabrielle Roy to Berthe Valcourt, Petite-Rivière-Saint-François, 14 July 1972 (SSNJM).
16. Clémence to Gabrielle, Otterburne, 4 November 1972, 16 October 1971, 15 July 1974 (NLC).
17. Gabrielle Roy to Berthe Valcourt, Quebec City, 29 November 1973 (SSNJM); Gabrielle to Antonia Houde-Roy, Quebec City, 14 March 1971 (Yolande Roy-Cyr Coll.).
18. Gabrielle Roy to Berthe Valcourt, Quebec City, 1 September 1971 and 14 December 1974 (SSNJM).
19. Clémence to Gabrielle, Otterburne, 4 February 1974 (NLC).
20. Gabrielle Roy to Berthe Simard, [Winnipeg] 7 September 1972 (NLC Berthe Simard Papers).
21. Clémence to Gabrielle, Otterburne, 4 November 1972 (NLC).
22. Gabrielle to Antonia Houde-Roy, Quebec City, 23 November 1972 (Yolande Roy-Cyr Coll.).
23. Gabrielle Roy to Simone Bussières, [Tourrettes-sur-Loup] 13 December 1972 (S. Bussières Collection).

24. Gabrielle Roy to Adrienne Choquette, Tourrettes-sur-Loup, 14 January [1973] (UQTR).

25. Gabrielle Roy to François Ricard, Quebec City, 24 March 1977 (F. Ricard Collection).

26. Gabrielle to Antonia Houde-Roy, Petite-Rivière-Saint-François, 15 June 1973 (Yolande Roy-Cyr Coll.).

27. Gabrielle Roy to Joyce Marshall, Petite-Rivière-Saint-François, 11 June 1973 (BUA).

28. Gabrielle Roy to Adrienne Choquette, Petite-Rivière-Saint-François, 24 July 1973 (UQTR).

29. Gabrielle Roy to Simone Bussières, Otterburne, 7 September 1973 (S. Bussières Coll.).

30. Gabrielle Roy to Berthe Simard, Otterburne, 10 September 1973 (NLC, Berthe Simard Papers).

31. Gabrielle Roy to Joyce Marshall, Otterburne, 15 September 1973 (BUA).

32. Gabrielle Roy to Victor Barbeau, Petite-Rivière-Saint-François, 7 [and 10] July 1969 (BNQ).

33. Gabrielle Roy to François Ricard, Quebec City, 24 October 1977 (F. Ricard Coll.).

34. Gabrielle Roy to Berthe Valcourt, Quebec City, 23 February 1974 (SSNJM).

35. Gabrielle Roy to Joyce Marshall, Quebec City, 15 March 1975 (BUA).

36. Gabrielle Roy to François Ricard, Petite-Rivière-Saint-François, 17 August 1974 (F. Ricard Coll.).

37. Gabrielle Roy to François Ricard, Quebec City, 27 September 1974 (F. Ricard Coll.).

38. Gabrielle Roy to François Ricard, Quebec City, 28 March 1975 (F. Ricard Coll.).

39. Gaétan Dostie, "Gabrielle Roy au bout de son monde," *Le Jour*, Montreal, 12 July 1975, p. 14; Robert Tremblay, "L'émouvant et beau retour de Gabrielle Roy," *Le Soleil*, Quebec City, 28 June 1975, p. D-8.

40. R. G. Scully, 1974; V.-L. Beaulieu, "Rien d'autre qu'un désert et qu'un manuscrit," *Le Devoir*, Montreal, 30 March 1974.

41. R. G. Scully, "La vieillesse, et l'Ouest triste," *Le Devoir*, Montreal, 21 June 1975, pp. 11–12; "La vallée Houdou" is reproduced on the same pages.

42. See Ronald Hatch, "Gabrielle Roy: Growing in the Wind," *Vancouver Sun*, Vancouver, 14 October 1977, p. 38L.

43. Rebecca Wigod, "*Garden in the Wind*," *The Province*, Vancouver, 23 September 1977; Mike Byfield, "*Garden in the Wind*," *Edmonton Report*, Edmonton, 17 October 1977; Kathleen O'Donnell, "No Divisions by Language in Roy," *Ottawa Citizen*, Ottawa, 10 September 1977; G. Woodcock, "Gabrielle Roy as Cultural Mediator," *Saturday Night*, Toronto, November 1977, pp. 69–72.

44. Gabrielle Roy to Joyce Marshall, Quebec City, 24 March 1977 (BUA).

45. Gabrielle Roy to François Ricard, Quebec City, 28 March 1975 (F. Ricard Coll.).

46. Gabrielle Roy to Gabrielle Poulin, 18 May 1978 (reproduced in *Revue d'histoire littéraire du Québec et du Canada français*, Ottawa, no. 12, 1986).

47. In the English translation by Alan Brown, which was approved by Gabrielle Roy (*Children of My Heart*, Toronto: McClelland & Stewart, 1979), the titles of the six stories are omitted and the book is divided simply into three "Parts"; the first contains the first four stories of the French edition, the second corresponds to "La maison gardée," and the third to "De la truite dans l'eau glacée."

48. Remarks of 15 March 1971, reported by M. Gagné, 1976, p. 364.

49. Remarks reported by J. Godbout, 1979, p. 32.

50. G. Marcotte, "Gabrielle Roy et l'institutrice passionnée," *Le Devoir*, Montreal, 24 September 1977, p. 16; Réginald Martel, "De vieux bonheurs encore tout neufs," *La Presse*, Montreal, 10 September 1977, p. D-3; Paul Gay, "Un monde merveilleux de chaleur humaine," *Le Droit*, Ottawa, 15 October 1977, p. 20; G. Poulin, "Une merveilleuse histoire d'amour," *Lettres québécoises*, Ottawa, November 1977, pp 5–9; F. Hébert, "*Ces enfants de ma vie*," *Liberté*, Montreal, January–February 1978, pp. 102–105; J. Godbout, "Les visages sous les mots," *L'Actualité*, Montreal, December 1977, p. 88.

51. Y. Thériault, "Les enfants de la vie de Gabrielle Roy," *Le Livre d'ici*, Montréal, 15 February 1978.

52. A. Brochu, "*Ces enfants de ma vie*," *Livres et Auteurs québécois 1977*, Quebec City, 1978, pp. 39–43.

53. Gabrielle Roy to B. Valcourt, Quebec City, 21 October 1977 (SSNJM).

54. R. Martel, "Honneur à Gabrielle Roy," *La Presse*, Montreal, 13 May 1978, p. D-19; J. Éthier-Blais, "*Fragiles Lumières de la terre*," *Québec français*, Quebec City, October 1978, pp. 48–49; Y. Thériault, "La finesse de Gabrielle Roy," *Le Livre d'ici*, Montreal, 28 June 1978.

55. Gabrielle to Clémence, Petite-Rivière-Saint-François, 19 July 1978 (NLC).

56. She was represented by her husband for the presentation of the Molson Prize (Ottawa, June 1978) and the Diplôme d'honneur of the Canadian Conference of the Arts (Ottawa, May 1980); by Alain Stanké for the Governor General's Award (Ottawa, May 1978); by me for the Canada Council Children's Literature Prize (Toronto, May 1980).

57. Gabrielle Roy to Joyce Marshall, Quebec City, 26 March 1976 (BUA).

58. See. D. Cobb, 1976; J. Godbout, 1979.

59. Gabrielle Roy to Margaret Laurence, Petite-Rivière-Saint-François, 4 June 1977 (YUT); Gabrielle Roy to Joyce Marshall, Petite-Rivière-Saint-François, 9 September 1977 (BUA).

60. See F.-A. Savard to Gabrielle Roy, 30 January 1978 (NLC).

61. *Enchantment and Sorrow*, "The Governor's Ball," XI, p. 111 (trans. P. Claxton).

62. Gabrielle Roy to Margaret Laurence, Petite-Rivière-Saint-François, 4 July 1977 (YUT).

63. See two texts from this period, "A Note to the Editor" (1977) and "Lettre de Gabrielle Roy à ses amis de l'ALCQ" (1979).

64. Copy of Gabrielle Roy to Solange Chaput-Rolland, Quebec City, 4 April 1980 (NLC).

65. In a letter of 12 November 1979 to Paul G. Socken (which is in the possession of the recipient), Gabrielle Roy stated that the story had been written "two or three years ago, I think"; but on 14 April 1977, she told Peter Newman, then editor of *Maclean's*, that the text had been written "a few years ago, without a purpose, simply to put down in words a curious adventure I had when, as a young journalist, I toured Canada in search of material to write a series on its ethnical groups" (NLC).

66. Gabrielle Roy to Margaret Laurence, Quebec City, 17 November 1979 (YUT).

67. Especially Pierre-Henri Simon, "*La rivière sans repos* de Gabrielle Roy," *Le Monde*, Paris, February 1972.

68. Around 1978, the Montreal publisher Stanké attempted to distribute his own edition of *Ces enfants de ma vie* in France, but with little success. After Gabrielle Roy's death, other attempts (*La détresse et l'enchantement* with Les Éditions Arléa in 1986; *Ces enfants de ma vie* with Les Éditions de Fallois in 1994) were also failures.

69. Gabrielle Roy to François Ricard, 21 March 1980 (F. Ricard Collection).

70. The adaptation appeared under various titles in the French-Canadian (June 1979), English-Canadian (August 1979), American (September 1979), Swedish (November 1979), Chinese (November 1979), Japanese (November 1979), British (December 1979), Portuguese (December 1979), German (December 1979), German Swiss (December 1979), Australian (January 1980), Brazilian (January 1980), Norwegian (January 1980), French (February 1980), French Swiss (February 1980), Indian (March 1980), Dutch (March 1980), New Zealand (April 1980), Arabic (April 1980), Danish (May 1980), and Korean editions of *The Reader's Digest*. Between 1976 and 1980, other adaptations of stories by Gabrielle Roy (excerpts from *La Rivière sans repos*, *Cet été qui chantait*, and *Ces enfants de ma vie*) were also published in the French-Canadian edition of the magazine.

71. She published *A Private Place* in 1975.

72. Gabrielle Roy to Joyce Marshall, Quebec City, 10 April 1973 (BUA).

73. After Gabrielle Roy's death, Alan Brown also translated *My Cow Bossie* (*Ma vache Bossie*), published by McClelland & Stewart in 1988.

74. Gabrielle Roy to Joyce Marshall, Quebec City, 23 December 1973 and 3 January [1974] (BUA).

75. Gabrielle Roy to Jack McClelland, Quebec City, 31 December 1975 (MMU).

76. In 1981, the new translation of *The Tin Flute* by Alan Brown was also published in the "New Canadian Library" series. As for *Children of My Heart*, a mass-market edition was published in the autumn of 1980 in the "Seal Books" series jointly owned by McClelland & Stewart and Bantam Books of New York.

77. In chronological order, these were *Cet été qui chantait* (1979), *Alexandre Chenevert* (1979), *La Rivière sans repos* (1979), *Rue Deschambault* (1980),

La Petite Poule d'Eau (1980), and *Fragiles Lumières de la terre* (1982). After
Gabrielle Roy's death, there appeared also *Ces enfants de ma vie* (1983), *La
Route d'Altamont* (1985) and *Un jardin au bout du monde* (1987).

78. Gabrielle Roy to Jack McClelland, Quebec City, 30 December 1976 (MMU).

79. On this subject, see Véronique Robert, "Bonheur d'occasion," *L'Actualité*,
Montreal, August 1982, pp. 27–32.

80. Copy of a letter from Gabrielle Roy to K. M. Glazier, Quebec City, 30
December 1975 (NLC).

81. Gabrielle Roy to Jack McClelland, Quebec City, 12 March 1976 (MMU).

82. From her income tax declarations (FGR), Gabrielle Roy's income was as
follows: in 1976, income $31,837 ($9,980 in net royalties, that is, after deduction of professional expenses + $20, 223 investment income +$1,634 pension
payments); in 1977, $38,382 ($10,617 + $24,352 + $3,413); in 1978, $47,206
($20,443 + $22,203 + $4,560); in 1979, $63,737 ($28,439 + $30,783 + $4,515); in
1980, $67,909 ($18,573 + $44,403 + 4,933); in 1981, $80,366 ($21,069 + $53,832 +
$5,465); in 1982, $86,104 ($21,382 + $58,596 + $6,126).

83. See P. Morency, 1992.

84. A second batch of manuscripts and documents that Gabrielle Roy had kept
for her own use and had not been included in the set acquired by the NLC in
1982–1983 was turned over to the NLC by le Fonds Gabrielle Roy in 1986 for
an additional sum of $35,000.

85. Clémence to Gabrielle, Otterburne, 18 January 1976 (NLC).

86. Gabrielle Roy to Berthe Valcourt, Quebec City, 29 December 1975 (SSNJM).

87. Doctor André de Roquigny to Gabrielle Roy, Winnipeg, 21 September 1977
(NLC).

88. Clémence to Gabrielle, St-Boniface, 18 September 1976 (NLC).

89. Clémence to Gabrielle, St-Boniface, 9 January 1982 (NLC).

90. Gabrielle Roy to Jack McClelland, Quebec City, 30 December 1976 (MMU);
the next day there appeared an interview in which Gabrielle Roy declared, "I
have no plans for memoires for the moment" (Alain Houle, 1976).

91. Gabrielle Roy to Léa Landry, Quebec City, 1 March 1961 (R. Jubinville
Collection).

92. Gabrielle Roy to Adrienne Choquette, St-Boniface, 23 March 1970 (UQTR).

93. There is an interesting variation in the French original, leading to a corresponding variation in translation: in "The Disparate Treasures of a Young
Girl Who Came From Deschambault Street" (1976, trans. A. Brown), after
young Gabrielle's performance the nun exclaims, "Puffed-up with pride,
eh?"; in *Enchantment and Sorrow* (1987, "The Governor's Ball," V, p. 57, trans.
P. Claxton), this rebuke becomes, "Get out of my sight, you little romancer!"

94. Gabrielle Roy to Léa Landry, Cardinal, 27 February 1930 (R. Jubinville Coll.).

95. Remarks reported by Céline Légaré, 1972.

96. Gabrielle Roy to François Ricard, 5 December 1973 (F. Ricard Coll.)

97. Gabrielle Roy to Berthe Valcourt, Petite-Rivière-Saint-François, 19 July 1978
(SSNJM).

98. Gabrielle Roy to Berthe Valcourt, Hollywood, 3 December 1978 (SSNJM).

99. Gabrielle to Antonia Houde-Roy, Hollywood, 7 December 1978 (Yolande Roy-Cyr Coll.).

100. Gabrielle to Marcel, Hollywood, 20 December 1978 (NLC).

101. Gabrielle Roy to François Ricard, Petite-Rivière-Saint-François, 20 July 1979 (F. Ricard Coll.).

102. Gabrielle Roy to Margaret Laurence, Quebec City, 11 March 1980 (YUT).

103. The Marie-Anna A. Roy Papers at the National Archives of Canada include a copy of *La Petite Poule d'Eau* heavily annotated with critical commentaries in Adèle's hand.

104. Gabrielle to Clémence, Quebec City, 16 March 1978 (NLC).

105. An unpublished and untitled manuscript that Gabrielle received from Adèle in 1978 (NLC).

106. The quotations in this paragraph are from an unpublished manuscript of Adèle's, "Grains de sable, Pépites d'or" (BNQ).

107. Adèle to Gabrielle, Montreal, 22 September 1978 (NLC).

108. Gabrielle Roy to François Ricard, Petite-Rivière-Saint-François, 7 August 1979 (F. Ricard Coll.).

109. Gabrielle Roy to Berthe Valcourt, Quebec City, 4 November 1979 (SSNJM).

110. Gabrielle Roy to Berthe Valcourt, [Quebec City,] 2 December 1979 (SSNJM).

111. Marie-Anna A. [Adèle] Roy, "Indulgence et Pardon," unpublished manuscript (MPA, BNQ).

112. Gabrielle Roy to Jack McClelland, Petite-Rivière-Saint-François, 19 July 1980 (MMU).

113. This second typed copy is today at the NLC with the manuscripts in their binders.

114. Gabrielle to Clémence, Quebec City, 19 February 1981 (FGR, dossier Clémence Roy).

115. The opening words of the sequel to *La détresse et l'enchantement* (*Enchantment and Sorrow*), *Le temps qui m'a manqué*, I, p. 13.

116. Gabrielle to Clémence, Quebec City, 22 February 1983 (FGR, dossier Clémence Roy).

117. Gabrielle Roy to Berthe Valcourt, Quebec City, 6 April 1983 (SSNJM).

NOTES TO EPILOGUE

1. Gabrielle Roy's last will was drawn up in 1981 and confirmed on 17 February 1982 (FGR and NLC).

2. Marie-Anna A. Roy, 1989–1990, episode 35; this article is one of a series of thirty-eight published between July 1989 and April 1990, which repeat substantially the same memories and the same recriminations contained in *Le Miroir du passé*.

Sources

I. Gabrielle Roy's Published Works

In each category (1. Books; 2. Newspapers, Periodicals, Collective Works), the items are listed in chronological order.

1. Books

For each title the following are given: (a) the first French-language edition published in Canada; (b) the first edition published in France; (c) the first English-language edition published in Canada, with its title and the name of its translator; (d) the first edition published in the United States; (e) the most recent French-language edition; and (f) the most recent English-language edition, the source of quotations contained in this book.

Bonheur d'occasion, fiction. (a) Montréal: Société des Éditions Pascal, 1945 [2 vols.]. (b) Paris: Flammarion, 1947. (c) *The Tin Flute*, trans. Hannah Josephson. Toronto: McClelland & Stewart, 1947. (d) New York: Reynald & Hitchcock, 1947. (e) Montreal: Boréal, 1993, Boréal Compact series no. 50. (f) trans. Alan Brown. Toronto: McClelland & Stewart, 1989, New Canadian Library series.

La Petite Poule d'Eau, fiction. (a) Montreal: Beauchemin, 1950. (b) Paris: Flammarion, 1951. (c) *Where Nests the Water Hen*, trans. Harry L. Binsse. Toronto: McClelland & Stewart, 1951. (d) New York: Harcourt Brace & Co., 1951. (e) Montreal: Boréal, 1993, Boréal Compact series no. 48. (f) Toronto: McClelland & Stewart, 1989, New Canadian Library series.

Alexandre Chenevert, fiction. (a) Montreal: Beauchemin, 1954. (b) Paris: Flammarion, 1955 [under the title *Alexandre Chenevert, caissier*]. (c) *The Cashier*, trans. Harry L. Binsse, Toronto: McClelland & Stewart, 1955. (d) New York: Harcourt Brace & Co., 1955. (e) Montreal, Boréal, 1995, Boréal Compact

series no. 62. (f) Toronto: McClelland & Stewart, 1990, New Canadian
Library series.

Rue Deschambault, fiction. (a) Montreal: Beauchemin, 1955. (b) Paris:
Flammarion, 1955. (c) *Street of Riches*, trans. Harry L. Binsse. Toronto:
McClelland & Stewart, 1957. (d) New York: Harcourt Brace & Co., 1957.
(e) Montreal: Boréal, 1993, Boréal Compact series no. 46. (f) Toronto:
McClelland & Stewart, 1991, New Canadian Library series.

La Montagne secrète, fiction. (a) Montreal: Beauchemin, 1961. (b) Paris:
Flammarion, 1962. (c) *The Hidden Mountain*, trans. Harry L. Binsse. Toronto:
McClelland & Stewart, 1962. (d) New York: Harcourt Brace & World, 1962.
(e) Montreal: Boréal, 1994, Boréal Compact series no. 53. (f) Toronto:
McClelland & Stewart, 1974, New Canadian Library series.

La Route d'Altamont, fiction. (a) Montreal: Éditions HMH, 1966, L'Arbre series no.
10. (b) Paris: Flammarion, 1967. (c) *The Road Past Altamont*, trans. Joyce
Marshall. Toronto: McClelland & Stewart, 1966. (d) New York: Harcourt
Brace & World, 1966. (e) Montreal: Boréal, 1993, Boréal Compact series no.
47. (f) Toronto: McClelland & Stewart, 1989, New Canadian Library series.

La Rivière sans repos, fiction [novel preceded by three "Eskimo stories"]. (a)
Montreal: Beauchemin, 1970. (b) Paris: Flammarion, 1972. (c) *Windflower*,
trans. Joyce Marshall. Toronto: McClelland & Stewart, 1970 [novel alone
without the "Eskimo stories"]. (e) Montreal: Boréal, 1995, Boréal Compact
series no. 63. (f) Toronto: McClelland & Stewart, 1991, New Canadian Library
series.

Cet été qui chantait. (a) Quebec City: Éditions Françaises, 1972 [illustrations by
Guy Lemieux]. (c) and (f) *Enchanted Summer*, trans. Joyce Marshall.
Toronto: McClelland & Stewart, 1976. (e) Montreal: Boréal, 1993, Boréal
Compact series no. 45.

Un jardin au bout du monde, short stories. (a) Montreal: Beauchemin, 1975.
(c) *Garden in the Wind*, trans. Alan Brown. Toronto: McClelland & Stewart,
1977. (e) Montreal, Boréal, 1994, Boréal Compact series no. 54. (f) Toronto:
McClelland & Stewart, 1989, New Canadian Library series.

Ma vache Bossie, children's literature. (a) Montreal: Leméac, 1976 [with illustrations by Louise Pomminville]. (c) and (f) *My Cow Bossie*, trans. Alan Brown.
Toronto: McClelland & Stewart, 1988 [with same illustrations as Leméac
edition]. (e) In *Contes pour enfants*. Montreal: Boréal, 1998.

Ces enfants de ma vie, fiction. (a) Montreal: Stanké, 1977. (b) Paris: Éditions de
Fallois, 1994 [preface by Yves Beauchemin]. (c) and (f) *Children of My Heart*,
trans. Alan Brown. Toronto: McClelland & Stewart, 1979. (e) Montreal:
Boréal, 1993, Boréal Compact series no. 49.

Fragiles Lumières de la terre, selected non-fiction texts 1942-1970. (a) Montreal:
Quinze, 1978, Prose entière series. (c) and (f) *The Fragile Lights of Earth*,
trans. Alan Brown. Toronto: McClelland & Stewart, 1982. (e) Montreal:
Boréal, 1996, Boréal Compact series no. 77.

Courte-Queue, children's literature. (a) Montreal: Stanké, 1979 [illustrations by
François Olivier]. (c) and (f) *Cliptail*, trans. Alan Brown. Toronto:
McClelland & Stewart, 1980 [with same illustrations as Stanké edition].
(e) In *Contes pour enfants*. Montreal: Boréal, 1998.

De quoi t'ennuies-tu, Éveline?, novella. (a) Montreal: Éditions du Sentier, 1982
[wood engraving and calligraphies by Martin Dufour]. (e) Montreal: Boréal,
1988, Boréal Compact series no. 8 [followed by *Ély! Ély! Ély!*].

La Détresse et l'Enchantement, autobiography. (a) Montreal: Boréal, 1984. (b) Paris:
Arléa, 1986 [preface by Jean-Claude Guillebaud]. (c) and (f) *Enchantment
and Sorrow*, trans. Patricia Claxton. Toronto: Lester & Orpen Dennys, 1987.
(e) Montreal: Boréal, 1988, Boréal Compact series no. 7.

L'Espagnole et la Pékinoise, children's literature. (a) Montreal: Boréal, 1986 [illus-
trations by Jean-Yves Ahern]. (c) and (f) *The Tortoiseshell and the Pekinese*,
trans. Patricia Claxton. Toronto: Doubleday Canada, 1989 [with same illustrations as Boréal edition]. (e) In *Contes pour enfants*. Montreal: Boréal, 1998.

Ma chère petite soeur, letters to Bernadette 1943-1970 [edited by François Ricard].
(a) and (e) Montreal: Boréal, 1988; (c) and (f) *Letters to Bernadette*, trans.
Patricia Claxton. Toronto: Lester & Orpen Dennys, 1990.

Le temps qui m'a manqué, sequel to *La Détresse et l'Enchantement* [edited by
François Ricard, Dominique Fortier, and Jane Everett]. (a) and (e) Montreal:
Boréal, 1997.

Contes pour enfants [*Ma Vache Bossie, Courte-Queue, L'espagnole et la Pékinoise,
L'Empereur des bois*]. (a) and (e) Montreal: Boréal, 1998 [with illustrations by
Nicole Lafond].

2. Newspapers, Periodicals, Collective Works

The following abbreviations are used in this section: LJ: Le Jour, *Montreal; RM:* La
Revue moderne, *Montreal; BdA:* Le Bulletin des agriculteurs, *Montreal.*

1926

"La survivance française." *La Liberté*, St-Boniface (15 December 1926) [prize-winning French composition].

1927

"À l'oeuvre!" *Bulletin de la Ligue des institutrices catholiques de l'Ouest*, St-Boniface (November 1927) [prize-winning French composition under the pen name Ardor].

1934

"The Jarvis Murder Case. By Gabrielle Roy, St. Boniface, Man. A Prize-Winning Short, Short Story." *The Free Press*, Winnipeg (12 January 1934) [short story].

1936

"La grotte de la mort." *Le Samedi*, Montreal (23 May 1936) [short story].
"Cent pour cent d'amour." *Le Samedi*, Montreal (31 October 1936) [short story].
"Jean-Baptiste Takes a Wife." *The Toronto Star Weekly*, Toronto (19 December 1936) [short story in English; see "Bonne à marier," June 1940].

1938

"Lettre de Londres. Choses vues en passant." *La Liberté et le Patriote*, St-Boniface (27 July 1938) [brief article].
"Lettre de Londres. Si près de Londres . . . si loin . . ." *La Liberté et le Patriote*, St-Boniface (5 October 1938) [brief article; see "Une grande personnalité anglaise," December 1938; and "La Maison du Canada," August 1939].
"Lettre de Londres. Londres à Land's End." *La Liberté et le Patriote*, St-Boniface (12 October 1938) [brief article].
"Les derniers nomades." *Je suis partout*, Paris (21 October 1938) [article].
"Lettre de Londres. Les jolis coins de Londres." *La Liberté et le Patriote*, St-Boniface (21 December 1938) [brief article].
"Une grande personnalité anglaise. Lady Francis Ryner." [sic] *Le Devoir*, Montreal (29 December 1938) [brief article; repeats part of "Lettre de Londres. Si près de Londres . . . si loin . . ." (5 October 1938)].
"Winnipeg Girl Visits Bruges." *The Northwest Review*, Winnipeg (29 December 1938) [brief article in English; repeats part of "Lettre de Londres. Choses vues en passant" (27 July 1938)].
"Noëls canadiens-français." *Je suis partout*, Paris (30 December 1938) [article].

1939

"Amusante hospitalité." *LJ* (6 May 1939) [brief article].
"Les logeuses de Montreal." *LJ* (20 May 1939) [brief article].
"Aperçus. Chacun sa vérité." *LJ* (27 May 1939) [brief article].
"Le week-end en Angleterre." *LJ* (3 June 1939) [brief article].
"Les chats de Londres." *LJ* (10 June 1939) [brief article].

"L'heure du thé en Angleterre." *LJ* (17 June 1939) [brief article].

"Nous et les ruines." *LJ* (24 June 1939) [brief article].

"Strictement pour les monsieurs . . . Un petit conseil." *LJ* (1 July 1939) [brief article].

"Ces chapeaux." *LJ* (8 July 1939) [brief article].

"L'instinct nomade même chez les Anglais." *LJ* (8 July 1939) [brief article].

"Quelques jolis coins de Montréal." *LJ* (22 July 1939) [brief article].

"Parmi ceux qui font la traversée." *LJ* (29 July 1939) [brief article].

"Histoire de France. Chez les paysans du Languedoc." *Paysana*, Montreal (August 1939) [article].

"La 'Maison du Canada'. " *La Revue populaire*, Montreal (August 1939) [article; repeats part of "Lettre de Londres. Si près de Londres . . . si loin . . ." (5 October 1938)].

"Les pigeons de Londres." *LJ* (5 August 1939) [brief article].

"Douce Angleterre." *LJ* (2 August 1939) [brief article].

"Comment nous sommes restés français au Manitoba." *Je suis partout*, Paris (18 August 1939) [article].

"Encore sur le sujet de l'hospitalité anglaise." *LJ* (19 August 1939) [brief article].

"La cuisine de madame Smith." *LJ* (9 September 1939) [brief article].

"La conversion des O'Connor." *RM* (September 1939) [short story].

"Le petit déjeuner parisien." *LJ* (30 September 1939) [brief article].

"Le monde à l'envers." *RM* (October 1939) [short story].

"Ceux dont on se passerait volontiers au cinéma." *LJ* (7 October 1939) [brief article].

"The Meet." *LJ* (14 October 1939) [brief article].

"Une trouvaille parisienne." *LJ* (21 Octobre 1939) [brief article].

"Londres à Land's End." *RM* (November 1939) [article; repeat of "Lettre de Londres. Londres à Land's End" (12 October 1938)].

"L'Anglaise amoureuse." *LJ* (4 November 1939) [brief article].

"Si on faisait la même chose au parc Lafontaine." *LJ* (11 November 1939) [brief article].

"En vagabondant dans le Midi de la France. Ramatuelle à Hyères." *LJ* (2 December 1939) [brief article].

"Le théâtre sans femmes." *LJ* (16 December 1939) [brief article].

"Noël chez les colons ukrainiens." *LJ* (30 December 1939) [brief article].

1940

"Une messe en Provence." *LJ* (27 January 1940) [brief article].

"Cendrillon '40." *RM* (February 1940) [short story].

"Nikolai Suliz." *LJ* (3 February 1940) [short story].

"De la triste Loulou à son amie Mimi." *LJ* (17 February 1940) [brief article].

"Une histoire d'amour." *RM* (March 1940) [short story].

"Ce que j'ai surtout aimé à Londres: les passants." *LJ* (2 March 1940) [brief article].

"L'hospitalité parisienne." *LJ* (16 March 1940) [brief article].

"Le roi de coeur." *RM* (April 1940) [short story].

"Gérard le pirate." *RM* (May 1940) [short story].

"Bonne à marier." *RM* (June 1940) [short story; French version of "Jean-Baptiste Takes a Wife" (December 1936)].

"Où en est Saint-Boniface?" *La Revue populaire*, Montreal (September 1940) [article].

"Avantage pour." *RM* (October 1940) [short story].

"Les petits pas de Caroline." *BdA* (October 1940) [short story].

"La dernière pêche." *RM* (November 1940) [short story].

"La belle aventure de la Gaspésie." *BdA* (November 1940) [feature article].

"Un Noël en route." *RM* (December 1940) [short story].

"Le joli miracle." *BdA* (December 1940) [short story under the pen name Aline Lubac].

1941

"La fuite de Sally." *BdA* (January 1941) [short story under the pen name Aline Lubac].

"Mort d'extrême vieillesse." *BdA* (February 1941) [feature article on the seigneurial régime].

"La ferme, grande industrie." *BdA* (March 1941) [feature article].

"La sonate à l'aurore." *RM* (March 1941) [short story].

"Nos agriculteurs céramistes." *BdA* (April 1941) [feature article].

"Le régime seigneurial au Canada français." *Aujourd'hui*, Montreal (April 1941) [repeat of "Mort d'extrême vieillesse" (February 1941)].

"À O.K.K.O." *RM* (April 1941) [short story].

"Une ménagerie scientifique." *RM* (May 1941) [feature article on a laboratory at the Université de Montréal].

"Tout Montréal [1]. Les deux Saint-Laurent." *BdA* (June 1941) [feature article].

"Tout Montréal [2]. Est-Ouest." *BdA* (July 1941) [feature article].

"Six pilules par jour." *RM* (July 1941) [short story].

"Tout Montréal [3]. Du port aux banques." *BdA* (August 1941) [feature article; republished in Nathalie Fredette, *Montréal en prose 1892-1992: anthologie*. Montreal: Hexagone, 1992].

"Un homme et sa volonté." *BdA* (August 1941) [feature article on J.-A. Forand].

"Tout Montréal [4]. Après trois cents ans." *BdA* (September 1941) [feature article].

"La côte de tous les vents." *BdA* (October 1941) [feature article on the North Shore].

"Vive l'Expo!" *BdA* (October 1941) [feature article on the Quebec agricultural exhibition].

"Embobeliné." *RM* (Octobre 1941) [short story; sequel to "Six pilules par jour" (July 1941)].

"Heureux les nomades." *BdA* (November 1941) [feature article on the Montagnais of Sept-îles].

"Ici l'Abitibi [1]. La terre secourable." *BdA* (November 1941) [feature article].

"Ici l'Abitibi [2]. Le pain et le feu." *BdA* (December 1941) [feature article].

1942

"Ici l'Abitibi [3]. Le chef de district." *BdA* (January 1942) [feature article].

"Ici l'Abitibi [4]. Plus que le pain." *BdA* (February 1942) [feature article].

"Ici l'Abitibi [5]. Pitié pour les institutrices!" *BdA* (March 1942) [feature article].

"Ici l'Abitibi [6]. Bourgs d'Amérique I." *BdA* (April 1942) [feature article].

"Ici l'Abitibi [7]. Bourgs d'Amérique II." *BdA* (May 1942) [feature article].

"La grande voyageuse." *RM* (May 1942) [short story].

"Peuples du Canada [1]. Le plus étonnant: les Huttérites." *BdA* (November 1942) [feature article; republished in *Fragiles Lumières de la terre*, 1978 ("The Hutterites" in *The Fragile Lights of Earth*, 1982)].

"Vers l'Alaska. Laissez passer les jeeps." *Le Canada*, Montreal (24 November 1942) [feature article].

"Peuples du Canada [2]. Turbulents chercheurs de paix." *BdA* (December 1942) [feature article on the Doukhobors; republished in *Fragiles Lumières de la terre*, 1978 ("Turbulent Seekers After Peace" in *The Fragile Lights of Earth*, 1982)].

"Regards sur l'ouest [1]. Si l'on croit aux voyages. . . ." *Le Canada*, Montreal (7 December 1942) [feature article].

"Regards sur l'ouest [2]. Notre blé." *Le Canada*, Montreal (21 December 1942) [feature article].

1943

"Peuples du Canada [3]. Femmes de dur labeur." *BdA* (January 1943) [feature article on the Mennonites; republished in *Fragiles Lumières de la terre*, 1978, under the title "Les Mennonites" ("The Mennonites" in *The Fragile Lights of Earth*, 1982)].

"Regards sur l'ouest [3]. Les battages." *Le Canada*, Montreal (5 January 1943) [feature article].

"Regards sur l'ouest [4]. Après les battages." *Le Canada*, Montreal (16 January 1943) [feature article].

"Peuples du Canada [4]. L'avenue Palestine." *BdA* (January 1943) [feature article on a Jewish colony in Saskatchewan; republished in *Fragiles Lumières de la terre*, 1978 ("Palestine Avenue" in *The Fragile Lights of Earth*, 1982)].

"La vieille fille." *BdA* (February 1943) [novella under the pen name Aline Lubac, presented as a "complete novel"].

"Peuples du Canada [5]. De Prague à Good Soil." *BdA* (March 1943) [feature article on the Sudeten colonists; republished in *Fragiles Lumières de la terre*, 1978, under the title "Les Sudètes de Good Soil" ("The Sudeten Germans of Good Soil" in *The Fragile Lights of Earth*, 1982)].

"Peuples du Canada [6]. Ukraine." *BdA* (April 1943) [feature article; republished in *Fragiles Lumières de la terre*, 1978, under the title "Petite Ukraine" ("Little Ukraine" in *The Fragile Lights of Earth*, 1982)].

"Peuples du Canada [7]. Les gens de chez nous." *BdA* (May 1943) [feature article on the French-Canadian colonists of Alberta].

"La grande Berthe." *BdA* (June 1943) [novella; presented as a "complete novel"].
"La pension de vieillesse." *BdA* (November 1943) [short story].

1944

"Horizons du Québec [1]. La prodigieuse aventure de la compagnie d'aluminium." *BdA* (January 1944) [feature article on the town of Arvida and the Alcan company].
"Horizons du Québec [2]. Le pays du Saguenay: son âme et son visage." *BdA* (February 1944) [feature article].
"Horizons du Québec [3]. L'Île-aux-Coudres." *BdA* (March 1944) [feature article].
"Horizons du Québec [4]. Un jour je naviguerai. . . ." *BdA* (April 1944) [feature article on Petite-Rivière-Saint-François].
"Horizons du Québec [5]. Une voile dans la nuit." *BdA* (May 1944) [feature article on the fishermen of the Gaspé; republished in *Fragiles Lumières de la terre*, 1978 ("A Sail in the Night" in *The Fragile Lights of Earth*, 1982)].
"François et Odine." *BdA* (June 1944) [short story under the pen name Danny].
"Horizons du Québec [6]. Allons, gai, au marché." *BdA* (Octobre 1944) [feature article on market gardening near Montreal].
"Horizons du Québec [7]. Physionomie des Cantons de l'Est." *BdA* (November 1944) [feature article on the Eastern Townships].
"Horizons du Québec [8]. L'accent durable." *BdA* (December 1944) [feature article on the growing Francophone communities in the Eastern Townships].

1945

"Horizons du Québec [9]. Le carrousel industriel des Cantons de l'Est." *BdA* (February 1945) [feature article on industrial development in the Eastern Townships (part one)].
"La vallée Houdou." *Amérique française*, Montreal (February 1945) [short story; republished in *Un jardin au bout du monde*, 1975 ("Hoodoo Valley" in *Garden in the Wind*, 1977)].
"Horizons du Québec [10]. Le carrousel industriel des Cantons de l'Est (deuxième partie)." *BdA* (March 1945) [feature article on industrial development in the Eastern Townships (part two)].
"Horizons du Québec [11]. L'appel de la forêt." *BdA* (April 1945) [feature article on a lumber camp].
"Horizons du Québec [12]. Le long, long voyage." *BdA* (May 1945) [feature article on log driving].
"Qui est Claudia?" *BdA* (May 1945) [novella under the pen name Danny, presented as a "complete novel"].
"La magie du coton." *BdA* (September 1945) [feature article on the cotton industry].
"La forêt canadienne s'en va-t'aux presses." *BdA* (October 1945) [feature article on the paper industry].
"Dans la vallée de l'or." *BdA* (November 1945) [feature article on the mining industry in northwestern Quebec].

1946

"Un vagabond frappe à notre porte." *Amérique française*, Montreal (January 1946)
[short story, published in English translation under the title "The Vagabond"
in *Mademoiselle*, New York (May 1948); republished in *Un jardin au bout du
monde*, 1975 ("A Tramp at the Door" in *Garden in the Wind*, 1977)].
"La source au désert." *BdA* (October 1946 and November 1946) [short story].

1947

"How I Found the People of St. Henri." *Wings, the Literary Guild Review*, New
York (May 1947); translated into French by M. Fisher as "Ma rencontre avec
les gens de Saint-Henri." *Cahiers franco-canadiens de l'Ouest*, St-Boniface,
1996].
"Feuilles mortes / Dead Leaves." *Maclean's*, Toronto (1 June 1947) [short story;
simultaneous publication in French and English; French version republished
in *La Revue de Paris*, Paris (January 1948)].
"La lune des moissons." *RM* (September 1947) [short story].
"Security." *Maclean's*, Toronto (15 September 1947) [short story; translation of
"Sécurité" (March 1948)].

1948

"Réponse de Mlle Gabrielle Roy." Société royale du Canada (Section française),
*Présentation de M. Léon Lorrain, Mlle Gabrielle Roy, M. Clément Marchand,
M. Maurice Lebel*, Ottawa (academic year 1947-1948) [acceptance speech; the
text also appeared under two other titles: "*Bonheur d'occasion* aujourd'hui,"
BdA (January 1948); and "Retour à Saint-Henri" in *Fragiles Lumières de la
terre*, 1978 ("Return to Saint-Henri" in *The Fragile Lights of Earth*); the speech
was also taken down in shorthand and published in five segments in succes-
sive issues of the magazine *Combat*, Montreal (1, 8, 15, 29 November and 6
December 1947)].
"La justice en Danaca et ailleurs." *Les oeuvres libres*, Paris, no. 23 (1948) [short
story].
"Sécurité." *RM* (March 1948) [short story; original French-language version of
"Security" (September 1947)].

1951

"Sainte-Anne-la-Palud." *La Nouvelle Revue canadienne*, Ottawa (April-May 1951)
[feature article; republished in *Fragiles Lumières de la terre*, 1978
("Saint-Anne-la-Palud" in *The Fragile Lights of Earth*, 1982)].

1952

"La Camargue." *Amérique française*, Montreal (May-June 1952) [feature article;
republished in *Fragiles Lumières de la terre*, 1978 ("The Camargue" in *The
Fragile Lights of Earth*, 1982)].

1954

"Souvenirs du Manitoba." *Mémoires de la Société royale du Canada*, 3rd Series, vol 48, June 1954 [autobiographical essay; versions with slight variations published in: *La Revue de Paris*, Paris, (February 1955); *Les Cloches de Saint-Boniface*, St-Boniface (1 August 1955); and *Le Devoir*, Montreal (15 November 1955)].

1956

"Comment j'ai reçu le Fémina." *Le Devoir*, Montreal (15 December 1956) [speech in response to the awarding of the Prix Duvernay; republished in *Fragiles Lumières de la terre*, 1978 ("How I Received the Fémina" in *The Fragile Lights of Earth*, 1982)].

"Préface" to a school edition of *La Petite Poule d'Eau*. Toronto: Clarke Irwin & Co., 1956. Edited and with an introduction by R. W. Torrens.

1957

"Préface" to a school edition of *La Petite Poule d'Eau*. London: George G. Harrap & Co., 1957. With an introduction and notes by J. Marks [republished in a deluxe edition of *La Petite Poule d'Eau*. Paris: Éditions du Burin et Martinsart, Les portes de la vie series, special *Canada* volume, 1967; subsequently in *Fragiles Lumières de la terre*, 1978, under the title "Mémoire et création" ("Memory and Creation" in *The Fragile Lights of Earth*, 1982)].

1960

"Grand-mère et la poupée." *Châtelaine*, Montreal (October 1960) [the translation by Joyce Marshall appeared simultaneously in the magazine's Toronto edition, *Chatelaine*, under the title "Grandmother and the Doll"; translation republished in Robert Weaver, ed., *Ten for Wednesday Night*. Toronto: McClelland & Stewart, 1961].

1962

"Quelques réflexions sur la littérature canadienne d'expression française." *Quartier latin*, Montreal (27 February 1962) [essay; republished in André Brochu, ed., *La Littérature par elle-même*, Montreal, Cahiers de l'AGEUM, no. 2, 1962].

"Les 'terres nouvelles' de Jean-Paul Lemieux." *Vie des arts*, Montreal (no. 29, Winter 1962) [essay].

"Le Manitoba." *Le Magazine Maclean*, Montreal (July 1962) [feature article; republished in *Fragiles Lumières de la terre*, 1978 ("Manitoba" in *The Fragile Lights of Earth*, 1982)].

"Sister Finance." *Maclean's*, Toronto (December 1962) [short story; translation of "Ma cousine économe" (August 1963)].

1963

"Ma vache." *Terre et Foyer*, Quebec City (July-August 1963) [children's story; republished as an illustrated children's book under the title *Ma vache Bossie*, 1976 (*My Cow Bossie*, 1988); and in *Contes pour enfants*, 1998)].

"Ma cousine économe." *Le Magazine Maclean*, Montreal (August 1963) [short story; original French-language version of "Sister Finance" (December 1962)].

"[Témoignage sur le roman]," in Paul Wyczynski, Bernard Julien, Jean Ménard and Réjean Robidoux (eds.), *Archives des lettres canadiennes*, Vol. III: *Le Roman canadien-français*. Montreal: Fides, 1963 [essay].

1967

"Le thème raconté par Gabrielle Roy / The Theme Unfolded by Gabrielle Roy," in *Terre des hommes / Man and His World* (trans. J. Marshall). Montreal and Toronto: Canadian Corporation for the World Exhibition, 1967 [essay; republished in full in *Fragiles Lumières de la terre*, 1978 (trans. A. Brown, under the title "Man and His World: A Telling of the Theme" in *The Fragile Lights of Earth*, 1982)].

"Préface." In *René Richard, oeuvres inédites*, exhibition catalogue. Quebec City: Musée du Québec, 1967 [essay].

1969

"Germaine Guèvremont, 1900-1968." *Mémoires de la Société royale du Canada*, Ottawa, 4th Series, vol. 7, 1969 [autobiographical essay; republished in *Études françaises*, Montreal (Winter 1997-1998)]

1970

"Mon héritage du Manitoba." *Mosaic*, Winnipeg (Spring 1970) [autobiographical essay; republished in *Fragiles Lumières de la terre*, 1978 ("My Manitoba Heritage" in *The Fragile Lights of Earth*, 1982)].

"L'arbre." *Cahiers de l'Académie canadienne-française*, no. 13: *Versions*. Montreal: 1970 [short story].

1973

"Jeux du romancier et des lecteurs" [excerpts], in Marc Gagné, 1973 [essay; speech to the members of the Alliance française de Montréal in December 1955].

"[Lettre à Judith Jasmin, 1972]." *Châtelaine*, Montreal (May 1973).

1974

"Le pays de *Bonheur d'occasion*." *Le Devoir*, Montreal (18 May 1974) [autobiographical essay; republished in Robert Guy Scully (ed.), *Morceaux du grand Montréal*. Montreal: Noroît, 1978].

1976

"Voyage en Ungava" [excerpts], in Marc Gagné, 1976 [essay].

"Mes études à Saint-Boniface." Text remains unpublished in French. ["My Schooldays in St-Boniface," trans. Alan Brown, was published under the title "The Disparate Treasures of a Young Girl Who Came from Deschambault Street." *Globe and Mail*, Toronto (18 December 1976).

1977

"A Note to the Editor." In Gary Geddes (ed.), *Divided We Stand*. Toronto: Peter Martin Associates, 1977 [letter].

1979

"Ély! Ély! Ély!" *Liberté*, Montreal (no. 123, May-June 1979) [short story].

"Lettre [. . .] à ses amis de l'ALCQ" [Association des littératures canadienne et québécoise]. *Studies in Canadian Literature*, Fredericton (1979).

1980

"Le Cercle Molière . . . porte ouverte." In Lionel Dorge, 1980 [autobiographical essay].

1984

"L'empereur des bois." *Études littéraires*, Quebec City (Winter 1984) [children's story; republished in *Contes pour enfants*. Montreal: Boréal, 1998].

1986

"[Lettres à Gabrielle Poulin (1977-1978) et à Annette Saint-Pierre (1970-1977)]." *Revue d'histoire littéraire du Québec et du Canada français*, Ottawa (no. 12, 1986).

1987

"Letters from Gabrielle Roy to Margaret Laurence." Edited by John Lennox, *Canadian Woman Studies / Cahiers de la femme*, Toronto (Autumn).

1988

"[Letters to W. A. Deacon (1946-1961)]." In John Lennox and Michèle Lacombe, 1988.

1991

"La légende du cerf ancien." Edited and with an introduction by François Ricard. *Cahiers franco-canadiens de l'Ouest*, St-Boniface (Spring 1991) [short story written about 1938].

"[Lettres à Tony Tascona (1963) et Antoine Gaborieau (1980)]." Ibid.

"Rose *en* Maria." *Elle-Québec*, Montreal (March 1991) [short story written about
　　1948].

1996

"[Lettre à Julien Hébert, 1976]." *Liberté*, Montreal (no. 223, February 1996).
"Ma petite rue qui m'a menée autour du monde." Edited and with an introduction
　　by François Ricard. *Littératures*, Montreal (McGill University, no. 14, 1996)
　　[autobiographical essay written about 1977].
"[Lettre à Marie Grenier-Francoeur, 1976]." In A. Fauchon (ed.), *Colloque interna-
　　tionale Gabrielle Roy*. Winnipeg: Presses universitaires de Saint-Boniface,
　　1996, p. 244.

1997

"Quatre lettres inédites de Gabrielle Roy [à Marcel Carbotte]." Edited and with an
　　introduction by Sophie Marcotte. *Études françaises*, Montreal (Winter 1997-
　　1998) [four unpublished letters from Gabrielle Roy to Marcel Carbotte].

II. Archives, Unpublished Manuscripts, Correspondence

1. "Gabrielle Roy Papers" (MSS 1982-11/1986-11) and "Gabrielle Roy and Marcel Carbotte Papers" (MSS 1990-17), Literary Manuscript Collection, National Library of Canada, Ottawa (NLC)

These two sets of papers contain all the archives preserved by Gabrielle Roy and
her husband; they have been one of the principal sources for this biography. They
include the working papers for most of the books published by Gabrielle Roy
(manuscripts, typewritten copies, corrected proofs, and translation manuscripts);
copies of her texts from various sources; official letters, press clippings, photographs, financial documents; various other personal papers; and three other types
of especially valuable documents:
(a) correspondence, contracts, and royalty statements documenting arrangements
　　between Gabrielle Roy (or Jean-Marie Nadeau as her representative) and her
　　publishers;
(b) almost all the unpublished manuscripts left by Gabrielle Roy, comprising
　　short stories, novels (including "La Saga d'Éveline"), dramatic texts, auto-
　　biographical writings (including the sequel to *La Détresse et l'Enchantement*),
　　accounts of her some of her travels, public addresses; for a description,
　　see F. Ricard (1992a);
(c) finally and especially, an abundance of personal correspondence, which divides
　　into two large categories:
　　　　i) – a few "complete" sets of correspondence, comprising both letters
　　written by Gabrielle Roy and a certain number of those she received from
　　her correspondent; this is the case with letters she exchanged with her

husband Marcel Carbotte (1947-1979), with her business manager Jean-Marie
Nadeau (1945-1958), and with her sisters Clémence (1947-1983) and
Bernadette (1943-1970);

ii) – "partial" correspondence, consisting only of letters received by
Gabrielle Roy. Of the very large number of her correspondents whose letters
fall into this category, those whose letters are the most numerous or interesting are: Victor Barbeau (1968-1978); Adrienne Choquette (1968-1973);
William Arthur Deacon (1954-1955); Germaine Guèvremont (1961-1967);
Margaret Laurence (1976-1983); Joyce Marshall (1967-1980); Pierre Morency
(1977-1980); Mélina Roy (1943); and Berthe Valcourt (1970-1983).

For a description of these two sets of papers and classification of the documents they contain, see Irma Larouche (1989), Johanne Beaumont (1991) and
F. Ricard (1992b).

2. Marie-Anna A. Roy Papers

This name applies to at least three sets of archives deposited by Adèle, Gabrielle
Roy's sister, in the following institutions: the National Archives of Canada in
Ottawa (NAC, MG30 D99 and 1991-245); the Manitoba Provincial Archives in
Winnipeg (MPA, MG9 A56); and the Archives nationales du Québec in Montreal
(ANQ-Montréal, P83), this last having been transferred to the Bibliothèque
nationale du Québec (BNQ, MSS 014 [Fonds M.-A. A. Roy]).

The papers at the NAC are the most complete and most interesting because
they contain original letters from Gabrielle to Adèle (1943-1954, sometimes annotated or mutilated by Adèle) and also photographs. Otherwise the three sets are
similar, consisting principally of typed copies of Adèle's unpublished writings,
especially those relating her personal history and that of her family. The most
common titles are: "À la lumière du souvenir"; "Journal intime d'une âme solitaire
(Reflet des âmes dans le miroir du passé)"; "En remuant la cendre des foyers
éteints et des coeurs"; "Généalogie des Roy-Landry"; "Les Deux Sources de l'inspiration: l'imagination et le coeur" (under the pen name Irma Deloy); "A vol
d'oiseau à travers le temps et l'espace"; "Otium cum dignitate"; "Grains de sable,
pépites d'or"; "Indulgence et Pardon"; "L'Arbre grandit"; "Les Entraves";
"Surgeons." The content of these unpublished works, with few exceptions, does
not differ appreciably from that of the works published by Adèle under the name
Marie-Anna A. Roy, which are listed in Section III below.

Published or unpublished, Adèle's writings contain valuable information,
although the facts she reports are often slanted by polemic intent.

3. Other Archival Collections

Archives nationales du Québec, Montreal (ANQ-Montréal)
Fonds Judith Jasmin (P143): letters from Gabrielle Roy to Judith Jasmin, 1947-
    1966; talk by J. Jasmin on "Quelques brèves rencontres," 1971.

Archives nationales du Québec, Quebec City (ANQ-Québec)
Fonds Alice Lemieux-Lévesque (P227): letters from Gabrielle Roy to Alice
    Lemieux-Lévesque, 1968-1971.

Archives des Soeurs des Saints Noms de Jésus et de Marie, Académie Saint-
    Joseph, St-Boniface, Manitoba (SSNJM)
Fonds Soeur Berthe Valcourt (FP4): letters from Gabrielle Roy to Berthe Valcourt
    (1970-1983) and to Bernadette (1970).
Fonds Gabrielle Roy (FP3): letters from Gabrielle Roy to members of the commu-
    nity, 1958-1982; press clippings; miscellaneous documents.
Chroniques de l'Académie Saint-Joseph (L7).

Archives des Ursulines, Quebec City
Fonds Gabrielle Roy: letters from Gabrielle Roy to Marguerite and Joseph Hargitay
    (1963-1972) and Thérèse Sasseville (1977); miscellaneous documents.

Bibliothèque nationale du Québec, Montreal (BNQ)
Fonds Victor Barbeau (MSS 411): letters from Gabrielle Roy to Victor Barbeau,
    1968-1977.
Fonds Paul Blouin (MSS 432): letters from Gabrielle Roy to Paul Blouin, 1975-1981.
Fonds Cécile Chabot (MSS 447): letters from Gabrielle Roy to Cécile Chabot,
    1949-1973.

Bishop's University Archives, Lennoxville, Quebec (BUA)
Joyce Marshall Papers: letters from Gabrielle Roy to Joyce Marshall, 1959-1980.

Frères Marianistes de Saint-Boniface, Winnipeg
Dossier Gabrielle Roy: letter from Gabrielle Roy to Brother Joseph Bruns, 1938.

Manitoba Provincial Archives, Winnipeg (MPA)
Department of Education Papers (GR 1628; GR 129A; GR 1231): Half-Yearly
    Returns of Attendance, districts 1188 (St-Boniface) and 964 (St-Louis);
    School Districts Half-Yearly Reports; Normal School Marks.
Winnipeg Little Theatre Papers (MG 10G16 and P390).
Department of Health and Public Welfare Papers (GR 267): Old Age Pension.

McMaster University, William Ready Division of Archives and Research
    Collections, Hamilton, Ontario (MMU)
McClelland & Stewart Limited Papers: letters from Gabrielle Roy to Jack
    McClelland and others, 1957-1980; documents concerning the publication of
    works by Gabrielle Roy in English translation.

National Archives of Canada, Ottawa (NAC)
Jori Smith Papers (MG30 D249): letters from Gabrielle Roy to Jori Smith and Jean
    Palardy, 1946-1973.

Robert Weaver Papers (MG31 D162): letters from Gabrielle Roy to Robert Weaver, 1959, 1978.

National Library of Canada, Ottawa (NLC)
Berthe Simard Papers (MSS 1989-8): letters from Gabrielle Roy to Berthe Simard, 1956-1982.

Jeanne Lapointe Papers (MSS 1990-16): letters from Gabrielle Roy to Jeanne Lapointe, 1948-1955; copy of a typewritten manuscript of *Alexandre Chenevert*.

Éditions Pascal Papers (MSS 1995-11): letters from Gabrielle Roy to Gérard Dagenais (1944-1945) and to Henri Girard (1944); an incomplete typewritten manuscript of *Bonheur d'occasion* and a corrected copy of the first edition.

François Côté Papers (MSS 1994-17): two unpublished texts by Gabrielle Roy (1940) found in the archives of Émile-Charles Hamel.

School Division of St-Boniface, Winnipeg (SDSB)
Gabrielle Roy File: correspondence between Gabrielle Roy and the St-Boniface School Commission, 1929-1938.

Société historique de Saint-Boniface, Winnipeg (SHSB)
Fonds Pauline Boutal (23): letters from Gabrielle Roy to Pauline Boutal, 1948-1951.

Fonds Cercle Molière (25): attendance lists and minutes of meetings, programs, press clippings, miscellaneous documents.

Fonds Marie-Thérèse Goulet-Courchaine (37): letter from Gabrielle Roy to Thérèse Goulet, 1947.

Fonds de l'Association d'éducation des Canadiens français du Manitoba (42): miscellaneous documents.

Université Laval, Division des archives, Québec
Fonds Gérard Dion (p117/10/1): letters from Gabrielle Roy to Gérard Dion, 1968-1969.

Université du Québec à Trois-Rivières, Trois-Rivières (UQTR)
Fonds Adrienne Choquette: letters from Gabrielle Roy to Adrienne Choquette, 1963-1973.

Université de Sherbrooke, Groupe de recherche sur l'édition littéraire au Québec, Sherbrooke
Fonds Éditions du Lévrier, dossier Marie-Anna A. Roy: correspondence and documents concerning the publication of *Le Pain de chez nous*, 1953-1954 (copies provided by Yvan Cloutier).

University of Toronto, Thomas Fischer Rare Books Library, Toronto (UOT)
William Arthur Deacon Collection (MS 160): letters from Gabrielle Roy to W. A. Deacon, 1946-1961; miscellaneous documents.

York University Archives and Special Collections, Toronto (YUT)
Margaret Laurence Papers: letters from Gabrielle Roy to Margaret Laurence, 1976-1980.

4. Private Collections

Fonds Gabrielle Roy, Montreal (FGR)
Dossiers Gabrielle Roy: Gabrielle Roy's income tax declarations and other financial documents; publishing contracts and business correspondence; will; miscellaneous documents.
Dossier Madeleine Bergeron et Madeleine Chassé: letters from Gabrielle Roy to the Madeleines, 1954-1979.
Dossier John Helliwell: letters from Gabrielle Roy to Renée Deniset, 1934-1942.
Dossier Antoine Sirois: letters from Gabrielle Roy to A. Sirois, 1963-1969.

Gabrielle Roy letters and other documents conserved by individuals
Ellen R. Babby (Washington): letter, 1982.
Simone and Pierre Boutin (Quebec City): letters, 1973-1979.
André Brochu (Montreal): letters, 1961-1980; manuscript.
Simone Bussières (Quebec City): letters, 1954-1978.
Richard M. Chadbourne (Calgary): letter, 1978.
Léonie Guyot (Winnipeg): letters, 1937-1945; an unpublished text (1934); miscellaneous documents.
Réal Jubinville (Hull, Que.): letters to Éliane Landry (1924-1943), to Léa Landry (1926-1981), and to Céline Jubinville (1979); letters from Mélina Roy to Éliane Landry (1922).
André Major (Montreal): letters, 1975-1981.
Eugénie Miko (Quebec): letters, 1968-1969.
Pierre Morency (Quebec): letters, 1974-1979; manuscript; miscellaneous documents.
François Ricard (Montreal): letters, 1973-1983; manuscripts; photographs; miscellaneous documents.
Yolande Roy-Cyr (Aylmer): letters to Antonia Houde-Roy (1968-1981); file concerning the publication of the text on "Terre des hommes / Man and His World" in 1967.
Jean Royer (Montreal): letter, 1983.
Ben-Z. Shek (Toronto): letters, 1970-1978; file on the story of Adèle's accusatory manuscript (1968-1969).
Paul G. Socken (Waterloo): letters, 1976-1980.
Jeannette Urbas (Toronto): letters, 1969-1982.
Pierre Vadeboncoeur (Montreal): letters, 1979.
Mel Yoken (New Bedford): letters, 1969-1981.

III. Books, Articles, Interviews

An asterisk indicates an entry containing remarks by or an interview with Gabrielle Roy. Systematic bibliographies on Gabrielle Roy and her works will be found in the following entries listed below: Gagné (1973), Ricard (1975), Socken (1979), Chadbourne (1984), and Saint-Martin (1998), and also in the articles on Gabrielle Roy's works contained in Volumes III to VI of the Dictionnaire des oeuvres littéraires du Québec *(Montreal, Fides, 1982-1994).*

* A.S.P. [Annette Saint-Pierre] (1970). "Gabrielle Roy au Manitoba." *Populo*, St-Boniface (November).

* Allaire, Émilia B. (1960). "Notre grande romancière: Gabrielle Roy." *L'Action catholique*. Quebec City (5 June).

Allaire, Émilia B. (1963). "Gabrielle Roy, première femme à la Société royale du Canada." In *Têtes de femmes: essais biographiques*. Quebec City: Éditions de l'Équinoxe.

* Ambrière, Francis (1947). "Gabrielle Roy, écrivain canadien." *Revue de Paris*, Paris (December).

* Anonymous (1947). "People Who Read and Write." *New York Times Book Review* (1 June).

* Audemar, Marguerite (1948). "Gabrielle Roy, romancière canadienne." *Eaux vives*, Paris (February).

* Avard, Lucille (1961). "Gabrielle Roy a lu Homère et part pour la Grèce." *La Presse*, Montreal (2 September).

Bahuaud, Cécile and France Lemay (1985). *Femmes de chez nous*. St-Boniface: Éditions du Blé.

Beauchamp, Colette (1992). *Judith Jasmin de feu et de flamme*. Montreal: Boréal.

* Beaudry, Pauline (1968-1969). "Répondre à l'appel intérieur." *Terre et Foyer*, Quebec City (December-January).

Beaulieu, André and Jean Hamelin (1982). *La Presse québécoise des origines à nos jours*, Vol. v: *1911-1919*. Quebec City: Presses de l'Université Laval.

Beaumont, Johanne (1991). *Fonds Gabrielle Roy et Marcel Carbotte 1990-17: Instrument de recherche*. Ottawa: National Library of Canada.

Benazon, Michael (to be published). "Gabrielle Roy's Montreal Years." In "Charting Their Territories: Montreal Writers and Their City" (manuscript transmitted by the author).

Bernier, T[homas]-Alfred (1887). *Le Manitoba, champ d'immigration*. Ottawa: self-published.

* Bessette, Gérard (1968). "Interview avec Gabrielle Roy." In *Une littérature en ébullition*. Montréal: Éditions du Jour [interview conducted in 1965].

Blay, Jacqueline (1987). *L'Article 23, les péripéties législatives et juridiques du fait français au Manitoba 1870-1986*. St-Boniface: Éditions du Blé.

Booth, Philip (1989). *The Montreal Repertory Theatre, 1930-1961: A History and Handlist of Production*. Master's Thesis, McGill University, Montreal.

* Bourbonnais, Marie (1947). "La femme du mois: Mme Gabrielle Roy." *Pour vous Madame*, Montreal (November-December).

Boutal, Pauline (1985). "Le théâtre laïque à Saint-Boniface et àWinnipeg, 1909-1929: le Cercle Molière, 1925-1974." In L. Dorge (1985).

Brandt, Yvette (1980). *Memories of Lorne, 1880-1980*. Somerset, Manitoba, The Municipality of Lorne.

Brown, Craig (ed.) (1987). *The Illustrated History of Canada*. Toronto: Lester & Orpen Dennys.

* Cameron, Don (1973). "Gabrielle Roy: A Bird in the Prison Window." In *Conversations with Canadian Novelists*, Vol. 2. Toronto: Macmillan (text published first in *Quill & Quire*, Toronto (October 1972) [a literal transcription of this interview is at the NLC].

Cercle Molière (1975). *Le Cercle Molière: 50e anniversaire*. St-Boniface: Éditions du Blé.

Chadbourne, Richard (1984). "Essai bibliographique: cinq ans d'étude sur Gabrielle Roy, 1979-1984." *Études littéraires*, Quebec City (Winter 1984).

Charbonneau, Robert (1972). "Gabrielle Roy." In *Romanciers canadiens*. Quebec City: Presses de l'Université Laval [text read previously on the radio program *Radio-Collège* during the season 1952-1953].

Charland, R.-M. and J.-N. Samson (1967). *Gabrielle Roy*. Montreal: Fides, series Dossiers de documentation sur la littérature canadienne-française.

Charpentier, Fulgence (1983). "Gabrielle Roy ou la condition humaine." *Le Droit*, Ottawa (23 July).

* Cobb, David (1976). "Seasons in the Life of a Novelist: Gabrielle Roy." *The Canadian*, Toronto (1 May).

Dagenais, Gérard (1967). "Gabrielle Roy." In *Nos écrivains et le français 1*. Montreal: Éditions du Jour.

* Dartis, Léon [Henri Girard] (1947). "La genèse de *Bonheur d'occasion*." *La Revue moderne*, Montreal (May).

* Deacon, William Arthur (1947). "Celebrity Hopes Fame Won't Interrupt Work." *Globe and Mail*, Toronto (2 February).

* Delson-Karan, Myrna (1986). "The Last Interview: Gabrielle Roy." *Québec Studies*, Hanover, no. 4 [interview conducted in 1982].

* Desmarchais, Rex (1947). "Gabrielle Roy vous parle d'elle et de son roman." *Bulletin des agriculteurs*, Montreal (May).

Dickason, Tony (1947). "Gabrielle Roy's Own Story Recalled by Sister Here." *Winnipeg Tribune* (1 March) [article based on an interview with Anna, Gabrielle Roy's sister].

Dioudonnat, Pierre-Marie (1973). *"Je suis partout" 1930-1944: les maurrassiens devant la tentation fasciste*. Paris: La Table ronde.

Dioudonnat, Pierre-Marie (1993). *Les 700 rédacteurs de "Je suis partout" 1930-1944: Dictionnaire des écrivains et journalistes qui ont collaboré au "Grand hebdomadaire de la vie mondiale" devenu le principal organe du fascisme français*. Paris: Sedopols.

Dorge, Lionel (1976). *Le Manitoba: reflets d'un passé*. Saint-Boniface: Éditions du Blé.

Dorge, Lionel, ed. (1980). *Chapeau bas, réminiscences de la vie théâtrale et musicale du Manitoba français* (Part One). St-Boniface: Éditions du Blé.

Dorge, Lionel, ed. (1985). *Chapeau bas, réminiscences de la vie théâtrale et musicale du Manitoba français* (Part Two). St-Boniface: Éditions du Blé.

* Dorion, Gilles and Maurice Émond (1979). "Gabrielle Roy." *Québec français*, Quebec City (no. 36, December).

* Duncan, Dorothy (1947). "Le Triomphe de Gabrielle." *Maclean's*, Toronto (15 April).

* Duval, Monique (1956). "Notre entrevue du jeudi: Gabrielle Roy." *L'Événement-Journal*, Quebec City (17 May).

* Elot, Maryse (1947). "Le Prix Fémina à Gabrielle Roy." *Les Nouvelles littéraires*, Paris (4 December).

Ferron, Jacques (1973). "Des sables, un manuscrit." *L'Information médicale et paramédicale*, Montreal (3 July) [article republished in *Du fond de mon arrière-cuisine*. Montreal: Éditions du Jour, 1973].

Frémont, Donatien (1947). "Gabrielle Roy du Manitoba." *Le Canada*, Montreal (26 September).

Frémont, Donatien (1980). *Les Français dans l'Ouest canadien*. St-Boniface: Éditions du Blé.

G.V.R. [Germain Roy] (1954). "Gabrielle Roy: La Petite Misère Comes Into Her Own." *St. Paul's Library Guild Bulletin*, Winnipeg (March).

* Gagné, Marc (1973). *Visages de Gabrielle Roy, l'oeuvre et l'écrivain*. Montreal: Beauchemin.

* Gagné, Marc (1976). "*La Rivière sans repos* de Gabrielle Roy: étude mythocritique" [Part 3]. *Revue de l'Université d'Ottawa*, Ottawa (July-September).

Gauvin, Lise (1986). "Réception et roman: *Bonheur d'occasion* et *Alexandre Chenevert* de Gabrielle Roy." *Actes du 6ᵉ Congrès international des études canadiennes*. Acireale, Italy: Schena Editore.

Genuist, Paul (1992). *Marie-Anna Roy, une voix solitaire*. St-Boniface: Éditions des Plaines.

Giguère, Richard (1983). "Amérique française." *Revue d'histoire littéraire du Québec et du Canada français*, Ottawa (no. 6, Summer-Autumn).

Giguère, Richard and Jacques Michon (eds.) (1985). *L'Édition littéraire au Québec de 1940 à 1960*. Sherbrooke: Université de Sherbrooke.

Giguère, Richard and Jacques Michon (eds.) (1991). *Éditeurs transatlantiques*. Sherbrooke and Montreal: Ex Libris and Triptyque.

* Gilbert Lewis, Paula (1984). "La dernière des grandes conteuses: une conversation avec Gabrielle Roy." *Études littéraires*, Quebec City (Winter 1984) [interview conducted in 1981].

* Godbout, Jacques (1979). "Gabrielle Roy: Notre Dame des bouleaux." *L'Actualité*, Montreal (January).

Grosskurth, Phyllis (1969). *Gabrielle Roy*. Toronto: Forum House, Canadian Writers & Their Works Series.

Groulx, Lionel (1933). *L'Enseignement français au Canada*, Vol. ii: *Les Écoles des minorités*. Montreal: Granger.

Grover, Sheila C. (1981). *375 Deschambault Street: Gabrielle Roy House*. Winnipeg: Historical Buildings Committee of Manitoba [brochure].

* Guth, Paul (1947). "Un quart d'heure avec Gabrielle Roy, prix Fémina 1947, auteur de *Bonheur d'occasion*." *Flammes*, Paris (no. 9, December) [republished under the title "L'interview de Paul Guth: Gabrielle Roy, prix Fémina 1947." *La Gazette des lettres*, Paris (13 December 1947)].

Harvey, Carol. J. (1993). *Le Cycle manitobain de Gabrielle Roy*. St-Boniface: Éditions des Plaines.

* Hind-Smith, Joan (1975). "Gabrielle Roy." In *Three Voices: The Lives of Margaret Laurence, Gabrielle Roy and Frederick Philip Grove*. Toronto: Clarke Irwin [contains remarks by Gabrielle Roy and excerpts from letters written by her].

* Houle, Alain (1976). "René Richard et Gabrielle Roy: le Nord fascinant." *La Presse*, Montreal (31 December).

* Jasmin, Judith (1961). "[Interview avec Gabrielle Roy]" on the television program *Premier Plan*. Radio-Canada, CBFT (30 January); production: Claude Sylvestre. [a transcription of this interview was transmitted to François Ricard by Jacques Blais].

* [Lafond, Andréanne] (1955). "Rencontre avec Gabrielle Roy." *Points de vue*, St-Jérôme (November).

Lanctot, Gustave (1947). "Allocution." In Société royale du Canada (Section française), *Présentation de M. Léon Lorrain, Mlle Gabrielle Roy, M. Clément Marchand, M. Maurice Lebel*, Ottawa (academic year 1947-1948).

Larouche, Irma (1989). *Gabrielle Roy, 1909-1983. Papiers, 1936-1983, MSS 1982-11/1986-11: Instrument de recherche*. Ottawa: National Library of Canada.

* Légaré, Céline (1972). "Gabrielle Roy, romancière de l'espoir et de la détresse." *Perspectives*, Montreal (7 October).

Lennox, John and Michèle Lacombe (eds.) (1988). *Dear Bill: The Correspondence of William Arthur Deacon*.Toronto: University of Toronto Press.

Linteau, Paul-André, René Durocher, and Jean-Claude Robert (1989). *Histoire du Québec contemporain*, Vol. I: *De la Confédération à la crise* (new edition). Montreal: Boréal.

Linteau, Paul-André, René Durocher, Jean-Claude Robert, and François Ricard (1989). *Histoire du Québec contemporain*, Vol. II: *Le Québec depuis 1930* (new edition). Montreal: Boréal.

Marshall, Joyce (1983). "Gabrielle Roy, 1909-1983." *The Antigonish Review* (no. 55, Autumn).

Marshall, Joyce (1984). "Gabrielle Roy, 1909-1983: Some Reminiscences." *Canadian Literature*, Vancouver (no. 101, Summer).

Marshall, Joyce (1990). "Remembering Gabrielle Roy." *Brick*, London, Ont. (no. 39, Summer).

Morency, Pierre (1992). "Un petit bois." In *Lumière des oiseaux*. Montreal: Boréal.

* Morissette, Robert (1970). "[Interview with Gabrielle Roy]." In *La Vie ouvrière dans le roman canadien-français contemporain*. Master's thesis, Université de Montréal [interview conducted in 1969].

* Murphy, John J. (1963). "Visit with Gabrielle Roy." *Thought*, New York (Autumn).

O'Neill-Karch, Mariel (1992). "Gabrielle Roy et William Arthur Deacon: une amitié littéraire." *Cultures du Canada français*, Ottawa (no. 9).

Pagé, Pierre, Renée Legris, and L. Blouin (1975). *Répertoire des oeuvres de la littérature radiophonique québécoise 1930-1970*. Montreal: Fides.

* Parizeau, Alice (1966). "Gabrielle Roy, la grande romancière canadienne." *Châtelaine*, Montreal (April).

* Parizeau, Alice (1967). "La grande dame de la littérature québécoise." *La Presse*, Montreal (23 June).

* Paterson, Beth (1945). "Gabrielle Roy's Novel of St. Henri Realizes Fragile Five-year Hope." *The Gazette*, Montreal (29 August).

Reeves, John (1975). "Gabrielle Roy." *Saturday Night*, Toronto (September).

Ricard, François (1975). *Gabrielle Roy*. Montreal: Fides, series Écrivains canadiens d'aujourd'hui.

Ricard, François (1984). "La métamorphose d'un écrivain." *Études littéraires*, Quebec City (Winter).

Ricard, François (1991). "La *Revue moderne*: deux revues en une." *Littératures* [McGill University], Montreal (no. 7).

Ricard, François (1992a). "Les inédits de Gabrielle Roy: une première lecture." In Yolande Grisé and Robert Major (eds.), *Mélanges de littérature canadienne-française et québécoise offerts à Réjean Robidoux*. Ottawa: Presses de l'Université d'Ottawa.

Ricard, François (1992b). *Inventaire des archives personnelles de Gabrielle Roy conservées à la Bibliothèque nationale du Canada*. Montreal: Boréal.

* Ringuet [Philippe Panneton] (1951). "Gabrielle Roy publie *La Petite Poule d'Eau*." *Flammes*, Paris (May) [republished under the title "Conversation avec Gabrielle Roy" in *La Revue populaire*, Montreal (October 1951)].

* Robert, Lucette (1951). "Gabrielle Roy, revenue au pays, retrouve un climat d'amitié." *Photo-Journal*, Montreal (19 July).

Robidoux, Réjean (1974). "Gabrielle Roy à la recherche d'elle-même." *Canadian Modern Language Review*, Toronto (March).

* Robillard, J.-P. (1956). "Entrevue-éclair avec Gabrielle Roy." *Le Petit Journal*, Montreal (8 January).

Robinson, Christine (1995). "*La Saga d'Éveline*: un grand projet romanesque de Gabrielle Roy." *Cahiers franco-canadiens de l'Ouest*, St-Boniface (Autumn).

Roy, Marie-Anna A. [Adèle] (1954). *Le Pain de chez nous, histoire d'une famille manitobaine*. Montreal: Éditions du Lévrier.

Roy, Marie-Anna A. [Adèle] (1958). *Valcourt ou La Dernière Étape, roman du Grand Nord canadien*. [Beauceville]: self published.

Roy, Marie-Anna A. [Adèle] (1969). *La Montagne Pembina au temps des colons. Historique des paroisses de la région de la Montagne Pembina et biographies des principaux pionniers*. Winnipeg: self published.

Roy, Marie-Anna A. [Adèle] (1970). *Les Visages du vieux Saint-Boniface*. St-Boniface: self published.

Roy, Marie-Anna A. [Adèle] (1977). *Les Capucins de Toutes-Aides et leurs dignes confrères*. Montreal: Éditions franciscaines.

* Roy, Marie-Anna A. [Adèle] (1979). *Le Miroir du passé*. Montreal: Québec-Amérique.

Roy, Marie-Anna A. [Adèle] (1988). "Cher visage." *Bulletin du Centre d'études franco-canadiennes de l'Ouest*, St-Boniface (no. 28, June).

Roy, Marie-Anna A. [Adèle] (1989-1990). "A l'ombre des chemins de l'enfance." *L'Eau vive*, Regina (38 episodes published between 6 July 1989 and 26 April 1990).

Roy, Marie-Anna A. [Adèle] (1993). "Vieux souvenirs de lumière." *L'Eau vive*, Regina (8 July).

Roy-Painchaud, Anna (1955). "A Drawerful of Porridge." *Chatelaine*, Toronto (November) [a story inspired by childhood memories].

Saint-Martin, Lori (1998). *Lectures contemporaines de Gabrielle Roy: Bibliographie analytique des études critiques (1978-1997)*. Montreal: Boréal, Cahiers Gabrielle Roy Series.

Savoie, Guy (1972). *Le Réalisme du cadre spatio-temporel de "Bonheur d'occasion."* Master's thesis, Université Laval, Quebec City.

* Scully, Robert Guy (1974). "Le monde de Gabrielle Roy." *Le Devoir*, Montreal (30 March).

Shek, Ben-Z. (1989). "De quelques influences possibles sur la vision du monde de Gabrielle Roy: George Wilkinson et Henri Girard." *Voix et Images*, Montreal (no. 42, Spring).

Socken, Paul G. (1974). "Gabrielle Roy as Journalist." *Canadian Modern Language Review*, Toronto (January).

Socken, Paul G. (1979). "Gabrielle Roy: An Annotated Bibliography." In R. Lecker and J. David (eds.), *The Annotated Bibliography of Canada's Major Authors*, Vol. 1. Downsview: ecw Press.

* Socken, Paul G. (1987). "Interview with Gabrielle Roy." In *Myth and Morality in "Alexandre Chenevert" by Gabrielle Roy*. Frankfurt: Peter Lang [interview conducted in 1979].

Stanké, Alain (1985). "Notes liminaires en guise de préface." In M. G. Hesse, *Gabrielle Roy par elle-même*, trans. from the English by Michelle Tisseyre. Montreal: Éditions Stanké.

* Tasso, L. (1965). "*Bonheur d'occasion* est le témoignage d'une époque, d'un endroit et de moi-même." *La Presse*, Montreal (17 April) [republished in *La Liberté et le Patriote*, St-Boniface (22 April 1965)].

Teboul, Victor (1984). *"Le Jour": émergence du libéralisme moderne au Québec*. Montreal: Hurtubise HMH.

* Thomas, A. Vernon (1947). "*The Tin Flute* Turns Out To Be a Pot of Gold for Its Author." *Saturday Night*, Toronto (12 April).

Thomas, Clara and John Lennox (1982). *William Arthur Deacon: A Canadian Literary Life*. Toronto: University of Toronto Press.

Trudeau, Mireille (1976). "*Bonheur d'occasion* et la presse française." Master's thesis, Université de Montréal.

Urbas, Jeannette (1988) "Not Enough Time." *Atlantis*, Halifax, (Autumn).

IV. Personal Recollections

Aimé Badiou (Notre-Dame-de-Lourdes, Manitoba); Madeleine Bergeron (Quebec City); Simone Bussières (Notre-Dame-des-Laurentides); M. C. (Quebec City); Marcel Carbotte (Quebec City); Léona Carbotte-Corriveau (Winnipeg); Cécile Chabot (Montreal); Hélène Chaput (Winnipeg); Madeleine Chassé (Quebec City); Guy Chauvière (Winnipeg); Bernard Dagenais (Quebec City); Françoise Dagenais (Montreal); Jacqueline Deniset-Benoist (Montreal); Lionel Dorge (Winnipeg); Paul Dumas (Montreal); André Fauchon (Winnipeg); Jacques Fortin (Montreal); Louis-Philippe Gauthier (Montreal); Thérèse Gauthier (Winnipeg); Léonie Guyot (Winnipeg); Réginald Hamel (Montreal); John Helliwell (New York); Gilles Hénault (Montreal); Antonia Houde-Roy (Ottawa); Réal Jubinville (Hull); Marcel Lancelot (Winnipeg); Jeanne Lapointe (Quebec City); Joyce Marshall (Toronto); Eugénie Miko (Quebec City); Jean Miko (Québec); Pierre Morency (Quebec); Yvon Quellet (Quebec City); Lucien Parizeau (Ottawa); Maria Pronovost (Winnipeg); Clelio Ritagliati (Winnipeg); Denise Rocan (Winnipeg); Adèle Roy (Montreal); Yolande Roy-Cyr (Aylmer); Ben-Z. Shek (Toronto); Berthe Simard (Petite-Rivière-Saint-François); Antoine Sirois (Sherbrooke); Jori Smith (Montreal); Jean Soucy (Quebec City); René Soulard (Montreal); Jeannette Urbas (Toronto); Berthe Valcourt (Winnipeg); Victorine Vigier (Notre-Dame-de-Lourdes, Manitoba).

Acknowledgements

The research and publication of this book would not have been possible without help from a great many people and institutions.

For their confidence in me, I would like first to thank all those who were kind enough to answer my questions and open their archives for my perusal. Their names appear in sections II and IV of the sources. Three of them – Lionel Dorge, Léonie Guyot, and the late Marcel Carbotte – made themselves available for consultation at all times and were real guides to me throughout my research. Without them, the book would surely not have escaped the pitfalls of superficiality and bookishness, as I dare to hope it has. Any errors in my narration of events are not the fault of any of these generous people, but mine alone.

I would like also to thank the staff members of the libraries and archives I consulted, where I was always received with the utmost consideration, especially from the guardians of the Literary Manuscript Collection at the National Library of Canada, whose curator at the time, Claude Le Moine, aided my research with patience and a depth of knowledge in his field that I shall not forget.

I owe a debt of gratitude also to my students – Anne-Marie Fortier, Marcel Fortin, Julie Potvin, Sophie Marcotte, Christine Robinson – who relieved me of certain specific areas of research and maintained an ongoing interest in my work, and to my friends and colleagues – Gilles Marcotte, Paul-André Linteau, Yvon Rivard, Jean Bernier – who kindly read my original French text before publication and gave me the benefit of their wisdom. I am also grateful to Paule Noyart for the sensitivity and attention to detail with which she corrected and polished my French manuscript, and to Patricia Claxton, who has been as conscientious, knowledgeable, and empathetic a translator as any author could hope to have.

Last but not least, I wish to thank the Humanities Research Council of Canada, the Killam Program of the Canada Council, and the Faculty of Graduate Studies of McGill University for their financial assistance.

F.R.

Index

Names of people and organizations and titles of books by Gabrielle Roy cited in the text (excluding the Notes and Bibliography).

Liberté, La (St-Boniface): 60, 79-80, 83,
93, 119, 127, 128, 131, 137, 138, 146, 147,
160, 165, 177, 179, 191, 269, 275
Librairie Beauchemin: *see* Éditions
Beauchemin
Librairie Ernest Flammarion: *see*
Éditions Flammarion
Lindley, Denver: 341
Lipton, Charles: 235
Literary Guild of America (New York):
264-65, 266, 267, 269, 280, 294, 342
Little Theatre: *see* Winnipeg Little
Theatre
Lockridge, Ross Jr.: 269
Loranger, Françoise: 382
Loranger, Jean-Aubert: 185
Lorrain, Léon: 283
Loti, Pierre: 123
Lottman, H. R.: 166
Louÿs, Pierre: 245
Luc d'antioche, Sister: *see* Beuglet,
Delphine
Lykochine, Antoine-Marie de (Father):
305
Lyman, John: 188, 234

Macdonell, John A.: 15
Machard, Alfred: 129
Mackinnon, Andrew: 155
Maclean's magazine (Toronto): 266,
270, 385, 434
MacLennan, Hugh: 261, 262, 264, 266,
473
Macmillan Canada (Toronto): 262
Madeleine (pseud. for Anne-Marie
Gleason-Huguenin): 187, 209
Mademoiselle (New York): 268
Maeterlinck, Maurice: 134
Magali: 187
Maheux, Arthur (Abbé): 209
Maillet, Adrienne: 245
Maillet, Andrée: 313
Maire, Marius: 313
Major, André: 408, 453, 474
Major, Luzina: 87, 88, 412

Malraux, André: 188, 400
Manitoba Provincial Archives: 77, 113,
156
Mansfield, Katherine: 368
Marcotte, Gilles: 313, 326-27, 343, 408,
452-53, 461, 474
Marion, Anna: 118
Marion, Berthe: 118
Marion, Séraphin: 271
Markowitz, Jacob: 261
Marquis, Julia: 44, 357-58
Marrin, Edward: 49-50
Marshall, Joyce: 266, 374, 379, 382-83,
405, 413, 414, 423-24, 434, 437, 449,
452, 454, 464, 468, 469
Martel, Réginald: 433, 462
Martin du Gard, Roger: 233, 264
Mason, Paula: 471
Massey, Vincent: 168, 317
Massey Commission: 317
Mathurins: *see* Théâtre des Mathurins
Mauffette, Guy: 193
Maugham, Somerset: 124
Maulnier, Thierry: 175, 287
Maupassant, Guy de: 83, 233
Mauriac, François: 233, 245, 267, 280,
368, 401
Maurois, André: 280, 401
Maurras, Charles: 175
Maxima, Sister: *see* Bellemare, M.-A.
McCarthy, J. R. (Senator): 268
McClelland, Jack: 294, 344, 377, 379,
423-24, 463, 469, 470, 471, 472, 473,
478, 487
McClelland & Stewart (Toronto): 262,
289, 317, 326, 342, 344, 375, 379, 383,
405, 414, 423-24, 434, 457, 469-70,
471
McDowell, Franklin: 261
McEachran, Blanche: 32, 227
McEachran, Edward: 32
McEachran, Imelda: 32
McEachran, Rosalie: *see* Landry, Rosalie
McGill University (Montreal): 449, 474
McIntyre, W. A.: 109, 113